Faunal Extinction
in an Island Society

Pygmy Hippopotamus Hunters
of Cyprus

CW01497577

INTERDISCIPLINARY CONTRIBUTIONS TO ARCHAEOLOGY

Series Editor: Michael A. Jochim, *University of California at Santa Barbara*
Founding Editor: Roy S. Dickens, Jr., *Late of University of North Carolina, Chapel Hill*

A Chronological Listing of Volumes in this series appears at the back of this volume.

A Continuation Order Plan is available for this series. A continuation order will bring delivery of each new volume immediately upon publication. Volumes are billed only upon actual shipment. For further information please contact the publisher.

Faunal Extinction in an Island Society

Pygmy Hippopotamus Hunters of Cyprus

ALAN H. SIMMONS

University of Nevada at Las Vegas
Las Vegas, Nevada

and Associates

KLUWER ACADEMIC / PLENUM PUBLISHERS
New York, Boston, Dordrecht, London, Moscow

ISBN 0-306-46088-2

©1999 Kluwer Academic/Plenum Publishers, New York
233 Spring Street, New York, N.Y. 10013

10 9 8 7 6 5 4 3 2 1

A C.I.P. record for this book is available from the Library of Congress.

Printed in the United States of America

Associates

Salvador Bailon • Laboratoire d'Anatomie Comparée, Muséum National d'Histoirie Naturel, Paris, France

Stephen R. Durand • Anthropology Program, Eastern New Mexico University, Portales, New Mexico 88130

Vincenzo M. Francaviglia • Istituto per le Tecnologie Applicate al Beni Culturali, Consiglio Nazionale delle Ricerche, Rome, Italy

Rolfe D. Mandel • Department of Geography, University of Kansas, Lawrence, Kansas 66045

Cécile Mourer-Chauviré • Centre du Paléontologie, Stratigraphique et Paléoécologie, Université Claude Bernard, Lyon 1, France

Michael Neeley • Department of Anthropology, Arizona State University, Tempe, Arizona 85287

Margaret E. Newman • Department of Archaeology, University of Calgary, Calgary, Alberta, AB T2N 1N4, Canada

Sandra Olsen • Quaternary Faunal Laboratory, Carnegie Museum of Natural History, Pittsburgh, Pennsylvania 15213

David S. Reese • Department of Anthropology, Field Museum of Natural History, Chicago, Illinois 60605

Kathy Roler • Anthropology Program, Eastern New Mexico University, Portales, New Mexico 88130

Mark Rose • *Archaeology,* New York, New York 10038

Martin R. Rose • Formerly of Biological Sciences Center, Desert Research Institute, Reno, Nevada 89506

Karel J. Steensma • Cjageldijk 71/C4, NL-3602 AY Maarssen, The Netherlands

Stuart Swiny • Department of Classics, State University of New York at Albany, Albany, New York 12222

Peter E. Wigand • Quaternary Sciences Center, Desert Research Institute, Reno, Nevada 89506

Introductory Note

The prehistory of Cyprus has held a particular fascination for scholars ever since the Swedish Cyprus Expedition discovered, some sixty years ago, the first evidence for a Neolithic settlement at Petra tou *Limniti* near the north coast. Subsequent research by P. Dikaios, A. Le Brun, and I. Todd on the Neolithic culture of the island has increased our knowledge of this early phase of Cypriot prehistory, but at the same time, it has raised the question whether the Neolithic was preceded by an earlier phase or not. Already in 1968, a suggestion was made by E. Stockton for the existence of a pre-Neolithic culture, but this suggestion was poorly documented and was not pursued as a viable proposition. Early in 1981, S. Swiny asked me to consider an investigation of what appeared to be a pre-Neolithic site at Akrotiri *Aetokremnos,* but I expressed certain reservation, and I was even more doubtful after visiting the site a few months later. My advice was that we should be extremely cautious, though I was favorably disposed to allowing a limited excavation if an experienced prehistorian could be found to undertake it. Alan Simmons accepted the challenge and over three years (1987, 1988, 1990), he and his collaborators excavated nearly the entire site, which is less than 40 sq m in extent. I have been "critical" throughout the excavation, not of the methods used but of the results of the stratigraphic study and of their interpretation. This criticism did not stem from a negative attitude, but I thought that an investigation of this kind—the results of which were to add at least 1,500 years to Cypriot prehistory—should be handled with extreme caution. Such an approach seemed even more imperative in view of the limited area of the excavation.

The excavation results are impressive and Simmons and his team are to be congratulated for not only publishing preliminary reports, but also for the prompt publication of the final report. An excavation in such a limited area of a period never before encountered on the island has surely not solved all the problems; indeed, it has raised a good number of questions. One cannot deny, however, that Akrotiri *Aetokremnos* is a cultural site, that the faunal and cultural material found there is of vital importance, and that the dating of the deposits to 1,500–2,000 years earlier than the previously known first occupation of Cyprus has opened new horizons for further investigations. The questions raised by the excavations should be considered together with the skepticism and criticism already expressed by certain scholars about the interpretation of Akrotiri *Aetokremnos* (and no doubt there will be further questions to address after this publication) as a positive phenomenon. For over fifty years, archaeologists have been excavating Late Bronze Age sites in Cyprus in order to attain a better understanding of merely some two to three centuries of the island's past, yet "the more we learn the less we know" about this period. An impressive start has been made at Akrotiri *Aetokremnos,* which should encourage systematic archaeological and paleontological surveys of the island. Even if this circa tenth millennium B.C. habitation were seasonal, surely it would not be the only one on Cyprus. The geographical location of Akrotiri *Aetokremnos,* together with its suggested seasonal occupation, gives it a uniqueness that can only be substantiated by careful documentation of comparable sites, for presumably the attraction (hippopotamus meat) was not confined only to this rather inhospitable spot. Despite the discovery of hippopotamus bone beds elsewhere, none seems to show an association with human activity. Fortunately, the island is exceptionally situated for research on the early prehistory of the Mediterranean.

VASSOS KARAGEORGHIS

Leventis Foundation, Nicosia, Cyprus
Former Director, Department of Antiquities,
Republic of Cyprus

Foreword

The multidisciplinary research program at Akrotiri *Aetokremnos* is important, in my opinion, for three reasons: two empirical and one conceptual. Quite apart from the archaeology, work at the site is a major contribution to island biogeography, in that the *Phanourios* sample—certainly the best from Cyprus and probably the best anywhere in the world—has already provided, and will continue to provide, important ecological and behavioral data on these intriguing creatures. Dwarfed island faunas are important to our understanding of the complex factors that shape natural selection in ecologically closed environments over the evolutionary long term. At *Aetokremnos*, we seem to have the "end" of a long sequence of hippo evolution on the island. With comparative studies of other Cypriot hippo faunas, we should be able to pin down the interval of initial colonization by what were, presumably, normal-sized hippos, and—if the other sites can be dated—document the dwarfing process in considerable detail. *Aetokremnos* would still be a significant paleontological locality, even in the absence of evidence of a human presence there.

While reading the text of the monograph, a number of questions strictly related to the paleontology occurred to me. One was how to model the colonization process. There seems to be little question that the large mammals colonized the island by swimming to it (because, I gather, Cyprus has not been connected to the mainland for roughly 5–6 million years). Moreover, the distance to the nearest land would have been at least 60–65 km, even during episodes of maximum sea-level regression, and considerably less than the 80–120 km that separates Cyprus from the Anatolian coast today. It might be possible to identify the source of the colonizing population and predict the colonization interval, given current, relatively refined knowledge of marine paleotemperature cores.

The dwarfing process itself is also interesting and remains very poorly understood. One might imagine that systematic relationships would obtain among (1) island surface area (or, more accurately, the area corresponding to hippo habitat); (2) the size of the initial, colonizing population (it must have been large enough to sustain a mating network); and (3) the time elapsed since initial colonization. Through Reese's (and other's) analyses, we already know something about diet preferences and the kinds of terrain to which the Cypriot pygmos were adapted. Extrapolating from modern research, we may also be able to say something about local group size and composition, because it appears that there are systematic differences between extant pygmy hippos and their larger relatives. Assuming that we can establish at least some of these parameters and make educated guesses about others, this becomes a classic simulation problem, the empirical credibility of which can be evaluated with the various hippo faunal samples found on the island. An island biogeographer could, no doubt, come up with many more intriguing questions that would maximize the research potential of the large and well-preserved *Aetokremnos* faunas.

The second major empirical contribution of the work is, of course, the archaeology. In my opinion, Simmons and his colleagues make an extremely strong case for contemporaneity of humans with *Phanourios*, even if the role of human agency in the extirpation of the species is not well understood. Moreover, the site is extremely well dated with 31 determinations from six laboratories establishing the period of use/occupation of the rockshelter in the tenth millennium B.C. (Simmons & Wigand 1994; anyone familiar with radiocarbon dating will recognize that it is practically a miracle to get so many coherent determinations on eight different kinds of samples from six different laboratories!). Simmons and his coworkers have conducted an exemplary excavation and analysis of *Aetokremnos* and have documented beyond a reasonable doubt the association of a large number of unequivocal artifacts with the faunas, the presence of informal hearths, and a high incidence of burnt bone. Even if we are not in a position to know the details of the archaeotaphonomic record at the site (and the question arises as to whether we know the detailed archaeotaphonomy of *any* site), it seems clear to me that humans were involved in the accumulation of the hippo, elephant, malacological, and avifaunas, and that alternative scenarios that seek to eliminate human agency stretch credulity to the breaking point. Interpretation of the *meaning* of this association will no doubt remain controversial (at least until we have a better understanding of the processes involved in ancient bone accumulations), but the association itself is beyond question.

The work at *Aetokremnos* also raises a number of conceptual issues, probably the most important one being the implications that the research has for the notion of a Neolithic colonization of the island by people already practicing domestication economies. These models are founded on work at the important site of Khirokitia, excavated over the years first by Porphyios Dikaios, and then by a French team headed by Alain LeBrun. Central tenets of these models are that there was no pre-Neolithic human presence on the island, and that Neolithic colonists brought with them not only domesticated ovicaprines and cereal grasses, but also wild species of potential economic importance (i.e., deer). It seems pretty clear that, whatever else it might mean, the *Aetokremnos* research documents a human presence on the island some 1.5–2 millennia earlier than Khirokitia, and with no indications (at least at *Aetokremnos* itself) of domestication economies. This situation fits a pattern of relatively late human colonization of the Mediterranean Islands (Sardinia—only technically an island—excepted) and raises the question of why humans began to occupy island niches when they did.

Being something of a demographic determinist, I think the answer to that question probably had a great deal to do with population-resource imbalances in the littoral regions of the eastern Mediterranean mainland, where the domestication process had already been underway for millennia, and where there is considerable evidence for dietary diversification and intensification prior to the appearance of domestication economies (see, e.g., Neeley and Clark 1994). When humans began to encounter dietary stress due to increased local population density as a consequence of sedentism (e.g., the Natufian), they initially responded to that stress by diversifying their diet to include more high-cost, low-yield resources (e.g., shellfish) and by intensifying the procurement of traditional dietary staples (e.g., gazelle, cereal grasses) (Cohen 1975, 1977; Redding 1988). When they began to "run out of options" for diversification and intensification, if they could emigrate, some did so.

Although humans probably reached the Mediterranean Islands from time to time throughout the Pleistocene, a sustained human presence on them is documented only around the Pleistocene/Holocene boundary. This is a significant piece of evidence that calls for an explanation. Domestication is a "process" not an "event" and, as a number of workers have clearly shown, it has roots deep in the Late Pleistocene (e.g., Clark 1987; Cohen 1977; Jarman *et al.* 1982). The *Aetokremnos* research must be seen in this broader intellectual context. It has profound implications for how we think about domestication, and how we weight the various causal factors (demographic, climatic, behavioral etc.) invoked to explain it.

Finally, it is worth remarking that any "interesting" results obtained from multidisciplinary research efforts at a site like *Aetokremnos* are bound to be controversial. It is naive to expect definitive resolution in the face of competing claims about evidence and competing views about the credibility of preferred approaches. Ultimately, these are epistemological issues, bound up in the different "packages" of biases and preconceptions that archaeologists bring to the research enterprise (see, e.g., Simmons 1991b). Given the lack of evidence accepted as decisive by all, different epistemologies result in conclusions that are fully warranted only within the boundaries of a particular conceptual framework. All conclusions are, therefore, conditional on the unstated assumptions that underlie a particular research protocol.

G.A. CLARK
Department of Anthropology
Arizona State University
Tempe, Arizona

Preface

The small size of Akrotiri *Aetokremnos* belies its significance. This has been a far more complex project than I imagined when we first started excavations, and when we concluded our field studies, I realized that *Aetokremnos* would not be easy to write up. I find it somewhat amusing—as well as ironic—that I have become an advocate for a human role in Pleistocene extinctions because I have never been overly convinced that in most parts of the world this was the case. In Cyprus, it appears that it was.

Aetokremnos is a controversial site, presenting many challenges. Our research there has resulted in a broadening of my understanding of what it really means to conduct true interdisciplinary archaeology. It is not easy, but it is rewarding. I should note that although this volume is the major report on our investigations, a second volume is planned by David Reese. This volume will provide much more detail on the faunal remains, especially those strange little animals, the extinct Cypriot pygmy hippopotamus (or the "pygmos" as they affectionately came to be called), that we all became so attached to in one way or another.

In a work such as this, there are numerous individuals who need to be thanked, even after all of my cajoling for timely submissions of individual authors' contributions. The research reported on here goes far beyond the contributors whose words and thoughts make up much of this volume. Many others contributed, knowingly or unknowingly, to what is reported here, and I can only list some of them. I must first thank the field staff of the project, all of whom were unpaid professionals, students, or amateurs. Without their untiring devotion, this project would never have happened. Even the occasional complaints about the *same* red wine offered at dinner are overlooked in light of their enthusiasm and skill. These individuals (not counting those who volunteered for only a day or so) include Gywnn Alcock, Bonnie Bazemore, Geoffrey Clark, Susan Dolezal, Steve Durand, William Farrand, Gerald Hennings, Susan Horne, Lena Kassianides, Elliot Lax, Rolfe Mandel, Françoise Martin, Gavin Muir, Michael Neeley, Sandra Olsen, Deborah Olszewski, Catheline Perlès, Kathy Roler, Phil Simkin, Shelly Smith, Thomas Strasser, Alessandra Swiny, Helena Swiny, Philip Swiny, Stuart Swiny, and Weihong Zhao. In addition, David Reese was with us for all three excavation seasons, as was Steve Held, who served as field director. I benefited immensely from their knowledge of Cyprus.

Aside from contributors, other individuals who gave of their time and wisdom, even if I might not have listened to the latter, include Olivier Aurenche, Ofer Bar-Yosef, Reuban Bullard, David Burney, John Cherry, Christopher Chippendale, Paul Croft, George Frison, Donald Grayson, Herbert Haas, Julie Hansen, Gary Haynes, Ellen Hersher, Alice Kingsnorth, Bernard Knapp, Alain and Odile LeBrun, Stephanie Livingston, Lee Lyman, Paul Martin (who I guess was right, at least for Cyprus!), Eric Meyers, Fred Nials, David Pearlman, Gary Rollefson, Avraham Ronen, David Rupp, Pat Shipman, Paul Sondaar, Joanna Smith, Alison South, Nicholas Stanley-Price, Mary Stiner, Ian Todd, Claudio Vita-Finzi, Alan Walker, and Fred Wendorf.

I also owe a great debt to the Department of Antiquities of the Republic of Cyprus. When initiated, Vassos Karageorghis was director, and his critical but fair assessment of the site is a tribute to the professionalism of the department. His successors (Athanasios Papageorghiou, Michael Louloupis, Demos Christou, and Sophocles Hadjisavvas, the present director) have been equally supportive. The former curator of the Kourion Museum, Socrates Savvas, made our stay there more pleasant than any field project has a right to expect. Members of the Western Sovereign Base Area Archaeological Society contributed to the project in many ways. Several Royal Air Force personnel, including Stewart Chapman, Frank Haggerty, Brian Hoskins, Brian Pile, and Julian Whitehead, also greatly facilitated the research. In particular, I must single out Gavin Muir and Phil Simkin who were "assigned" to us and probably did not know what they were getting into; they deserve enormous credit for their support and knowledge of "the system."

There are many others without whom this project would never have been started and completed, and I owe them a particular debt of gratitude. From the Cyprus American Archaeological Research Institute (CAARI), Vathoulla Moustouki was always a source of great assistance. Stuart Swiny, former director of CAARI, and his talented family was an inspiration for the project; and in those days when we did not even know if *Aetokremnos* was cultural, he put his professional reputation on the line with characteristic good humor. I hope the results of this work justify his confidence in the site. The wonderful hospitality of all of the Cypriot people we encountered made this a delightful introduction to Cyprus for me. I only hope that the future brings a lasting peace to this often troubled island.

In the United States, various individuals formerly with the Desert Research Institute (DRI) supported the project in many ways. Mona Reno aided considerably with early reports on the site. I must single out Susan Sawatsky for her untiring effort in producing the computer-generated profiles in Chapter 4 and other figures in Chapter 5, which were made using *Interleaf.* The late Cynthia Irwin-Williams, former director of the Quaternary Sciences Center at DRI, was an enthusiastic supporter. The project would not have been completed without the great support of Dale Ritter, Cythnia's successor at DRI until his retirement in 1995. Various individuals at the University of Nevada, Las Vegas, have also helped with the project, and I especially thank Margaret Lyneis and Claude Warren for their insights. The figures were drawn by Geoffrey Clark (chipped stone), Renee Corona-Kolvet (chipped stone, maps), Michael Neeley (chipped stone), Deborah Olszewski (chipped stone), Janie Ravenhurst (ground stone), and Russell Hapke (Fig. 13.1). Some of the final photos in Chapter 7 are reproduced by courtesy of the Field Museum of Natural History. Eliot Werner of Plenum Press has been more than patient throughout the process of publishing this volume. Finally, my wife Renee Corona-Kolvet has been a constant source of inspiration for dealing with the "pygmos." I'm sure that she, as am I, is now happy that they may finally rest in peace.

No modern archaeological project can be undertaken without adequate funding. *Aetokremnos* was no exception, and involved "creative financing" on several levels. The National Geographic Society provided the bulk of the funding. Other agencies that also supported the project included the Desert Research Institute, the Institute for Aegean Prehistory, the Leakey Foundation, the Lindley Foundation, the National Endowment for the Humanities, and the National Science Foundation.

A brief word on site names as used in this volume: As is customary in Cyprus, archaeological sites normally have two names, the first after the nearest village and the second referring to the nearest toponym. The second word should be italicized. In most cases, a site is known by its second name alone; thus *Aetokremnos*. Sometimes, however, particularly well-known sites (such as the Aceramic Neolithic village of Khirokitia *Vounoi*) are frequently referred to by their village name, that is, Khirokitia in this example. This scheme can often be confusing to non-Cypriot specialists, and I have tried to be consistent throughout this volume.

Contents

Chapter 1

Introduction and Research Context

THE PROBLEM

It is easy to see how Akrotiri *Aetokremnos* (or "Vulture Cliff" [erroneously referred to as "Eagle's Cliff" in earlier publications[1]]) received its name. The site, located on the southern coast of the Mediterranean island of Cyprus (Fig. 1-1) is precipitously perched on a cliff with a dramatic plunge into the Mediterranean Sea (Fig. 1-2). The first time I saw *Aetokremnos* in July 1985 I had little idea that it would change our understanding of Mediterranean prehistory, let alone have far wider implications regarding the role of humans in the extinction of Pleistocene faunas. It was a hot July day, one of those crystal clear Mediterranean summer days during which the intense sun dominated everything else. Stuart Swiny, then director of the Cyprus American Archaeological Research Institute (CAARI), had been to the site several times and knew the way well. Accompanied by David Reese, who also was seeing the site for the first time, I tentatively followed Swiny down the steep cliff side to the site. Its wind-swept surface was severely eroded, and it seemed that any intact materials would have long ago been lost to the tumultuous sea below. It is fair to say that my first opinion of *Aetokremnos* was far from favorable, although one could not deny the drama of its location.

Aetokremnos was first discovered in 1961 by the son of a British serviceman stationed on the Royal Air Force (RAF) Western Sovereign Base Area, on which it is located. David J. Nixon, an 11-year-old, was exploring the steep cliffs of the southern face of the Akrotiri Peninsula. Undoubtedly, his parents would not have approved of this endeavor, as the drops to the sea are formidable. During his explorations, he came across the deposit at *Aetokremnos*, which we now know is a collapsed rockshelter. There he found strange looking bones and a few chipped stone artifacts, several of which he collected, after dutifully noting the site's location, which he designated "Site E." When his family returned to Great Britain, he took these objects with him, ultimately bringing them to the British Museum (Natural History) in London, where the late Kenneth Oakley indicated that the flints

---

[1]Swiny (1995:9, footnote 11) discussed the naming of the site in more detail, noting that the correct transliteration of the toponym is *Atokremnos* (Vulture Cliff) and not *Aetokremnos* (Eagle Cliff). However, since *Aetokremnos* is now established in the literature, we retain this designation.

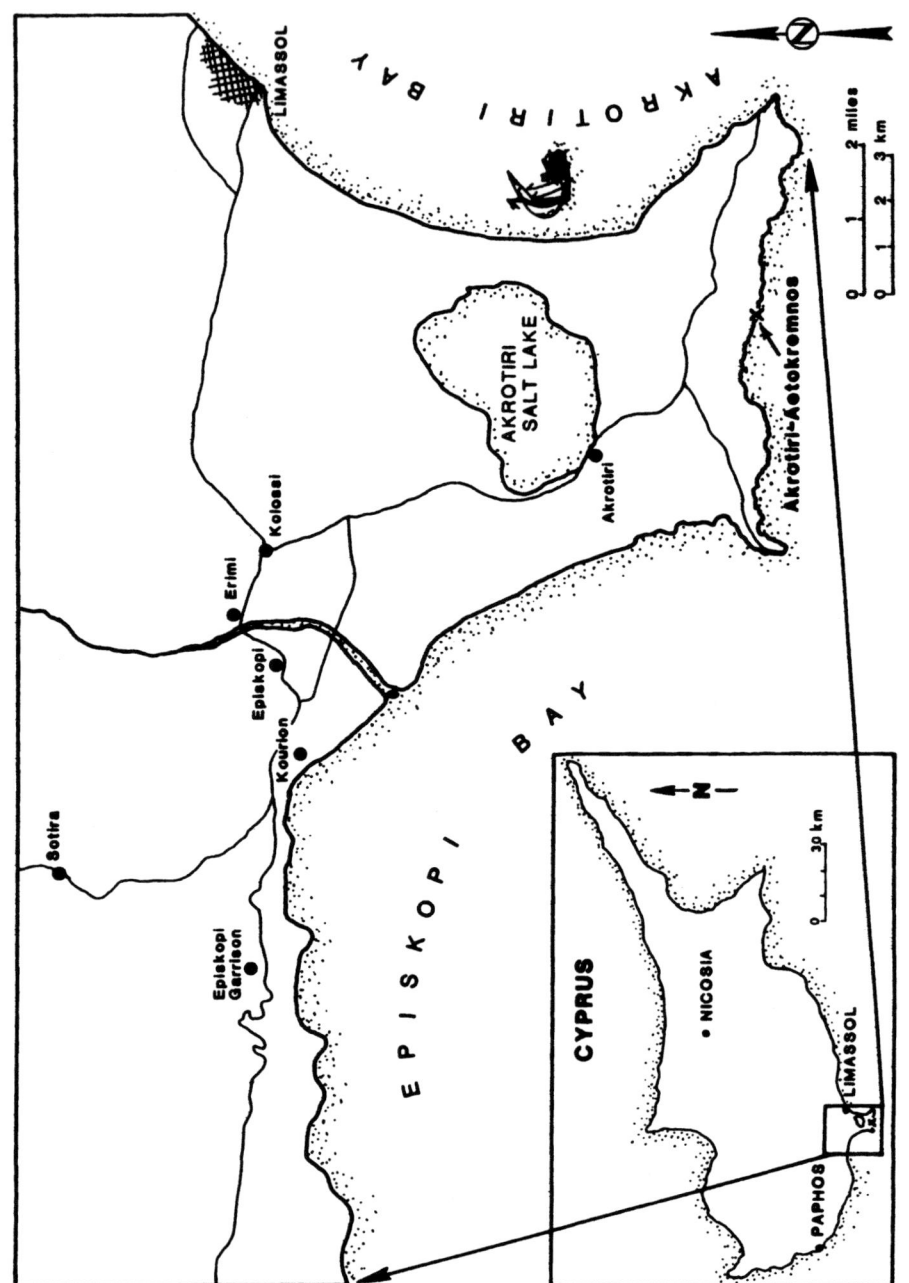

Figure 1-1. Location map of Akrotiri *Aetokremnos*.

Figure 1-2. *Aetokremnos,* showing cliff-side location.

appeared "Neolithic." The bones also were identified as coming from the endemic and quite extinct Cypriot pygmy hippopotamus, whose earlier taxonomic classification of *Phanourios minor* (Boekschoten and Sondaar 1972:306) has since been amended to the current usage of *Phanourios minutus* Cuvier (Faure *et al.* 1983). Nixon wrote a letter to the Cypriot Department of Antiquities in Nicosia, informing them of his discovery.

It was not until 1981 that interest in *Aetokremnos* resurfaced. This time, a British flight lieutenant (now squadron leader) and amateur archaeologist, Brian Pile, conducted an archaeological survey of portions of the Akrotiri Peninsula. He rediscovered *Aetokremnos,* ironically naming it Site E, just as Nixon had done. Pile, too, thought this an interesting locality and informed local archaeologists of the discovery. These individuals included Swiny, who examined the site and was equally intrigued.

Aetokremnos was not an impressive site, especially by Cypriot standards, where archaeology has tended to concentrate on those remains with architectural features. All that was visible were a few pieces of chipped stone, abundant amounts of *Phanourios* and other bone (including pygmy elephant, or *Elephas cypriotes* Bate), and an apparently thin layer of marine shell. Numerous paleontological sites containing *Phanourios* occur in Cyprus, and it was questionable whether or not *Aetokremnos* was even archaeological. It could very easily have represented another paleontological locality, with the artifacts being fortuitous associations, eroded onto the rockshelter's ledge from sites located along the cliff tops. Still, the association was tantalizing, and the presence of a layer of marine shell some 40 m above the present sea shore was curious as well.

After this rediscovery, several other archaeologists were invited to visit the site. Visiting is not as simple as it seems because access to the high-security RAF base is restricted. Many who examined the chipped stone were piqued by their somewhat unusual appearance, at least in comparison to other Cypriot materials. Unfortunately, lithic analyses have long been neglected in Cyprus, so it was difficult to make any precise comparisons. During one visit to the site, Swiny collected some of the exposed marine shell as well as some of the *Phanourios* bones. He submitted three samples for radiocarbon dating. The results were surprising, exhibiting a remarkable range: the oldest, on shell, was 11,000 ± 100 B.P. (Pta-3112), and the most recent, on bone, was 3700 ± 60 B.P. (Pta-3435). Realizing that there are potential problems with dating surface remains, especially of marine shell and bone, the oldest determination was, nonetheless, intriguing. If accurate, and *if* it represented a cultural episode, *Aetokremnos* would be the oldest archaeological site on Cyprus, predating the Aceramic Neolithic period by some 2,000 years.

Thus *Aetokremnos* was beginning to pose an interesting problem from at least two perspectives. First, if it dated to the late ninth millennium B.C., it had serious implications for the first human occupation of Cyprus. Previously, most researchers believed that the earliest settlement was during the Aceramic Neolithic, which began circa 6500–7000 B.C., despite some unsubstantiated claims for an earlier "Paleolithic" occupation (see later). Second, if the association of *Phanourios* remains and artifacts was valid, it could have significant implications for a possible human role in the extinction of these unique Pleistocene fauna. All known paleontological sites containing these remains apparently predated human occupation of the island, and conventional wisdom was that these species went extinct long before the arrival of humans. Indeed, the significance of *Aetokremnos* spread beyond Cyprus because few of the Mediterranean islands have compelling evidence for either pre-Neolithic occupation or the association of humans with extinct Pleistocene fauna. The extinction scenario was particularly intriguing and significant beyond the Mediterranean, given that the role of humans in the extinction of Pleistocene animals is one of the most controversial issues in contemporary archaeology. Thus *Aetokremnos* had considerable promise—if it was, indeed, an archaeological site.

The only way to determine if *Aetokremnos* was cultural was to conduct professional excavations, preferably by an archaeologist familiar with early, pre-Neolithic hunter-gatherer archaeology and with sites lacking architecture. An added complication was the site's location on a British military facility. It soon became apparent that if any professional excavations were to be conducted, they would have to be done by either British or American archaeologists. As luck would have it, I heard about the site initially from my colleague Gary Rollefson. I corresponded with Swiny, who suggested that I visit the site myself to assess it. Having had considerable experience in both Neolithic and earlier archaeology, including a focus on small surface sites, I was intrigued by the possibility. It was thus after a season of excavations at the Aceramic Neolithic settlement of 'Ain Ghazal in Jordan that I first made that fateful side trip to Cyprus.

My initial impression was less than overwhelming. But there was something about *Aetokremnos* that was not right . . . it just did not seem to be a fortuitous constellation of bones and artifacts. I had certainly seen far less impressive, but clearly cultural, sites on the mainland, both in the Near East and in the United States. I was fortunate enough to be offered the site for excavation. Over the next two years, after frustrating attempts to obtain funding failed, I was able to assemble a small research team, and we conducted a limited test excavation in 1987. We were surprised and overwhelmed by the results. Our excavation of only four small units demonstrated that substantial subsurface deposits were present, to a depth approaching 1 m in some areas. Furthermore, chipped stone artifacts were found in direct, primary context with *Phanourios* remains. The incredible number of *Phanourios* remains also became readily apparent. Finally, additional radiocarbon determinations supported the early occupation. We obtained support from the National Geographic Society for a more thorough season in 1988, followed by another season in 1990, with additional funding from National Geographic, the Lindley Foundation, the L. S. B. Leakey Foundation, and the Desert Research Institute (University and Community College System of Nevada), with which I was affiliated during the excavations and much of the analysis. During the 1990 season, virtually the entire site was excavated. Following excavation, additional funding from the National Science Foundation, the Institute for Aegean Prehistory, and a travel grant from the National Endowment for the Humanities allowed for the analyses of recovered materials. Several preliminary reports or general articles have been published (Held 1989b:39–63; Reese 1988, 1989b, 1992b; Simmons 1988a,b, 1989a,b,c, 1991a,c, 1992a,c,d, 1993; Simmons and Reese 1993; Simmons *et al.* 1989; Swiny 1995), as have a series of specialized reports (Mandel and Simmons 1997; Reese 1992a, 1996; Simmons 1991b, 1992b, 1996; Simmons and Wigand 1994).

The results of these investigations, documenting the "Akrotiri Phase," are presented here. We feel that *Aetokremnos* has dramatically changed the face of Mediterranean prehistory. Because this is not an immodest claim, we invite readers to form their own opinions of the importance of *Aetokremnos*. The remainder of this chapter provides a contextual framework for our investigations. It first examines the environmental context of *Aetokremnos*, followed by a summary of previous archaeological investigations on the Akrotiri Peninsula. Attention then turns to a discussion on the early prehistory of both Cyprus and the Mediterranean islands, and the chapter concludes by examining island biogeography and the impact of humans on endemic faunas. Chapter 2 describes the site and outlines the research design and methodology. Chapter 3 presents the geoarchaeological analysis of *Aetokremnos*, while Chapter 4 discusses the archaeological stratigraphy. Chapters 5 and 6 provide detail on the cultural features and artifactual materials recovered. Chapter 7 describes the faunal assemblages, while Chapter 8 addresses chronology. In Chapter 9, the results of specialized analyses are presented. Chapter 10 provides data on additional investigations conducted on the Akrotiri Peninsula as part of the project. Chapter 11 compares the *Aetokremnos* chipped stone materials to other sites, both in Cyprus and on the adjacent Levantine mainland. Finally, Chapter 12 synthesizes the previous chapters, assessing the cultural context of *Aetokremnos*, while Chapter 13 examines the significance of the site, not only to Cyprus but to the Mediterranean and beyond.

A point regarding the data from *Aetokremnos* needs to be made here. Modern interdisciplinary archaeology inevitably results in the accumulation of far more data than can be reasonably published in a format such as this. We felt, however, that the site's importance deserved the wide dissemination that this series can provide. The author may be contacted for disk copies of the more detailed data.

ENVIRONMENTAL AND ECOLOGICAL CONTEXT

The Present Environment

Cyprus, covering some 9,550 sq km, is the third largest island in the Mediterranean Sea (Fig. 1-3). It lies just outside the Gulf of Iskenderun, about 65 km south of Turkey and 105 km west of Syria. The geological history of the island is complex and well documented. There was no post-Miocene land bridge connecting Cyprus with the mainland, and the island is oceanic in origin (Constantinou 1982; Gass 1968). The Cypriot landscape has been modified by geomorphic processes, including erosion, alluvation, and eolian deposition throughout the Quaternary (Knapp *et al.* 1994:393–394; Poole and Robertson 1991).

Four primary topographic provinces comprise the island: the coastal belt, the Kyrenia (or Northern) Range, the Troodos (or Southern) Range, and the Mesaoria (or Central Plain). The coastal belt is low almost everywhere, although cliffs occur in some areas. For the most part, the shores are rocky, but small sandy bays are present all around the island, sometimes with extensive strands backed by sand dunes or salt flats. Salt lakes, fringed by salt marshes and other saline habitats, are present near Larnaca and Limassol. In the north, the coastal belt is narrow, nowhere greater than 5 km wide. The Kyrenia Range (also known as the *Pentadaktylos*) is a spectacularly precipitous ridge approximately 80 km long. It runs west to east and is roughly parallel with and adjacent to the north coast. It is composed of hard Permo-Carboniferous-Cretaceous limestone and marbles, with scattered basaltic sills and dykes. The Troodos Range is predominately igneous, with rounded masses of "pillow" lavas in its lower reaches. Higher are peaks of gabbro, diabase, and serpentine (or "picrolite"—an important raw material for prehistoric artisans). The highest point in Cyprus is in the Troodos: Mount Khionistra (Olympus) at 1,950 m. Finally, the Mesaoria Plain is a fertile, treeless feature in the middle of the island. It separates the Kyrenia and Troodos Ranges. A large part of the Mesaoria Plain consists of recently deposited alluvium, while the remainder is composed of Pleistocene sands, marls, gravels, and conglomerates interspersed with older formations of chalk and gypsum. The Mesaoria is crossed by several rivers, all seasonal and normally dry during the summer (Meikle 1977:1–3).

The climate of Cyprus is an arid Mediterranean type, with relatively short, cool, and wet winters, followed by long, dry, and very hot summers. The annual rainfall for the entire island is, on average, about 500 mm, most of which falls between November and March, although local differences are considerable. Not only is variation in rainfall considerable, prolonged droughts are frequent. Temperature varies with season and altitude, ranging from 15.7° C in January to about 36.9° C in August. Snow covers the upper slopes of the Troodos for an average of 10 weeks during the winter. The change from cool, moist conditions in the winter to the warmth and dryness of the summer generally is rather abrupt (Meikle 1977:3-4).

Some portions of Cyprus are relatively moist. The narrow northern coastal range, for example, receives a fair amount of rainfall and also has perennial springs. There also are several rivers, some of which were perennial until recently, draining to the sea. There are a number of springs throughout the Cypriot countryside, dependent on the proper geological conditions. These conditions clearly have affected human settlement both in modern and ancient times (Swiny 1982:2). Many believe, however, that most of the modern sources of fresh water in Cyprus are snowfall in the Troodos and rainfall elsewhere (Knapp *et al.* 1994:394–395).

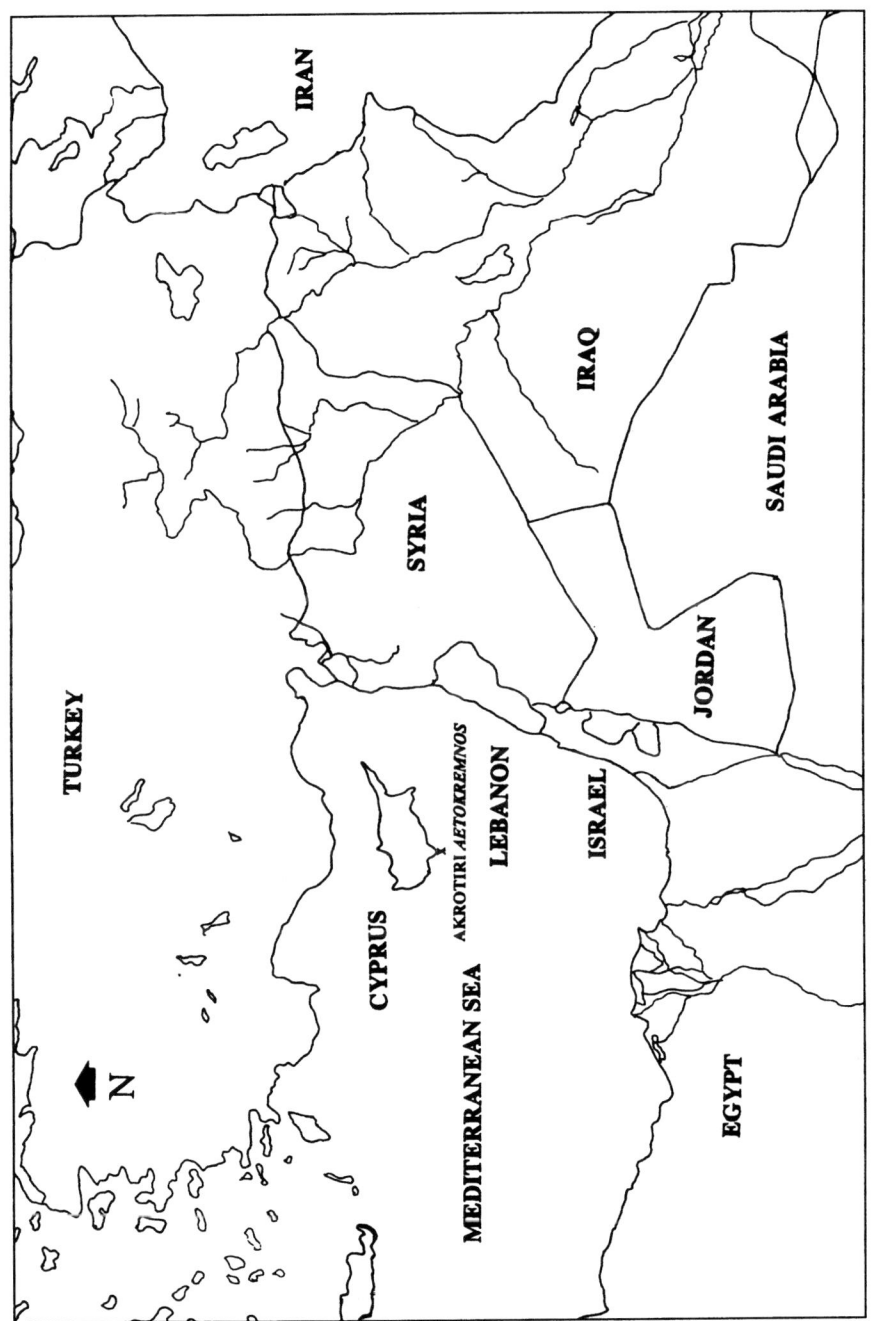

Figure 1-3. Map of Cyprus and the Mediterranean region.

The diversity of topography and the presence of microclimates in Cyprus have resulted in an unexpectedly large range of flora (Meikle 1977, 1985). In the hot and dry lowlands, grass, dwarf shrubs, and xerophytic weeds characterize the vegetation. There is also broadleaf cactus, which is a recent introduction, and juniper, carob, olive, and date palm. Within the foothills of the Kyrenia and Troodos Ranges, some xerophile shrub communities have been established, along with carob, fig, almond, and pistachio trees. Isolated stands of cedar and cypress exist along the Kyrenia Range, while grapevines cover the southern and southeastern flanks of the Troodos. Deciduous hardwood trees today occur only above 1,200 m in the Troodos, where conifers or evergreens are dominant. These latter trees include pine, cedar, wild cypress, and evergreen Cyprian oak (Knapp *et al.* 1994:395).

Although extremely rich in flora, indigenous fauna is more impoverished. Most of the faunal species presently on the island were introduced by humans. The most notable mammalian endemic fauna were the Cypriot pygmy hippopotamus and pygmy elephant. No carnivores are endemic to Cyprus (Boetschoken and Sondaar 1972; Swiny 1988). There are only ten "indigenous" species, all presumably introduced by humans. These are the moufflon (*Ovis orientalis*), fox (*Vulpes vulpes*), hare (*Lepus capensis*), rat (*Rattus rattus*), shrew (*Crocidura russula*), hedgehog (*Hemienchinus auritus*), two forms of mice (*Mus musculus, Acomys dimiadiatus*), Persian fallow deer (*Dama mesopotamica*), and wild boar (*Sus scrofa*) (Bate 1903a,b, 1906; Swiny 1982:4). Held (1990:16) expanded this list to 23 mammals for the Late Holocene, but this inventory included 12 species of bats. Regardless, it is clear that even after human occupation of the island, faunal constellations remained low.

The Akrotiri Peninsula

The Akrotiri Peninsula, on which·*Aetokremnos* is located, is roughly 12 km north-south by 9 km east-west and is the dominant feature of the southern coast of Cyprus. The area can broadly be defined as a shallow syncline of Miocene, Pliocene, and Quaternary rocks with an east-west axis. The Peninsula represents a former island that is now joined to the mainland by a tombolo. There is a shallow salt lake between the two spits that formed the tombolo.

The Peninsula is flanked by Akrotiri Bay and Cape Gata to the east and Episkopi Bay and Cape Zevgari to the west (Heywood 1982:162; Swiny 1982:1–2). It can be divided into three areas: the southern, central, and northern. The southern portion, where *Aetokremnos* is situated, rises from the shallow waters of the Mediterranean in sandstone and marl cliffs to a maximum height of 64 m above sea level (Heywood 1982:164).

The Peninsula is hilly to the north and gently inclines toward the sea. From the northern boundary, which follows the 700 ft (or 213 m) contour, the ground surface slopes gently toward the villages of Erimi, Kolossi, and Ypsonas. From there, the slope becomes very gentle southward toward the Akrotiri Salt Lake and the sea. The hilly portion consists mostly of chalks and marls, with intrusions in the river valleys of calcareous siltstones and alluvium. Many plateaus and ridges have a thick deposit of *havara* (a Cypriot terms that broadly translates as "limestone"), sometimes containing pockets of red terra rossas. Havara more properly represents a surface layer, often several meters thick, of "secondary" limestone deposited through the evaporation of calcium rich groundwater during the summer (Elliott and Dutton 1962:75; Swiny 1982:2). It often is capped by a hardpan calcrete, locally known as *kafkalla*, which is formed through the accumulation of calcium carbonate.

The greater part of the cliff section at *Aetokremnos* exposes Pliocene-age rocks of the Athalassa and Nicosia Formations. The Athalassa Formation, which forms the upper 10–12 m of the section, consists of a highly fossiliferous series of brown and yellowish-brown bioclastic limestones. The underlying Nicosia Formation is a marine littoral facies, consisting of pale brown bioclastic limestones and calcareous sandstones and microbreccias (Morel 1960). The Nicosia beds are largely composed of comminuted shell fragments, with rare fragments of Mamonia hornstone, basic igneous rock, and subordinate quartz and chert grains. Many rockshelters, including *Aetokremnos,* are associated with this stratigraphic unit. The buff-white marls of the Miocene-age Pakha Formation compose the lower 15 m of the cliff section. A distinct unconformity separates the Pakha from the overlying beds of the Nicosia Formation.

Holocene and Late Pleistocene eolian sand sheets and dunes are banked up against and over some of the cliffs in the area of *Aetokremnos* (Morel 1960; Poole and Robertson 1991). Also, there are modern dunes on narrow beaches that are scattered along the southern shoreline of the Akrotiri Peninsula. However, most of the sea cliffs, including the one at *Aetokremnos,* descend directly to the water.

The overhanging rock ledge that formed *Aetokremnos* apparently developed in a manner similar to the numerous rockshelters presently existing along the cliffs of the Akrotiri Peninsula. Specifically, differential weathering of the bioclastic limestone produced an indentation in the cliff. A deepening of this feature occurred as the back wall was attacked by physical and chemical weathering. As enlargement of the hollow progressed, it would have provided shelter for prehistoric people. During this time, sandy sediment accumulated on the shelter floor, thereby protecting it from further attack by weathering or erosion. Excavations revealed that the extant interior of the shelter covered an area of approximately 35 m^2. Portions of the shelter, however, may have been lost as a result of slope retreat. Eventually, the entire roof collapsed, burying the rockshelter deposits and cultural materials contained within.

No major streams cross the Akrotiri Peninsula. North of the village of Episkopi, however, off the Peninsula proper, the Kouris River, which was perennial until quite recently, is one of the largest streams on Cyprus. Other nearby streams, including the Garyllis to the east and the Paramali to the west, are insignificant by comparison and contain little water, especially during the summer. Springs supply water to some areas of Cyprus, but none have been documented on the Peninsula itself (Cadastral Survey of Cyprus 1988). Although the Akrotiri Salt Lake obviously contained water, at least seasonally, it clearly was not potable for humans. Thus it is likely that fresh water was always a problem for the early occupants of the Peninsula.

The Akrotiri Peninsula shares the semiarid Mediterranean climate common to the rest of Cyprus. Over 80 percent of the precipitation falls during December, January, and February (Swiny 1982:3). Today, the local flora is dominated by carobs (*Ceratonia siliqua*) and olives (*Olea europaea*). Localized stands of Cypriot Aleppo pine (*Pinus brutia*) are common. Inland, the southern part of the Akrotiri Peninsula is covered by the remains of the so-called Akrotiri (or Episkopi) Forest, a marquis vegetation consisting mainly of cypress and junipers (*Cupressacea*). Spiny burnet (*Poterium spinosum*), lentisc (*Pistacia spinosum*), and thorny broom (*Calycotomo infesta*) are the principal constituents of the local *garrigue* or marquis (Heywood 1982:164; Swiny 1982:3–4). In antiquity, most of the peninsula was covered with open forest or park land, an ideal habitat for the small selection of indigenous animals discussed earlier (Christodoulou 1959:47; Swiny 1982:4).

The Akrotiri Salt Lake is the dominant feature of the Peninsula, and it may have been an ideal habitat for *Phanourios*. The lake is located in the center of the Peninsula. It lies in the center of a subsea depression and covers an area of about 11 sq km. At times the sea transgresses and joins with the lake, however, making it difficult to draw the exact lake boundaries. The lake bed is about 2.7 m below mean sea level, and the water level in the lakes achieves its maximum height when connected with the sea (Hadjistavrinou and Constantinou 1977: 46).

As noted earlier, the Peninsula was at one time an island. Although the geological facts regarding the formation of an "Akrotiri Island" are established, when this occurred is not. It is certain that the eastern end of the Akrotiri Salt Lake was open to the sea as recently as the Roman period, and probably later. Many early maps of Cyprus clearly show that the lake is open to the sea. This includes "Isola di Ciprio" maps, such as the 1538 Matheo Pagano woodcut and a circa 1562 anonymous Roman or Venetian rendering. One of the oldest maps, "Cypri Insula," by Henricus Martellus Germanus (ca. 1480) actually showed the southern portion of the Peninsula as a near island, with the supposed salt lake area completely open to the eastern sea (Stylianou and Stylianou 1980:185, 195, 207). Even later, presumably more accurate, maps, such as Johann Paul Reinhard's 1766 "Cypri Facies Antiqua," show the salt lake with an opening to the sea (Stylianou and Stylianou 1980:396). In fact, at least one map, E. Michalet's 1693 "I(sle) De Chipre," showed the Akrotiri Peninsula as an island (Stylianou and Stylianou 1980:353).

Of course, one must allow for a "cartographic illusion" effect in early mapping, in which topographic features may not have been accurately rendered. As Stylianou and Stylianou (1980:128) noted in their discussion of the 1693 depiction of the Peninsula as an island: "In fact, owing to the low marshes of the area it [the Peninsula] does look detached from a certain distance out at sea."

More precise evidence for the salt lake being open to the sea is the presence of a Hellenistic or Roman shipwreck discovered near the lake, some 150 m from the present shoreline (Heywood 1982:164). This certainly indicates that the area was open, at least periodically, quite recently.

In any case, whether or not the Peninsula was an island clearly is dependent on several factors, including, obviously, sea level and tectonic activity. It is likely that at times in the past, at least the southern portion of the Peninsula was separated from the mainland. This separation, though, undoubtedly was minimal. With present evidence, it is simply impossible to tell if the area where *Aetokremnos* is located was an island at the time of its occupation. There is a long history of sea-level regressions and transgressions in the Mediterranean throughout the Quaternary, although it is generally accepted that the main rise began by about 15,000–14,000 B.P., and that by about 9000 B.P. the coastal paleogeography approached its present configuration (van Andel 1989, 1990; van Andel and Shackleton 1982; Flint 1974:558). If the sea level already had completed its major rise by the time of *Aetokremnos'* occupation, the possibility of an island may be unlikely. Stanley-Price (1979a:8–9), however, believed that the Akrotiri Peninsula may have been "no more than a shallow gulf between the mainland and the offshore island of Cape Gata" until relatively recently (i.e., the late Roman period). Thus the matter of whether or not the southern edge of the Akrotiri Peninsula was an island when *Aetokremnos* was occupied must remain unresolved at the present time.

Paleoenvironment

Paleoenvironmental data for both Cyprus in general and the Akrotiri Peninsula specifically are limited. One of the best comprehensive examinations of paleoenvironmental topics for Cyprus is an unpublished manuscript by Held (1983). In that document, the author addressed geography, Quaternary geology and geomorphology, Quaternary eustasy, soils and land use, climate, and natural vegetation (Held 1983:17–163). Held also summarized much of this information in his doctoral dissertation (Held 1989b).

A critical issue, that of shoreline reconstruction consonant with fluctuations in sea-level changes, is clearly relevant to our study, especially regarding both animal and human colonization of the island. Unfortunately, little is known about the paleoshorelines of Cyprus, and less is known about those of the Akrotiri Peninsula. A recent article by Gomez and Pease (1992), however, provides some insight.

The examination of Pleistocene sea-level fluctuations began in the Mediterranean (Gomez and Pease (1992:1), and several studies have considered the effects of related shoreline changes on human settlement patterns (e.g., van Andel and Lianos 1983; van Andel and Shackleton 1982; van Andel and Sutton 1987; Flemming *et al.* 1978; Kraft *et al.* 1977; Shackleton *et al.* 1984). Most researchers believe that the main postglacial rise in sea level occurred between about 15,000/14,000 and 9000 year ago. Gomez and Pease (1992:1) noted, however, that Early Holocene eustatically driven changes in palaeogeography were subtler than previous ones.

Successfully reconstructing Holocene coastal palaeogeography requires considerable knowledge of the relative roles of eustatic and tectonic controls on sea level (Gomez and Pease 1992:2). For the western and central Mediterranean, tectonically induced submergence generally is considered to be subordinate to eustatic changes in sea level (Flemming 1972; Shackleton *et al.* 1984), and the coastline is assumed to have attained a semblance of its present configuration in the Early Holocene (ca. 9000 B.P.) For the eastern Mediterranean, including Cyprus, however, it has been more difficult to isolate the effect that localized tectonic activity has had on the coastline's configuration during the Holocene (Flemming *et al.* 1978; Neev *et al.* 1987, cited in Gomez and Pease 1992:2).

Gomez and Pease (1992:2) noted that the nature and implications of changes in Cyprus's palaeogeography have been addressed only in quite broad terms (e.g., Gifford 1978; Held 1989b). Poole and Robertson (1991) had delimited the coastal palaeogeography of the island for circa 18,000 B.P., but this is too early to be of direct significance for human occupation. Gomez and Pease's (1992) study provided palaeogeographic maps for the Cypriot coastline for circa 9000 and 5000 B.P. Unfortunately, this earlier period postdates human occupation at *Aetokremnos*. Thus we still have no direct evidence for the position of the shoreline during the crucial period when the site was occupied.

According to Gomez and Pease (1992), mean sea level in the eastern Mediterranean was about 120 m lower at circa 18,000 B.P. than its present level (following Shackleton *et al.*'s 1984 research). By circa 9000 B.P., mean sea level had risen to about –35 m, and by 5000 B.P. it was within –1 m of its present elevation (Flemming and Webb 1986). Gomez and Pease (1992:2) noted, however, that this general trend may mask regional variations resulting from localized, tectonically induced displacements (cf. Dreghorn 1981). There also appears to have been no major uplift of the Troodos ophiolite during the Holocene (Poole and Robertson 1991; Poole *et al.* 1990). Because of local variations in the relative rates of uplift and submergence (Flemming 1978), it is therefore difficult to precisely determine the rate of sea-level rise and delimit the exact position of the Cypriot shoreline at any given time in the Holocene. In Flemming and Webb's (1986) analysis of tectonic and eustatic changes for deriving best-fit eustatic curves for the Mediterranean, the sea level for Cyprus at circa 5000 B.P. was about –6 m. Gifford (1978) had estimated about –8 m for southeast Cyprus, thus these two figures accord relatively well (Gomez and Pease 1992:2).

Using recent studies and data digitized from 1:300,000 and 1:100,000 bathymetric charts, Gomez and Pease (1992) constructed palaeogeographic maps for the Cypriot coastline. These maps suggest that there were pronounced differences in the position and configuration of the palaeoshoreline for the two periods studied. At 9000 B.P., the shoreline along the southern coast of Cyprus is estimated to have been about 1.5 to 2.5 km further seaward than it currently is, and by circa 5000 B.P., the present configuration of the shoreline had been reached (Gomez and Pease 1992:4).

Gomez and Pease (1992:4) addressed *Aetokremnos* specifically, believing that during the site's occupation the shoreline was likely to have been greater than 1.5 km farther seaward from its present position. Furthermore, coastal erosion initiated by the rising sea level along the south coast of Cyprus has modified the contemporary coastline's configuration to an unknown extent. They noted, additionally, that Poole and Robertson (1991) found no evidence of tectonically induced displacement during the Holocene.

Leaving the issue of sea level, we may now focus attention on terrestrial environmental reconstruction. Certainly historical information suggests an island greatly different from today's. Modern Cyprus consists largely of a severely eroded landscape, no doubt largely culturally induced by overgrazing and overcultivation, which has left an indelible scar. If the comments of Eratosthenes (275–195 B.C.) are true, however, most of Cyprus, including the Mesaoria, was heavily forested in antiquity. Where forests have been destroyed, tall shrub marquis occasionally survives, but even this is uncommon (Meikle 1977:4).

It is often surmised that in antiquity, the interior of Cyprus was heavily forested (Meiggs 1982), although actual paleobotanical data are rare. In a general reconstruction of the Early Holocene vegetation of Cyprus, it is assumed that the island experienced the same reforestation generally agreed to have occurred in the less arid zones of the Near East by circa 10,000 B.P. Meikle (1977:4–8) divided the Late Holocene vegetation of Cyprus into eight phytogeographic regions. The nature of this climax vegetation probably was entirely oak-pine Mediterranean woodland in character (Zohary 1973, Map 7), falling under the broad classification of "Mediterranean Evergreen Oak Belt Formation." Jones *et al.* (1958:24) believed that "there is no doubt that the whole island, including the Central Plains, was at one time covered by Mediterranean evergreen sclerophyllous forest in which oaks, juniper and cypress were the dominant species in different areas." At least the central lowlands, however, should be considered as semiarid, and therefore a marquis cover rather than a true forest may have characterized the vegetation (Stanley-Price 1979a:13–14).

The traditional notions of floral succession have been questioned by Blumler (1993:289–291), who suggested that "climax" vegetation may also have included large-seeded annuals or dense, shrubby vegetation, the former occurring on fertile soils and the latter on rock soils. Blumler also noted that early successional plants often create conditions unfavorable to the establishment of their offspring (Knapp *et al.* 1994:395). Indeed, what limited pollen data that do exist for Cyprus show low percentages of arboreal pollen and high percentages of herbaceous pollen (Renault-Miskovsky 1985, 1989). These findings cannot, however, be considered representative of the entire island.

Regarding fauna, we have already noted the impoverished nature of prehuman Cyprus. While endemics such as *Phanourios* and *Elephas* have been documented extensively in the paleontological literature (see Held 1992; Reese 1989b, 1995; and Sondaar 1986 for summaries), these did not survive long into the Holocene. Their coexistence with humans, of course, is a major thrust of this volume.

Cyprus, overall, has largely been ignored by paleoenvironmental researchers despite numerous archaeological investigations on the island. Even in more broadly focused studies, such as Brice's (1978) comprehensive study of the environmental history of the Near East, Cyprus was barely mentioned. Stanley-Price (1979a:1–15), however, did provide a useful, if general, overview of the Early Holocene geography of the island. The situation has improved with the inception and implementation of multidisciplinary projects, and Held (1983:1–16) provided a thorough discussion of the status of such research. Especially significant have been studies on land use and catchment analysis with reference to ethnographic data (Legge 1982a), geomorphology (Gifford 1978; Koucky and Bullard 1974; Morrison 1982), faunal remains and paleoethnobotany (Colledge 1980, 1981, 1982; Croft 1989a,b; Cutler 1982; Davis 1984, 1987a; Hansen 1989, 1991; Kyllo 1982; Legge 1982b; Miller 1984; Schwartz 1973a,b; Stewart 1974), and palynology (Bottema 1966, 1976; Renault-Miskovsky 1985, 1989).

All this is very well, but when it comes to the Akrotiri Peninsula, virtually no paleoenvironmental data exist. In particular, a paleogeographic study of the Akrotiri Salt Lake, similar to what Gifford (1978) did for the Larnaca Salt Lake to the east, is sorely needed. Even more directly relevant to *Aetokremnos* would be a series of paleogeographic studies aimed specifically at shoreline reconstruction and other coastal attributes as they affect resource distribution, as has been done at Franchthi Cave in the Argolid of Greece (e.g., van Andel 1987; van Andel and Sutton 1987; Shackleton 1985). Gomez and Pease's (1992) recent study made a significant contribution, but remains generalized. Presently, we can only make generalizations in attempting to reconstruct the Akrotiri Peninsula's paleoenvironment.

If Akrotiri Salt Lake caused a near islandlike microenvironment on the Peninsula, a lagoon biotope of the type often associated with such coastal configurations may have been present at the time that *Aetokremnos* was occupied. The cliffs in which the site is located may have been attached to the emerging Limassol Plain by only a narrow spit of alluvium. The marshy, lagoonal environment that would have existed around the salt lake would have made an attractive habitat for *Phanourios* and the apparently sympatric *Elephas* (Held 1989a:9). As noted earlier, an assumption has been that much of Cyprus was forested prior to human overexploitation. Beach zones, however, are a natural barrier for many plants (Cox *et al.* 1973:94), so some of the arboreal species included in Cyprus's maritime scrub forest climax are not likely to have been abundant on the Akrotiri Peninsula. These may have formed a coastal forest on the higher landforms near Limassol (Held 1989a:map G; 1989b:11). The critical unknown variable here is the level of the sea at the time of occupation. The assumption of a lower sea level at circa 9000 B.P. (cf. Gomez and Pease 1992) would, in a sense, contradict this reconstruction. On the other hand, the tectonic instability of the Akrotiri Peninsula might have counteracted any effects of sea-level change (although, as noted earlier, Poole and Robertson [1991] did not find evidence for local tectonic displacement during the Holocene). In other words, we simply do not know with a comfortable degree of confidence what the precise paleoenvironmental conditions were like at any particular point or area in Cyprus during much of the Holocene. Only a program of systematic paleoenvironmental research will begin to address these issues on a locale basis.

In summary, paleoenvironmental research has not characterized Cypriot archaeology. It is, however, becoming more common with the realization that

> (a) the evidence is there but will not reveal itself unless searched for by . . . geologists, botanists, and paleontologists, and (b) the methodological principles of cultural ecology need to receive much more explicit treatment in Cypriot prehistoric archaeology than in the past if the reciprocal causality between culture and insular environment . . . is to be understood. (Held 1983:329)

SUMMARY OF PREVIOUS ARCHAEOLOGICAL INVESTIGATIONS ON THE AKROTIRI PENINSULA

Although Cyprus has been studied by archaeologists for decades, only limited investigations have occurred on the Akrotiri Peninsula. The area adjacent to the Peninsula is extraordinarily rich in archaeological remains, with perhaps the Roman complex of Kourion being the best known. But the Peninsula itself has not been well studied, due in no small part to the fact that most of it is home of RAF Akrotiri, a high-security military establishment. In particular, much of the area along the southern end of the Peninsula, where *Aetokremnos* is located, is a restricted zone.

Despite these restrictions, there have been a few archaeological investigations on the Akrotiri Peninsula prior to the *Aetokremnos* project, although there is an overall lack of systematic information available. These studies are well summarized in a volume edited by H. Swiny (1982). Many of the investigations that have been conducted on the Peninsula have been undertaken by amateur archaeologists associated with the Western Sovereign Base Area Archaeological Society. These studies indicate that the Peninsula has been occupied for millennia. In particular, the area witnessed an abundant Roman occupation, including large settlements, tombs carved into the Akrotiri cliffs, and at least one harbor. There also is evidence for earlier occupation, much of it obtained by the survey of Pile, the "rediscoverer" of *Aetokremnos*, who documented numerous artifact scatters, including some dating to the Chalcolithic and earlier.

RESEARCH ON THE EARLY PREHISTORY OF CYPRUS AND THE QUESTION OF THE INITIAL OCCUPATION OF THE MEDITERRANEAN ISLANDS

Introduction

We believe that *Aetokremnos* is the oldest well-documented archaeological site in Cyprus, and amongst the oldest on any of the Mediterranean islands. Given this claim, it is necessary to examine in some detail the archaeological evidence and context for early occupations of these islands. We first examine the Neolithic period of Cyprus. Such a summary is necessary since the earliest, Aceramic, phases of the Neolithic could conceivably have been related to the occupation of *Aetokremnos*. We then take a wider, pan-Mediterranean approach, summarizing evidence for pre-Neolithic occupations in the region. Finally, we return to Cyprus and will examine in some detail the few claims that have been made for pre-Neolithic cultural materials.

The Cypriot Neolithic

Cyprus, having witnessed successive occupations for thousands of years, has a rich archaeological heritage. Not surprisingly, much research has focused on Bronze Age and later sites, which tend to contain substantial remains. There is, however, an abundant, if less well known, earlier occupation to Cyprus. Knapp *et al.*'s (1994) recent review of the early periods includes a revised chronological scheme, where both the Neolithic and Chalcolithic are considered as "Early Prehistoric" while the Late Chalcolithic and Bronze Age are considered as "Late Prehistoric" (summarized in Table 1-1). They provide an excellent overview of early developments on the island, presenting these within a comprehensive theoretical framework.

As is typical with the adjacent Levantine mainland, two Neolithic phases are recognized in Cyprus: Aceramic and Ceramic. The Aceramic Neolithic frequently is referred to as the Khirokitia Culture (KCU) (Knapp *et al.* 1994:404), clearly demonstrating that site's significance as well as the site-specific biases so common in Cypriot archaeology. There are at least a dozen Aceramic sites known (Stanley-Price 1977a, 1979a), although Watkins (1973:38) claimed that this number is closer to twenty, and Held (1982:8) believed that over fifty sites may belong to the Aceramic Neolithic. Summaries of the Aceramic Neolithic include those by Cherry (1990:154–157), Knapp *et al.* (1994:398–409), LeBrun (1989, 1993), LeBrun *et al.* (1987), Todd (1987b,c), and Watkins (1981a). More detailed description may be found in the gazetteers compiled by Held (1989b:287–379) and Stanley-Price (1979a). Only a very few sites have been systematically investigated. Khirokitia *Vounoi*, Rizokarpaso *Cape Andreas Kastros*, Kalavasos *Tenta*, Kholetria *Ortos*, and Limnitis *Petra tou Liminiti* have been thoroughly excavated or intensively sampled, while more limited test excavations and/or surface collections have been conducted at only a few other sites (Knapp *et al.* 1994:404–405). Most evidence for the Aceramic Neolithic comes from habitation sites, and smaller, limited activity sites have not been the focus of critical research. Recent survey work, however, has begun to record nonarchitectural sites as well (e.g., Kardulias *et al.* 1992; Rupp 1981,

Table 1-1. Suggested Chronological Scheme for the Early Prehistoric Period in Cyprus (modified from Knapp *et al.* 1994:381)

Revised	Traditional	Dates BC (calibrated)
Akrotiri Phase	"pre-Neolithic"?	10,000–?
Khirokitia culture (KCU)	Aceramic Neolithic	7,000/6,500–5,800/5,500
Gap?		5,800/5,500?–5,000?
Sotira culture (SCU)	Ceramic Neolithic	5,000–3,900/3,700
Erimi culture (ECU)	Chalcolithic	3,900/3,700–2,400

1987a,b; Rupp *et al.* 1984), and test excavations have recently been conducted at two small sites in the west (Simmons 1998b). Nonetheless, the emphasis on villages has resulted in a distorted understanding of the Aceramic Neolithic, and it also has produced a bias against systematic investigation of limited activity sites (e.g., Simmons 1991b).

The Aceramic Neolithic is followed by an apparent cultural hiatus, after which the Ceramic Neolithic, or Sotira Culture, is documented. The Sotira Culture is widespread (Cherry 1990:157; Karageorghis 1982:26–30; Knapp *et al.* 1994:406–409) and some sites are built over Aceramic Neolithic remains, but there is little evidence for cultural continuity, leading some researchers to posit recolonization of the island (Cherry 1981:60–61; Stanley-Price 1977a:34–37, 1979b).

The Aceramic Neolithic is the phase most relevant to the *Aetokremnos* project, and a brief summary is appropriate here, because one might propose a continuity. Cypriot Aceramic Neolithic chipped stone assemblages bear virtually no similarities to roughly contemporary mainland artifacts and frequently are referred to as nondescript, "unremarkable" (Held 1989b:59, 1990:21) or "d'un secteur technologique neglige et peu creatif" (Cauvin 1984:86). However, systematic studies have been rare, and the lack of such analyses is a significant research gap (Held 1990:17–18). Even at major sites, only cursory information has been published (e.g., Cauvin 1984; Coqueugniot 1984; Hordynsky and Todd 1987:17–18; LeBrun 1981:31–41). At two sites, however, more detailed information is available. These are *Cape Andreas Kastros* (LeBrun 1981:31–41) and *Ortos* (Cooper 1997:61–96; Simmons 1994a:4–8, 1994c:40–42). Studies at the later indicate a fairly sophisticated chipped stone technology, as do recent excavations at Aceramic Neolithic *Shillourokampos* (Guilaine *et al.* 1993, 1995) and *Ais Yiorkis* (Fox 1987:20–21; Simmons 1998b), both of which are relatively small sites with limited evidence for architecture. It is my feeling that if systematic analyses were conducted on more of the Aceramic Neolithic assemblages, the results might surprise many researchers.

Despite the rather uninspiring nature of the chipped stone, other stone artifacts are more impressive. Elaborate polished ground-stone artifacts, including axes, and a very sophisticated stone vessel industry are characteristic of the Aceramic Neolithic. Ornaments of picrolite or other polished stone also are common at many sites.

It also is informative to examine Aceramic Neolithic subsistence strategies in relation to *Aetokremnos,* because the later indicates a radically different economic base. Unfortunately, we know less about Aceramic Neolithic subsistence than might be expected. Particularly lacking are paleobotanical data. Despite extensive excavation at a few sites, there is very little systematically collected paleobotanical information available for the Aceramic Neolithic (Hansen 1987, 1989, 1991). There are several reasons for this, including traditionally poor preservation of botanical remains, but early excavations were conducted without benefit of state-of-the-art data recovery methods. Analysis of pollen also has been limited, although one such study at Khirokitia provided important information on vegetation reconstruction and human impacts (Renault-Miskovsky 1989), if not paleoeconomy.

Neither Khirokitia nor *Tenta* produced a wide variety of paleobotanical material, with einkorn wheat being the most common species. Lentils and other small legumes also were present. The only other Aceramic Neolithic sites in Cyprus that have produced plant remains are *Cape Andreas Kastros* (van Zeist 1981) where, like Khirokitia, samples were few and selective, and Dahli *Agridhi* (Steward 1974), where very few remains were identified from a small number of samples (that site was only tested in a limited fashion). The recent excavations at Kholetria *Ortos* conducted extensive floatation. Despite this, paleobotanical remains there are limited, although analysis is still underway (Simmons 1994a:10).

Fauna from Cypriot Aceramic Neolithic sites are better preserved than are botanical remains. The fauna are interesting in that they contain not only domesticated species, but also fallow deer, which is not believed to have been an endemic species. In addition to deer, other economic species include sheep, goat, and an early breed of domestic pig. Mouse, shrew, dog, and possibly cat (at Khirokitia and *Ortos*) also occur (Croft 1982, 1989b, 1995; Davis 1984, 1989, 1994). Recently, there also have been claims for cattle at two sites (Guilaine *et al.* 1995:25, 30–31; Simmons 1998b), which is particularly significant as this species was previously felt to be an early Bronze Age introduction (Knapp *et al.* 1994:418). At *Cape Andreas Kastros,* there is also an emphasis on marine resources, as seen in the presence of fish (Desse 1984; Desse and Desse-Berset 1989, 1994) and marine shell (Cataliotti-Valdina 1994).

An overall picture that emerges is an economy that was based on farming two varieties of wheat, barley, lentils, peas and broadbean; on the raising of sheep, goat, pig, and possibly cattle; and the hunting of Persian fallow deer. Various subsidiary food resources also were exploited. These include wild plants and fruits (e.g., vetch, fig, olives, pistachio), fish, marine invertebrates, and birds. The domesticated plants and animals were almost certainly imported from the Levant (Carter 1989; Croft 1989b; Davis 1994:305; Hansen 1989, 1991; Held 1982:9; Miller 1984; Stanley-Price and Christou 1973; Waines and Stanley-Price 1977).

Of particular significance to the *Aetokremnos* project is that no traces of pygmy hippopotamus or pygmy elephant have been uncovered in association with archaeological sites. The only exceptions to this are single bones recovered from two Aceramic Neolithic and one Chalcolithic sites. The first, a metacarpus, is from *Cape Andreas Kastros*, and the second, a worked fossilized long bone, is from Akanthou *Arkosyko* (Reese 1989b:29, 1992a). A *Phanourios* left lower molar from Chalcolithic *Mosphilia* also has been recorded (Reese 1995:181). The association of these bones with cultural materials is questionable, and Davis (1987b:125, 1989:189) suggested that these single bones could have been collected from fossil sites by Neolithic "paleontologists." The absence of these animals from the archaeological record suggests that these indigenous species either were extinct or rapidly became so when man colonized the island, probably due to hunting and competition from introduced animals (Davis 1984:124–125).

Chronological refinement of the entire Cypriot Neolithic sequence is a major issue, especially in light of the findings from *Aetokremnos*. This subject has been dealt with in extreme detail by Held (1989b:211–284, 497–695) and Knapp *et al.* (1994:379–390). Despite the presence of numerous radiocarbon determinations from the Aceramic Neolithic, there are substantial problems in the period's chronology (Cherry 1990:156). These problems involve issues of calibration, C-13 correction, and a host of other difficulties. Held (1989b:278) provided a reasoned estimated of circa 7,000/6,500 to 5,700/5,5000 calendar years B.C. for the duration of the Khirokitia Culture. Knapp *et al.* (1994:383) suggested an Aceramic Neolithic "floruit" in the mid-late seventh–early sixth millennium B.C.[2]

Equally daunting is both the duration of the Sotira Culture and the presumed hiatus between it and the Khirokitia Culture (Knapp *et al.* 1994:406–409), the so-called "gaping

---

[2]Current research at *Shillourokambos* (Guilaine *et al.* 1995) may extend the Aceramic Neolithic back by approximately a thousand years, but precise details have not yet been published.

chasm" (Watkins 1981b:10) or "occupational hiccup" (Held 1990:22) of about 1000 years. The existence of this gap is a subject of some controversy, and although it is outside of scope of discussion here, it clearly has important implications for the origin of the Ceramic Neolithic and later cultures (Cherry 1990:157).

In summary, our knowledge of the Cypriot Neolithic is coming into clearer focus, and much current research is taking a problem-oriented approach. Identified problem areas include examination of the island's early colonization, the gap in occupation between the Aceramic and Ceramic Neolithic (Cherry 1981; Stanley-Price 1977a), and the duration and extent of the Sotira Culture (Dikaios 1961; Peltenburg 1978, 1982b; and Stanley-Price 1979a:77–81). In addition, studies such as those undertaken by Todd (1977, 1978, 1979, 1982, 1989a) on the Vasilikos Valley Project, LeBrun's (1994) detailed studies at Khirokitia, and Stanley-Price's (1977a,b, 1979a,b) broader attempts at theoretical treatment have contributed substantially to a better understanding of the Cypriot Neolithic.

Pre-Neolithic Human Occupation of the Mediterranean Islands: Fact or Fiction?

Although the broad outlines of Neolithic settlement of Cyprus are known and accepted, what, if anything, came before is not. The possibility of an earlier occupation is one of considerable controversy, an issue that *Aetokremnos* has fueled. Prior to our investigation, consensus opinion was that the first occupation of most of the Mediterranean islands, including Cyprus, was relatively late, occurring during the Neolithic (e.g., Cherry 1979, 1981, 1984, 1985; Stanley-Price 1977a,b). There have, however, been claims for earlier occupations, and it is instructive to summarize these. Cherry's (1990, 1992) excellent treatments provided thorough and thoughtful discussion on this controversial issue. Vigne (1987a, 1989, 1992) also has addressed this issue in a systematic fashion, as have Lewthwaite (1989) and Patton (1996).

Over the years, there have been many claims for pre-Neolithic occupation of several of the Mediterranean islands. Stanley-Price (1977:69) provided two simple criteria for evaluating such claims: (1) the reported material must exhibit features exclusively characteristic of Paleolithic or Mesolithic (Epipaleolithic) materials, and (2) the materials' context must be clearly of Pleistocene age. Although useful, Stanley-Price's caveats need clarification. Depending on where one draws the boundary line, pre-Neolithic material need not necessarily be "Pleistocene"—it could include materials from the Early Holocene. Certainly, however, any claims for pre-Neolithic materials must demonstrate both a chronological antecedence to the Neolithic and an artifact assemblage sufficiency distinct from the Neolithic to warrant separate cultural classification.

One obvious aspect of proposing human occupation of any island is the need to postulate sea travel by those responsible. Extensive geological research shows that subsequent to the Late Miocene, Cyprus has always been isolated by several kilometers of open sea (Held 1989a:12; Hsü 1977; Stanley-Price 1977b:69). If the maximum recession of sea level during the Pleistocene was nearly 130 m (Millman and Emery 1968), Stanley-Price (1977a:29) believed that there always was a gap of at least 60 km between Cyprus and Anatolia (Stanley-Price 1977a:29); slightly over 100 km today separates Cyprus from Latakia in Syria (Adovasio *et al.* 1978:39). Both Held (1989a:12) and Swiny (1988:3) have calculated slightly lower figures of about 30–40 km separating northeastern Cyprus from a now-submerged northern Levantine coast via the so-called "Klidhes Strait." These figures clearly reflect optimal conditions as well; throughout the Pleistocene and Early Holocene, it is likely that sea levels fluctuated.

Distance is not the sole variable involved here. Held (1989b:66–104) has dealt with this issue in great detail, providing a provocative discussion, drawing largely on, and refining, the approaches espoused by MacArthur and Wilson's *Theory of Island Biogeography* (1967). Held considered the relative ease or difficulty of island colonization. Much of his discussion has to do with the size of islands as well, with the theory being that the larger islands, presenting better "targets," are usually those initially occupied. Held's analysis included developing a "target/distance ratio" (T/D ratio), providing a standardized numerical quantification by which to measure how difficult a particular island may have been to reach.

Held noted that although the Klidhes Strait may have been the shortest distance between Cyprus and the mainland, it may not have been the easiest route; the distance advantage may have been offset by the fact that "Cyprus would not have been visible from the paleocoastline . . . hence requiring a 'blind' crossing" (Held 1989b:73). He further calculated that the under Late Holocene conditions, the smallest water gaps between Cyprus were as follows: 69 km between Cape Anomer (Anatolia) and Cape Kormakiti, 81 km between Cape Ovacik (Anatolia) and the northern seaboard, 101 km between Cape Ras al Ibn Hani (Syria) and Cape Andreas in the northern panhandle of Cyprus, and 108 km between Cape Ras al Basit (Syria) and Cape Andreas. During glacial maxima, these distances would have been less: 65, 64, 81, and 81 km, respectively. These changes would have resulted in a shift in optimal crossing points and easier accessibility from the northern Levant (Held 1989b:73).

Although we cannot do justice to Held's elaborate analysis here, he concluded that Cyprus was a rather difficult and isolated "colonization target" (for both humans and animals) due partially to a lack of "stepping-stone islands." He believed, in fact (Held 1989a:15, 1989b:78–104), that the occupation of Cyprus by humans was a major feat, despite the fact that the actual distance separating Cyprus from the mainland is not huge—in clear weather, Cyprus is visible from both southern Anatolia and Syria (Stanley-Price 1977b:76). Although a voyage from the mainland to Cyprus was not necessarily an easy task, Held (1989b:104) conceded that "in the Mediterranean, of course, boat voyages— even where primitive water craft are involved—are unlikely to exact endurance records from the occupants." (Patton [1996:35–42] provided additional discussion on this issue.)

Any pre-Neolithic colonizers of the island had to possess a relatively efficient knowledge of seafaring. Certainly, even by the time of the occupation of *Aetokremnos*, marine travel already was known in the Mediterranean—obsidian from the island of Melos recovered at Franchthi Cave in Greece indicates this as early as circa 12,000 B.P. (Perlès 1979). The types of vessels used by these early seafarers is unknown, but Johnstone (1980) believed that boats or rafts made from reed bundles were likely.

Cherry (1981, 1984, 1985, 1987, 1990, 1992) has examined many of the pre-Neolithic claims from throughout the Mediterranean, providing a compelling argument that almost all are poorly documented and do not stand up to critical scrutiny. Portions of Runnels (1995) and Patton (1996:35–62) also addressed this issue. A few of the more frequently cited claims include Maroula on Kythnos in the Cyclades (Honea 1975), presumed Upper Paleolithic skeletal remains (Facchini and Giusberti 1988) or pre-Neolithic occupation (discussed and generally dismissed by Broodbank and Strasser [1991] and Lax and

Strasser [1992]) on Crete, three localities in Corsica (Bonifay 1983; Camps 1988:22–23; Lanfranchi 1967, 1974; Lanfranchi and Weiss 1973, 1977), Corbeddu in Sardinia (Hofmeijer and Sondaar 1992; Hofmeijer *et al.* 1987, 1989; Sondaar *et al.* 1986,1989, 1991), and possible Lower Paleolithic finds in northern Sardinia (Acra *et al.* 1982a,b; Martini 1992; Martini and Pitzalis 1980). The Paleolithic (especially Upper) and Mesolithic are well represented in Sicily (Garcia 1972:23; Pianese 1968; Tagliacozzo 1993; Tusa 1985), but this island is close to the mainland, and a land bridge existed during the Upper Pleistocene (Cherry 1990:189; Sondaar 1987:162). A similar argument may be made for many claims from the Aegean islands, where islands with presumed Paleolithic materials, such as Corfu, are quite close to the mainland (cf. Runnels 1995).

Some better supported claims come from the Balearic and Pitiussae Islands, where over 200 radiocarbon determinations provide a sequence reaching back to initial colonization (Alcover 1991; Lewthwaite 1989; Waldren 1982, 1991, 1994; Waldren and Kennard 1987; Waldren *et al.* 1984, 1991). In Mallorca, excavations at Muleta produced 36 radiocarbon determinations spanning circa 2000 to 45,000 B.P. (Waldren 1982). Not all the deposits there are cultural, but it is likely that humans were on Mallorca by circa 7000 B.P. If the determinations from Ca'n Canet (Kopper 1984) are correct and date human associations, occupation as early as circa 9000 B.P. is possible. There are, however, difficulties with these sites (Cherry 1990:184–189).

A brief consideration of two other cases, more thoroughly discussed by Cherry (1990:175–178, 1992) and Simmons (1991b:286–287), may be instructive here. One of the better documented claims for a pre-Neolithic settlement is that made for Corbeddu Cave in Sardinia (Hofmeijer and Sondaar 1992; Hofmeijer *et al.* 1987, 1989; Sondaar *et al.* 1986; Spoor and Sondaar 1986, 1987).

Corbeddu Cave initially was investigated for its paleontological interest. Professional archaeologists only became associated with the project at a relatively late stage in its investigation. Cultural material is present, including clear Neolithic remains in upper strata. Below the Neolithic level, the remains of the ochotonid hare (*Prolagus sardus*) and extinct deer (*Megaceros cazioti*) were reported with apparent traces of human activity (but no artifacts) and human bone. Below this, another pre-Neolithic occupation dating to circa 14,000 B.P. was claimed. This layer contained abundant deer; various taphonomic variables and modifications to the bone were attributed to human causation. In fact, it has been implied that the ancestors of those responsible for the Corbeddu deposits could have immigrated to Sardinia during the Middle Pleistocene, some 200,000–300,000 years ago. Despite an impeccable excavation of an obviously significant paleontological resource with some intriguing taphonomic questions, the Corbeddu evidence simply is not very robust (Cherry 1990:175–177, 1992; Vigne 1987a:168–170).

The second example, also from Sardinia, is even less convincing. Some of the presumed earliest sites in the Mediterranean are claimed to come from the Perfugas district of Sardinia, along the Rio Altana and at Pantillinu (Arca *et al.* 1982a,b; Martini 1992; Martini and Pitzalis 1980, 1981, 1982). Sites here have been claimed to date to the Lower Paleolithic, largely based on the presence of large, hard, hammer-struck "Clactonian-looking" artifacts. These "sites" are huge surface lithic scatters or are heavily abraded or rolled surface finds. Although many of the artifacts could indeed be Lower Paleolithic implements, they also could represent specialized activities of much later groups. Furthermore, the presence of these artifacts in highly disturbed contexts, such as plowed fields, raises the very real possibility of postoccupational disturbance, including the possibility of very recent "manufacture" by modern agencies. What is particularly disturbing about the situation is that despite obvious contextual problems, Perfugas is now enshrined as an integral part of the Sardinian archaeological heritage, with finds being represented in museums as examples of the Lower Paleolithic occupation of Sardinia without mention of possible distorting factors.

The point of this digression is simply to observe that it is not an easy task to precisely document the "archaeological signature" of early hunter-gatherer remains. Caution must be used before jumping to conclusions based on sparse or equivocal data from questionable contexts, and alternative scenarios for presumed associations should be considered (Cherry 1992; Simmons 1991b:287).

Pre-Neolithic Claims from Cyprus

Let us now examine pre-Neolithic claims from Cyprus, of which there have been four specific cases, as well as a few hints from other localities. The two most widely cited claims for pre-Neolithic occupation in Cyprus are by Stockton (1968) and Vita-Finzi (1973). Critical examination of both, however, shows them to be less than convincing. Slightly more compelling, yet still unverified, claims have been made by Adovasio et al. (1975, 1978) and by Baudou (1982, 1983; Baudou and Engelmark 1983; Baudou et al. 1985).

Stockton's claim of early flint artifacts from three locations near Kyrenia in northern Cyprus is based on surface materials with little or no context that were not diagnostic of any known early assemblages. These materials were reanalyzed as part of the *Aetokremnos* project (see Chap. 10). Stockton noted abundant waste materials as well as over a hundred tools. These primarily were a variety of "scrapers," "knives," and "backed flake tools." He also noted the presence of a heavily patinated bifacial "chopper-like" tool, a possible awl, and two small geometrical pieces, one of which was triangular and the other rectangular. The last was "quite the more convincing" (Stockton 1968:18). If these were real microlithic artifacts, they would be important because such artifacts often are a diagnostic implement of the Epipaleolithic; unfortunately, the illustrations (Stockton 1968:Plate VII) show very crude objects unlikely to be microliths. Also recorded were 12 cores "all irregularly knapped on a plain platform and all showing an acute angle (about 45°) between the platform and bulbar face. The flakes, too, generally showed a corresponding angle and a prominent bulb of percussion. There was no evidence of blade-making at all" (Stockton 1968:18). Many of these presumed artifacts were heavily patinated, but a smaller number were "fresher."

Of particular interest is Stockton's mention of round "thumbnail" scrapers. This is significant because the most diagnostic artifacts of the *Aetokremnos* assemblage are thumbnail scrapers. Stockton's illustrations of two of these (1968:Plate V) are, unfortunately, not very compelling.

The illustrations of these "artifacts" (Stockton 1968:Plates V–VII) are far from convincing. Much of the material is so undiagnostic as to even question its human origin. It also appears that most of Stockton's flints were collected on the property of the Australian archaeologist J. R. Stewart. Stewart's widow has indicated that these collections were made from road gravels that had been brought in from various beaches, and thus were not in situ deposits (Swiny, personal communication 1985). Many of the so-called artifacts may have been naturally fractured cobbles; all were from highly disturbed deposits. Those that are artifacts are likely *dhoukani* flints from modern threshing platforms (Held 1990:21; Pearlman 1984). In short, there is nothing to verify Stockton's claim that this material "certainly antedates what was previously the earliest known cultural remains of Cyprus, and could antedate it up to 40,000 years" (Stockton 1968:19).

Likewise, Vita-Finzi (1973), a researcher with more formal training in archaeology than Stockton, who was an avocational archaeologist, believed that several flint artifacts found on a fossil beach and within a red clayey silt near the mouth of the Moronou River east of Zyyi, on the south coast of the island, could be of pre-Neolithic (possibly Middle Paleolithic) age. He based this conclusion on the location of the artifacts in a geological context of some antiquity. Once again, however, the five illustrated artifacts (Vita-Finzi 1973:Fig. 1 a–e) are undiagnostic. Two appear to be elongated flakes (a and b), one an amorphous flake (e), one a rather globular core (d), and one a possible microlithic core, or flake with several scars removed (c). None look like "typical" Middle Paleolithic implements. Given their context, they could be natural rather than human-made, and in any event, they are not suitably distinct to warrant a pre-Neolithic status.

Another study in which a pre-Neolithic presence was suggested was the survey conducted by Adovasio and his colleagues in the northwest part of Cyprus. Adovasio *et al.* (1975, 1978) undertook a systematic survey of the Khrysokhou River drainage, specifically seeking early materials. They noted possible pre-Neolithic spot finds and also believed that one large site, Androlikou *Ayios Mamas*, might be Upper, or even Middle, Paleolithic.

The assemblage from *Ayios Mamas*, originally recorded by Dikaios (1936), was compared with another collected by the surveyors at *Myrmikoph*, a presumed Aceramic Neolithic site (Adovasio *et al.* 1975:361). The sample size from both was small: 156 (62 tools) and 89 (23 tools). A typological and technological comparison yielded the following results: The assemblage from *Myrmikoph* had a generalized blade technology and a relatively lower number of distinct tool types, while the artifacts from *Ayios Mamas*, though based on flakes, was typologically more specialized and therefore thought to resemble Upper or Middle Paleolithic assemblages. Furthermore, the use of faceted platforms on the *Ayios Mamas* assemblage (15.56%), as opposed to a high frequency of punctiform platforms (26.32%) at *Myrmikoph*, supported this conclusion, since faceted platforms are a common technological element of Middle Paleolithic (Mousterian) assemblages (Adovasio *et al.* 1975:356–361). Most of these were eroding from gravel deposits and were not associated with other artifactual materials (Adovasio *et al.* 1978:42–44).

In addition to *Ayios Mamas*, several spot finds also were believed to represent pre-Neolithic implements. These included "a bifacially worked chopper made on a partially decorticated cobble of pebble chert, a remarkably Levallois-like chalcedony uniface with a faceted platform, a unifacial side-scraper of Middle Paleolithic appearance, and a large nucleus [core], again with a faceted platform" (Adovasio *et al.* 1978:44). These materials were found eroding out of gravel deposits and were not associated with other artifacts (Adovasio *et al.* 1975:362).

Although Adovasio and his colleagues present a reasonable argument, careful consideration reveals it to be less than compelling. There are a number of difficulties. First, all of their observations are made on unstratified surface or eroded materials. Second, none of the artifacts in question are illustrated. Third, the representativeness of the assemblages from *Ayios Mamas* and *Myrmikoph* must be questioned. Fourth, *Ayios Mamas* (and *Myr-*

mikoph) also contain a large quantity of probable Neolithic ground-stone implements (Adovasio et al. 1975:361). The presence of ground stone strongly argues for, at a minimum, a Neolithic component at Ayios Mamas and introduces the chimera of assemblage mixing.

Finally, the technological and typological analysis is less than convincing. A basic problem is the small sample size. Although both the Ayios Mamas and the Myrmikoph assemblages have large percentages of scrapers (25.81% and 30.39% respectively), Ayios Mamas exhibits considerable tool diversity, which might be typical of a pre-Neolithic, hunter-gatherer assemblage (interestingly, the most common tools at Aetokremnos are scrapers). Unfortunately, so little has been published on Cypriot chipped stone assemblages that useful comparisons are difficult. The argument for platform types is equally unconvincing. Although faceted platforms do occur at Ayios Mamas, flat (i.e., unprepared) platforms were predominant at both sites (75.56% at Ayios Mamas and 68.42% at Myrmikoph). There clearly are some differences between both sites, but an argument claiming that one is possibly Middle Paleolithic cannot be supported with the data provided. To deliver the coupe de grâce is Held's (1990:21, fn. 10) observation that resurveys of Ayios Mamas by Stanley-Price (1979a:140) and Peltenburg (1979a:78) failed to confirm a "Paleolithic" character of the chipped stone and, in fact, recorded quantities of Formative ceramics.

A final claim for pre-Neolithic sites comes from another survey, conducted in 1980. This survey was in the Tremithos Valley, some 10 to 20 km west and northwest of Larnaca (Baudou 1982, 1983; Baudou and Engelmark 1983; Baudou et al. 1985). Three sites were located that were considered "Stone Age sites, probably lacking pottery. The find material consists of flint flakes and implements. No Stone Age pottery, axes or fragment of stone vessels were found" (Baudou et al. 1985:369).

In 1981, a trial excavation was conducted at one of the sites, Ayia Anna 3 (or Ayia Anna Perivolia). A total of 328 chipped stone artifacts was found in three small trenches. These were distributed in all levels, from the surface to the uppermost part of the river sand at a depth of 2.1 m. Chipped stone tools included 11 scrapers, 6 knives, 5 borers, 4 gravers, and 9 tanged blades. The bulk of the artifacts were flakes, with few blades or cores. None showed silicate gloss. Because these items were found in all levels, the excavators felt that they could not represent dhoukani flints. Also found in these same deposits, but only to a depth of 75 cm, were 44 (or 52 in the 1985 report) potsherds, dating from Iron Age to Roman times (Baudou and Engelmark 1983:5; Baudou et al. 1985:370).

In 1982, another nine trenches were excavated, in which the same distribution of chipped stone and potsherds was observed. Apparently "ca. 55" artifacts were recovered, and another "ca. 550" were distributed over the slope of the site and up to another site, Ayia Anna 2. These were mostly flakes and a "few blades and cores" (Baudou and Engelmark 1983:6).

Baudou et al. (1985:371) believe that all of this material has been redeposited. Based on geological evidence, they argue that the younger erosional phase, which contains the potsherds, dates to Roman or post-Roman times and coincides with what Vita-Finzi (1969:101) and Bintliff (1977:35) have termed a Younger Fill. The underlaying gravel bed, which contains chipped stone, could not be dated with certainty, but they place it in Vita-Finzi's (1969:92) and Bintliff's (1977:35) Older Fill, which is of "paleolithic" age (Baudou and Engelmark 1983:7; Baudou et al. 1985:370–371). They conclude that Ayia Anna 3, and possibly the other two nearby aceramic sites, belong to the Upper Paleolithic (Baudou and Engelmark 1983:7).

There are many problems with the Tremithos sites that make them suspect. Once again, the familiar difficulties of redeposited materials is present. The fact that artifacts occur at up to a depth of over 2 m is of interest, but given the location of the test trenches near a river, and the possibility of rapid sedimentation, this is not a convincing argument for antiquity. The illustrated artifacts do little to help convince one of the familiarity of the authors with chipped stone typology. The so-called tanged blades are particularly problematic (Baudou and Engelmark 1983:6, Fig. 5, nos. 3 and 4). There appears little question that they are human-made, but they do not, as illustrated, represent convincing tanged pieces. Furthermore, tanged pieces are known from the Cypriot Aceramic Neolithic (e.g. Simmons 1994a:5, 1994c:41–42; Stekelis 1953:411). In addition, the illustrated "gravers" (Baudou and Engelmark 1983:6, Fig. 5, nos. 1 and 2) look more like burins. There are inconsistencies in the number of artifacts reported. Discarding the chipped stone as possible *dhoukani* flints, simply because some were buried, is not convincing either. The geomorphological correlations are questionable, as is the applicability of the Vita-Finzi valley fill model to this particular situation. The control over stratigraphy during excavation also must be questioned; the nine trenches excavated in 1982 were partially dug with a tractor (Baudou and Engelmark 1983:4). Finally, one might question the analytical reasoning of the authors. For example, they state the Ayia Anna 3 is older than other Aceramic Neolithic sites in Cyprus because of the lack of stone vessels. They admirably allow for an alternate hypothesis of a specialized function in which stone vessels were not required, but they appear to disregard this rather casually by observing that "it is hard to imagine any special function which would preclude such artifacts. The location and the other finds are typical of a dwelling site of hunters and gatherers" (Baudou and Engelmark 1983:7). This type of reasoning is not conducive to a problem-oriented analysis of the issue at hand, and the Tremithos sites should be considered as interesting but offering no proof of great antiquity.

In examining these claims for early sites, it is important to note that although the level of survey sophistication in Cyprus has steadily improved and (e.g., Rupp 1987a,b; Rupp *et al.* 1984; Sørenson and Rupp 1993; Todd 1982), recent surveys have failed to locate clearly pre-Neolithic sites, and there presently is no evidence on Cyprus for a Paleolithic occupation (Herscher 1995:261). Nonetheless, it is important to keep in mind that such occurrences would undoubtedly be represented by extremely low-visibility archaeological remains. It is unlikely that they were major settlements. Locating such sites requires intensive and systematic survey and the services of trained lithic analysts. One must be wary of falling into a trap that a site without ceramics or groundstone represents something "pre-Neolithic." Without systematic analytical treatment, isolated chipped stone, or even groups of chipped stone, cannot a priori be placed into a specific cultural category. Far more detailed analysis of Cypriot chipped stone assemblages is required to understand the range of variability present in the well-documented cultural periods before we can even begin to consider such assemblages reflecting a pre-Neolithic stage.

Before concluding this rather negative section on previous claims of possible pre-Neolithic sites, we should note that there also are hints of early cultural materials from at least two paleontological sites containing *Phanourios* bone. If these can be verified, Swiny's (1989:180) observation that "several so-called Pleistocene faunal deposits that have also yielded artifacts, shells, and burnt bones must now be reinvestigated" is well taken. The first site is Xylophagou *Spilia tis Englezous*, in southeastern Cyprus, which contains *Phanourios* and some *Monodonta* shell. This cave also suggests cultural deposits in the form of some charcoal and two pieces of chert mixed with small fragments of burnt (*Phanourios?*) bone (Held 1989b:407–408, 1990:21; Reese 1995:139). Ironically, this is one of the original sites investigated by Dorothea Bate, who first scientifically documented the hippopotamus of Cyprus. Having visited the locality, my assessment is that the supposed cultural materials are questionable, although the site should be systematically examined. A radiocarbon determination of 6650 ± 95 B.P., or 5640–5480 cal B.C. (OxA-3562) was obtained on the charcoal. This determination could (barely) suggest an Aceramic Neolithic use of the cave, but this remains problematic.

The other paleontological site that may contain both *Phanourios* and cultural remains is Akanthou *Arkhangelos Mikhail* in northern Cyprus (Reese 1995:86–131). It is a collapsed cave or rockshelter located in a gully not far from the Aceramic Neolithic site of Akanthou *Arkosyko*. It was originally recorded as "Akanthou" by Gunnis (1936) and rerecorded by Reyment as Afodision (published in Boekschoten and Sondaar 1972); Bromage *et al.* (1988) also have conducted some work at the site. It contains abundant remains of *Phanourios*; pygmy elephant also is present. What is intriguing about the site is that Boekschoten and Sondaar (1972) report a bone bed up to .75 m thick and about 20 m long. Although much of the deposit is brecciated, apparently some is in a loose matrix, a situation paralleled at *Aetokremnos*. At least one bone also is burned. Nearly all of the reported *Phanourios* sites in Cyprus do not contain a soft matrix. Finally, another interesting element of *Arkhangelos Mikhail* was the presence of about ten possible chipped stone artifacts. These were collected by D. Reese in 1973 and turned in to the Cyprus Museum in 1974 (D. Reese, personal communication 1991). Unfortunately, after the Turkish invasion of 1974 and the subsequent confusion, they apparently were lost, so I have not been able to examine them. In addition, Sondaar and Spaar found "about a dozen chipped stones" in 1994 (Reese 1995:86), but I also have not seen these. There are three dates for the site (see Chap. 8, Table 8-6); these are intriguing, as they suggest a rough contemporanity with *Aetokremnos*.

Although at present there is little to convincingly indicate that *Arkhangelos Mikhail* is a cultural site, it is one of the few fossil localities that falls out of the normal pattern and contains tantalizing hints of a cultural association. Unfortunately, there is little likelihood of any major systematic investigation in the foreseeable future, due to its location in the occupied northern part of the island.

The possible co-occurrence of cultural materials at these paleontological sites is tantalizing, for they suggest parallels with *Aetokremnos* from markedly different parts of the island. Unfortunately, until systematic studies can be conducted, they remain little more than intriguing hints of a more widespread occurrence of the Akrotiri Phase.

Conclusions

Although there have been numerous claims for pre-Neolithic occupation of many of the Mediterranean islands, few can stand up to critical scrutiny. When such remains are claimed to be associated with extinct Pleistocene fauna, the evidence is even more limited, as will be discussed in the next section.

In searching for early remains, it is important to keep several issues in mind. There is a tendency among many in archaeology to look for the "oldest" of something, ignoring the implications behind such claims. This is clearly an inappropriate approach; as Cherry (1990:203) has noted "the quest is not for some elusive 'earliest island site,' but for a better understanding of the general pattern and process of island colonization; truth will not simply emerge with more and better data, and it is more profitable to get on with the job of trying to make sense of what we know now."

From a more explanatory perspective, Cherry (1981:45–64; 1990:198–199) made an important distinction between actual colonization of an island, resulting in a permanent settlement and the potential "founder populations," and mere utilization of an island's resources on a temporary or seasonal basis. Successful colonization implies permanent (and year-round?) habitation. Cherry noted that *colonization* is perhaps a misleading term because it implies well-planned expeditions by groups intending to establish a permanent base. He believes that a more realistic perspective should regard early seafaring in the Mediterranean as "many, tentative, impermanent, short-distance reciprocal movements by mere handfuls of individuals" (Cherry 1981:60). Such groups would probably have produced ephemeral, low-visibility sites, if indeed their remains would be detectable at all. *Aetokremnos*'s limited visible remains fit well into this scenario. (The question of whether or not *Aetokremnos* represents a "successful colonization" is discussed in Chap. 12.)

In critically examining the question of early occupation, it is instructive to note Evans's (1977:14–15) and Cherry's (1981:58–59) observations that Mediterranean islands are generally unsuitable as home bases for hunters and gatherers. This is due to the islands' small sizes and consequent limited exploitation territories; furthermore, they frequently also are faunally impoverished. Cherry (1981:59) noted that only with the inception of agriculture, allowing increased production from decreased amounts of land, would the islands be perceived as appropriate places for *permanent* settlement. He apparently has, however, somewhat modified this view (Cherry 1990). The flaw that I find with the argument of resource scarcity is that we know of the remarkable resilience of humans adapting to extreme environments: if preagriculturalists could live in, for example, the deserts of the American West or Australia, it is hard to believe that hunters and gatherers could not have eked out some existence on many of the Mediterranean islands.

While true Paleolithic occupation of Cyprus may, in fact, be unlikely, the possibility of antecedent Neolithic groups must be considered, especially because the Neolithic appears with little or no suggestion of developmental phases. Watkin's (1981a; Morrison and Watkins 1974) notion of a "para-Neolithic" as a possible precursor deserves attention. His suggestion that such a "culture" might not represent an orthodox Neolithic pattern is important. Along the same lines, Held's (1982:6, 1989a:8) suggestion of a "proto-Neolithic," pre-Khirokitia phase, is well taken. In either situation, the archaeological remains from such groups, reflecting adaptation to the unique resources available on an island, might be dissimilar to contemporary mainland developments.

In summary, if pre-Neolithic sites exist in the Mediterranean, they probably will be in the form of ephemeral, nonarchitectural, occupations. To convincingly document a pre-Neolithic occupation of any of the Mediterranean islands requires fulfilling a minimal set of data expectations and requirements. Previous claims that have been made do not meet these and are unsubstantiated. It is not easy to deal with archaeological sites producing fossil or subfossil material, to distinguish reliably between natural and cultural patterns or bone fragmentation, to recognize and date surface scatters of crude lithic finds that represent only very transient episodes in the past, or to see in the modern landscape the signs of earlier paleogeographies that make it much more worthwhile to search for sites in one setting than another (Cherry 1990:202–203).

Although the explanatory value of small surface sites is well known (e.g., Doyel and Debowski 1980; Simmons 1981; Ward 1978), they do have their limitations. To be thoroughly convincing, stratified and geochemically datable deposits with clear cultural associations and the presence of undoubtable artifacts are required. Furthermore, these artifacts must be of an adequately sized and representative sample retrieved under systematic conditions. *Aetokremnos* represents such a site.

ISLAND BIOGEOGRAPHY IN THE MEDITERRANEAN: THE QUATERNARY FAUNAL RECORD, EXTINCT ENDEMICS, AND THE ROLE OF HUMANS IN THE EXTINCTION PROCESS

Islands are often viewed as controlled laboratories for the study of cultural and ecological processes (cf. Evans 1973, 1977; MacArthur and Wilson 1967; Terrell 1976, 1977). A considerable literature exists on island biogeography, and the explanatory potential posed by these environments has been recognized by archaeologists for many years (Cherry 1995; Keegan and Diamond 1987; Kirch 1988; Patton 1996).

The Mediterranean islands are one region where considerable archaeological and biological research has been conducted. The endemic fauna of these islands and their unique adaptations have fascinated scholars for years. Dwarfed and gigantic forms of mainland species are well documented here. The strange menagerie of Pleistocene creatures included "giant" (squirrellike) dormice, swans, vultures, owls, tortoises, and lizards. Dwarfed forms also were common, including pygmy deer, pigs, elephants, hippopotami, and unique "mouse-goats" (antelope-like creatures). These animals lived on many of the Mediterranean islands (or former islands), including Cyprus, Crete, Sicily, Malta, Corsica, Sardinia, and the Balearics (Davis 1985; Reese 1989b; Reyment 1983; Sondaar 1986). Of particular interest to this study are the extinct pygmy hippopotami and pygmy elephants of Cyprus.

Despite its large size, Cyprus is one of the most geologically and biogeographically isolated of the Mediterranean islands. Its origin is oceanic, and the island is separated from the southern seaboard of Anatolia and the Syro-Palestinian littoral by two deep submarine features, the Adana Trough and the Latakia Basin, respectively. Geological and geophysical evidence provide a complex, but persuasive argument against a Quaternary land bridge (Held 1989a:12; Hsü 1977; Lort 1977; Stanley 1977). Current opinion is that even at times of minimum sea levels during the Pleistocene glaciations, Cyprus remained separated from the mainland by at least 30–40 km of deep water (Swiny 1988:3).

It is therefore unlikely that the endemic animals arrived on most of the islands by a Pleistocene (or Quaternary) land bridge, contrary to suggestions by some researchers (Audley-Charles and Hooijer 1973; Kuss 1973). Only Sicily has clear evidence of such a connection (van Andel 1989:737, 1990, Fig. 1; Azzaroli 1980:425; Shackleton *et al.* 1984:310), although some also believe that Sardinia, Corsica, and the Balearics may have been connected at the beginning of the Tertiary (Azzaroli 1981; Azzaroli and Guazzone 1979; Boccaletti and Manetti 1978). In addition to geological evidence, Sondaar (1977:673–679) presentd a convincing argument against the land-bridge theory, noting that it does not account for the composition of island fauna. Instead, the so-called "Island Sweepstakes" route proposed by Simpson (1940, 1965) seems more likely (Sondaar 1986). In such instances, animals venture far from the coast, reach an isolated island from which they cannot return, and are forced to settle there. This sweepstakes dispersal means that "the geographic route is impossible for most species and possible only on rare occasions for others. In most cases, dispersal on such a route is a one-way affair" (Sondaar 1986:52). The actual mechanism by which mammals that occur in the fossil record of the Mediterranean Islands,such as the deer, hippopotamus, and elephant, initially got to the islands probably was by swimming; "only overseas dispersal can explain the uniform composition of the endemic island faunas" (Sondaar 1977:674). As improbable as this image may seem, these land animals are known for their swimming abilities. Elephants love water, and several reports exist of them island hopping in the open sea off India and Sri Lanka; their trunks make excellent snorkels. Deer will flee to water if threatened and have been observed swimming (Carrington 1962; Johnson 1980, 1983; Sondaar 1977, 1986). Hippopotami have been known to swim from the Tanzanian mainland in East Africa to Zanzibar, a distance of more than 35 km (Sondaar 1986:52).

Although little biogeographic research has been conducted on Cyprus itself (but see Held 1989a,b), comparative data from other parts of the world show that pronounced isolation reduces the colonization rates of species with low dispersal ability, such as reptiles and mammals; increasing island size coupled with the high persistence ability of these species produces enhanced endemism among the successful colonizing populations (Case and Cody 1987). Because, according to equilibrium theory of island biogeography (MacArthur and Wilson 1967), the balance between immigration rate and extinction rate in island biotas is a function of size and isolation, the "island effect" in the case of Cyprus predictably accounts for poor species diversity and high endemicity in terrestrial mammals, while bird and plant species are marked by a much smaller number of endemics. This biological pattern is confirmed by the island's flora (Zohary 1973) and Quaternary faunal assemblages, whose two salient features are a pronounced lack of species diversity and the presence of evolutionary dwarfism. This would explain why Pleistocene fossil and subfossil sites on the island consist almost exclusively of the remains of two terrestrial mammals, *Phanourios* and *Elephas*.

The Mediterranean island pygmy species of hippopotamus and elephant were considerably smaller than their mainland counterparts, the dwarfism being an evolutionary response to both the lack of predators and to the limited resources available on the islands (Sondaar 1977). The occurrence of nanism also has been attributed to degeneration, the evolutionary deterioration or loss of function or structure; degeneration occurred as the result of the inbreeding inevitable in small isolated populations (Sondaar 1986:50). Interestingly, many of the morphological traits of the extinct pygmy hippopotami bear greater similarity to the living full-sized hippopotamus (*Hippopotamus amphibius*) than they do to the modern pygmy hippopotamus (*Choeropsis liberiensis*). It is, therefore, incorrect to assume that the Pleistocene island pygmy hippopotami were "carbon-copies" of modern pygmy forms; the extinct forms were smaller and had numerous specialized adaptive characteristics.

Some of the more significant characteristics of *Phanourios* include their small size (about that of a large pig), lophodont dentition, bone fusion (syndactyly) and shortening in the lower limbs, placement of the eyes and nose on a lower plane than in modern hippopotami, and loss of foot pads. The "low gear" locomotion of *Phanourios*, in which the animal moved its limbs primarily in a fore-aft direction, but not sideways, suggests it was better adapted to walking than swimming. Coupled with the loss of foot pads—the extinct hippopotami apparently walked on the tips of their toes—these morphological changes in the lower limbs, resulting in heavier built legs with stouter bones, allowed for greater mobility and access to the mountainous terrain characteristic of the Mediterranean islands (Houtekamer and Sondaar 1979). The dentition changes were in the number and shape of teeth, and, coupled with wear patterns of the jaws, indicate that the molars were adapted to grinding (Reese 1989b:23; Sondaar 1977, 1986:53–54).

These adaptations are important behaviorally, for they suggest that pygmy hippopotami may have had different food requirements than modern counterparts. A reduced dependency on aquatic resources is indicated; nonaquatic resources found in rugged grazing areas may have been important dietary components (Sondaar 1977:680–686, 1986:53–54), and Boekschoten and Sondaar (1977:336) suggested "a mode of living like a leaf-eating pig."

Although largely ignored by archaeologists, at least before the discovery of *Aetokremnos,* sporadic paleontological research since the beginning of this century has produced a respectable, albeit incomplete, body of knowledge about the occurrence and osteology of these unique creatures (Bate 1903b, 1904b, 1906; Boekschoten and Sondaar 1972; Caloi and Palombo 1983; Davis 1985; Faure *et al.* 1983; Houtekamer and Sondaar 1979; Reese 1975a,b, 1988, 1989b, 1995; Swiny 1988). Available evidence suggests that large numbers of *Phanourios* were present on Cyprus during the Pleistocene (Reese 1995; Sondaar 1977:687). Whether *Phanourios* descended from *H. amphibius* is not certain, but it underwent more morphological changes than any other island hippopotami (Boekschoten and Sondaar 1972:335). The demonstrable absence of carnivores and other terrestrial megafauna from Pleistocene Cyprus indicates the island's *Phanourios* and *Elephas* populations were not subject to selective pressures and resource competition, thus contributing to their persistence ability and survival—now documented archaeologically—into the Early Holocene.

Excluding *Aetokremnos* and possible associations at the sites previously mentioned, *Phanourios* and/or *Elephas* occur in at least 37 confirmed ossiferous sites and/or isolated or unverified finds throughout Cyprus. It is likely that intensified systematic field surveys will locate additional sites (Held 1989b:381–418; Reese 1989b, 1995; Swiny 1988). The total assemblage is weighed heavily in favor of *Phanourios*, with *Elephas* remains present at only 21 sites or as isolated finds, and in consistently small quantities. The disproportionate number of hippopotami to elephants is discussed by Held (1989b:142–145). Analysis of the location of fossil sites shows a frequent association with aquatic microenvironments at the time of their occupation, although sites located in the mountains also occur (Held 1992:196, Fig. 1).

Many of the bone beds occur in caves or rockshelters, as well as near rivers or ponds and on alluvial fans. Nearly all of the remains are in breccia deposits and are heavily fossilized. With few exceptions (e.g., Kato Dikomo *Vokolosspilios,* [Reese 1995:22–32] or Akanthou *Arkhangelos Mikhail* [Reese 1995:86–131], both caves, and Ayia Irini *Dragontovounari* [Reese 1995:58–77], possibly a former rockshelter), these deposits are exposed bone beds with little or no stratigraphy. Significantly, none of these fossil sites display the abundance of bone seen at *Aetokremnos.*

Overpopulation and starvation stress are two possible extinction scenarios. Sondaar (1986:54) noted that in the Mediterranean, the fossils of some of these animals frequently occur in caves and fissures, where the animals sought shelter or into which their remains were washed. In Crete, he cited evidence of a site containing the remains of more than a hundred endemic deer, which were mainly newborns, one-year-olds, or very old individuals. Sondaar believed that this age distribution suggests they all died around the same time, probably in a bad season, and that only the strongest individuals survived. He also cited the case of Dragon Mountain (i.e., Ayia Irini *Dragontovounari* [Reese 1989b:26, 1995:58–77]) in Cyprus as another example of a rich bone bed, perhaps part of a small river or pool, containing hippopotami. Sondaar believed this site also reflects a mass die occurring as a single event, pointing to a mass starvation. Unfortunately, Sondaar (1986:54) incorrectly stated that endemic deer also were there; this most assuredly is not the case, as endemic Pleistocene deer have never been found on Cyprus; they are believed to have been brought to the island with Neolithic colonizers (Davis 1984:152, 1989:206, 1994:305). This is a regrettable error; Sondaar continued to state that the pygmy deer remains at Dragon Mountain, as well as those from Crete, exhibit osteoporosis, a bone defect caused by chronic malnutrition (Sondaar 1977:694–696, 1986:54). He appears to have, in this instance, confused a Cretan site for a Cypriote one. In fact, this defect is only found on some Cretan deer. Nonetheless, Sondaar's point is valid, and he continues this argument, stating that

> [t]his type of evidence suggests that overpopulation, followed by food shortage, was the principal selective pressure on the islands. The absence of carnivores probably allowed herbivore populations to grow out of balance with the environment, causing overgrazing and destruction of otherwise suitable habitats. This may have been a recurring phenomenon, causing drastic changes in population size and thus favoring a quick rate of evolution. (Sondaar 1986:54)

By implication, such a scenario also could lead to a relatively rapid rate of extinction, although there is little evidence from Cyprus pointing to nutritional stress. One or two bones in the Utrech collection do, however, show some evidence of disease (D. Reese, personal communication December 1995). As Held (1989b:145) noted, this could be determined by systematic investigation of signs of group morbidity and abnormal mortality rates in the fossil record. Such data may exist, for the Cypriot fossil remains have, in general, been poorly studied. Looking for such patterns certainly should be a priority for future paleontological investigations, although preliminary studies suggest that they are very rare.

The role of humans in extinctions must be considered, of course, although it is problematic, controversial, and difficult to document archaeologically. Although numerous examples exist of the extinctions of endemic island fauna by invading or colonizing human groups during historic or protohistoric periods, *Aetokremnos* provides a time depth to extinction set against the Late Pleistocene/Early Holocene. A staggering literature exists on this disputed topic (e.g., Axelrod 1967; Diamond 1989b; Donovan 1989; Grayson 1989, 1991; Martin and Wright 1967; Mead and Meltzer 1985; Nitecki 1984; Stanley 1987; and especially Martin and Klein 1984 [and references therein]). Detailed discussion is clearly beyond the scope of this volume, but given the claims being made for *Aetokremnos*, it is useful to summarize the issue, at least as relevant to the Mediterranean islands (see additional discussion in Chap. 13).

Several claims have been made for the association of cultural materials with extinct Pleistocene animals from many of the Mediterranean islands; indeed, the "islands appear to be especially strategic places to study extinction as well as evolution of insular forms" (Martin 1984:391). Some of these claims come from Mallorca, Tilos, and Sardinia (Acra *et al.* 1982a,b; Bachmayer and Symeonidis 1974; Bachmayer *et al.* 1976; Burleigh and Clutton-Brock 1980; Sondaar 1986, 1987; Sondaar *et al.* 1984, 1986; Spoor and Sondaar 1986;

Symeonides 1972, 1988; Symeonides *et al.* 1973; Theodorou 1990; Waldren 1982, 1994; Waldren *et al.* 1984). Most involve animals that are smaller than the pygmy hippopotami and elephants; in the Tilos case, however, pygmy elephants at Charkadio Cave may have lived until about 3,500 years ago, and Theodorou (1990:19) believed that it is "possible that man met the Tilos elephant eye to eye since we find some strange pieces of tusk that may have been fashioned by primitive man to be used as tools." In most instances, including Tilos, these claims are tenuous and poorly documented.

Certainly the best documented example is from Mallorca, where the antelope-like *Myotragus balearicus*, whose origins extend back 5.5 million years, survived as recently as circa 4000 B.P. and were an economic resource for humans at least two or three millennia previously (Burleigh and Clutton-Brock 1980; Cherry 1990:194; Clutton-Brock 1984; Clutton-Brock and Burleigh 1983; Waldren 1994; Waldren *et al.* 1984). As discussed previously, Corbeddu Cave in Sardinia also suggests an association of humans and endemic Pleistocene fauna. None of these claims, however, match *Aetokremnos* with well-documented antiquity, and although humans have exploited hippopotami in the Levant for millennia (e.g., Horwitz and Tchernov 1990; Uerpmann 1987), there was no evidence, prior to our investigations, for an association of humans with pygmy hippopotami or pygmy elephants. The only such possible association is from Madagascar, where human and pygmy hippopotami may have coexisted as recently as roughly 1,000 years ago (MacPhee and Burney 1991).

In the few well-documented Mediterranean island cases where there is a temporal overlap between human populations and extinct fauna, it invariably is short and associated with Neolithic or later occupations. In most instances, though, the assumption is that these species were extinct before peoples' relatively recent arrival (although see Martin 1984:390–391). A human hand in extinctions, when it can be documented, is complex, being either direct and quick, or indirect and long term (Diamond 1989b). If humans were responsible, this could have been by means of two mechanisms: either they hunted the fauna, resulting in overkill, or they changed the habitat of the animals by the introduction of cultivation and the importation of potential animal competitors (Boekschoten and Sondaar 1972:336; Davis 1987:124–125), or both.

In Cyprus, if *Phanourios* was still viable by the time of Neolithic settlement, its closest competitor would have been the feral pig (an early breed of domestic pig is documented in Aceramic Neolithic contexts, and the assumption is that some escaped, giving rise to feral populations) (Davis 1987:124). But, as pointed out earlier, until the investigations at *Aetokremnos,* there has never been a clear association of cultural remains with the extinct pygmy hippopotamus or pygmy elephant.

In conclusion, although humans ultimately are believed to have caused the extinction of several Mediterranean endemics (Vigne 1987a), only a handful of sites document this. These existed later than *Aetokremnos,* and claims for Late Pleistocene/Early Holocene sites remain unverified (Cherry 1990:194–197; Vigne 1987a). Barring the possibility of an overlap between the remnant population of Pleistocene fauna and the Aceramic Neolithic culture of Cyprus *as it is currently defined* (Dikaios 1962; Held 1982; LeBrun *et al.* 1987; Stanley-Price 1977a,b, 1979b), the absence of pygmy hippopotami and elephants from the Neolithic faunal record supports the argument that these "mini-megafaunas" were hunted into extinction earlier by the island's first occupants, during what we have termed the *Akrotiri Phase.*

Chapter *2*

Site Description, Research Design, and Methodology

SITE DESCRIPTION

From surface appearances, *Aetokremnos* is distinctly unimpressive. This is a testament to the potential for incorrect interpretations based solely on surface remains (cf. Simmons 1998a). Given the focus of Cypriot archaeology on architectural sites, it is no wonder that *Aetokremnos* failed to arouse the interest of many who visited it. Our excavations demonstrated, however, that the surface was not an accurate mirror for what was buried. The following, taken largely from the thorough description provided by Held (1989b:39–44), depicts the site's surface prior to any excavation.

Aetokremnos is located on a steep sedimentary talus of the cliffs that form the south coast of the Akrotiri Peninsula (Fig. 2-1). This talus plummets into the sea below an eroding cliff face that was marked *Aetokremnos* on R. E. Kitchener's 1885 survey maps . The site is situated on a flat bench area of the talus, some 40 m above the Mediterranean Sea and 30 m below the top of the cliffs (Figs. 2-2 and 2-3). This bench plunges dramatically into the sea on its west end. To the south and east, the fall is less steep but no less dangerous.

The surface of this relatively flat area contained a scattering of weathered bones, chipped stone, pottery, and shell. An exposed section of apparently intact sediment contained additional bones and was overlaid by a thick layer of broken shells ("Area C") (Fig. 2-4).

Aetokremnos has been subjected to erosion and deflation that affected the site's composition. The relatively severe winters that bring heavy rains, a near continuous and stiff sea breeze, and eolian sandblasting all were factors affecting *Aetokremnos*, and steady deterioration was visible over a period of even a few years. It was clear that much of the site already had fallen into the sea, and that this erosion was accelerating with the passing of each year.

The bench on which the site is located consists of a bedrock formation of biocalcarenite and sandy marls of the Lower Pleistocene Athalassa Formation and a thin (about 50 cm) mantle of unstratified and poorly sorted colluvium. The central slope profile has a gradient of approximately 30 degrees; on the western side directly below the site, this gradient

33

Figure 2-1. *Aetokremnos,* showing cliffs.

increases to nearly 45 degrees for approximately 20 m before reaching a vertical drop to the sea. Most of the site is on top of this steep slope.

Immediately above and behind the exposed section of shell and bone is an approximately 10-m-long bedrock ledge. This represents the break line of a former overhang, whose original extent we can only estimate. This ledge and the presence of large rock debris directly in front and below it indicates that *Aetokremnos* is a collapsed rockshelter (see Chap. 3). This same process of collapse is visible in numerous rockshelters along adjacent cliffs. Wind erosion forms cavities in the porous bedrock, deepening the evolving shelter until the caprock breaks off. Roof debris then buries the floor of the shelter or falls into the sea. The remaining rooffall traps windblown sand until the residual shelter is choked off, sealing its floor. Because mechanical and chemical weathering simultaneously affect the entire talus, the outer edge of the buried shelter floor eventually reappears when the slope profile has receded sufficiently.

At *Aetokremnos,* this cutting back of the slope led to the exposure of two separate areas of bone (Areas A and B on original plans) not containing shell or artifacts, as well as a stratified section of bone and shell (Area C). The bone in Areas A and B appeared heavily fossilized and calcified, as is typical of paleontological sites on Cyprus. These lie directly on a formation of *kafkalla* and held little promise of intact deposits. Area C, however, suggested limited in situ deposition. It was a wedge-shaped section approximately 2 m in length and 35 cm thick at the north, upslope, end. The south end had been truncated by the slope. Area C was *Aetokremnos*'s most intriguing feature because it suggested a stratified deposit. It was bounded on two sides by large rooffall boulders. In front and downs-

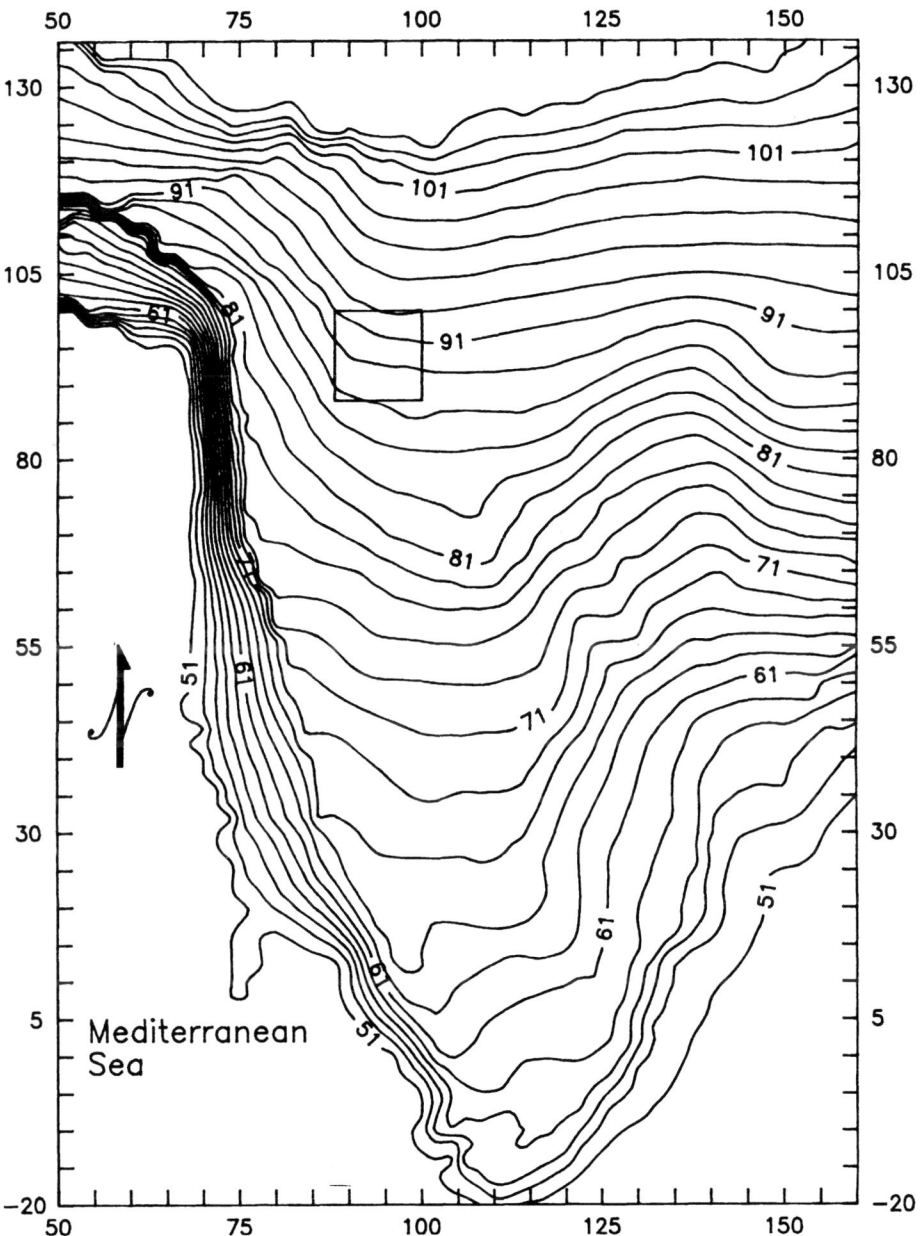

Figure 2-2. Site area topographic map. (Prepared by S. Durand and K. Roler)

lope was a scree deposit with low evergreen ground cover. The area behind Area C was believed to offer the best opportunity of containing intact deposits.

The visible stratification in Area C consisted of a layer of burned and cracked marine
mollusks. These were primarily *Monodonta turbinata* Born, with a few specimens of *Patella*

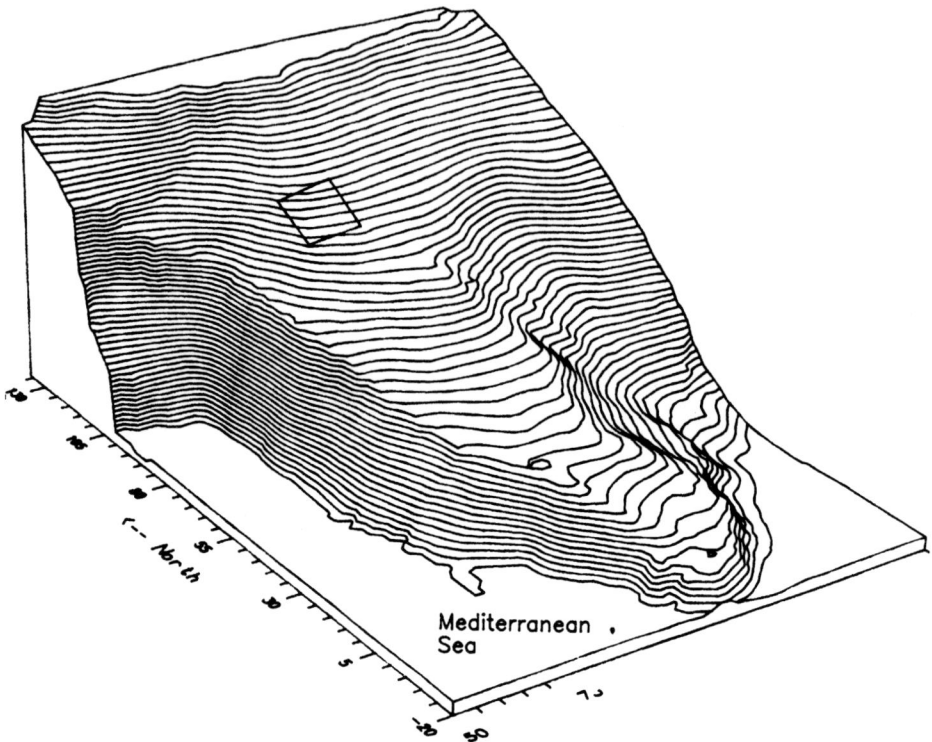

Figure 2-3. Site area orthographic map. (Prepared by S. Durand and K. Roler)

species as well. The shell occurs over a layer containing bones; one chert artifact also was visible in this layer. The matrix in which this material was located was ashy. The depth of the bone layer could not be determined because it was obscured by the scree covered slope surface. Indications, however, were of a limited depth with the shelter's presumed floor near the bottom of the exposed bone.

Among the scree was an extensive scatter of bones, shell, and over 30 nondescript chipped stone artifacts. Preliminary identification of the bone established that the majority was *Phanourios*. Pygmy elephant also was represented by a fragmentary adult molar and a radius/ulna. All of this material was localized around Areas A, B, and C in such a manner that it appeared to have originated in them. No chipped stone, bones, or other cultural material, with the exception of a thin scatter of Roman pottery, was found on either side or above the site area, suggesting that these materials did not wash down from above.

Thus the surface indications at *Aetokremnos* were vague but intriguing. Once excavation began, however, it rapidly became apparent that much more intact deposition was present than initially imagined. In particular, the scree below Area C contained a substantial amount of depth before reaching the bedrock floor. As excavation progressed, we felt that the shelter was sizable, continuing, as it did, all along the ledge noted earlier, with a south-facing orientation. Subsequent excavation, however, revealed that the shelter was smaller

Figure 2-4. Preexcavation surface of *Aetokremnos,* showing shell layer (later identified as Feature 5).

than originally believed, having a west-southwest orientation (Fig. 2-5). What we initially believed to be rooffall in the presumed center of the shelter turned out, in fact, to represent the shelter's eastern edge. Some of the interior of the shelter, that portion to the west, had fallen into the sea. The extent of this portion is difficult to estimate; what is presently intact is a former interior surface area less than 35 sq m.

RESEARCH STRATEGY

Introduction

Given the controversial nature and the implications of *Aetokremnos,* one of our principal objectives was straightforward: to demonstrate whether or not the site was, in fact, cultural. If it was, its primary significance was twofold: First, it would be the oldest site documented on Cyprus, and, indeed, one of the oldest sites on any of the Mediterranean islands. Second, it would be an archaeologically supportable example of humans being directly associated with, and possibly involved in, the extinction of a Late Pleistocene fauna.

Conceptual Framework

The immediate goal of the project was to conduct a precise interdisciplinary investigation of *Aetokremnos* to document if it was anthropogenic, and how old it was. Excavation was all the more pressing because the site was rapidly eroding into the sea.

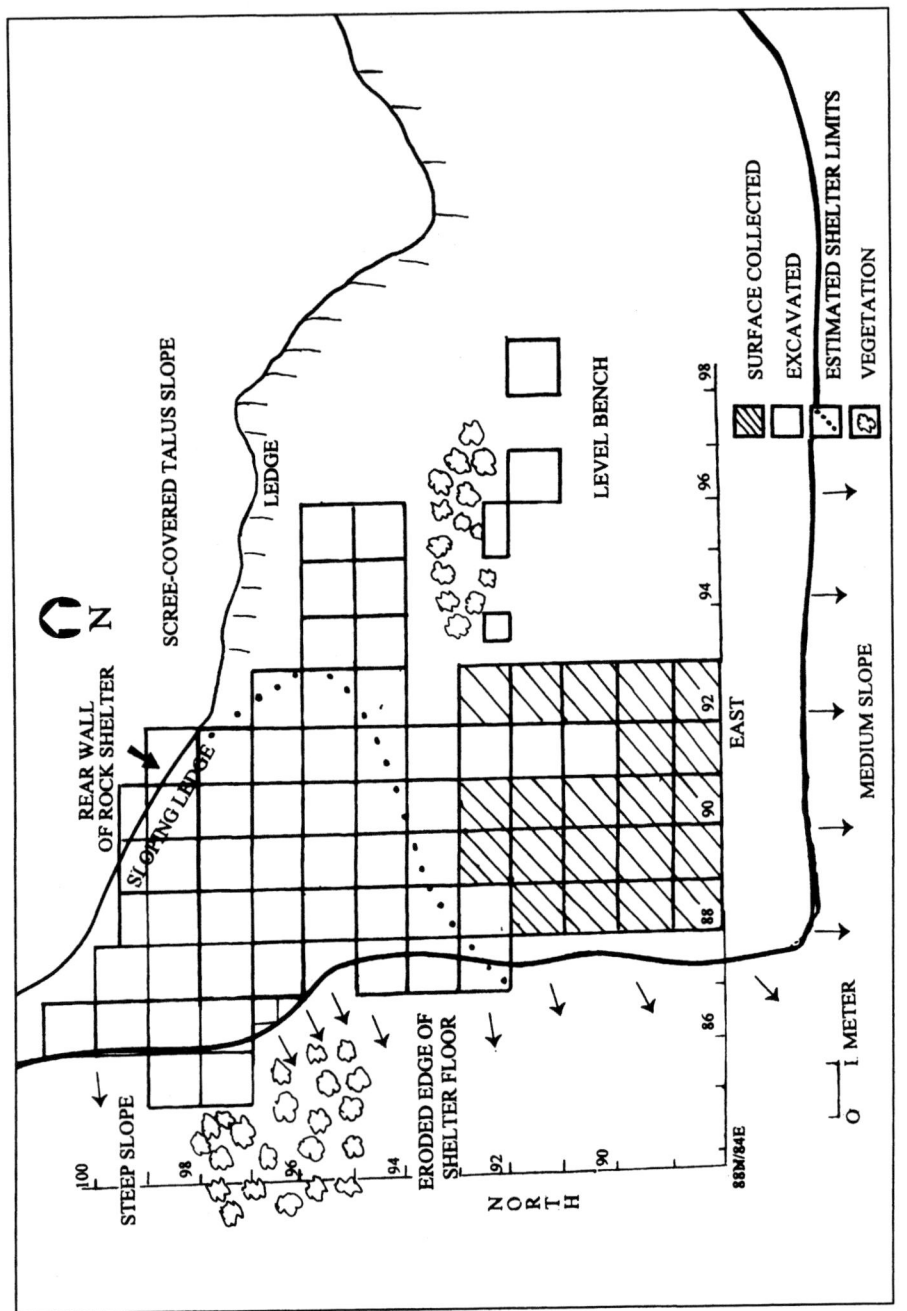

Figure 2-5. Akrotiri *Aetokremnos* plan map.

Prior to our excavations, several archaeologists had visited the site with Stuart Swiny. One systematic examination was by Avraham Ronen of Haifa University in 1981. Ronen saw two major issues: (a) Were the deposits in situ? (b) What were the origin and genesis of both the bone bed and the ashy shell layer, and what was the relationship between them? He concluded that *Aetokremnos* was in situ by observing that

1. it was too much of a coincidence for a solid layer of bone fragments to underlie a shell midden by chance;
2. if material came from a higher point, it probably would not have been concentrated where it presently was, directly below a small cliff, because going over that cliff would cause it to proceed farther downslope; and
3. if the material came from above, the shell and ash would have most likely been dispersed and separated rather than being comingled as they were.

Ronen believed there was little doubt of the ash deposit's human origin because chipped stone artifacts were clearly embedded in it. The underlying bed of bone also appeared to be cultural because many of the bones were burned, disarticulated, and fractured. This would be unlikely in a natural deposit. It also was unlikely that a natural deposit of bone would occur on such a steep cliff (Ronen 1981).

The issue of natural deposition is, of course, an extremely important aspect of the argument that *Aetokremnos* is anthropogenic, and it is worthwhile considering it in some more detail here. One of the many researchers who examined the site during its excavation was Catherine Perlès (CNRS, Paris). Her observations were based on data available at the time of her visit during the 1988 season. She was specifically interested in the taphonomic processes that could have produced the bone deposit, and she developed an elegant, yet simple, argument (Perlès 1988) that bears repetition in some detail here.

Perlès noted that the bone deposit was unusually dense within a small area; it also showed an abundance of individual animals, at least several *Phanourios* individuals within a surface limited to a few square meters; and it was located on a narrow, flat surface on the upper third of a steep cliff. One scenario for explaining this deposit was that it reflected an accretional paleontological deposit. This scenario supposes that individual animals or small groups of animals repeatedly died on the site, a situation that could correspond to the natural death of, presumably, aging or sick animals, or to the accidental occurrences of animals falling over the cliff or into a sinkhole. Perlès makes several arguments against this interpretation.

First, although accretional sites are well known, they are rarely if ever found in locations as precipitous as *Aetokremnos*. The site also lacks both vegetation and water resources that would have been attractive to animals. It is doubtful that the shelter was ever deep enough to offer thorough protection from the elements; it is equally unlikely that sick animals, even as adapted to mountainous terrains as *Phanourios* presumably was, could have easily climbed down the vertical upper portion of the cliffs to reach *Aetokremnos*, a steep climb even for healthy animals. One might argue for access to the shelter from the beach below if sea level were lower than at present (Held 1989b:47), but the same argument for accessibility still remains. In addition, if one argues that the bone is a result of some sort of behavioral preference on the part of *Phanourios*, an explanation as to *why* this one shelter was selected must be offered. There is nothing at the locality of *Aetokremnos* that would appear to be particularly attractive to *Phanourios*.

A second argument against a natural deposition is anatomical. In an undisturbed natural die site, one might expect some articulation, which is not the case at *Aetokremnos* (although see Haynes 1991 for considerable discussion of this issue). There is no evidence for predators in Cyprus prior to the arrival of humans, so postoccupational disturbance by scavenging carnivores may be ruled out. Other nonhuman disturbance processes that could have caused disarticulation are the collapse of the shelter's roof, natural agents such as rain or wind, and pedoturbation by plants or small burrowing animals (Held 1989b:47). It is, however, unlikely that these processes would have caused the extent of disarticulation apparent at the site. Geomorphic examination of the deposits also revealed no evidence of major water transport (see Chap. 3). Finally, there are many shelters all along the southern coast of the Akrotiri Peninsula that would have provided similar conditions and should therefore show evidence of *Phanourios* remains. As confirmed by later survey, this was not the case.

Third, although animals falling over the cliffs above *Aetokremnos* is possible, there is no feature of the plateau on the cliff top that would account for a repeated jump at this very point and not elsewhere along the peninsula. If accidental jumps or falls occurred, they should be distributed more or less randomly along the horizontal bottoms of the cliffs. Furthermore, it is difficult to explain how the bones came to be deposited inside the shelter.

Finally, the sinkhole scenario can be discounted as the geomorphological nature of the Akrotiri Peninsula argues against their formation. Furthermore, in natural sinkholes, sedimentation occurs in between the various animals falls. At *Aetokremnos*, this was not the case.

If the hypothesis of an accretional paleontological deposit can be discounted, what of the possibility of a natural mass death site? Again, Perlès effectively discounts this at *Aetokremnos*. This scenario could suppose a mass jump of one or several *Phanourios* herds, presuming that this type of behavior was possible for the species. There are a number of reasons that make this unlikely. First, it is likely that more than one major episode is responsible for the bone bed. Furthermore, the earlier observations that there were no features on the plateau that could account for several falls at just this point are equally valid. If this scenario were true, the animals would have rolled down the cliff and spread throughout the slope. There is no natural feature that could have stopped them from rolling down to the bottom of the cliffs and into the sea. This is particularly true for an animal as rotund as *Phanourios*. The distribution of bones at *Aetokremnos* was far too concentrated for such a phenomenon to occur.

If such a situation occurred, one might expect that not all the bones would have been covered by sediment immediately, and at least some would show surface weathering. Although many of the bones are differentially weathered, their weathering appears to have been caused by postdepositional erosion of the deposit, resulting in differential exposure to the elements.

Finally, a mass death site does not explain the fact that the bones were located, primarily, under the original shelter. If they had fallen or jumped from the cliffs en masse, it is physically impossible for them to have accumulated inside of the shelter. Of course, an alternate explanation involving a natural mass death is that the animals concentrated at the shelter of their own volition. This was a situation that only careful excavation could determine, and, as is argued throughout this volume, it is a scenario we do not believe can be supported (see Chap. 12 for additional discussion).

In summary, the lack of lateral spreading of the bones along the cliff precludes an ac-cretional death site, while the lack of vertical spreading of the bones precludes a mass death site. The special feature of *Aetokremnos* that must be accounted for in any explanation is the lateral and vertical concentration of the bones. Very few natural agents can account for such a concentration, and at *Aetokremnos* neither water movement, nor displacement by carnivores, which are absent from Cyprus, are potential explanations. A human origin for the bone deposit therefore becomes the most parsimonious explanation. Even so, however, this explanation had to be verified by rigorous testing (Perlès 1988).

Thus, if *Aetokremnos* was anthropogenic, as we believed the evidence suggested, what was its anthropological significance? As far back as the early 1980s, Held (1983:219–233) proposed alternate hypotheses regarding *Aetokremnos*, largely based on the radiocarbon determinations then available.

The first hypothesis was that *Aetokremnos* was occupied over one thousand years prior to the first documented Aceramic Neolithic settlement in Cyprus and was roughly contemporary with the Natufian of the Levant. If this were true, the initial occupation of Cyprus took place much earlier than previously believed, breaking the colonization pattern postulated by Cherry (1981) for the Eastern Mediterranean. Furthermore, the occupants of *Aetokremnos* represented a possible founder population ("Proto-Neolithic") for the Ace-ramic Neolithic.

The alternate hypothesis was that *Aetokremnos* was among the earlier representation of the Aceramic Neolithic in Cyprus and was roughly contemporary with the Pre-Pottery Neolithic B (PPNB) in the Levant. In this scenario, the occupants of *Aetokremnos* and of other Cypriot Aceramic Neolithic sites represented coexistent yet discrete groups with lit-tle or no mainland contact and with different adaptive patterns (see Ronen 1995 for a re-lated argument). *Aetokremnos* would represent a highly specialized early Aceramic Neolithic site with no archaeological precedent in Cyprus (i.e., a seasonal camp used for shellfish and other marine resources exploitation and the butchering of, minimally, *Phanou-rios* and *Elephas*).

Held (1983:232) favored the first hypothesis, and, in his 1989 dissertation (Held 1989b), after two excavation seasons at *Aetokremnos*, he elaborated on these ideas and concluded that at least Area C was a primary deposit. This section was firmly embedded in the original slope of the talus, and its position immediately in front of and below the bedrock ledge gave it protection from vertical slope movements and rocks breaking loose from the cliffs above. It also was clear that the bone layer was beneath the shell layer, sug-gesting an earlier deposition. The occurrence of the marine shell some 40 m above present sea level also had to be considered. It could be explained in only two ways: Either the shells were part of a fossil beach, or they were left by humans. Although such a high beach can-not be ruled out, it seems unlikely; if such a beach existed, it most certainly would have de-stroyed the underlying bone layer and its ash matrix. The alternate explanation of a human agency in its deposition seemed more plausible, especially given the documented subsis-tence and ornamental use of similar shells by Early Holocene groups throughout the Near East (e.g., Reese 1978, 1982; Stanley-Price 1976). Thus the presence of a shell midden de-posit reflecting the exploitation of aquatic resources seemed likely (Held 1989b:45–46).

Held further discounted the possibility that the chipped stone had washed in from above and concluded that Areas A–C were the only possible sources for these artifacts. This conclusion also was in accordance with the observation that bones on the surface were in various stages of calcification, indicating that they were in the process of eroding out of the slope and had not been transported from elsewhere (Held 1989b:46).

Held (1989b:45; also see Chap. 3 and Mandel and Simmons 1997) also noted that the coastal topography of the Akrotiri Peninsula supported the conclusion that *Aetokremnos* was a collapsed rockshelter. The alternative scenario of depressions or sinkholes in which the animals might have been trapped was not supported by an examination of the relevant geomorphology.

Finally, Held (1989b:45) concluded that if the deposits at *Aetokremnos* were cultural, animal remains should be disarticulated, and the burning evident on some these remains must be shown not to have resulted from a later occupation or from a natural brush fire. Additionally, further radiometric dates from excavated contexts would have to be more consistent than the initial set of surface dates, and they ought to be consistently early.

Research Objectives

Thus, it was within the research contexts provided by scholars such as Held, Pérles, and Ronen that we approached our investigation at *Aetokremnos*. They had posed a number of tantalizing scenarios that could only be verified by precise excavation. Their observations guided a series of specific research objectives.

Clearly, a primary objective was simply to determine whether or not *Aetokremnos* was cultural. If this could be verified, the next goal was to document the site's chronology. There were three chronological possibilities: It was either pre-Neolithic, Neolithic, or post-Neolithic. Radiocarbon determinations obtained prior to excavation supported its antiquity but also posed some problems. The range of determinations could suggest a multiple occupation, but the homogeneity of the material remains argued against this interpretation. It seemed more likely that the dates simply were unreliable, as the samples were obtained from surface contexts that could have affected their carbon isotope content. Clearly, the age of *Aetokremnos* was a critical issue that required geochemically defensible resolution, and we hoped, through excavation, to obtain determinations on charcoal, a more reliable material than either shell or bone.

Demonstrating the association, or lack thereof, of extinct fauna with cultural remains at *Aetokremnos* was, of course, an extremely significant aspect of the project. Both *Phanourios* and *Elephas* generally were believed to have been extinct prior to the arrival of humans on Cyprus. *Aetokremnos,* however, appeared to contradict this, regardless of the site's age. If the site was pre-Neolithic, it would document human predation of these two species, demonstrating that they were not extinct prior to the arrival of people. If the site was Neolithic, it would be the first clear association of these fauna with cultural remains during this period, and it would again point to human predation into the Neolithic. If the site was post-Neolithic, it would be clear evidence that these species were not extinct until after the Neolithic. Even if excavation failed to verify the association of cultural and faunal materials, the significance of *Aetokremnos* as a paleontological resource was uncontested.

Another goal of the project was to systematically analyze the artifact assemblage from *Aetokremnos*. The chipped stone artifacts collected prior to excavation were undiagnostic and did not appear to fall within either Levantine, Anatolian, or Cypriot Aceramic Neolithic (or other) typologies. Of course, as Held (1983:224) noted, if *Aetokremnos* represented colonization by Levantine groups, for example, the adaptive strategy that they may have developed in Cyprus would not necessarily have required the same diagnostic artifacts or parallel settlement patterns associated with their original homelands. Admittedly, this is somewhat speculative, but it is a serious argument, one also suggested by Watkins (1981a). All indications were that the assemblage from *Aetokremnos* was distinct from anything else known in Cyprus, and a thorough analysis would help in its definition and in constructing functional interpretations.

Excavations at *Aetokremnos* also would provide information on the adaptive strategies that were used by (depending on the site's age) pre-, post-, or Neolithic inhabitants of Cyprus. The site appeared to represent a specialized site type that emphasized the exploitation of both marine resources and certain faunal species. Such specialization had not previously been well documented in the prehistory of Cyprus.

Other project objectives related to environmental and geomorphic issues. Paleoenvironmental data generally are lacking for Cyprus, and our excavations would, if only in a small way, help fill in this deficiency. In additional, geomorphic investigation was necessary to more fully understand formation processes, subsequent occupation and abandonment episodes, and the stratigraphic correlation of faunal elements with cultural materials at *Aetokremnos*.

Finally, although attention was to focus on *Aetokremnos*, we also wanted to examine other sites located by Brian Pile during his survey to see if there might be a relationship to the main site. Of particular interest was the recovery of a "PPNB"-like projectile point at a site (Site 23) containing a possible stone-ringed hearth, a large knife, and several undiagnostic lithics (Swiny 1988:5, 10–11). The point shares some morphological similarities to Levantine Byblos types. Thus the testing of a few of these sites was an ancillary objective of the project; we also wished to conduct a systematic survey of portions of the Akrotiri Peninsula. Although much of the Peninsula had been thoroughly covered by Pile, it was desirable to supplement his data with a survey conducted by professionally trained archaeologists.

Testable Models

With these goals in mind, we formulated several alternate explanatory models that investigations at *Aetokremnos* would test. These are summarized as follows:

MODEL 1: *Aetokremnos* was not anthropogenic, but rather it represented the results of natural processes.

COROLLARY 1: The artifacts associated with the bone resulted from fortuitous circumstances.

MODEL 2: *Aetokremnos* was cultural and predated the documented Cypriot Aceramic Neolithic. As such, it was the oldest known site in Cyprus, representing a landfall of people, probably from the Levant or Anatolia.

COROLLARY 1a: This landfall, either unintentional or planned, was short lived and ultimately unsuccessful, having little impact on future development of the island.

COROLLARY 1b: This landfall, either unintentional or planned, was antecedent to the Aceramic Neolithic, possibly representing a "founder population."

COROLLARY 2: The association of *Phanourios* and *Elephas* with cultural remains indicated that these species were not extinct prior to man's arrival in Cyprus.

MODEL 3: *Aetokremnos* was cultural and was contemporary with the Aceramic Neolithic. It represented a functional site type previously unidentified (marine and terrestrial fauna resource procurement camp), and indicates that *Phanourios* and *Elephas* did not become extinct until the Aceramic Neolithic.

MODEL 4: *Aetokremnos* was cultural and was later than the Aceramic Neolithic. Again, this would represent a site type previously undocumented. It would also indicate that *Phanourios* and *Elephas* did not, in fact, become extinct until well after human colonization of Cyprus.

MODEL 5: *Aetokremnos* was cultural and represented an occupation by people who settled above preexisting bone deposits containing the extinct species. Their subsequent activities may have resulted in the bones becoming burned. There would not, though, be a direct association between the human occupation and the extinct fauna.

After four seasons of excavation and survey, we have concluded that Model 2 best fits the available data. This conclusion will be developed throughout this volume.

Finally, beyond the goals relating specifically to the excavation of *Aetokremnos*, there were two broader issues that concerned us, as well: First, we wished to address the broader topic of island colonization, and the ramifications of it in light of *Aetokremnos's* presumed antiquity. Second, if a Late Pleistocene fauna was indeed directly associated with cultural materials, this would have substantial implications for the controversial role of human involvement in Pleistocene extinctions. Our success at addressing these issues can be gauged by the readers of this volume.

METHODOLOGY

An examination of the surface at *Aetokremnos* did not promise abundant in situ remains; it appeared that most of the intact deposits had already eroded into the sea. We believed that if such deposits existed, they probably would cover a limited horizontal extent, with the best chance of preservation being the area behind the presumed shell layer (that is, Area C). Excavation has shown, however, how incorrect our assessment was: Over a meter of intact deposition existed in some portions of *Aetokremnos* (Fig. 2-6).

Given the limited and fragile nature of the site, it was necessary to implement a precise data recovery program capable of retrieving as much material as possible. Furthermore, the degree of erosion occurring every year was substantial and was clearly having an impact on the site. I first visited *Aetokremnos* in 1985; by the time of our first excavations in 1987, some of the previously intact western portions already had been damaged, being subjected to the often violent gales that occur in the winter on the Akrotiri Peninsula. This necessitated nearly complete excavation of the site, leaving unexcavated only portions of two 1-by-1-m units. Thus in a sense our excavations assumed a rescue dimension, and it required a cost- and time-efficient approach.

The excavation of *Aetokremnos* was conducted over three field seasons, in 1987, 1988, and 1990, with the last representing the most intense investigation. In addition, a survey was conducted in 1991. We excavated the site in units that might be considered small for most excavations in Cyprus. *Aetokremnos*, however, is one of the "smallest" sites ever excavated on the island, and given its controversial nature, a precise data retrieval program was essential. Without the comforting confines of architecture, it was necessary to de-

Figure 2-6. Site stratigraphy, postexcavation. Rod is 50 cm. long.

velop recovery strategies more consistent with Paleolithic sites than with those related to later periods.

The first step in our investigation of *Aetokremnos* was to establish a "safety net" along the precipitous west edge of the small shelf on which the site is located. This consisted of placing a security fence along the very edge of the drop-off into the sea. After doing this, a site datum point was established, and a site area map was constructed. Several excavation datum points were established for elevations; all these points were tied to the master datum.

One-by-one-m squares were the basic recovery units. These often were subdivided into 50-by-50-cm quadrants. All data retrieval, including surface collection, was conducted within this grid. The only exception to this was surface collection downslope immediately to the southwest of the shelter. This precipitous area was littered with bone that had eroded from the shelter. Early on in the investigation, in 1987, when we were uncertain if there was much intact deposition, we collected as much bone as possible, including this obviously displaced material. Due to safety considerations, the grid was not implemented on this steep surface, which had a direct drop of some 40 m into the Mediterranean Sea.

Once the grid had been established over all of the site, a surface collection was made (Fig. 2 7), both in areas in the shelter and outside of it. Prior to excavation, 31 $^1/_2$ grid units were collected. The majority of these were to the immediate south of the shelter, where surface materials that had eroded downslope were plentiful. An additional area to the southwest was collected, but this fell outside of the grid, due to the safety considerations noted earlier.

After surface collection, the excavation strategy was to start at the eroded shallow edges of the shelter (Fig. 2-8) and work our way into the deeper, inslope and intact de-

Figure 2-7. Surface collection unit at *Aetokremnos;* note the density of the bone.

Figure 2-8. Excavation into the eroded western edge at the site.

Figure 2-9. Excavation into intact interior deposits, showing the last unit excavated.

Figure 2-10. In situ chipped stone artifacts associated with faunal materials in Stratum 4.

posits, until only a few interior units remained to be excavated (Fig. 2-9). This method allowed maximal stratigraphic control, as we worked from the known to the unknown. We
also excavated several units outside of the main area to determine the horizontal area of the
shelter. These units rapidly reached bedrock, confirming the small size of *Aetokremnos*.

Excavation was stratigraphic, following visible layers when possible. We used "level"
designations during excavation; these were subsequently incorporated into specific strata
within the master site stratigraphy. In cases when a stratum was relatively thick, it was subdivided into smaller vertical units. Features and loci were excavated separately from the levels and unit(s) within which they were located.

As excavation progressed, it became clear that a large amount of rooffall capped much
of the intact deposits. Several immense rocks had to be removed to continue excavation,
and there was no way to do this without inflicting some damage on the underlying and surrounding matrix. Fortunately, because of the skill, persistence, and ingenuity of the crew,
we were successful in removing all of the offending rooffall. This part of the project was not
without its exciting moments. In those areas that were damaged, material was recorded as
being possibly mixed, even in cases in which it was obvious that most of the material was
from a particular stratum.

With a site as controversial as *Aetokremnos*, careful provenience was a necessity, as it
should be with any site. We initially intended to map in three dimensions every artifact retrieved. When it became apparent that the site was richer than anticipated, and that artifacts
were directly associated with bone (Fig. 2-10), we abandoned this strategy. Accordingly,
most artifacts were provenienced by the unit and level, and most often by the quadrant, in
which they were located. In some instances, however, point plotting was done, generally on
tools recovered in situ. We made no effort to point-plot individual bones. Nearly a quarter
of a million fragments were recovered, and such a strategy would have been unworkable.
As with any excavation, compromise is always required. The compromise that we made at
Aetokremnos was to precisely excavate as much of the site as possible within our resources.
This decision did not allow for a point-plotting methodology. We do not feel, however, that
a great deal of information was lost, and most artifacts can be placed within a particular
stratum within a 50-sq-cm horizontal space.

All excavated material was dry-sieved using $\frac{1}{4}$-inch mesh screening. Flotation and
other samples were taken from features and other relevant deposits. All material was
recorded with a "field number" (FN) designation on a master FN sheet and on individual
level forms. This provided a useful cross-check. Samples were recorded in a similar manner
with "sample field number" (SFN) designations.

All material was brought in from the field daily and processed in the laboratory established at the Kourion Museum in Episkopi village. This material was washed and cataloged
there, and preliminary analysis also was conducted. The detailed chipped stone analyses
were conducted by Alan Simmons, Deborah Olszewski, and Geoffrey Clark and by David
Reese on the megafauna and shells after the field seasons. Specialized analyses were so-
licited from various experts whose reports appear in this volume.

Chapter 3

Stratigraphy and Sedimentology

Rolfe D. Mandel

INTRODUCTION

Geologic investigations at *Aetokremnos* focused on the sedimentary strata that encompass all of the physical space within and immediately above the collapsed rockshelter. In addition to defining and describing strata, sediments were studied to determine their source and mode of transport and to identify postdepositional modification. Collectively, this information helps explain how the faunal remains and associated artifacts were buried in situ by sediment prior to being sealed beneath the collapsed roof of the shelter. It also allows us to make statements about the duration of human occupation at the site and the magnitude of site disturbance after the period of occupation. Although the sedimentological information from *Aetokremnos* cannot be used to reconstruct regional paleoclimates, it sheds light on past environments that existed at and near the site.

This chapter is divided into four major sections. The first section describes field methods and laboratory analyses used in the geologic investigation. The second section focuses on depositional processes that contributed sediment to the site before and after the roof of the rockshelter collapsed. The third section presents the results of field observations and laboratory analyses, including detailed descriptions of strata and sediments. The last section summarizes the history of sediment accumulation within rockshelter and considers how geologic processes affected the archaeological record during and after the period of human occupation at *Aetokremnos*. Additional detailed discussion may be found in Mandel and Simmons (1997).

METHODS

Field Methods

Field investigations at *Aetokremnos* went through several stages. Work was initially hindered by the presence of large roof-fall blocks mantled by a veneer of colluvium. During the 1987 field season, excavation units were concentrated along the fringes of the shelter in order to avoid these obstacles. Several large roof-fall blocks were removed in 1988 to allow excavation within the interior of the shelter. However, one massive roof-fall block remained in place over a large area of the site. Hence, the full thickness and lateral extent of the underlying deposits could not be determined until the final field season. Complete removal of the collapsed roof in 1990 exposed a package of unconsolidated sediment that was about 1 m thick (Fig. 3-1). The thickness of this package was fairly consistent from the outer edge to the back of the shelter. The sediment rested directly on the bedrock floor of the shelter.

Because the excavation of *Aetokremnos* progressed from the surface downward over a period of three years, we did not follow geologic protocol and number stratigraphic units sequentially from the bottom of the shelter upward. Instead, we followed archaeological convention in numbering our units from the surface downward; that is, the lowest numbered unit is at the top of the stratigraphic sequence and is also the youngest deposit. Bone and artifact provenience was keyed into this numbering system during the excavation.

Four stratigraphic units were identified on the basis of presence/absence of in situ cultural deposits. Arabic numerals (1–4) were used to identify these "archaeological" units, beginning with the uppermost zone, Stratum 1. The stratigraphic units were subdivided into sedimentary units that were designated by the addition of an upper-case letter after the stra-

Figure 3-1. View of the interior of the *Aetokremnos* rockshelter during the 1990 field season. Note the bone bed (Stratum 4B) at the bottom of the excavation units. There is a basin-shaped feature in Stratum 2A (right-center). The rod is 50 cm long.

tum number, for example, Stratum 2A. The sedimentary units were rock terms defined by lithologic characteristics, such as color, texture, and bedding.

After describing the physical characteristics of the sedimentary units at *Aetokremnos*, we collected sediment samples for laboratory analysis. Rockshelter sediments were usually sampled from a single type section in the site that characterized all the strata. At *Aetokremnos*, this sampling strategy was not feasible because all strata were not present in a single section. In order to interpret the stratigraphy across the site, it was necessary to sample sediments from several profiles. Sediment samples weighing approximately 500 g each were collected from the middle of each sedimentary unit represented in the profiles.

Several localities outside the rockshelter were sampled to provide comparative data for possible sources of sediments within the shelter. Colluvial deposits mantling the roof at the back of the rockshelter were sampled from two profiles. Also, samples were taken from deposits of eolian sand on slopes above and below the rockshelter. In addition, one sample was collected from the littoral zone of a sandy beach along the shore of the Akrotiri Peninsula. The beach sample was used to characterize the mineralogy and granulometry of sediment in the primary source area for eolian deposits on the slopes surrounding *Aetokremnos*.

Laboratory Methods

Particle size distribution was determined using a modification of the pipette method developed by Kilmer and Alexander (1949) and the Soil Survey Staff (1982). Organic matter contents were low enough that the samples did not require pretreatment for organic matter removal. The clays were separated by centrifuge precipitation of the silts and sands and decantation of the suspended clay fraction. Sands were separated from the silts using a 300-mesh sieve. The sands were oven dried and separated into five fractions by sieving.

Total phosphorous (P) was determined by digesting samples with a salicylic-sulfuric acid mixture in a Technicon Model BD-20 Block Digester (Technicon Industrial Method 334-74W/B). The digested solutions were made to volume with distilled water, and P was determined with a Technicon Autoanalyzer II, using the colorimetric method.

Calcium carbonate ($CaCO_3$) equivalent was determined by the rapid titration method (Piper 1942). This procedure involves digesting samples in 1 normal solution (1 N) hydrochloric acid and titration with 1 N sodium hydroxide.

The mineralogy, sphericity, and roundness of sand grains was studied by Teresa Silence at the University of Nebraska-Omaha. The very coarse (2.0–1.0 mm), coarse (1.0–0.5 mm), and medium (0.5–0.25 mm) fractions were examined, using a binocular microscope at 3× magnification. Percentages of carbonates, quartz, igneous clasts, and other minerals were visually estimated. Sphericity and roundness were determined, using a visual comparison chart (Tucker 1988). Grains from the fine (0.25–0.125 mm) and very fine (0.125–0.0625 mm) fractions were placed on glass slides and immersed in type A, nondrying immersion oil, having a refractive index of 1.5150. A cover slip was placed on all samples, and the grain mounts were examined under a petrographic microscope at 10× and 20× magnification.

DEPOSITIONAL PROCESSES

Interpretation of rockshelter sediments usually is complicated by the fact that several different depositional processes operated simultaneously, and sediments came from multiple sources (Farrand 1985). Field observations revealed that this was certainly the case at *Aetokremnos*. These observations were corroborated by the results of laboratory analyses, which will be discussed later.

Four major processes contributed sediment to the floor of the rockshelter prior to the collapse of its roof: rock fall, grain-by-grain disintegration (attrition) of the bioclastic limestone that formed the roof and walls of the shelter, eolian deposition, and slopewash. Following its collapse, colluvial and eolian processes deposited sediment above the roof of the shelter. Sedimentary facies resulting from these depositional processes were recognized by (1) sedimentary features observed in the walls of excavation units, (2) grain-size distributions determined through standard laboratory procedures, and (3) mineralogy and morphology of grains determined by optical analyses.

Rockfall

Angular fragments of bioclastic limestone with diameters ranging from a few centimeters to several meters were scattered through the fine-grained matrix of deposits within the rockshelter (Fig. 3-1). The presence of these fragments in all strata indicate that they were sporadically released from the walls and ceiling of the rockshelter. The release of rock fragments may be attributed to (1) widening of joints and bedding planes by water movement through openings in the bedrock (see Bjerrum and Jorstad 1968) and/or (2) hydration spalling (see Farrand 1985). With the first process, instantaneous release of the fragments occurs when joints or bedding plains expand and cause failure along zones of weakness. With hydration spalling, sudden release of rock fragments also occurs, but the rock fall is produced by solution weathering along joints and bedding plains. Although the role of freeze/thaw in producing rockfall has been stressed in other studies (e.g., Laville *et al.* 1980), *Aetokremnos* is in a climate that presently is without frost. Moreover, it is unlikely that frost occurred during the Early Holocene, as it would require a drop of about 13° C during winter to bring freezing temperatures to the southern coast of Cyprus. Regardless of what caused rockfall, large and small clasts were probably produced when the fragments struck the floor of the shelter (see Farrand 1985: 25).

Attrition

Solution weathering, including hydration and carbonation, causes grain-by-grain disintegration of bioclastic limestone; it probably produced a steady rain of sediment to the floor of the *Aetokremnos* rockshelter. This process was referred to as "granular disintegration" by Carson and Kirkby (1972), and it is recognized as an important sediment-generating mechanism in rockshelters of the eastern Mediterranean (Farrand 1985: 25–28). We chose the term *attrition* for this weathering process (after Donahue and Adovasio 1990). As Donahue and Adovasio (1990) pointed out, grain-size distribution of sediments produced by attrition are controlled entirely by the size range of clasts within the source rock. Based on particle-size analyses, the bioclastic limestone at *Aetokremnos* consisted of grains that are mostly 2.0–0.5 mm in diameter (Table 3-1); hence, sediment generated by attrition is predominantly that size.

Eolian Deposition

Eolian sand sheets mantle some of the slopes adjacent to *Aetokremnos*, and sand dunes occur on top of the sea cliffs above the site. Hence, eolian deposition has greatly affected the southern coast of the Akrotiri Peninsula, and it is a process that contributed sediment to the rockshelter.

There are two principle sources of eolian sediment near *Aetokremnos:* (1) sandy beach deposits along the shoreline and (2) weathered sandstone and bioclastic limestone that is eroding on the slopes above the shoreline. The sandy beach deposits are presently restricted to very narrow zones at the base of steep sea cliffs, and at many places the cliffs descend directly to the sea. However, according to Gomez and Pease (1992), a broad, relatively flat beach extended out about 1.5 km beyond the modern shoreline during low sea levels. They suggested that this broad beach was exposed as recently as 10,500 years ago, providing an abundant supply of fine sand for eolian transport.

A second major source of eolian sediment is the weathered sandstone and bioclastic limestone exposed in slopes above the shoreline. Granular disintegration of this rock produces fine sandy and silty sediment that is entrained and transported by the wind. Even today, strong sea breezes usually raise clouds of fine sediment when they sweep across the barren slopes immediately south of *Aetokremnos*. As these clouds drift upslope, eolian sediment derived from the weathered bedrock is deposited at high positions in the landscape. It is likely that this process also operated during the Early Holocene, providing bedrock-derived eolian sediment to the rockshelter.

Although the grain sizes of eolian sediments derived from the beach and bedrock are similar, the mineralogy is different. Both the beach deposits and bedrock contain many small shell fragments (bioclasts) and calcite grains that are readily transported by wind. However, the beach deposits contain abundant silt- and sand-sized olivine, plagioclase, serpentine, pyroxine, sulfide, oxide, and multicrystal grains that are extremely rare (< 1%) in the bioclastic limestone. Thus, an abundance of "exotic" clasts within eolian deposits indicates a beach source for some of the sediment.

Slopewash

During and immediately after major rainfalls, sediment is entrained and transported down the slopes by surface runoff. Although much of the runoff moves as sheets of water (sheet wash), some is contained in rills and gullies. The term *slopewash* is used here to include sediment deposited on slopes by all of these forms of surface runoff.

Two types of slopewash were recognized at *Aetokremnos:* (1) massive, poorly sorted surface deposits (colluvium) that mantle what is left of the rockshelter's roof and (2) laminated, well-sorted deposits within the rockshelter. The colluvium on the roof of the rockshelter consisted of very poorly sorted sediment, ranging in size from boulders to clay-sized particles. This material was transported downslope by gravity and water. However, some of the surface runoff was funneled into small solution cavities that drained into the back of the

Table 3-1. Particle Size Distribution of Samples from Sand Dunes, Beach Deposits, and Bedrock at Akrotiri *Aetokremnos*

| | Weight (%) | | | | | | | | | | | | | |
| | Sand | | | | | | Silt | | | | Total clay | Textural class[a] | Mean size (mm) | Standard deviation |
Provenience	VC	C	M	F	VF	Total	C	M	F	Total				
Bedrock[b]	20.3	37.7	19.7	14.4	7.9	76.8	8.4	10.7	1.7	20.7	2.5	LS	0.54	0.5
Beach[c]	1.1	2.8	4.8	81.7	9.6	85.0	1.8	2.4	3.5	7.6	7.5	LS	0.19	0.17
Sand dune[d]	0.1	3.1	13.4	72.7	10.7	91.6	1.7	0.7	1.3	3.7	4.8	S	0.20	0.13
Sand sheet[e]	0.0	0.9	7.7	87.2	4.2	94.7	0.7	0.8	0.3	1.8	3.5	S	0.19	0.09

Note: Particle-size limits (mm): Sand: Total = 2.0–0.05, VC = 2.0–1.0, C = 1.0–0.5, M = 0.5–0.25, F = 0.25–0.10, VF = 0.10–0.05; Silt: Total = 0.05–0.002, Coarse = 0.05—0.02, Medium = 0.02–0.005, Fine = 0.005–0.002; Clay: Total = < 0.002.

[a]Texture classes: S=sand, Si=silt, C=clay, L=loam.

[b]Sample of weathered bioclastic limestone collected from the roof of the rockshelter.

[c]The sample was collected from the littoral zone of the narrow beach about 35 m downslope from *Aetokremnos*.

[d]The sample was collected from the upper 20 cm of a sand dune located on a beach near the southeast tip of the Akrotiri Peninsula.

[e]The sample was colleted from the upper 20 cm of an eolian sand sheet that is banked against a talus slope about 50 m east of *Aetokremnos*.

Figure 3-2. View of the back of the rockshelter. Note the solution cavity immediately below the brow of the shelter. The rod is 1 m long.

rockshelter (Fig. 3-2). Deposits resembling cones and alluvial fans developed at the mouths of these solution cavities. Some of the slopewash also accumulated in a small channel near the north wall of the shelter. All of the slopewash deposits within the shelter were laminated, and sediment within each lamina was well sorted.

RESULTS

Stratigraphy and Sedimentology

Detailed descriptions of the stratigraphic and sedimentary units are provided in this section. One unit, identified as Stratum 5 in the field and occurring in only portions of a few excavation units, is not addressed here; it is best considered as part of Stratum 4C (see additional discussion in Chap. 4). As noted earlier, the major stratigraphic units are defined on the basis of cultural context, whereas the sedimentary units are defined by lithologic characteristics.

Stratum 1

Stratum 1 is the uppermost stratigraphic unit and includes (1) colluvium that mantles intact and collapsed portions of the rockshelter's roof and (2) colluvium, laminated slopewash, rooffall, and attrition sediment above Stratum 2. Stratum 1 does not contain any in situ cultural materials, thus, despite the presence of redeposited glass, Roman pottery, and chert flakes, it is considered a culturally "sterile" package of sediment. Faunal remains were found in Stratum 1, but only where bones from Stratum 2 had obviously been displaced upward by the impact of roof-fall blocks. Also, erosion of bone-rich strata within and along the fringes of the collapsed rockshelter has contributed faunal remains to sheetwash and colluvial deposits that compose Stratum 1.

Five sedimentary units were identified in Stratum 1: Stratum 1A through 1E. These strata are described in sections that follow.

Stratum 1A. Stratum 1A is 25 to 50 cm thick and consists of colluvium derived from slopes above the rockshelter. This unit mantles the large roof-fall blocks above the archaeological deposits, and it overlies stratum 1B on the bedrock overhang at the back of the rockshelter. Angular limestone cobbles and boulders are scattered through a calcareous, fine-grained matrix, and sedimentary features are absent. A very thin surface soil with A–C horizonation developed in the upper part of Stratum 1A. The A horizon is 13 to 20 cm thick and is light yellowish-brown (10YR 6/4, dry) sandy loam. Loose, single grains (structureless) within the underlying C horizon replaced the weak, fine, granular structure within the A horizon. Also, the C horizon is slightly lighter in color (very pale brown, 10YR 7/4, dry) than the A horizon.

The proportion of sand in Stratum 1A ranges from 61.7 to 68.5%, with modes in the fine and very fine fractions (Table 3-2 and Fig. 3-3). Mean particle size (0.30–0.39 mm) is relatively fine in this stratum, and the standard deviation (0.44–0.49) indicates that the < 2 mm fraction is well sorted. The abundance of fine and very fine sand is attributed to an incorporation of primary and reworked eolian sediment in the colluvium. The mineralogy of the sand indicates that most of the eolian sediment was derived from weathered bioclastic limestone that was exposed in slopes adjacent to the rockshelter. All of the sand fractions contain ≤ 5% noncarbonates, and although there is a slight increase in the amount of quartz in the fine and very fine fractions, igneous and metamorphic grains, as well as other minerals characteristic of eolian sediment from the beach source, are very rare (Mandel and Simmons 1997:Table III). It is likely that the wind added fine-grained sediment to Stratum 1A as the colluvium accumulated. In addition, deposits of calcareous eolian sand on the slopes and bluffs above *Aetokremnos* have been severely eroded by surface runoff and probably contributed sediment to debris flows.

Stratum 1B. Stratum 1B is restricted to the bedrock overhang at the back of the rockshelter. This sedimentary unit rests directly on bedrock and is mantled by Stratum 1A. It is 25 to 40 cm thick and, like Stratum 1A, consists of a poorly sorted colluvium derived from the slopes above the site. The boundary between 1A and 1B is marked by a buried soil that was developed in the upper part of Stratum 1B; therefore, colluviation was interrupted by an episode of landscape stability and soil formation before Stratum 1A aggraded. The buried soil is distinct but weakly developed (A–AC profile). The Ab horizon is 20 to 30 cm thick and is dark brown (10YR 4/3, dry), sandy clay loam. There is weak, fine and medium granular structure within the Ab horizon, and the matrix is strongly calcareous. The ACb is a brown (10YR 5/3, dry) to pale brown (10YR 6/3, dry), sandy loam.

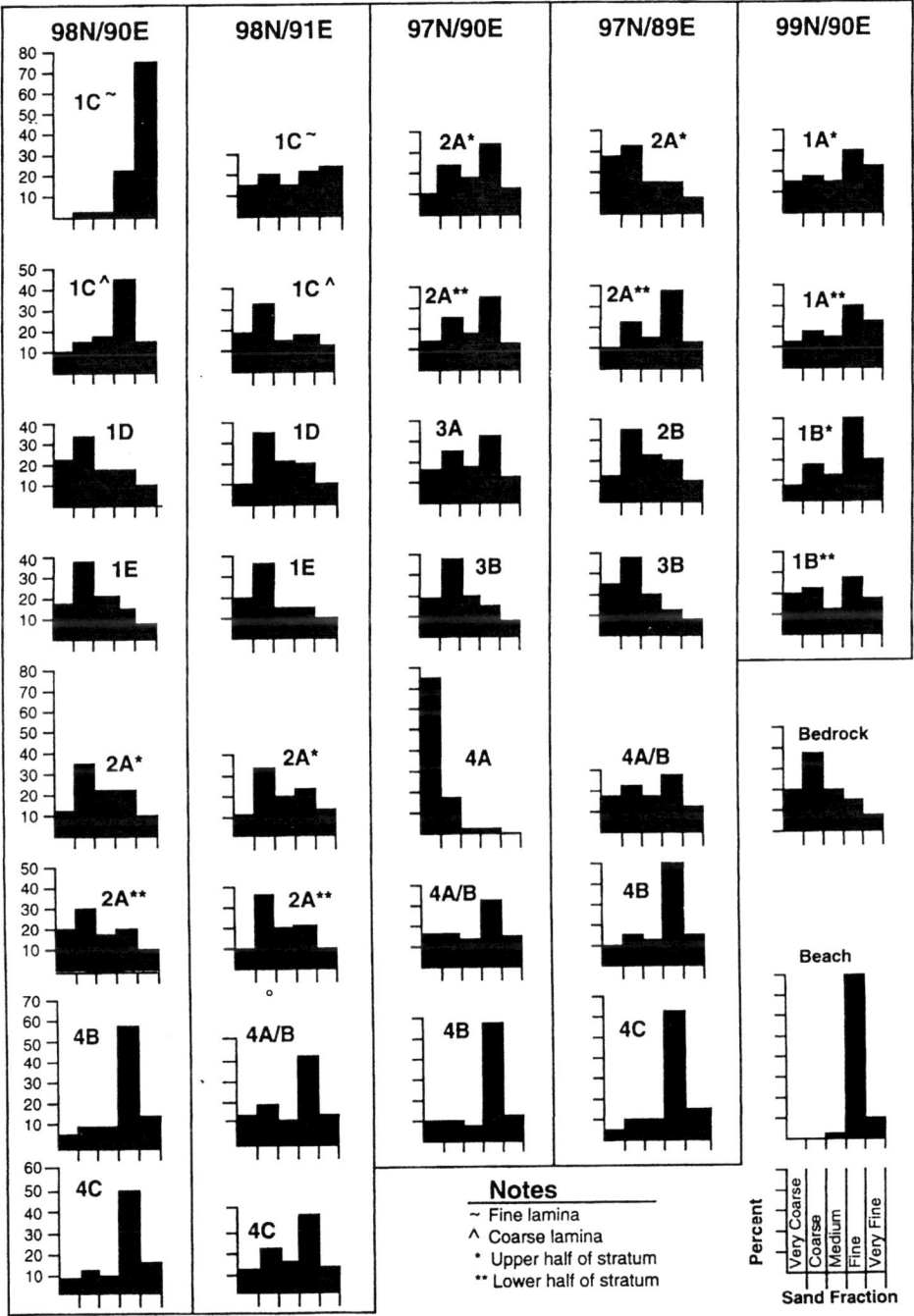

Figure 3-3. Granulometric histograms of the sand fractions.

Table 3-2. Particle Size Distribution of Samples from the Aetokremnos Rockshelter

Stratum	Depth[a]	Weight (%)										Total clay	Textural class[b]	Mean size (mm)	Standard deviation
		Sand						Silt							
		VC	C	M	F	VF	Total	C	M	F	Total				
99N/90E (above the shelter): East wall															
1A	0–13	14.5	16.0	14.5	31.5	23.5	61.7	5.8	10.2	8.4	24.4	13.9	SL	0.30	0.44
1A	13–32	13.7	16.9	14.7	31.8	22.9	66.1	4.7	9.1	6.3	20.2	13.7	SL	0.32	0.44
1B	32–50	7.3	18.6	13.7	39.8	20.6	57.9	4.5	8.6	8.0	21.2	21.0	SL	0.23	0.35
1B	50–70	20.4	21.8	13.0	26.2	18.6	58.2	4.8	8.7	8.6	22.1	19.8	SL	0.34	0.48
99N/89E (above the shelter): North wall															
1A	0–20	18.2	14.6	13.0	32.0	22.8	68.0	4.4	8.0	1.2	13.6	18.4	SL	0.35	0.48
1A	0–35	18.6	20.3	16.1	28.0	17.0	68.5	3.5	8.1	6.4	18.0	13.5	SL	0.39	0.49
1B	35–45	11.6	16.8	13.5	36.5	21.6	56.7	4.3	10.4	8.0	22.6	20.7	SCL	0.25	0.40
1B	45–55	17.3	22.5	14.5	26.1	19.6	52.0	4.9	11.9	9.5	26.3	21.7	SCL	0.29	0.45
98N/91E: East wall															
1C[c]	0–28	14.0	25.2	15.1	22.1	23.6	34.4	8.8	16.9	17.4	43.1	22.5	L	0.19	0.36
1C[d]	28–57	18.5	32.8	17.4	19.4	11.9	65.1	4.8	10.8	5.2	20.9	14.0	SL	0.42	0.49
1D	57–74	10.7	35.0	22.4	21.2	10.7	66.5	4.5	9.9	5.9	20.4	13.1	SL	0.37	0.42
1E	74–113	19.1	36.3	17.4	16.6	10.4	63.6	5.5	12.0	5.9	24.4	12.0	SL	0.44	0.49
2A	113–133	11.8	33.9	19.8	22.6	11.9	64.1	6.4	13.8	4.5	24.8	11.1	SL	0.37	0.43
2A	133–154	10.2	37.2	20.0	21.3	11.3	63.9	5.0	14.9	5.1	24.9	11.1	SL	0.36	0.42
4A/B	154–176	13.2	19.1	11.3	42.9	13.5	55.8	5.5	9.1	5.9	20.6	23.7	SCL	0.27	0.41
4C	176–184	11.2	22.7	14.9	38.8	12.4	58.0	5.1	9.4	5.5	20.0	22.0	SCL	0.28	0.40

98N/90E: North wall

1C[c]	0–22	0.3	1.2	1.0	22.0	75.5	20.9	13.8	24.4	14.8	53.1	26.0	SiL	0.04	0.07
1C[d]	22–44	10.2	14.6	15.8	44.0	15.4	74.0	3.3	6.1	4.9	14.3	11.7	SL	0.31	0.40
1D	44–68	22.7	33.2	17.1	17.1	9.9	63.3	4.2	9.7	6.5	20.3	16.4	SL	0.44	0.51
1E	68–107	18.4	38.3	21.3	15.0	7.0	75.8	4.2	10.3	3.3	17.8	6.4	SL	0.52	0.49
2A	107–128	12.0	34.3	21.2	21.5	11.0	63.4	6.2	14.1	5.1	25.4	11.1	SL	0.37	0.43
2A	128–149	19.9	30.8	18.0	20.2	11.1	64.8	5.5	12.8	5.3	23.6	11.6	SL	0.42	0.49
4B	149–172	7.1	8.9	8.8	58.5	16.7	49.7	4.1	11.4	7.0	22.6	27.8	SCL	0.17	0.34
4C	172–131	8.6	13.4	10.2	51.1	16.7	51.8	5.6	10.1	6.1	21.7	26.5	SCL	0.20	0.34

97N/89E: East wall

2A	0–15	28.8	33.7	15.8	14.5	7.2	71.2	4.1	9.3	5.4	18.8	10.0	SL	0.56	0.55
2A	15–28	10.7	22.1	15.9	38.5	12.8	70.9	6.4	9.0	4.8	20.1	9.0	SL	0.34	0.41
2B	28–31	11.0	36.5	22.4	20.6	9.5	72.0	6.4	11.3	4.2	21.8	6.3	SL	0.41	0.43
3B	31–47	24.6	37.0	19.8	12.5	6.1	78.3	4.1	9.0	2.9	16.0	5.8	LS	0.59	0.52
4A/B	47–71	17.1	23.9	17.5	28.4	13.1	76.8	7.5	6.4	2.9	16.8	6.4	SL	0.44	0.48
4B	71–89	9.7	14.0	12.1	50.2	14.0	75.8	5.5	5.9	3.5	15.0	9.2	SL	0.31	0.40
4C	89–96	4.8	9.0	9.6	62.3	14.3	75.9	3.8	4.7	3.5	12.0	12.1	SL	0.24	0.31

97N/90E: North wall

2A	0–18	10.1	24.6	17.4	34.4	13.5	67.3	7.4	11.6	4.3	23.3	9.4	SL	0.33	0.41
2A	18–36	12.9	24.6	15.8	34.8	11.9	72.0	5.8	9.8	3.6	19.3	8.7	SL	0.38	0.44
3A	36–51	14.6	25.7	16.0	31.4	12.3	60.9	5.5	11.5	5.6	22.6	16.5	SL	0.34	0.44
3B	51–59	18.4	38.3	21.3	15.0	7.0	75.8	4.2	10.3	3.3	17.8	6.4	SL	0.52	0.48
4A	59–73	76.4	16.6	3.3	3.0	0.7	85.7	3.8	3.2	2.1	9.2	5.2	LS	0.35	0.46
4A/B	73–86	16.2	16.5	13.9	36.6	16.8	67.4	10.0	9.1	4.2	23.3	9.3	SL	1.11	0.58
4B	86–97	10.3	10.7	9.0	57.0	13.0	66.0	4.7	6.3	4.3	15.3	18.7	SL	0.26	0.38

Note: Particle-size limits (mm): Sand: Total = 2.0–0.05, VC = 2.0–1.0, C = 1.0–0.5, M = 0.5–0.25, F = 0.25–0.10, VF = 0.10–0.05; Silt: Total = 0.05–0.002, Coarse = 0.05–0.02, Medium = 0.02–0.005, Fine = 0.005–0.002; Clay: Total = < 0.002.

[a] Depth below the surface of the uppermost stratum in the profile.

[b] Textural classes: S=sand, Si=silt, C=clay, L=loam.

[c] Only fine-grained laminae were sampled.

[d] Only coarse-grained laminae were sampled.

The sand content is high (52–58%) in Stratum 1B, with fine sand dominating the sand fraction and coarse sand forming a second mode in the lower half of the unit (Table 3-2 and Fig. 3-3). Like Stratum 1A, the sand fraction in 1B is dominated by grains derived from bioclastic limestone, and most of the fine and very fine sand represents primary and reworked eolian sediment (Mandel and Simmons 1997: Table III). However, the mean particle size (0.23–0.34 mm) is finer in Stratum 1B compared with 1A. Also, clay content is relatively high in 1B, ranging from 19.8 to 21.7%. This may be due to a longer duration and/or a greater intensity of weathering for Stratum B compared with 1A.

Stratum 1C.   Stratum 1C consists of laminated, sandy and silty slopewash that was deposited near the north wall of the rockshelter (Fig. 3-4). The surface of this unit slopes southwestward, away from the back of the shelter. Several solution cavities along the top of the north wall of the shelter provide points of entry for the slopewash (Fig. 3-2). As sediment-laden water flowed through these cavities and out of the shelter; it cut a small channel through Strata 2, 3, and 4 and into the underlying bedrock. This channel was subsequently filled with the laminated sediment that composes Stratum 1C. Individual laminae are from 1 to 4 mm thick and gently dip to the southwest. The coarse-grained laminae consist of very pale brown (10YR 7/4, dry), sandy loam; sand content is as great as 74%, and mean grain size ranges between 0.31 mm and 0.42 mm (Table 3-2). In contrast, the fine-grained laminae consist of very pale brown (10YR 7/3, dry) and pale brown (10YR 6/3, dry), silt loam and loam with mean grain size ranging between 0.04 mm and 0.19 mm.

Figure 3-4. Laminated slopewash deposits (Stratum 1C) above Stratum 1E in the northwest corner of the rockshelter. The rod is 50 cm long.

Preservation of primary sedimentary features and the paucity of rooffall within Stratum 1C indicate that the slopewash accumulated rapidly. Although some bones of *Phanourios* and other fauna were found in Stratum 1C, they were widely scattered through the slopewash. Also, their frequency decreased as the distance from concentrations of bones in Strata 2 and 4 that were truncated by Stratum 1C increased. Hence, all of the bones in Stratum 1C were eroded from in situ cultural deposits, as water flowed out from the back of the rockshelter prior to the collapse of the roof.

In the extreme northeast corner of the rockshelter, Stratum 1C mantles Stratum 1D. However, it overlies 1E or bedrock in the northwest quarter of the shelter. Large roof-fall blocks that were deposited prior to the aggradation of Stratum 1C affected the flow of water and emplacement of the slopewash. This influence is most apparent in excavation units N99E88, N98E88, and N97E88 (see Fig. 4-6 in Chap. 4), where a massive roof-fall block diverted flowing water to the north, thereby protecting cultural deposits to the south and west of the obstruction. However, Feature 1 and Strata 2, 3, and 4 are truncated by Stratum 1C immediately north of the roof-fall block.

Stratum 1D. Stratum 1D consists of laminated, dark brown (10YR 4/3, dry), slopewash above Stratum 1E. It is restricted to the extreme northeast corner of the shelter, and its surface, like that of Stratum C, slopes southwestward, away from the back of the shelter. The gradient was established by deposition of slopewash spilling out of a solution cavity located high up on the wall in that corner. The dark sediment was traced up through the cavity to its source: the buried soil developed in Stratum 1B. Stratum 1D prograded only a short distance to the west-southwest before it was buried by Stratum 1C. Individual laminae are 1 to 2 mm thick and have a sandy loam texture (Table 3-2). Bedding is distinct, and there are relatively few rock-fall fragments. Hence, deposition of this "soil sediment" appears to have been rapid.

Stratum 1E. Stratum 1E is a culturally sterile body of sediment that was generated largely by rooffall and grain-by-grain disintegration (attrition) of the bioclastic limestone. Angular fragments of rooffall from 5 to 75 cm in diameter are scattered through a homogeneous, very pale brown (10YR 7/4, dry), sandy loam matrix (Fig. 3-4). Stratum 1E is about 30 cm thick and has not been modified by soil development. The < 2 mm fraction is highly calcareous (74–75%) and dominated by sand (Tables 3-2 and 3-3). The sand has a unimodal grain-size distribution, with a distinct peak in the coarse fraction (Fig. 3-3). This distribution resembles that of the bioclastic limestone that composes the roof and walls of the rockshelter. However, about 5% of the very fine sand in Stratum 1E consists of subrounded to rounded igneous and metamorphic grains that were derived from beach deposits (Mandel and Simmons 1997:Table III). Also, shell fragments and the skeletal remains of foraminifera observed in the fine and very fine sand fractions are not from the bioclastic limestone and could have only come from a beach source (Silence 1996). These findings indicate that the wind contributed a small volume of sediment to Stratum 1E.

Stratum 2

Stratum 2 is the uppermost cultural zone within the collapsed rockshelter. This unit largely consists of attrition and eolian sediment, though large and small fragments of rock-

Table 3-3. Phosphorous (P) and Calcium Carbonate (CaCO₃)
Contents of Samples from *Aetokremnos*

Stratum	Depth (cm)	P (ppm)	CaCO₃ (%)	Stratum	Depth (cm)	P (ppm)	CaCO₃ (%)
99N/90E (above the shelter): East wall				99N/89E (above the shelter): North wall			
1A	0–13	225	62.2	1A	0–20	191	64.8
1A	13–32	236	63.7	1A	20–35	206	69.3
1B	32–50	326	62.9	1B	35–45	263	59.8
1B	50–70	368	62.2	1B	45–55	233	67.2
98N/91E: East wall	98N/90E: North wall						
1C^a	0–57	405	62.9	1C^a	0–44	338	57.4
1C^b	0–57	435	72.9	1C^b	0–44	244	57.3
1D	57–74	495	70.7	1D	44–68	263	68.1
1E	74–113	574	74.4	1E	68–107	510	74.9
2A	113–133	986	70.1	2A	107–128	578	72.3
2A	133–154	1,058	72.6	2A	128–149	1,691	70.3
4A/B	154–176	5,625	37.2	4B	149–172	5,190	24.0
4C	176–184	3,750	40.1	4C	172–181	3,990	26.0
97N/89E: East wall	97N/90E: North wall						
2A	0–15	544	71.9	2A	0–18	1,163	59.6
2A	15–28	1,800	54.1	2A	18–36	3,120	58.7
2B	28–31	1,200	74.1	3A	36–51	799	56.3
3B	31–47	1,095	79.7	3B	51–59	720	79.2
4A/B	47–71	6,300	48.3	4A	59–73	9,000	26.5
4B	71–89	6,465	32.6	4A/B	73–86	6,375	41.5
4C	89–96	2,925	14.6	4B	86–97	3,330	16.8

^{a}Only fine-grained laminae were sampled.
^{b}Only course-grained laminae were sampled.

fall are scattered through it. The thickness of Stratum 2 is extremely variable, ranging between about 10 and 50 cm. This unit mantles a culturally sterile zone (Stratum 3) within most of the shelter, but directly overlies Stratum 4 in places at the front of the shelter. The lower boundary of Stratum 2 is usually abrupt. Stratum 2 is subdivided into Stratum 2A and 2B. These strata are now described.

Stratum 2A.   Stratum 2A is at the top of Stratum 2 and is 15 to 45 cm thick. The upper two-thirds of Stratum 2A consists of calcareous, dark grayish brown (10YR 4/2, dry), sandy loam. The matrix is loose and interspersed with cobble- and boulder-size clasts representing rooffall. There is a large volume of fine, disseminated charcoal in the upper part of 2A, giving the matrix an ashy appearance. The lower half of 2A also is calcareous sandy loam, but it is not as enriched with charcoal; hence, it is has a lighter color (grayish-brown [10YR 5/2, dry] to light brownish gray [10YR 6/2, dry]). There is no evidence of soil development in Stratum 2A, and its upper and lower boundaries are abrupt.

Stratum 2A is the most distinct cultural zone in the sequence of rockshelter deposits. In addition to containing several cultural features, it has a high density of chipped stone, ornamental pieces, and shell. There are also a substantial number of *Phanourios* and other vertebrate remains.

Sand dominates the < 2 mm fraction in Stratum 2A, with proportions ranging between 64 and 72% (Table 3-2). The mean particle size ranges from 0.33 mm to 0.56 mm, and the standard deviation (0.41–0.55) indicates that the < 2 mm fraction is well sorted to moderately well sorted. The grain-size distribution of the sand fraction in most samples from Stratum 2A is bimodal, with peaks in the coarse and fine fractions (Fig. 3-3). These data suggest that the sediment composing Stratum 2A has two sources. The bulk of the coarse sand probably came from attrition of the bioclastic limestone. However, some of the sediment was blown in from the beach. This interpretation is supported by the mineralogical analysis. The proportion of igneous and metamorphic grains increases from less than 1% in the very coarse and coarse sand fractions to 2–5% in the fine and very fine sand fractions (Mandel and Simmons 1997:Table III).

The $CaCO_3$ content of Stratum 2A is relatively high, ranging between 60 and 72% (Table 3-3). These values indicate that sediment composing Stratum 2A was not leached after it was deposited. Hence, it is likely that this stratum was exposed to subaerial weathering for a relatively short period before it was mantled by large roof-fall blocks.

Stratum 2A is rich in phosphorous (P), with concentrations ranging between 544 and 1,800 ppm (Table 3-3). In all but one of the sections that were analyzed, P increased from the upper to the lower half of Stratum 2A. This trend corresponds with an increase in the density of bones and artifacts.

Stratum 2B.   Stratum 2B is a thin, discontinuous layer of calcareous, reddish-brown (5YR 5/4, dry) sandy loam immediately below 2A. It is 1 to 5 cm thick and limited to areas where there is evidence of burning within 2A. A good example of this spatial relationship is the reddish zone (Stratum 2B) beneath the pile of ash composing Feature 1 in Stratum 2A. The color of Stratum 2B clearly is a result of thermal alteration of the sediment.

The mean particle size in Stratum 2B is 0.41 mm; hence, it is slightly coarser than 2A. The fine-grained matrix has a high proportion of sand (72%), with coarse grains dominating the sand fraction (Table 3-2 and Fig. 3-3). Analysis with a binocular microscope revealed that the abundance of coarse sand is a result of fusing of smaller grains. Given that Stratum 2B only occurs beneath hearths, the fusing of grains is attributed to intense heat generated by fires in the overlying cultural features.

Stratum 2B is above Stratum 3 within much of the area of the collapsed rockshelter. However, it is above Stratum 4 where 3 is missing. The distribution of Strata 3 and 4 is discussed later.

Stratum 3

Stratum 3 is a sterile zone that often separates Stratum 2 from the bone midden (Stratum 4) at the bottom of the sedimentary sequence (Fig. 3-5). This unit is 15 to 30 cm thick across most of the site, but it is much thinner or absent in several areas, especially near the front and back of the shelter. At a few places, cultural features in Stratum 2 truncate Stratum 3 and intersect Stratum 4. However, no cultural materials were found in situ within Stratum 3.

Stratum 3 consists of loamy sand and sandy loam that represent accumulations of sediment by attrition and eolian processes. Also, large and small fragments of rockfall are

Figure 3-5. View of Stratum 2 (dark unit at top), Stratum 3 (light unit in middle), and Stratum 4 (dark, bone-rich unit at bottom). Note the hippopotamus mandible protruding from Stratum 4B. The rod is 50 cm long.

scattered through the fine-grained matrix. Stratum 3 is subdivided into two sedimentary units: Stratum 3A and 3B.

Stratum 3A.   Stratum 3A is a homogeneous layer of loose, pale brown (10YR 6/3, dry), sandy loam immediately below Stratum 2. The proportion of sand in 3A is about 60%, with modes in the fine and coarse fractions (Fig. 3-3). Stratum 3A also is characterized by relatively high proportions of silt (22.6%) and clay (16.5%). The mean particle size is 0.34 mm, with a standard deviation of 0.44 (well sorted). Altogether, the grain-size data suggest that 3A is composed of a fairly large volume of wind-blown sediment in addition to material generated by attrition and rooffall. The relatively high proportion of igneous and metamorphic mineral grains within the sand fraction supports this interpretation (Mandel and Simmons 1997:Table III). Most notably, noncarbonate grains compose up to 20% of the very fine sand fraction.

The CaCO$_3$ content of Stratum 3A is 56.3%, which is lower than that of the unweathered strata above it (Table 3-3). Although this content suggests that some leaching has occurred in 3A, there is no evidence of soil development. Hence, Stratum 3A probably was exposed to subaerial weathering for a few hundred years or less.

The P content of Stratum 3A (799 ppm) is greater than that of the sedimentary units that compose Stratum 1, but not as great as the bone- and ash-rich units of Strata 2 and 4 (Table 3-3). It is likely that Stratum 3A has been enriched with P leached out of cultural deposits immediately above it. This would account for the moderate concentration of P.

Stratum 3B. Stratum 3B is a homogeneous layer of loose, very pale brown (10YR 7/4, dry), sandy loam immediately below 3A, or below 2B where 3A is missing. Stratum 3B was distinguished from 3A in the field on the basis of texture. The proportion of sand in 3B is 78%, with modes in the coarse and very coarse fractions (Fig. 3-3). This bimodal grain-size distribution resembles the one for the bedrock sample. Mean particle size for 3B ranges from 0.52 mm to 0.59 mm, and the standard deviation (0.48–0.52) indicates that the < 2 mm fraction is well sorted to moderately well sorted. Although some of the sand grains are rounded, the proportion of igneous and metamorphic grains is 1% or less in all of the sand fractions. Hence, 3B appears to be largely composed of attrition sediment, with only a small amount of wind-derived material.

There is no evidence of soil development in 3B, and the high CaCO$_3$ content (79%) indicates that this stratum has not been greatly affected by postdepositional weathering. The P content of Stratum 3B ranges from 720 to 1095 ppm, with the highest amount occurring where Stratum 2 is immediately above Stratum 3B (Table 3-3). This placement supports the interpretation that some phosphorous has been leached out of the ash- and bone-rich cultural deposits within Stratum 2 and illuviated in Stratum 3.

Stratum 4

Stratum 4 is the lowest stratigraphic unit in the collapsed rockshelter. It consists of an extremely dense accumulation of bones, primarily *Phanourios,* resting directly on the bedrock floor of the shelter (see, for example, Figs. 4-5 and 4-9–4-11 in Chap. 4). The bones are in a loose, sandy loam matrix that has been darkened by fine, powdery charcoal (Fig. 3-5).

Stratum 4 is 10 to 50 cm thick and is distributed throughout most of the interior of the collapsed rockshelter. The bulk of the sediment that composes this unit accumulated through attrition and eolian deposition. However, boulder-size and smaller clasts representing rooffall are common.

Stratum 4 is subdivided into four sedimentary units: Stratum 4A, 4B, 4A/B, and 4C. These strata are described in the following sections.

Stratum 4A. Stratum 4A is a laterally discontinuous unit of loose, light brownish-gray (10YR 6/2, dry), sandy sediment above the main bone bed within Stratum 4. It is 10 to 35 cm thick and was easily distinguished by its color and granular structure. The presence of strong, coarse, crumb-shaped aggregates was initially interpreted as a product of soil development. However, inspection of the aggregates with a binocular microscope revealed that individual grains of calcium carbonate were fused together, presumably by intense heat, entrapping small (< 0.25 mm) carbonate and noncarbonate grains. Hence, the granular structure is not a pedogenic feature. Instead, it is attributed to high temperatures generated by hearth fires in Stratum 4.

The texture of the < 2 mm fraction in Stratum 4A is loamy sand, with a sand content of 85%. The mean particle size is 1.1 mm, making 4A the coarsest stratum in the rockshelter (Table 3-2). Very coarse sand composes 76.4% of the total sand fraction, which is more than three times greater than the proportion of very coarse sand in any other stratum. The texture of 4A, like the granular structure, is attributed to postdepositional modification of sediment by fires in the shelter during the period that this stratum was a living surface. Heat generated by the fires not only fused silt- and clay-sized grains, thereby forming many sand-sized aggregates, but also fused fine sand grains into larger particles.

Three other lines of evidence point to modification of sediment composing Stratum 4A: $CaCO_3$ and P content and sand-grain morphology. The $CaCO_3$ content ranges from 26.5 to 48.3%, which is much lower than that of the unweathered strata above it (Table 3-3). It is likely that some $CaCO_3$ has been lost in this stratum as a result of intense heat generated in hearths. As noted earlier, many of the mineral grains in Stratum 4A have been fused by heat. Hence, it is likely that temperatures exceeded the threshold for oxidation of $CaCO_3$.

Concentrations of P are extremely high in Stratum 4A, with values ranging between 6,300 and 9,000 ppm (Table 3-3). As noted earlier, Stratum 4 contains the greatest volume of bones in the stratigraphic sequence, and the sediment has been darkened by fine, powdery charcoal. Phosphorous enrichment in 4A and the underlying strata is attributed to the weathering of the bones and charcoal.

The shape of sand grains also suggests that weathering has affected Stratum 4A. Nearly all of the bioclasts within this stratum are well rounded or subrounded (Silence 1996). Although roundness may be produced by mechanical abrasion during sediment transport, only chemical weathering could wear down and smooth the sharp angles and edges of bioclasts derived from attrition within the shelter (Mandel and Simmons 1997).

The presence of rounded and subrounded igneous and metamorphic grains entrapped within the fused calcium carbonate grains indicates that Stratum 4A contains eolian sediment derived from the beach. The mineralogical analysis also detected relatively high proportions (15–20%) of noncarbonate mineral grains within the fine and very fine sand fractions (Mandel and Simmons 1997). Hence, the < 2 mm fraction is a mixture of eolian and attrition sediment.

Stratum 4B. Stratum 4B is 10 to 45 cm thick and consists of a loose matrix of bones, wood ash, and sediment. Simmons (1991a, this volume) refers to 4B as a "bone midden" because of the tremendous volume of burned and unburned bone concentrated in this stratum. It is also designated as a sedimentary unit because geologic processes have contributed mineral grains to this portion of Stratum 4. Except in areas where it has been truncated by Stratum 1C, 4B is present throughout the site. However, it thins toward the back of the rockshelter and has been eroded in places along the shelter's outer edge.

The fine-grained sediment (< 2 mm) in 4B is grayish-brown (2.5Y 5/2, dry), sandy loam. Rooffall is scattered through this stratum, and most clasts are cobble sized or smaller. Fine sand strongly dominates the sand fraction (Fig. 3-3), with proportions ranging from 50 to 57% (Table 3-2). The mean particle size is relatively fine, ranging from 0.17 to 0.31 mm.

Hence, there appears to be a significant eolian component in 4B. The high proportion of igneous and metamorphic minerals (35–40%) and quartz grains (20–30%) in the fine and very sand fraction supports this interpretation (Mandel and Simmons 1997:Table III).

The $CaCO_3$ content of 4B ranges from only 16 to 32% (Table 3-3). The relatively low amount of $CaCO_3$ is attributed primarily to oxidation, the result of the high temperatures generated in hearths. It is also likely that the large amount of noncalcareous eolian sediment in this stratum has diluted the $CaCO_3$ content. The P content is very high in Stratum 4B, with concentration ranging from 3,300 to 9,000 ppm (Table 3-3). The P is derived from bone, organic residues, and charcoal in this stratum.

Stratum 4A/B. In some portions of the rockshelter, there are small inclusions of crumb-shaped aggregates typical of Stratum 4A within grayish brown (2.5Y 5/2, dry), bone-rich sediment typical of Stratum 4B. Where this occurs, the stratigraphic unit is designated as 4A/B. The grain-size distribution of the sand fraction in 4A/B is bimodal, with primary and secondary modes in the fine and coarse fractions, respectively (Fig. 3-3). The proportion of igneous and metamorphic grains increases from < 1% in the very coarse sand fraction to 35–40% in the very fine sand fraction. The proportion of quartz grains similarly increases from 1 to 2% in the very coarse sand fraction to 20–25% in the fine sand fraction (Mandel and Simmons 1997:Table III). These findings clearly indicate that Stratum 4A/B is a mixture of eolian and attrition sediment.

Stratum 4A/B has the highest clay content in the stratigraphic sequence, with values ranging from 23 to nearly 28%. The abundance of clay-sized particles in Stratum 4A/B may be due to its position near the bottom of the stratigraphic sequence. It is likely that 4A/B received fine-grained sediment that was translocated out of the overlying strata by water percolating down through the loose, sandy matrix. Also, the accumulation of water in the lowest strata favors weathering processes that generate clay-size grains.

The chemical properties of Stratum 4A/B are similar to those of Stratum 4B (Table 3-3). Specifically, $CaCO_3$ content is relatively low (24.0–40.1%), and the P content is high (5,190–5,625 ppm). The low $CaCO_3$ content is attributed to (1) oxidation resulting from high temperatures generated by numerous hearth fires and (2) the dilution effect of the noncalcareous eolian sediment. The P is derived from bone, organic residues, and charcoal within and above 4A/B.

Stratum 4C. Stratum 4C is common between the bone midden (4B or 4A/B) and the bedrock floor of the rockshelter. Although 4C contains faunal remains, the density of bones in this stratum is not as great as that in 4B. Also, 4C does not contain a large volume of wood ash.

Stratum 4C is usually less than 10 cm thick and consists of light olive brown (2.5Y 5/3, dry), sandy loam or sandy clay loam. The olive color of 4C is due to poor drainage and concomitant reduction of organic matter and iron-bearing minerals at the bottom of the package of sediment within the rockshelter. The bedrock floor not only restricts the vertical movement of water, but depressions in the floor tend to retain water.

The grain-size distribution in 4C is similar to that in 4B and 4A/B. The mean particle size ranges from 0.20 mm to 0.28 mm, with a standard deviation of 0.31 to 0.40 (very well sorted to well sorted). Fine sand strongly dominates the sand fraction, and there is a second mode in the coarse fraction of some samples (Fig. 3-3). The abundance of fine sand suggests that there is a significant eolian component in Stratum 4C. This interpretation is supported by the mineralogy of the sand fraction. The proportion of noncarbonate mineral grains increases from 5 to 10% in the coarse fraction to 40–50% in the very fine fraction (Mandel and Simmons 1997:Table III).

The clay content is relatively high in most of the samples from Stratum 4C (Table 3-2). Like Stratum 4A/B, the abundance of clay probably reflects weathering in the moist sediment at the bottom of the profile. It is also likely that clay has been translocated down from overlying strata.

CONCLUSION

Geological investigations at *Aetokremnos* focused on site stratigraphy and the granulometry, mineralogy, morphology, and geochemistry of sediment stored in the collapsed rockshelter. Information gleaned from these investigations was used to determine (1) the nature and depositional sequence of the sedimentary units, (2) the origin and mode of transport of the sediments that compose various strata, and (3) the magnitude of sediment modification after deposition. This approach emphasized the processes of site formation rather than simply describing artifact-bearing strata. It also helped resolve the following questions that are related to the archaeology of the rockshelter: Were the lithic artifacts and/or faunal remains (bones of *Phanourios* and other animals) eroded off adjacent slopes and washed into the rockshelter? Were the faunal remains in place long before the rockshelter was occupied by people? Has there been significant vertical mixing of sediment and, most importantly, are the artifacts located where people left them, that is, in situ? Conclusions based on the results of the geologic investigations at *Aetokremnos* follow:

• Most of the sediment stored in the collapsed rockshelter is a product of rockfall, attrition, and eolian deposition. Although boulder-size clasts generated by rockfall have disturbed some of the archaeological deposits, sediments that accumulated through attrition and eolian processes sealed features, bones, and stone artifacts in a sandy matrix.

• A small volume of slopewash entered the back of the rockshelter through solution cavities. These laminated deposits (Strata 1C and 1D) are restricted to the extreme northern quarter of the shelter and occupy less than 5% of the total area within the shelter. Hence, the presence of artifacts and bones in other parts of the shelter cannot be attributed to redeposition, that is, archaeological materials eroded off the slopes above *Aetokremnos* and washed into the rockshelter. It is also important to note that slopewash deposits had the lowest concentration of artifacts and bones compared with the other strata in the rockshelter. This would not be the case if the slopewash was the primary source of the cultural materials in the rockshelter.

• A large proportion of the fine and very fine sand in Strata 2, 3 and 4 consists of igneous and metamorphic grains that were transported by wind. It is likely that the primary source of this eolian sediment was a broad, sandy Early Holocene (ca. 10,500–10,000 B.P.) beach about 40 m below the elevation of *Aetokremnos*. This interpretation is consistent with Gomez and Pease's (1992) contention that the circa 10,500 B.P. shoreline near *Aetokremnos* was at least 1,500 m farther seaward than it is today. With such a large area of the coastal plain exposed during the Early Holocene, there would have been an abundant supply of sand available for eolian transport.

• High phosphorous contents in Strata 2 and 4 indicate that they have been enriched with P from wood ash and bones. The soft tissue of animals is another likely source of P. This evidence strongly supports the argument that Strata 2 and 4 were greatly influenced by intense human activity, especially the processing and cooking of game, while these units were aggrading.

• There is no evidence of soil development in any of the stratigraphic units within the rockshelter. Instead, it appears that the sediment and associated cultural materials (bones and artifacts) rapidly accumulated on the floor of the shelter soon before the roof collapsed and isolated the underlying deposits from subareal weathering.[1] This finding supports radiocarbon data suggesting that the duration of human occupation, as represented by cultural deposits in Strata 2 and 4, was relatively short (perhaps a few hundred years or less). Also, the boundaries between the stratigraphic units in the rockshelter are generally razor sharp. The presence of such abrupt boundaries indicates that there has been little or no mixing of sediment by humans (e.g., digging pits), small animals (burrowing), large animals (trampling and digging), and plants (root growth). Hence, there has been very little mixing of artifacts and bones between Strata 2 and 4. In most places, these two units are clearly separated by an archaeologically sterile zone (Stratum 3). Where Stratum 3 is missing, Strata 2 and 4 are separated by an abrupt boundary. When these finding are considered with the archaeological evidence, the argument is unsurmountable that most of the cultural materials at *Aetokremnos* are in situ.

---

[1] Measurements taken at reference points in a modern rockshelter upslope from *Aetokremnos* indicate that eolian and attrition sediment is accumulating on the floor of the shelter at rates of 1.4–1.8 cm/yr. If sedimentation occurred at these rates during the Early Holocene, the entire package of fine-grained sediment in the *Aetokremnos* rockshelter may have accumulated in less than 100 years.

Chapter *4*

Archaeological Stratigraphy

ALAN H. SIMMONS AND ROLFE D. MANDEL

ARCHAEOLOGICAL STRATIGRAPHY

A precise understanding of the stratigraphy at *Aetokremnos* clearly is crucial to its interpretation. Mandel (Chap. 3) already has provided a detailed and precise analysis of the stratigraphy, sedimentology, and geomorphology of *Aetokremnos*. The purpose of this chapter is to relate the stratigraphy more directly to the site's archaeological context. We also provide several stratigraphic profiles that cross-cut the interior of the *Aetokremnos* rockshelter.

A number of critical issues are involved here, and these can be addressed, in part, by a comprehension of the site's stratigraphy. These issues include the following:

1. It was necessary to demonstrate whether or not the bone deposits at the site were a result of natural or cultural activity.
2. The presence of artifacts associated with the bone had to be demonstrated to reflect an in situ occurrence.
3. Even if an in situ cultural presence could be established at the site, it was necessary to determine the chronological relationship of this presence to the bones.
4. If more than one cultural occupations could be demonstrated, it was necessary to determine their chronological relationships.

STRATIGRAPHIC DESCRIPTIONS—AN OVERVIEW

Although initial impressions of *Aetokremnos* were that there was limited stratigraphy present, three excavation seasons have clearly demonstrated the fallacy of this. We now know that there is a very complex and rich stratigraphic record at the site. Table 4-1, derived from Mandel's detailed analysis, summarizes the final master stratigraphy of the site. Note that this table includes several mixed strata (e.g., Stratum 1/2) used in the analysis of materials from *Aetokremnos*.

Table 4.1. Master Stratigraphy for *Aetokremnos*

Undisturbed Strata

Stratum 1A: Colluvium limited to shelf above main excavation area.

Stratum 1B: Soil (A horizon) developed into colluvium.

Stratum 1C: Laminated sandy and silty sheetwash deposited into the back of the shelter.

Stratum 1D: Primarily sheetwash, restricted to northeast corner of shelter.

Stratum 1E: Mixture of sediment contributed from wind, rooffall, and attrition of bedrock.

Stratum 2A (upper 2A and lower 2A): Arbitrary division within cultural zone, applied when this zone was thick; coarse and fine grained; fine, disseminated charcoal; highly phosphorous.

Stratum 2B: "Red zone"; thin and discontinuous.

Stratum 3: "Sterile" zone; pale brown, very friable.

Stratum 4A: Granular zone at the top of Stratum 4 bone bed; individual grains fused by heat.

Stratum 4B: Ashy bone bed; grayish-brown friable sediment.

Stratum 4A/B: Granular aggregates within grayish brown sediment typical of Stratum 4B; may represent some Strata 4A and 4B mixing.

Stratum 4C: Olive-greenish sandy loam and sandy clay loam at the base of Stratum 4, olive color is a product of reduction; contains bones and is in contact with the bedrock floor.

Stratum 5: Very localized laminated sediment, fine-grained, sterile.

Mixed Strata (These are thin "transitional" zones that do not represent primary deposition.)

Stratum 1/4: Mixed zone of Strata 1 and 4 outside of shelter.

Stratum 1–4: Mixed zone containing Strata 1–4; outside and inside shelter, mixed disturbed zone; similar to Stratum 1/4, but may include material from Strata 2 through 4.

Stratum 1/2: Mixed zone of basal Stratum 1 and upper Stratum 2A.

Stratum 2/4: Mixed zone of Strata 2 and 4 (primarily 2A and 4B).

Stratum 2B/4A: Red base capping midden.

S: Surface, includes deflated and eroded materials on present site surface.

Three comments are necessary to supplement Table 4-1. First, it is important to realize that although *Aetokremnos* represents an intact and relatively undisturbed prehistoric occupation, this does not mean that more recent cultural materials are absent from the site. Roman potsherds and glass and metal fragments were found in the rockshelter, but these are clearly intrusive. Roman sites litter the southern Akrotiri coastline, and tombs are present in many of the cliffs adjacent to *Aetokremnos*. Two probable tombs are, in fact, immediately above the site, and others are nearby. Hence, it is not surprising that there are some later materials on the site. Without exception, these artifacts are confined to either Stratum 1 or to outer margins of the rockshelter, where mixing with intact deposits can be demonstrated.

A second point concerns Stratum 4A. This is termed a *granular stratum* due to the nature of its matrix. Crumb structure in this stratum is attributed to burning (see Chap. 3). Associated with Stratum 4A is, as expected in the bone midden, a large number of bones. In some instances, the bone is extremely burned and brittle. Burned bone, however, is not restricted to Stratum 4A, and in some cases it underlies the stratum. Also, there are portions of Stratum 4A in which not all the bone is burned.

A final point to make regards the bedrock floor of the shelter. The bone midden rests directly on top of this floor. The floor is extremely "clean," almost as if it had been swept. Given the constant accumulation of sediment on the floor as a result of rockfall, attrition of the bioclastic limestone that formed the roof and wall of the rockshelter, eolian deposition, and sheetwash, it is inconceivable that the bone could have been deposited naturally on such a clean surface.

For analytical purposes, the strata frequently were combined. We also employed a few mixed categories for situations in which materials were either clearly mixed or had the potential for this. This "analytical stratigraphy," consisting of the individual strata identified by Mandel (Chap. 3), is summarized in Table 4-2 and used frequently in subsequent chapters.

Given the complexity of the deposits at *Aetokremnos,* it is instructive to examine several stratigraphic vignettes from different positions within the site. This can best be done by examining the stratigraphy as it was known during each of the three seasons, beginning with 1987, when we had a rather naive view of the deposits. Next is an examination of two sections from the 1988 excavations, followed by a consideration of several of the sections exposed in 1990, the final season. Looking at the stratigraphy in this fashion will clarify our evolving perception on the occupation of the site. In the 1987 and the 1988 descriptions, we rely primarily on one of the principal excavator's observations, which are detailed in his doctoral dissertation (Held 1989b:49–56); the nomenclature has been updated to reflect our final interpretation of the sequence. In the descriptions for the 1987 and 1988 seasons, we essentially are looking at sections near the eroded western face of the shelter. For the 1990 descriptions, the sections are primarily in the center and rear of the shelter. Figure 4-1 shows the location of the stratigraphic descriptions; each profile is labeled with a section number, beginning with the 1987 illustration as "Section 1." This numeric designation is for heuristic purposes only and does not imply a consecutive excavation sequence. Figure 4-2 provides a key for the stratigraphic sections.

1987

During 1987, only 3 square meters were excavated to depth (N94E88, N95E88, and N98E87/88-mid unit). Other units were excavated, primarily near the edge of the shelter, but these were essentially composed of mixed Stratum 1–4 deposits with no stratigraphic integrity. In a few instances, Stratum 4 was recorded for areas we now know are outside of the shelter's limits (e.g., in N91E91 and N92E93). These should properly be regarded as disturbed Stratum 4 deposits.

Excavation of the three main units was enough, however, to demonstrate the presence of intact deposits at *Aetokremnos,* something of which we were initially uncertain. Of these

Table 4-2. Analytical Stratigraphy at *Aetokremnos*

Pure Strata
Stratum 1
Stratum 2
Stratum 3
Stratum 4
Mixed Strata—Surface
Stratum 1/2
Stratum 2/4
Stratum 1–4 (includes, as appropriate, Stratum 1/4)[a]

[a]See Table 5-1.

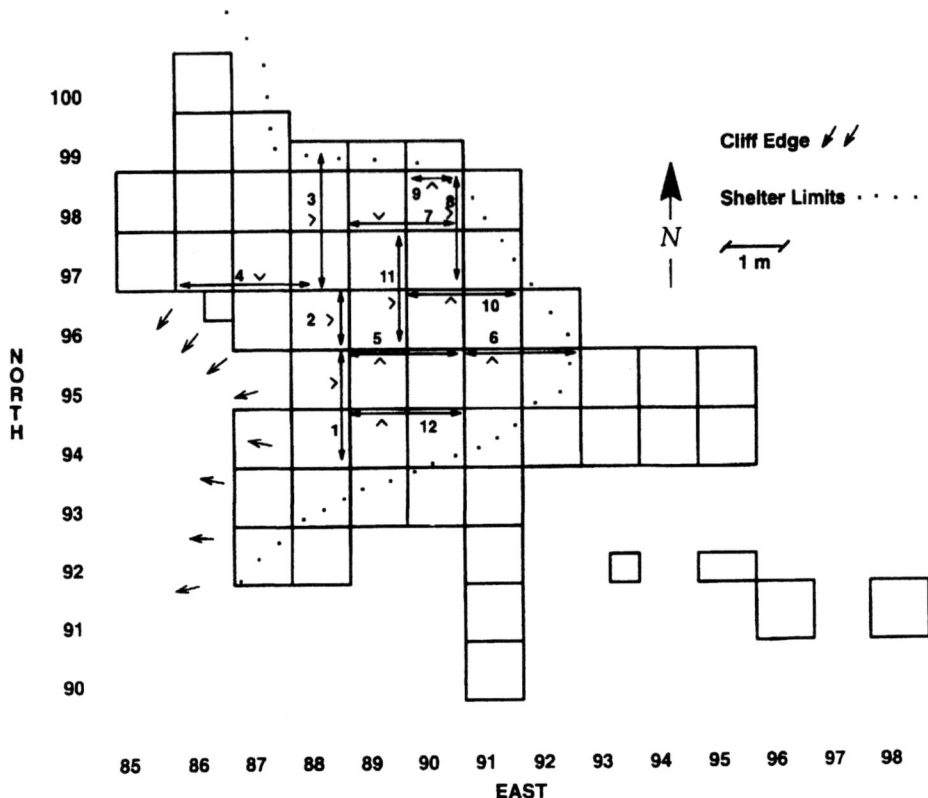

Figure 4-1. Location and orientation of stratigraphic sections.

three excavation units, one (N98E87/88) located near the northwest edge of the site was a relatively deep "telephone booth" that revealed a thick stratified deposit. Excavation to the west of this unit exposed more of the bone deposit originally visible in section and subsequently designated as a midden. This excavation led to the discovery that although the bones closest to the eroding edge of what appeared to be the shelter's floor were covered with calcium carbonate as a result of evaporation, those still covered by topsoil were not calcified. These bones appeared much lighter and "fresher" than those commonly found in paleontological sites in Cyprus.

The density of faunal remains in this basal stratum (originally designated "Levels 3 and 4" and now termed Stratum 4) was so high that the bones formed the matrix for the dark, ashy sediment. Numerous rocks of varying size found embedded in Stratum 4 represent rooffall. The thickness of the bone midden ranged from more than 50 cm in the interior of the shelter to less than 5 cm along the outer fringe.

Stratum 4 was mantled by a 10–15-m-thick layer of marine shells, which we now know is not a separate stratum but rather a feature (Feature 5) within Stratum 2. This shell deposit was capped by colluvium (Stratum 1), which was sterile in all excavated areas of the site except for a few pieces of intrusive Roman pottery and glass (see earlier discussion). Faunal remains were, in a few instances, found in the postoccupational context of Stratum

STRATA   KEY

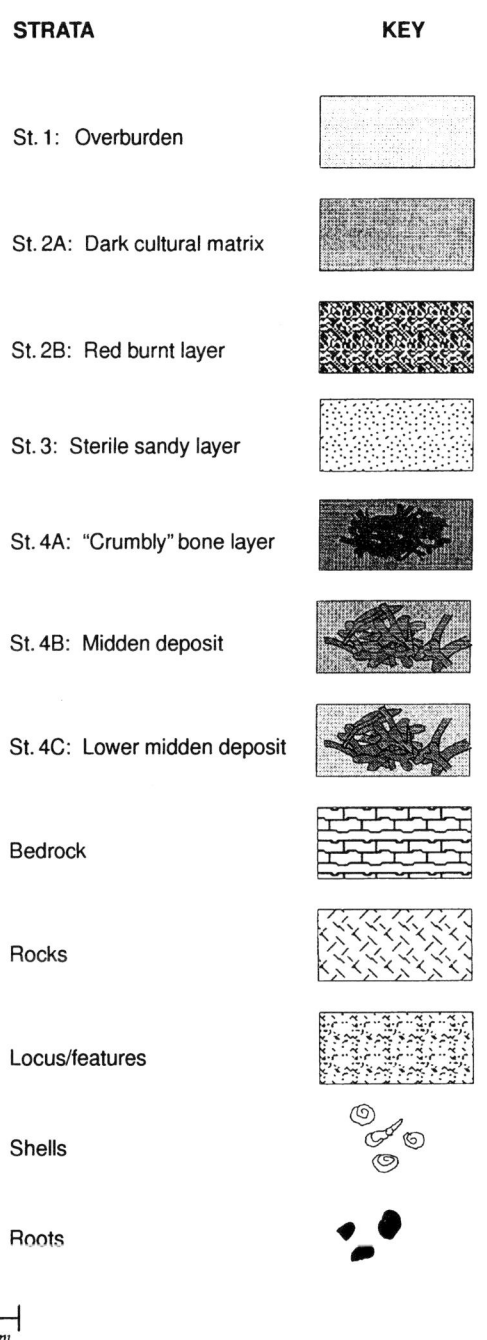

St. 1: Overburden

St. 2A: Dark cultural matrix

St. 2B: Red burnt layer

St. 3: Sterile sandy layer

St. 4A: "Crumbly" bone layer

St. 4B: Midden deposit

St. 4C: Lower midden deposit

Bedrock

Rocks

Locus/features

Shells

Roots

10 cm

Figure 4-2. Key for stratigraphic profiles.

1, but only where the main bone deposit had obviously been forced up into the colluvium by the impact of rooffall, or where the deposit had been truncated by Stratum 1. The role of these two natural, postdepositional disturbance processes is crucial to the argument that the stratification of the materials is by and large intact, and that reworking, where probable, did not result from a later human occupation of the site. This stratigraphic sequence is illustrated in Figure 4-3 (Section 1).

In summary, the stratigraphy at the end of the 1987 season appeared to consist of a dense bone deposit with little or no internal stratification. The bone deposit rested directly on the bedrock floor of the shelter. A thin layer of shell (within Stratum 2) mantled the bone deposit and was, in turn, sealed by colluvium (Stratum 1). This indicated that both Strata 2 and 4 were deposited in fairly rapid succession on a bedrock floor that was as clean as if it had been swept. Coupled with the composition of bone and shell layers, in which burned and unburned faunal remains and some artifacts cooccur, the evidence was, even in 1987, compatible with an interpretation supportive of a cultural, rather than a natural deposition of all the deposits at the site, including the bone midden.

1988

During the 1988 season, the stratigraphic complexity of *Aetokremnos* became apparent. After more intact deposits were excavated, it was obvious that the relatively simple sequence recognized in 1987 was far too naive. The best exposure in 1988 was an expansion of the 1987 "phone booth" excavation in N98E88/87 to include N99 and N97. It was here that the basic stratigraphic sequence for the site was determined, and it was little changed even after more thorough excavations in 1990. Accordingly, this sequence is described in some detail here.

The units in which the stratigraphic sequence was established are located in the northwestern portion of the site. Here, large rooffall blocks have preserved thick, stratified deposits. Because this small (4 m²) area of the site is located near the back wall and the eroded edge of the shelter, it encapsulates the entire transition from thick, sealed, and protected interior deposits to thin, eroded deposits at the outer fringe. Figures 4-4 (Section 3) and 4-5 (Section 4) illustrate this stratigraphic sequence. These sections are perpendicular to each other, so that the right edge of Section 3 meets the left edge of Section 4 at a 90 degree angle to form the southeast corner of the excavation unit. This positioning provides a view of the unit's east (Section 3) and south (Section 4) sides. In Section 3, which is viewed looking east toward the center of the shelter, the thickness of deposits is observable. A ledge of bioclastic limestone that projects above the area in the upper left-hand corner of Figure 4-4 marks the underside of the remnant roof where it joins the back wall of the shelter. The stratigraphy in these sections is described as follows.

A dense accumulation of bones, primarily of *Phanourios*, rests directly on the clean bedrock floor of the shelter. This layer (Stratum 4) contains fine, dark gray sediment filtered in among the bones. Although individual pieces of charcoal were not present, the matrix is extremely ashy. Some rooffall also is present, as are a number of rocks with very smooth, pitted, and slightly red surfaces. These look oddly worn and are so different in color and texture from the surrounding rocks that Held (1989b:55) interpreted them as "old rocks" that might be linked to the human use of the shelter. Examination with a binocular microscope, however, revealed that these rocks have been smoothed and pitted by solution

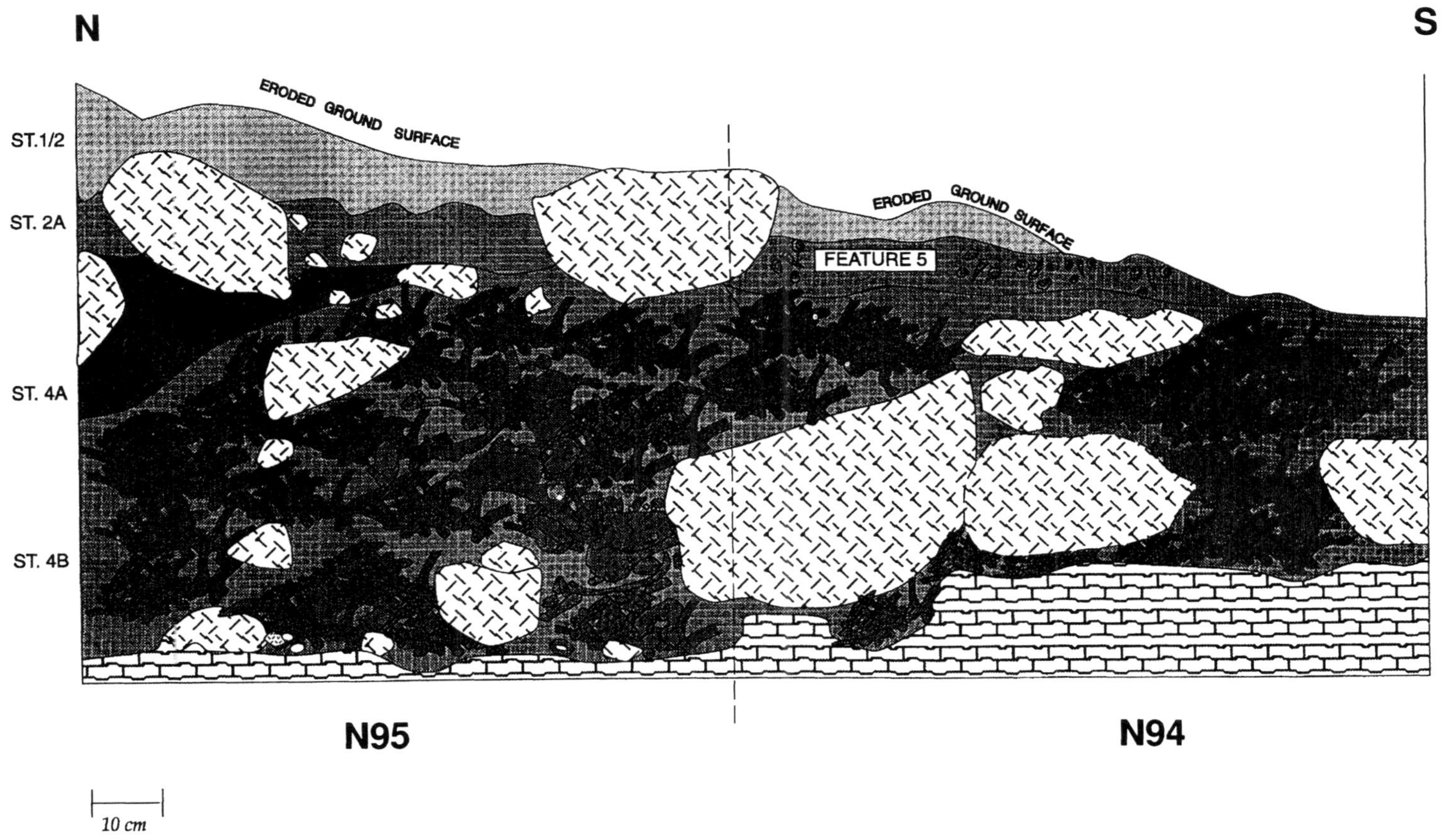

S

N94

N95

N

ST.1/2

ST. 2A

ST. 4A

ST. 4B

ERODED GROUND SURFACE

ERODED GROUND SURFACE

FEATURE 5

10 cm

Figure 4-3. Section 1: N94E88 and N95E88 (east section).

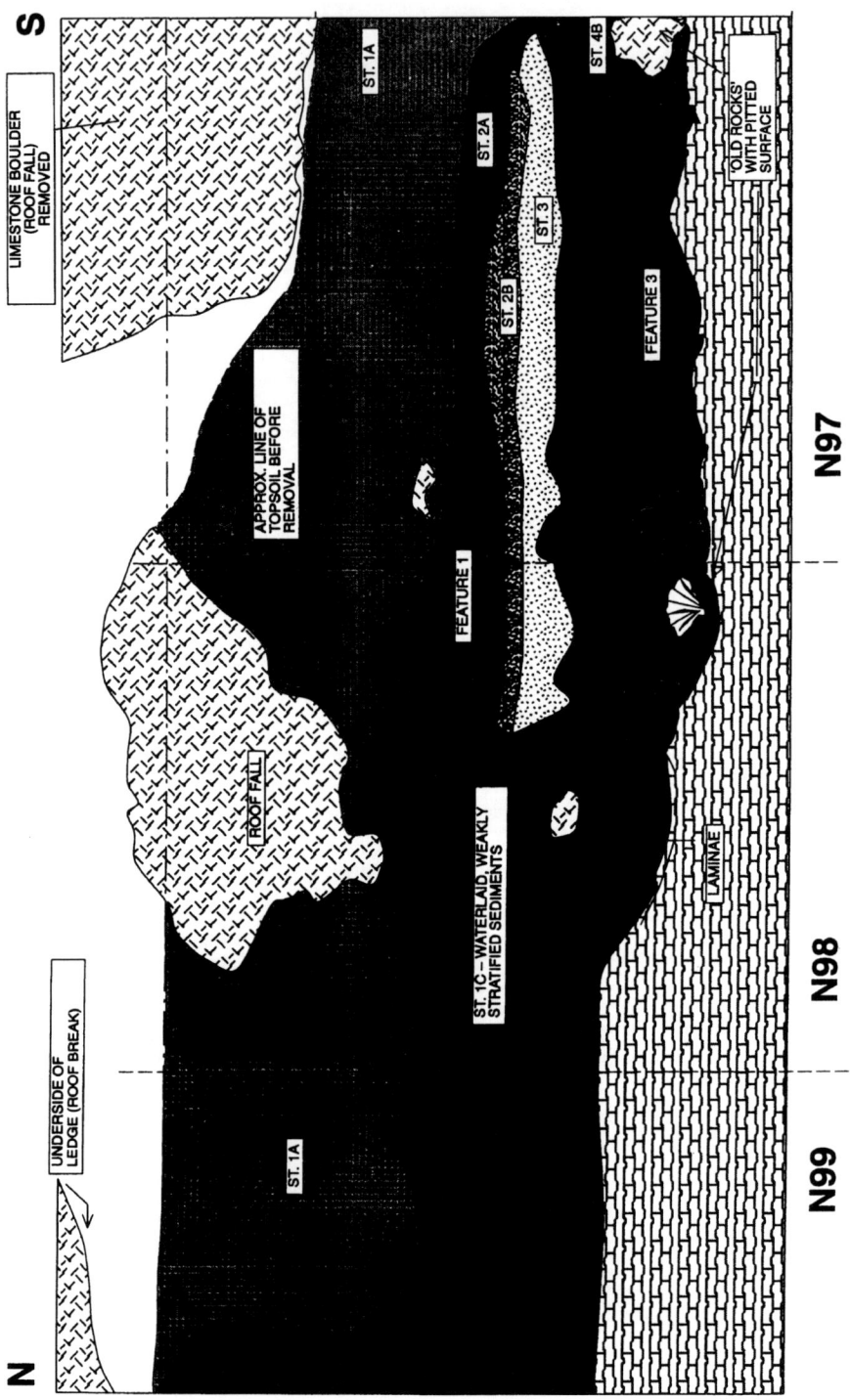

S

LIMESTONE BOULDER (ROOF FALL) REMOVED

ST. 1A

ST. 2A

ST. 3

ST. 2B

ST. 4B

"OLD ROCKS" WITH PITTED SURFACE

APPROX. LINE OF TOPSOIL BEFORE REMOVAL

FEATURE 1

FEATURE 3

ROOF FALL

ST. 1C—WATERLAID, WEAKLY STRATIFIED SEDIMENTS

LAMINAE

UNDERSIDE OF LEDGE (ROOF BREAK)

ST. 1A

N99   N98   N97

N

Figure 4-4. Section 3: N99E88, N98E88, and N97E88 (east section, midunit).

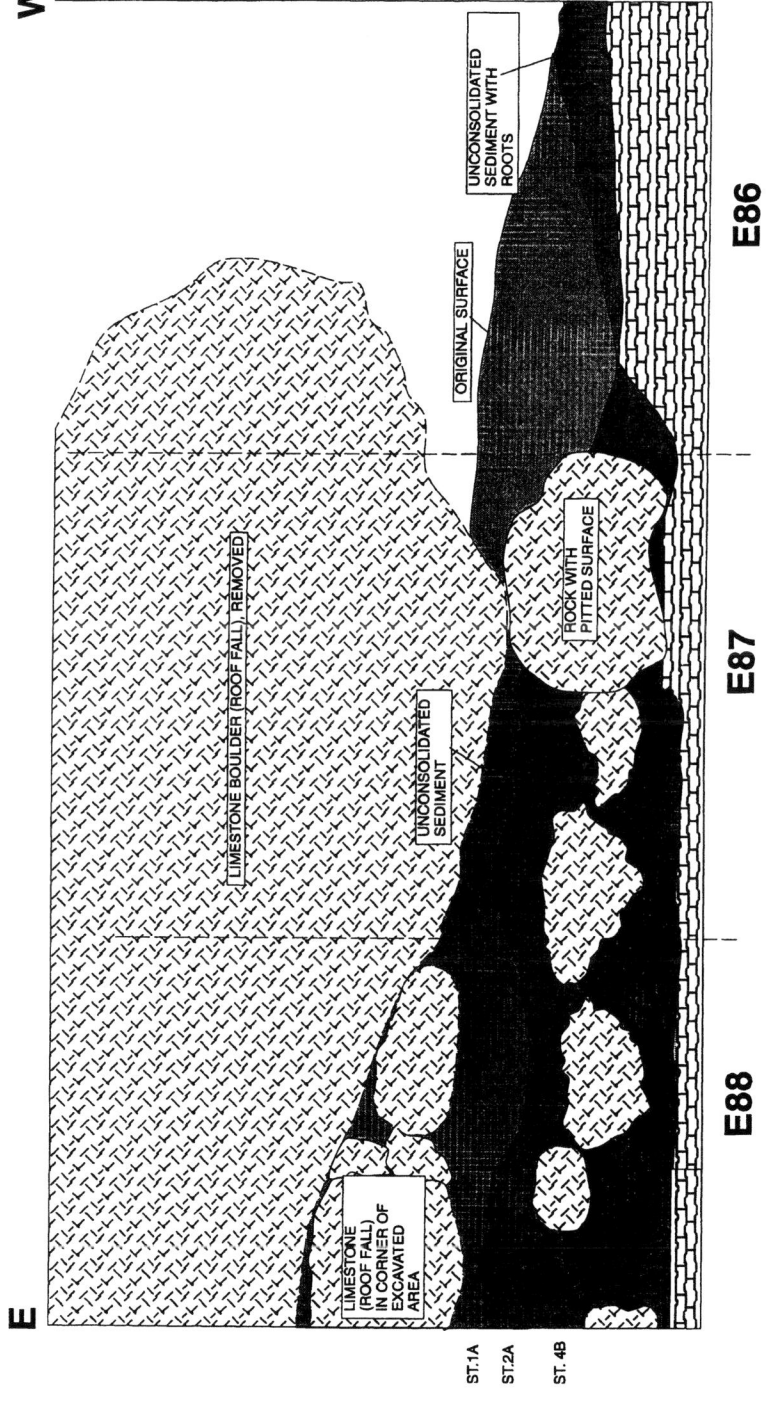

W

E86

E87

E88

E

UNCONSOLIDATED SEDIMENT WITH ROOTS

ORIGINAL SURFACE

LIMESTONE BOULDER (ROOF FALL) REMOVED

ROCK WITH PITTED SURFACE

UNCONSOLIDATED SEDIMENT

LIMESTONE (ROOF FALL) IN CORNER OF EXCAVATED AREA

ST. 1A
ST. 2A
ST. 4B

Figure 4-5. Section 4: N97E86–E88.

weathering. Nevertheless, it is clear that these rocks are not part of the bedrock floor because they rest on a thin layer of bones rather than the floor. Whatever the explanation, the rocks are curiously patterned around Feature 3. This feature, which occurs within Stratum 4, is a discrete concentration of heavily charred bone. Immediately above the charred bone, and still part of Feature 3, is a row of blackened stone capping the midden in this spot. Although these stones are not heat fractured, they probably were blackened during burning.

The next higher stratigraphic unit, Stratum 3, is archaeologically sterile. In the section illustrated in Figure 4-4, Stratum 3 seals the bone midden (Stratum 4) from the subsequent cultural deposit represented by Stratum 2.

Stratum 3 is mantled by a thin layer of reddish brown sandy loam; this loam becomes somewhat patchy toward the southern end of Section 3. This distinctive layer (Stratum 2B) is the intensely burned bottom of Stratum 2. The source of this heat is found in the overlying sedimentary unit, Stratum 2A, which corresponds to the clearest cultural deposit at *Aetokremnos*. Stratum 2A has an ashy matrix with a high density of chipped stone, ornamental pieces, shell, and a limited, but still substantial, number of *Phanourios* (and other vertebrate) remains. It is within this stratum that Feature 1 is located (Fig. 4-4). Although this feature's principal characteristic is a conical heap of ash, it also is a more widespread deposit. Its bottom is formed by Stratum 2B.

Above Stratum 2A is a thick layer (Stratum 1A in Fig. 4-4) of loose sediment that shows signs of disturbance, including root penetration and rodent burrowing. The impact of rooffall also is apparent here.

In Section 4 (Fig. 4-5), it can be seen that the bone midden is directly below the rich deposit of Stratum 2A without being separated by the sterile Stratum 3, or, in fact, Stratum 2B. As this section shows, the impact of several tons of rooffall, as represented by one large slab, led to compression and subsidence of the upper half of the deposit. In spite of this disturbance, the stratigraphic units remained intact.

Held interpreted the stratigraphic sequence in Section 4 as the changeover from a two-phase occupation (above and below Stratum 3) in the rear of the shelter to a single phase occupation at the front (Held 1989b:.5). Based on the information available in 1988, he further believed that Stratum 2A in this portion of the shelter corresponded to what at the time was considered a separate layer of shell (i.e., Feature 5). We now know that, in fact, this "shell layer" was a smaller concentration of shell located within Stratum 2A; thus Held's original interpretation remains essentially unchanged except that the shell "layer" has been "demoted" to a feature.

Subsequent excavation and careful consideration of the stratigraphy at the site indicate that the sequence in Section 4 does not represent a changeover from a two-phase to a one-phase occupation. Rather, the deposits toward the front of the shelter, interpreted by Held as a one phase occupation, represent some mixed materials from Strata 2 and 4. Despite the mixing, the strata maintain their integrity as two phases of occupation. What has occurred, and is clearly visible in Figures 4-4 and 4-5, is that as one moves southwest toward the exposed front of the shelter, the deposits become reworked by erosion processes and bioturbation. This reworking is limited to the outer fringe of the rockshelter. We hasten to stress the minimal impact of the reworking. What is illustrated in Figure 4-5 still reflects the two primary cultural Strata, 2A and 4. What appears likely is that in the less-protected western portion of the site, erosion and abundant rooffall resulted in the obliteration of both Strata 2B and Strata 3, if, indeed, these deposits were ever present in the area illustrated by Figure 4-5. Both of these strata are discontinuous throughout the site (see Chap. 3), and their absence in this section, so close to their very clear presence less than a meter to the northeast, is indicative of the stratigraphic complexity at *Aetokremnos.*

In summary, by the end of 1988, we believed that several activities were reflected in the western portion of the site that were contemporaneous (or nearly so) with the deposition of the bone midden. Our investigations indicated that the cultural materials toward the back of the shelter were more abundant, heterogeneous, and spatially structured within the deposits than those associated with the midden area. Interpretation of the stratigraphic significance of the sterile Stratum 3 was reserved until more of the deposits could be excavated. Held (1989b:56–57) felt that if Stratum 3 consisted of eolian materials that accumulated on top of the bone midden, this could suggest a partial abandonment of at least the east sector of the shelter before it came into use again as an ash dump. Alternately, the sterile stratum could have simply represented a bed of sandy loam spread intentionally over the burned stones that cap Feature 3 in Stratum 4 to make a level surface on the bone midden for the deposition of hot ashes from Feature 1 (in Stratum 2). If that were the scenario, it would mark a functional discontinuity in the use of this part of the site rather than a chronological one. Radiocarbon determinations did not clarify the matter, because even if two discrete occupational phases were represented, the break between them would be too short to be detected radiometrically (see Chap. 8).

1990

Excavations in 1990 finally clarified the stratigraphic situation at *Aetokremnos,* at least as far as was possible. They demonstrated that Stratum 2 and Stratum 4 deposits were not absolutely contemporaneous, and that the perceived complexity of activities toward the back of the shelter was not synchronous with the deposition of the bone midden. The evidence suggests that even Stratum 2 was not the result of a single occupational episode; several microstratigraphic events can be detected there. However, the time gap between the two major occupations of the site was minor; it certainly cannot be measured in radiocarbon years. It is our belief that the same people were responsible for these occupations, an argument that will be developed throughout this book.

Several sections (Figs. 4-6–4-14) are used to illustrate the stratigraphy uncovered in 1990. These figures essentially show variants of the same thing, and in most cases, they are an enhancement of the basic sequence first exposed in 1988. Because this basic site sequence was described in detail earlier, the following discussion describes each section in summary fashion as stratigraphic vignettes.

Excavation of N96E88 (Fig. 4-6; Section 2) linked southern and northern portions of the site. The shell layer (now Feature 5) first identified in Stratum 2 in the adjacent southern unit is no longer present. Additionally, Stratum 3 is now present in patches, as are fragments of Stratum 2B. Strata 4A and 4B are well represented. Note that rooffall is present in these lower strata. A feature (Number 8) has disturbed the stratigraphic integrity of this section.

Section 5 (Fig. 4-7) is a typical east-west cross section through the center of the site. If linked with Section 6 (Fig. 4-8), the entire east-west section of the site is illustrated. Portions of Stratum 1 are present in Section 5. These were only preserved in the western section; abundant rooffall essentially replaced Stratum 1 in this section. Medium-sized pieces of rooffall are present throughout this section. The heterogeneity of Stratum 2A is clearly visible here. Note the superimposed nature of Features 6 and 7, as well as the presence of a

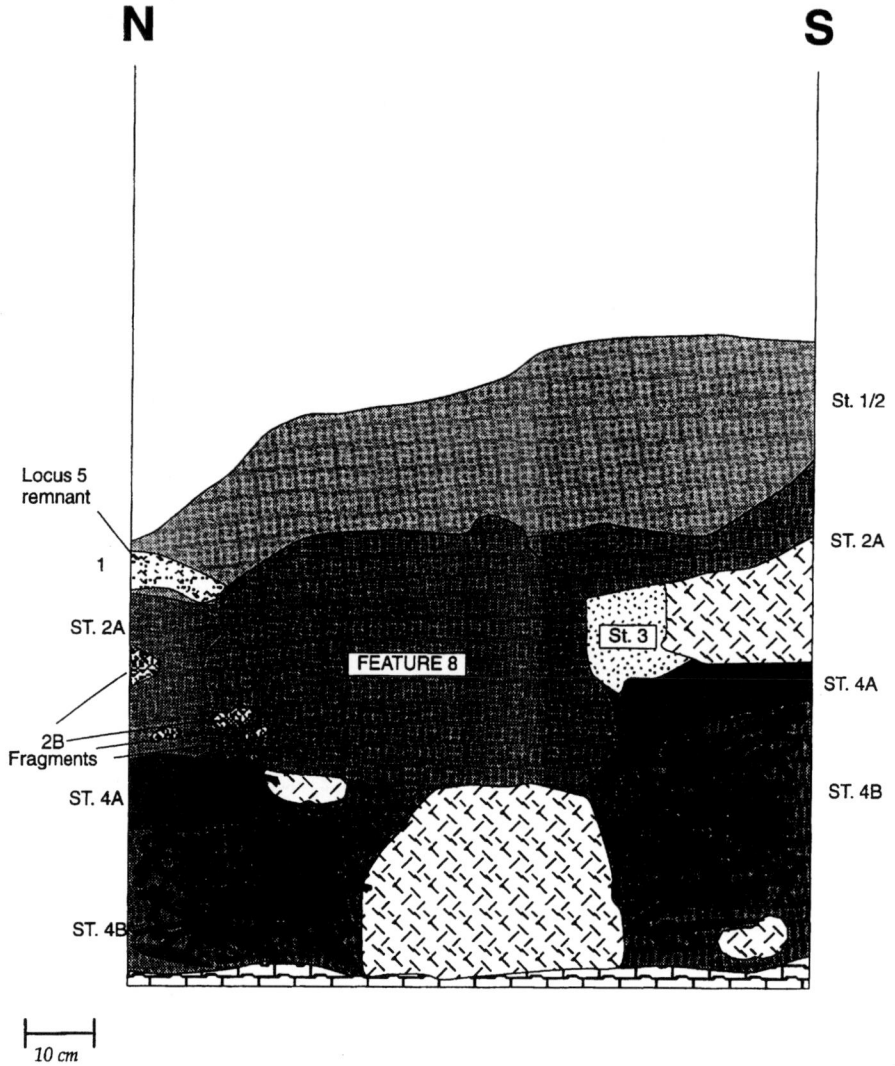

N   **S**

St. 1/2

Locus 5
remnant

1

ST. 2A

ST. 2A

St. 3

FEATURE 8

ST. 4A

2B
Fragments

ST. 4A

ST. 4B

ST. 4B

10 cm

Figure 4-6. Section 2: N96E88 (east section).

small lenses of shell immediately over Feature 6. Stratum 3 is quite thick here. Stratum 4A is apparent, but it becomes less distinct as one moves west toward the mouth of the shelter. Stratum 4B is well represented.

Section 6[1] (Fig. 4-8) is a continuation of Section 5. This section shows the far eastern end of the shelter, including the back edge. A thick, undisturbed portion of Stratum 1 (Strata

---

[1]N95E91 was one of the few units not completely excavated, and this section is a "mirror image" of what was actually drawn. In other words, as originally drawn, this is the south profile of N96E91. As reversed, the view is the north section of N95E91, viewed to the north from "within" the unexcavated unit. The section has been reversed to provide a direct linkage with Section 5.

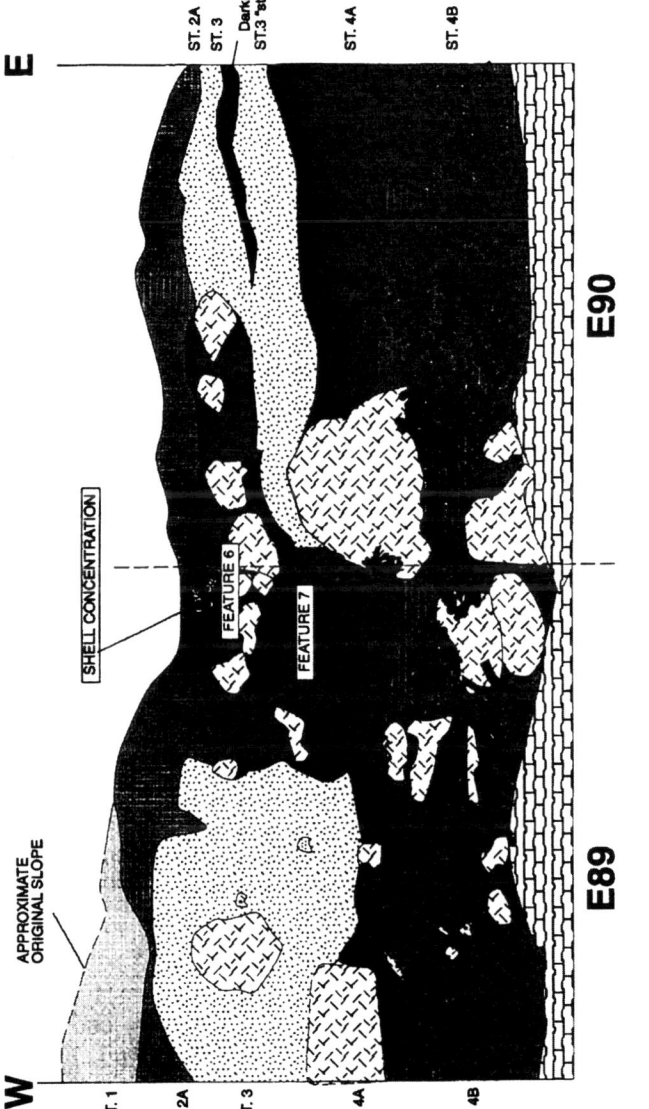

Figure 4-7. Section 5: N95E89, E90 (north section).

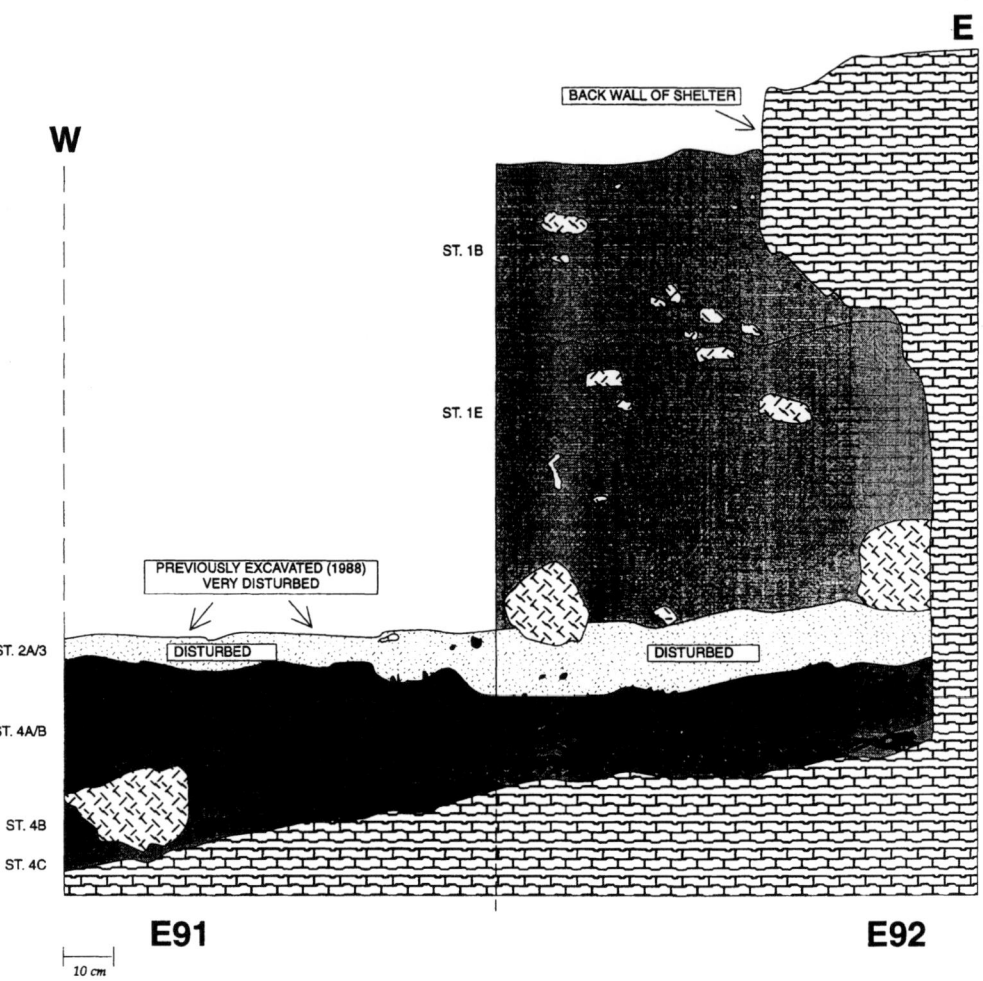

Figure 4-8. Section 6: N95E91, E92 (north section).

1B and 1E) is preserved here. The articulation between terminal Stratum 1 and Stratum 2A is clear, as shown in the eastern part of Section 6 (even though Stratum 2 is disturbed here). This portion of the shelter contains only traces of Stratum 3. This absence is not surprising, especially toward the back of the shelter, considering the composition of Stratum 3, a mixture of sediment contributed by wind, rockfall, and attrition of bedrock. Thus, the back of the shelter is an unfavorable environment for the formation of Stratum 3.

The area noted as "previously excavated" in Section 6 was the 1988 trench that cut north-south through this part of the shelter. Disturbance was considerable here, even in 1988, due to excessively large pieces of rooffall. Despite being covered at the end of the 1988 season, there was some disturbance to the exposed top of the deposits.

There is no Stratum 2B present in Section 6. Immediately beneath Stratum 2A is the bone midden. Stratum 4A/B is present only in the western section of this profile (where it links with Stratum 4A immediately to the west, as seen in Section 5). The main bone midden, Stratum 4B, is well represented. Note that it continues directly to the rear wall of the shelter, although it thins to about 15 cm. The abundance of bone also decreased toward the rear, but bone did occur right up to this edge. Stratum 4C also is well represented in this section, although it thins and almost disappears as one moves to the west, toward the mouth of the shelter.

Section 7 (Fig. 4-9) is an east-west profile of an area near the back of the shelter. This section clearly shows the undulating nature of the deposits at *Aetokremnos*. As with most of the sections illustrated, postoccupational Stratum 1 deposits have already been removed; many of these were severely disturbed, primarily by rooffall. In Figure 4-9, the thickness and complexity of the Stratum 2A deposits can clearly be seen; these are subdivided into "upper" and "lower" Strata 2A. Basal Stratum 2B also is visible in the western side of the section, but it rapidly diminishes as one moves east. Disturbed "patches" of Stratum 2B occur, as do sporadic portions of various loci.

Section 7 also shows the indistinct nature of some portions of Stratum 3, which is present in this part of the shelter, but not as clearly as it is elsewhere. Stratum 3 is well defined in the western end of the section, but as one moves to the east, it becomes less apparent, "melting" into the bottom of Stratum 2A and the top of Stratum 4A. This portion is Locus 1, as described for N97E90 (see Chap. 5). Stratum 3 is well preserved when it occurs under Stratum 2B; where Stratum 2B is absent, Stratum 3 also disappears. This probably is a fortuitous occurrence. Also note the presence of an ash lens in Stratum 3, confirming that this stratigraphic unit is not entirely sterile.

Stratum 4A is well represented in Section 7, underlying Stratum 3 to the west and Stratum 2A to the east. The granular nature of Stratum 4A is more apparent to the west; in the east, this granularity is less pronounced, and the distinction between Strata 4A and 4B is less clear. Note the presence of Locus 2 (in N97E90), a krotovina filled with sheetwash, in the far eastern portion of the section. Finally, Stratum 4C forms a thin layer in the eastern portion of this section, occurring immediately above the shelter's floor.

Sections 8 and 9 (Figs. 4-10 and 4-11) form a 3-m-long profile of the northeastern back of the shelter. Figure 4-11 is a north view, while the remaining 2m (Fig. 4-10) are at a right angle, forming the east face of the same unit. As can be seen, parts of these sections are sandwiched between the shelter's floor and a "lip" of the back wall of the shelter. It is in this wedge that intact portions of Stratum 1 are preserved (only in Section 9).

Immediately underlying these sections is a thick portion of Stratum 2A (subdivided into upper and lower 2A). It is in this area of the site, that the thickest portion of Stratum 2A is preserved, exceeding 50 cm in some cases.

Stratum 3 is not present in Sections 8 and 9. Stratum 3 only appears in the southwest quadrant and the western portion of the southeast quadrant of N97E90; it also occurs as traces in N98E90. In Section 8, Locus 1 represents a replacement for Stratum 3. In Section 9, the boundary between Stratum 2A and Stratum 4 is poorly defined. There is some evidence for Stratum 4A, but it is not as clear as it is elsewhere. This lack of clarity may be due to the presence of the east extremity of Feature 3, a concentration of burned bone (not illustrated in Section 9) that may have partially obscured Stratum 4A. Clearly visible in Section 8 at the top of Stratum 4 is Locus 2, a krotovina. Stratum 4C also is well defined in this section.

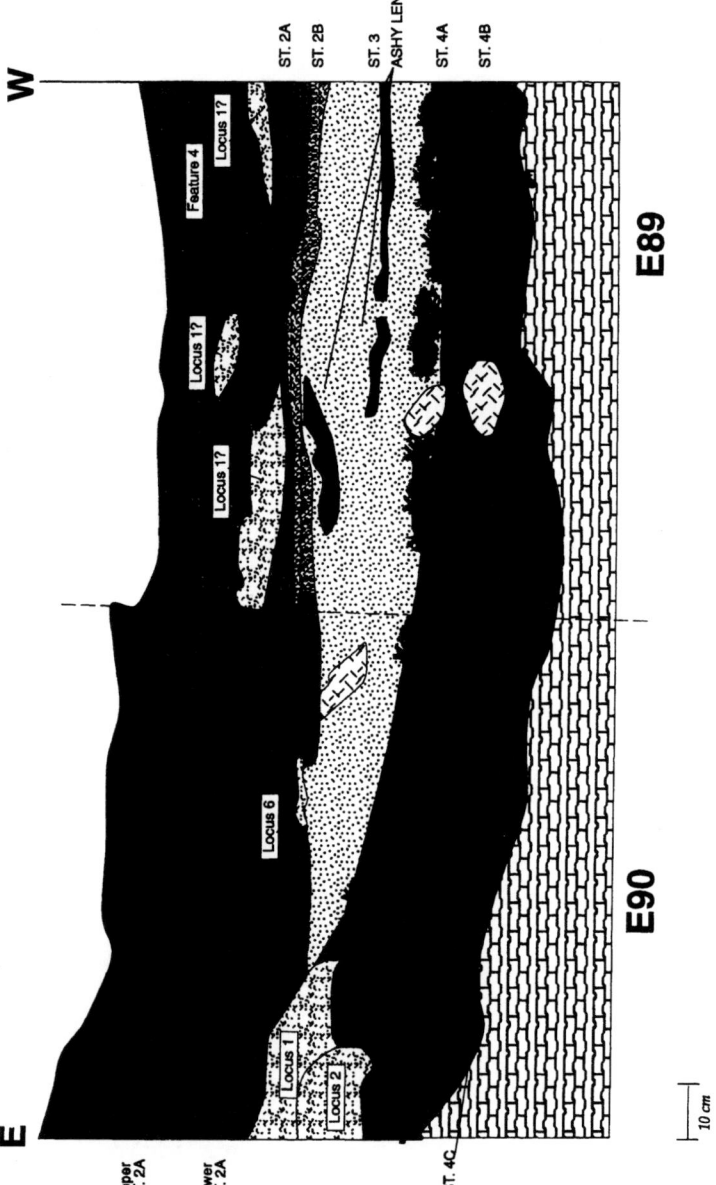

Figure 4-9. Section 7: N98E90, E89 (south section).

W

E89

E90

E

ST. 2A
ST. 2B
ST. 3
ASHY LENS
ST. 4A
ST. 4B

Feature 4

Locus 17

Locus 17

Locus 6

Locus 1

Locus 2

Upper
ST. 2A

Lower
ST. 2A

ST. 4C

10 cm

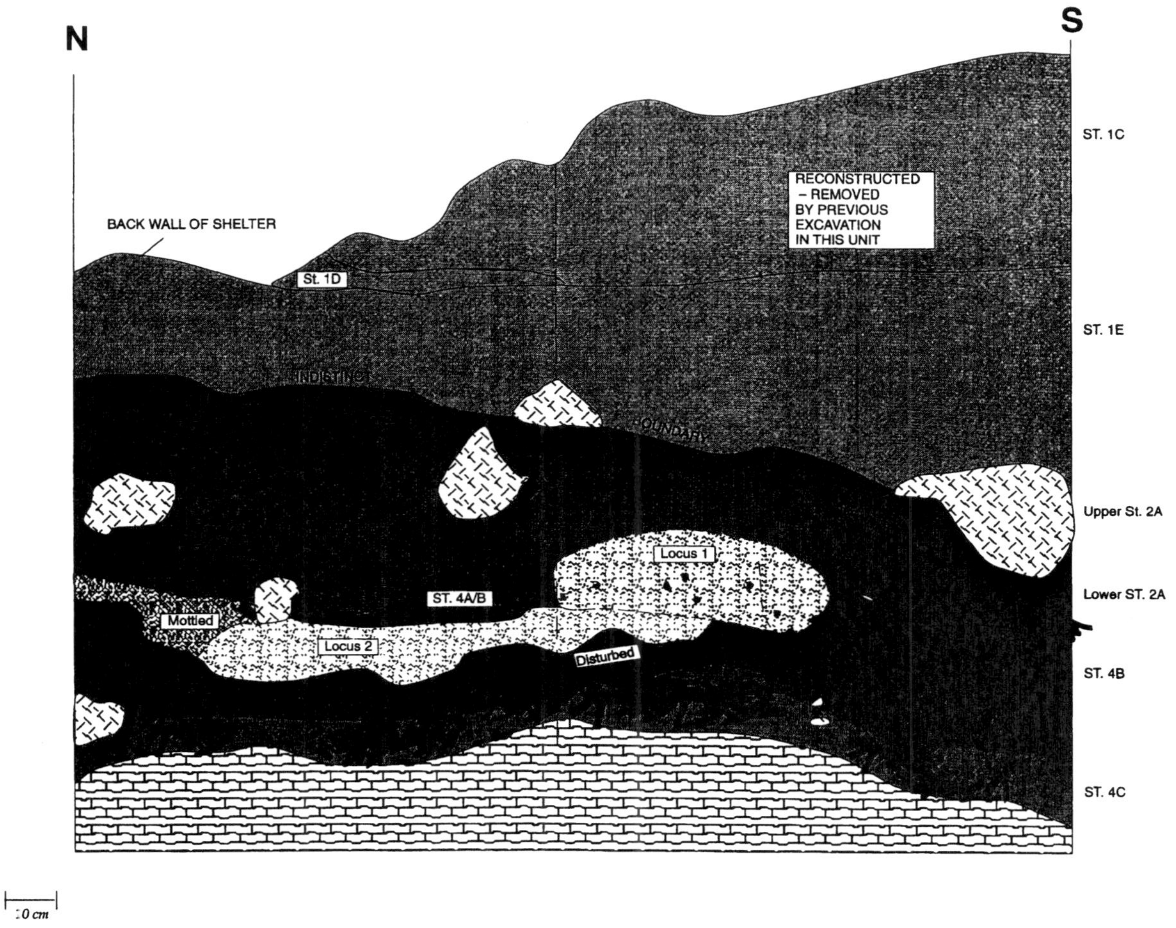

S

ST. 1C

ST. 1E

Upper St. 2A

Lower ST. 2A

ST. 4B

ST. 4C

RECONSTRUCTED
– REMOVED
BY PREVIOUS
EXCAVATION
IN THIS UNIT

Locus 1

Disturbed

ST. 4A/B

Locus 2

Mottled

GRINDING

BACK WALL OF SHELTER

St. 1D

N

≈0 cm

Figure 4-10. Section 8: N98E90 and N97E90 (east section).

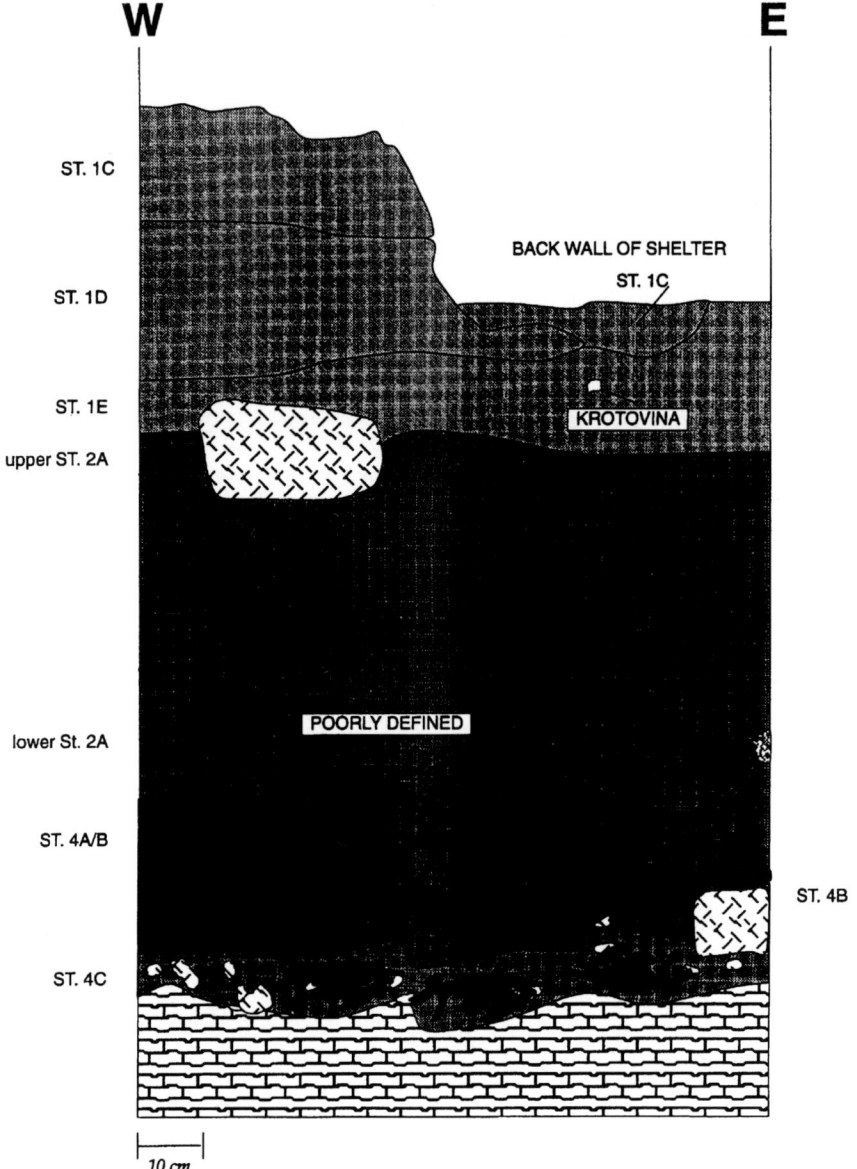

Figure 4-11. Section 9: N98E90 (north section).

     Section 10 (Fig. 4-12) is an east-west profile from the center rear of the shelter. Part of it is directly opposite Section 6, and a comparison of these two sections illustrates the stratigraphic differences that can occur within a small area (less than 1 m) of the intact deposits at *Aetokremnos*. While the bone midden and Stratum 2 are relatively flat in the latter section, a more complex situation is apparent a mere meter to the north, as seen in Section 10.

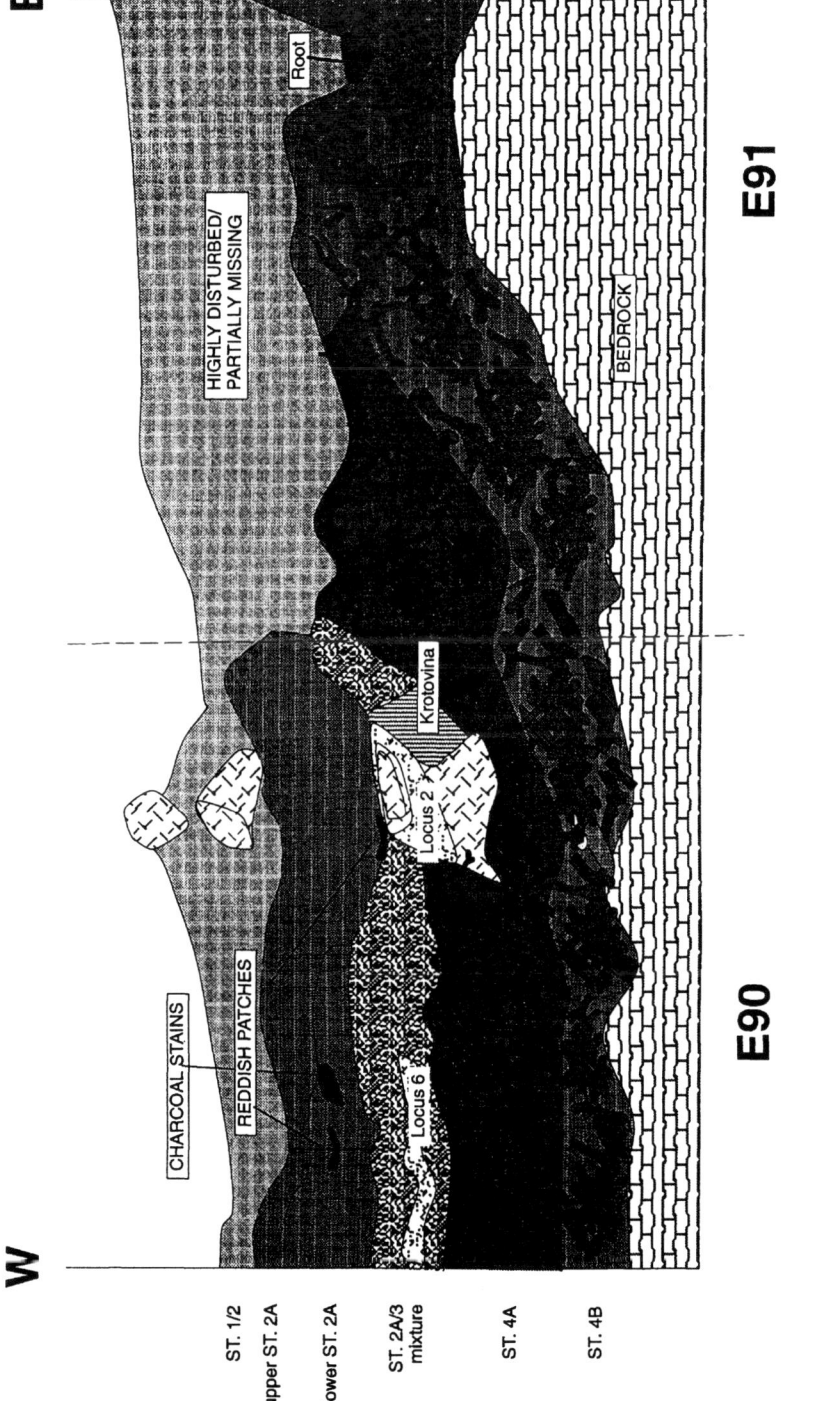

Figure 4-12. Section 10: N96E90, E91 (north section).

In that section, a disturbed area of the bottom of Stratum 1 contains a mixture of Stratum 2A and immediately overlies Stratum 4 in the eastern half of the profile. Continuing west, however, a small portion of upper Stratum 2A is immediately below Stratum 1. The lower portion of Stratum 2A in Section 10 is not clearly defined, and it is mixed with patches of Stratum 3. Portions of Loci 2 and 6 (as described for N96E90) are visible here, with Locus 2 appearing as a thick "pocket." Small patches of a reddish matrix, probably related to Stratum 2B, are visible in the western half of this section as well.

Stratum 4B is well represented in Section 10, as is Stratum 4A. The latter, however, is inconsistent in that it contains some very densely packed granular portions. Also of interest is the fact that even in Stratum 4B much of the bone was fragmented. This is more common in Stratum 4A.

The extreme eastern portion of Stratum 4 is somewhat odd as well in that it appears disturbed. This may, however, be due to a relatively sharp rise in the bedrock here. Also, some of the bone here was cemented by calcium carbonate to the bedrock floor. Finally, what sets this small area aside from the remainder of Stratum 4 deposits is the presence of pockets of dark yellow sand about 1–2 cm thick, which were immediately on the bedrock (not visible in Section 10), usually under the bone.

Section 11 (Fig. 4-13) is the north-south profile of the center of the shelter that best illustrates the stratigraphic placement of several of the loci defined at *Aetokremnos* as well as the complexity of Stratum 2. Stratum 1 is not illustrated in this section, having been removed prior to the section's drawing. Stratum 2A is as much as 35 cm thick in Section 11. Interbedded within Strata 2 and 3 are several loci.

As can be seen in Section 11, several ephemeral inclusions are present throughout Strata 2 and 3. Not all of these were given individual locus designations. Stratum 3 here is well defined, but portions of it contain Locus 6. The presence of this locus indicates that not all of Stratum 3 can be considered sterile. In addition, small portions labeled Stratum 3 consist of a darker than normal matrix for this layer. Some very small patches of reddish matrix, probably related to Stratum 2B, also are clearly visible in this section. The possibility that some of these represent disintegrated burned (oxidized red) stones also cannot be overlooked, but Stratum 2B is very clear when it immediately underlies, and may be part of, Locus 3.

Stratum 4 is well represented in Section 11. All three subdivisions are clearly present. As is common with Stratum 4A, some portions are more granular than others. This condition is a reflection of the edge of Feature 3. Stratum 4B is typical midden fill, consisting of well-preserved and intact bones. Stratum 4C also is present, but only in the northern portion of the section.

The final section, 12 (Fig. 4-14), is an east-west profile of the south-central portion of the shelter. This section only illustrates Strata 4 and 5 and is provided here to show the location of the latter, which has an extremely limited distribution. Stratum 4A is absent here, but the clay-rich Stratum 4C is common and thicker here than elsewhere. This thickness may have something to do with the formation of Stratum 5.

Stratum 5 was subdivided into three microstrata. Stratum 5A is pale brown (10YR 3/3) and is a thin, laminated stratum beneath the bone midden (i.e., Stratum 4C). It is fine grained, with very small pebbles, possibly water deposited. Stratum 5B is gray-brown (2.5Y 5/2) and is another thin, laminated deposit that is fine grained. Finally, Stratum 5C is a gray brown (2.5Y5/2), laminated deposit immediately over bedrock. It is a grainy, compacted deposit, containing even finer sediments than Strata 5A and 5B.

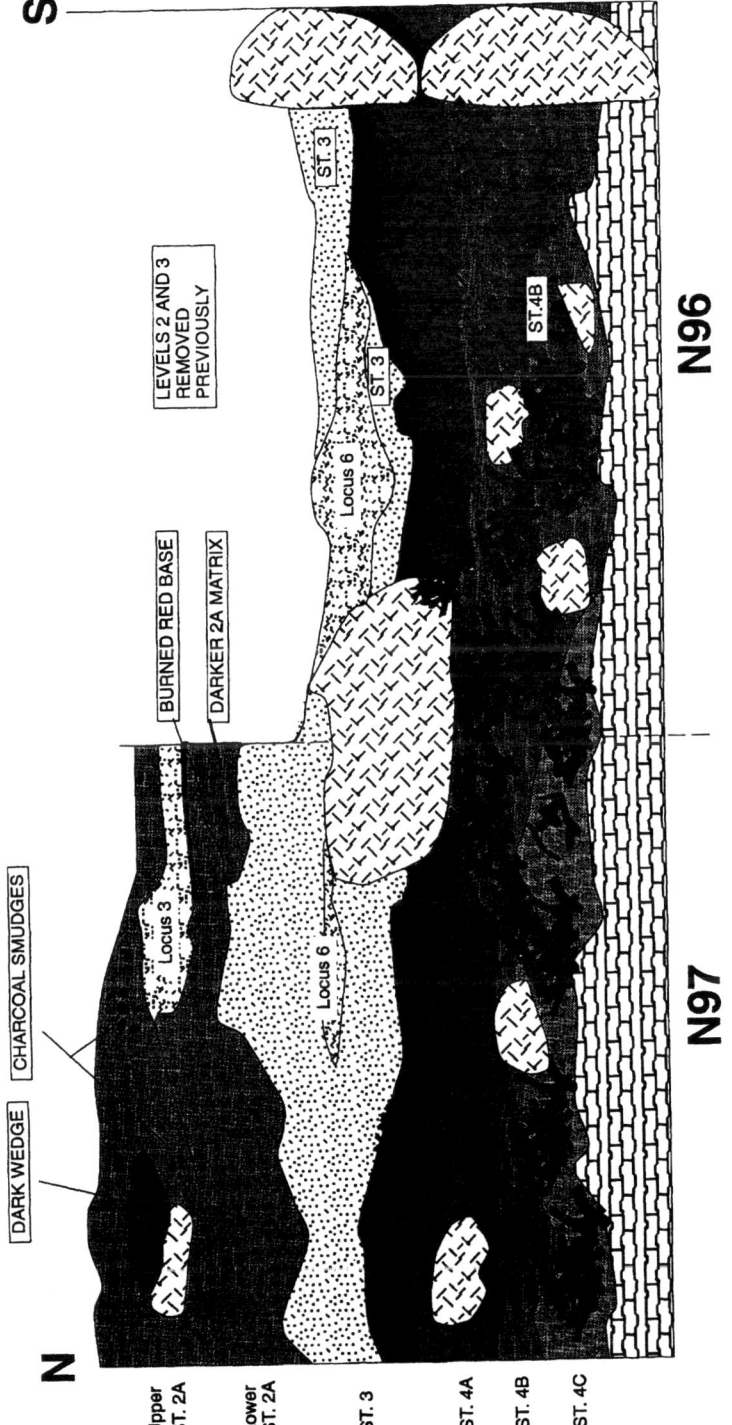

Figure 4-13. Section 11: N97E89 and N96E89 (east section).

S

N

LEVELS 2 AND 3
REMOVED
PREVIOUSLY

BURNED RED BASE

DARKER 2A MATRIX

CHARCOAL SMUDGES

DARK WEDGE

Locus 3

Locus 6

Locus 6

ST. 3

ST. 3

ST. 3

ST.4B

ST.4B

Upper
ST. 2A

Lower
ST. 2A

ST. 3

ST. 4A

ST. 4B

ST. 4C

N97

N96

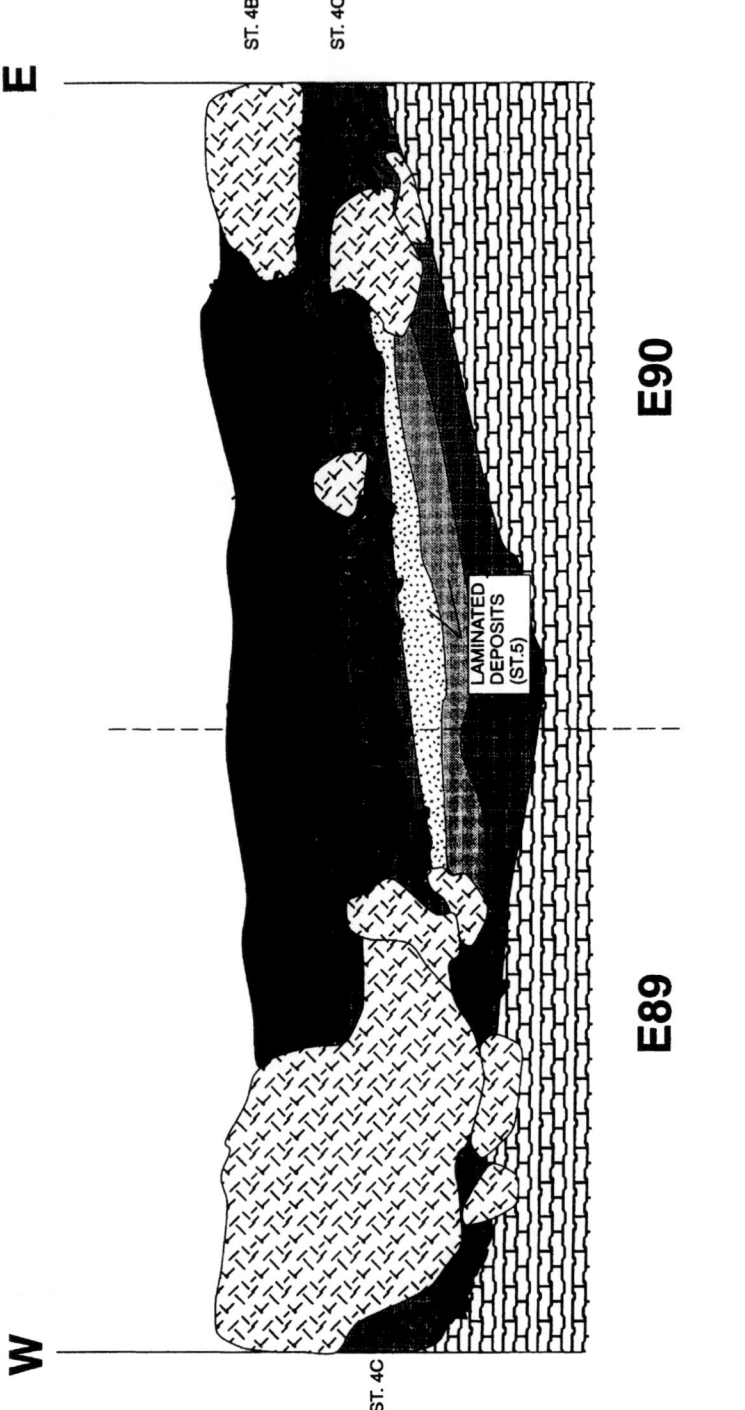

Figure 4-14. Section 12: N94E89, E90 (north section, Stratum 2 removed).

Stratum 5 occurs only in the lowest portion of the section illustrated here and is extremely localized. It is nearly sterile, containing only 15 bones, 4 *Monodonta*, and 1 *Patella* (burnt), and appears to have been deposited by water (sheetwash). Analytically, it is best considered as part of Stratum 4C. Mandel (Chap. 3) did not consider Stratum 5 as a separate stratigraphic unit. Its areal extent is limited to portions of N95E89 and N95E90, with a very small incursion into the N94 units. In N95E89, it covers an area of approximately 7 × 40 cm in the southeast quadrant, while in N95E90, it covers an area of about 11 × 55 cm of the southern quadrants. Stratum 5 is situated on a low point of bedrock, and much of it is under a small lip of bedrock floor, which may have acted as a natural trap for these sediments.

STRATIGRAPHIC SUMMARY

The foregoing discussion has described the stratigraphy at *Aetokremnos*. We have attempted to provide both general and detailed information that illustrates the relatively thin, yet complex, stratigraphy of the site. Although it is clear that rooffall and postoccupational disturbances have caused some damage to the deposits, it is equally clear that much of *Aetokremnos* is relatively intact. Although some reworking has occurred, it has been minimal in extent. It is clearly evident that, for example, the deposits at *Aetokremnos* were not redeposited by water action. We have identified areas where water action has occurred, but this action was always localized. Likewise, possible root, rodent, and insect action occurs on a limited basis and may have reworked some material, but not to a significant degree.

One is left with the inescapable conclusion that the bulk of the deposits relating to the occupation of the Akrotiri Phase, that is, Strata 2 and 4, are intact. An intervening stratum, Stratum 3, consists of a usually sterile pale brown, sandy loam. This condition is not, however, consistent throughout the site; Stratum 3 does not always form a separating unit between Strata 2 and 4. For the most part, Stratum 3 appears to have accumulated as a result of aeolian deposition and the gradual disintegration of the roof (see Chap. 3). In some cases, however, there could also be some anthropogenic reworking of this stratum, as was suggested as the reason for its occurrence between Features 1 (Stratum 2A) and 3 (Stratum 4B).

We feel that the stratigraphic evidence at *Aetokremnos* argues compellingly for the direct association of *Phanourios* with cultural materials. This supports other evidence from a constellation of data, presented throughout this volume, all of which lead to the same conclusion.

Chapter *5*

Cultural Features and Loci

ALAN H. SIMMONS AND DAVID S. REESE

FEATURES

Introduction

The identification and interpretation of cultural features at limited activity sites lacking proper architecture often is a difficult and frustrating task. This situation is no less troublesome at *Aetokremnos*, where we have documented 11 features. These are summarized in Table 5-1, and their horizontal distribution is plotted in Figure 5-1. Earlier preliminary reports indicated the presence of 12 features (e.g., Simmons 1991a); however, we have eliminated one of these as too problematic to be considered a feature.

More often than not the features at *Aetokremnos* are ephemeral and lack clearly defined boundaries. One of their distinguishing characteristics is that they occur in a context distinctly different from the surrounding matrix. This context frequently took the form of what we have termed *casual hearths*. These are burned areas, sometimes with oxidized red bases and with a fill of burned cobbles (primarily igneous); they are also sometimes composed simply of ash stains and/or burned rocks. They probably functioned as informal burning areas, either for cooking or some other activity.

Feature Descriptions

Feature 1

Feature 1 was the first feature documented at *Aetokremnos*. It was initially revealed as a cone-shaped ash formation with it broadest point some 30 cm across at the bottom in a section only 1 m in length (Fig. 5-2); it was interpreted as a hearth or roasting pit. During subsequent excavation more of the feature was revealed, indicating that the cone portion tapered to a longer, but much less distinctive, strip of dark material. Stratigraphically, the feature lies in Stratum 2 (with small parts blending into the upper portion of Stratum 2/4) (see Fig. 4-4, Chap. 4). We now know that Feature 1 represents an activity area that functioned either as a hearth, or more likely, an area where hot ashes were dumped onto a clean surface, forming the distinctive "cone" of the feature.

95

Table 5-1. Summary of Features at *Aetokremnos*

Feature number	Principal units	Primary stratum	Type
1	N98E88, N98E87, N97E88, N97E87	2	ash heap/hearth area
2	N94E90	4B	casual hearth
3	N97E88, N97E89, N97E90, N98E89, N98E90, N98E88	4A–B	burnt fauna concentration
4	N98E88, N98E89	2	hearth, activity area
5	N95E89, N95E88, N94E89, N94E88	2A	shell concentration
6	N95E89, N95E90, N96E89, N96E90	1/2 + 2	casual hearth (stone lined)
7	N95E89, N95E90	2	casual hearth (stone lined)
8	N96E88	2/4	bell-shaped pit
9	N96E89	4	casual hearth
10	N97E89	2	casual hearth
11	N97E90	2	casual hearth

The thickest portion of the feature is the cone, which has a maximum depth of ca. 31 cm. Moving away from this area, however, its thickness diminishes rapidly, to approximately 10 cm or less. Portions of the bottom of Feature 1 are a thin red oxidized surface (about 5 cm maximum thickness), indicative of intense heat. This could represent intentional heating, as in a hearth in which burning formed the red base. It also could reflect unintentional formation, caused by the deposition of hot ashes onto a sterile surface. Finally, in some instances where this appears, especially as patchy loci, it could represent disintegrating stones, although in most cases this explanation appears unlikely. This red, burned base, termed Stratum 2B, is clearly seen at the bottom of the cone; it also continues adjacent to the cone and occurs in sporadic patches in several units adjacent to Feature 1. We believe that it does reflect burning, although its wide occurrence throughout Stratum 2 argues against its being the bottom of any specific feature, such as a hearth.

In the conical area, where Feature 1 is most pronounced, it immediately overlies Stratum 2B and the sterile Stratum 3, which below the cone is some 11 cm thick. Stratum 3, however, rapidly thins and ultimately disappears to the south and west; here the bottom of Feature 1 occurs in Stratum 2/4 in the absence of Stratum 3.

The fill of Feature 1 is composed of a fine black ashy matrix. It covers approximately 2 square meters, but its precise boundaries are difficult to determine, as portions have suffered considerable postoccupational disturbance. The most traumatic such disturbance was the removal of an entire portion of deposit immediately north of the cone. This truncation was caused by water movement from the back of the shelter, which formed a small, but apparently powerful, channel moving from the rear to the front (Fig. 5-3, Fig. 4-4 in Chap. 4; also see Mandel, Chap. 3, for more detail). This entirely removed a portion of both Strata 2 and 4, including some of Feature 1. In addition, the feature is located near the exposed west face of the intact deposit, and it is likely that some of it was lost to erosion. Rooffall also has caused some disturbance.

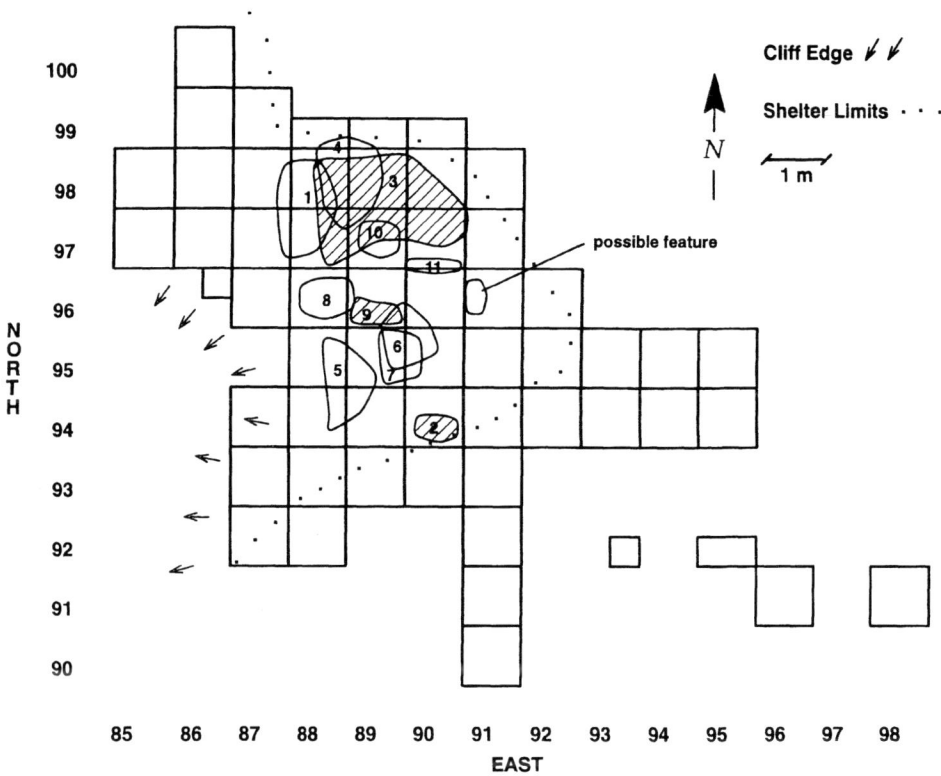

Figure 5-1. Horizontal plot of features by strata. Cross-hatching indicates Stratum 4.

Four radiocarbon determinations came from Feature 1 or adjacent to it. Three were on a single sediment sample from the cone (9240 ± 420 B.P., Tx-5833C; 9490 ± 120 B.P., Tx-5833A; 10150 ± 120 B.P., and Tx-5833B), while the fourth was on shell from adjacent Stratum 2/4 (10,840 ± 60 B.P., SMU1991).

If one views Feature 1 as covering a wide activity area within Stratum 2, the number of chipped stone artifacts (and other materials, such as shell and beads) is impressive, because most of these occur in Stratum 2 in a few units surrounding and including Feature 1. However, in the principal area of Feature 1, the cone itself, only one artifact, a tertiary flake, was present (near the truncated edge). Another 59 chipped stone artifacts, including 5 tools, were directly adjacent (that is, within 1 m) to the cone (Table 5-2). Nine of these occur at the bottom of Stratum 2, while 7 are located in the upper portion of Stratum 2/4 adjacent to the feature. In addition, two igneous cobbles, both water worn and broken, one of which appears burned, also are present around the cone, as are a picrolite pendant and 19 nonfood marine shells; the latter probably were ornaments. Of these, 10 are *Columbella* (1 worked into a bead and 8 stringable), 5 are *Dentalium* (3 beads), 3 are *Conus* (all holed at the apex), and 3 are burnt *Glycymeris* fragments, and an operculum. Finally, a single ceramic sherd also occurs in the vicinity of the feature, in the upper portion of Stratum 2. This clearly is intrusive, probably deposited by the water action that truncated part of N98E88-87.

Figure 5-2. Feature 1 exposed in section prior to excavation.

Abundant food shell also is present, most adjacent to the conical area. This food includes over 668 (149, or 22.3%, burnt) *Monodonta*, 17 *Patella* (3 burnt), and two *Helix*. Of these shells, 31 (28 *Monodonta* and 3 *Patella*) are within the cone itself, and 20 *Monodonta* (64.5%) and 2 *Patella* are burnt. The actual number of *Monodonta* is greater, as one uncounted sample of these shells was used for a radiocarbon determination. Finally, a large number of bones are present around the feature, although none occurred directly in the cone. There were 1,880 *Phanourios* bones in and around the feature, with 670 (35.6%) burnt. This bone sample includes 224 bones (125, or 55.8%, burnt) from in and south of the Feature in Stratum 2, and 1,656 (including 545, or 32.9%, burnt pieces) from Stratum 2/4. The majority of these bones occur in the lower portion of Stratum 2/4. We believe this bone was deposited slightly earlier than the construction of Feature 1. There are also 196 (44, or 22.8%, burnt) bird bones from at least three *Otis* and three *Anser* present, all in Stratum 2, in and adjacent to Feature 1.

Figure 5-3. Feature 3 (note Feature 1 on top). Rod is 50 cm long.

The presence of abundant *Phanourios* bone in the area around Feature 1 (at least 6 individuals) is a strong argument for their direct association with Stratum 2. One could argue, alternatively, that the construction of features such as Feature 1 could have uprooted previously deposited *Phanourios* bone from Stratum 4, resulting in a mixing of deposits. This uprooting is unlikely, however, because much of Feature 1 is separated from the bone midden (i.e., Stratum 4) by a sterile layer (Stratum 3). This indicates that the construction of the feature did not disturb bone from the midden, and that the *Phanourios* fragments associated with the feature are in situ.

Making any functional interpretations based on the material culture associated with Feature 1 is not easy. Certainly the abundance of food remains is indicative of subsistence activity. Over 30 individual shells (71% burnt) occur within the cone, suggesting that this portion of the feature served as a site for the cooking of these mollusks. Cooking could have occurred directly at the cone, or these remains could represent secondary deposits from more formal cooking areas located elsewhere. The presence of *Phanourios* and bird bones is more problematic, as these occur throughout Stratum 2. However, the concentration of these bones around Feature 1 also suggests a preparation activity.

Turning to the chipped stone, there is no apparent pattern that distinguishes this area of Stratum 2 from others. Of the 60 pieces adjacent to the feature, 5 are tools. A range of waste materials is present, including 2 cores. These materials suggest that reduction could have occurred in the immediate vicinity of Feature 1. The 2 scrapers, 3 retouched flakes and blades, along with 27 flakes and blades, could have functioned as cutting implements

Table 5-2. Chipped Stone Artifacts Associated with Feature 1

Class	Stratum 2	Stratum 2, Lower	Stratum 2/4	Total
Tools				
Thumbnail scraper	1			1
Sidescraper	1			1
Retouched blade	1			1
Retouched flake	1			1
Retouched bladelet	1			1
Debitage				
Cortical flake			1	1
Secondary flake	2	1	1	4
Tertiary flake	11	2	1	14
Tertiary blade	5			5
Bladelet		2	1	3
Other waste materials				
Microflakes	5	1	2	8
Debris	14	3	1	18
Core globular	1			1
Core fragment	1			1
TOTAL	44	9	7	60

during processing. These possible activities, however, remain speculative, especially when considering that abundant chipped stone materials in roughly the same proportions occur throughout Stratum 2.

In summary, Feature 1 is a large feature with a smaller focal point, the conical heap. A large number of artifacts and bones occur adjacent to the feature, although few pieces were actually within the cone. Although a majority of the *Phanourios* bones in the vicinity of Feature 1 occur below it, several are stratigraphically associated with it, and there seems little question of their contemporaneity.

We believe that Feature 1 represents an activity area that encompassed a large, but undetermined, portion of Stratum 2, one that is contingent with Feature 5, a concentration of shells 2 m to the south. The conical focal point of the feature could have been a hearth that was used extensively, resulting in the thick ashy deposit, with the horizontal thinning to the south representing postuse dispersal. The cone's inverted morphology, however, does not suggest a hearth. More likely, Feature 1 functioned as an ash dump or a secondary refuse deposit where hot ashes were placed, perhaps after cleaning out hearths.

Feature 2

Feature 2 is a poorly defined casual hearth within the upper portion of Stratum 4B. The feature is located at the southern edge of the shelter; it was probably near its open face. This portion of the shelter has been disturbed by erosion and by rooffall. The feature underlies Stratum 1/2; no "pure" Stratum 2 is present, nor is the sterile Stratum 3. It is a roughly oval concentration of dark gray/black fine sediment that contains charcoal stains. The feature overlies a slab of rooffall that might have been the hearth's bottom because the surface of the rock is blackened. The feature's dimensions are approximately 50 by 100 cm, and it is about 5 cm thick.

Two microflakes were recovered near the feature. Forty-four *Phanourios* bone fragments (39, or 88.6%, burnt) also were present (representing two individuals), as were 24 *Monodonta* (3 burnt) and 6 *Helix* shells. The direct association of this material is, however, questionable, given the feature's indistinct character.

Feature 2 is typical of the casual hearths found at *Aetokremnos*. It appears to have functioned as an informal burning locus, which was constructed either during or shortly after the deposition of the Stratum 4 bone midden. The fact that the feature's base may have consisted of a piece of rooffall suggests that the shelter continued to be occupied after portions of the roof collapsed.

Feature 3

Feature 3 is a concentration of extremely burnt bone located in Strata 4A and 4B that minimally covers 6 square meters. This feature is directly below Feature 1, but it is very clearly separated from it by Stratum 3, the sterile level that covers much, but not all, of the shelter's interior (Fig. 5-3, and Fig. 4-4 in Chap. 4), as well as by a large piece of rooffall. Portions of the feature are capped by large burned stones, which appear on top of Stratum 4B. As one moves toward the interior of the shelter, the abundance of the burned rocks decreases, replaced by Stratum 4A, which is absent in the more western reaches of the feature. In most instances, the burned bone of Feature 3 continues down to bedrock; it is not resting atop unburned bone.

A few large "pitted" stones also occur in Feature 3. These have a very smooth surface, as compared with the rough rooffall. They are clustered around the western edge of the feature. Although they could have been imported into the site, William Farrand, one of the project's geomorphologists, feels these could easily be differentially weathered rooffall. Regardless of origins, they could have served as impromptu "benches."

Almost all of Feature 3 is capped by Stratum 3. The presence of this stratum demonstrates that the burned bone concentration comprising the feature could not have been burned as the result of later activities in Stratum 2. Burning (Features 1 and 4) occurs in Stratum 2 in some areas overlying Feature 3; however, if as a result of these activities bone was burned in Feature 3 by heat penetration, Stratum 3 also should be burned, and that is not the case.

Nearly all of Feature 3 consists of extremely burned bone, most of it *Phanourios*. This bone is so burned that it has often assumed a "crinkly" appearance and is very friable. The boundaries of Feature 3 can be plotted by the extent of this burning. Although burnt bone is common throughout the deposit, both in Strata 2 and 4, the overwhelming abundance of it in concentrated form is what defines Feature 3. Over 62,500 *Phanourios* bones representing at least 50 individuals make up the feature. Many of these are almost charred beyond recognition. This massive amount of bone represents 28.6% of all *Phanourios* remains recovered from the site.

In addition to *Phanourios*, limited numbers of other animals also are present in Feature 3. These include 5 *Elephas* bones, 5 *Vipera* bones, 3 ?*Geochelone* and ?*Testudo* samples, and 49 bird bones from two individuals (*Otis, Athene*). Also present are 195 *Monodonta* (45, or 23.1%, burnt) and 12 *Patella*. Ornamental shells include one *Dentalium* and two *Columbella*.

Twenty-two chipped stone artifacts also occur (Table 5-3), but none are tools. These include 7 tertiary flakes, 1 core trimming element, 1 secondary flake, 1 bladelet, 7 microflakes, and 5 pieces of debris, and they represent nearly 20% of all chipped stone from Stratum 4. Four pieces of igneous rock also are present. It is significant that none of these artifacts occur within the "heart" of the feature. Rather, when plotted, all are located around the periphery of the feature. This same pattern also is true for the ornamental shell.

The roughly oval distribution of chipped stone around the feature suggests that preparation activities occurred on its edges, and bone was then discarded into the feature's core for burning. The proximity of the pitted stone to much of the chipped stone also is intriguing. If these stones served as "benches," one might expect to find chipped stone around them.

Feature 3 is easily defined. Interpreting it is another matter. It is clear that it functioned as an area where bone was intensively burned. It is unlikely that the feature represents redeposition of bone burned elsewhere, because the burned bone is present, in most instances, down to bedrock. The severe burning, resulting in thousands of friable fragments, argues against a cooking function . . . certainly such intense burning would have destroyed any meat. Perhaps once meat had been obtained, and the bones were discarded, they were then burned for some other purpose. It is tempting to think of a use of the bone as a fuel, used either for cooking or heating. The presence of bone from the remainder of the midden, most of it unburned, would have provided a ready fuel supply, and the artifacts surrounding the feature may represent an activity area in which unburned bone was prepared for subsequent burning.

Feature 4

Feature 4 was initially identified as a casual hearth. More thorough excavation, however, revealed it to be a relatively large area of dark ashy matrix with poorly defined edges. It is located in Stratum 2A and is best considered in conjunction with Feature 1, with which it is contiguous.

Feature 4 is variable in thickness, ranging from roughly 4 cm to over 15 cm. Its fill is an extremely ashy dark black/gray matrix. The upper boundaries of the feature are not as

Table 5-3. Chipped Stone Artifacts from Feature 3

Type	No.
Core-trimming element	1
Secondary flake	1
Tertiary flake	7
Bladelet	1
Microflakes	7
Debris	5
TOTAL	22

well defined as is the lower portion. The feature can first be detected in the lower portion of Stratum 1/2, where the matrix is not quite as dark as in Stratum 2A. The bottom of the feature consists of patches of Stratum 2B, the red, burned surface that terminates Stratum 2. Immediately below Stratum 2B is the sterile Stratum 3, which occurs abundantly in this area of the site.

The western edge of Feature 4 joins the eastern edge of Feature 1. Indeed, if one considers Feature 1 as more than its core cone area, both Features 1 and 4 are on the same surface. The boundaries of Feature 4 are somewhat arbitrary and are roughly defined by the extent of its extremely dark matrix. To the south, this matrix becomes lighter in color. The southern edge overlaps, very slightly, Feature 10, a hearth stain in the lower portion of Stratum 2A. The southern boundary of Feature 4 is further confused by its sporadic occurrence. To the north, the feature ends at the back of the shelter. To the east, it diminishes some 1.5 m from the eastern wall of the shelter, where the adjacent Stratum 2A matrix is not as dark as it is farther to the west. In all likelihood, the feature is larger than we have described it. If Stratum 2B, in fact, marks some sort of burned surface terminating all of Stratum 2, it may be that any material above it should be considered as "greater" Feature 4. By restricting our definition of the feature to the extremely dark matrix, we have opted for a conservative explanation of it.

Material associated with Feature 4 has been divided into two contexts. The first occurs within the feature itself, while the second consists of immediately adjacent materials to the south and east, where the edge of the feature "bleeds" into a "cleaner" Stratum 2A and is thus rather indistinct. We also have identified materials immediately overlaying the feature in Stratum 1/2 separately. The numbers that follow do not include items from the adjacent Feature 1.

There is a considerable amount of bone associated with the feature. One hundred and eight *Phanourios* bones have been identified (104, or 96.3%, burnt), representing an MNI of two. In addition, 300 (103, or 34.3%, burnt) bird bones, representing at least seven birds (3 *Otis*, 3 *Anser*, 1 *Anas*), are present. Eggshell also is present. When examining the associated south and east edges, 123 (80, or 65.0%, burnt) *Phanourios* bones of two individuals, and 68 bird bones (14, or 20.6%, burnt) of five birds (2 *Otis*, 1 *Anser*, 1 *Anas*, 1 *Phalacrocorax*) can be added. There also is one partly burnt *Sus* phalanx 3. In the Stratum 1/2 section over the feature, there are 43 *Phanourios* bones (32, or 74.4%, burnt), 71 bird bones (27, or 38.0%, burnt) of 1 *Otis*, and 4 *Vipera* bones.

There is an equally abundant amount of shells associated with the feature. There are 440 (135, or 30.7%, burnt) *Monodonta* and 22 (13, or 59.1%, burnt) *Patella* individuals directly in it, while 1,813 (339, or 18.7%, burnt) *Monodonta* and 46 *Patella* (6, or 13.0% burnt) are in the south and east margins. In the overlying portion of Stratum 1/2, 706 (96, or 13.6% burnt) *Monodonta* and 27 (10, or 37.0%, burnt) *Patella* are present.

Ornamental items also are common, with two *Dentalium* (1 a bead) in the feature itself. A picrolite pendant also is present in the feature. In adjacent units, there are 3 *Dentalium* beads, 3 holed *Conus*, 3 *Columbella* (2 open apex, 1 unmodified), 1 holed *Cerithium*, and 2 *Glycymeris* (1 holed) in the adjacent units. Over the feature, in Stratum 1/2, are 3 *Dentalium* (1 a bead), 1 *Columbella* with an open apex, and 1 unmodified *Conus*.

Of possible functional significance is a large number (27) of igneous cobbles in the adjacent units of the feature, as well as a shallow "mortar." Also present is one of the two pumice pieces from the site. The concentration of these items suggests that they were used for specific activities associated with the feature. One such use may have been in food processing of shell. They also could have been used to smash bones in the extraction of extract marrow (although the bones are largely complete).

Nearly 200 chipped stones artifacts are associated with the feature (Table 5-4). This is a conservative number; it does not include items from Feature 1 (an additional 60 artifacts), nor those from nearby Stratum 2A units. Of the approximately 40 square meters comprising the shelter's interior, Feature 4 covers about 1.5 square meters, only 3.8%. Yet the amounts of chipped stone are proportionally high. The majority (78.6%) of the artifacts occur around the edges of Feature 4, rather than in its interior.

When one examines all the associated chipped stone from this feature, some interesting patterns emerge. At first glance, the proportional occurrence of various classes mirror those from the site as a whole. The percentage of tools (11.6%), for example, is nearly identical to the overall site percentage of 12.5%. In breaking down classes, however, there is a

Table 5-4. Chipped Stone Associated with Feature 4

Type	Directly associated	Peripheral	Above	Total
Tools				
Thumbnail scrapers		6		6
Side/end scrapers	2	1		3
Burins		4		4
Burin/scraper		1		1
Notches		1		1
Retouched blades	1	1		2
Retouched flakes	1	3		4
Microlith-truncation	1			1
Microlith-retouched bladelet	1			1
Total tools	6	17		23
Debitage				
Core tablet		1		1
Cortical flake		1		1
Secondary flakes	2	10		12
Tertiary flakes	5	12		17
Secondary blade	1			1
Tertiary blades		7		7
Bladelets	7	3		10
Total debitage	15	34		49
Other waste materials				
Burin spalls	3	2		5
Microflakes	18	25	2	45
Debris	21	45	5	71
Cores		3		3
Core fragments	1	1		2
Total other waste materials	43	76	7	126
TOTALS	64	127	7	198

concentration of burins in this small area. Twenty-five percent of all burins recovered from the site occur around Feature 4; examining only Stratum 2, this figure jumps to 45%. Thirty-one percent of all burin spalls also occur with Feature 4, strong evidence for the in situ nature of the deposits and the relationship of burin spalls to burins. The most common (39%) tool class associated with Feature 4 is a variety of scrapers, including 17% of all thumbnail scrapers recovered from the site. One-third of all microlithic tools also come from Feature 4. The clustering of both burins and scrapers in an area covering less than 4% of the shelter's interior argues persuasively for a functionally specific focus involving these tools. The same observations can be made regarding debitage and other waste materials. There is, for example, a high proportion of microflakes associated with Feature 4 (23% of all chipped stone artifacts associated with the feature and 25% of all microflakes from the site). All of these data indicate an intense usage of this specific area of the shelter.

In summary, Feature 4 probably is best viewed as a continuation of Feature 1. These two features together contain a substantial number of the artifacts recovered from Stratum 2, although they only cover about 7% of the shelter's interior. We cannot determine specifically what activities occurred toward the back of the shelter, but given the abundance of chipped stone, igneous cobbles, ornamentals, and faunal remains, it is likely that food preparation and general maintenance were major foci.

Feature 5

Feature 5 was one of the most prominent aspects of *Aetokremnos* prior to its excavation. It was visible in the eroded face of the west end of the intact deposits and initially was interpreted as a shell layer (see, e.g., Simmons 1988a:555). It was not recognized as a feature until subsequent excavation revealed that its horizontal extent was far less than first believed. It is located in Stratum 2A, and undoubtedly a portion has been lost to erosion (Figs. 4-3 in Chap. 4 and 2-4 in Chap. 2). Even after limited excavation in 1987 and 1988, the concentration appeared to form a level capping the bone midden (Stratum 4). Subsequent and more extensive excavation in 1990, however, revealed that this "layer" had a limited horizontal extent of 1 square meter. Accordingly, we now view it as a shell concentration within Stratum 2A. It is at the same general elevation as the other Stratum 2 features.

Feature 5 is about 6 cm thick in its most definable core area. Although shell is abundant throughout Stratum 2A, the large amount present within the small area covered by Feature 5 is the reason for its definition as a feature. Within the 6-cm-thick core of the feature 1,874 *Monodonta* (188, or 10%, burnt) and 48 *Patella* (8, or 16.7%, burnt) are present. Also present are one *Columbella* (open apex) and one *Dentalium*. Also present are 217 (54, or 24.9%, burnt) *Phanourios* bones of 2 individuals, 184 (34, or 18.5%, burnt) bird bones of eight individuals (5 *Otis*, 2 *Anser*, 1 Anseriform). Eggshell also occurs.

Although the concentration is very obvious, exactly where it begins vertically is not. Materials indirectly associated with Feature 5 are difficult to define, given the feature's poor horizontal and vertical boundaries. During excavation, the upper portion of Stratum 2A overlying Feature 5 contained 333 *Monodonta* (39, or 11.7%, burnt) and 21 *Patella* (3, 14.3%, burnt) shells; these may reflect the top of the feature.

A similar situation exists with the bottom of the feature. Abundant materials also were present below Feature 5, both in the lower portion of Stratum 2A (Strata 2B and 3 are absent) and in Stratum 4. In the lower portion of Stratum 2A, there are 24 (14, or 58.3%, burnt) *Phanourios* bones representing one individual. Also here are 105 bird bones of eight *Otis* individuals and one *Anser*. In addition, 74 *Monodonta* (12, or 16.2%, burnt) and 2 *Dentalium* are present. In the underlying Stratum 4B, 341 *Monodonta* (133, or 39%, burnt) and 9 *Patella* (4, or 44.4%, burnt) occur, as does 1 *Columbella* fragment. Numerous vertebrate remains also occur here (4,539 *Phanourios* bones, 47 *Elephas* bones, and 25 bird bones); these clearly are not associated with the feature. Certainly shell occurs elsewhere in both Strata 2 (especially) and 4, so it is perhaps best not to regard these materials below Feature 5 as part of it.

More material comes from what might be termed a *mixed* Feature 5 context, from Stratum 2/4, located at the original exposed section. Here we have 1,405 *Phanourios* bones (17.9% burnt), representing four individuals. There also are 9 *Elephas* bones, 69 bird bones (47.3% burnt) of 3 *Otis* and 1 *Anser*, 1 *Vipera* vertebra (burnt), ?*Geochelone* remains, 292+ *Monodonta* (11.3%+ burnt), 5+ *Patella* (60%+ burnt), and 2 *Dentalium*. It is important to note, however, that these remains probably are not directly associated with the feature.

Thirty-eight chipped stone artifacts are associated, at least indirectly, with this feature (Table 5-5). Most (35) occurred at its top; only 2 (a microflake and a piece of debris) were actually in the feature. Two tools were present (1 thumbnail scraper, 1 retouched flake); the majority of the material consisted of debitage, including 1 core trimming element, 2 cortical flakes, 5 secondary flakes, 6 tertiary flakes, 1 secondary blade, and 5 tertiary blades. Other materials included 2 burin spalls, 4 microflakes, 9 pieces of debris, and 1 core. One waterworn igneous cobble fragment also was present.

In summary, Feature 5 is a relatively thin and horizontally restricted concentration of shell. It undoubtedly functioned as a shell-processing area. Only 10% of the *Monodonta* is

Table 5-5. Chipped Stone Artifacts Associated with Feature 5

Artifact	Top of feature	Below feature	In feature	Total
Tools				
Thumbnail scraper	1			1
Retouched flake	1			1
Debitage				
Core-trimming element blade	1			1
Cortical flakes	2			2
Secondary flakes	5			5
Tertiary flakes	6			6
Secondary blade	1			1
Tertiary blades	5			5
Other waste materials				
Burin spalls	2			2
Microflakes	3		1	4
Debris	7	1	1	9
Core	1			1
TOTAL	35	1	2	38

burned, however, and may argue against this resource being cooked in Feature 5. Initial preparation may have occurred here, prior to cooking, perhaps extracting the meat from the shell and discarding the latter, forming the feature. Such a process could suggest that the shellfish were eaten raw. Given the abundance of burned shell at the site, this would be atypical.

Feature 6

Feature 6 is a casual hearth in lower Stratum 2A. The feature is approximately 8 cm thick, although its top is poorly delineated. Its matrix is dark gray/brown and is fine grained. This matrix is not very ashy, except at the bottom of the feature, where an ash lens caps some fire-altered stones. Several burned stone cobbles (about 5 cm in diameter) occur in the northeast portion of the feature, and fire-cracked rock is present in its fill and at the bottom. Feature 6 is very close to Feature 7 in horizontal and vertical space. They are partially separated from each other by a thin (2–5 cm) lens of a brown/yellow sandy matrix. This separation is particularly clear around the center of the units in which the features occur; in other areas, the boundary between the bottom of Feature 6 and the top of Feature 7 is blurred (see Fig. 4-7 in Chap. 4).

The feature itself contains no *Phanourios* remains, 8 unidentifiable bird bones (1 burnt), 150 *Monodonta* (12, or 8%, burnt), 3 *Patella* (2 burnt), and eggshell fragments. If the immediately overlying matrix that may form the top of the feature is included, then 14 *Phanourios* bones (3 burnt, 1 individual), 53 bird bones of three birds (1 *Otis*, 1 *Columba*, 1 *Corvus*), 2 *Vipera* vertebrae, 573 *Monodonta* (88, or 15.4%, burnt), 12 *Patella* (3 burnt), 2 *Columbella*, 2 *Dentalium* (1 a bead), and 1 holed *Conus* may be added, although this material is not clearly associated. Likewise, 14 *Monodonta* (but no *Phanourios*) occur immediately below the feature.

Artifacts from the feature are restricted to 6 chipped stone items: 1 unifacial knife, 3 tertiary flakes, 1 secondary flake, and 1 microflake. Including the matrix above the feature adds another secondary flake. This upper portion also includes 2 waterworn igneous cobbles and 5 shell beads (2 *Columbella*, 2 *Dentalium*, and 1 *Conus*).

Several additional remains may be associated with the feature. These are either at the bottom of Feature 6 or the top of Feature 7, and we include them here. Although the features are separated by the thin layer described earlier, that layer is not sterile. Found between the features are the following: From N95E90, there are 21 *Phanourios* bones (16, or 76.2%, burnt), 4 bird bones (2 *Otis* individuals), 2 *Vipera* vertebrae, 404 *Monodonta* (39, or 9.7%, burnt), 7 *Patella* (1 burnt) and 1 *Columbella* (holed). Artifacts include 8 pieces of chipped stone (2 bladelets, 3 debris, and 3 microflakes) and 2 igneous cobbles. From N95E89, there are 247 *Phanourios* bones (193, or 78.1%, burnt), representing one individual, 12 bird bones (1 *Otis*), 3 *Monodonta*, and 1 *Patella*.

That so little of the shell is burned suggests that it may not be directly associated with the feature. Indeed, much of the shell may be remnants of Feature 5, the shell concentration. The small proportions of burned bone also argues against its being directly associated with the feature.

This feature is one of the better defined casual hearths at *Aetokremnos*. It appears to have a base of burned cobbles and ash; fire-cracked rock also occur within the feature. It probably functioned as an "opportunistic" hearth area.

Feature 7

Feature 7 is nearly a carbon copy of Feature 6. It, too, is a stone-filled casual hearth. Located immediately below Feature 6 (see Fig. 4-7 in Chap. 4), it is still in lower Stratum 2A. The feature is an oval ash stain whose core area is some 67 × 50 cm. It is about 20 cm thick. A number of stones are arranged so as to form a basin or stone-lined base. These stones are present only in the northwest end of the feature, however, and do not cover the entire base, thereby giving the impression of a less than elaborate preparation. A large basin-shaped stone, however, is present in the southeast end. These stones are all ash stained. Some *Phanourios* fragments (28) are at the very bottom of this area, where the ash stain is very well delineated.

The ashy matrix of the feature is dark gray/brown and fine grained. The bottom of the feature is not as clearly defined as it is at the top, and the feature cuts into the top of the bone midden in Stratum 4. As such, some of the bone associated with the feature may not represent a direct relationship; the feature, in cutting into the midden, may have churned up some underlying bone.

The core of the feature contains 344 *Phanourios* bones (338, or 98.2%, burnt), representing three individuals, and 53 bird bones (50, or 94.3%, burnt) (1 *Otis* and 1 Anseriform), and no chipped stone. The very bottom of the feature contains 28 *Phanourios* bones (see earlier); these may be intrusive from Stratum 4.

As with Feature 6, Feature 7 contains a cobble-lined bottom and fill. This attests to some preparation, if not elaborate construction. Feature 7 was deposited before Feature 6, but it is probable that only a very short period of time separated the construction and use of both features.

Feature 8

Feature 8 is the highest feature documented at *Aetokremnos*. It is a poorly delineated pit, beginning at the bottom of Stratum 1/2 (as does Feature 4, although in terms of absolute elevations Feature 8 is slightly higher) and cutting into the bone midden. It is about 35 cm deep. The western edge of the pit has been damaged by erosion, and this is where the feature is most poorly defined. It appears, however, to have been roughly bell shaped, although its edges are indistinct.

The stratigraphic situation of the pit is complex, for its construction disturbed underlying deposits and subsequent post-occupational erosion has confused the situation even more. The top of the pit is difficult to discern, but it appears to have been constructed at the bottom of Stratum 1/2, as noted earlier. It then cuts into Stratum 2A and apparently went through Stratum 2B and Stratum 3. Finally, the pit terminated in Stratum 4, cutting through a thin section of the crinkly Stratum 4A and into a small portion of the "proper" bone midden, Stratum 4B. Part of the feature's bottom is on top of a piece of rooffall that is seated almost on the floor of Stratum 4 (see Fig. 4-6 in Chap. 4). The edges of the feature are best defined in its eastern section, where its walls are quite steep.

The fill of Feature 8 is extremely loose unlike the surrounding matrix, which is much more compacted. The fill is dark brown/gray. A fair amount of root activity has probably darkened the matrix and contributed to its amorphous shape.

A relatively large amount of material was recovered from the feature's fill. We have divided the feature's contents into materials directly associated with its interior and those materials from the probable top of the feature and around its poorly defined edges.

From the interior, 168 (57, or 33.5%, burnt) *Phanourios* bones of one individual, 57 (16, or 28.1%, burnt) bird bones of two birds (1 *Otis*, 1 unidentified), 1 *Vipera* vertebra, and ?*Testudo* bones were recovered. Shells also were abundant, including 148 (13, or 8.8%, burnt) *Monodonta*, 5 (1 burnt) *Patella*, and 5 *Helix*. The area around the feature's edges and top contained 1,261 (338, or 26.8%, burnt) *Phanourios* bones of six individuals, 30 (9, or 30%, burnt) bird bones of six individuals (4 *Otis*, 2 Anseriforms), and 291 (19, or 6.5%, burnt) *Monodonta*, 17 (2 burnt) *Patella*, and 3 *Columbella* (1 burnt, all 3 stringable).

Thirty-five chipped stone artifacts were recovered in association with the feature (Table 5-6). These include 6 tools (2 thumbnail scrapers, 3 retouched blades, and 1 microlith-a truncation), which is a high proportion. Other materials include 2 secondary flakes, 1 tertiary flake, 2 secondary blades, 2 tertiary blades, 1 bladelet, 1 burin spall, 8 microflakes, 1 core, and 11 pieces of debris. One *Columbella* bead also was recovered from the mixed edge. Two waterworn igneous cobbles (1 broken) were present within the feature's fill as well.

Feature 8 is a confusing entity that was constructed late in the occupation of *Aetokremnos*. It is a deep pit, probably bell shaped, that cuts through several layers, terminating in the upper portion of the bone midden. The extremely ashy and dark nature of the

Table 5-6. Chipped Stone Artifacts from Feature 8

Type	In feature	Mixed	Top of feature	Total
Tools				
Thumbnail scrapers		2		2
Retouched blades	3			3
Microlith-truncation		1		1
Total tools	3	3		6
Debitage				
Secondary flakes	1		1	2
Tertiary flake	1			1
Secondary blades	1	1		2
Tertiary blades			2	2
Bladelet	1			1
Total debitage	4	1	3	8
Other waste materials				
Burin spall		1		1
Microflakes	4	1	3	8
Debris	3	2	6	11
Core			1	1
Total other waste	7	4	10	21
TOTAL	14	8	13	35

feature's matrix suggests a burning (cooking?) function, yet few of the food remains recovered from it are burned. This indicates a storage or disposal function. The presence of the dark matrix may support the latter interpretation to a slight degree. If the feature served as a disposal pit, it is likely that ashes and other charred matrix would have been included in the deposition of trash into the feature. This, however, is admittedly speculative. The indistinct nature of the feature's boundaries have been compounded by erosion. This feature is suitably distinct from the casual hearths at *Aetokremnos* to warrant a different functional interpretation, but one that we cannot convincingly explain.

Feature 9

The top of this small feature begins in Stratum 4A, and its bottom is within Stratum 4B; it is roughly 17 cm thick. The feature is primarily a concentration of bone within a very dark sand matrix. It is distinctive from its surrounding area both by this dark color and by the high density of bone as compared with the areas immediately surrounding it. The overall structure of this feature is quite similar to that of Feature 3, located approximately 1 m to the north. Feature 9 may represent a continuation of this feature. Its most striking difference from the other feature, however, is that the bone is not as burned or friable as it is in Feature 3.

Recovered from within the feature were 1,291 (596, or 46.2%, burnt) *Phanourios* bones of four individuals. From the area directly above the feature, and possibly intruding into it, were 217 (162, or 74.7%, burnt) (3 individuals) *Phanourios* bones and 20 (5 burnt) bird bones of three birds (2 *Otis*, 1 *Turdus*). One unburned *Monodonta* shell also was recovered. No chipped stone artifacts were associated with this feature. By way of comparison, the surrounding areas outside of the feature proper contained 878 (272, or 31%, burnt) (southern) and 117 (36, or 30.8%, burnt) (northern) *Phanourios* bones. The area below the feature is nearly solid bone, being part of the bone midden.

Feature 9 is an area of localized burning. It may have functioned as a casual hearth, although it differs from other of these features at *Aetokremnos* in that it contains no burned rock. It is in many ways more similar to a smaller version of Feature 3, a large area of intensely burned bone. Feature 9 may represent a southern extension of this concentration, separated by approximately 1 m of "normal" midden deposit.

Feature 10

Feature 10 is a well-defined ash stain (Fig. 5-4) that probably represents the bottom of a hearth. It is first visible at the bottom of lower Stratum 2A, and it cuts into Stratum 2B. It rests on top of the sterile Stratum 3, and it is approximately 9 cm thick. The stratigraphic situation of Feature 10 is somewhat complex in that it is associated with Locus 6, a probable patchy remnant of Stratum 2B (a burned red base), and Locus 7, a yellow matrix similar in color to Stratum 3, but not sterile.

Feature 10 is circular, with a diameter of 55 cm. It has a thin red edge along its northeastern perimeter. This edge is indistinct in the northwestern perimeter and absent in the southern edge. It probably is the result of burning. A large flat stone, about 55 × 30 × 14 cm, is located adjacent to the western periphery of the feature; the portion of it in Feature 10 is charred. This stone appears to be part of the feature, as the ash stain does not continue

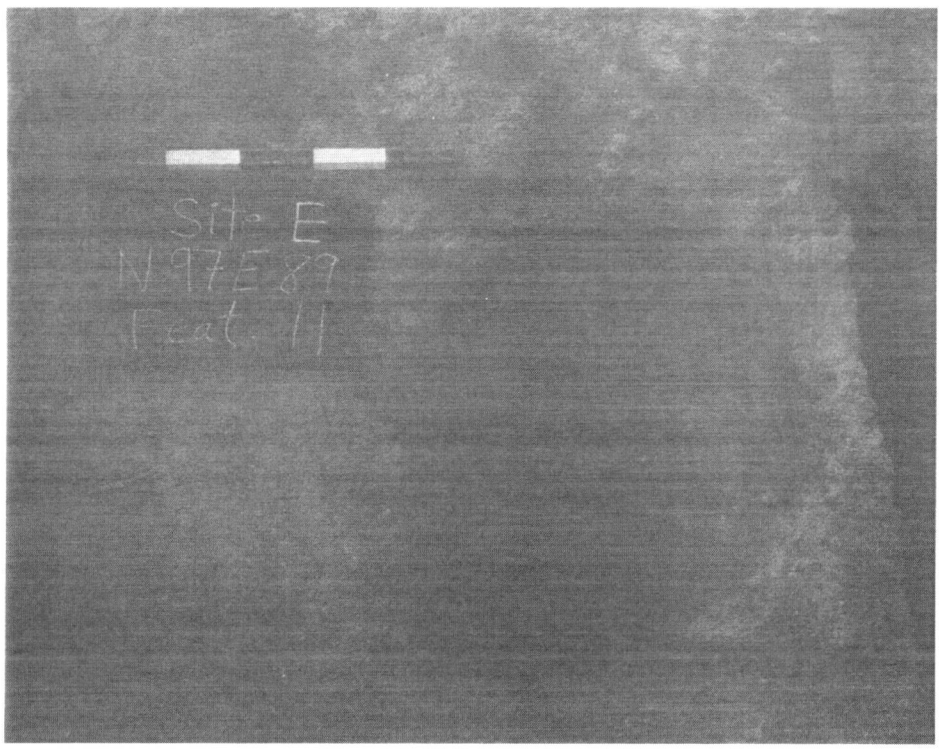

Figure 5-4. Feature 10 (field labeled as "Feature 11")—ash stain. Rod is 50 cm long.

under it. The feature's matrix is fine grained, ashy, and dark and yielded the oldest date at *Aetokremnos* (11,720 ± 240 years B.P., on charcoal, Beta-40380).

Beyond ash, the feature's content was limited. Two (both burned, 1 individual) *Phanourios* bones were recovered. The only *Mus* from the site was also found here, including burnt bones. There are 11 unburnt bird bones (1 individual, small passeriform) as well. One holed *Cerithium* (unburnt) also was present in the feature. No chipped stone is associated with the feature.

Feature 10 is the most "classic" hearth from *Aetokremnos* in that it is circular, well defined, and has a burned red edge partially preserved. Unlike other casual hearths at the site, it is distinct in that it is thin and does not contain burned stone.

Feature 11

Feature 11 is similar to Feature 10, but much more poorly preserved. It is located in lower Stratum 2A. Feature 11 is so poorly defined that we debated as to whether or not we should designate it a feature. It is suitably distinct from its surrounding areas, however, to warrant designation as a feature. The feature is a dark ash stain with traces of a burned, red base (Stratum 2B). It has a maximum thickness of about 13 cm. Much of the surrounding matrix is complicated by a stratigraphic situation in which Stratum 3, the sterile yellow layer, appears mixed with portions of lower Stratum 2A (and patches of Stratum 2B). Root activity also has disturbed the area encompassed by Feature 11.

Although the areas surrounding Feature 11 are rich in material, there is relatively little from the feature itself. No *Phanourios* remains, but 3 (all burnt) unidentifiable bird bones, 134 (112, or 84%, burnt) *Monodonta*, and 9 (8 burnt) *Patella* were recovered. That so much fauna are burned supports the interpretation of the area as a feature, probably a hearth. One microflake was recovered; this probably is intrusive.

Feature 11 probably functioned as a small hearth, as did Feature 10. As with that feature, it is defined by a circular ash stain rather than by the presence of burned rocks. Feature 11's poor preservation hampers a clearer understanding of its morphology or function. It does, however, contain a substantial amount of burned shell, suggesting that it functioned in the cooking of resources.

Possible Feature

One additional area was initially designated as a feature (originally Feature 5). It is located in a stratigraphically unclear area of the southeastern quadrant of N96E91. One source of the stratigraphic confusion was the presence of a huge piece of rooffall above the feature, which had disturbed and compacted the underlying deposits. It was first identified at the end of the 1988 season and was not excavated beyond a brief probe, largely owing to its inaccessibility because of the rooffall.

In 1988, the "feature" was described as a very dark (black), loose, and sandy matrix some 25 cm thick at its maximum. It appears to be directly related to the bone midden, but was distinct from it in that its matrix was much darker. A fairly large number of shell and chipped stone artifacts were associated, but due to limited exposure it was not known if there was a direct relationship. Root activity also was noted, which could have at least partially been responsible for the dark color.

Subsequent excavation in 1990 could not satisfactorily distinguish this feature's area from the surrounding area enough to warrant a feature designation. Although we initially thought that the "feature" was located at the top of the bone midden, we now could determine that this was not as clear as first believed. It appears more likely that it is a continuation of the cultural surface encompassed by Stratum 2A; as such, it could represent a continuation of Feature 4. The original assumption of a Stratum 4 association was due to the admixture and compaction of deposits, most of which was caused by rooffall and root activity. We have, thereby, decided to err on the conservative side and not consider this as a proper feature.

Feature Stratigraphy and Functional Relationships

A major question regarding the features at *Aetokremnos*, in addition to their specific functions, is their contemporaneity. Radiocarbon determinations were only directly available from two features (1 and 10); these fit comfortably within the range represented by all of the site's determinations. We have maintained elsewhere (see Chaps. 8 and 12) that although there are two primary occupations at *Aetokremnos*, represented by Strata 2 and 4, the chronological separation between these was brief and cannot be measured in radiocarbon years.

It is useful to compare the absolute elevations of the *Aetokremnos* features, especially their tops, in an attempt to establish a stratigraphically defensible construction chronology. This chronology can be used in determining a rough contemporaneity. We realize, of course, that people do not live on flat surfaces, just as they do not live in meter squares. The surfaces at *Aetokremnos* undulate. Part of this undulation is no doubt due to the distortion caused by massive rooffall, but even the floor of the shelter is not perfectly flat, thus a direct comparison of absolute elevations can be misleading. The natural slope of the shelter is such that the center-interior portion is lower than the southwestern edge, where a slight rise can be detected. Thus similar deposits on these surfaces will obviously have differing elevations, and one-to-one comparisons must be made cautiously. Furthermore, a comparison of the beginnings of the features is less than a precise measure because these tops are in many cases not clearly demarcated; indeed, in some instances (notably Feature 10), what is archaeologically present is probably the bottom of the feature. These caveats aside, it still is instructive to look at the absolute elevational range represented by the features. In Figure 5-5, we have plotted the absolute elevations of the approximate tops and bottoms of the features at *Aetokremnos,* irrespective of their horizontal location. The dashed lines are approximations.

The stratigraphic situation of the *Aetokremnos* features is relatively tight. Those features located in Stratum 2 cluster together, as do those in Stratum 4, and a pattern suggesting contemporaneity may be discerned. Features with the same top elevations, within an arbitrary ± 5-cm range, form four groups: 1, 4, and 7; 5, 6, and 8; 2 and 10; and 3 and 9. Only in Features 2 and 10 is this pattern inconsistent, because Feature 2 occurs in the upper portion of Stratum 4, and Feature 10 occurs in lower Stratum 2A. The upper elevations of Feature 2 are more consistent with a Stratum 2 placement. This can be explained in two ways. First, Feature 2 is located on the extreme southern edge of the shelter, where there is a rise in absolute elevation; consequently, all of the deposits there are higher than are those from within the interior. Second, Feature 2, excavated in 1988, had elevations taken from Datum C. We were unable to take a direct EDM reading on this datum, because it was located on a large piece of rooffall that had been rolled into the sea to provide access to underlying deposits. Consequently the "translation" to the EDM master elevation was based on measurements obtained using line levels, and some degree of inaccuracy may have been introduced.

Although the majority of the Stratum 2 and Stratum 4 features occur at roughly the same top elevations, it is clear from an examination of Figure 5-5 that both Features 10 and 11 were constructed earlier in the occupation of Stratum 2, with Feature 10 being the earliest (a fact supported by a radiocarbon determination). Those Stratum 2 features that intrude into Stratum 4 can be clearly identified in Figure 5-5, numbers 7 and 8. Note that the appearance of the bottom of Feature 10 cutting into Stratum 4 is an illusion, because Stratum 4 is lower in this portion of the site in terms of absolute elevations.

One can examine these data in more detail by comparing functional interpretations given to stratigraphically corresponding features. Given the small and restricted confines of the shelter, it is unlikely that only a portion of it was occupied during any one time. It is more likely that the entire shelter's area was used. Nonetheless, spatial patterning is apparent by looking at the stratigraphic and horizontal distributions of the features.

The uppermost features, numbers 5, 6 and 8, are all functionally distinct. All are located nearly adjacent to one another in the center of the shelter. Feature 5 is a shell

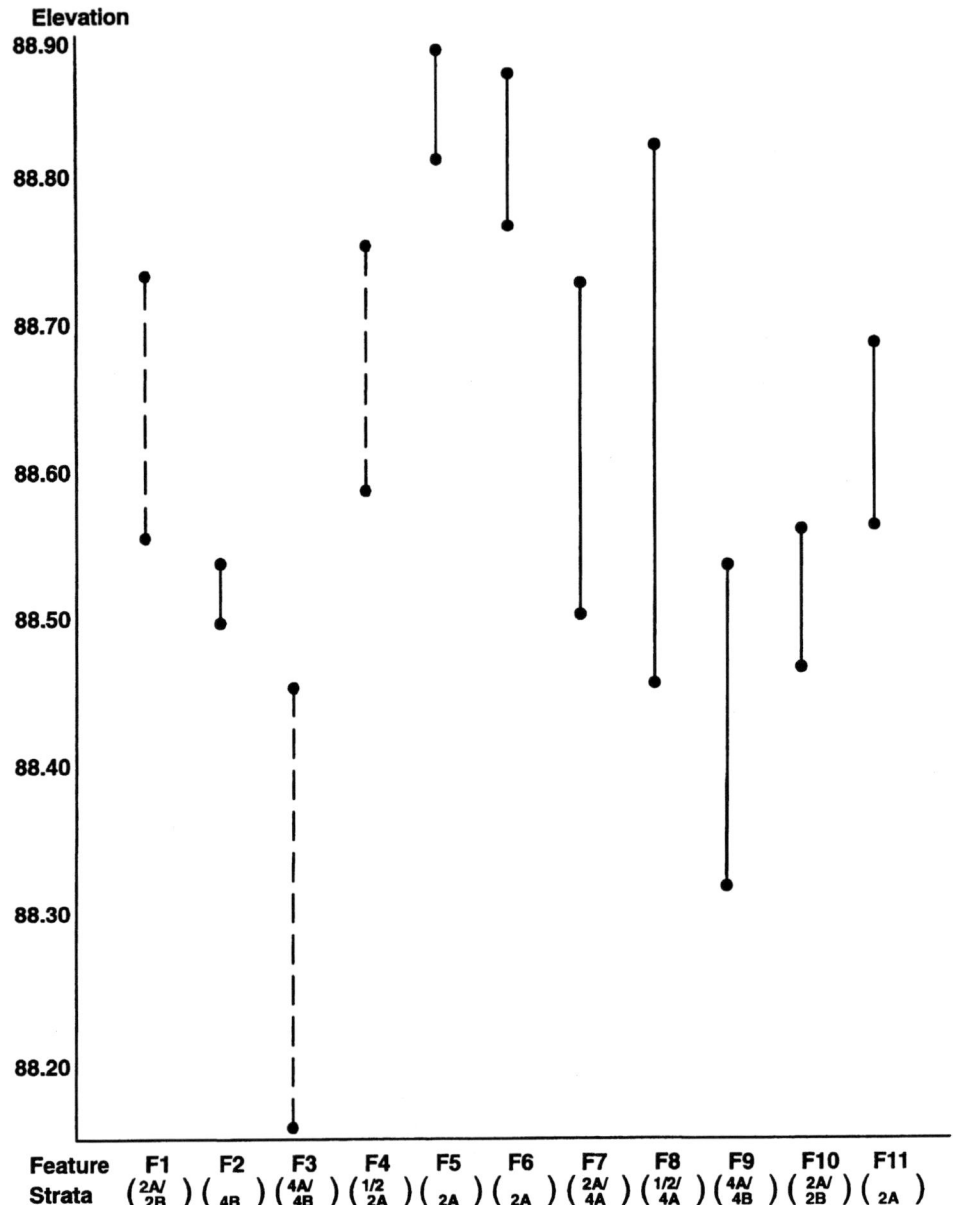

Feature Absolute Elevations

Figure 5-5. Feature absolute elevations. Dashed lines (⋮) are approximations.

concentration, Feature 6 is a casual hearth, and Feature 8 is a relatively deep pit. It is tempting to see a direct relationship between the shell deposit and the casual hearth because both contain abundant shell and are immediately adjacent. Shellfish may have been prepared in Feature 6, and once the meat was consumed, the shells could have been discarded, forming Feature 5. Or, depending on preparation techniques, meat to be cooked in Feature 6 may have been removed from the shells prior to cooking, forming the shell concentration (Feature 5). Feature 8 also is directly to the north and may have been functionally related as well.

A similar pattern can be seen with Features 1, 4, and 7, which also are all different from one another. Feature 1 is an ash heap and associated burned surface; Feature 4 is a probable continuation of 1, consisting of a burned surface and suggesting generalized activities by its lack of a specific focus; and Feature 7 is a casual hearth located over 1 m to the south, close to the front of the shelter. There is an inconsistency in the radiocarbon determinations between Feature 1 and 4, but it may be explained by the materials dated (see Chap. 8). If these features were deposited at the same time, they indicate functional segregation during this phase of occupation, suggesting cooking activities toward the front of the shelter, with deposits of ash and general maintenance activities toward the rear.

The remaining Stratum 2 features are stratigraphically separated, although we again caution that the time represented by this separation was very short. These features probably represent the first occupation that resulted in the formation of Stratum 2. Interestingly, these isolated features (numbers 10 and 11) are both hearth remnants that are distinct from the "rock-filled" casual hearths represented by Features 6 and 7. This differentiation could suggest a slightly less intense use of the shelter during its initial Stratum 2 occupation.

The three features located in Stratum 4 also are functionally distinct. One (Feature 2) is a casual hearth similar to the Stratum 2 rock-filled features; it is located near the southern edge of the shelter. This casual hearth is similar to those in Stratum 2 and supports an interpretation that similar activities took place during the short separation of the two strata. Feature 9 is a small concentration of burned bone located in the center of the shelter. It may be related to the other feature in Stratum 4 (no. 3), which is a widespread concentration of extremely charred bone located near the rear of the shelter. Feature 3 represents a much more intense activity, while Feature 2 and 9 reflect more limited, probably short-term (single?) episodes. If Feature 3 functioned as some sort of postconsumption bone-processing area, it is tempting to regard Feature 2 as an area where actual cooking of meat occurred, with the bones later being processed in Feature 3.

This discussion has offered some explanation of the vertical and horizontal spatial distribution of features at *Aetokremnos*. Certainly, alternate explanations may be equally plausible, but our reconstruction fits observed data patterns. These suggest functionally discrete areas of the site at various times during its short occupation. These areas are all related, in one way or another, to food processing, but they suggest differential spatial use through time, rather than a single pattern. There appears to be more diversity, as reflected by the features, during the latter occupation of the site, a period when we suspect that a wider range of resources were, indeed, being exploited.

In summary, the elevations of the features at *Aetokremnos* assist in determining their sequence of deposition. In some cases, features overlay others in the same units, but the absolute separation between them is small, suggesting only a short period between depositions. In other instances, the features appear to have been constructed in essentially the same occupational episode. The stratigraphic separation of features also has revealed some interesting patterns relating to their uses. A more complex, or at least diverse, usage pattern can be seen in the later occupations. This pattern may be related to a broadening of the resource base during this phase.

LOCI

Introduction

In addition to features, we identified several loci during the excavations. As used here, a *locus* is a stratigraphic abnormality, something that does not quite fit in with its surroundings. These abnormalities usually are thin lenses that are very poorly defined, difficult to trace, and cover only a small area. They are not formal enough to be considered features, having no clear patterning. Loci were identified in only four units, all contiguous and all in the most intact part of the shelter. Each locus was numbered by individual excavation unit.

Table 5-7. Chipped Stone Artifacts Associated with Loci

| | Unit/Locus | | | | | | |
| | N97E89 | | | | N97E90 | | |
Class	L. 1[1]	L. 2/7	L. 6[2]	L. 8	L. 1	L. 3	Total
Tools							
Side/end scrapers	2						2
Retouched blade	1		1				2
Retouched flake	1						1
Retouched bladelet	1						1
Total tools	5		1				6
Debitage							
Secondary flakes	1					2	3
Tertiary flakes	4		1			1	6
Secondary blades	1						1
Bladelets	6					1	7
Total debitage	12		1			4	17
Other waste materials							
Burin spalls	1	2	1	1		1	6
Microflakes	9		3			10	22
Debris	14		4		1	7	26
Core fragment	1						1
Total other waste	25	2	8	11	18	55	
TOTAL	42	2	10	1	1	22	168

[1]This material also was included in the summary for Feature 4.
[2]Includes material from all units.

Thus, Locus 2 in one unit does not equal Locus 2 in another. Table 5-7 lists chipped stone associated with loci, while Table 5-8 provides the same information for faunal remains.

Locus Descriptions

N97E89

Locus 1. Locus 1 is directly associated with Feature 4 and represents a patchy remnant of that feature. It occurs only in the northern half of the unit, and consists of a very ashy and loose matrix, with a thin red base. The red base appears to represent the remnants of Stratum 2B, as well as the base of Feature 4. The thin portion of red matrix that makes up most of Locus 1 is relatively well defined and is possibly the result of a single burning episode.

There is a fair amount of cultural material associated with this locus; this is not unusual considering the general richness of Feature 4. No faunal remains were directly associated with the locus. After all of N97E89 and adjacent units had been excavated, and

Table 5-8. Faunal Remains from Loci

Type	Unit / Locus							
	N97E89							
	1	2/7	3	4	5	6¹	8	
Phanourios			9 (7)	4 (2)			19 (19)	8 (1)
Bird			34 (12)		6 (2)		53 (14)	21 (3)
Eggshell				+ (+)			+	
Snake							2	
Monodonta			18 (10)	1 (1)	1 (1)	7 (1)	673 (145)	1
Patella			1				5 (2)	
Helix			1					
	N96E90							
		2	3	6				
Phanourios				9				
Bird		1 (1)	1					
Monodonta		1	4 (4)					
Patella			1 (1)					
	N97E90							
		1	2	3				
Phanourios		98 (89)		29 (29)				
Sus				2 (2)				
Bird				11 (4)				
Eggshell				+				
Monodonta		12 (2)	24 (2)	106 (73)				
Patella			1	1 (1)		7		

Note: Numbers in parentheses (x) refer to burned bones or shells and + refers to presence.
¹Includes material from all units.

loci information could be compared, it seems likely that Locus 1 is a segment of the widespread Locus 6. The major difference between the two loci is that Locus 1 is directly adjacent to Feature 4.

Locus 2.   Locus 2 is located in the southwestern portion of the unit. It is a yellow silty matrix that resembles the sterile Stratum 3. This locus, however, is clearly in Stratum 2A and is not sterile. After the unit was completely excavated, a comparison of all loci information indicated that Locus 2 was, in fact, a continuation of Locus 7, which occurs in the southeastern quadrant of the unit. Locus 7 is slightly higher in absolute elevation than is Locus 1, but there is no horizontal separation between the two. At the same approximate elevation and adjacent to these loci is Feature 10. Given that Loci 2 and 7 are essentially the same, we have combined materials from both Tables 5-7 and 5-8.

Locus 3.   This locus was identified in the western quadrants of the unit. In section it appeared as a yellow sandy lens, but on excavation its matrix was more like that of the "normal" Stratum 2A deposits. It underlies Locus 1 and overlies Stratum 2B in this unit.

Locus 4.   This locus was initially identified in the eastern section of N96E89 as an ash lens. It covers only a small portion of the northwestern quadrant (primarily in the southwestern portion of that quadrant). This locus is a very thin and ephemeral "stain."

Locus 5.   This is another very thin locus. It consists of a yellow matrix, appearing as a wedge-shaped lens in the southwestern corner of the southwestern quadrant of the unit.

Locus 6.   Locus 6 is the most widespread locus identified at the site, occurring in the center portion of four adjacent units. It consists of a compacted red patchy and sandy matrix with a silty composition. In all likelihood, it represents a mixture of lower Stratum 2A, Stratum 2B (the red base of Stratum 2), and the yellow sterile matrix of Stratum 3. Portions of Locus 6 actually occur in a disturbed, or mixed, Stratum 3. As noted earlier, it is likely that Locus 1 (in the northern portion of the unit) is a part of Locus 6, although the latter is stratigraphically higher by approximately 2 cm. On excavation, these two loci blended into one another. Locus 6 "proper," however, is slightly higher in the western units in which it occurs, sloping slightly downward to the east. This sloping suggests that it was not a level surface but rather undulated.

Locus 7.   Locus 7, situated in the southeast quadrant of the unit, consists of a fine yellow sand. It is stratigraphically below Locus 6 and, as noted previously, appears to represent a continuation of Locus 2. Both of these loci are adjacent to Feature 10, the circular remnants of a hearth. Both loci resemble Stratum 3, but they are not sterile.

Locus 8.   Locus 8 is a gray lens immediately below Stratum 2B and on top of Stratum 3. Like Loci 2 and 7, it may be associated with Feature 10; a few fire-cracked cobbles occur within its matrix. The locus occurs only in the western half of the unit. It is very thin in the northwest area of the unit, where it is underlain by a thin portion of Stratum 3. Moving south, it covers the top of Stratum 4A where there is no Stratum 3.

N96E90

Locus 1. Locus 1 occurs in the southwest quadrant of the unit. It consists of a light reddish-brown matrix that may be a segment of Stratum 2B, although it could be the remnants of a few decayed (and heated?) stones of the same color. Several small, unburned stones (about 5 cm in diameter) are present around this locus.

Locus 2. Locus 2 occurs in the north half and is a yellowish-brown, hard-packed matrix. It contains some fleks and stains of charcoal and is fine grained. Both Loci 1 and 2 also contain some "chunks" of sediment—about 1 cm in diameter—and both appear to be directly on top of Stratum 3, which is present in traces in this unit.

Locus 3. Locus 3 is a small but relatively thick (roughly 7 cm) locus situated in the eastern half of the unit. It is fine-grained, gray/brown ashy sediment that occurs beneath the main Stratum 2A deposits but above Stratum 4. The thickness of this locus and its contents suggest that it may have been the locus of a small single burning episode.

Locus 6. Locus 6 here is a continuation of the same locus initially identified in N97E89. It occurs only in the western 5 cm of the northwest quadrant of the unit; a small portion extended into the southwest quadrant as well. Unlike its richer expression in N97E89, only nine *Phanourios* bones occur here.

N96E89

Locus 6. Locus 6 is the only locus in this unit. It occurs in the north half of the unit as a very patchy and thin (2–4 cm) red lens.

N97E90

Locus 1. Locus 1 occurs in the northeast quadrant of the unit, primarily toward the eastern end. It forms a contact between lower Stratum 2A and the top of Stratum 4; Stratum 3 is present in this unit, but only in the western quadrants. In a sense, Locus 1 replaces Stratum 3 here, but it is not sterile, nor is it clearly defined. Its yellowish matrix consists of a somewhat compacted soil; this is clayey at the lowest point of the locus, where it forms the top of Stratum 4. Locus 1 overlies Locus 2, but its western end is level with that noncultural locus (see below). A relatively large amount of material is associated with this locus.

Locus 2. Unlike the other loci, Locus 2 in this unit is not the result of cultural activity. It is a north-south running channel of yellow matrix that appears to be waterlaid. It was first apparent in the east section of N98E90, but it is most clear in the east half of N97E90. It has a hard-packed clayey composition, is yellow in color (Munsell 2.5Y 6/4), and is sterile. To the south, the matrix becomes very soft and darker (Munsell 10 YR 4/2); this darkening is at least partially due to root activity. It is approximately 15 cm wide in the northeast corner and widens to about 25 cm to the south. In the southeast quadrant, it is disturbed. The channel cuts through the bottom of Stratum 2 and top of Stratum 4 in this unit. Locus 2 is similar to the area of water-lain activity (not given a locus number) that truncated Feature 1 in N98E88, but it affected a much smaller area and is better defined. The presence of a manifestation such as Locus 2 is evidence for the cause of some of the stratigraphic disturbance that can be seen in this portion of the site. It is nearly certain that the 24 *Monodonta* and 1 *Patella* associated with this locus are redeposited and not in situ.

Locus 3. Locus 3 occurs in the southwest quadrant of the unit, forming the separation between upper and lower Stratum 2A. It is patchy and discontinuous and is formed primarily by a red matrix similar to Stratum 2B. Despite its ephemeral nature, a relatively large amount of material is associated with Locus 3. The occurrence of such a large number of artifacts in a very restricted area supports a relationship with the artifact-rich Stratum 2A. The concentration of shell may suggest that localized shell-food preparation involving burning was a function within this locus.

Locus 6. Locus 6 in this unit is a continuation of the locus first identified in N97E89, therefore we have retained its "Locus 6" designation. It is a thin, dark band sandwiched within Stratum 3, which occurs only in the western portion of N97E90. Note that Locus 6 in the other units occurs in Stratum 2. The locus covers only the western half of the southwest quadrant of the unit.

Discussion

We have described a number of loci recorded within the interior of the *Aetokremnos* rockshelter. These loci are less distinct than features but nonetheless vary substantially enough from their surrounding matrices to be considered different. The loci most often are visible as thin lenses within the lower portions of Stratum 2. Only Locus 6 is relatively widespread, covering portions of four units. All of the loci (except a small portion of Locus 6) are clearly related to the Stratum 2 occupation of the site.

A major interpretive question is, What do the loci represent? Two scenarios come to mind immediately. First, they all are manifestations of a singular occupation; the fact that they are stratigraphically separated can be explained as being due to postoccupational disturbances, including roof-fall, root activity, water action, erosion, and deflation. All of these processes combined to produce an undulating and broken surface, with remnants of the principal activity area of Stratum 2 being represented by the loci, which are now not in situ. In other words, all the loci represent essentially the same occupational episode.

An alternate explanation is the one favored here. In this scenario, the loci are regarded as individual occupational episodes within the overall occupation of Stratum 2. The microstratigraphic separation is viewed as maintaining its integrity, with the majority of the loci reflecting the remnants of various short-term Stratum 2 occupations.

Resolving these alternate interpretations may be impossible. The time span involved is too short to be measured in radiocarbon years, as is readily evident by the series of determinations available for the site. A compelling argument against the disturbance hypothesis can be mounted, however. First, the generally intact nature of most of the loci must be considered. Although they may be ephemeral, they also are readily identifiable surfaces that do not evince massive disturbance. Furthermore, given the relative thickness of Stratum 2, it is unlikely that it was deposited in a single episode. This argument is further supported by the features, both in Strata 2 and 4, in which clear stratigraphic separation without intervening disturbance is apparent. Although the caveats against radiocarbon dating cited earlier must be borne in mind, the lowest feature (Feature 10) in Stratum 2 also has the site's oldest determination. If postoccupational disturbance had caused the stratigraphic imbalance between the loci, it is unlikely that features such as Feature 10 would have been preserved as intact as they are without undergoing the same disturbances. Likewise, although there is evidence for localized disturbance (such as Locus 2 in N97E90), the overall structure of the strata at *Aetokremnos* indicates in situ deposits. Although the patchy nature of most of the loci (as well as of some of the features) suggests that the deposits have been impacted to some degree, we feel that this impact was relatively minimal.

Given a careful examination of the available evidence, most of the loci at *Aetokremnos* seem to reflect individual intact depositions. The time span separating these, as with the features, may have been minimal, perhaps only a few years or less. Combined with the evidence from the features, the stratigraphic occurrence of the loci suggests a repeated occupation of the shelter over a relatively short time span.

If this is the case, one might ask how many individual episodes are represented. Given the stratigraphic evidence alone, based on absolute elevations, we suggest that at least five microstratigraphic episodes occurred. We calculated this by providing a plus or minus range of 5 cm to the top of each locus and examining the corresponding vertical separation and overlap. This plus or minus factor actually may be generous given that all of the loci occur within a range of approximately 40 cm.

Coupled with evidence from the features, these stratigraphic observations indicate that Stratum 2 was not deposited during a single occupational episode. Much more likely is a sequence of limited occupations relatively early in the formation of Stratum 2. This sequence culminated with the major occupation resulting in the widespread formation and deposition of Stratum 2.

Chapter 6

The Artifact Assemblage from Aetokremnos

CHIPPED STONE ARTIFACTS

Introduction and Terminology

There are no known Cypriot counterparts to the chipped stone assemblage from *Aetokremnos*. One might expect to find the closest assemblages to *Aetokremnos* from the Cypriot Aceramic Neolithic, but there are few similarities. As noted in Chapter 1, chipped stone has received little systematic attention in the Cypriot literature. Thus, because we are defining a new cultural phase at Akrotiri *Aetokremnos,* it is important to provide a thorough description of the most common cultural materials there, which consist of chipped stone artifacts.

The analytical method used on the *Aetokremnos* assemblage is technological and typological in nature (Bordes 1961; Brézillon 1971). It is based on the detailed Levantine classifications that deal with both Neolithic (cf. Gebel and Kozłowski 1994; Rollefson 1985:46–48; Rollefson and Simmons 1988:399–407; Simmons 1980) and earlier, primarily Epipaleolithic, materials (cf. Marks 1976; Marks and Simmons 1977; Tixier 1963).

Our description of the *Aetokremnos* chipped stone assemblage is based on a techno-typological system that considers reduction sequence as a primary analytical unit. This system is schematically illustrated in Figure 6-1. These categories, which include a variety of waste materials, are largely self-evident; definitions may be found in the references cited in the previous paragraph. Two groups, however, do require definition here. The first group is within debitage. As used here, a *primary* flake or blade is an artifact with at least 50% of its exterior surface covered with cortex. A *secondary* flake or blade has less than 50% cortex, while *tertiary* blades or flakes have no cortex. The amount of cortex on a blank relates to its place within the reduction sequence. Blanks containing substantial cortex suggest that initial core reduction occurred on site, while tertiary elements indicate more final blank production. Most of the tools from *Aetokremnos* were manufactured on tertiary blanks.

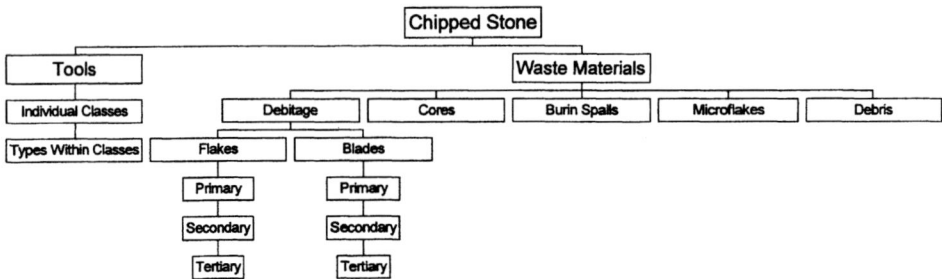

Figure 6-1. Schematic diagram of chipped stone typological system.

The second group is *microflakes*. Microflakes have an important interpretative element, suggesting either final tool manufacture or the resharpening of tools. In our usage, microflakes are less than 15 mm in length (cf. Chapman 1977:421; Schutt and Vierra 1980:47; Simmons 1982:193) and display characteristic debitage attributes, such as tiny bulbs and platforms.

Although waste materials make up the majority component in any chipped stone assemblage, tools are the most diagnostic component. In this analysis, a formal tool must exhibit deliberate modification in the form of retouch. In many Near Eastern assemblages, scrapers are a common tool class, and the most diagnostic element in the *Aetokremnos* assemblage is a type of scraper we have termed a *thumbnail* scraper. These tools are characterized by their small size and consistent edge retouch. A variety of other scraper types also occur in the assemblage. In our usage, a scraper must exhibit relatively invasive retouch on either the end or side of a blank. Unlike some analyses, the retouch must be well formed in order for a piece to qualify as a scraper. The presence of retouch alone is not enough; this retouch must be distinct.

A number of other tools classes also occur at *Aetokremnos*. These include a variety of burins, which are defined by their distinct beveled morphology, produced by striking a "burin spall" from an edge. Backed pieces exhibit abrupt, heavy retouch along an edge. Truncations are defined by the presence of lateral retouch across a distal end. Unifaces show retouch that covers an entire face of a blank. Bifaces, which exhibit complete retouch on both interior and exterior surfaces, are missing from the *Aetokremnos* assemblage, with the exception of one large bifacial axe made on a core. Multiple tools are those that contain elements of more than one type; at *Aetokremnos*, these take the form of burins combined with another type. Notches exhibit a characteristic retouched indentation somewhere along the surface.

A large category of tools includes retouched blades and flakes. These are perhaps the least diagnostic of tools and represent opportunistically manufactured expedient implements. The retouch forming these tools often is quite marginal, and, in some instances, it could be caused by use rather than by intentional modification. Indeed, another term for these tools could be *use modified pieces*, although we prefer the more neutral *retouched* designation. To qualify as such an implement, the retouch had to be visible to the naked eye. Microscopic wear analysis was not attempted on the *Aetokremnos* assemblage (although see discussion on Shea, following).

The final category of tools is microliths, which include several types. Microlithic implements are diagnostic elements in Epipaleolithic assemblages, and their presence can hint at a cultural affiliation. In the *Aetokremnos* assemblage, however, only 6 (4.7%) of the tools are microliths, 2 truncations, 1 trapezoid, 1 atypical lunate, and 2 retouched bladelets.

Attributes Monitored

In order to fully describe the *Aetokremnos* assemblage, we monitored several metrical and nonmetrical attributes on waste materials and the tools. Metrical attributes included standard length, width, and thickness measurements on tools and debitage. These attributes were not measured on debris or microflakes. Debris ("chips and chunks" or "shatter") by definition lacks clear length and width criteria. We did analyze a sample (from the 1990 excavation) of debris by three size categories: less than 5 mm, 5–15 mm, and greater than 15 mm. Microflakes, by definition less than 15 mm long, are invariably thin and narrow.

Several nonmetric attributes also were monitored. Three attributes were monitored on all chipped stone: raw material, burning, and patination. Raw material can indicate sources and trade. Heavily patinated pieces might suggest long surface exposure. Accordingly, if many buried pieces were patinated, it could indicate the mixing of deposits. The presence of burning could suggest intentional heat treatment. It also could indicate that some artifacts were either lost or intentionally disgarded in areas where burning occurred.

When present, the type of platform also was monitored. Platform type is a valuable clue to technological sophistication. On artifacts with platforms, the presence of lipping also was monitored.

The *Aetokremnos* Chipped Stone Assemblage—
A Descriptive Analysis

Table 6-1 summarizes the entire *Aetokremnos* chipped stone assemblage, while Figure 6-2 illustrates the breakdown of principal classes. Not included on Table 6-1, because they are not "chipped stone" sensu stricto, are two hammerstones. Both of these were recovered from the site's surface. The table provides artifact counts by stratum. In the following discussion, the assemblage is described as one unit. Although there is stratigraphic separation, we feel that the chipped stone materials from *Aetokremnos* represent a single assemblage. There is no discernible difference in either technology or typology between levels. In examining the two "pure" strata (Strata 2 and 4) with simple chi-square statistics, we were unable to detect any significant differences between major artifact classes (Table 6-2) from the two principal strata (2 and 4); we feel confident in describing this collection as one assemblage, produced by the same cultural group.

In some cases, the number of artifacts given for a particular class or grouping in the subsequent discussion may not exactly match that indicated in Table 6-1. This is because some pieces may inadvertently not have been included in a particular statistical analysis; they may have been out of the collection for illustration, or on display, for example. Finally, for length measurements, the number of specimens in some categories may exceed that given for complete pieces (theoretically the only pieces measured for length). However, in a few instances, given the orientation of a piece, it was possible to estimate approximate length without actually having the complete length present.

Table 6-1. Chipped Stone Assemblage Recovered from *Aetokremnos*

| | Stratum | | | | | Mixed Strata | | | | | |
Class	Surface	1	2	3	4	1/2	2/4	1–4	N	%	R%*
Tools											
Scrapers											
Thumbnail	3	2	20		4	5	2		36		28.1
Side			4			1	2		7		5.5
End			3						3		2.3
End/side			4						4		3.1
Scraper/plane	1								1		0.8
Scraper/knife			1						1		0.8
Burins	1	3	8			2		1	15		11.7
Burin on truncation			2				2		4		3.1
Burin on scraper			1						1		0.8
Backed pieces			1				1		2		1.6
Truncations					1	2			3		2.3
Unifacial knives			1					1	2		1.6
Pièce esquillée					1				1		0.8
Notches			2		1				3		2.3
Axe	1								1		0.8
Retouched blades	1	2	6		1	1	4	1	16		12.5
Retouched flakes	2	2	11		3	3	1		22		17.2
Microliths											
Trapezoid			1						1		0.8
Truncation			1				1		2		1.6
Lunate			1						1		0.8
Retouched bladelet			2						2		1.6
SUBTOTAL									128	12.5	100.1
Debitage											
Core trimming		1	2		2			1	6		
Core tablets			1						1		
Primary flakes	2		7		2		2		13		
Secondary flakes	10	9	40		11	2	5	2	79		
Tertiary flakes	7	8	92		26	20	7	4	164		
Secondary blades		1	6	1	2	1	2		13		
Tertiary blades	7	1	43		3	5	2	4	65		
Bladelets			24	1	7	4	4	2	42		
SUBTOTAL									383	37.5	
Other waste											
Burin spalls			14		1		1		16	1.6	
Microflakes	1	7	122	1	20	11	14	2	178	17.5	
Debris	3	11	196		34	30	13	9	296	29.0	
Cores	3		12		1	2	2		20	1.9	
SUBTOTAL									510	50.0	
TOTAL									1021	100.0	

*R% refers to tools only.

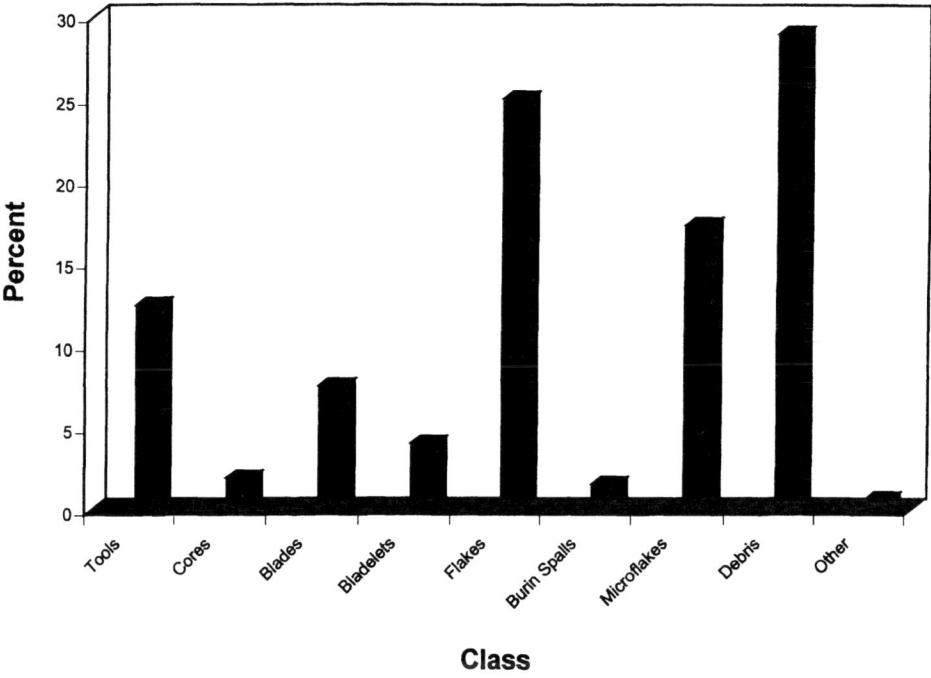

Figure 6-2. Breakdown of chipped stone classes, using bar graph.

Nonmetric Technological Observations

Debris.   Most of the debris falls into the two smaller size classes. Only slightly over 10% is larger than 15 mm. Although debris from 1987 and 1988 was not recorded in this manner, it, too, conformed to this general pattern. The size of debris suggests that the technological emphasis at *Aetokremnos* was toward final, rather than initial, reduction. This observation is born out by the relatively small number of primary elements. The presence of cores, however, indicates that some initial reduction probably also occurred at the site.

Raw Material.   No exotic materials that indicate a non-Cypriot source, such as obsidian, occur at *Aetokremnos.* All of the material is locally available. It is important to note, though, that the Akrotiri Peninsula contains no sources of raw material; the closest sources would be to the north, at the beginning of the Peninsula. Here, on the western side of the Peninsula, the Kouris (Lykos) River empties into Episkopi Bay, while on the eastern side, the Garyllis River enters Akrotiri Bay. Both rivers, which at present only sporadically contain water, could have brought suitable raw materials down from the Troodos Range. Conceivably, nodules also could have been washed onto beaches of the Peninsula after having been "flushed" out of the rivers.

Table 6-2. Chi-Square Statistics by Major Stratum on Tools (Upper) and Debitage (Lower)

	Tools			
Strat	OT	SC	Total	
2	38	31	69	
	(55.1)*	(44.9)	(100.0)	
4	7	4	11	
	(63.6)	(36.4)	(100.0)	
Total	45	35	80	
	(52.3)	(43.7)	(100.0)	
	Value	Degree of Freedom	Prob	
Pearson chi-square	0.283	1	0.595	
Yates corrected chi-square	0.042	1	0.838	

	Debitage						
Strat	BL	BS	CO	DE	FL	MF	Total
2	75	14	14	198	143	125	569
	(13.2)	(2.5)	(2.5)	(34.8)	(25.1)	(22.0)	(100.0)
4	12	1	1	34	39	20	107
	(11.2)	(0.9)	(0.9)	(31.8)	(36.5)	(18.7)	(100.0)
Total	87	15	15	232	182	145	676
	(12.9)	(2.2)	(2.2)	(34.3)	(26.9)	(21.5)	(100.0)
	Value	Degree of Freedom	Prob				
Pearson chi-square	7.135	5	0.211				

Key: OT = Other tools, SCR = scrapers, BL = blades, BS = burin spalls, CO = cores, DE = debris, FL = flakes, MF = microflakes.
*Raw % in parentheses.

There are essentially five general raw material types available to flint knappers in Cyprus: cherts from the Lefkara chalks, the Mamonia formation, the Perapedhi Formation, jaspars, and silicified umbers. By far the most widespread is the Lefkara formation, which occurs in three units: lower, middle, and upper. Cherts from the lower unit often occur in large nodules and thin beds and are pink to brown in color. Those from the middle units also occur in large nodules (but not as large as in the lower unit) and thin beds; they are often white, gray, or light brown in color. The upper unit consists of massive marly chalks and contains virtually no cherts. There is, thus, a wide range of color variability within the Lefkara cherts. Lefkara cherts are favored raw materials because they occur in large nodules and have not been deformed since their formations. Mamonia cherts occur in smaller nodules and often are deformed and brittle; thus they occur less commonly in archaeological assemblages. Cherts from the Perapedhi Formation are rare, occurring only in the southwest. Jaspars occur in three color varieties: reds, greens, and yellows. They are igneous and are found between the pillow lavas of the Troodos. Finally, the silicified umber is quite the rarest material; it also occurs in the Troodos, sitting on the pillow lavas (Xenophontos, personal communication 1991).

Some researchers have recorded the presence of the specific types of flint mentioned earlier in Cypriot assemblages. For example, Fox observed that Lefkara and Moni flints are the dominant types at the Aceramic Neolithic site of Kholetria *Ortos* (Fox 1988:29-30). Note that Fox separated Moni from Mamonia cherts, although Xenophontos felt that Moni was essentially a clay deposit with incorporated mamonia rocks in it (Xenophontos, personal communication 1991). In the present analysis, we did not feel that sufficient information existed to specify particular types. Accordingly, we monitored the color of the raw material, without giving it a particular type name

Dr. Costas Xenophontos, of the Cyprus Geological Survey, examined a sample of the *Aetokremnos* chipped stone. The vast majority is Lefkara, while a few pieces are Mamonia cherts. Rare, but present, are pieces of silicified umber, serpentinite, dense limestone, chalk, and at least one piece of chalcedonized silica, from an igneous formation.

It is clear that a wide range of raw material was used by the inhabitants of *Aetokremnos*, although most were from Lefkara cherts. Overall, the material is fine grained and easily knappable. Table 6-3 shows the range of raw materials present, by debitage, cores, and tools. There is no pattern readily apparent. The only preference is for gray flint, which comprises nearly 20% of the debitage and over 25% of the formal tools. Within debitage types, gray materials are again the most preferred. Tan cherts do show a higher occurrence on

Table 6-3. **Raw Material Selection for Debitage, Cores, and Tools**

Type	Debitage		Tools		Cores	
	N	%	N	%	N	%
Red	75	8.6	13	10.1	4	20.0
White	97	11.1	16	12.5	2	10.0
Gray	173	19.9	33	25.8	2	10.0
Pink	63	7.2	1	0.8	0	0.0
Tan	96	11.0	16	12.5	1	5.0
Brown	92	10.6	18	14.1	4	20.0
Caramel	32	3.7	8	6.3	0	0.0
Cream	8	0.9	2	1.6	0	0.0
Mottled black	11	1.3	0	0.0	0	0.0
Mottled red	45	5.2	7	5.5	1	5.0
Mottled gray	49	5.6	2	1.6	0	0.0
Mottled white	34	3.9	3	2.3	1	5.0
Mottled pink	16	1.8	1	0.8	2	10.0
Mottled tan	17	2.0	3	2.3	1	5.0
Red brown	5	0.6		0.0		0.0
Mottled brown	7	0.8		10.8		15.0
Banded white	1	0.1	0	0.0	0	0.0
Banded red	0	0.0	1	0.8	0	0.0
Banded black	1	0.1	0	0.0	0	0.0
Quartzite	13	1.5	0	0.0	1	5.0
Limestone	4	0.5	0	0.0	0	0.0
Other	32	3.7	3	2.3	0	0.0
TOTAL	871	100.0	128	100.1	19	100.0

bladelets than noted for this material in other classes. There is a high number (23%) of microflakes that occur on gray cherts; this is consistent with the large number of tools manufactured from the same material.

Although the number of cores at *Aetokremnos* is small (*N*=20), the pattern of raw material selection used in these artifacts does not closely match that seen in debitage and tools. For example, 20% of the cores are brown cherts, while only slightly over 10% of the debitage and 14% of the tools were manufactured from this material. Furthermore, 10% of the cores are on a mottled pink chert, while less than 2% and 1% of debitage and tools, respectively, occur on the same material. Given the small sample size of cores, however, these can only be general observations.

Table 6-4 shows the raw material preferences for the major tool classes. Once again, the gray cherts form approximately 25% of each category. Nonthumbnail scrapers, however, show an even higher (43.8%) preference for this material. Although only six microlithic implements were recovered, all were manufactured on high-quality materials. Two of the six were manufactured from a fine caramel-colored chert, which is perhaps the finest quality raw material in the entire assemblage. Thumbnail scrapers figure prominently in the *Aetokremnos* assemblage. There is, however, no special raw material preference, with the majority being manufactured on gray and white cherts.

It is also useful to compare burins with burin spalls. One might reasonably assume that there would be a concordance of raw materials here because burin spalls occur in the manufacture of burins. In general terms, this is the case. For example, 20% of the burins are on white chert, as are 18.8% of the burin spalls. This pattern also occurs with gray and brown cherts, but it is less marked. There are, however, some more pronounced differences.

Table 6-4. Raw Material Preference for Major Tool Classes

	TS		OS		B		RF		RB		ML	
Type	N	%	N	%	N	%	N	%	N	%	N	%
Red	4	11.1	1	6.2	1	5.0	4	18.2	1	6.3	1	16.7
White	6	16.6	0	0.0	4	20.0	1	4.5	4	25.0	0	0.0
Gray	9	25.0	7	43.8	4	20.0	6	27.3	4	25.0	1	16.7
Pink	1	2.8	0	0.0	0	0.0	0	0.0	0	0.0	0	0.0
Tan	4	11.1	1	6.2	3	15.0	3	13.6	1	6.3	1	16.7
Brown	6	16.6	3	18.8	2	10.0	4	18.2	1	6.3	1	16.7
Caramel	2	5.7	2	12.5	0	0.0	1	4.5	0	0.0	2	33.3
Cream	0	0.0	0	0.0	0	0.0	0	0.0	2	12.5	0	0.0
Mottled red	2	5.7	1	6.2	1	5.0	1	4.5	0	0.0	0	0.0
Mottled gray	0	0.0	0	0.0	1	5.0	1	4.5	0	0.0	0	0.0
Mottled brown	0	0.0	0	0.0	1	5.0	0	0.0	0	0.0	0	0.0
Mottled white	1	2.8	0	0.0	1	5.0	1	4.5	0	0.0	0	0.0
Mottled pink	0	0.0	0	0.0	0	0.0	0	0.0	1	6.3	0	0.0
Mottled tan	0	0.0	1	6.2	1	5.0	0	0.0	0	0.0	0	0.0
Banded red	0	0.0	0	0.0	0	0.0	0	0.0	1	6.3	0	0.0
Other	1	2.8	0	0.0	1	5.0	0	0.0	1	6.3	0	0.0
TOTAL	36	100.0	16	99.9	20	100.0	22	99.8	16	100.3	6	100.1

Key: TS = thumbnail scrapers, OS = other scrapers, B = burins, RF = retouched flakes, RB = retouched blades, ML = microliths.

For example, 18.8% of the burin spalls are on red chert, while only one burin (4.8% of burins) is. The same pattern also occurs with mottled white chert.

Overall, we see little patterning reflected in raw material selection. The most commonly available materials were those most frequently used in the manufacture of tools. The wide range of materials present in the assemblage suggests an expedient technology in which easily available materials were used, as long as they were of sufficient quality.

Other Nonmetric Attributes.   Table 6-5 summarizes other nonmetric attributes. Burnt artifacts may indicate heat treatment or simply reflect fortuitous situations in which artifacts were discarded into trash or hearth areas where burning occurred. Between 20 and 30% of tools, debitage, and cores was burned. These data do not appear to reflect specialized heat treatment.

Patination suggests prolonged exposure on an open surface, although patinated artifacts also could have been produced from already patinated raw materials. If a large number of

Table 6-5.   Miscellaneous Attribute Information, Burning, Patination, Completeness of Debitage and Tools

	Debitage		Cores		Tools	
Burning	*N*	%	*N*	%	*N*	%
Burned	261	30.0	4	20.0	33	26.0
Not burned	610	70.0	16	80.0	94	74.0
TOTAL	871	100.0	20	100.0	127	100.0
Patination	Debitage		Cores		Tools	
Patinated	78	9.0	4	20.0	18	14.2
Not patinated	793	91.0	16	80.0	109	85.8
TOTAL	871	100.0	20	100.0	127	100.0
Completeness	Debitage		Tools			
Complete	176	46.4	45	35.4		
Broken	203	53.6	82	64.4		
TOTAL	379	100.0	127	100.0		

Tool completeness	TNS		OS		Burins		RB		RF		ML	
Complete	21	58.3	5	31.3	7	36.8	1	4.5	3	18.8	5	83.3
Broken	15	41.7	11	68.7	12	63.2	21	95.5	13	82.1	1	16.7
TOTAL	36	100.0	16	100.0	19	100.0	22	100.0	16	100.0	6	100.0

Debitage completeness	Flakes		Blades		Bladelets		Others	
Complete	123	48.4	26	33.8	20	48.8	7	100.0
Broken	131	51.6	51	66.2	21	51.2	0	0.0

Key: TNS = thumbnail scrapers, OS = other scrapers, RB = retouched blades, RF = retouched flakes.

artifacts were patinated, it could indicate contamination from open-air surface sites. The proportions of patinated artifacts are relatively small, although they exceed 10% in each class. We do not interpret this as indicative of contamination from other localities.

By far the most common type of platform was the simple, single platform, accounting for nearly 50% of both tools (42.4%) and debitage (45.7%). Punctiform platforms also were common (8.5% tools, 13.0% debitage), attesting to the precise bladelike nature of some of the assemblage, and suggesting that indirect percussion flaking was a common occurrence. A variety of other platform types, such as dihedral, multiple, and cortical, were present in low frequencies. Crushed platforms were relatively common (10.2% tools, 21.9% debitage), as were unidentifiable types (35.6% tools, 13.4% debitage).

If platform lipping implies a soft-hammer technique (Crabtree 1972:44, 74), use of this technique was a rarity at *Aetokremnos*. Only 15.5% of the debitage and 7.1% of the tools were lipped, suggesting that such a technique, which can result in the production of long and thin blanks (Bordaz 1970:25), was not favored at the site. In fact, however, several such blanks are present, although they are not lipped, which calls into question the reliability of this attribute as a precise marker for the production of these blanks, at least for the *Aetokremnos* assemblage.

A large percentage of the *Aetokremnos* tools and debitage is broken (Table 6-5). The fact that proportionally more tools are broken than debitage may suggest that tools were discarded once broken. The high number of broken implements supports the idea that the site functioned primarily as a work area.

It is useful to look at this variable in more detail. Of the major tools classes, only thumbnail scrapers and microliths (hampered by a small sample size of only six) contain a more than 50% proportion of complete pieces (58.3% and 83.3% respectively). This percentage may indicate that the scrapers were more valuable tools and that, if broken, they may have been rejuvenated for further use, which also could help to account for their small overall size. Other tools, perhaps easier to expediently manufacture, were possibly discarded immediately on being broken.

Among the debitage classes, there is no immediately discernible pattern between broken and complete pieces. Approximately half of the flakes and one-third of the blades are complete, thus resulting in a relatively large number of usable, complete blanks that were not further modified into formal tools. Most of the cores are complete, and few are exhausted. These observations imply that raw material conservation and efficient reduction were not primary concerns, which is somewhat surprising, considering that the nearest sources of raw materials were at the beginning of the Akrotiri Peninsula, some 15 km to the north of *Aetokremnos*.

Debitage Metric Observations

Table 6-6 provides summary statistical information on key metrical observations on the *Aetokremnos* debitage. Although flakes outnumber blades and bladelets by more than two to one (2.1:1), there is no denying the bladelike character of this assemblage. That the distinction between blade and flakes is "real" is clearly born out by comparing the metric observations on these artifacts. Those blades that do occur in the *Aetokremnos* assemblage are generally long and thin. This is clear by examining the length, width, and thickness measurements (Table 6-6A), as well as those for the platforms (Table 6-6B). Blade and

Table 6-6. Debitage Length, Width, and Thickness and Platform Attributes

(A) *Debitage metrics*	Blades			Bladelets			Flakes		
	Length	Width	Thickness	Length	Width	Thickness	Length	Width	Thickness
N	26	73	76	20	41	41	138	188	253
Mean	44.2	16.2	4.4	23.1	9.0	2.9	28.9	23.2	5.7
SD	14.6	3.6	2.3	6.5	2.1	1.2	13.2	8.7	3.4
Minimum	22.0	7.9	1.2	13.3	4.7	0.9	8.4	8.5	1.4
Maximum	84.9	27.8	12.6	34.4	12.0	6.4	76.3	68.3	20.1

(B) *Platform metrics*	Blades	Bladelets	Flakes
Length			
N	19	8	69
Mean	7.3	4.4	11.2
SD	4.6	1.9	7.0
Minimum	1.6	2.2	2.7
Maximum	20.8	7.9	33.1
Width			
N	19	8	77
Thickness			
Mean	3.4	2.3	4.9
SD	2.4	0.5	3.1
Minimum	0.9	1.7	0.9
Maximum	11.2	2.9	15.5

Note: Measurements are in mm. In some instances, length *N* may exceed number of complete pieces because this variable could be measured on nearly complete artifacts (p. 000).

bladelet platforms are always narrower and thinner than are flake platforms. These observations attest to a true blade technology rather than the fortuitous production of blades. The ratios of width to length amongst blades (0.37), bladelets (0.39), and flakes (0.91) further confirm that blades were an intentional end product.

The sample of cores from *Aetokremnos* is small (Table 6-7). Considering their scarcity, metric observations are less meaningful than are those for debitage. Cores tend to be large, but there is a wide range in all measurements (mean length = 45.1, mean width = 35.1, mean thickness = 18.1, *N* = 19). What is unusual about the *Aetokremnos* cores is that 25% are bladelet forms; if one includes the fragmentary and exhausted specimens, this figure jumps to 45%. Although bladelets are common in the assemblage, they are not as abundant as these figures would suggest. It may be that some of the cores classified as bladelet forms actually represent extremely reduced or exhausted cores. This, however, does not appear to be the case, as the bladelet cores recorded exhibit clear bladelet scars. Furthermore, the typology of cores represents a wide range, with 15% being simple "test for material" cores, which have had only one or two flakes removed. It may be that some of the *Aetokremnos* cores were being efficiently reduced to a point of exhaustion, but this certainly is not the case for all specimens. This condition is in marked contrast to the tested sites, where exhausted cores are extremely abundant.

Only two hammerstones are present in the *Aetokremnos* assemblage. Both are from surface contexts and had been collected prior to our excavations; both are gray chert. One

Table 6-7. Core Typology

Type	N	%
Single platform	1	5
Globular	3	15
Multidirectional	3	15
Bladelet	5	25
Subdiscoial	1	5
Fragment/exhausted	4	20
Material test	3	15
TOTAL	20	100

hammerstone is spherical in morphology and is severely battered. Its dimensions are 56 × 51 × 37 mm. It is patinated but not burned. The other hammerstone is elongated, with a chipped end that may have functioned as a chopping tool. It is 92 × 52 × 30 mm; it is not burned or patinated.

Tools

Formal, retouched, tools comprise 12.6% of the *Aetokremnos* assemblage. By contemporary Levantine or Anatolian standards, there is little that this tool assemblage stands apart in; typologically, it would fit comfortably within late Epipaleolithic or early Neolithic assemblages (see Chap. 11). When compared with Cypriot chipped stone tools, however, the *Aetokremnos* tools have few counterparts.

A detailed typology of all the tools from *Aetokremnos* is provided in Table 6-8, while Table 6-9 gives summary metrics. The tools are dominated by thumbnail scrapers, which form nearly 30% of the tools. Burins also are common, as are other scraper forms. Together, retouched blades and flakes make up nearly 30% of the assemblage. Perhaps most distinctive in this assemblage, apart from the thumbnail scrapers, is the low but consistent number of microlithic tools (nearly 5% of tools). These tools suggest intriguing links to contemporary mainland cultures.

Tools as a group were manufactured on a wide variety of debitage blanks, and there is no specific preference. For example, 31.2% of the tools were made on blades (all tertiary) and 4.7% on bladelets, while 63.3% were made on flakes (0.8% cortical, 21.9% secondary, and 40.6% tertiary). These proportions match rather closely those of usable but unretouched debitage blanks.

By far the most common form of retouch are invasive types, comprising over 55%. This situation is not unexpected because scrapers also make up about 40% of the tools, and this type of retouch is a defining criteria for scrapers in the approach used here. Semisteep and steep forms of retouch also are common (18.3%), as is abrupt retouch (12.9%). Marginal retouch, which some researchers equate with "use-wear" rather than formal retouch, is frequent, but accounts for only slightly over 10% of the retouch types.

All of the retouch types identified here are based on observations made with the naked eye. We did not conduct an microscopic wear studies for a variety of reasons, including

Table 6-8. Detailed Tool Typology

Type	N	% of Class
Thumbnail scrapers		
Side	1	
End	5	
Side/end	25	
Variant 1	4	
Variant 2	1	
Subtotal	36	28.1
Other scrapers		
End	3	
Side	7	
Side/end	4	
Scraper plane	1	
Scraper/knife	1	
Subtotal	16	12.5
Burins		
Single blow, straight	8	
Multiple blow, straight	2	
Single blow, angle	3	
Multiple, dihedral	1	
Dihedral	1	
Single, on truncation	3	
Double, on truncation	1	
Angle, on side scraper	1	
Subtotal	20	15.6
Truncations		
Straight	2	
Convex	1	
Subtotal	3	2.3
Notches	3	2.3
Axe	1	0.8
Unifacial knife	2	1.6
Backed pieces	2	1.6
Pièce esquillée	1	0.8
Retouched blades	16	12.5
Retouched flakes	22	17.2
Microliths		
Lunate	1	
Trapezoid	1	
Truncation	2	
Retouched bladelets	2	
Subtotal	6	4.7
TOTAL	128	100.0

Table 6-9. Metrics on Major Tools Classes, Excluding Thumbnail Scrapers

Class	Complete			Broken		
	Length	Width	Thickness	Length	Width	Thickness
Other scrapers		$N = 5$			$N = 9$	
Mean	47.7	26.8	11.1	25.4	21.1	6.8
SD	24.6	14.0	11.2	7.1	6.0	2.1
Minimum	31.5	16.0	3.8	16.0	13.9	2.8
Maximum	90.1	48.7	30.3	34.0	32.0	9.2
Burins		$N = 7$			$N = 10$	
Mean	43.6	20.8	8.5	31.3	20.5	6.0
SD	11.1	4.7	3.3	15.4	5.3	2.1
Minimum	23.0	12.7	4.8	11.0	12.2	2.5
Maximum	54.4	26.8	13.9	62.0	31.2	9.4
Retouched blades		$N = 3$			$N = 13$ (12 for Length)	
Mean	75.5	29.1	11.8	43.1	22.2	6.1
SD	26.6	9.9	8.5	15.2	4.9	3.1
Minimum	57.2	20.6	6.1	16.0	13.1	2.6
Maximum	106.0	40.0	21.6	72.0	29.6	14.4
Retouched flakes		$N = 1$			$N = 19$	
Mean	34.1	20.4	7.4	22.2	19.7	7.2
SD	—	—	—	9.6	6.5	3.2
Minimum	34.1	20.4	7.4	9.0	9.5	2.2
Maximum	34.1	20.4	7.4	41.0	36.7	12.4

financial considerations, and the fact that it is difficult to remove large numbers of artifacts from Cyprus, which would have been necessary for such specialized studies. We did, however, have a small sample (three artifacts) examined Dr. J. Shea (1989). The sample consisted of 1 pointed blade (not classified as a tool), 1 thumbnail scraper, and 1 side scraper. His observations are of some interest and are summarized as follows.

On the distal part of the right edge of the pointed blade, Shea noted a concentration of small feather-terminated flakes arrayed in a close patterns. Although these scars are not pronouncedly rounded, there appears to be a band of matte-reflecting abrasion running along this edge. Such a wear pattern is matched on experimental tools used to cut thick or dried hide/leather. From these observations, Shea felt confident in interpreting the artifact as a "hand-held knife" worn from skin cutting. He noted that such a wear pattern usually does not appear until after more than 15–20 minutes of concentrated use. Turning to the thumbnail scraper, he noted a pattern of edge rounding and striations that suggest scraping activities. Typically, scraping a dry hide or dehairing an animal skin for only a brief period (less than 10 minutes) would result in a much more pronounced degree of rounding, thus leading Shea to conclude that the tool was used to scrape a very fresh skin, in which case the presence of animal fats might retard the rate at which edge abrasion formed. The tool's small size also suggested to Shea that it might have been hafted. Finally, on the side scraper, there is a very weak pattern of matte-reflecting abrasion that suggests it was used in longitudinal cutting. Although he could not match this pattern on an individual worked-material category in his experimental reference collection, Shea felt that it was probably used to cut some material of "medium" resistance, possibly cartilage, dry skin, or softer fresh wood (Shea 1989).

Although the sample size was abysmally low, these results are consistent with an interpretation of cutting fresh hide (the thumbnail scraper) and dry hide or leather. The fact that the blade exhibited some wear also indicates that many of the formally unretouched debitage blanks may well have functioned as expedient cutting implements.

The remainder of this discussion refers to individual tool classes.

Thumbnail Scrapers. Because thumbnail scrapers are such a distinctive element of the assemblage, they are described in greater detail here than are other tools. These tools are consistently well manufactured. They fall into five specific types (see Table 6-8 and Figs. 6-3 and 6-4), with side/end forms being dominant (nearly 70% of this class) (Fig. 6-3). The

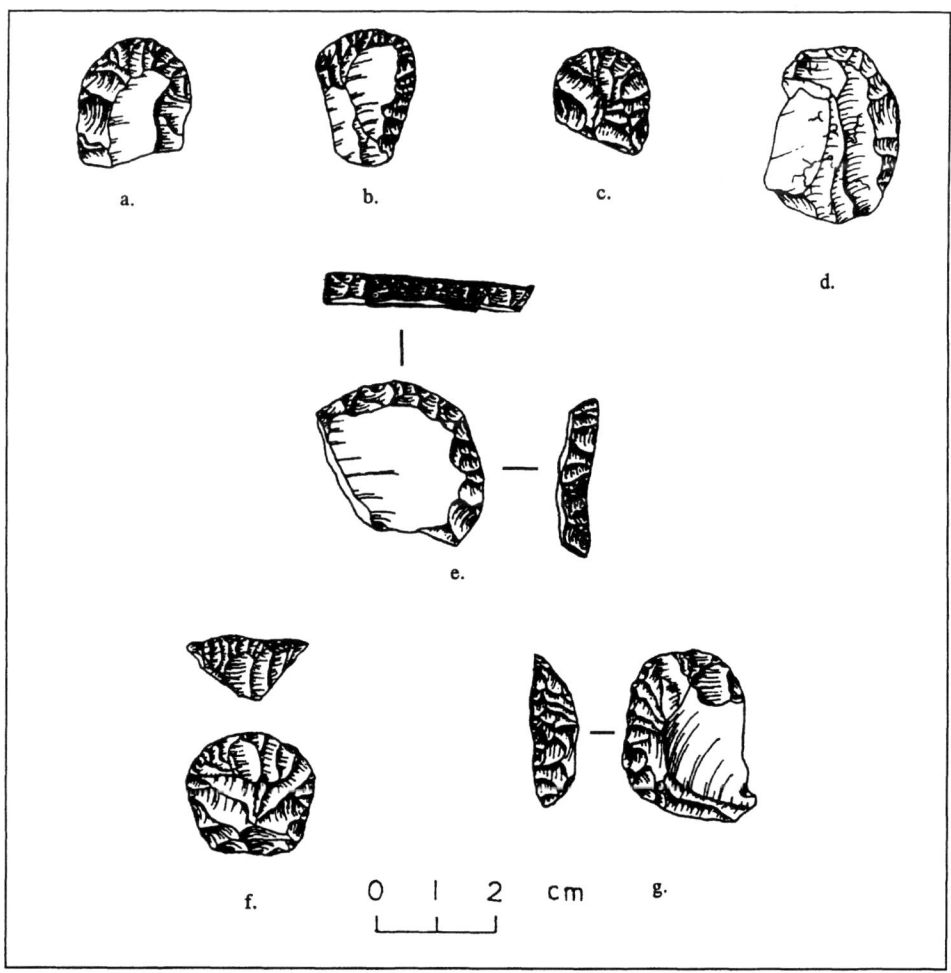

Figure 6-3. Thumbnail scrapers from *Aetokremnos* (a–g = side/end).

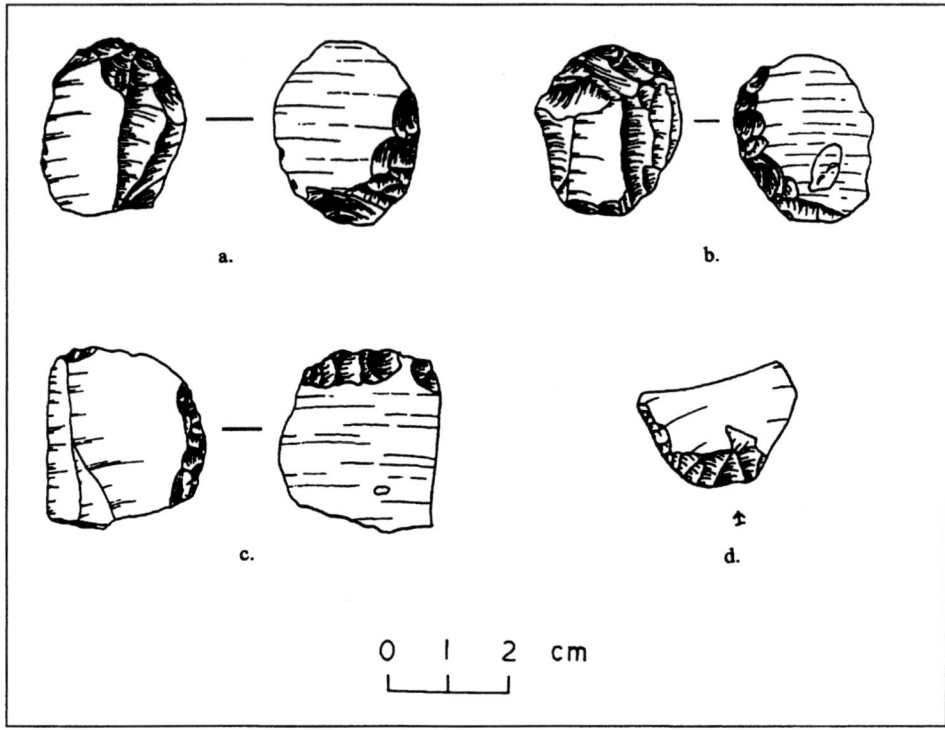

Figure 6-4. Thumbnail scrapers from *Aetokremnos* (a,b,c = Variant 1; d = interior only).

Variant 1 forms are interesting in that the scraper retouch is interior as well as exterior (Fig. 6-4:a,b,c); in one case, it is only interior (Fig. 6-4:d). The single specimen of Variant II is a piece in which retouch covers the entire surface. Table 6-10 provides attribute information on these artifacts.

Some of the smaller thumbnail scrapers resemble small exhausted cores. One example in particular (Fig. 6-3:f) has such steep and invasive retouch that it could have been classified as a small subdiscoidal or pyramidical core. This distinction becomes more important in examining the chipped stone assemblages from two of the three tested sites, where a great number of small, exhausted cores are present (see Chap. 10).

All of the thumbnail scrapers are manufactured on flakes, with tertiary forms being the preferred blank. Similar proportions exist for the larger scrapers, with 62.4% manufactured on tertiary flakes, 18.8% on tertiary blades, and the remaining 18.8% on secondary flakes. Invasive or steep invasive retouch is responsible for over 80% of the retouch on the thumbnail scrapers.

The percentage of patinated scrapers is slightly higher than for all tools as a whole (19.4% compared with 14.2% for all tools). The same is true for burning, where 30.6% of the thumbnail scrapers are burned compared with 26% when all tools are considered as a group.

Unlike other tools, a higher percentage of thumbnail scrapers are unbroken (21 of 36). If one compares the figures of complete and broken pieces, however, it is apparent that

Table 6-10. Thumbnail Scraper Metric and Nonmetric Attributes

	Complete (N = 21)			Broken (N = 13)		
	Length	Width	Thickness	Length	Width	Thickness
(A) Metric						
Mean	24.9	21.5	7.5	21.5	190	7.0
SD	3.5	3.3	2.0	5.2	5.0	1.9
Minimum	16.4	15.0	4.4	15.0	13.9	3.8
Maximum	30.3	27.0	11.1	30.2	31.8	9.8
Blank type	N	%				
(B) Non-Metric						
Secondary flake	15	41.7				
Tertiary flake	21	58.3				
Retouch type						
Invasive	11	30.6				
Steep invasive	19	52.8				
Abrupt	1	2.8				
Steep	4	11.1				
Unidentified	1	2.8				
Burning						
Burned	11	30.6				
Not burned	25	69.4				
Patination						
Patinated	7	19.4				
Not patinated	29	80.6				

there is little difference between them, suggesting either that broken artifacts could still have been used and were perhaps even manufactured on broken blanks. The size consistency of these artifacts is very tight, and this is one of their distinguishing aspects. In overall morphology, they are rounded or ovoid, being only slightly longer than they are wide. For their small size, they are rather thick.

Observations on wear visible to the naked eye were made on both thumbnail and other scrapers (Table 6-11). These observations included the degree of wear visible on the retouched edge of the artifact, as well as on the entire piece. The thumbnail scrapers exhibit a considerable degree of wear, which might be attributed to use, whereas none of the other scrapers show "extensive" wear. These observations suggest that the thumbnail scrapers were principal artifacts at *Aetokremnos* and were used frequently and heavily.

Other Scrapers.   The nonthumbnail scrapers form a diverse class, with side scrapers being the most common form. These are followed by combination side and end scrapers. Many of these scrapers resemble the thumbnail forms but are simply larger. All but three of these artifacts are manufactured on flake blanks (10 on tertiary flakes and 3 on secondary flakes). The three others are manufactured on tertiary blades. Only one of these

Table 6-11. Scraper Wear

	Thumbnail scrapers				Other scrapers			
	Edge		Overall		Edge		Overall	
Wear degree	N	%	N	%	N	%	N	%
None	8	24.3	13	39.4	6	50.0	8	66.7
Moderate	11	33.3	7	21.2	6	50.0	4	33.3
Extensive	14	42.4	13	39.4	0	0.0	0	0.0
Total	33	100.0	33	100.0	12	100.0	12	100.0

scrapers is patinated, and three are burned. Of the 16 artifacts in this class, 13 exhibit invasive retouch.

The size range of these scrapers varies considerably (see Table 6-9). Eleven of the 16 pieces are broken. Complete pieces are substantially longer than the thumbnail forms, while the length of broken pieces is similar to that of the thumbnail scrapers. These scrapers also are wider than thumbnail forms. Unlike the thumbnail scrapers, there is a considerable difference in length, width, and thickness between broken and complete forms. Of these scrapers, the most unusual is a "scraper/plane" that was recovered from the surface and could possibly be intrusive. This patinated piece is not burned and has the general morphology of a "preform." It is the largest scraper in the assemblage (length 90.1 mm, width 48.7 mm, thickness 30.3 mm). The scraper retouch is invasive and irregular.

Burins. Burins (Fig. 6-5) form a relatively large tool class and have not been commonly reported in Cyprus. Several types are present, with single blow straight forms being the most common (Fig. 6-5:a–c). Other types include dihedral, multiple blow straight (Fig. 6-5:e), and single-blow angle forms. Eight of the 20 burins are manufactured on flakes (2 on secondary flakes and 6 on tertiary flakes), 12 on blades (3 on secondary blades and 9 on tertiary blades). Only one is patinated; three are burned. Thirteen of the burins are broken.

Burin spalls occur in low (1.6% of all chipped stone) but consistent proportions. Although functional interpretations of burins are open to question, we cannot ignore the possibility that burin *spalls* were actually the tools, with burins being either waste materials or additional tools (Vaughan 1985). Specifically, the possibility that some burin spalls may have been used as retouched drill bits (cf. Baird 1992) should be considered.

Accordingly, we examined the burin spalls from *Aetokremnos* to see if any of these tiny artifacts exhibited signs of retouch or use. None of the spalls showed retouch. We monitored several other variables, including shape, end morphology, cross section, and wear (Table 6-12).

If spalls were being used for drills or perforators, we might expect a selection for pointed ends. As can be seen, one-half of the spalls had at least one pointed end. Conceivably, these could have been used as some sort of piercers. Only three burin spalls exhibited any sort of visible wear, however. One of these had some chipping on its pointed end and what could be an impact fracture, but this is inconclusive.

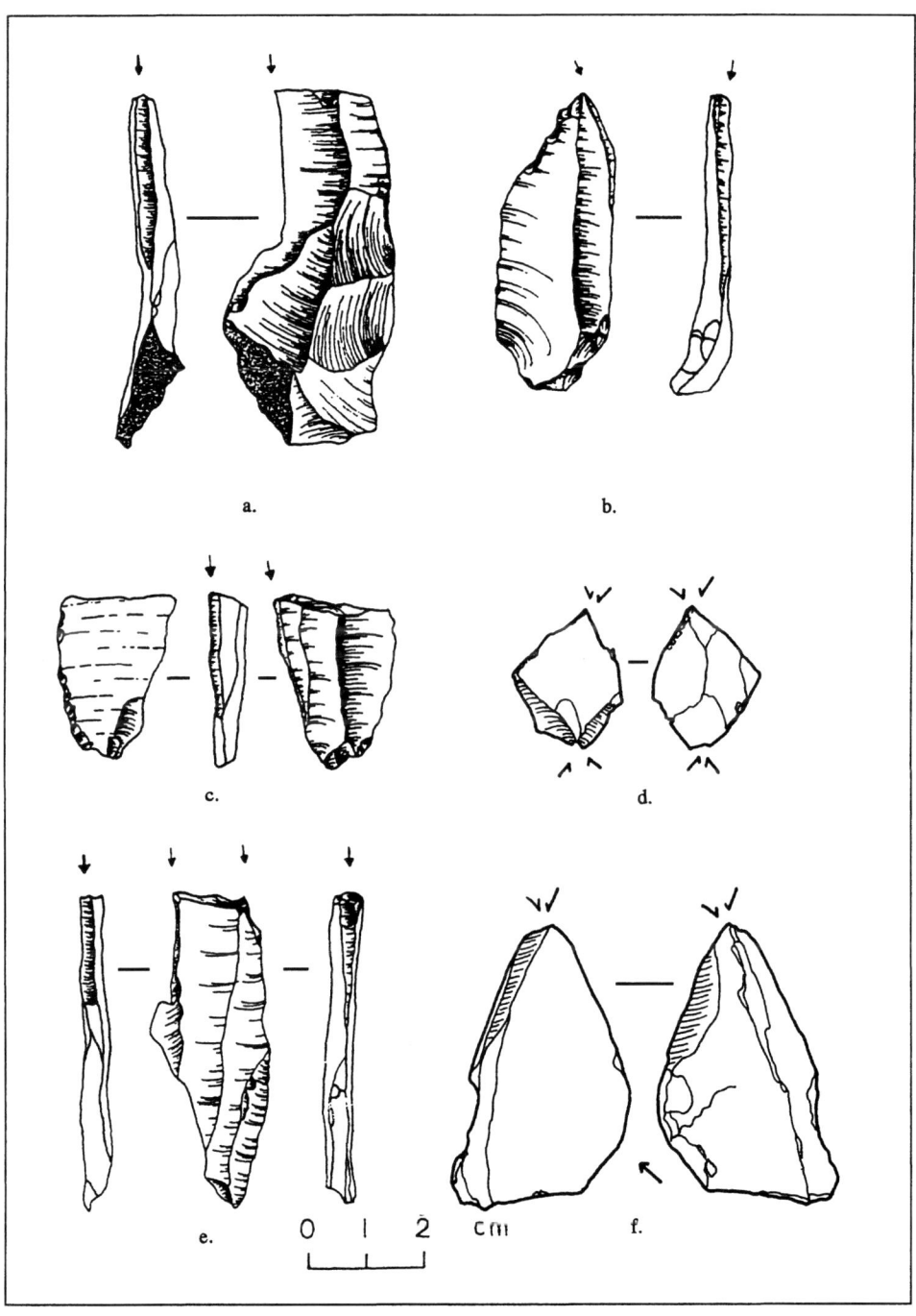

Figure 6-5. Burins from *Aetokremnos* (a,b,c = straight, single blow; d = multiple dihedral; e = multiple, straight; f = multiple, dihedral).

Table 6-12. Burin Spall Attributes

Shape	End	Cross Section	Wear
Twisted	Blunt/broken	Triangular	None
Straight, incurvate	Flat/broken	Flat	1
Straight, incurvate	Blunt/blunt	Trapezoidal	None
Straight	Blunt/broken	Flat	None
Straight	Flat/pointed	Trapezoidal	2
Incurvate	Flat/pointed	Right angle	None
Incurvate	Flat/pointed	Triangular	None
Straight	Broken/pointed	Triangular	None
Incurvate	Flat/pointed	Flat	None
Straight	Flat/pointed	Triangular	None
Straight	Blunt/broken	Right angle	None
Twisted	Blunt/broken	Triangular	3
Straight	Blunt/broken	Trapezoidal	None
Straight	Blunt/broken	Trapezoidal	None
Straight	Pointed/broken	Right angle	None
Straight	Blunt/pointed	Triangular	None

Key: Wear indications: 1 = possible nibbling on broken end; 2 = some chipping on pointed end, impact fracture; 3 = possible "battering" on broken end.

Taken collectively, the evidence is not very compelling that burin spalls at *Aetokremnos* were used as tools. Although one-half of the spalls had a pointed end, their use as tools seems unlikely. One argument against tool usage is the limited thickness of the spalls—any amount of pressure applied to these thin artifacts would have broken them. Furthermore, even on burin spalls exhibiting retouch or use, Vaughn (1985:494–495) has observed that this could be the result of use *prior* to detachment from a blank.

Functionally, we do not preclude the possibility that some of the *Aetokremnos* burin spalls may have been used as informal piercing or prying implements; they would have been particularly useful in removing meat from the abundant marine shell assemblage. As such, they could have been expediently produced (and used) tools, but there is no evidence to indicate either intentional modification (i.e., retouch) or use (i.e., wear) to strongly support this proposition.

Retouched Pieces.   Retouched pieces make up nearly 30% of the formal tools (Fig. 6-6:g,h). When the retouch is of the marginal variety, it is always possible that it was not intentional but rather the result of use. We should also note that we do not exclude the possibility that unretouched blades or flakes could have functioned as tools (see earlier discussion on Shea's analysis). These blanks often have sharp edges that would have been suitable for cutting tasks. However, if there was no visible retouch, even of the marginal variety, on a piece, it was not classified as a tool.

Of the 16 retouched blades, 7 are burned and 3 are patinated. Retouch type on these tools is generally marginal (7 pieces) or semisteep (3 pieces). Twelve are manufactured on tertiary blades, while the remainder are on secondary blades. Thirteen are broken. Of the 22 retouched flakes, 5 are patinated and 6 are burned. Thirteen are manufactured on tertiary flakes, 8 on secondary flakes, and 1 on a cortical flake. All but one are broken, although two of the broken pieces only had a small piece missing, thereby allowing mea-

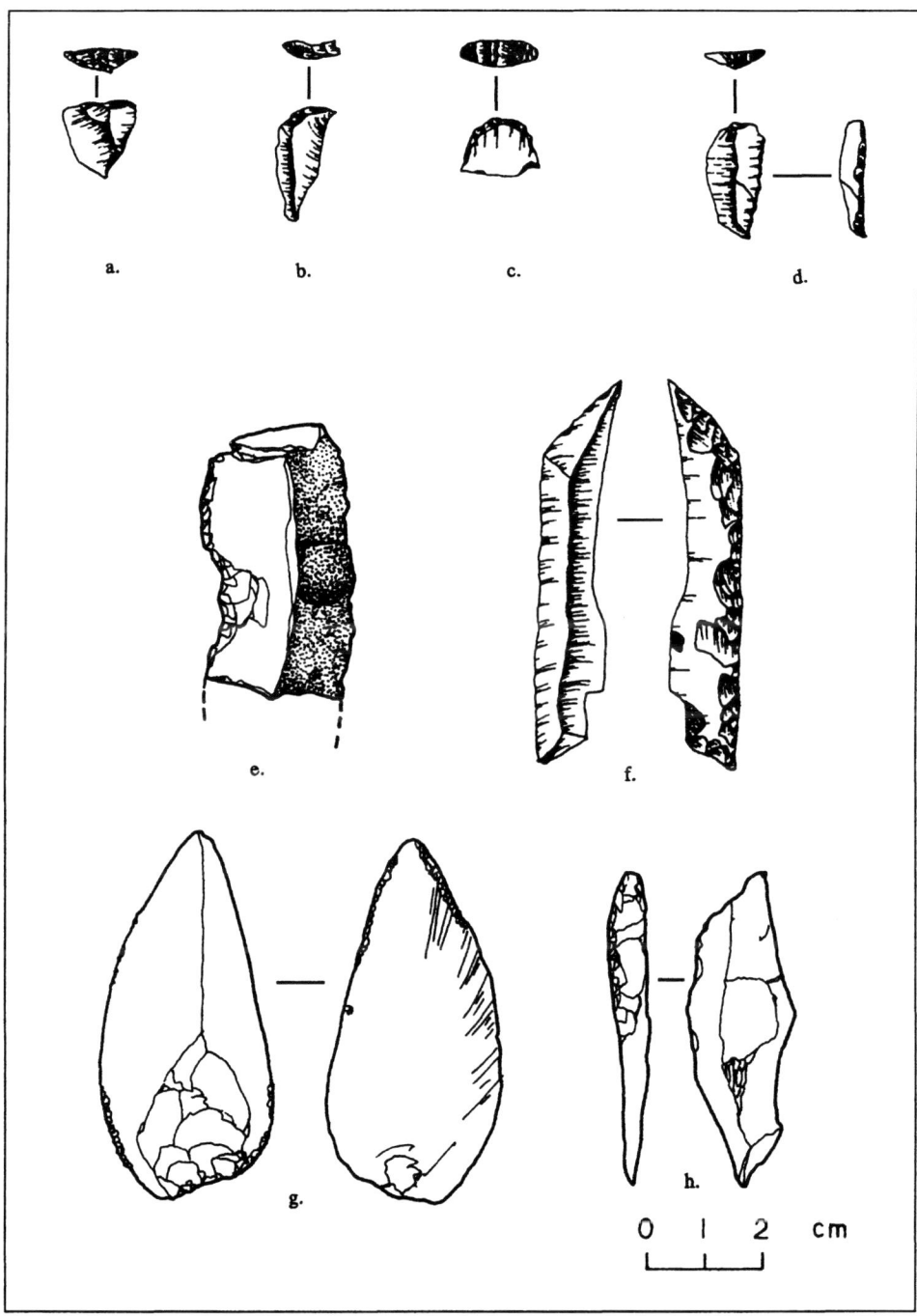

Figure 6-6. Miscellaneous tools from *Aetokremnos* (a,b = microlith, truncation; c = microlith, lunate; d = microlith, retouched bladelet; e = notch; f = unifacial knife; g = retouched flake; h = retouched blade).

surements as complete (see Table 6-9). More of the retouched flakes have substantial retouch than do the blades. Four pieces exhibit invasive retouch (but not enough to be classed as a scraper), while three have abrupt retouch.

One of the retouched blades is a curious piece. It is, unfortunately, a broken specimen and is quite small. It has both abrupt and a scaled type of retouch on one end only and is somewhat reminiscent of a poorly formed "tang," possibly representing a projectile point base. If this were the case, it would be important, since projectile points are a rarity in Cyprus. Alternatively, tangs are reported as tool types at Khirokitia (Stekelis 1953:411) and Kholetria *Ortos* (Simmons 1994a:5). Of related interest is the pointlike tool recovered from one of the surface sites tested in conjunction with *Aetokremnos* (see Chap. 10).

Truncations. Only three truncated pieces were recovered (but see also multiple tools and microliths). Of these, one each is burned and patinated. The truncation is formed by simple retouch across a broken edge. All three pieces are on broken tertiary blades.

Notches. Notches are defined by the presence of a distinct grooving, or notching (Fig. 6-6:e). Only three such artifacts were recovered, all manufactured on blades (two secondary and one tertiary). None are burned nor patinated. One is complete and two are broken.

Backed Pieces. Only two backed pieces are present in the *Aetokremnos* assemblage, both manufactured by abruptly retouching the edge of a tertiary blade. Neither piece is burned nor patinated. One is broken and one is complete.

Unifacial Knives. Two distinctive artifacts in this assemblage have been classified as unifacial knives (Fig. 6-6:f). Both pieces exhibit steep invasive retouch that covers nearly the entire surface. One is manufactured on a tertiary flake, one on a tertiary blade. Both pieces are broken, and none are patinated. One is burned.

Pièce Esquillée. One artifact is classified as a pièce esquillée. This is a broken tertiary flake with scaled retouch. It is not patinated, nor is it burned.

Axe. Although the *Aetokremnos* assemblage consists of relatively small tools, one large piece was recovered. This was an unbroken axe or pick found on the surface of the site, slightly downslope from the shelter. It is not burned, nor is it patinated. It is 120.0 mm in length, 39.4 mm in width, and 15.5 mm in thickness.

Multiple Tools. All of the multiple tools are burin forms, and the observations made above for burins includes the five forms represented here. One of the multiple tools is a single-blow angle burin on a side scraper, manufactured on a secondary blade. The burin blow on this piece is on the interior surface. Three of these tools are single-blow burins on truncations, and one is a double burin on a truncation.

Microlithic Tools. The six microliths (Fig. 6-6:a–d) recovered from *Aetokremnos* are unique for Cyprus. Although one might be tempted to equate microlithic implements with a Natufian or similar Epipaleolithic mainland development, this must be done cautiously, for microliths occur in early Neolithic contexts on the mainland, as well. Furthermore, their limited number at *Aetokremnos* precludes any serious comparative statements. Nonetheless, their presence may hint at a Late Epipaleolithic or Early Neolithic origin.

Of the six implements, one is a "aberrant" lunate (Fig. 6-6:c) in that it is quite thick. This piece has abrupt retouch that is bipolar. The presence of a lunate is suggestive of Natufian affiliation, but again this can only be considered as observation because it is based on a single artifact. The trapezoid is the other specialized microlith. It has unequal sides and is almost lunate in proportions. The remaining four pieces are either truncations or retouched bladelets. One of the truncations is a convex form on a laterally retouched bladelet (Fig. 6-6:b). The retouched edge is semisteep and continuous. The other truncation is on an unretouched wide bladelet (Fig. 6-6:a). The truncation is straight and is formed by abrupt retouch. Of the two laterally retouched bladelets, one is continuous retouched with semisteep retouch and is also partially truncated (Fig. 6-6:d), while the other has discontinuous (approximately half of one edge) marginal retouch.

None of the microliths are patinated, and only one (the lunate) is burned. One of the retouched bladelets is broken; the other microliths are complete.

Summary

The chipped stone assemblage from *Aetokremnos* is unlike any described for Cyprus. The closest island parallels are found in the Aceramic Neolithic, but published descriptions of chipped stone assemblages from such sites do not suggest many similarities, either in tool types or debitage. Although it might be incorrect to say that the assemblage represents a true blade technology, there certainly is a blade aspect to it. Blades are well manufactured true blades, often quite long and thin. Metrically, they are quite distinct from flakes, having proper blade proportions. The large number of bladelets also indicates a blade-oriented technology, as does the abundance of punctiform platforms. Over 35% of the tools were manufactured on blades or bladelets, indicating that these were desired tool blanks. Although there are more than two times as many flakes as there are blades at *Aetokremnos*, flakes are quite common even in well-documented Aceramic Neolithic assemblages, which often are considered as representing a blade technology. In fact, the ratio of blades to flakes at *Aetokremnos* is higher than at Cypriot Aceramic Neolithic sites. Even on the mainland, where Aceramic Neolithic blade technologies are well documented, flakes are very common (see additional discussion in Chap. 11). As such, *Aetokremnos* represents more of a blade technology than do Cypriot Aceramic Neolithic sites.

Cores are often excellent indicators of technological parameters. Unfortunately, the sample from *Aetokremnos* is small, and true blade cores are not represented. The presence of so many bladelet cores, however, supports the conclusion that a bladelike technology was in use at the site. The ratio of all debitage to cores (19.15:1) also indicates a relatively high degree of technological efficiency.

Tools from *Aetokremnos* stand out from those at other Cypriot assemblages. Tertiary elements (76.5%) were preferred for tool manufacture; this again supports a conclusion of technological efficiency. Perhaps the most distinctive element of the *Aetokremnos* assemblage is the abundance of well-manufactured thumbnail scrapers. These certainly are the most common tool type and may well represent a diagnostic element for the Akrotiri Phase. The presence of numerous burins also is of considerable interest, as are other scraper forms.

All of these variables indicate that the technology represented at *Aetokremnos* was far from an expedient, flake-based one. The site's occupants clearly possessed the knowledge and skills necessary for the production of a sophisticated and efficient blade-based technology.

GROUND STONE ARTIFACTS (*STUART SWINY*)

Introduction

The nonchipped lithic finds from *Aetokremnos* may be classified in three broad categories: artifacts, cobbles, and pebbles. Considering the difficulty of accurately dating most categories of ground stone tools, only the stratified finds will be discussed here (i.e., Strata 2, 2A, 2/4, 4A/B, and 4B). There are numerous concentrations of Chalcolithic material on the Akrotiri Peninsula (Heywood 1982:167; Heywood *et al.* 1981:24, 31), and it is quite possible that the occasional ground stone tool could, along with quantities of much later Roman pottery, have found its way to *Aetokremnos*. Their distribution is summarized in Table 6-13.

An additional 66 cobbles and pebbles were recorded from the general area of the shelter and mixed strata, all but three of which are unworked. Field Numbers (FNs) 43 and 92 could have been fragments of saddle querns, but they are too small to enable unequivocal identification; FN 62 is a unique object that will be discussed later.

Of the 87 stratified lithics recorded, only 5 can be described as artifacts, in addition to a single object of dubious attribution. The remaining assemblage consists mainly of broken, fractured igneous cobbles and a few intact pebbles.

Artifacts

Carefully shaped axes, pounders, pestles, mortars and querns are conspicuously absent from *Aetokremnos,* which sets the site apart from all other major prehistoric settlements on the island. From Stratum 2A, four unaltered cobbles with faint signs of use-wear on one or several faces were recorded. A cobble from the same stratum with an oval cavity 30 × 40 mm in diameter barely qualifies to be classified as a mortar (Swiny 1986:21), and it is more accurately described as a "cobble with a pecked depression." Type III mortars

Table 6-13. Distribution of Stratified Artifacts, Cobbles, and Pebbles

Stratum	Artifact	Cobble	Pebble
2	5	56	7
2/4		3	1
4A/B		1	6
4B		8	
Total	5	68	14

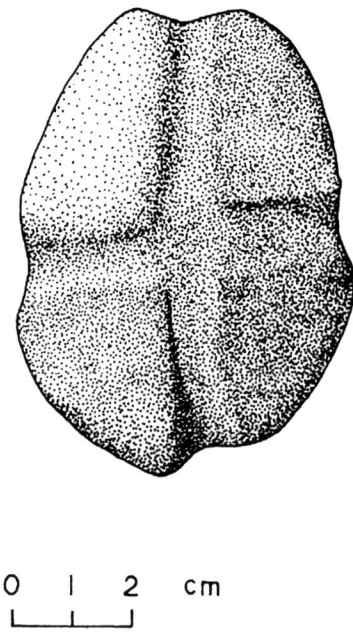

Figure 6-7. Grooved "cruciform" stone from *Aetokremnos.*

published by Dikaios (1953:259, Pl. LXIV:68) from Khirokitia *Vounoi* and similar pieces from the same site published by LeBrun (1984, Fig. 63:2, 7; 1989, Fig. 51:2, 3) provide the best Cypriot parallels for this type.

It is unfortunate that the most diagnostic ground stone artifact, FN 62 (Fig. 6-7), is a surface find from the scree several meters *below* the shelter. The findspot and erosion patterns noted at the site strongly suggest it originated from the Akrotiri Phase deposit. It is a flattened, oval beach cobble with carefully pecked grooves encircling its longitudinal and transverse medial planes. The groove is sufficiently deep at both extremities to prevent a securely attached twine or thong from slipping off the rounded stone.

No parallels for this object exist on Cyprus, although a cobble with intersecting shallow grooves forming a cross pattern does resemble the plan view of FN 62 when observed from above (Elliott 1985b:92, Fig. 68:2), but here the similarity ends. Elliott (1985b:92) noted that it "conceivably could have been used as a weight," and the *Aetokremnos* piece may have served a similar function or, better still, as a net sinker.

Cape Andreas Kastros, like *Aetokremnos,* is ideally located to exploit local marine resources, therefore the former could be expected to yield net or line sinkers if such were in use during the Aceramic Neolithic. Indeed, LeBrun (1981:74, Fig. 45:8–12; 1984:6, Fig. 5:14, 17, 18) interpreted a series of *galets a gorge* (waisted cobbles) and perforated cobbles as probable fishing accessories. FN 62 would certainly not look out of place in this assemblage.

Cobbles

By far the most striking feature of the assemblage is the fragmentary and shattered condition of 64 out of the 68 stratified cobbles recorded. Igneous and dense limestone cobbles do not shatter easily, even when exposed to fire.[1] At *Aetokremnos*, most are reduced to sharp-edged fragments less than one-third of their original size, which must have happened as the result of considerable mechanical stress.

If the cobbles had been intentionally shattered through percussion, some of the "hammerstones" used to perform this operation should have been recovered by the excavation, yet only two were recorded. The use-wear marks on the four previously discussed cobbles are certainly too ephemeral to have functioned as hammerstones. A few of the cobble fragments show discoloration, perhaps due to heating in a fire. They also could have served as "pot boilers" (Barfield 1991; Barfield and Hodder 1991). Although igneous cobbles are not easily fire cracked, repeated reheating and rapid cooling may have caused their eventual fragmentation.

The ratio of intact to broken cobbles at Early and Middle Cypriot (i.e., Bronze Age) sites, such as Sotira *Kaminoudhia* (personal observation), Alambra *Mouttes* (Coleman *et al.* 1996), and Episkopi *Phaneromeni* (Swiny 1986), where the writer was able to study the entire assemblages, is the opposite to *Aetokremnos*. These sites had few broken cobbles in relation to the number of intact ground stone tools and unworked cobbles. Recent publications of Neolithic (Cluzan 1984:111–124) and Chalcolithic (Elliott 1985a:271–275; Elliott, personal communication) ground stone assemblages fail to note significant numbers of shattered "blanks" littering the sites.

All the cobbles at *Aetokremnos* were water worn and rounded in shape, with often rough and lightly pitted surfaces. This erosion pattern suggests that few if any had been collected from a beach or riverbed, where their surface would have been ground smooth, even to a dull luster. Most cobbles at *Aetokremnos* are diagnostic of material from exposed Pleistocene fanglomerate deposits. Although there are no major Pleistocene fanglomerates in the vicinity of the site—the nearest being 7 km to the north—cobbles with pitted surfaces are scattered over the southern sector of the Akrotiri Peninsula, which seems to have been the preferred source for these lithics.

Pebbles

In contrast with the cobbles, all 14 stratified pebbles are intact, but without signs of use-wear. Twelve had been collected from a beach, as they are smooth and shiny; the remainder had probably originated from the plateau above the site. Five additional pebbles were recorded in unstratified contexts.

---

[1]In the course of a 26-year residence on Cyprus, the author, Stuart Swiny, frequently built camp fires in river valleys and on beaches that were composed entirely of igneous and limestone pebbles and cobbles. Large igneous and dense limestone fieldstones (average size 30 x 20 x 20 cm) do sometimes split when exposed to the heat of a fiercely burning camp fire, but smaller cobbles or either material are usually unaffected, even if, for example, water is poured on them to extinguish the fire. Fieldstones of Pakhna Formation chalk and marl do not stand up well to fire and readily crack and shatter if used in the construction of a hearth, if the latter is not protected by a layer of mud mortar.

In order to check whether heated igneous cobbles would crack on contact with cold water, three were heated on a gas burner for 20 minutes and then dropped into a bucket of water. In this experiment, none of the cobbles cracked. All three were collected from the Pedieos riverbed in Nicosia.

Conclusions

Very little can be said about the nonchipped stone lithics excavated at *Aetokremnos*. No well-formed ground stone tools were abandoned at the site, and the others only show light signs of wear. By far, the most unusual aspect of the assemblage is the shattered condition of most cobbles, for which, at this stage, there is no obvious explanation.

STONE ORNAMENTS (*DAVID REESE*)

In addition to several worked ornamental shell artifacts (see Chap. 7), we recovered six worked picrolite artifacts. These are: 3 pendants (Fig. 6-8); 1 bead, 1 pendant fragment (Fig. 6-9, left); and 1 worked piece (Fig. 6-9, right). Preliminary reports on the 1988 season at *Aetokremnos* mention two "serpentinite" beads (Peltenburg 1991:123; Simmons 1989b:815, 1989c:42). These are actually a picrolite pendant and bead. The most logical source of the *Aetokremnos* picrolite is the lower Kouris River (Peltenburg 1991:112). I would imagine, however, that small picrolite cobbles or pebbles might be washed out of the mouth of the Kouris River and naturally find their way to the beach below *Aetokremnos*. Xenophontos agreed that picrolite cobbles can probably be found along the beach south and east of the Kouris River (personal communication 1991).

The *Aetokremnos* picrolite ornaments are the earliest stone ornaments found on the island. They are, however, quite similar to some of the stone ornaments known from Neolithic Cyprus.

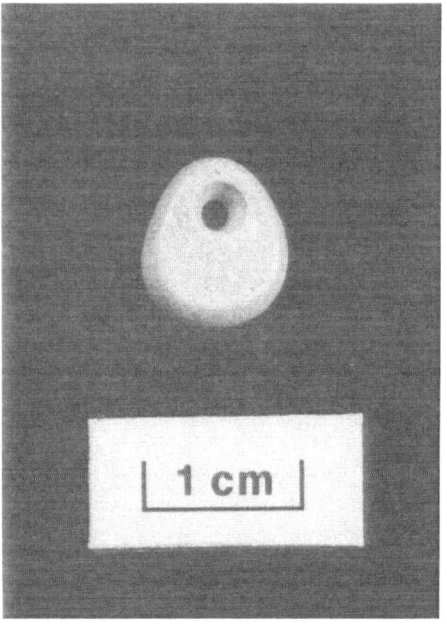 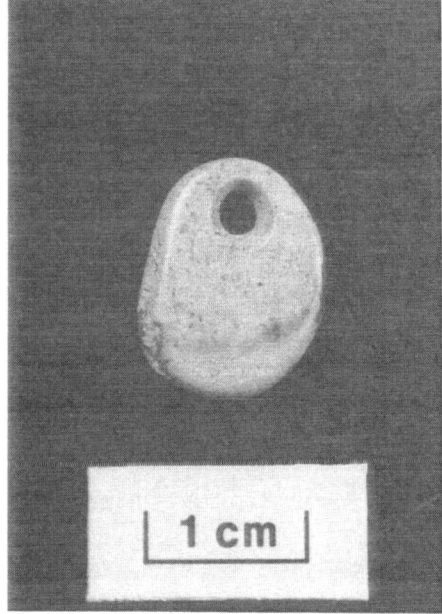

Figure 6-8. Two of the picrolite pendants from *Aetokremnos*.

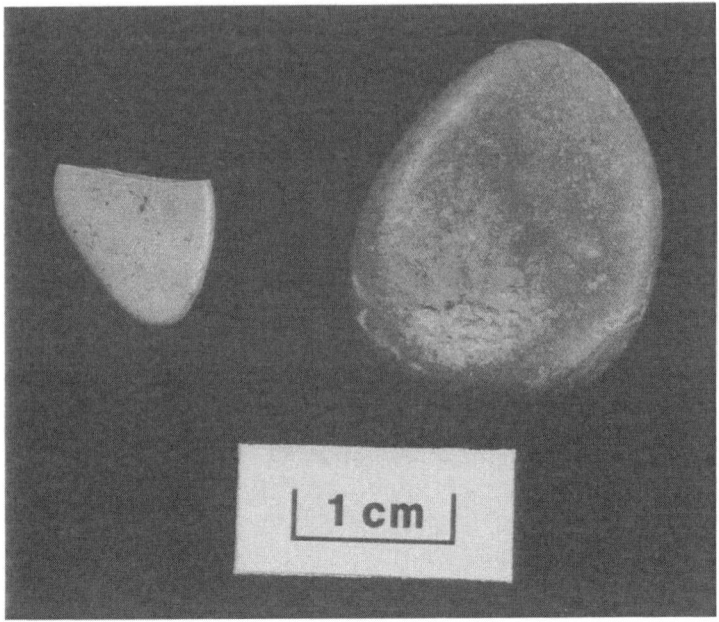

Figure 6-9. Picrolite pendant fragment (left) and worked piece (right) from *Aetokremnos.*

THE PIERCED CALCARENITE DISK (*DAVID REESE*)

This disk (Fig. 6-10) was found in Stratum 2/4, in unit N98E87. It is made of a yellow calcarenite, and is half preserved. It had a length of 105 mm and is 7 mm thick. The exterior edge has been roughly chipped on the obverse side to make a circle. The central hole has been drilled from both sides. The beveled area around the hole on the obverse side is 8.5 mm and around the reverse hole, 7.5 mm. The hole itself has a diameter of 4.75 mm. The obverse side also has five parallel, deeply incised lines and four other lines.

Gjerstad suggested that a similar artifact from Aceramic Neolithic *Petra tou Limniti* was used as a sinker, probably in fishing. Dikaios suggested that the two smaller examples from Khirokitia *Vounoi* may have been used as stoppers, possibly for containers made of some perishable material. The two larger examples may have been used in a similar fashion, as net-sinkers or as mace heads (Dikaios 1953:285). Similar pierced or perforated disks are found at Late Neolithic Sotira *Teppes* in southern Cyprus. Here there are five examples, with four of limestone and one of sandstone, some having a beveled hole, which range in diameter from 45 to 75 mm. It has been suggested that they may be spindle whorls (Dikaios 1961: 202, Pl. 91; 103:75, 217, 267, 378, 518; 1962:94, Fig. 47).

I do not agree with any of the previously suggested uses of these items (net sinkers, vessel stoppers, mace heads, spindle whorls). I suggest that they were used as platforms for making stone and shell beads or pendants, with the piece to be worked placed in the beveled hole in the disk. The incisions seen on the *Aetokremnos* disk and *Vounoi* disk 528 are probably evidence that these disks were also used for scoring or cutting stone or shell, as in cutting off sections of *Dentalium* and *Columbella* shells and ring or cylindrical stone beads.

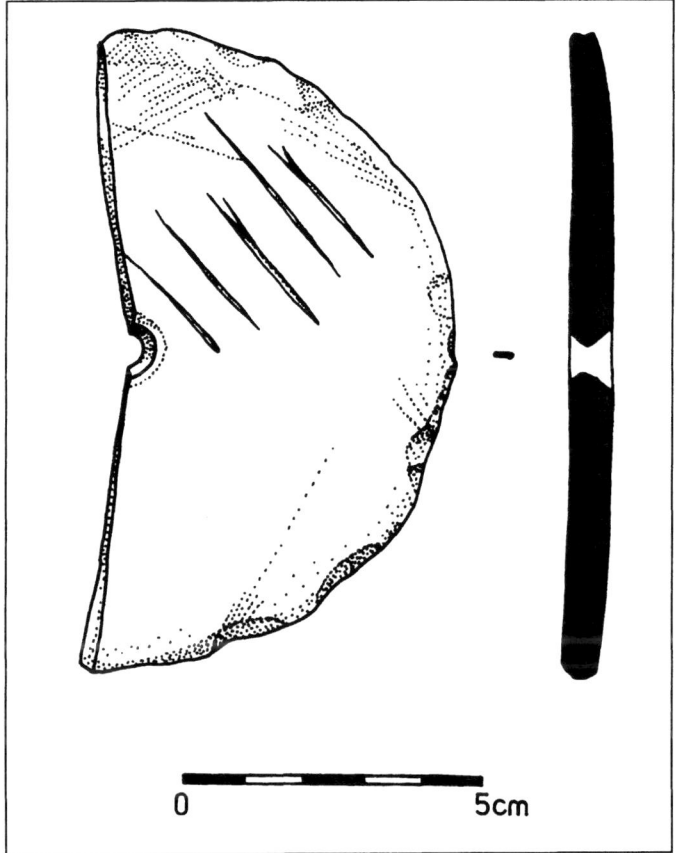

Figure 6-10. The *Aetokremnos* pierced disk.

WORKED BONE (*DAVID REESE*)

One worked *Phanourios* bone was recovered from *Aetokremnos* (Reese 1992a). This was from Stratum 4B in N96E87. It is the probable upper incisor of a young *Phanourios* that has been cut through and smoothed at the preserved end and has two parallel incised lines. The artifact is 20.5 mm long and 8 mm wide. This tooth may have been tied and worn as a pendant, given the presence of other ornaments at the site.

INTRUSIVE ARTIFACTS

Several artifacts that are considered intrusive were recovered from *Aetokremnos*. These artifacts are primarily ceramics, but they also include glass and metal items. They are summarized in Table 6-14. Most of the ceramics are Roman. Nearly all of the intrusive items are from the upper or mixed strata of the site. The majority occur in Strata 1–4,

Table 6-14. Intrusive Objects at *Aetokremnos,* Summary by Strata

Stratum	Ceramics	Glass	Metal	N	%
	Artifact Type			Total	
Surface	4	2	1	7	10.6
1	17	3	1	21	31.8
2	2	0	0	2	3.0
4	2	0	0	2	3.0
1–4	20	8	1	29	43.9
1/2	3	2	0	5	7.7
TOTAL	48	15	3	66	100.0

Note: Numbers in *N* refer to specific FNs, which in a few cases may have had more than one item.

which, it will be recalled, consists of badly mixed deposits. In only a few instances were materials recovered from Stratum 4. The two potsherds from this stratum are from units near the original exposed section (units N94E88 and N94E89), and although they are recorded as "Stratum 4," this designation undoubtedly does not represent their proper context.

We note the presence of numerous Roman and other, later period sites throughout the Akrotiri Peninsula (Heywood 1982:169), including one site (a small Roman structure) located on the cliff top immediately over *Aetokremnos.* In addition, several Roman tombs are cut into the nearby cliffs. The presence of these materials, we are confident, can easily be explained as being the result of materials eroding over the edge of the cliff, or from the tombs, down onto the shelf on which *Aetokremnos* is located.

Chapter 7

The Faunal Assemblages

PRESERVATION AND ANALYTICAL PROCEDURES

We recovered a huge faunal assemblage from Akrotiri *Aetokremnos* (Fig. 7-1), comprised of nearly 300,000 remains. Most (over 98% of the vertebrate remains, or about 218,000+ bones of 505+ individuals) of this consisted of *Phanourios minutus*, the endemic pygmy hippopotamus, which, of course, is one of the most controversial aspects of the site. Beyond the *Phanourios*, however, other faunal materials were present, including 3,207 bird bones (75+ individuals), over 73,000 marine shell fragments (21,500+ individuals), and smaller amounts of other species. In this chapter, we provide information on the fauna recovered from the site. Table 7-1 provides an overview of the faunal collection.

The reader should be aware that the portion of this chapter devoted to *Phanourios* and *Elephas* remains is summary in fashion. The detailed accounting of these remains will be published in a separate volume by David Reese, which will include detailed taphonomic analyses, an examination of body-part composition and distribution, measurements, and comparisons with other collections. The size of the assemblage presented a daunting analytical challenge. Thus what follows relating to *Phanourios* must be considered preliminary. Certain aspects are bound to change on completion of the study. We believe, however, that the overall configuration of the assemblage will not change, and additional analysis certainly will not alter our conclusions regarding the association of the cultural materials with the faunal remains. We provide enough data in this chapter for readers to draw their own conclusions.

The preservation of faunal material at *Aetokremnos* is exceptional. Although much of the material is fragmentary, mainly due to burning and postoccupational disturbances such as roof fall, the bones were generally in excellent condition. Despite the disturbances, complete *Phanourios* skulls (Figs. 7-2–7-3) and many other whole or nearly complete elements were recovered (Fig. 7-4). Only bones from the surface and the rockshelter's floor were concreted. Buried deposits contained bone in remarkably good condition, although fossilization was setting in.

Figure 7-1. Excavated bones during preliminary processing in laboratory.

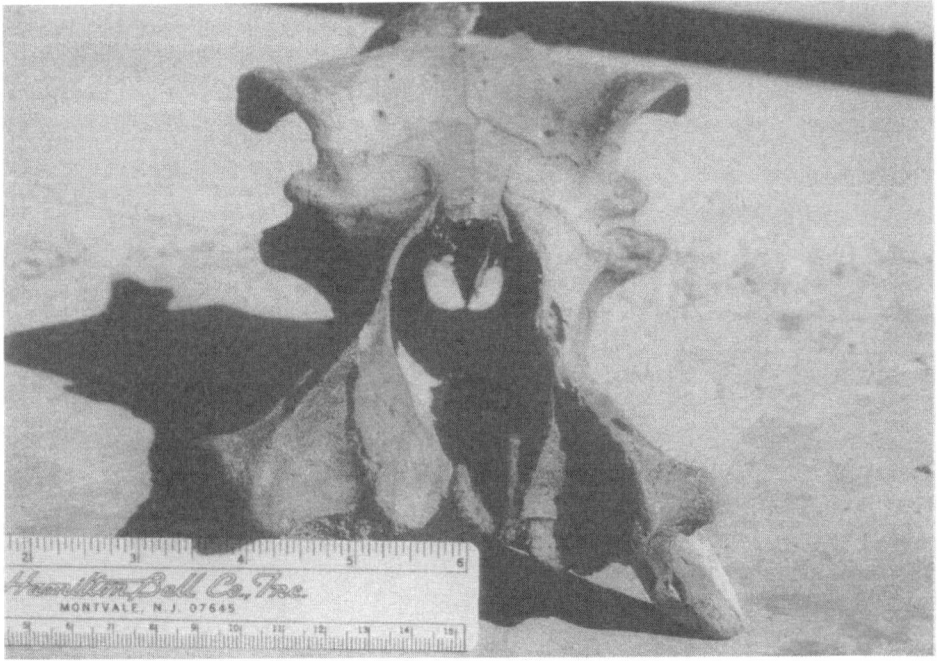

Figure 7-2. Complete *Phanourios* skull: frontal view.

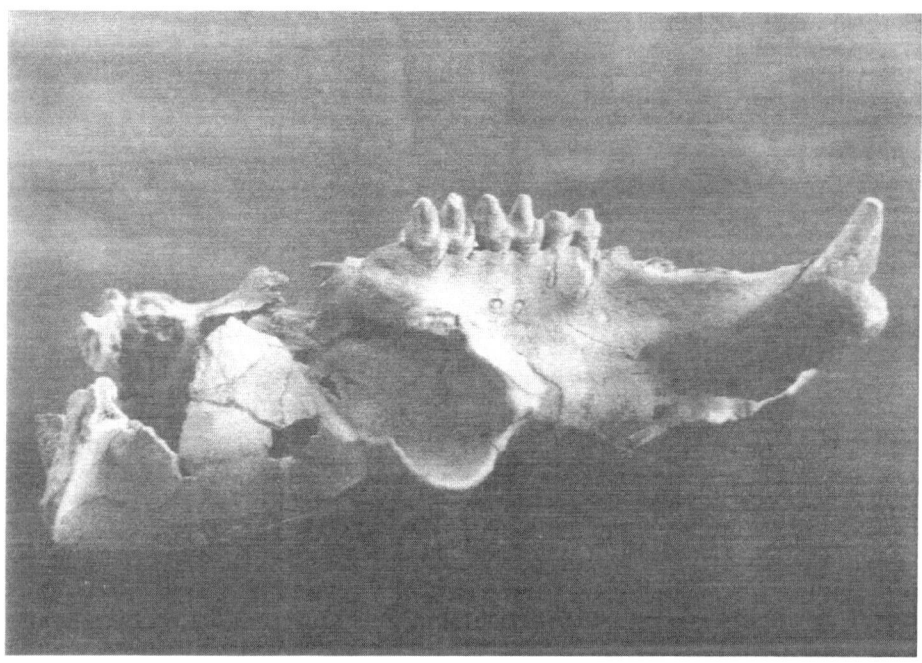

Figure 7-3. Complete *Phanourios* skull: side view.

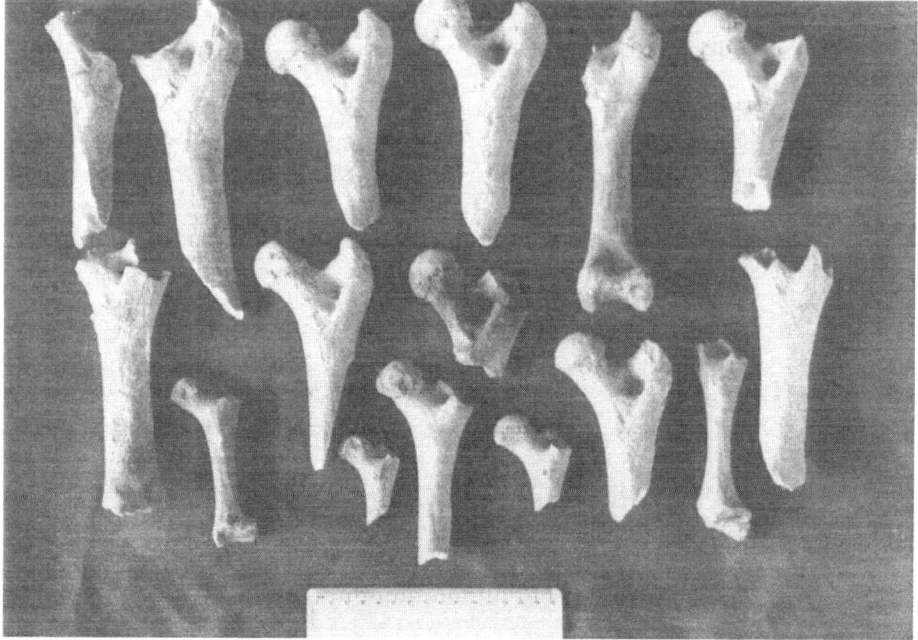

Figure 7-4. Various *Phanourios* femora.

Analysis of the *Phanourios*, *Elephas*, shells, and some other remains was undertaken by Reese. Birds, mouse, and fish remains were sent to specialists. To date, the analysis of *Phanourios* remains from all features, loci, and Strata 1, 1/2, 2, 3, and 4C has been completed. A preliminary, rough count was made of the remaining *Phanourios* bones from Strata 1–4, 2/4, and 4A and B. The values for burned bones, identifiable elements, and Minimum Number of Individuals (MNI) for these strata are the result of this initial analysis and are likely to increase when the analysis is completed. Our examination of the *Phanourios* sample suggests that the data gathered so far are adequate to characterize the entire assemblage.

Prior to analysis, the *Phanourios* and other remains were first washed in water; those badly encrusted with calcium carbonate were also washed in a dilute HCL solution. They were then separated into identifiable species. Following this, each species was separated into identifiable and unidentifiable fragments and sorted by feature and/or stratum. To facilitate analysis, bones from FNs (Field Numbers) within the same unit and stratum were combined into a single FN that best characterized a particular feature or excavation unit. The basic data collected for all assemblages include: Number of Identified Specimens (NISP), element, side, burning presence/absence, and bone fusion or teeth eruption information. The element, side, and age data were used to compute the MNI statistics.

MAMMALIAN FAUNA

Pygmy Hippopotamus (*David Reese and Kathy Roler*)

Introduction

The endemic pygmy hippopotamus was first scientifically collected by Dorothea M. A. Bate in the early 1900s (Bate 1906; Forsyth Major 1902), and subsequently named *Phanourios minutus* (Cuvier, 1824). Space constraints in this volume do not permit us to examine the fascinating history of this species. Additional information on *Phanourios* may be found in Bate (1906), Boekschoten and Sondaar (1972), Faure *et al.* (1983), Forsyth Major (1902), Houtekamer and Sondaar (1979), and Reese (1975b, 1989b, 1995).

At *Aetokremnos*, nearly a quarter of a million *Phanourios* remains were recovered. This is a remarkable number, not only for an archaeological site, but also for a paleontological one (see Reese 1995 for numbers from other sites). Most of the Cypriot paleontological sites have small quantities of bone, although a few do contain substantial numbers (Reese 1995). These latter sites, however, do not have cultural material, and their context is not similar to *Aetokremnos*. In particular, the large amount of burning seen at *Aetokremnos* is not paralleled elsewhere. Only Akanthou *Arkhangelos Mikhail* has burning, and this only on one bone (Reese 1995:86, 89, Pl. 29). Although burning of faunal materials is found at Cypriot (e.g., King 1953:432–453; Schwartz 1974a:104ff) and Levantine archaeological sites (Klein 1995:416; Köhler-Rollefson *et al.* 1988:424), what sets *Aetokremnos* apart is the extent of burning.

Aetokremnos is the largest such assemblage yet documented anywhere. For the remains from features, loci, and strata that have been fully analyzed, 35.9% were identifiable as to element. A minimum of 63,490 (29.1%) of the *Phanourios* bones were burned; this number will no doubt increase as the remaining bones are analyzed. The following discus-

Table 7-1. Summary of Faunal Remains from *Aetokremnos*

Fauna	NISP	%	MNI
Vertebrates			
Pygmy hippopotami (*Phanourios*)	218,459	98.3	505+
Pygmy elephants (*Elephas*)	229	0.1	3
Deer (*Dama*)[1]	4	—	1–4
Pigs (*Sus*)	13	—	ca. 4
Genets (*Genetta*)	2	—	1
Mice (*Mus*)	5	—	1
Birds	3,207	1.4	75+
Snakes (*Vipera/Natrix*)	ca. 245	0.1	14–40
Tortoises (*Testudo*)	25+	—	9–14
Toads (*Bufo*)	1	—	1
Fish	1	—	1
Total vertebrates	222,191	99.9	—
Marine invertebrates	73,365	—	21,576
Land snails	90*	—	97
Total Invertebrates	73,455		
TOTAL FAUNA	295,646	—	—

*Does not include Surface, Strata 1, 1/2, or 1–4.

sion summarizes these remains. Additional context information was provided in Chap. 5, where *Phanourios* remains from features were discussed. Table 7-2 presents a summary of these remains by stratum.

Phanourios Remains by Stratum

The MNI has been calculated for all features (see Table 7-4 following), and those strata that have been fully analyzed (Table 7-2), but they are not yet available for the entire collected sample. Full details on the calculation of MNI, as well as complete tables of elements and age estimates for each stratum, will be provided in the faunal volume. In brief, MNI values given here were calculated using data concerning element, side, portion present (whole, proximal, distal), and age (unfused/fused, tooth eruption and wear). The maximum of the right or left value for an element or element portion was used as the base MNI value. Age estimates also were considered before calculating final MNI values: Two adult left humeri and one juvenile right humeri would represent 3 MNI. Because many of the elements used were complete or in excellent condition, some of the difficulties associated with refitting fragmented elements (Binford 1984; Ringrose 1993) have not adversely impacted this study. The forthcoming faunal volume will clearly identify the aggregation method used to calculate the final MNI values, as the aggregation method has been shown to have a dramatic effect on those values (Grayson 1984).

Because there are no relevant data available for living or extinct pygmy hippopotami, we have used pig fusion and tooth eruption information to estimate age of the *Phanourios* remains. Using this information, it is easy to determine the age of individuals at either end of the range (under 1 year or over 3.5 years), but difficult to accurately determine the age

Table 7-2. Distribution of *Phanourios* Remains by Stratum, Showing Percentages Identifiable and Burned

Stratum	*Phanourios* remains NISP (MNI)		Minimum number burned		Number of identifiable specimens		
	N	%	N	%/Stratum	N	%[1]	%[2]
Surface	4,387 (31)	2.0	NYC[3]	NYC	276	0.8	6.4
1–4	4,566 (15)	2.1	NYC	NYC	71+	0.2+	1.6+
1/2	1,151 (6)	0.5	265	23.0	512	1.5	44.5
2/4	11,428 (45)	5.2	1,309[4]+	—	2,275+	6.5+	19.9+
1	123 (2)	0.1	33	26.8	31	0.1	25.2
2	3,966 (29)	1.8	1,837	46.3	1,556	4.4	39.2
3	503 (5)	0.2	460	91.5	92	0.3	18.3
4A/B	176,707 (322)	80.9	57,305[5]+	32.5[5]+	24,716+	71.2+	4.0+
4C	15,628 (52)	7.2	2,281	14.6	5,684	16.4	36.4
TOTAL	218,459	100.0	63,490	—	34,735	99.9	—

[1]Percentage of identifiable body parts in relation to total number of identifiable parts.
[2]Percentage of identifiable body parts in relation to total number of *Phanourios* bones per stratum.
[3]NYC = Not Yet Calculated.
[4]Only a portion of the bones from Stratum 2/4 have been examined for burning.
[5]Only a portion of the bones from Stratum 4A/B, primarily those from features, have been examined for burning.

of individuals between these ranges. The preliminary age estimates for the *Aetokremnos* *Phanourios* remains are given in Table 7-3.

It should be understood that the figures presented here represent minimal numbers. Thus there are at least 505 individual *Phanourios* represented at *Aetokremnos*. This number will increase when all of the *Phanourios* remains have been completely analyzed.

Clearly the majority of the *Phanourios* remains (88%) come from Stratum 4 (Table 7-2). Most *Phanourios* bone in Stratum 4 comes from Strata 4A and B (176,707), while 15,628 come from Stratum 4C (Table 7-2). When the mixed strata are removed from consideration, the proportion of *Phanourios* in Stratum 4 is even higher, at 95.5%. A total of 201,314 *Phanourios* bones (92.1%) come from unmixed contexts.

Equally significant is the number of *Phanourios* remains in Stratum 2. Although the overall percentage is small (less than 2%), this nonetheless represents 3,966 bones. This observation becomes more important when examining the relationship of *Phanourios* remains to other animals, particularly birds. Here we see a dramatic increase in the number of bird remains in Stratum 2 that is in inverse relationship to the number of *Phanourios* remains. The implications of this are discussed in Chap. 12.

Over a third (36.4%) of the *Phanourios* bones from Stratum 4C could be identified as to element (Table 7-2). A similar frequency of identifiable elements was found in most of the other strata that have been fully analyzed (Stratum 1, 25.2%; Stratum 1/2, 44.5%; Stratum 2, 38.8%; Stratum 3, 18.1% [but only 92 bones]). The frequency of identifiable elements in the remaining strata, including Strata 4A and B, which contain the vast majority of the *Phanourios* remains, is expected to dramatically increase once the remains from each have been fully analyzed.

Table 7-3. Preliminary Age Estimates of *Phanourios* Remains by Strata (Youngest and Oldest)

	Age			
	< 1 Year	+ 3.5 Years	Other	Total
Surface	7+	19+	1+	27+
1–4	2	12	—	14
1/2	3	2	1	6
2/4	6+	27+	1+	34+
2	5	4	4	13
3	1	—	1	2
4A/B[1]	45+	126+	2+	173+
4C	16	26	—	42
TOTAL	85+	216+	10+	311+

[1]These figures are based on only a sample of *Phanourios* remains from Stratum 4A/B; not all have yet been analyzed for aging.

Burned bone was found in almost all layers in widely varying frequencies. Stratum 4C had the lowest amount of burned bone (14.6%). Higher frequencies of burning were found in all of the strata above this level, but they were highest in Strata 3 (91.5%) and 2 (46.3%). As Stratum 3 was a sterile layer, the few burned bones it contained (460) would have been intrusive, either from Strata 2 or 4.

Phanourios Remains by Feature

Approximately one-third of all *Phanourios* remains were recovered from features (Tables 7-4 and 7-5). A point made in Chapter 5 regarding features must be reiterated here: Due to the often relatively indistinct nature of the features at *Aetokremnos,* the numbers of *Phanourios* remains given in various tables include bones directly associated with the features as well as those found immediately adjacent to them.

Ten features at the site contained *Phanourios* remains (see Table 7-4); seven of these were hearths, and one, Feature 3, was a concentration of burned bone that may have been an informal hearth or fire pit. High frequencies of burned bone were found in these 8 features, making up 89.6% of all the burned bone identified thus far. When burned bone immediately adjacent to these 8 features is added, the figure makes up 90.9% of all the burned bone presently identified from the site. The lowest frequencies of burned bone were found in Feature 5 (a shell concentration in Stratum 2) and Feature 8 (a bell-shaped pit).

The element frequencies for Features 3, 7, and 9 (those with the greatest number of *Phanourios* remains) are given in Table 7 6. Examination of this table reveals that all elements of the body are present; there is no evidence for any sorting or *schlepp effect* (Perkins and Daly 1968). This conclusion is further supported by the similar frequencies of the elements, particularly in Feature 3. Many elements from this feature fall in the range of 39–49 paired and 19–30 unpaired elements. Thus it appears that entire carcasses were processed at the site, with most of the bones being disposed of in situ.

Table 7-4. Summary of *Phanourios* NISP, MNI, and Burned by Feature

Feature number	Stratum	In feature NISP (MNI)	Burned N (%)	Immediately adjacent NISP (MNI)	Burned N (%)
1	2	224 (2)	125 (55.8)	1,656 (6) [from St. 2/4]	545 (32.9)
2	4	44 (2)	39 (88.6)	—	—
3	4	62,587 (48)	55,452 (88.6)	—	—
4	2	108 (2)	106 (98.1)	166 (3)	111 (66.9)
5	2	217 (2)	54 (24.9)	1,429 (5) [1,405 from St. 2/4]	262 (18.5)
6	2	282 (4)	212 (75.2)	—	—
7	2	344 (3)	342 (99.3)	—	—
8	2/4	168 (1)	57 (33.9)	1,261 (6)	338 (26.8)
9	4	1,291 (3)	596 (46.2)	217 (3)	162 (74.7)
10	2	2 (1)	2 (100.0)	—	—
TOTAL		65,267 (68)	56,985 (87.3)	4,729 (23)	1,453 (30.7)

Table 7-5. Distribution of *Phanourios* Remains by Stratum and Association with Features

Stratum	Not Associated with features		Associated with features/Loci		Total
	N	%	N	%	
Surface	4,387	100.0	0	—	4,387
1–4	4,566	100.0	0	—	4,566
1/2	1,094	95.0	57	5.0	1,151
2/4	6,811	59.6	4,617	40.4	11,428
1	123	100.0	0	—	123
2	2,586	65.2	1,380	34.8	3,966
3	495	98.4	8[1]	1.6	503
4	127,913	66.5	64,422	33.5	192,335
TOTAL	147,975	67.7	70,484	32.3	218,459

[1]Locus 8, N97E89.

Horizontal Distribution

No detailed analyses have yet been completed on the horizontal distribution of specific *Phanourios* body elements at *Aetokremnos*. Horizontal distribution of all *Phanourios* remains are discussed in Chapter 9 (Durand), where it is demonstrated that the highest con-

Table 7-6. *Phanourios* Body Parts Used in MNI Calculations for Features 3, 7, and 9

Element	Feature 3	Feature 7	Feature 9
Head/Neck			
Occipital condyle	46	2	0
Vomer	33	1	1
Posterior skull	19	1	2
Palate	47 (9 juv)*	0	3
Temporal	44	0	2
Lacrymal	29	0	2
Mandible	37 15 juv)	1	3 (1 juv)
Upper canine	15	0	2
Lower canine	12	0	0
Atlas	26	0	1
Axis	29	0	0
Forelimb			
Scapula	48 (14 juv)	1	1
Humerus	49 (14 juv)	1	2
Radius/ulna	50 (9 juv)	0	1
Hindlimb			
Sacrum	18	1	1
Pelvis	39 (7 juv)	1	1
Femur	39 (14 juv)	3 (2 juv)	1
Patella	6	0	0
Tibia	49 (11 juv)	0	0
Fibula	14	0	1 (juv)
Calcaneus	45	1 (subadult)	2
Astragalus	19	0	0

*juv = juvenile.

centration of bones occurred toward the front and center of the rockshelter in Stratum 4 and in the southeast corner in Stratum 2.

Conclusions

The sheer number of *Phanourios* is unparalleled, posing a daunting analytical challenge. The information provided here is only a summary of the recovered materials. We are convinced, however, that this assemblage is the result of human activity. Given the modifications to much of this bone, particularly in the form of burning, it is difficult to imagine how such a large assemblage could accumulate as the result of natural processes. Detailed arguments supporting this contention are provided elsewhere in this volume, especially in Chaps. 12 and 13.

Pygmy Elephant (*David Reese*)

Aetokremnos produced 332 pygmy elephant bones. From the head/neck, these included 60 skull fragments (from one skull), 2 mandibles, 20+ incisor (tusk) fragments, (primarily from 1 incisor), 6 molars, 1 atlas, and 1 axis. Forelimb elements include 3 scapula, 4 humerus, and 6 radius/ulna fragments, while hind limb elements consist of 2 pelvis, 2 sacrum, 8 femur, 7 tibia, and 1 fibula fragments. From the lower leg, there were 2 astragalus, 1 calcaneus, 1 tarsus, 2 cuneiform, 1 scaphoid, and 5 metapodial elements. In addition to these, there are 26 vertebrae fragments, 34 rib fragments, and 36 unidentifiable fragments. Of these, the mandible is spectacularly well preserved (Fig. 7-5); when reconstructed, the tusk also is nearly complete (Fig. 7-6). The Pleistocene and Early Holocene pygmy elephant of Cyprus was first described by Bate in the early 1900s and named *Elephas cypriotes* Bate, 1903 (Bate 1903a, 1904a–d). This species is not as commonly found as the contemporary *Phanourios*. Although *Phanourios* is known from at least 33 sites, only 20 sites (including *Aetokremnos*) have yielded any elephant remains. Of these, 10 have only a single bone, 2 have two bones, 2 have three bones, and only 5 sites have five or more bones. Localities producing both species produced mainly *Phanourios* remains. Five sites have produced elephant teeth of a larger size than *E. cypriotes*, and their geologic context suggests that they are ancestral to *E. cypriotes*. Full site-specific details may be found in Reese 1995.

   Almost all of the *E. cypriotes* remains from *Aetokremnos* come from Stratum 4B. There are three individuals present based on the very young molar from the Surface and the two right mandibles, two left scapulae (one unfused), two right acetabulae, two right femora (Fig. 7-7), and two right tibia. All bones are unfused except for a left and right scapula (which fuse under one year) and the proximal radius (fused by 1.5 yrs; the distal end of this bone is unfused). Several bones are burnt: a distal humerus epiphysis frag-

Figure 7-5. *Elephas* mandible, in situ.

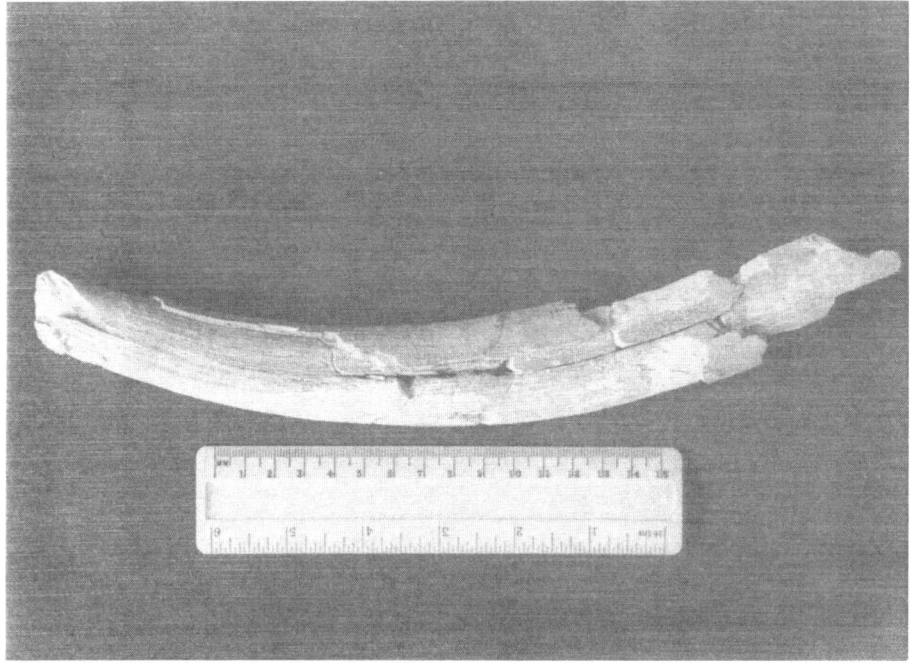

Figure 7-6. *Elephas* tusk.

ment (partly burnt), a distal radius epiphysis (probably partly burnt), two vertebrae, and three ribs.

The majority of skull and tusk fragments come from N95E88, as do the only atlas and axis. Also, the atlas articulates with the occipital condyles of the skull from this unit. Most of the mandible and molar remains come from N94E90, particularly FN 375. A left tibia proximal epiphysis and fibula come from N95E89 (northeast quadrant). However, the tibia diaphysis comes from N93E89. A left femur comes from N94E89 (southwest quadrant), while the probably associated distal epiphysis comes from N95E89 (west half). An astragalus, calcaneus, and tarsus, all hind limb elements, come from N94E89. Probably associated with these bones are the left tibia and fibula noted earlier. All three carpals come from N95E89 (south half).

Some of the broken but attaching or unattached epiphyses come from separated units: a right femur comes from N93E88 (distal epiphysis) and N95E88 (diaphysis); a left tibia comes from N93E89 (diaphysis), N95E89 (northeast quadrant) (proximal epiphysis), and N97E87-88 (north) (upper shaft fragment); a right humerus comes from N94E89 (disphysis) and N95E89 (northwest) (distal epiphysis), a right tibia comes from N94E89 (diaphysis and proximal epiphysis) and N98E87 (distal epiphysis); and probable joins of a left humerus come from N93E88 (proximal end) and N94E89 (distal shaft). All of the above joins are within Stratum 4B.

There is also a right femur join between N97E87-88 (south half) in Stratum 4B (distal shaft) and N96E87 (west half) in Stratum 1/2 (proximal shaft). It is even possible that this right femur and the right tibia from N96E86 (east half, Stratum 2/4) come from the same

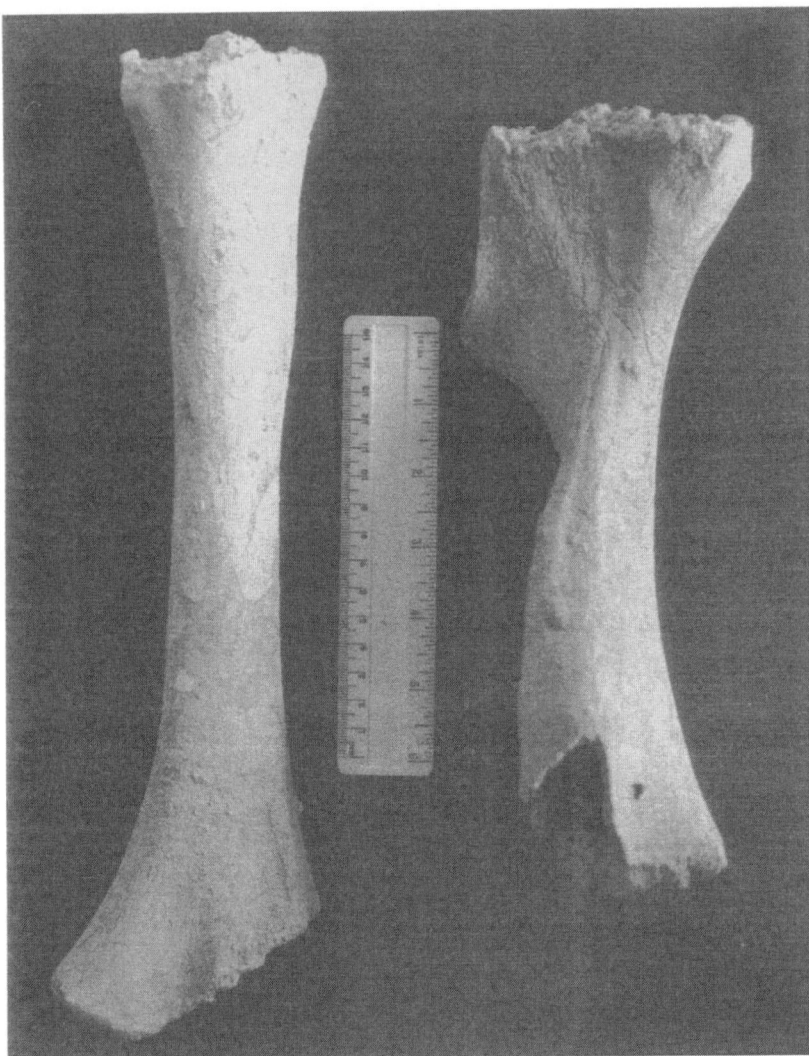

Figure 7-7. *Elephas* femur and humerus.

hind limb. Although this presents a potential stratigraphic problem, it probably represents the results of some mixing between strata, possibly caused by rooffall.

Pig (*David Reese*)

The 14 pig (*Sus scrofa* Linnaeus, 1758) remains from *Aetokremnos*, noted on Table 7-7, are probably wild boar (Fig. 7-8). They probably come from four individuals; four bones are from Stratum 4 and the remainder are from Stratum 2. The domestic pig is not

Table 7-7. Data on Additional *Aetokremnos* Fauna (all measurements in mm)

A. PIG
Stratum 2 (upper)

FN 1138	N97E90	(Locus 3; SW quad)
		phalanx 2 (II/V): F, burnt, GLpe 24, Bp 12.25, SD 8, Bd 9.25
		phalanx 3: broken, burnt (2 MNI by size)
FN 422	N98E89	(Feature 4, mixed/peripheral)
		phalanx 3: left, partly burnt, DLS 24.5, Ld 22

Stratum 2

FN 320	N96E91	
		metatarsus V: right, UF, preserved length 54 mm
FN 1022	N98E90*	
		incisor
		2 metapodial II/V: 1 mc II UF (maximum length 49), other broken
		phalanx 2: UF and epiphysis

Stratum 2 (lower)

FN 866	N96E89	(south half)
		phalanx 3

Stratum 4B

FN 367	N97E87-88	(N quads)
		metapodial II/V: F, maximum length 59.75
		phalanx 3: left, DLS 23.5, Ld 22
FN 385	N99E87	(SW quad)
		phalanx 3: left, broken DLS, Ld 23.25
FN 506	N99E87	(NW quad)
		phalanx 2: UF, broken, maximum length 20
		phalanx 3: left, DLS 24.25, Ld 21.25

B. DEER (or Pig—see footnote 1) MEASUREMENTS
Strata 1/2

FN 402	N96E87	(west half)
		phalanx 1: F, longitudinal fragment, eroded, GL 39 (acided)

Stratum 2

FN 1021	N99E89	(south half)[†]
		phalanx 1: JF, GLpe 35, Bp 17.25, SD 13, Bd 19.25

Stratum 2 (lower)

FN 340	N96E91	
		phalanx 3: right, DLS 33.75, Ld 32.25

Stratum 3

FN 914	N96E89	(southeast quadrant)
		phalanx 3: right, DLS 33, Ld 29.5 (acided)

C. *GENETTA GENETTA* (NNML, NO. 1685) AND *GENETTA* CF. *PLESICTOIDES*
FROM *AETOKREMNOS* MEASUREMENTS

		G. genetta	*G.* cf. *plesictoides*
dP^3	length	7.1	8.3
	width at protocone	2.9	2.7
	width of blade[1]	1.8	2.0
dP^4	length[2]	4.0	4.5
	width	4.9	4.9
	length C-dP^{4}[3]	25.0	25.5

[1]At junction of paracone and metastyle.
[2]Parallel to paracone and metacone; width perpendicular.
[3]Alveolar length.
*Shown in Fig. 7-8.
[†]Shown in Fig. 7-10.

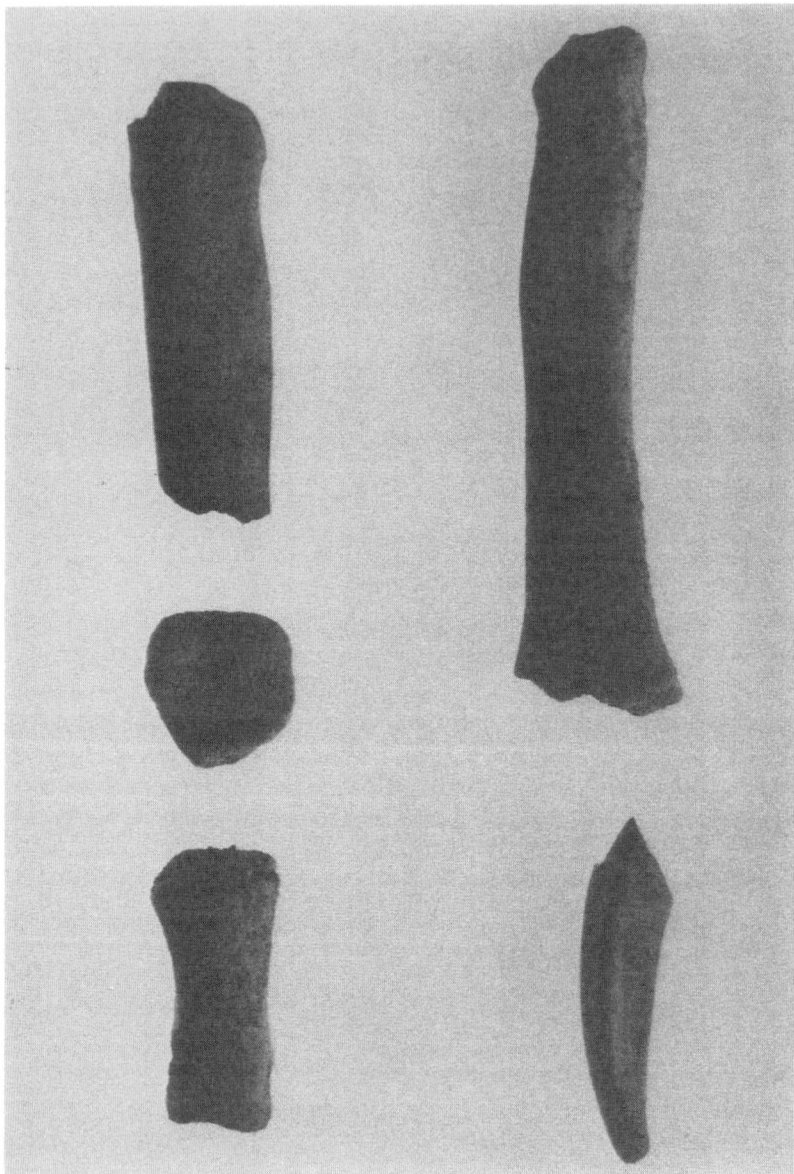

Figure 7-8. Various *Sus* elements.

present at this time on the mainland. All of these remains must have been brought to the island from the mainland by those hunting at *Aetokremnos*.

Wild pig or boar has been reported from Khirokitia, Dhali *Agridhi* (Schwartz 1973b:216, 1974a:105ff.; Lehavy 1974:96), and Erimi *Pamboula* (King 1953:435). Recent work, however, suggested that these pigs were domestic, but a "primitive" breed (Croft

1991:66–67; Davis 1984:156, 1989:207). Boar have not been reported in any other faunal collection. J. H. Schwartz (personal communication March 20, 1995) now accepts that the pig is a primitive domestic breed.

As with the possible deer (see below), the fact that most of the *Aetokremnos* pig remains are phalanges (nine bones) or metapodials (three) may indicate that they are bones that were left in a piece of fur or skin that was used as clothing or bedding. Such a suggestion has been used to explain similar remains from a number of Mediterranean and mainland sites. For example, two phalanx 2 of a possible *Rupicapra rupicra* (Linnaeus, 1758), the chamois, from Aceramic Neolithic *Vounoi* (Watson *et al.* 1977:233, 235, 245) are interpreted as clothing or bedding. Likewise, a Leopard (*Panthera pardus*) phalanx 2 from Late Natufian Salibiya I in the Jordan Valley, which on the plantar surface "shows skinning marks made with a flint tool, providing evidence for the use of pelts" (Crabtree and Campana 1990a:113, 1990b:22). They also found 115+ phalanges, mainly terminal phalanges (claws) of a large raptorial bird, which may have a similar nonfood explanation. Most of the bear bones at Neolithic Magula Pevkakia in Thessaly are of the foot (Hinz 1979:79–80), and the two bear bones from Late Neolithic Dimini, also in Thessaly, are phalanges (Halstead 1987:77, 1992:36). Both collections may be from skins or pelts. There are several abnormally high concentration of deer phalanges in pre-Neolithic levels at Corbeddu cave in Sardinia. In Locality T in Hall III there are 1,268 deer bones, with 832 phalanges (65.6%; 302 1st, 308 2nd, 222 3rd) (Sondaar *et al.* 1984:37, 41). In Hall I here, there are 89 deer bones with 56 phalanges (62.9%), and many terminal phalanges of large birds of prey (Sondaar *et al.* 1986:20).

Deer (*David Reese*)[1]

Four (Mesopotamian) fallow deer (*Dama mesopotamica* Brooke, 1875) remains from four deposits were recovered at *Aetokremnos*. These are described in Table 7-7; note that none are from Stratum 4. Their presence was unexpected, as most researchers felt that deer were first brought to Cyprus by the Aceramic Neolithic colonizers. The fact that all of the *Aetokremnos* deer remains are phalanges may again indicate that they are bones left in a piece of fur or skin that was used as clothing or bedding. Therefore, these remains were probably not imported to *Aetokremnos* as live animals, but rather in the form of pelts.

Genet (*Karel Steensma and David Reese*)[2]

Aetokremnos produced two bones of a young genet (Family Viverridae). These bones initially were referred to as "possibly from a juvenile cat or fox" (Simmons 1991a:862) in a preliminary report. There is a left maxilla fragment (Stratum 4B, FN 720, N95E89, NW

---

[1]François Poplin (Muséum national d'Histoire naturelle, Paris) and Jean-Denis Vigne (Centre National de la Recherche Scientifique, Paris), both of whom have also examined these four bones, disagree with Reese and his colleagues in their identification. Poplin and Vigne feel that the bones in question are in fact pig (*Sus*), although Poplin (1999, personal communication) concedes that specimen FN 402 "looks rather cervid." Whether or not these bones are deer or pig does not alter our interpretation that they came from clothing rather than live animals.
[2]Dr. C. Smeenk of the Nationaal Natuurhistorisch Museum, Leiden, is gratefully acknowledged for giving access to the recent genet specimens. Thanks are due to Dr. H. de Bruijn, Dr. P. Y. Sondaar, and Mr. A. Spaan for their comments on an earlier version of the manuscript. Mr. J. P. Brinkerink cleaned the maxilla fragment. The photograph is by Steensma.

quadrant; Fig. 7-9) and a proximal tibia fragment (FN 727, NE quadrant of the same unit). The palate fragment has a maximum length of 29 mm and a width of 9 mm. The tibia fragment has a preserved length of 37 mm and an unfused proximal end. The two remains probably come from the same young individual.

The only carnivore remains found in a fossil deposit on Cyprus are about a dozen bones of two adult individuals referable to endemic genet (*Genetta plesictoides* Bate, 1903e) from the 1902 collections of Bate at Kato Dhikomo *Vokolosspilios* (Bate 1903c:121–124, Pl. X:1–6, 1903e). This site produced quantities of *Phanourios* bones as well as the bones of bats, rats, mice, shrews, pig, goat, birds, and fish. There is some question as to the date of the genet and the other small animals at this site; they are likely to be Holocene intrusions (Boekschoten and Sondaar 1972:332; Vaufrey 1929:187).

The *Aetokremnos* maxilla fragment contains an almost complete upper milk dentition; the milk canine (dC) and the two first milk premolars (dP^1 and dP^2) are missing. The tips of the successors of dC and dP^2 are visible in the alveoles. The animal must have reached at least 44 days old, the date of eruption of the complete upper-milk dentition (Volf 1959:170).

Comparison of this fragment with the skull of a juvenile specimen of extant *Genetta genetta* (Linnaeus, 1758) in the Nationaal Natuurhistorisch Museum, Leiden (NNML, no.

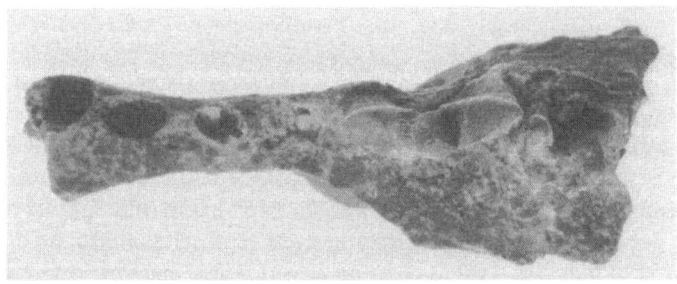

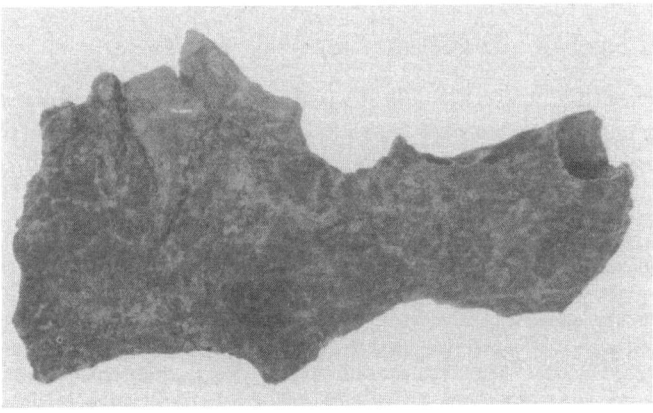

Figure 7-9. *(above) Aetokremnos* genet, left maxilla, top view; *(below)* left maxilla, side view.

1685, locality unknown) by Steensma revealed the following similarities and differences (see Table 7-7):

1. The dP^3 and dP^4 are slightly larger in the Cypriot specimen.
2. The milk carnassials (dP^3) are morphologically identical.
3. The dP^4 of the Cypriot specimen is slightly longer but not wider, and, consequently, it shows a more robust outline; the parastyle is stronger, more ridgelike, and separated from the paracone by a notch; the metastyle is better developed; the anterior margin of the dP^4 of the Cypriot specimen is extended at the paracone and parastyle, causing a large tangent plane with the dP^3; the protocone is situated farther posteriorly, and the lingual gap between dP^3 and dP^4 is accordingly larger; there is no sharp ridge between the protocone and paracone along the anterior edge of the tooth as there is in the *G. genetta* specimen, but there is an obtuse elevation farther posteriorly.

The *Aetokremnos* specimen is, especially in the morphology of the dP^4, somewhat different from the specimen of extant *G. genetta*. Bate (1903c) described her *Vokolosspilios G. plesictoides* mainly on the basis of an adult left mandibular ramus with P$_2$–M$_1$. Comparison of the *Aetokremnos* specimen with the type material is therefore impossible. We assume, however, that the *Aetokremnos* genet bones belong to the same species. Consequently, these specimens are assigned to *Genetta* cf. *plesictoides*.

There are no reports of any fossil genets from the Levant or Anatolia, although it is possible that *G. plesictoides* also lived on the mainland and is therefore not endemic to Cyprus. Today, the closest occurrences of genets are in south Arabia and Libya. The genet is said to be easy to tame (Kowalski and Rzebik-Kowalska 1991:145), and they can be kept as pets. It is known that the genet was domesticated in France during the Early Middle Ages, where it was later replaced by the domestic cat, which was introduced into Europe by crusaders returning from Palestine in the tenth century (Chauvin 1975).

The genet of Cyprus may have arrived with the first inhabitants of the island or may have traveled on their own, possibly by rafting on floating vegetation. The only wild carnivore living on the island today is the (Cypriot) red fox, *Vulpes vulpes indutus* Miller, 1907.

Mouse (*David Reese*)

Aetokremnos produced several mice remains from a water-sieved sample from a Stratum 2 casual hearth (Feature 10; FN 978, N97E89, east quads). Some of these bones are burnt. They have been examined by Dr. Jean-Christophe Auffray (Institut des Sciences de l'Evolution, Université Montpellier II). The shape of the anterior part of the M^1 suggests that this mouse could be more closely related to *Mus macedonicus* Petrov and Ruzić, 1983, the (Macedonian) mouse/East Mediterranean house mouse than *Mus musculus domesticus* Schwarz and Schwarz, 1943.

Four Cypriot Pleistocene sites have produced unspecified murid remains (Bate 1903b:344, NHML nos. M 8630-36, M 10690-91; Boekschoten and Sondaar 1972:314, 321, 327, 332), although it is possible that some of these remains are Holocene intrusions. Numerous *Mus* cf. *musculus* or *Mus musculus* remains also have been identified from

Aceramic Neolithic and later sites (e.g., Davis 1987a:308, 1989:194; Helmer 1981:Fig. 57; Watson *et al.* 1977:235, 237).

AVIFAUNA (*CÉCILE MOURER-CHAUVIRÉ*)

Introduction

The *Aetokremnos* bird bone collection is the oldest avifaunal collection known from Cyprus. The only bird bones from any of the Late Pleistocene fossil sites are several bones found in 1902 at Kato Dhikomo *Vokolosspilios* (NHML nos. M 8629, M 9635), and three small passeriform bones from Xylophagou A*yii Saranda* found in 1969, but these may all be Holocene intrusions. The *Aetokremnos* sample also is one of the largest bird bone collections from any Early Holocene East Mediterranean archaeological site.

There are 3,205 bird bone fragments (529 identifiable) from a minimum of 73 individual birds. The majority (2,074, 64.7%) come from Stratum 2, although 547 (17.1%) were retrieved from Stratum 4. Their stratigraphic distribution is given in Table 7-8. Horizontal distribution within the two major strata are discussed in Chap. 9.

Identified Species and Comments

The bird bone collection from *Aetokremnos* is characterized by an extraordinary abundance of *Otis tarda*, the great bustard. This species has been found relatively frequently during the Holocene, mainly in localities in the southern part of Europe, where it is generally represented by a small number of remains. At *Aetokremnos*, it is represented by 349 fragments from 65 units, which indicates that it was extensively hunted by the first inhabitants of the island. The list of identified species, arranged in order of zoological nomenclature, and the occurrence of the different taxa by strata is given in Table 7-9.

Table 7-8. Bird Bone Distribution at *Aetokremnos* by Stratum

Stratum	Number of fragments	Number of excavation units (squares or portions of)
Surface	24	4
1	42	3
1/2	235	12
1–4	53	5
2 (upper)	496	11
2	1,009	14
2 (lower)	569	17
2/4	190	7
3	40	6
4A	26	2
4A/B	135	6
4B	350	17
4C	36	4

Table 7-9. Identified Bird Species by Stratum

Species	Number of Bones	MNI	Strata*
Podiceps nigricollis (Brehn, 1831)	1 (burnt)	1	2
Puffinus puffinus (Brünnich, 1764)	1	1	2/4
Phalacrocorax aristotelis (Linnaeus, 1761)	8 (5 burnt)	1	2
Anser anser (Linnaeus, 1758) or *Anser fabalis* (Latham, 1787)	24 (2 burnt)	8	1, 1/2, 1/4, 2 (3), 2/4, 4
Anser sp.	54 (11 burnt)	4	2 (2), 4 (2)
Mid-sized Anseriform	4 coracoid bones	3	2 (2), 2/4
Anas crecca (Linnaeus, 1758)	5	2	2
Order Anseriforme	5	1	2
cf. *Circus*	1	1	4B
Rallus aquaticus (Linnaeus, 1758)	1	1	2
Otis tarda Linnaeus, 1758 (males)	181 (22 burnt)	24	Surface, 1 (2), 1/2 (3), 1/4 (2), 2 (9), 2/4 (2), 3, 4 (4)
Otis tarda Linnaeus, 1758 (females)	152 (24 burnt)	14	Surface, 1, 1/2, 1/4, 2 (4), 2/4 (2), 3, 4 (3)
Otis tarda Linnaeus, 1758 (unsexed)	25	Indeterminate	
Otis tarda Linnaeus, 1758 (juvenile)	2	1	2
Columba livia (Gemlin, 1789) or *Columba oenas* (Linnaeus, 1758)	5	3	1/2 (2), 2, 4B, 4C
Asio flammeus (Pontopiddan, 1763)	1	1	2
Athene noctua (Scopoli, 1769)	22	1	4A/B
Turdus iliacus (Linnaeus, 1766) or *Turdus philomelos* (Brehm, 1831)	1 (burnt)	1	4A/B (Feature 9)
Family Turdidae	5	1	4A/B (Feature 9)
Corvus corone (Linnaeus, 1758) or *Corvus frugilegus* (Linnaeus, 1758)	9 (1 burnt)	4	1/2, 2, 2/4, 4B
Small Passeriformes	1	1	2 (Feature 10)

*Numbers in parentheses refer to MNI; if not listed, MNI for Stratum is 1.

Podiceps nigricollis, the Black-necked Grebe, is only represented by a proximal part of a burnt humerus from Stratum 2. Its present distribution is discontinuous Holarctic and Ethiopian in a great number of climatic zones, but rarely in deserts and never in tundras or tropical rainforests (Voous 1960:11). It was breeding on Cyprus at the beginning of the century, but today it occurs mainly as a winter visitor (Flint and Stewart 1983:41). Its preferred habitat is freshwater marshes or brackish lagoons, and thus it could have occurred on the nearby Akrotiri salt lake; in the Early Holocene, this lake may have been connected to open sea.

Puffinus puffinus, the Manx or Levantine Shearwater, is only represented by a distal ulna from Stratum 2/4. Its distribution is discontinuously semicosmopolitan in temperate, Mediterranean, and steppe climatic zones (Voous 1960:13). It is found mainly on the coasts of western Europe and on oceanic islands. At the present time, it is reported as a passage migrant on Cyprus (Flint and Stewart 1983:41), but it probably bred on Cyprus in the past.

Phalacrocorax aristotelis, the Shag, is represented by 8 bone fragments, all from Stratum 2 in nearby areas (N96E90-91 and N98E89 NW). Five bones are burnt; probably only one individual is present. Its distribution is West Palearctic, in tundra, boreal, temperate, and Mediterranean climatic zones (Voous 1960:15). It is a resident breeder on Cyprus, in particular on the Akrotiri Peninsula (Flint and Stewart 1983:42). Its habitat is mainly rocky sea coasts with steep cliffs and small offshore rocky islets (Voous 1960:15).

Anser anser, the Greylag Goose, or *Anser fabalis,* the Bean Goose, and *Anser* sp., an undetermined goose, are represented by 78 bones, mainly from Stratum 2. Their dimensions were compared to those given by Bacher (1967:75) for Recent geese. Unfortunately, the material from *Aetokremnos* is very fragmentary, and there are very few pieces on which it is possible to take measurements.

There is great overlap in the dimensions of the two large species *A. anser* and *A. fabalis,* and of *A. albifrons* (the White-fronted Goose), which is on average slightly smaller. On 25 dimensions that it was possible to measure on the *Aetokremnos* material, 11 fall within the variation range of the three species (*A. anser, A. fabalis,* and *A. albifrons*), and 14 are larger than the corresponding dimensions of *A. albifrons* and only agree with *A. anser* and *A. fabalis* (Table 7-10). Therefore, I think that these 14 fragments can be attributed to *A. anser* or *A. fabalis* and the others to *Anser* sp. The presence of *A. albifrons* cannot be entirely ruled out.

In the *Aetokremnos* material, the best preserved elements, such as the humeri and the coracoids, are distinctly smaller than in *C. equitum,* and the only measurable phalanx 1 of the major digit of the wing is 36.6 mm long, which agrees with my Recent comparative material of *A. anser* or *A. fabalis.* It does not indicate a reduction of flying ability. The phalanx of *C. equitum* is from 33 to 42 mm long (*N*=9) (Northcote 1988:732), but it differs from the *Aetokremnos Anser* phalanges by its stoutness and shortened aspect.

The present-day breeding distribution of *A. anser* is discontinuous in boreal temperate steppe, and desert climatic zones. According to Voous (1960:46), its breeding area must have extended in the past over the whole of Europe, and "the disintegration of the breeding

Table 7-10. Dimensions of the Large Anseriforms (mm) from *Aetokremnos* and Recent *A. anser*, *A. fabalis*, and *A. albifrons* (After Bacher 1967)

	Aetokremnos A. anser or A. fabalis	*Aetokremnos* Anser sp.	Recent A. anser	Recent A. fabalis	Recent A. albifrons
Coracoid					
Internal length			n=102	n=62	n=48
	est.* 63.0, 64.0, 69.0		59.2–73.1	58.9–72.6	53.5–61.7
Humerus					
Proximal width			n=96	n=54	n=48
	33.0, 35.2		30.6–37.8	30.7–37.7	29.0–32.7
Min. width, shaft	11.2, 12.6	10.7	10.0–12.4	10.0–12.6	8.8–10.9
Min. depth, shaft	9.5, 10.0	9.0; 9.0	8.1–10.4	8.1–10.8	7.7–9.1
Distal width	25.3, 25.5, 26.1	23.1, 23.5, 23.7	22.5–27.0	22.6–27.8	21.0–24.4
Tibiotarsus					
Min. width, shaft			n=20	n=23	n=16
	7.8, 7.9		6.9–9.1	6.5–8.5	5.0–7.6
Min. depth, shaft		5.7, 5.7	5.0–7.0	5.0–6.7	3.8–5.8
Distal width		15.1	14.8–17.6	14.4–17.8	13.6–15.5

*Est. = estimated measurement.

range probably has resulted exclusively from direct persecution by man, disturbance of the nests, and cultivation of the suitable nesting grounds." During historic times, it was still nesting in southern Europe and even in northeast Algeria. It is possible that it nested throughout Turkey, and as it winters directly south of the breeding range and particularly along the coasts, it is possible that it wintered on Cypriot coasts or on the shores of the Akrotiri salt lake.

A. fabalis has a trans-Palearctic breeding distribution, in boreal and tundra climatic zones. It winters in Europe and Asia as far south as 30°–40° N (Voous 1960:48).

A. albifrons breeds predominantly in the tundra and winters mainly in coastal regions with extensive estuaries, but also in other low-lying and swampy grassy plains (Voous 1960:47). It is reported as wintering in Turkey, the coastal part of Syria, Iraq, and the Nile delta (Cramp and Simmons 1977:405). It is more frequent on Cyprus than the other two geese: "many hundreds" were seen in 1925 and "hundreds" in 1974 (Flint and Stewart 1983:47).

In their wintering grounds, the three species of geese are found on muddy seashores, wide estuaries, low-lying and swampy grassy plains, and wet meadows (Voous 1960:46–48). At the present time *A. anser* and *A. fabalis* are considered to be accidental or occasional visitors to Cyprus; *A. albifrons* is considered a winter visitor (Cramp and Simmons 1977:404; Flint and Stewart 1983:47; Neophytou 1976:4).

A. anser has been reported at three Natufian sites in the Near East (Hayonim and Mallaha in Israel and Mureybet in Syria) and at PPNB Jericho (Pichon 1984a:43; Tchernov 1993:140), but the dimensions of the bones can also correspond to *A. fabalis*.

A midsized Anseriform is represented by 4 coracoid fragments, 3 of them from Stratum 2 and the fourth from Stratum 2/4. This material does not allow a more accurate determination, but comes from at least three individuals.

Anas crecca, the Teal, is represented by 5 bones of two individuals from Stratum 2. Its distribution is Holarctic in various climatic zones, ranging from tundra to Mediterranean. In its breeding range it usually lives on small freshwater pools and lakes, but in winter it appears in estuaries and coastal lagoons (Voous 1960:22). This duck is a very common winter visitor and passage migrant on Cyprus from October/November to early March, and the peak numbers are usually in January/February, with up to 5,000 birds wintering on the Akrotiri salt lake (Flint and Stewart 1983:48).

A cf. *Circus*, Harrier, an Accipitriform (low-flying woodland hawks), is represented by a coracoid fragment from Stratum 4B. The Harriers' habitat ranges from marshes and more or less humid lowland plains to dry steppes. The occurrence of a Harrier would be quite normal in the *Aetokremnos* context. The four Recent European species occur on Cyprus either as winter visitors or passage migrants (Flint and Stewart 1983:55–56).

Rallus aquaticus, the Water Rail, is represented by a proximal part of a femur from Stratum 2. Its distribution is discontinuously trans-Palearctic, mainly in boreal, temperate, Mediterranean, and steppe climatic zones (Voous 1960:84). At the present time, it is a common passage migrant and winter visitor to Cypriot marshes and an occasional breeder (Flint and Stewart 1983:65). It frequents mainly freshwaters with dense, fairly tall aquatic vegetation (Cramp and Simmons 1979:538).

Otis tarda, the Great Bustard, is the most common bird at *Aetokremnos*. Among the first elements received for identification from the 1987 excavation was a distal part of a tarsometatarsus, which presented a foramen on the anterior face just above the middle

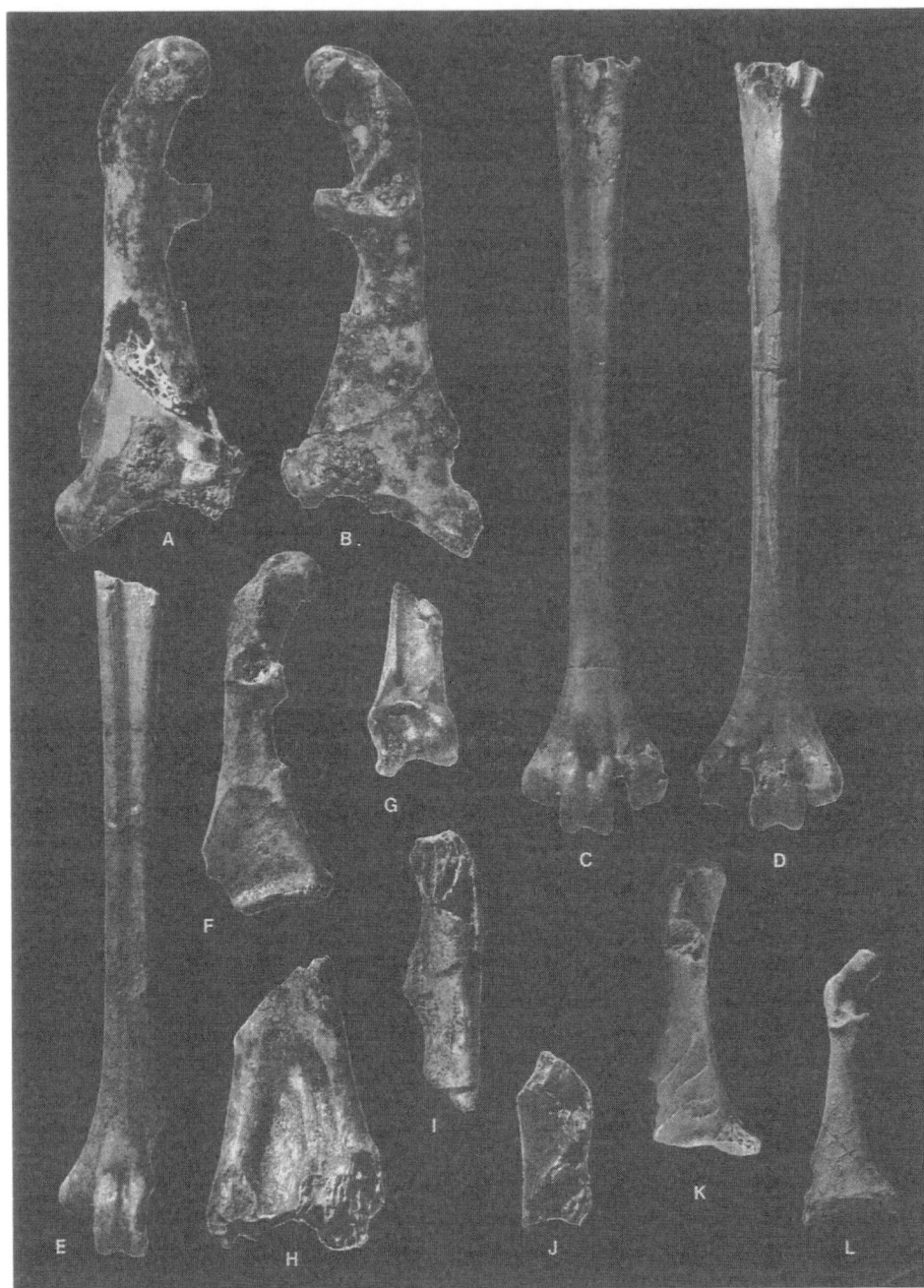

Figure 7-10. Bird bones from *Aetokremnos*. (a) *Otis tarda*, male size, right coracoid. Stratum 2 (lower), FN 524, anterior view, × 1; (b) as "a," posterior view, × 1; (c) *Otis tarda*, male size, left tarsometatarsus with a foramen above the middle trochlea. Stratum 2 (upper), FN 426, anterior view, × 1; (d) as "c," posterior view, × 1; (e) *Otis tarda*, male size, left tarsometatarsus without foramen.

trochlea (Fig. 7-10:c). This foramen does not exist in Recent forms. However, the tarsometatarsi from later seasons did not exhibit such a foramen (Fig. 7-10:e), and it was probably a pathological feature. The dimensions of the *Aetokremnos* bones fall within the variation range of the Recent *O. tarda*, and it is possible to refer them to the Recent species. Great Bustards have been reported on other Mediterranean islands: Pleistocene Malta (Bate 1916:422, 430) and Ibiza (Alcover *et al.* 1992:277; Florit *et al.* 1989:38), and Late Neolithic Rhodes (Halstead and Jones 1987:138).

Its present distribution is very discontinuous, in the Palearctic province, in the boreal, temperate, Mediterranean, and steppe climatic zones, but it was certainly much more widespread before the expansion of humans. In historic times, it was exterminated in Scotland, England, Denmark, southern Sweden, France, Switzerland, the former Yugoslavia, and Greece (Cramp and Simmons 1979:661; Voous 1960:88). It is still breeding in the Asian part of Turkey, and it is considered a scarce and irregular visitor on Cyprus (Flint and Stewart 1983:68). However, in early February 1974, 50 to 60 Great Bustards, together with flocks of White-fronted Geese, appeared at Rizokarpaso *Apostolos Andres Kastro* in northwest Cyprus after a severely cold winter (Neophytou 1976:xi, 16). Its habitat consists of extensive flat or hilly arid land with grass and weeds and steppes with short grass (Voous 1960:88).

The Great Bustard is the largest bird of the Recent European avifauna. There is a strong sexual variation in size, and it is possible to distinguish the bones of the males from those of females. The males weigh from 8 to 16 kg and are up to 1.05 m long; the females weigh from 3 to 4 kg (Cramp and Simmons 1979:659, 668).

During the occupation of *Aetokremnos*, *O. tarda* must have been numerous and was probably sedentary on Cyprus. Their extermination was probably furthered by the fact that they are highly gregarious for much of the year (Cramp and Simmons 1979:663). It Stratum 4, the MNI is about the same for males as for females, while in Stratum 2 there are about twice as many males as females. It is possible that males, which have much more meat, were selectively hunted.

Otis tarda, or a closely related form, has been reported from the Middle Pleistocene of Europe (e.g., Mourer-Chauviré 1975a) and the Late Pleistocene in Europe (e.g., Alcover *et al.* 1992) and the Levant (e.g., Kersten 1991;Tchernov 1980). It is even more frequently found in the Holocene at a large number of localities in Europe (e.g., Clot and Mourer-Chauviré 1986; Mourer-Chauviré 1981) and in Turkey (Boessneck and von den Driesch 1987:47; Stahl 1989), Syria (Buitenhuis 1988:61), Israel (Pichon 1984a, 1987:117, 124, 135, 141, Pl. III:5), Jordan (Boessneck and von den Driesch 1978; Köhler-Rollefson 1989:203; Köhler-Rollefson and Rollefson 1990:5; Köhler-Rollefson *et al.* 1988:428), Iraq (Solecki 1977), and Iran (Jánossy 1977, Meadow 1983:399–400).

Stratum 2, FN 1022, anterior view, × 1; (f) *Otis tarda*, female size, left coracoid. Stratum 4A/B, FN 878, posterior view, × 1; (g) *Otis tarda*, female size, left tibiotarsus, distal part, burnt. Stratum 4B, FN 878, anterior view, × 1; (h) *Otis tarda*, male size, left humerus, distal part, burnt. Stratum 4B, FN 357, palmar view, × 1; (i) *Otis tarda*, male size, left coracoid, anterior part, burnt, with two broad traces of burning. Stratum 4B, FN 357, anterointernal view, × 1; (j) *Otis tarda*, male size, right coracoid, anterior part, burnt, Stratum 4B, FN 357, internal view, × 1; (k) *Anser* sp., left coracoid. Stratum 2 (lower), FN 320, posterior view, × 1; (l) *Anas crecca*, left coracoid. Stratum 2 (upper), FN 791, posterior view, × 1.5.

Columba livia, the Rock Dove, or *Columba oenas*, the Stock Dove, are only represented by 5 remains of at least three doves from Strata 2, 4 and 1/2. These two species are practically the same size and are very difficult to distinguish osteologically (Fick 1974; Mourer-Chauviré 1975a; Vilette 1983; Weesie 1988:27–28).

The distribution of *C. livia* is Palearctic, Asian, and North Ethiopian, mainly in temperate, Mediterranean, steppe, desert, savanna, and tropical climatic zones. It inhabits rocky regions with adjacent stony or grassy plains without a prominent growth of trees (Voous 1960:136).

The distribution of *C. oenas* is West and Central Palearctic, in boreal, temperate, and Mediterranean climatic zones. It is the ecological substitute of *C. livia* in wooded regions. It inhabits broad-leaved and mixed forests with numerous old and hollow trees. It usually nests in trees and sometimes in small caves in steep rocky walls (Voous 1960:136).

C. livia is a resident breeder on Cyprus and nests on its rocky seacoasts, while *C. oenas* is an irregular winter visitor (Flint and Stewart 1983:83–84). In the *Aetokremnos* context, the presence of *C. livia* would be more likely, but it is not possible to be more positive about it.

Asio flammeus, the Short-eared Owl, is represented by an anterior part of a scapula, which is morphologically and metrically very characteristic. Its distribution is Holarctic and discontinuously Australian and South American, in the tundra, boreal, temperate, and Mediterranean climatic zones, and in mountains. It mainly frequents open marshes and bogs, wet or dry grasslands, and coastal salt marshes (Voous 1960:158). It is a winter visitor to Cyprus (Cramp 1985:590).

Athene noctua, the Little Owl, is represented by numerous fragmentary elements that come from the same individual in Stratum 4A/B. These elements include two small skull fragments, which is exceptional for the site. The bird probably died inside the rockshelter, and its bones remained almost undisturbed here.

Weesie (1982:32) described an endemic extinct species from the Pleistocene of Crete, *Athene cretensis*. This species is characterized by its dimensions, which are larger than the Recent *A. noctua*, and particularly by its proportionally more elongated legs, which correspond to an adaptation to a more terrestrial way of life. In the *Aetokremnos* material, it is not possible to measure the total length of the bones, but only the width of the shaft in the middle. In *A. cretensis*, the width of the midshaft is larger than in the Recent *A. noctua* (Weesie 1982:Fig. 2). By its dimensions, the form at *Aetokremnos* corresponds to the mainland *A. noctua*.

The distribution of *A. noctua* is trans-Palearctic and partially Ethiopian, in temperate, Mediterranean, steppe, and desert climatic zones. Its habitat ranges from lightly forested regions and meadows with scattered clumps of trees to rocky semideserts and steppes (Voous 1960:159–160). It is a resident breeder on Cyprus (Cramp 1985:590).

The Turdidae (Thrushes) are represented by 3 fragments from Stratum 2, a complete humerus (burnt) from Stratum 4A/B, and a fragmentary humerus from Stratum 4B, from at least two individuals. The complete humerus belongs to the genus *Turdus*, and according to its size (27 mm), it can be attributed either to *Turdus iliacus* (Redwing) or to *T. philomelos* (song thrush) (Weesie 1988:41). The distribution of *T. philomelos* is West and Central Palearctic, in boreal and temperate climatic zones and in mountains. Its habitat is made up of mixed broad-leaved and coniferous forests (Voous 1960:200). *T. iliacus* is trans-Palearctic and almost totally confined to the boreal zone. It lives in less dense forests than the song thrush (Voous 1960:200). Both species are northern breeding birds, but they can be found during the winter on Cyprus (Hüe and Ethecopar 1970:577).

Corvus corone (including *C. corone corone*, the carrion crow, and *C. corone cornix*, the hooded crow) and *Corvus frugilegus*, the rook, are very difficult to distinguish by their osteological characteristics (Weesie 1988: 46). The *Aetokremnos* material includes 9 fragments of 8 bones from at least four individuals. It is not possible to give a more accurate determination.

C. corone have a trans-Palearctic distribution, in boreal, temperate, Mediterranean, steppe, and desert climatic zones, and in mountains. Its habitat is very varied but usually associated with trees (Voous 1960:266). At the present time, the hooded crow breeds on Cyprus (Hüe and Ethecopar 1970:521).

C. frugilegus also has a trans-Palearctic distribution, mainly in boreal, temperate, steppe, and desert climatic zones. Its habitat consists of wide, grassy river valleys with meadows and riverine forests (Voous 1960:266). It is sedentary and migratory; some populations winter in the Mediterranean, and it is reported as a winter visitor to Cyprus (Bannerman and Bannerman 1958:5; Hüe and Ethecopar 1970:523). As with *Columba livia* or *C. oenas*, the presence of *C. c. cornix* is more likely, but the possibility of *C. frugilegus* cannot be ruled out.

There is also a single unidentifiable small passeriform (song bird) bone from Stratum 2B. Three small unidentifiable passeriform bones were found in 1969 by Boekschoten and Sondaar at the Cypriot Late Pleistocene site of Xylophagou *Ayii Saranda* (personal analysis), but these may be Holocene intrusions.

It is worth noting that the *Aetokremnos* avifauna does not include any Phasianidae (game birds), which makes it very different from the Pleistocene/Early Holocene avifaunas on the mainland. The midsized Phasianidae, such as the representatives of the genera *Alectoris* and *Francolinus*, which are present today on Cyprus, did not exist in the past on the isolated Mediterranean islands and were introduced there by humans (Alcover *et al.* 1992:275). The only Phasianidae that is found on the islands is *Coturnix coturnix* (the quail), which is also the only migratory phasianid in western Europe. *C. coturnix* has been found at Early Chalcolithic Kissonerga *Mylouthkia* and contemporary *Mosphilia* in southwestern Cyprus (Croft 1989b:209, and personal communication to D. Reese May 22, 1994). At the present time, it is both a breeder and a passage migrant on Cyprus (Flint and Stewart 1983:64).

Also, the *Aetokremnos* avifauna does not include any endemic extinct species. This sample, however, may not be representative of the complete Early Holocene avifauna in Cyprus; it is probable that it only corresponds to the biotope restricted to the immediate surroundings of the rockshelter.

Ecological Significance and Variation of the Avifauna According to the Strata

The majority of the identified bones are from species that are aquatic or live in open countries. The aquatic forms are *Podiceps*, *Puffinus*, *Phalacrocorax*, midsized Anseriform, *Anas* and *Rallus*. The open country dwellers are *Anser*, *Circus*, *Otis*, *Asio*, and *Athene*.

The only forms that could indicate a forested environment are the Turdidae, which live in woods or bushes; *Corvus corone* or *C. frugilegus*, which live in cultivated areas and parklands, but nest in trees; and *A. noctua*, which also live in lightly forested regions.

In Stratum 4, the avifauna is only composed of forms living in open or sparsely wooded areas, and there are no aquatic forms. The aquatic forms *P. nigricollis, P. aristotelis,* midsized Anseriform, *A. crecca,* and *R. aquaticus* are only found in Stratum 2, with the exceptions of *P. puffinus* and one of the midsized Anseriforms (both from Stratum 2/4). Most of the marine invertebrates (67.8%) also come from Stratum 2. Stratum 2 also contains the majority of the *O. tarda* remains, while it only contains 2.1% of the *Phanourios* remains. This indicates that during the deposition of Stratum 2, the inhabitants of the rockshelter exploited a much wider range of resources than during the deposition of Stratum 4. The MNI and the percentages of the different types of environment are given in Table 7-11.

According to the information provided by birds, the environment of *Aetokremnos* appears as very open, with grasslands and marshes, and with seabirds nesting in the cliff and migratory birds wintering on the shores of the Akrotiri salt lake or lagoon. This restoration must be limited to the immediate surroundings of the locality and cannot be extended for the entire island of Cyprus.

A few Aceramic Neolithic sites on Cyprus have yielded bird bones. The number of identified species is low and does not allow us to make comparisons with the *Aetokremnos* avifauna. Khirokitia produced 2 bones of *Columba palumbus* (Wood Pigeon), and single bones of *Corvus corone* and *Ciconia ciconia* (White Stork) (Pichon 1984b). Older excavations there yielded 2 *Columba livia* bones from one locus and the bone of a small duck (Watson *et al.* 1977:236). Dhali *Agridhi* produced 3 first phalanges of a medium-sized bird (Schwartz 1974a:115) and a humerus of a pigeon-sized bird (Croft 1989a:270, no. 4). Kalavasos *Tenta* had a probable *C. palumbus* and a small passerine (Croft 1989b:71). Birds also have been recovered from Ceramic Neolithic sites: Sotira *Teppes* produced a single bird bone from House 27, Floor II–III (Zeuner and Ellis 1961:236), and Ayios Epiktitos *Vrysi* produced 16 unidentified bird bones (Legge 1982b:76, 86).

Taphonomic Study

Fragmentation

The number of bird bone fragments recovered at *Aetokremnos* is 3,205, of which 529, 16.5%, were identified. The degree of fragmentation of the material is very high, which may by partly due to the trampling of the living floor by the inhabitants of the shelter, the burn-

Table 7-11. **Minimum Numbers of Individuals (MNI) and Percentages, by Major Strata, Corresponding to Different Types of Environments**

	Stratum 2		Stratum 4	
Environment	MNI	%	MNI	%
Waters	7	22.6	0	—
Open country	20	64.5	11	73.3
Rocks or forests (*Columba*)	1	3.2	1	6.7
Woods or bushes (*Turdus, Corvus*)	2	6.5	3	20.0
Unknown (small Passerine)	1	3.2	0	—
TOTAL	31	100.0	15	100.0

ing of many of the bones, the ancient collapse of the roof of the shelter, and breakage during excavation, washing, and shipment to France. The number of undeterminable splinters is very high compared with the number of determined remains.

Burning

Among the 529 identified remains, the number of burnt of charred fragments is 65, 12.3%, and among the undetermined remains, the number of burnt or charred fragments is 527—19.9%. The total number of burnt or charred determined and undetermined fragments is 592 or 18.5% of the total collection.

This percentage is very high: When bird bones are submitted to the action of fire, they are usually completely destroyed. That a bird bone was burnt but not destroyed—and was preserved until the present time—is probably a rare event. It is most probable that a much larger number of bird bones were completely burnt and therefore disappeared completely.

In *O. tarda,* the traces of burning are more frequent on the femora (29.2%) than on the radii (20.9%) and humeri (19.1%) (Table 7-12). For the Geese, because the number of fragments and traces of burning are low, the percentages do not have a great significance. In total, for the Great Bustard and for the Geese, 14% of the fragments show traces of burning.

Differential Preservation

In archaeological sites and in natural (nonhuman) fillings, the different elements of the bird skeleton are not always preserved in the same way. The pattern of preservation makes it possible to draw some conclusions about the agent of accumulation of the bones (Baales 1992:18–20; Mourer-Chauviré 1975a:305, 1975b:107, 1983:111–124).

For *O. tarda,* the minimum number of the main postcranial elements was worked out by taking into account the best-represented parts. It has been very difficult to calculate the minimum number of bones for the ulnae and the radii because they are represented by a very few proximal and distal parts, mainly by small fragments of the shaft. The minimum numbers of bones was estimated by taking into account the degree of fragmentation of the

Table 7-12. Location of Burning/Charring on *O. tarda* and *Anser* Sp. Bones

Bones	*O. tarda*			*Anser* sp.		
	Number of fragments	Number burnt	% burnt	Number of fragments	Number burnt	% burnt
Coracoids	47	6	12.8	14	1	7.0
Scapulae	16	0	—	7	0	
Humeri	47	9	19.1	25	3	12.0
Ulnae	14	0	—	3	2	67.0
Radii	43	9	20.9	5	0	—
Carpometacarpi	9	0	—	4	1	25.0
Femora	24	7	29.2	0	0	—
Tibiotarsi	12	1	8.3	4	1	25.0
Tarsometatarsi	28	2	7.1	1	1	100.0

shafts. The same problem arises for the tarsometatarsi of females, which are also mostly represented by shaft fragments.

The best-preserved bones are the coracoids, often represented by their scapular part, and the humeri. The scapular part of the coracoid is the most robust part of the skeleton. However, there is differential preservation according to sex. In the males, the most numerous bones are the coracoids, while in the females the most numerous bones are the humeri. The bones the least preserved proportionally are the carpometacarpi, ulnae, and tibiotarsi.

The minimum number of wing bones (humerus, radius, ulna, carpometacarpus) is 48, or 36%. The elements of the wing are represented by an average of 12 bones. The minimum number of leg bones (femur, tibiotarsus, tarsometatarsus) is 36, or 27%. The elements of the leg are also represented by an average of 12 bones. Thus in the case of *O. tarda*, compared with the leg bones, the wing bones are not better preserved. The elements of the shoulder girdle (scapula, coracoid) are represented by 50 bones, thus an average of 25 bones. The elements of the proximal segment of the limbs (humerus, femur) are represented by 37 bones, an average of 17.5 bones. The elements of the distal segments of the limbs (radius, ulna, carpometacarpus, tibiotarsus, tarsometatarsus) are represented by 47 bones, an average of 9.4 bones. In conclusion, the elements of the shoulder girdle are approximately three times, and the elements of the proximal segment of the limbs approximately twice, as well preserved as the elements of the distal segments of the limbs.

For the large Anseriforms (*Anser anser* or *A. fabalis* and *Anser* sp.), the elements of the wing (average 4 bones) are much better preserved than the elements of the leg (average 1 bone). The elements of the shoulder girdle are represented on average by 8 bones, the elements of the proximal segment of the limbs on average by 6 bones, and the elements of the distal segments of the limbs on average by 1.75 bones. Therefore, in the case of the geese, the elements of the shoulder girdle are four times, and the elements of the proximal segment of the limbs three times, as well preserved as the elements of the distal segments of the limbs.

These proportions of preservation of the proximal and distal elements of the limbs are very different from those that are found when the birds have been hunted by large nocturnal raptors such as the Eagle Owl (*Bubo bubo*) or the Snowy Owl (*Nyctea scandiaca*). In the Snowy Owl, on the contrary, the distal elements of the legs and wings are strongly overrepresented (Baales 1992: 19–20; Mourer-Chauviré 1975a:305, 1975b:107, 1983:111–124).

The differential survivorship of avian bones in naturally deposited versus archaeological localities has also been studied by Ericson (1987) and Livingston (1989). If one takes into consideration the three main elements of the anterior limb (humerus, ulna, carpometacarpus) and the three elements of the posterior limb (femur, tibiotarsus, tarsometatarsus), and if all these elements are preserved in the same way, one should obtain a percentage of 50% for the anterior elements compared with the sum of anterior and posterior elements.

Livingston (1989:543–546) showed that the differential survivorship of bird bones is not only related to possible human action, but also depends on the relative robustness of the bones, this robustness being related to the way of life of the birds. In geese and dabbling ducks, strong fliers with robust wing elements, the percentage of anterior elements varies from about 62 to 86%, while in diving ducks, coots, and grebes, which have more lightly built wing elements, the percentage of anterior elements varies between 24 and 48%.

In the case of *Aetokremnos*, the percentage of anterior elements for *O. tarda* is 50.7%, which is very close to the anatomically expected ratio, while for the *Anser* forms the percentage of anterior elements is 83%. This value is very close to the percentage found for geese and dabbling ducks from two archaeological sites in North America studied by Livingston (1989:542), while in the geese from northern European archaeological sites, the percentage of anterior elements is on average 53%, which is not statistically different from the anatomically expected ratio (Ericson 1987:71).

In conclusion, it is not possible to study the survivorship of bird bones globally because this survivorship depends on several factors: (1) whether the birds were living in the site or whether they were brought to the site by predators, human or nonhuman (Mourer-Chauviré 1975a: 305, 1975b:107), (2) the size of the birds, in particular with regard to the size of the predator (Mourer-Chauviré 1983: 114, 117), and (3) the taxonomic composition of the bird assemblages (Livingston 1989), to which can be added the action of humans (Ericson 1987).

Seasonality

The avifauna has some implications for seasonality at *Aetokremnos*. Some species are sedentary at the present time or were probably sedentary at the time of the site's occupation. These are *P. nigricollis, P. puffinus, P. aristotelis, R. aquaticus, C. livia, A. noctua, C. corone. Otis tarda* also was probably sedentary on Cyprus; the presence of juvenile individuals at *Aetokremnos* confirms that the Great Bustard was breeding on the island. These species may have been present the entire year. *A. anser,* whose presence is not completely assured, is migratory and was probably only at the site during its breeding period in the spring and summer. The other species, *A. fabalis,* the presence of which is also not completed assured; *A. albifrons* (?); *A. crecca; Circus* sp.; *A. flammeus;* and *T. iliacus* or *T. viscivorus* are migratory and were probably wintering on Cyprus. Thus we may conclude that the birds recovered from *Aetokremnos* indicate that the site probably was occupied throughout the entire year.

OTHER FAUNA

Eggshell (*David Reese*)

Aetokremnos produced eggshells from 13 separate deposits (i.e., FNs), most from Stratum 2. From Stratum 1/2, there was one FN in residue (i.e., from a water-sieved sample) from N94E90. In upper Stratum 2 there were two FNs—one from Feature 4 in N97E89 (northwest quadrant) and the other from Locus 3 in N97E90 (southwest quadrant). From Stratum 2 contexts, there were six FNs. These were from N94E88 and N94E89 (southwest quadrant), Feature 5 residue; residue from N97E87 (northeast quadrant); N97E89 (southwest quadrant, some partially burnt); N97E89 (southeast quadrant), Locus 6 (some partially burnt); and N97E89 (northwest quadrant), Locus 4, (partially burnt). From lower Stratum 2, there were three FNs. The first was from N97E90 (northwest quadrant), while the second was from the southwest quadrant of the same unit; the third was from Feature 6 residue in N93E90 (northwest quadrant). Finally, from Stratum 4A/B, there was one FN from the southern quadrants of N96E89.

The species of bird producing the eggshells have not yet been identified, but it is likely that they are the same species represented in the bird bone collection, particularly the Great

Bustard and Geese. Some of the eggshells from Stratum 2 have been burnt. Eggshells have only rarely been found on prehistoric sites, and these are usually of the thick-shelled ostrich.

Toad and Snake (*Salvador Bailon, translated from the original French by Stuart Swiny*)

Introduction

Research on amphibian and reptilian remains from archaeological sites is still uncommon and has only resulted in a few publications. These species, however, can provide valuable information on the environment in which people lived and on human relationships with these animals. *Aetokremnos* provides an example of the information yielded by these vertebrates when retrieved from an archaeological context. Furthermore, both forms are intrinsically interesting from a zoological point of view, because they provide information on the recent origins of the current herpetofauna and on paleobiogeography and the mechanisms that lead to its reconstitution.

Systematics

The following forms are present at *Aetokremnos: Bufo viridis* Laurneti, 1768 (Green Toad), *Vipera lebetina* Linnaeus, 1758 (Blunt-nosed Viper or Levant Viper), *Natrix natrix cypriaca* ([Cypriot] Grass Snake) and *Coluber jugularis* Linnaeus, 1758 (Large or Persian Whip-Snake or Black Snake). Of the 264 skeletal fragments studied, 260 (98.5%) belong to *V. lebetina*.

Amphibians.   *B. viridis:* Sample, 1 femur (Stratum 1C, FN 493, N98E90). This femur was a long bone, slightly sigmoidal in section, with a partially subdivided femoral ridge that consists of a pronounced, sharp inner ridge with a lesser outer ridge. The overall morphology of the bone, specifically that of the femoral ridge, closely corresponds to that of the living *B. viridis,* the only member of this family currently living in Cyprus. Its presence has been noted at Khirokitia (Watson *et al.* 1977:236, 237; 1 vertebra). A sample has been recorded in a possibly Pleistocene deposit at Cape Pyla (*Bufo* sp.; Sanchiz 1984:65).[3]

Snakes.   *V. lebetina:* Sample, 232 vertebrae and an undetermined number of rib fragments (Table 7-13). This viper is by far the best represented form; it comprises 98.3% of the identifiable sample. It is only represented by vertebrae and rib fragments. A relatively large number of vertebrae (30%) show traces of burning, some of it heavy.

From a morphological point of view, the vertebrae (Fig. 7-11) differ little from contemporary specimens of this species. The length of the centrum for 134 vertebrae ranges from 3.9 mm for the smallest to 10.07 mm for the largest, with an average value of 6.1 mm (variation ± 1.093). By comparison, these values correspond to a total body length in contemporary specimens that ranges from 110 to 170 cm. The overall length of contemporary specimens of this species does not appear to exceed 150 cm (LeGarff 1991).

---

[3]Xylophagou-*Ayii Saranda* is the only Cape Pyla site with amphibian remains (nos. PY-301 to 304 in Dr. A. van der Meulen's office, Room W324, Tray P58, Faculteit Aardwetenschappen, Universiteit Utrecht, The Netherlands).

Table 7-13. Distribution of Reptile Bones at *Aetokremnos*

Stratum		Bones
A. SNAKE		
Stratum 1		
FN 778	N96E92	*V. lebetina:* 13 vertebrae
Stratum 1/2		
FN 657	N96E88	*V. lebetina:* 4 vertebrae
FN 827	N96E89 (Feature 6, top; S quads)	*V. lebetina:* 1 vertebra
FN 1132	N97E90 (SW quad)	*V. lebetina:* 2 vertebrae
FN 709	N98E89 (Feature 4, over feature)	*V. lebetina:* 2 vertebrae
FN 905	N99E88 (SW quad)	*V. lebetina:* 1 vertebra
Stratum 1–4		
FN 759	N97E85	*V. lebetina:* 3 vertebrae
Stratum 2 (upper)		
FN 967	N96E90 (SW quad)	*V. lebetina:* 3 vertebrae
FN 822	N97E89 (SW quad)	*V. lebetina:* 1 vertebra
FN 856	N97E89 (NE quad)	*V. lebetina:* 1 vertebra
FN 1099	N97E90	*V. lebetina:* 3 vertebrae (at least 1 burnt)
FN 788	N98E89	*V. lebetina:* 11 vertebrae
Stratum 2		
FN 208	N94E91	*V. lebetina:* 1 vertebra fragment
FN 982	N96E89 (NE quad)	*V. lebetina:* 6 vertebrae
FN 871A	N96E92	*V. lebetina:* 22 vertebrae
FN 294	N97E87 (NE quad)	*V. lebetina:* 2 vertebrae
FN 902	N97E89 (Locus 6, SE quad)	*V. lebetina:* 1 vertebra
FN 517	N97-98E98 (W half)	*V. lebetina:* 4 vertebrae
FN 1022	N98E90	*V. lebetina:* 25 vertebrae
		Natrix: 1 dorsal vertebra
Stratum 2 (lower)		
FN 651	N95E90 (bottom of Feature 6 or top of Feature 7)	*V. lebetina:* 1 vertebra
FN 866	N96E89 (S half)	*V. lebetina:* 1 vertebra
FN 987	N96E90 (NW and SE quads)	*V. lebetina:* 2 vertebrae
FN 340	N96E91	*V. lebetina:* 53 vertebrae (1 burnt)
		C. jugularis: 1 vertebra
FN 1115	N97E90	*V. lebetina:* 10 vertebrae
Stratum 2/4		
FN 344	N95E88 (Feature 5, mixed feature) (broken, burnt)	*V. lebetina:* 1 vertebra
FN 960	N96E89 (Feature 8, NW quad)	*V. lebetina:* 1 vertebra
Stratum 3		
FN 610	N96E91	*V. lebetina:* 37 vertebrae
FN 1156	N97E90 (Locus 6, SE quad)	*Natrix:* 1 vertebra

(continued)

Table 7-13. (Continued)

Stratum		Bones
Stratum 4A/B		
FN 878	N96E89 (S half)	*V. lebetina:* 1 vertebra
Stratum 4B		
FN 532	N96E87 (E half)	*V. lebetina:* 1 vertebra
FN 729	N96E88 (NW quad)	*V. lebetina:* 2 vertebrae
FN 1092	N96E90 (NE quad)	*V.lebetina:* 1 vertebra
FN 654	N96E91	*V. lebetina:* 4 vertebrae
FN 556	N97E86	*V. lebetina:* 1 vertebra
FN 367	N97E87-88 (N half)	*V. lebetina:* 2 vertebrae, both partly burnt
FN 684	N97E88 (Feature 3, E quads)	*V. lebetina:* 4 vertebrae
FN 1059	N97E89 (Feature 3, NW quad)	*V. lebetina:* 1 vertebra
Stratum 4C		
FN 737	N96E88	*V. lebetina:* 1 vertebra
B. TORTOISE		
Stratum 2 (upper)		
FN 982	N96E89 (NE quad)	*?Testudo,* diaphysis of left humerus, very young (not twisted)
Stratum 2		
FN 294	N97E87 (NE quad)	*?Testudo:* carapacial fragments
Stratum 2 (lower)		
FN 427	N96E91	*?Testudo:* carapacial fragments
Stratum 1–4		
FN 553	N95E89 + N96E88	*?Testudo:* diaphysis of left femur
Stratum 2/4		
FN 77	N95E88 (Feature 5, mixed debris)	*?Testudo s.l.:* carapacial and plastral fragments
FN 680	N96E88 (Feature 8)	*?Testudo:* carapacial fragments
Stratum 4A/B		
FN 819	N98E88 (Feature 3, SE quad)	*?Geochelone s.l.:* one (?) fragment of caudal vertebrae, burnt green
FN 891	N98E89 (NW quad)	*?Geochelone s.l.:* diaphysis of fibula
Stratum 4B		
FN 357	N95E88	*?Testudo:* peripheral fragments *?Geochelone:* ?plastral fragment
FN 803	N93E90 (NE quad)	*?Testudo:* proximal head of right humerus
FN 684	N97E88 (Feature 3,	*?Testudo:* carapacial fragments, E quads) diaphysis of left femur *?Geochelone s.l.:* several bones: hands/feet of young with coracoid (stout) and tibia (stout), metatarsus (stout), caudal vertebrae
FN 1169	N97E90	*?Testudo:* fragment of peripheral

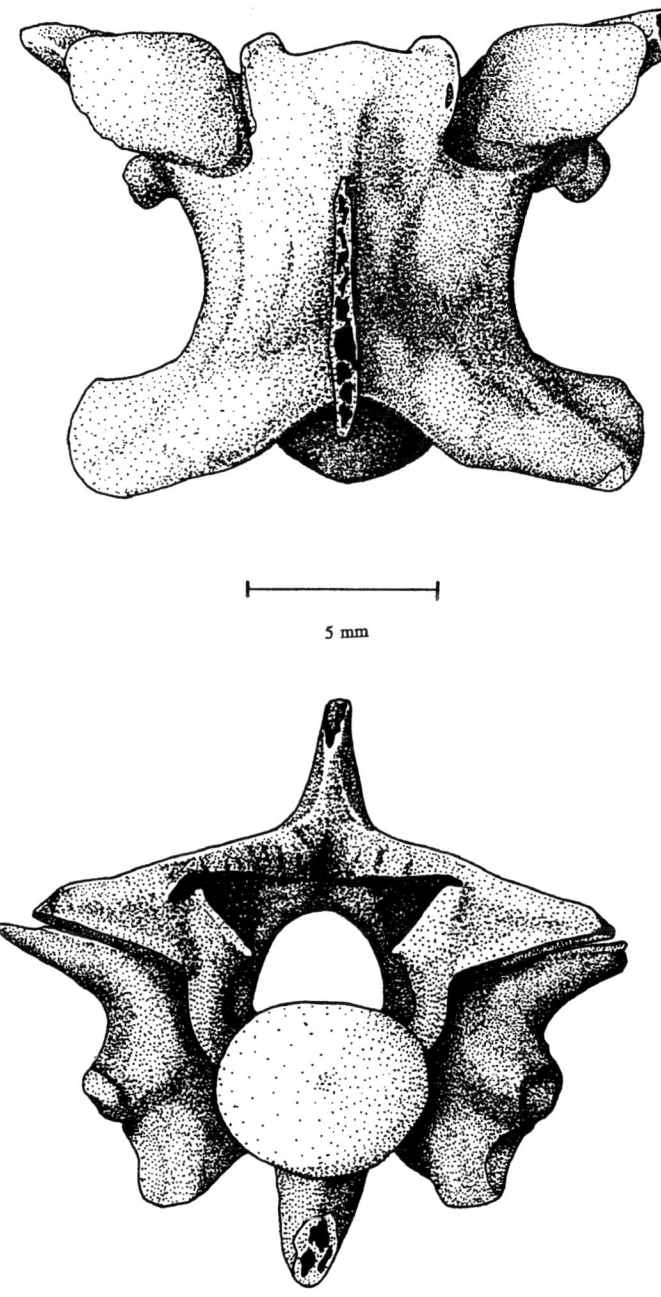

5 mm

Figure 7-11. *Vipera lebetina*, dorsal vertebra.

The Levantine Viper was represented in all strata; however, its stratigraphic distribution is very heterogeneous, with Stratum 2 yielding 63% and Stratum 4, 7.8% of the total assemblage. This is the first reference to the existence of the species on Cyprus.

Natrix natrix cypriaca: Sample, 2 dorsal vertebrae (Stratum 2, FN 1022; Stratum 3, FN 1156). The vertebrae have the usual characteristics of this species, among which should be noted the presence of hypapophyses (despite the fact that these vertebrae are not upper dorsals), a vaulted neural arch, a subacetabulum process, and a laterally well-delimited ventral surface of the centrum (Bailon 1991; Szyndlar 1984). The attribution is based on the presence of a hypophyse with an obtuse distal end. This feature was noted by Szyndlar (1984) as a means of distinguishing *N. natrix* from other European natricines (*N. tesselata* and *N. maura*). *N. natrix cypriaca* currently lives on the island, and its presence at *Aetokremnos* is the first time it was recorded at a site (Hadjisterkotis and Reese 1994; Teschner *et al.* 1992).

C. jugularis: Sample, 1 dorsal vertebra (Stratum 2B, FN 340). This is a medium-sized vertebra with a centrum 5.36-mm long and a neural arch that is vaulted when viewed from the rear. The ventral view of the centrum, devoid of a hypopophysis, is elongated, quite narrow, and well defined laterally. The subcentral grooves are little developed, and the central ridge is thin and high, with a flat ventral edge that exhibits a slightly spatulated distal end. These characteristics correspond to those of the living *C. jugularis* and differentiate it from the other Cypriot Colubridae. This species has been recorded at Khirokitia (Watson *et al.* 1977:236, 237).

Discussion

The large amount of *V. lebetina* remains at *Aetokremnos*, especially in the strata considered to be of cultural origin; its random distribution; the high percentage of burnt remains; and, to a lesser extent, the absence of cranial bones argue in favor of their presence being caused by cultural factors. Humans seem to have hunted Levantine Vipers at *Aetokremnos*. It could have been a food resource, or its presence may be explained by the desire to eliminate an undesirable venomous species, or perhaps it was connected with some undetermined cultural activity. Vipers must have been hunted mainly in the spring and autumn whey they are diurnal and thus easier to locate.

Twenty-four species of amphibians and reptiles are currently recorded on Cyprus: 3 species of anorus amphibians, 18 species of squamates, and 3 species of turtles (Bons *et al.* 1984; Wiedl and Eugster 1991). Only one of these species, *Coluber cypriensis*, is endemic to the island (Schätti 1985), while the others are well represented on the mainland (Europe, Asia, and Africa).

Paleontological information on Cypriot amphibians and reptiles is quite sparse. Sanchiz (1984) mentioned the presence of *Bufo* sp. at "Cabo Pyla," while Watson *et al.* note the presence of *B. viridis*, *C. jugularis*, *Agama stellio cypriaca* Daan, 1967 (Cypriot Agama lizard or Starred Agama), and *Eumeces schneideri* Daudin, 1802 (Schneider's Skink or Spotted Skink) in Aceramic levels at Khirokitia. To this list should be added the four species from *Aetokremnos*: *B. viridis*, *V. lebetina*, *N. natrix Cypriaca* and *C. jugularis*. All of these species are still present on the island, and no Quaternary extinctions of amphibians or snakes have been recorded.

The Consumption of Snakes on Cyprus (*David Reese*)

Certainly, it is not out of the question that snakes could have been eaten at *Aetokremnos*. There is a reference to the consumption of snakes on Cyprus by the Abbe Giovanni Mariti, who was on the island from 1760–67. In his 1769 book, *Viaggi per l'Isola di Cipro*, published in Lucca, he wrote, "There is also a black snake five or six feet long. This is not venomous, and may be handled without offense. It is sometimes skinned and cooked, and said to be a savoury morsel" (Cobham 1909:15). Mariti is probably referring to *C. jugularis*.

Tortoise (*David Reese*)

Aetokremnos produced terrestrial turtle (tortoise) remains from 12 units: Stratum 2 (3), Strata 1–4 and 2/4 (3), and Stratum 4 (6) (Table 7-13). These remaines were kindly identified by Dr. Roger Bour, Laboratoire des Reptiles et Amphibiens, Muséum National d'Historie Naturelle, Paris. Unlike the snake remains, most turtle remains are from Stratum 4, but the sample is quite small. It is worth noting that many of the remains come from Feature 3, the largest deposit at the site, and that both Strata 4A/B samples come from unit N98E89. It is unclear if the remains are food debris, although several are burnt. It is possible that turtle carapaces were used as small containers. Bour suggested that the *Testudo* remains (9 samples) are *T. graeca* Linnaeus, 1758 (or the newly elevated species *T. ibera* of Turkey), the Spur-thighed Tortoise, which are today found in Turkey, Syria, and Israel. Others (5 samples) are assigned to ?*Geochelone (sensu lato)* on the basis of size or the heavily built morphology.

Fossil and archaeological turtle remains from Cyprus have recently been surveyed (Hadjisterkotis and Reese 1994). Boulenger (1888:505) queried Unger and Kotschy's listing of *Testudo marginata* as present on Cyprus. Two small Pleistocene (probable) turtle carapace fragments were found by Boekschoten and Sondaar (1972:321) in 1969 in the lignitic clay at Kythrea *Kephalovrysi*.

There are few reports of turtle remains from Aceramic Neolithic sites on Cyprus. The 1970 season at *Cape Andreas Kastros* produced the proximal half of a left humerus of ?*Testudo* (CAK no. 110-3; pathological or distorted) and a ?*Geochelone sensulato* carapace fragment with scapula insertion (CAK no. 153-2; analyzed by Bour). Dhali *Agridhi* yielded one tortoise femur (Croft 1989a:270, n.4). For the Ceramic Neolithic, Ayios Epiktitos *Vrysi* produced 14 samples of a marine turtle (Legge 1982b:85).

Fish (*Mark Rose*)

Only 1 fish bone was found, from N97E87-88, Level 4. This is a distal fragment of a caudal vertebra (perhaps no. 19 on the vertebral column) of a Gray Mullet (Mugilidae, species indeterminate). It has a vertical diameter (posterior) of 9.2 mm and a horizontal diameter (posterior) of 9.8 mm. The fish may have been about 50 cm or more in length and about 1 to 1.2 kg in weight (Deese *et al.* 1987). Six species of Gray Mullet are native to the eastern Mediterranean. Medium-sized fish (25 to 100 cm), they school in coastal waters, entering lagoons, estuaries, and river to filter feed on minute plants, invertebrates, and detritus (Whitehead *et al.* 1986:1197–1204).

Marine Invertebrates (*David Reese*)

In addition to the bone sample, *Aetokremnos* produced the largest marine shell collection ever excavated on Cyprus, although they are present at many Aceramic Neolithic Cypriot sites (e.g., Catoliotti-Valdina 1994; Demetropoulos 1984; Gjerstad 1934:8; Lehavy 1989:209, 215, Fig. 13c, Pl. 8c; Peltenburg 1979b:23, 24, 34, Fig. 3:17; Reese 1978; 1993:207–208), as well as on the mainland (e.g., Bar-Yosef 1994; Bate 1937:224; Reese 1982, 1989a, 1991; van Regteren Altena 1962; J. Shackleton *et al.* 1988; N. Shackleton 1968, 1969). The *Aetokremnos* sample is the largest shell collection for its time period from anywhere in the Mediterranean Basin.

The vast majority of the 73,365 fragments, representing 21,576 individuals (Table 7-14), are food debris, mainly the Topshell (*Monodonta*, 20,750 individuals, 96.2%) and the Limpet (*Patella*, 640, 3.9%). The next most common shells, the 88 *Columbella*, 49 *Dentalium*, 25 *Conus*, and several of the rarer forms, are largely human-modified or naturally made shell beads.

There are 265 complete and 71,054 fragments of *Monodonta*, coming from at least 20,750 individuals. These are mainly *M. turbinata*, but *M. articulata* is also present. There are 1,860 *Patella* fragments, representing at least 640 individuals. The majority of *Monodonta* and *Patella* individuals come from Stratum 2. A summary of the marine shells used as a food resource is given in Table 7-15.

In addition to *Monodonta* and *Patella*, there are a number of much rarer marine invertebrates that were also probably food remains (5 shells, 3 crabs, and 1 example each of echinoid and cuttlefish): crab pincers from Strata 1 and 1/2; a fresh *Cerithium* with an open mouth and slightly broken apex and a fresh *Arca* hinge fragment from Stratum 1–4; a fresh

Table 7-14. Marine Invertebrates

20,750 (4,366)*	Topshell: *Monodonta turbinata* (Born, 1778); *Monodonta articulata* (Lamarck, 1822)
640 (192)	Limpet: *Patella caerulea* Linnaeus, 1758; *Patella lusitanica* Gmelin, 1790
88	Dove shell: *Columbella rustica* (Linnaeus, 1758)
49	Dentalium shell: 21 "beads", *Dentalium dentalis* Linnaeus, 1767 (48 examples); *Dentalium rubescens* (Deshayes, 1825) or *Dentalium vulgare* (da Costa, 1778) (1 shell)
25	Cone shell: 23 holed, *Conus mediterraneus* "Hwass" in Bruguière, 1792
8	Horn shell: 5 holed, *Cerithium vulgatum* Bruguière, 1792
6	Dog cockle: 1 holed, *Glycymeris glycymeris* Linnaeus, 1758; *Glycymeris pilosa* Linnaeus,1767
1	(Noah's) Ark shell, Stratum 1–4: *Arca noae* Linnaeus, 1758
1	Turret shell, Stratum 2 (upper): *Turritella communis* Risso, 1826
1	(Rough) Venus shell, Stratum 2: *Venus verrucosa*
1	Operculum (Stratum 2)
1	Whelk, Stratum 4C: *Euthria cornea* Linnaeus, 1758
3	Crabs, Strata 1, 1/2, 2 (lower)
1	Sea urchin, Stratum 2: *Paracentrotus lividus* Lamarck
1	Cuttlefish, Stratum 4B: *Sepia* sp.

TOTAL: 21,576 individuals

*Numbers in parentheses refer to number burnt.

Table 7-15. Summary of *Monodonta* and *Patella* MNI at *Aetokremnos*

				Stratum				
Shells	Surface	1	1/2	1–4	2	2/4	3	4
Monodonta	194	594	1,822	680	14,174	1,208	99	1,979
	(33)	(97)	(268)	(170)	(3,143)	(132)	(11)	(456)
	0.9%	2.9%	8.8%	3.3%	68.3%	5.8%	0.5%	9.5%
Patella	22	33	75	33	325	52	5	95
	(3)	(14)	(25)	(11)	(105)	(13)	(3)	(24)
	3.4%	5.2%	11.7%	5.2%	50.8%	8.1%	0.8%	14.8%

Note: First number is total number of individuals present. Lower number in parentheses is the number of these that are burnt. Percentage is for each species by stratum.

Turritella broken at the apex from Stratum 2 (upper); a fresh umbonal fragment of *Venus* and *Paracentrotus* remains from Stratum 2; a burnt crab pincer from Stratum 2 (lower); a *Sepia* cuttlebone fragment from Stratum 4B; and a fresh *Cerithium* apical fragment from Stratum 4C.

At *Aetokremnos*, the *Monodonta* and *Patella* were either eaten raw or roasted on the fire. *Monodonta* were often smashed (probably using the waterworn igneous cobbles found in the excavation) to remove as much of the meat as possible (see Swiny, Chap. 6).

About 18% of all *Monodonta* complete shells and fragments (or 4,310 individuals, 21.0% of the total *Monodonta* individuals) are burnt, and 40% of all *Patella* fragments (or 198 individuals, 30.9% of the total *Patella* individuals) are burnt. It is clear from examining the partially burnt shells that this burning largely took place by roasting the shells directly on an open fire. The distal end (lip/mouth area) of *Monodonta* and the edges of *Patella* are the most frequently burnt parts of the shells. Such burning also has been seen on the *Monodonta*, *Patella*, and the larger helicid land snails at the Upper Paleolithic/Mesolithic Addaura cave near Palermo in western Sicily (personal analysis). Shells found in features and loci are noted in Chap. 5.

Nonfood, ornamental (or utilitarian) shells also were recovered. Often these ornamental shells were found in groups, and it is interesting to note that two of the five stone pendants came from Stratum 2 units, which also produced shell beads (Fig. 7-12).

Of 88 *Columbella*, 33 shells (37.5%) come from Stratum 2 and 29 (33%) from Stratum 4. At least 51 shells were collected dead, being clearly waterworn and often having small waterworn pebbles stuck in the mouth of the shell. Seventy-five of these shells (85%) were stringable as beads. Nine shells have been burnt. The 13 unstringable shells included at least 4 shells that were collected dead and 4 that were burnt. Five shells had been cut into beads resembling the picrolite and *Dentalium* beads. They are 4–5 mm long and have a diameter of 6.25–8 mm. They come from Strata 1/2 (1), 2 (1), and 4B (3).

For the 49 *Dentalium*, 31 (63.3%) are from Stratum 2, with 4 shells from Stratum 4 and 6 each from Strata 1/2 and 2/4. All are *Dentalium dentalis* (the largest Mediterranean species), except for 1 *Dentalium rubescens/vulgare* bead from Stratum 2/4. Of the 26 rather complete dentalia, 1 is waterworn, 5 are burnt, and two have pigment on them: orange (Stratum 2) and red/orange (2/4).

Twenty-four of the *Dentalium* are considered to be "beads"; all measure 14 mm or less in length. Half of the dentalia beads are from Stratum 2. At least 8 of these beads are made

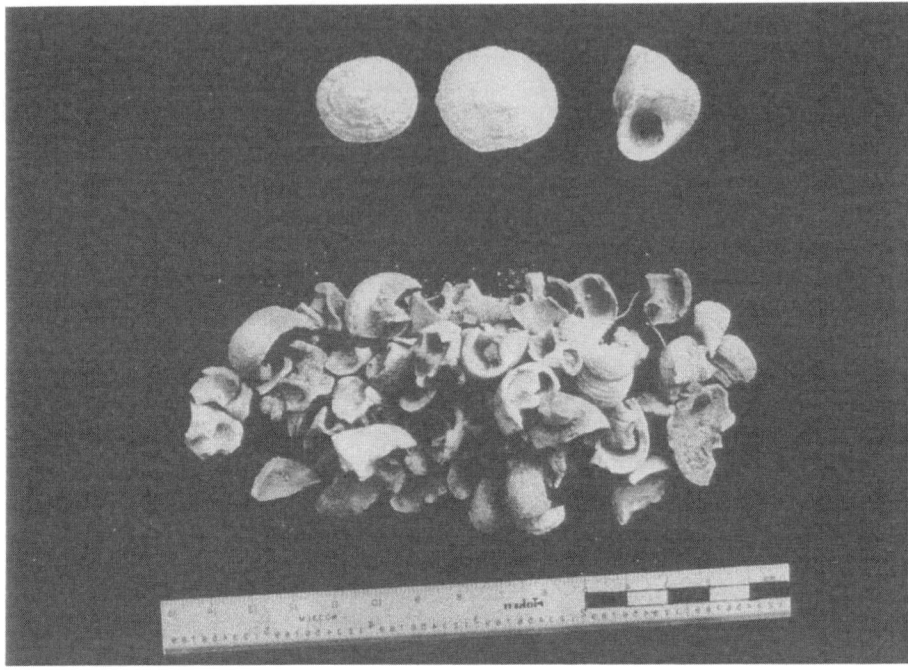

Figure 7-12. Marine invertebrates from *Aetokremnos*.

from shells that were collected dead on the beach. Two of them have cleanly cut edges, evidence that they were cut from more complete shells. Three beads (from Strata 2 [upper], 2, 4B) have orange pigment on them. One from Stratum 2 (upper) is burnt brown.

Most of the 25 *Conus* are of small size for the species, about the size of *Columbella*. Twelve are from Stratum 2 and 8 from Stratum 4. Fifteen of the shells are waterworn; some of them have small waterworn pebbles in the mouth like the *Columbella*. Twenty-three *Conus* are holed in some way and could be strung; most have naturally made holes at the apex. Four of the shells are burnt, 2 black and 2 gray.

There are 6 *Glycymeris*, with 5 from Stratum 2. Two are waterworn, and 3 are burnt. One from Stratum 2 (upper) has a naturally made hole at the umbo (bivalve "beak") and may have been used as a pendant.

There are 5 *Cerithium* that could have been strung as ornaments. Four of the 5 were collected dead on the beach (i.e., waterworn), and 4 come from Stratum 2.

To summarize, the 155 shells probably used as beads or pendants include 75 *Columbella*, 50 *Dentalium*, 23 *Conus*, 5 *Cerithium*, 1 *Glycymeris*, and 1 *Euthria*.

Monodonta are found in the splash/littoral zone on rocky shores and in shallow tidal pools. *Patella* also are common in the littoral and sublittoral zones on rocky shores and in shallow tidal pools. *Columbella* are found in the littoral and sublittoral zones, particularly in shallow rocky areas. *Dentalium* live buried in sandy or muddy bottoms and are often found washed up on beaches. *Conus* are found in the littoral zone on rocky shores. *Cerithium* are found in the littoral zone on down, on stony, sandy, or muddy bottoms.

The vast majority of the shells (99.7%) are species found living in the littoral zone on rocky shores. The exceptions are 49 *Dentalium*, 1 *Turritella*, 1 *Venus*, and 1 *Sepia*.

In conclusion, at *Aetokremnos* the *Monodonta*, *Patella*, crabs, sea urchin, cuttlefish, and a small number of other shells are food remains. *Columbella*, *Dentalium*, *Conus*, *Glycymeris*, and most of the *Cerithium* were not food items; they are often in a waterworn condition and were collected already dead on the beach. The single fish bone found suggests that although fishing was practiced, it was rare, and that the collection of marine invertebrates high up on the rocky shore was the more common means of coastal exploitation.

The *Aetokremnos* marine invertebrate forms compare closely with the collections from various Aceramic Neolithic sites on Cyprus, although at Khirokitia the majority of shells were found in burial contexts. *Cape Andreas Kastros* yielded the same species as *Aetokremnos*, with *Monodonta* being the major food shell and *Columbella* the major ornamental. One major difference between *Aetokremnos* and these two Neolithic sites (and also Kholetria *Ortos*) is the lack of worked triton/trumpet shell (*Charonia* sp./*Cymatium* sp.) vessels and "spoons" at *Aetokremnos* (Demetropoulos 1984; Reese 1978 and unpublished additions, 1993:207; Stanley-Price 1976; Wilkins 1953). Also, at most Aceramic Neolithic sites that have been excavated and the shells published, the range of species exploited is much greater than at *Aetokremnos*.

Land Snails (*David Reese*)

The *Aetokremnos* faunal sample includes a small number of land snails. Most of these come from the surface and Stratum 1; they are very fresh and have bright color bands. These are considered to be intrusive and very recent in date. In this study, analysis is restricted to Stratum 2 and below. Most numerous are 73 *Helix*, one of the larger helicids found on Cyprus. These are referable to *H. cincta*, *H. pomatia*, or *H. pachya*. There are 11 from Stratum 2 (upper), 23 from Stratum 2, 11 from Stratum 2/4, 3 from Strata 4A/B, 21 from Stratum 4B, and 4 from Stratum 4C. Two individuals from one Stratum 2 unit (N97-98E88, W quads) are burnt. This unit also produced a large sample of marine food shells, many of which are burnt (1,106 *Monodonta* individuals [369 burnt] and 28 *Patella* [14 burnt]).

The next most commonly found land snail are 14 *Helicella* sp., with 11 small specimens from one unit in Stratum 4B. At least four species of *Helicella* are known from the island (Reese 1978:102). Finally, there are 2 *Rumina decollata* (from Strata 2 and 4B), 1 burrowing form, and 1 unidentifiable land snail from Stratum 2 (lower).

Helix, larger *Helicella* species, and other forms (such as *Eobania vermiculata*) are eaten today on Cyprus; they are a speciality of Boghaz (Famagusta Bay) and other villages of the Karpas peninsula (Thurston 1971:107). It is possible that the burnt *Helix* is evidence that these shells are to be considered a food item. In any case, the small quantity of land snails recovered suggests that these shells were very rarely consumed. Land snails were certainly eaten roasted (along with *Monodonta* and *Patella*) at the Upper Paleolithic/Mesolithic Addaura cave in western Sicily (personal analysis).

Cape Andreas Kastros produced about 150 *Helix* shells, mainly in the upper levels. Only 1 shell had been burnt, and this was from Burial 540 (Reese 1978:17, 76). There were 19 *Helix cincta* from the 1977–81 excavations at Khirokitia; 9 were from Levels I or II (Demetropoulos 1984).

Chapter 8

The Dating of Akrotiri Aetokremnos

PETER WIGAND AND ALAN H. SIMMONS

INTRODUCTION

The chronology of *Aetokremnos* is clearly of paramount importance to the site's interpretation. Archaeological sites may be dated by either relative or absolute means, and the latter is especially crucial on a site as controversial as *Aetokremnos*. Fortunately, we have excellent stratigraphic control and numerous radiocarbon determinations for constructing a radiometrically secure and geochemically defensible chronology for *Aetokremnos* (see Simmons and Wigand 1994 for a summary). In this chapter, we discuss several aspects of the site's chronology. After briefly examining relative dating methods, we address the absolute radiocarbon chronology established for the site. Doing so involves a brief examination of the materials dated and how the determinations obtained relate to the site's stratigraphy. Another, briefer, section addresses *Aetokremnos's* significance in helping to establish an eastern Mediterranean correction factor for the Reservoir Effect. Finally, we provide an interpretation of the reliability of the radiocarbon determinations from *Aetokremnos*.

RELATIVE DATING

Relative dating is of limited utility for evaluating *Aetokremnos's* chronology. Available relative methods are not fine grained enough to allow even the semblance of a precise placement. There are four relative methods that can be used in the interpretation of the site: paleontology, stratigraphy, artifact typology, and geomorphology. Individually, none are very robust.

Paleontology

The presence of *Phanourios* (and other faunal) remains in association with cultural materials suggests their contemporaneity. If our understanding of the Cypriot faunal record were better, their presence would be a useful, if general, tool in interpreting *Aetokremnos's* chronology. Unfortunately, little systematic examination of the paleontological record has occurred, and its chronology is only broadly interpreted (e.g., "Late Pleistocene").

Unfortunately, the most controversial aspect of *Aetokremnos* is the association of cultural and fossil faunal materials. It would, therefore, be tautological to use this association as a means of dating the site, especially when the site is unique in being the only well-documented association of Pleistocene fauna with cultural materials in Cyprus.

Geomorphology and Stratigraphy

Geomorphology also offers a means of relative dating, but in the case of *Aetokremnos*, it is of limited value. Because recent erosion has been extensive, the nature and rate of deposition of noncultural material (i.e, primarily Stratum 1) over the cultural deposits (Strata 2 and 4) cannot be determined to provide a clue to the site's age. As geological testing around the site (see Mandel, Chap. 3) has indicated, deposition rates in the microenvironment of the Akrotiri cliffs can be as rapid as recent erosion rates. As a result, the unconsolidated nature of the cliffs and their situation on an eroding headland do not offer much opportunity for comparative dating using geomorphology.

The stratigraphic record at *Aetokremnos* is, of course, related to the site's geomorphologic location and its erosional and depositional history. The presence of superimposed deposits indicates some passage of time, but as first noted, this could occur rapidly. In fact, the time difference between the two major strata is not measurable in radiocarbon years (see later). Absence of paleosols or tephra layers for regional cross-correlation also limits the use of site stratigraphy for establishing the site's chronology.

Artifact Typology

A traditionally archaeological approach to the relative dating of *Aetokremnos* would be to make use of comparative artifact typology. If the artifacts from the site could be shown to resemble those from other, dated, sites we would have an idea of *Aetokremnos's* chronological placement. Unfortunately, the assemblage from *Aetokremnos* is unique in Cyprus (at least thus far and possibly excluding the tested sites: see Chap. 10). However, some general comparisons to the mainland may be appropriate. These comparisons suggest a generalized "Epipaleolithic" or "Early Neolithic" placement, which provides little assistance in a more precise tuning of the site's chronology, especially because subsequent developments in Cyprus, such as the Aceramic Neolithic, generally occurred later than are those on the mainland.

Summary

Traditional means of relative dating are of little use in assessing *Aetokremnos's* chronology. The major problem in using paleontological, geological, or archaeological methods is the general absence in Cyprus of comparative data. Therefore, relative methods of dating the site are not very useful. Fortunately, numerous radiocarbon determinations from which a strong chronology can be established have been obtained. Although not answering all of the chronological questions at *Aetokremnos*, this chronology addresses many of the more important ones. Ironically, *Aetokremnos* is now one of the best-dated early archaeological sites on any of the Mediterranean islands.

AN EXAMINATION OF THE ABSOLUTE CHRONOLOGY
OF *AETOKREMNOS*

Introduction

Much of the controversy surrounding *Aetokremnos* concerns its chronology. We have obtained 31 radiocarbon determinations from the site (Tables 8-1 and 8-2, and Figs. 8-1 and 8-2).

Because these determinations lie just outside of the tree-ring calibration curve, and to avoid confusion caused by mixing calibrated and uncalibrated dates in our discussion, the dates reported here are uncalibrated (but see Manning 1991 and below). As a point of reference, however, we also include calibrated dates (Stuiver and Braziunas 1993) in parenthesis behind the $\delta\ ^{13}C$ corrected radiocarbon determination. This is provided for those who feel comfortable with the new calibration curves. Following standard convention, uncalibrated dates are reported as B.P. or B.C., while calibrated estimates are reported as B.P. or B.C. All of our early dates lie within the period of major Early Holocene increases in atmospheric carbon dioxide. Because this resulted in changes in the rate of production of ^{14}C in the atmosphere, we are being extra cautious in the application of ^{14}C calibrations, for example, the coral calibration (Stuiver and Becker 1993).

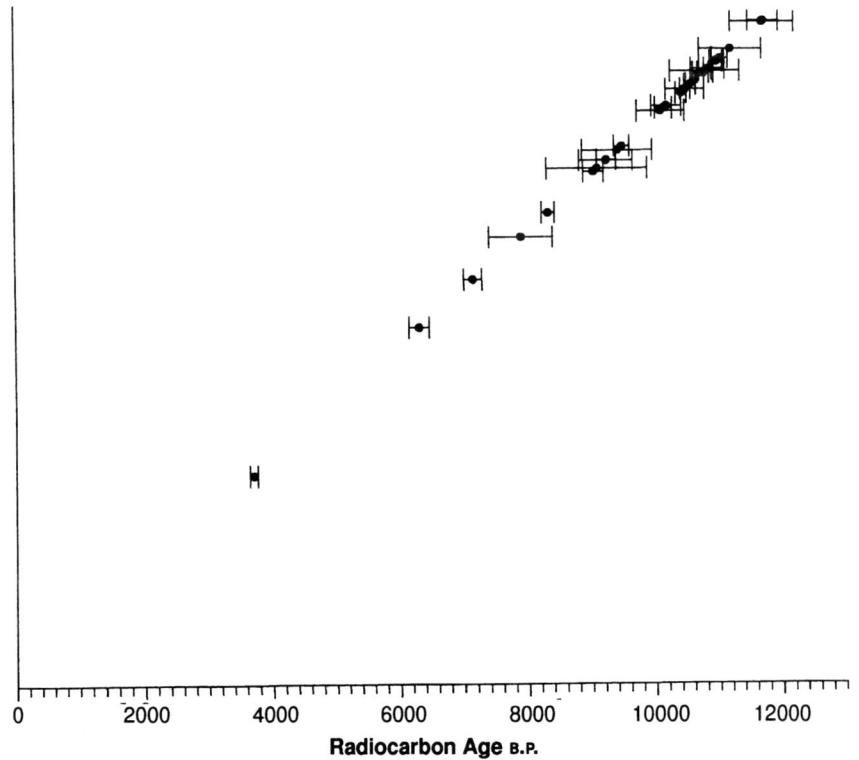

Figure 8-1. Distribution of *Aetokremnos* radiocarbon determinations at one standard deviation.

Table 8-1. Radiocarbon Determinations from Akrotiri *Aetokremnos* as Originally Reported by Radiocarbon Dating Laboratories

Date (B.P.)	Laboratory	Material	Provenience/Comments
3700±60	Pta-3435	Bone collagen	Surface: removed prior to excavation; date unreliable; 50.4 grams of collagen and sand dated (Vogel 1984)
6310±160*	Beta-3412	Burnt bone	Surface: removed prior to excavation; of 0.3 grams of carbon extracted, 0.3% was noncarbonate carbon; date unreliable
7150±140*†	Beta-43174	Burnt bone	N96E91, Stratum 4B: clear stratigraphic association; 0.5 gram of unidentified carbon dated (Tamers 1991)
7900±500*	UCL-304	Shell (10 ml sample)	N97E87-88, Stratum 4B: first-order method processing; small sample with large error; possibly contaminated
8330±100	Pta-3281	Burnt bone	Surface: charred portion of Pta-3435; 4.6 grams of alkali soluble fraction; possibly contaminated
9040±160	TX-5976A	Bone apetite	N95E88, Stratum 2/4: apetite fraction of TX-5976B; from 7 bone fragments
9100±790	ISGS-1743	Bone carbon	N95E88, Stratum 2/4: total carbon of 7 bone fragments; only 0.2 grams of total organics dated
9240±420	TX-5833C	Humins¹ fraction	Soil matrix from conical Feature 1, N98E88-87, Stratum 2A; same sample as TX-5833B and TX-5833A
9250±150	Pta-3128	Burnt bone	Partially (recently?) exposed, Stratum 2/4 beneath shell layer (Feature 5 in Stratum 2A); removed prior to excavation; 1.4 grams of alkali soluble fraction dated
9420±550	TX-5976B	Bone collagen	N95E88, Stratum 2/4: scanty collagen fraction of TX5976A
9490±120	TX-5833A	Bulk organic carbon	Soil matrix from conical Feature 1, Stratum 2A, N98E87-88; same sample as TX-5833C and TX-5833B
10,100±370*	UCL-203	Shell (20 ml sample)	N97E86, Stratum 4B: first-order method processing
10,150±130	TX-5833B	Humic acid fraction	Soil matrix from conical Feature 1, Stratum 2A, N98E87-88; same sample as TX-5833C and TX-5833A
10,190±230†	Beta-41405	Charcoal	N97E88, Stratum 2A: same sample as Beta-41406; only 0.22 grams of carbon available for analysis

Date	Lab number	Material	Context
10,420±85	Beta-41000/ETH-7188	Charcoal	N97E89, Stratum 2A (AMS sample)
10,480±300†	Beta-41407	Charcoal	N96E89, Stratum 2A: same sample as Beta-41408; only 0.16 grams of carbon available for analysis
10,485±80	Beta-41406/ETH-7331	Charcoal	N97E88, Stratum 2A (AMS sample): same sample as Beta-41405
10,560±90	Beta-40382/ETH-7160	Charcoal	N97E89, Stratum 4C (AMS sample)
10,575±80	Beta-41408/ETH-7332	Charcoal	N96E89, Stratum 2A (AMS sample): same sample as Beta-41407)
10,770±90	Beta-41002/ETH-7189	Charcoal	N96E89, Stratum 2A (lower) (AMS sample)
10,770±160*	Beta-43176	Burnt bone	N96E90, Stratum 4B: oldest bone determination; scanty unidentified organic residue dated (Tamers 1991)
10,800±550*	UCL 201	Shell (20 ml sample)	N97E90, Stratum 2A (lower): first-order method processing
10,810±110	Beta-22811	Shell (conventional)	N95E88, Stratum 2/4 (in dark midden): like matrix containing bone and artifacts below exposed shell layer (Feature 5)
10,840±60	SMU-1991	Shell (conventional)	N98E88/87, Stratum 2/4; associated with bone, artifacts, and Feature 1: shells from parts of Strata 2, 2/4, and possibly 4, but mainly from the upper part of Stratum 2/4
10,840±270†	Beta-40655	Charcoal	N96E90, Stratum 2A (lower): composite of three small, adjacent samples; only received acid wash pretreatment
10,970±100	Pta-3322	Shell (conventional)	Exposed shell layer (Feature 5), Stratum 2A: dated prior to excavation of the site; inner shell fraction of Pta-3112
11,000±100	Pta-3112	Shell (conventional)	Exposed shell layer (Feature 5), Stratum 2A: dated prior to excavation of the site; outer shell fraction of Pta-3322
11,030±130	Beta-28795	Shell (conventional)	N98E89, Stratum 2A
11,200±500*	UCL 194	Shell (20 ml sample)	N96E87, Stratum 4B: first-order method processing
11,700±500*	UCL 192	Shell (20 ml sample)	N98E90, Stratum 2A: first-order method processing
11,720±240†	Beta-40380	Charcoal	N97E89, Stratum 2A, Feature 10: a casual hearth; only .53 gr. of charcoal present; only received acid wash pretreatment

Note: Asterisked (*) determinations are those reported without δ^{13}C corrections by the laboratories (see text and Table 13-2). Shell dates in this table do not include a Reservoir Effect correction; All samples, except for Pta dates and Beta-3412 (which were obtained from the surface prior to the 1987 excavations and are unprovenienced) were obtained from sealed contexts. Samples marked with a dagger (†) were given extended counting time. Large standard deviations reflect extremely small sample size.

Table 8-2. *Aetokremnos* Radiocarbon Sample δ¹³C Correction Factors
with Corrected and Uncorrected Dates

δ ^{13}C %	Uncorrected Date (B.P.)	Corrected Date (B.P.)	Laboratory Number
−22.3	3655±60	3700±60	Pta-3435
−22.75[1]	6310±160	6350±160	Beta-3412
−22.75[1]	7150±140	7190±140	Beta-43174
2.72[1]	7900±500	8350±500	UCL-304
−23.0	8295±100	8330±100	Pta-3281
−15.03	8875±160	9040±160	TX-5976A
−24.7	9095±790	9100±790	ISGS 1743
−25.47	9250±420	9240±420	TX-5833C
−22.5	9210±150	9250±150	Pta-3128
−16.0	9270±550	9420±550	TX-5976B
−24.56	9485±120	9490±120	TX-5833A
2.72[1]	10,100±370	10,550±370	UCL-203
−23.65	10,130±130	10,150±130	TX-5833B
−24.4	10,180±230	10,190±230	Beta-41405
AMS[2]	—	10,420±85	Beta-41000/ETH-7188
−25.1	10,480±300	10,480±300	Beta-41407
AMS	—	10,485±80	Beta-41406/ETH-7331
AMS	—	10,560±90	Beta-40382/ETH-7160
AMS	—	10,575±80	Beta-41408/ETH-7332
AMS	—	10,770±90	Beta-41002/ETH-7189
−22.75[1]	10,770±160	10,805±160	Beta-43176
2.72[1]	10,800±550	11,250±550	UCL-201
2.7	10,350±110	10,810±110	Beta-22811
3.2	10,380±60	10,840±60	SMU-1991
−25.2	10,850±270	10,840±270	Beta-40655
2.7	10,520±100	10,970±100	Pta-3322
2.3	10,555±100	11,000±100	Pta-3112
2.7	10,570±130	11,030±130	Beta-28795
2.72[1]	11,200±500	11,650±500	UCL-194
2.72[1]	11,700±500	12,150±500	UCL-192
−24.1	11,710±240	11,720±240	Beta-40380

[1]Estimated ¹³C correction factor; see text for explanation.
[2]AMS = accelerator mass spectrometry date; δ ¹³C correction is automatically included.

In most cases, the radiocarbon determinations were provided with δ ¹³C values and corrected determinations when they were reported. However, in some cases, only the uncorrected determination was provided (e.g., the UCL shell dates). For calculation of weighted averages (following Ward and Wilson 1978) discussed later, these dates were standardized using an estimated δ ¹³C correction. This was accomplished by using a value of +2.72 (the average δ ¹³C correction of the other six previous shell dates) as the correction factor for shell determinations and applying it in a formula derived from those presented by Stuiver and Polach (1977). The formula was tested against samples that had uncorrected and δ ¹³C corrected determinations, and for which the correction factor was known. A value of -22.75 (the average δ ¹³C correction of the other bone dates) was used for the bone dates for which

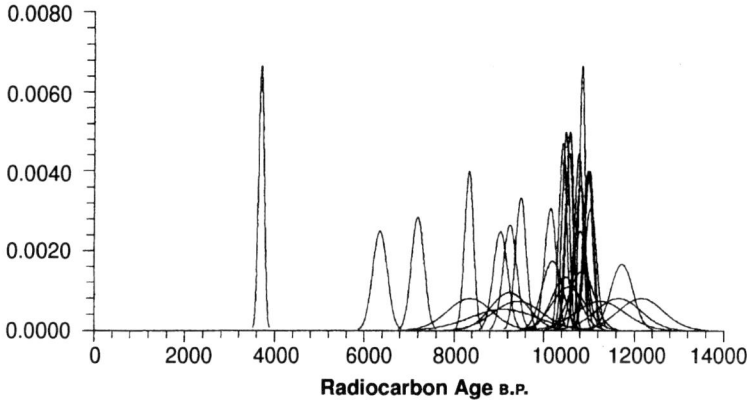

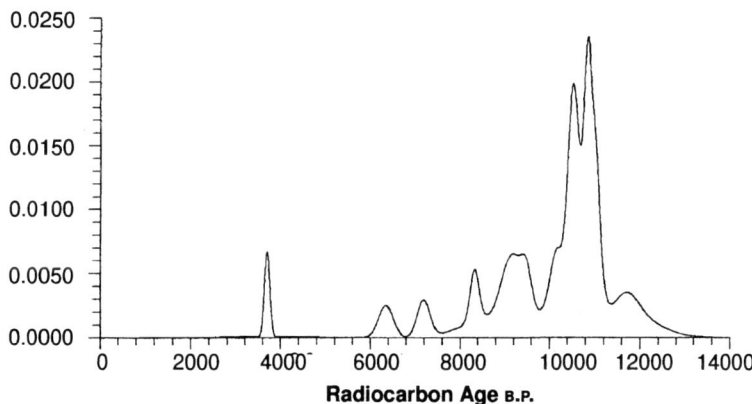

Figure 8-2. (Above) *Aetokremnos* radiocarbon determinations (all $\delta^{13}C$ corrected) as Gaussian distributions at one standard deviation centered around the mean, with the area beneath each curve held constant (Geyh 1980). (Below) Summation of these curves in order to show the concentrations of determinations through time.

corrections had not been provided. These newly generated values were used in conjunction with those already available to calculate the weighted averages presented later. Finally, all averaged dates referred to in the text are rounded to the nearest 5 years by convention.

The determinations were obtained from marine shell, *Phanourios* bone, sediment from a feature, and charcoal (Fig. 8-3). Some of the *Aetokremnos* determinations are clearly more contextually and geochemically defensible than are others. For example, both bone and shell have a reputation of being notoriously difficult to date, and some researchers have questioned the *Aetokremnos* chronology because of the unreliability of these materials. It is our feeling, though, that the consistency in the grouping of dates on all materials and their stratigraphic relationships and associations meet those criteria that are usually required for archaeological acceptance.

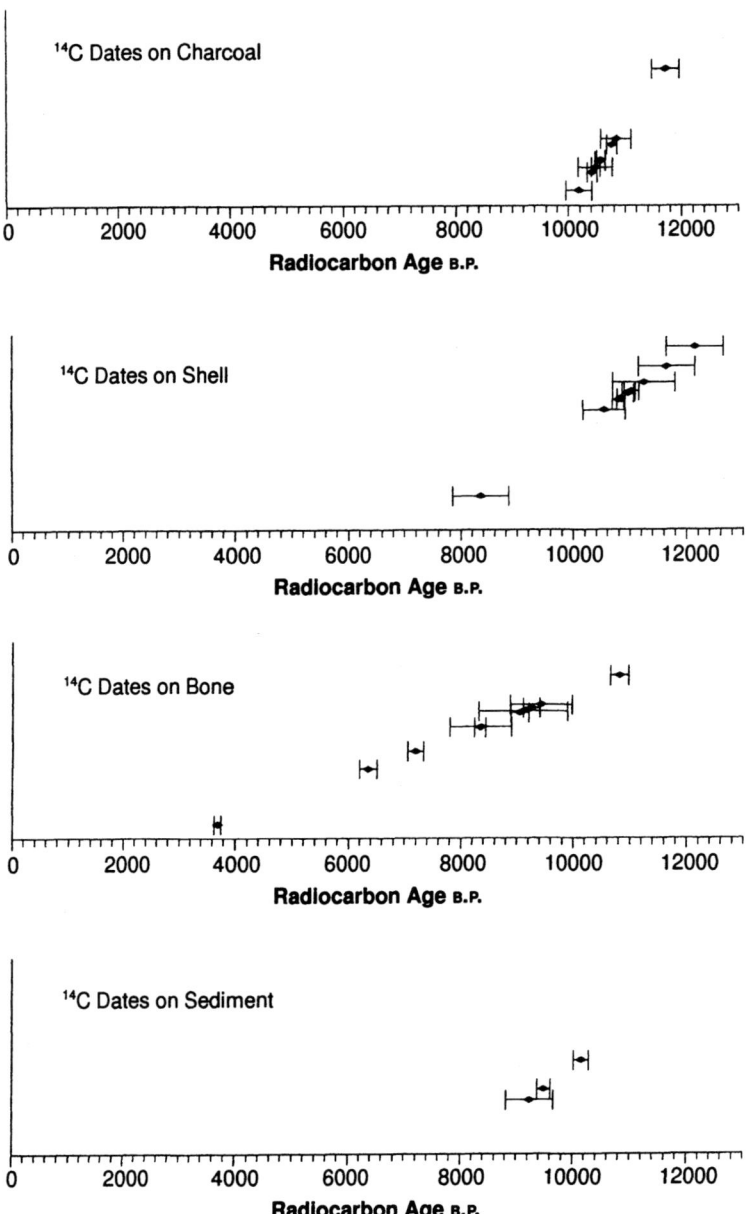

Figure 8-3. *Aetokremnos* radiocarbon determinations by material type.

Materials Dated

Given the controversial nature of *Aetokremnos,* it is necessary to discuss each material type and the problems of some of the individual determinations. Much of the detail provided here is based on comments made by the appropriate radiocarbon laboratory personnel when the samples were dated. For shell determinations, *no* Reservoir Effect correction is included (see separate discussion later). The determinations are all based on a half-life of 5,568 years and are reported as radiocarbon years before present (A.D. 1950).

Bone

All bone dated from *Aetokremnos* is from pygmy hippopotamus. Given the problems of dating bone, as a group, the bone dates are probably the least reliable (Table 8-1 and Fig. 8-3). For example, Beta-43174 and Beta-43176 are from the same stratum separated by barely 1 m and yet differ in age by over 3,500 radiocarbon years. This case highlights the need for careful assessment of *Aetokremnos* bone determinations.

Bone specimens exposed at the surface were likely contaminated due to weathering processes, and rendered unreliable for dating. Bones redeposited into younger contexts were subjected to interstitial contamination by organic and carbonate carbon (difficult to remove during standard pretreatment) from the soil matrix and potentially subjected to chemical fractionation as well. Carbon may have been leached from other sources and precipitated in bone intersticies during periods of wetter climate, when alkali soil solutions could mobilize soluble carbons (humic and folvic acids) and transport them through site sediments. This process could invalidate alkali bone fraction dates. In general, bone apatite is a poor material to date, whereas bone collagen is a reliable material to date. Unfortunately, burning of bone destroys most if not all of the collagen. For bone radiocarbon date details see Table 13-1.

Sediment

The 3 sediment determination (Table 8-4 and Fig. 8-3) all are from the same sample, which was associated with soil matrix from Feature 1. Although this sample initially was large, it did not contain any charcoal chunks and once processed resulted in only a minimal amount of carbon. The greater age of the humins sample (TX-5833C) compared with the other TX-5833 specimens (Tx-5833A and TX-5833B) may be due to the absence of younger (i.e., mobile) carbon derived from humic acids, originating from the decay of younger organic materials, for example, rootlets, in the sediment.

Shell

The shell determinations from *Aetokremnos* represent a major contribution to Mediterranean chronology (Fig. 8-3). Although shell dates, especially marine shell, often are not considered extremely reliable, we are convinced of their accuracy in this case because of their dense clustering and their general concordance with stratigraphically associated charcoal dates.

Several (those with a "UCL" number) of the shell determinations were processed using the "first-order" method, usually with a 20 ml sample size (only one used a 10 ml sample size, possibly contributing to the departure of its date from the rest; Vita-Finzi, personal communication 1991). This technique offers a quick and inexpensive determination that is considered good to the "first order" of magnitude (Glover *et al.* 1990). The agreement of the "first-order" determination with "normal" conventionally processed shell determinations provides good evidence for the accuracy of this method. The UCL determinations were *not* reported with δ ^{13}C corrections; however, we have corrected them using the average correction factor from the other shell dates (Simmons and Wigand 1994, and earlier). *Aetokremnos* shell determinations provided a means of establishing a Reservoir Effect for the eastern Mediterranean for the Early Holocene (Simmons and Wigand 1994, and see later).

Charcoal

The charcoal determinations from *Aetokremnos* provide perhaps the most reliable dates for the site (Fig. 8-3). Charcoal, in general, is not well preserved in many Cypriot archaeological sites (S. Swiny, personal communication 1991), so we were fortunate in retrieving any at all. Although the samples from *Aetokremnos* are small, and many required extended counts, their consistency is striking. Several of the charcoal specimens that were dated conventionally were confirmed using an accelerated mass spectrometer (AMS). All AMS determinations reported here are δ ^{13}C corrected. The ^{13}C, ^{14}C and ^{12}C were measured concurrently in the accelerator, allowing precise corrections (Beta Analytic 1991).

DISCUSSION

Material Types and Weighted Averages

Despite the problematic nature of some of the dated materials, there is a remarkable clustering of the determinations, especially by material type. The three surface determinations, all of which are on bone, were removed from consideration as possibly contaminated due to long exposure to weathering. The weighted average of the remaining 28 δ ^{13}C corrected determinations is 10,465±25 B.P. (cal B.C. 9703). We feel that this is a minimal date for the site (see later). Manning (1991, discussed later), using another approach with fewer dates, arrives at a somewhat older site age.

It is instructive to examine these determinations more closely, by material type, in particular. The weighted averages of the materials dated at *Aetokremnos* with δ ^{13}C correction are for shell (10 samples), 10,900±40 B.P. (cal B.C. 10,470); for charcoal (9 samples), 10,575±35 B.P. (cal B.C. 9955); for bone (6 samples, minus the surface specimens), 8955±75 B.P. (cal B.C. 7580); and for sediment (3 samples), 9770±85 B.P. (cal B.C. 8550). The charcoal and shell determinations are very close. The bone and sediment determinations, however, differ considerably. Almost two thousand years separates the weighted averages of shell and bone determinations, with the weighted average of the sediment determinations lying midway between the two.

We have received some criticism because of our use of the bone determinations, and, indeed, they represent the most variable of the *Aetokremnos* dates. If these were our only data, we would be more skeptical of the site's true age. We are, however, impressed by the relative clustering of these determinations when the surface samples are removed. Although outwardly apparently well preserved, the *Aetokremnos* bone contains only minimal amounts of collagen, which ideally is what we would prefer to date. In lieu of collagen, we had hoped to obtain dates on bone amino acids (cf. Stafford *et al.* 1988). With this in mind, a small sample was sent to Dr. T. Stafford at the University of Colorado. Unfortunately, the amount of nitrogen preserved was far below the minimum required for such analysis, so Stafford considered it unlikely that accurate amino acid dates could be obtained on these samples. Let us illustrate how "small" the carbon content is on some of these bones. On one of the more recent determinations (Beta-43174), a sample that weighed approximately 3.6 kg yielded only about 0.5 g of organic carbon. This measurement translates to a total organic carbon content of less than $\frac{1}{10}$ of 1%. Normally, bone contains about 12% carbon. This percentage suggests extremely poor organic preservation of the *Aetokremnos* bones and an increased possibility of contamination from outside sources and certainly requires caution in their use as a dating material. Their clustering with sediment determinations, however, suggests that an event of some kind is being measured. It is clear that these determinations date organic residue from a specific source. Whether this source is organic carbon associated with a period of soil formation or some other event is unclear.

It is apparent that an older and younger group is formed by the radiocarbon determinations, based on the type of material that has been dated. The older group comprises the charcoal (weighted mean of 10575 B.P.) and shell determinations (weighted mean of 10,900 B.P.). If the shell determinations are corrected for Reservoir Effect (see later), they also would cluster around 10,575 B.P. The younger group is made up of the bone (weighted mean of 8955 B.P.) and sediment determinations (weighted mean of 9770 B.P.).

Shell Date Problems

The accurate dating of shell encompasses a number of problems; the primary one involves isotopic fractionation (mainly the manner in which the three main forms of carbon, ^{12}C, ^{13}C and ^{14}C, are assimilated) (Polach and Golson 1966). In the oceans, the proportions of the various carbon isotopes may not be the same as those in the contemporary atmosphere because of the slower diffusion rate of carbon in the water column (the Reservoir Effect). Therefore, organisms near the surface may be in closer equilibrium than those at greater depth. This situation is complicated by deep water currents and upwelling in coastal areas. In addition, setting up modern standards has been further complicated by the enrichment of modern organisms in ^{14}C by atomic weapons testing. Finally, postdepositional contamination of shell through the formation, re-solution, and precipitation of younger carbonates within the sediment column during soil-water movement may result in the deposition of carbonates that contain younger carbon on the surface or in the pores of porous older shell material.

At *Aetokremnos*, each of these problems could play a role in skewing marine shell ^{14}C determinations. The dominant invertebrate species are the Topshell (*Monodonta* sp.) and Limpet (*Patella* sp.). The Topshell is found most frequently in the splash/littoral zone on rocky shores and in shallow tidal pools, where the mixing of atmospheric carbon with ocean waters is facilitated. The same mixing conditions would exist in the environment that the limpet inhabits, which includes the littoral and sublittoral zones on rocky shores and shallow tidal pools. The dilemma is that the carbon residence time in the eastern Mediterranean, and how that may have varied in the past, is unknown.

The other major complication is that shells may have been subjected to contamination in the postdepositional environment. Contamination would be most common during periods of moister climate. There is evidence of later carbonate deposition (carbonate coatings) on some bone within the site, suggesting that there was potential for such contamination to occur. However, the clear association of the charcoal and shell materials and the similarity of the ^{14}C determinations suggest that younger carbonate contamination is not a problem, except in the case of perhaps one shell determination (UCL-304, 7900±500 B.P.) from Stratum 4B. This determination lies well outside the Chavenet criteria for rejecting samples differing from the average of five samples by more than 1.65 standard deviations (Long and Rippeteau 1974), so we have accordingly rejected this shell date. All the remaining nine shell determinations have been retained. It should be noted that this shell determination was a "first-order" determination and used only 10 ml for the process (cf. Glover *et al.* 1990).

Although one "first-order" date was rejected, we should note the remarkable consistency of the other "first-order" samples (designated by "UCL") with the more conventional determinations. These confirm the robustness of the method.

Sediment Date Problems

All three sediment determinations are from the same sample. The determinations are skewed toward older values by the two fractions that consist of "alkali soluble" carbon (humic acid and humins). These are easily mobilized by soil water of high pH and easily move up or down the sediment profile. These two fractions could reflect decomposition products from organics higher in the profile, that is, decaying bone, rootlets or wood, or plant material that was incompletely carbonized. The "solid carbon" fraction of the sediment sample dated to 9490±120 B.P. (cal B.C. 8180). This radiocarbon determination may date a period of greater vegetation cover that occurred long after the site sediments were deposited. Rootlets from this vegetation could have penetrated the site from above, have been carbonized, and formed the bulk of the sample that was dated, thereby giving it an anomalously younger date.

Bone Date Problems

The bone determinations are highly variable, reflecting the fractions dated and differing degrees of contamination. Two determinations—Pta-3128 (9250±150 B.P.) and Pta-3281 (8330±100 B.P.)—are on soluble carbon humate fractions that could reflect mobilized carbon from the decay of materials outside the bone itself. Sample TX-5976 (9040±160 B.P.) is on bone apatite from a specimen whose "collagen" had dated to 9420±550 B.P. (TX-5976B). The bone apatite fraction is poor material for dating bone (Polach 1971; compare carbonate, apatite, and collagen fraction determinations from the same bone). Collagen is the only fraction that does not exchange carbon during digenesis. Therefore, we also question the reliability of the bone apatite determination. After excluding the rejected samples, the new weighted average is calculated, and the Beta-43174 determination of 7190±140 B.P. is rejected as an outlier, according to Chavenet's criteria for rejection. The resulting weighted average for the remaining bone determinations is 10,640±150 B.P. (cal B.C. 10,100), a figure that agrees with the weighted averages calculated for the charcoal and shell determinations.

Stratigraphic Problems

Conceivably, based on the earlier discussion, one could use the range in dates to argue for two discrete occupations. We do not, however, believe this to be the case. There are two major strata, both of which are cultural. In some cases, but not all, these strata are separated by a thin sterile layer of sediment, suggesting a brief hiatus. The upper stratum (Stratum 2) contains about 75% of the chipped stone artifacts and less than 1% of the *Phanourios* bones (although this still amounts to over 1,500 individual pieces); the lower stratum (Stratum 4) is interpreted as a "midden." This deposit contains the majority of *Phanourios* and nearly 12% of the chipped stone. In areas where the intervening sterile stratum (Stratum 3) is not present, Strata 2 and 4 directly adjoin (i.e., Stratum 2/4).

Radiocarbon Ages before Sample Rejection and without Reservoir Correction

Fifty-five percent of the 31 determinations (17 samples) are from Stratum 2. Five are from the Stratum 2/4 interface, 6 are from Stratum 4, and the remaining 3 are from surface contexts (Fig. 8-4). These last three have been rejected from the sample. Using the 28 remaining radiocarbon determinations, the weighted average from Stratum 2 is 10,640±30 B.P. (cal B.C. 10,095), from Stratum 2/4 it is 9960±75 B.P. (cal. B.C. 8,930), and from Stratum 4 it is 9835±65 B.P. (cal B.C. 8,640). These figures present us with an interesting case of reverse stratigraphy (note that shell materials do not yet have a Reservoir Effect correction). There is about an 800-year difference between the two major strata in radiocarbon years. The difference between the lower stratum (4) and the "mixed" Stratum (2/4) is, however, minuscule. Given the similarity of the Stratum 2 determinations and those of the charcoal (from all strata), which may be the most reliable, we should perhaps view the Stratum 2 dates as the most accurate and consider that postdepositional digenesis processes may have slightly affected the ages of the stratigraphically lower dates, reflecting the possibility that the lower strata were the areas in the site profile where humates and folvic acids that had been leached from Strata 1 and 2 were deposited during episodes of weathering. Furthermore, note that the Stratum 2 dates very closely mirror the weighted average of all dates from the site (except the Surface samples), being separated by only 175 radiocarbon years.

Radiocarbon Ages after Sample Rejection and without Reservoir Correction

If we take into consideration the earlier discussion that rejected questionable bone and sediment dates, the resulting weighted averages for each of the strata are much more in agreement. The weighted average of the remaining samples without reservoir effect correction (see later) from Stratum 2 is 10,670±30 B.P. (cal B.C. 10,150), from Stratum 2/4 it is 10,725±110 B.P. (cal B.C. 10,240), and from Stratum 4 it is 10,600±75 B.P. (cal B.C. 10,010) (Table 13-3). Therefore, no difference. The weighted average of all radiocarbon determinations that omit the rejected bone and sediment samples is 10,665±25 B.P. (cal B.C. 10,145).

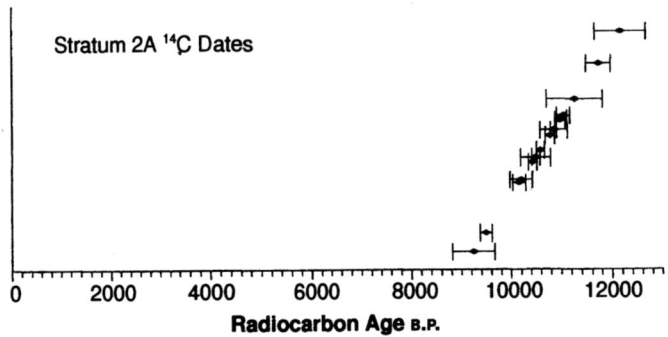

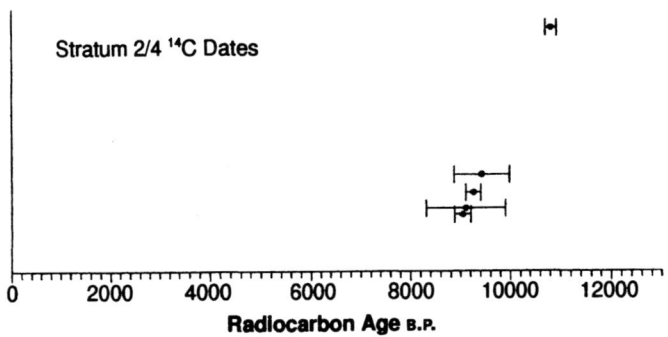

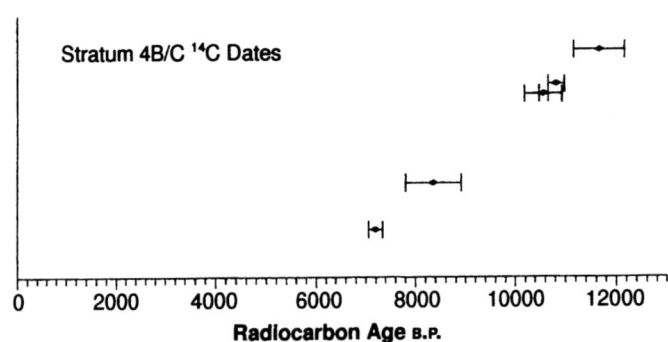

Figure 8-4. *Aetokremnos* radiocarbon determinations by strata.

An additional argument for no major chronological gap between the strata is the similarity of the lithic assemblages from the two strata. Typologically and technologically there is no difference in materials; and chi-square tests show there is no distinction between the strata (see Chap. 6). We believe that this result clearly indicates a minimal separation in time between these two strata, and indeed, the project geomorphologist has argued that the accumulation of the sterile Stratum 3 could have occurred over a very short time.

Summary

Held (1989b:223–226) had discussed the discrepancy between the *Aetokremnos* bone, charcoal, shell, and sediment determinations. As we have mentioned earlier, we are in general agreement with him with regard to the possibility of contamination from the migration of humates through the sediment column. In fact, the consistent centering of both "bone" humate and sediment humate determinations between 9200 B.P. and 9400 B.P. (cal B.C. 7920 and 8070) may reflect a climatic event at that time during which humic and folvic acids that were being formed as decay products in an incipient soil (A horizon) were leached downward through, and deposited within, the sediment column. Such migration of humates is a common process in sediments of high pH, such as those found at *Aetokremnos*. The filling of the interstices within the bone with this material would give a false age to the "whole bone" or "bone" humate determinations. These false data would skew such determinations toward a younger age if there were datable material remaining in the bones. If the original carbon in the bones had been destroyed, the age obtained would date the event. Because the sediment and bone determinations are nearly identical, we suggest that these dates may indicate a period of greater organic production (vegetation growth) at the site at around 9400 to 9200 B.P. (~cal. B.C. 8070–7920).

This growth may reflect a period of wetter climate that can be traced around the Mediterranean, associated with the Holocene "Thermal Maximum." Movement of the Intertropical Convergence Zone northward into Saharan Africa at this time created large pluvial lakes in northwestern and north-central Africa (Nicholson 1978; Nicholson and Flohn 1980: especially Fig. 9 and its discussion). This event coincided with the movement of sub-Saharan flora and fauna into North Africa as far north as the Tibesti and the

Table 8-3. Weighted Means of Radiocarbon δ ^{13}C Corrected Determinations from Akrotiri *Aetokremnos*

	All w/o Reservoir[1]	W/o Reservoir, Minus Rejected Dates[2]	W/Reservoir Effect[3]	Cal B.C. date and 1 Sigma Range[4]
All (N=31)	10,119 ± 18	10,670 ± 26	10,529 ± 26	9825 (10005–9702)
Charcoal	10,577 ± 36	10,577 ± 36	10,577 ± 36	9960 (10114–9777)
Shell	10,898 ± 39	10,911 ± 40	10,577 ± 40	9960 (10118–9773)
Bone	6228 ± 41	10,639 ± 151	10,639 ± 151	10,090 (10352–9723)
Sediment	9770 ± 86	9490 ± 120	9490 ± 120	8180 (8353–8042)
All Str 2	10,641 ± 28	10,671 ± 28	10,508 ± 28	9778 (9957–9643)
All Str 4	9835 ± 66	10,640 ± 76	10,618 ± 76	10,050 (10230–9801)
All Str 2/4	9958 ± 76	10,726 ± 107	10,423 ± 107	9600 (9876–9380)
Str 2 charcoal	10,581 ± 40	10,581 ± 40	10,581 ± 40	9969 (10126–9780)
Str 4 charcoal	10,560 ± 90	10,560 ± 90	10,560 ± 90	9920 (10152–9671)
Str 2 shell	10,926 ± 43	10,926 ± 43	10,592 ± 43	9995 (10150–9795)
Str 4 shell	10,353 ± 262	10,939 ± 297	10,605 ± 297	10,020 (10480–9376)
Str 2/4 shell	10,810 ± 110	10,810 ± 110	10,476 ± 110	9720 (10018–9472)
Str 4 bone	8758 ± 105	10,805 ± 160	10,805 ± 160	10,360 (10554-10,082)
Str 2/4 bone	9161 ± 106	9316 ± 451	9316 ± 451	8010 (8547–7516)

[1]Weighted averages without Reservoir Effect correction and included surface samples.
[2]Weighted averages without Reservoir Effect correction after rejection of several dates (see text for detail).
[3]Weighted averages with Reservoir Effect correction after rejection of several dates (see text for detail).
[4]The calibrated B.C. dates and the 1 sigma range following Stuiver and Braziunas (1993) and Bard *et al.* (1993).

Hogar Mountains of the Sahara. A coincident northward deflection of the Atlantic storm track, which is normally centered across the north coast of Africa, perhaps to a position over Cyprus may have occurred. During this brief interval, perhaps no more than 500 years or at the outside about 1,000 years, vegetation cover may have become more dense, stabilizing sediment surfaces and allowing the formation of incipient soils. Decay products formed in these soils would have gone into solution because of the high pH of these limestone-derived sediments and then have been transported down the sediment column by rains.

Held (1989b:225) had suggested, as had Manning (1991) and ourselves (Simmons and Wigand 1994:251–253), that the discrepancy between the charcoal and shell determinations reflects Reservoir Effect. This discrepancy may range as high as the 481±56 years used by Manning (1991:871). Using more dates, all with δ ^{13}C corrections, we have suggested a 334-year correction. The need for and scale of this Reservoir Effect correction becomes clear when the δ ^{13}C determinations are plotted as a dispersion diagram (lower Fig. 8-2). In fact, our weighted average age for *Aetokremnos* of 10529±26 B.P. (all samples, Table 8-3) compares favorably with the 10100 B.P. of Held (1989b:226) and the 10316±24 B.P. of Manning (1991:876, fn.), especially when considering that we had more samples than either of them.

DURATION OF SITE OCCUPATION AT *AETOKREMNOS*

In reviewing the earlier discussion, two key questions emerge: When was *Aetokremnos* occupied, and for how long? We believe that the data point to a relatively short-term occupation during the tenth millennium B.C., centered around the calibrated calendar age of 9825 B.C. (range of 9702–10,005, single standard deviation). This is based on 26 samples, omitting the three surface determinations and the two other determinations that were excluded as being outliers. The uncalibrated age is 10,529 B.P.

Manning (1991) endeavored with great effort to place the occupation of *Aetokremnos* into real calendar years, an exercise that we have not emphasized, both in order to avoid confusion and because of the current tentative nature of the ^{14}C calibration curve for the earliest Holocene. In any event, Manning arrived at only a somewhat older determinations than we have. He did so by an elaborate statistical treatment, attempting an approximate, or first-order, calibration of the determinations. He compared the *Aetokremnos* materials with chronologies established via dendrochronology, varves, Uranium-Thorium ages from Barbados coral, and other methods. Without going into detail, Manning determined that

> the relatively short-lived habitations(s) of Site E should lie *somewhere within* the interquartile range, or *floruit*, of the calibrated data (= central 50%); these are, respectively [depending on what calibration data base was used]:
>
> (i) 8547–10744 BC (with an estimated error of ± 382 calendar years);
>
> (ii) 8890–10375 BC (±487 calendar years); or
>
> (iii) 8224–9958 BC (±365 calendar years). (Manning 1991:874)

These estimates of the *floruit* overlap with the two sigma (standard deviation) range of our estimated site age (from 9554 to 10,146 calendar years B.C.).

Manning was, however, not entirely satisfied with this reconstruction. Because not all of the determinations from the site are of equal quality or from the same stratum, he attempted to better define the upper phase of the site, that is, Stratum 2. He used 15 samples from this stratum, but omitted the bone samples as unreliable. He concluded that, depending on the choice of calibration curve (either coral or varve/dendrochronology), a calendar date for Stratum 2A is in either the later eleventh, or earlier tenth millennium B.C. He favored the latter calibration, based on Stuiver *et al.* (1991) (Manning 1991:875).

Manning also felt uncomfortable in averaging dates of different materials: "a set of dates which does not consist of homogeneous samples (and contexts) cannot be assumed to form a normal distribution around a single real age (radiocarbon or calendar). It should not be averaged (*except in terms of an approximate 'exploratory' statistic*)" (Manning 1991:876, italics added for emphasis).

We have no serious disagreement with Manning's general conclusions. He was being cautious by not using the bone determinations, but he also omitted a substantial number of determinations by restricting himself to Stratum 2. As argued earlier, we feel that the archaeological and stratigraphic evidence suggests an insubstantial time gap between Strata 2, 2/4, and 4; certainly one that is not measurable in radiocarbon years. Although we appreciate his caution in not averaging determinations from differing materials, we have averaged samples by both material type and by lumping all of them together. Because the differences are not appreciable, we use the weighted average for all determinations obtained from sealed contexts as a *general* (or "exploratory" in Manning's sense) value.

Manning (1991) conducted a painstaking exercise in his attempt to derive a real calendar age for the occupation of *Aetokremnos*. However, such exercises may be premature because of the wide deviations of the radiocarbon calibration curve during the millennia around the transition from glacial to postglacial climates (due in part to radical shifts in atmospheric ^{14}C that occurred at that time). In addition, although later sites in Cyprus have been assigned calendar ages, other sites around the Mediterranean of comparable age to *Aetokremnos* are still analyzed using their uncalibrated radiocarbon determinations. However, it is clear from his, and our, analysis that there is considerable time between the occupation of *Aetokremnos* and the beginning of Aceramic Neolithic of Cyprus.

In summary, then, we propose that *Aetokremnos* was not occupied for a long period of time. It is likely that occupation was seasonal (see discussion in Chap. 12), and it probably occurred over a span of less than a few hundred years. The nature of the chronological data preclude a finer resolution.

ESTABLISHING A RESERVOIR EFFECT FOR THE EASTERN MEDITERRANEAN

There is another issue of interest that may be addressed with the *Aetokremnos* radiocarbon determinations, that is, the Reservoir Effect in the dating of marine shells. Marine shell determinations are subject to several complicating factors in their interpretation, the most important of which is the number of years that need to be subtracted from shell dates to account for the Reservoir Effect. This term applies to an estimated correction that takes into account long residence times of old water in the oceans; 400 years frequently is used (Vogel and Visser 1981), but regional calibrations can vary considerably.

The local Mediterranean correction, which compensates for upwelling and evaporation effects, has previously had only one point listed for the entire Mediterranean Sea, off the coast of Algeria. This figure is –135±85 years from a single shell sample dating to 357 B.P. (Stuiver *et al.* 1986:1019, Table 1). There has been, therefore, very little baseline information from which to interpret the *Aetokremnos* dates.

In large basins, such as the Mediterranean Sea, radiocarbon activity levels can vary substantially from those in the contemporaneous atmosphere. Reservoir activity values vary significantly through time due to a multitude of conditions including (1) lag in the exchange of ^{14}C between the atmosphere and the oceanic surface waters, (2) changes in oceanic circulation, and (3) incorporation of waters previously outside the basin (for the Mediterranean Sea those could include glacial melt waters from the continental ice sheet in Russia spilling through the Black Sea and those from the glaciated Alps). Establishment of a Reservoir Effect is particularly crucial for the radiocarbon determinations from *Aetokremnos* because they are from the period during which dramatic changes in the ^{14}C composition of the atmosphere and the oceans were occurring (Stuiver *et al.* 1991). What is required for such correction factors are paired dates on shells and other materials (preferably charcoal), as well as modern standards for the area. *Aetokremnos* offers such comparisons.

In earlier publications of the *Aetokremnos* determinations, we used a calibrated age of 690 years older than the ^{14}C age. This was an estimate, based on various interpolations, and we now believe it was too great a sum, based on the recently obtained charcoal determinations from *Aetokremnos* and on more precise calculations.

For *Aetokremnos*, the weighted average of all the δ ^{13}C corrected shell dates were compared with the weighted average of all the δ ^{13}C corrected charcoal dates. The correction factor that must be added to the shell dates to make them equivalent to the charcoal dates is +334 years. If the same comparison is made between the weighted averages of eight δ ^{13}C corrected charcoal and six δ ^{13}C corrected shell determinations from just Stratum 2, the result is +345 years.

Using a similar approach, Manning (1991:871, Table 1) arrived at a slightly different correction. In calculating his correction, he

> adopts a crude exploratory approximation . . . and compares the weighted average of the 11 dates on charcoal/sediment from Stratum 2A (10439 ± 36 B.P.) with the weighted average of the 6 (uncorrected) dates on shell from the same stratum (10920 ± 43 B.P.), the correction appears to be about 481 ± 56 years (calculation of weighted averages follows the method in Ward and Wilson 1978. (Manning 1991:871)[1]

Although Manning's method of calculation is the same as used here, his results differed from ours for two reasons. First, we did not incorporate sediment dates because the possibility of mobile carbon contamination in an alkali rich soil was too great. Second, we had two additional shell determinations from Stratum 4. For Stratum 4, the same comparison between the single δ ^{13}C corrected charcoal and the two δ ^{13}C corrected shell determinations (a third—UCL 304—was rejected as an outlier, see earlier) resulted in a difference of 379 years (if the third, rejected, determination is used, this figure is –207 years). Although

---

[1]Determinations UCL 203 and UCL 304 were obtained subsequent to Manning's calculations. Both, however, are from Stratum 4 and would not affect his results.

this 379-year figure is not greatly different from our preferred 334-year correction, we reject it on statistical grounds because only one charcoal sample and two shell samples are being compared, making the potential error too great. In addition, although the charcoal sample comes from the bottom of the unit and the shell samples come from the top of the unit, we do not feel that this difference reflects the amount of real time separating the top and bottom of the deposit.

There are obviously several ways to manipulate these data. Clearly, additional paired dates are needed from this region, but the *Aetokremnos* specimens provide a crucial beginning for a poorly calibrated area; they should be of use in interpreting marine shell dates from other Early Holocene archaeological contexts in the eastern Mediterranean.

INTERPRETATION OF THE *AETOKREMNOS* RADIOCARBON DETERMINATIONS

As we have shown and as numerous others authors have noted, not all radiocarbon dates are created equal. In an attempt to provide more accurate interpretations of dates, Meltzer and Mead (1985) have developed a rating system based on two criteria: the nature of the material dated and the strength of association of the ^{14}C determination and the material to be dated. Their system appears designed to specifically assess dates on extinct animals, which of course is appropriate to the case at hand. The system, however, also is useful for assessing radiocarbon data from archaeological contexts.

As an additional test of the *Aetokremnos* chronology, we have applied the Meltzer and Mead (1985) ranking method (Table 8-4) to our data. The first category, that of

Table 8-4. Radiocarbon Date Rating System*

	Score
1. Material dated	
A. Derived from extinct taxon	
Body perishables (dung, keratin, etc.)	6
Primary humates or amino acids	5
Collagen	4
Apatite	3
Whole bone	1
B. Derived from other material	
Charcoal (elemental carbon)	6
Wood (logs, twigs, leaves)	5
Peat	3
Organic mud (includes gytjja)	3
Soil	3
Shell (freshwater/terrestrial)	2
Terrestrial carbonate (marl/tufa)	1
2. Strength of association	
Strong	3
Medium or unknown	2
Weak	1

*Adapted from Meltzer and Mead (1985:161).

material dated, separates dates derived directly from extinct faunal remain from dates run on other materials; each material type within these categories is then ranked according to presumed reliability. The second category measures the strength of the association between the material dated and the target taxa. A strong association is one in which materials are in unequivocal association with the target taxa or material that is of the target taxa itself (Meltzer and Mead 1985:160–162). This category clearly relies strongly on archaeological context. The first category ranges from 1 to 6, while the second ranges from 1 to 3. For any particular date, the two scores are added together, for a maximum "best" score of 9.

Table 8-5. *Aetokremnos* **Radiocarbon Determinations, as Scored Using the Meltzer and Mead (1985) Method**

Date (B.P.)	Laboratory	Material	Association	Rank
3700±60	Pta-3435	4	1	5
6310±160	Beta-3412	1	1	2
7150±140	Beta-43174	3	1	4
7900±500	UCL-304	1	3	4
8330±100	Pta-3281	1	1	2
9040±160	TX-5976A	3	2	5
9100±790	ISGS-1743	1	2	3
9240±420	TX-5833C	3	3	6
9250±150	Pta-3128	1	2	3
9420±550	TX-5976B	4	2	6
9490±120	TX-5833A	3	3	6
10,100±370	UCL-203	1	3	4
10,150±130	TX-5833B	3	3	3
10,190±230	Beta-41405	6	3	9
10,420±85	Beta-41000 (ETH-7188)	6	3	9
10,480±300	Beta-41407	6	3	9
10,485±80	Beta-41406 (ETH-7331)	6	3	9
10,560±90	Beta-40382 (ETH-7160)	6	3	9
10,575±80	Beta-41408 (ETH-7332)	6	3	9
10,770±90	Beta-41002 (ETH-7189)	6	3	9
10,770±160	Beta-43176	1	3	4
10,800±550	UCL-201	1	3	4
10,810±110	Beta-22811	1	2	3
10,840±60	SMU-1991	1	3	4
10,840±270	Beta-40655	6	3	9
10,970±100	Pta-3322	1	2	3
11,000±100	Pta-3112	1	2	3
11,030±130	Beta-28795	1	3	4
11,200±500	UCL-194	1	3	4
11,700±500	UCL-192	1	3	4
11,720±240	Beta-40380	6	3	9

Summary of radiocarbon rankings from *Aetokremnos*.

Rank	2	3	4	5	6	9	TOTAL
Number	2	6	9	2	3	9	31
Percent	6.5	16.1	29.0	6.5	12.9	29.0	100.0

Meltzer and Mead (1985:162) concluded that "reliable dates" are those rating either 8 or 9. Grayson (1989), in dealing with the chronology of North American Pleistocene extinctions, used this same scoring system. He chose rank 6 as a "basal" level in order to provide a sample of dates sufficiently large for statistical analysis, while at the same time eliminating the weakest dates. He, too, regarded ranks of 8 or 9 as the most accurate and considered that "ranks 6 and 7 include dates that are extremely likely to be invalid" (Grayson 1989:155).

It is instructive to apply this scoring system to the *Aetokremnos* determinations. A few words of explanation on how this has been done follow: A major category of dated materials from *Aetokremnos* is marine shell. Meltzer and Mead's system only deals with freshwater/terrestrial shell, which has a low rank of only 2. Given that marine shell may be even more unreliable, especially in areas such as the Mediterranean where inadequate data exist for a Reservoir Effect correction factor (but see discussion earlier), we have chosen to give the marine shell a rank of only 1 for this analysis. This choice represents a conservative approach and makes all the *Aetokremnos* marine shell dates suspect using this ranking system because the highest rank could be only 4 (that is, 1 for material type and 3 for a strong association). We feel that the remarkable clustering of shell determinations, both internally and when considered in relation to other dated materials, in fact, makes them much more robust. If we had only one or two shell dates, we would be much more suspicious; however, the tight range given by 10 dates gives us more reason for confidence. For the purposes of this analysis, however, we will take the conservative approach.

The strength of association criterion used here was based on the stratigraphic nature of the dated sample. A strong association was indicated by materials from either Stratum 2 or 4, a medium association by materials from Stratum 2/4, and a weak association by surface materials.

Using these variables, the ranking of each date is given and summarized in Table 8-5. These data must be interpreted cautiously. Using the strict criteria set forth by both Meltzer and Mead and Grayson, only 29% (*n*=9) of the *Aetokremnos* dates would be considered "reliable," with only another 9.7% even falling into the category of rank 6 or above established by Grayson. However, the shell dates were automatically eliminated, as discussed earlier. If one removes the shells dates from consideration at all, reducing the sample to 21, the proportion of reliable dates increases to 42.9%. Clearly, one can take a variety of approaches with these figures, but it is more important to realize that nine determinations result as "reliable" using this conservative approach. In many archaeological situations, nine dates would be considered an adequate sample to date a site as small as *Aetokremnos*.

ADDITIONAL DATES FROM PALEONTOLOGICAL SITES IN CYPRUS

Most of the paleontological sites in Cyprus containing *Phanourios* are undated by absolute methods. It often has been assumed that these are "Pleistocene" in age, and that they could be several hundred thousand years old. Absolute dates on dwarfed fauna from other Mediterranean islands confirm this antiquity (Reese 1995). Recent dates, primarily through amino acid racemization (AAR) and electron spin resonance (ESR) methods, on some of the Cypriot deposits, however, have suggested that some may in fact be roughly contemporary with *Aetokremnos*. This conclusion is significant in that it suggests that

Table 8-6. AAR and ESR Dates of Cypriot Pygmy Mammals*

Site Name	Method	Source and/or Sample Number	Date B.P.
Aetokremnos	AAR	FN 359, N98E86, Str. 2/4	Used as 10,000 standard
	AAR	FN 490, N98E87, Str. 4B	8400–5560
	AAR	FN 367, N97E87-88, Str. 4B	12,600–8000
	AAR	FN 375 N94E90*, Str. 4B	15,650–10,400
Kata Dhikimo *Vokolosspilios*	AAR	NHML, M 9300a	16,250–9750
	ESR	FAUU, C-DM	13,104–8736
Ayia Irini *Pervolia*	AAR	MNH, Ay loc. 5	10,000–6000
	ESR	FAUU, C-AY I	10,170–6780
Ayia Irini *Dragontovounari*	AAR	MCZ, 8110b	11,250–6750
	ESR	FAUU, C-AY II	8166–5444
Liveras *Mandres Virilas*	AAR	MC^b, 8161b	10,000–6000
	ESR	FAUU, C-MDVL	11,946–7964
Kormakiti *Krommyon*	AAR	PMU (specimen collected in 1930)	3600–2400
Akanthou *Arkhangelos Mikhail*	AAR	MCZ, 8131b	15,000–9000
	AAR	Bromage collection	13,750–8250
	ESR	FAUU, C-AK	9030–6020
Kissonerga *Kleitoudes*	ESR	FAUU, C-KS	21,960–14,640

*Adapted from Reese 1995.
Note: All dates are on *Phanourios* molars, unless otherwise noted (a=*Elephas* molar plate; b= *Phanourios* lower canine fragment).
Key
AAR   Amino Acid Racemization (performed by Dr. Giorgio Belluomini, Centri di Studio per il Ouaternario e l'Evoluzione Ambientale, Dipartimento di Scienze della Terra, Università degli Studi "La Sapienzi," Rome).
ESR   Electron Sin Resonance (performed by Dr. Motoji Ikeya, Department of Earth and Space Science, Osaka University, Toyonake, Osaka, Japan). These dates are based on a tentative dose rate:radiation assessment of the samples. Radiation assessment of the site is also necessary to determine the accurate age. The ESR ages only suggest the order of magnitude, as described by Ikeya (1993).
FAUU   Stratigraphy/Paleontology Department, Faculteit Aardwetenschappen, Universiteit Utrech, The Netherlands.
MCZ   Department of Vertebrate Paleontology, Museum of Comparative Zoology, Harvard University, Cambridge, Massachusetts.
MNH   Department of Vertebrate Paleontology, Muséum d'Histoire Naturelle, Geneva, Switzerland.
NHML   Department of Paleontology, Natural History Museum, London.
PMU   Paleontologiksa Museet Uppsala, Uppsala Univeristy, Sweden.

Phanourios populations may have been more widespread than previously believed. Although outside the scope of the present discussion, we provide some of these dates for comparative purposes (Table 8-6). Given the experimental nature of these technqiues, one should not rely on them too heavily, but they do provide rough estimations.

Note that three AAR dates also are available for *Aetokremnos* (Table 8-6); these were not discussed earlier in this chapter due to the potential limitation of the method. They do, however, fall into the range of our radiocarbon dates.

CONCLUSION

Although *Aetokremnos* is among the best absolute-dated archaeological sites on any of the Mediterranean islands, there are limitations to its chronosequence. The series of radiocarbon determinations confirm the site's antiquity. Due to the nature and postdepositional alterations of the materials dated, we cannot expect ever to be able to give a true absolute calendar date for the site. However, we are not uncomfortable with the results of the bulk of the determinations from *Aetokremnos*. More of the dates cluster than not, and if one applies the commonly used method of invoking two standard deviations, the grouping of most dates becomes stronger. The radiocarbon method is perhaps best regarded as a "relative" absolute method—it will never achieve the precision or accuracy of a tree-ring sequence.

We cannot say exactly in what year *Aetokremnos* was occupied, nor can we give the duration of its occupation. It may have been as long as the floruit indicated by Manning (1991), but we suspect a much shorter span, based on the archaeological data. As noted earlier, the similarity of determinations from all strata suggests a short duration, as does the similarity of the artifact assemblage. We can say, however, that the people who inhabited *Aetokremnos* throughout its relatively short life belonged to the same cultural tradition, and that they antedated what was previously considered to be the earliest evidence of humans on the island, the Aceramic Neolithic.

Given the nature of many of the materials dated, if we had only a few radiocarbon determinations from *Aetokremnos,* we would be much more hesitant in its dating. However, the remarkable similarity of all the determinations leads us to the conclusion that *Aetokremnos* does indeed represent at least an early ninth to mid-tenth millennium B.C. occupation. Although some critics may not be convinced, the sheer number and the sealed context of the *Aetokremnos* determinations exceeds what is normally considered necessary to adequately date an archaeological site. Although it is a primary objective to obtain geochemically defensible dates on any archaeological site, the nature of the archaeological remains must also be considered, especially for early prehistoric sites. Sometimes, datable materials are not preserved. We initially feared that this might be the case with *Aetokremnos,* but after painstaking data recovery, we were able to retrieve datable materials. Although the reliablity of the dates obtained on these materials may not satisfy everyone, we do not feel that any more accurate determinations could have been obtained, nor that any further calibration is necessary. As Manning pointed out, "[N]either the quality of the chronometric data from Site E, nor the quality of the approximate calibration data, justify further, more sophisticated calibration analysis" (1991:876).

We realize that in making a claim for the earliest site in Cyprus, it is incumbent upon us to present as compelling an argument as possible. The preceding pages have done so.

In summary, the chronology of Akrotiri *Aetokremnos* has added substantial new information to a sparse data base. Coupled with new dates from paleontological sites, evidence is building that *Phanourios* existed far later than previously believed. Although some have voiced concern over the *Aetokremnos* determinations, we need to consider these not in isolation, but in their proper archaeological and regional context. We remain convinced that they are an accurate reflection of the site's true age.

Chapter 9

Specialized Analyses

SURFING HIPPOS—THE DISTRIBUTION OF ARTIFACT AND SUBSISTENCE REMAINS (*Stephen Durand*)

In this section, we present a visual picture of the distributions of artifact and subsistence remains at *Aetokremnos*. The intent is primarily descriptive, though the distributions will be assessed for their fit with the proposed behavioral reconstructions at the site. Although archaeologists are beginning to undertake complex analyses of artifact distributions (e.g., Lang 1992), our approach is more in line with the perspective of Tukey (1977) and is exploratory in nature (see also Tufte 1983). We will focus on the two principal strata at the site: Strata 2, 4; we will also make reference to Stratum 2/4.

Combined, all chipped stone artifacts from Strata 2, 2/4, and 4 are densest toward the back of the shelter, which is also the location of the most undisturbed cultural material. When stratigraphically separated, artifacts in Stratum 2 tend to be concentrated toward the back of the shelter, while those in Stratum 4 tend to be concentrated on the west side of the shelter (Fig. 9-1). This general patterning corresponds well with the faunal remains from these strata. The distribution of artifacts in Stratum 2/4 has a pattern similar to that of Stratum 4, suggesting that 2/4 is differentially mixed from the unit below (Stratum 4) rather than from the unit above (Stratum 2).

Figure 9-2 differentiates between the tools and the debitage in Stratum 2. The tool and debitage patterns are similar, and there does not appear to be any differential clustering. Likewise, when the distribution of the different tool classes is plotted, differential clustering does not appear (Fig. 9-3). The primary cluster of artifacts in Stratum 2 contains all tool classes, and all classes also occur outside this cluster, though in smaller numbers. A single, major behavioral locus is suggested with a light scatter of tools that occurs outside this area. Elsewhere in this volume, this stratum has been interpreted as having been a relatively short duration occupation, and these artifact distributions are not inconsistent with that conclusion.

The tools in Stratum 4 are shown in Figure 9-4. The tools here follow the debitage distributions, as is the case with Stratum 2. One might argue that the scrapers in the unit are clustered together, though the small sample size makes this interpretation problematic. As

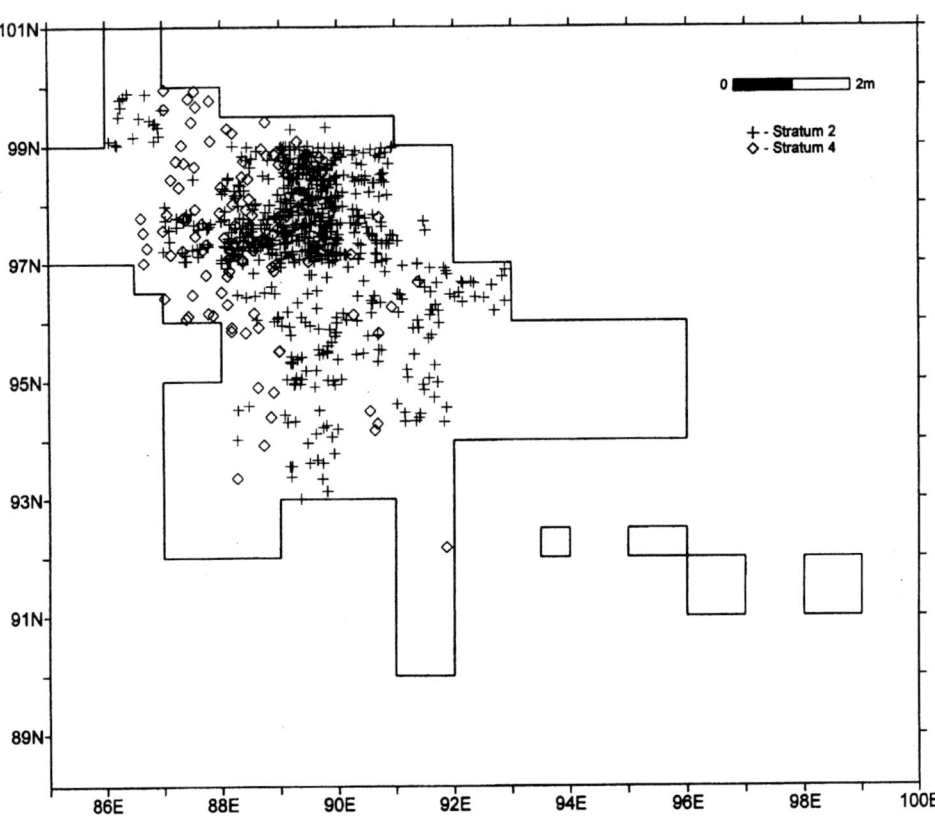

Figure 9-1. The distribution of all stone artifacts with Stratum 2 and Stratum 4 differentiated.

with the debitage, when we plot the distribution of tools from both Strata 2 and 4 (Fig. 9-5), there is not significant overlap.

Given the abundance of subsistence remains, it was not realistic to plot the tens of thousands of bones and shells that make up this assemblage. We chose, instead, to use contour maps of shaded relief to depict these distributions. The advantage of shaded relief maps over contour lines is that the patterning is instantly recognizable. The contour intervals for each category are based on the strata with the highest frequency. It should be kept in mind when viewing these maps that they depict the general patterns. Objects of each kind can occur outside the distributions depicted, but the nature of the techniques that generate the maps have eliminated these low-frequency occurrences.[1]

Shell is abundant in Stratum 2, and the shell midden (i.e., Feature 5) located this stratum conforms well with the artifact distribution here (Fig. 9-6). There are three small con-

---

[1]SURFER, Version 6.01 (Keckler 1994), was used to generate all of the maps in this section. The artifact distribution maps were constructed by posting the location of each artifact on a base map of the areas excavated. The shaded contour maps were constructed by gridding the area from the raw frequency data for each artifact class. Kriging interpolation was used. The same base map of area excavated was used for the shaded contour base map.

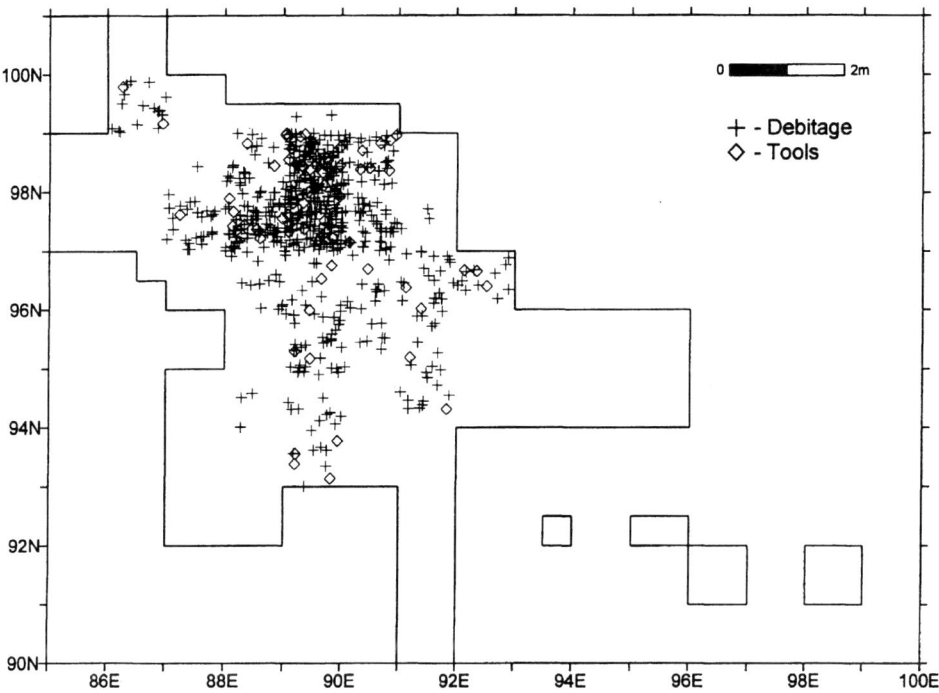

Figure 9-2. The distribution of all stone artifacts in Stratum 2, distinguishing between debitage and tools.

centrations of shell in Stratum 4, and these could be the result of mixing from the deposits above. Shell is present in Stratum 2/4 but in very small numbers.

The highest frequencies of avifauna are also in Stratum 2 (Fig. 9-7). There are three main clusters of bird remains and one minor cluster. As with the shell and the artifacts in Stratum 2, the bird remains tend to be at the back of the shelter. However, there are also significant numbers of bird remains at the front of the shelter in this stratum. Bird remains are also present in Stratum 2/4 and in Stratum 4 (Fig. 9-8). Stratum 2/4 is probably mixed from above and below, though the bird bones here do not overlap substantially with the similar remains from the strata above and below. The bird remains in Stratum 4 are located toward the front of the shelter, and though less dense than in Stratum 2, they are probably not the result of mixing from above. The distribution of the bird remains is similar to the artifact distribution in this stratum.

Stratum 4 in dominated by *Phanourios* bones, and the distribution reveals a main cluster and two minor clusters (Fig. 9-9). The other strata do not contain appreciable numbers of *Phanourios* and provide little interpretative value. It is important to note, however, that *Phanourios* in Stratum 2 is concentrated toward the front and center of the shelter and does not overlap with the Stratum 4 distribution. This pattern provides additional support against mixing of deposits. The *Phanourios* bones in Stratum 4 are located out from the back wall of the shelter and conform well with distribution of stone tools from this stratum.

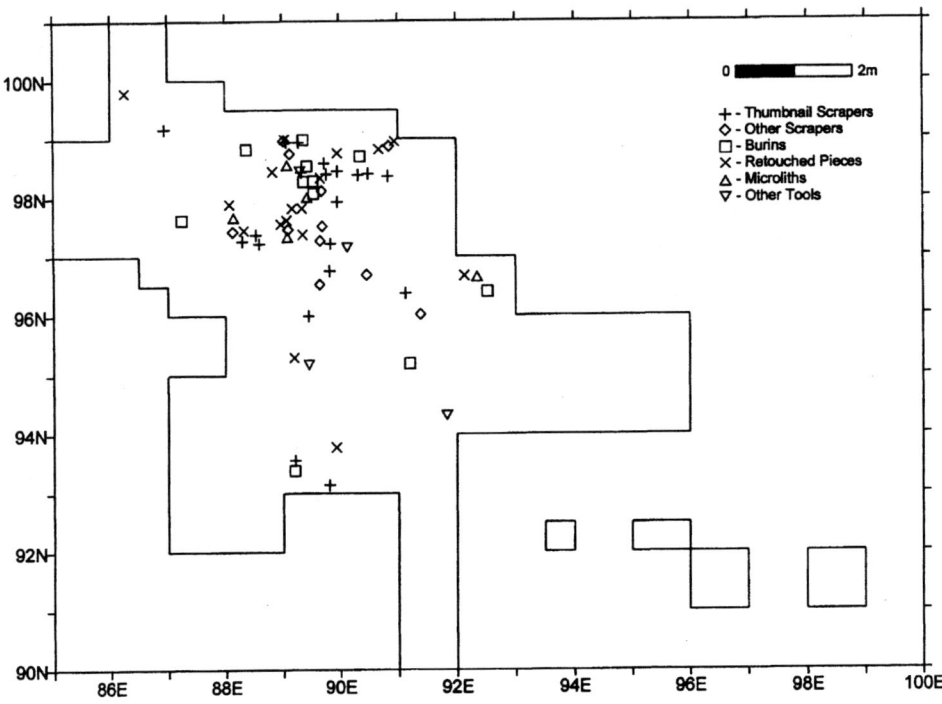

Figure 9-3. The distribution of stone tools by class in Stratum 2.

This presentation of the artifact and subsistence remains clearly demonstrates a consistent pattern for the two behavioral strata at *Aetokremnos*. Interpreting these patterns culturally is somewhat of a problem as the site may have been altered somewhat by natural processes since it was occupied. Nevertheless, some possible scenarios can be suggested.

The Stratum 4 remains are concentrated at the front of the shelter and closer to the cliff edge than the remains in Stratum 2. The back wall of the site is not completely vertical, and the juncture of the back wall and the floor is sloping rather than perpendicular. Thus the shape of the shelter may somewhat have controlled the location of much of the initial deposition of bones and artifacts.

Artifacts and subsistence remains in Stratum 2 are concentrated toward the back of the shelter. With the *Phanourios* bone bed as a surface, the juncture of the back wall of the shelter may have been vertical, thus permitting the later occupants of the shelter to use the entire surface. Alternatively, if the back portion of the shelter was not habitable due to a low roof or other factors, the living surface may have been toward the front of the shelter, with the back portion of the shelter serving as a refuse area. The features in Strata 2 do appear to be out from the back wall and are consistent with this possibility.

Another possible explanation for the different distributions in the two strata may be climatic/environmental. Though Cyprus is a Mediterranean island, the winters can be on the cool side. The back of the shelter would have afforded the occupants some protection from winter storms. Stratum 2 may be the remains of a winter occupation, while Stratum 4 may represent an occupation at a different time of the year.

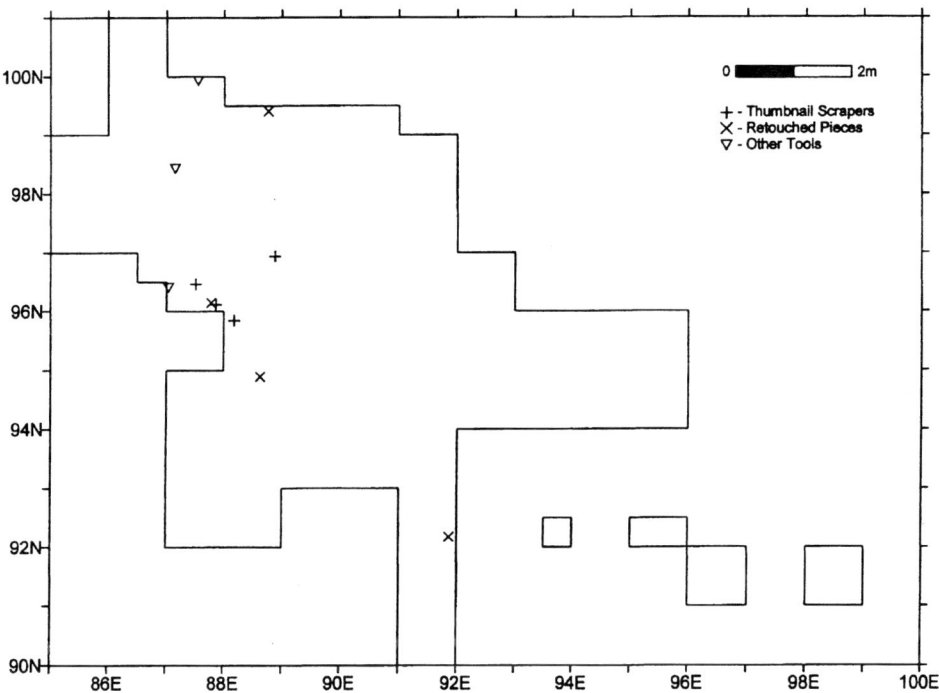

Figure 9-4. The distribution of stone tools by class in Stratum 4.

The mixed stratum (2/4) is consistent with a mixed or disturbed stratigraphic unit. It is localized in specific areas of the site and does not follow the same sort of pattern as the strata above and below in either the artifact or subsistence remains.

Certainly, the behavioral interpretations of *Aetokremnos* are primarily dependent on data other than the distributions of the artifacts and the subsistence remains. The benefit of this presentation is to provide the reader with a visual sense of the these distributions, and we conclude that these distributions are not inconsistent with the interpretations that are offered elsewhere in this volume.

BLOOD RESIDUE ANALYSIS OF SAMPLE ARTIFACTS
(*Margaret Newman*)[2]

In recent years, it has been recognized that lithic and ceramic artifacts often retain traces of organic residues from the time of their original use. Studies have demonstrated that by the use of biochemical and immunological methods, the species of origin can be identified (Briuer 1976; Broderick 1979; Downs 1985; Fredericksen 1988; Hyland *et al.*

[2]The production of species-specific antisera is funded by a University Research Grant awarded to Toward Ceri, Department of Biological Sciences, University of Calgary (Ceri and Newman, principal investigators). The anti-pygmy hippopotamus serum was generously donated by Jerold Lowenstein, University of California, San Francisco.

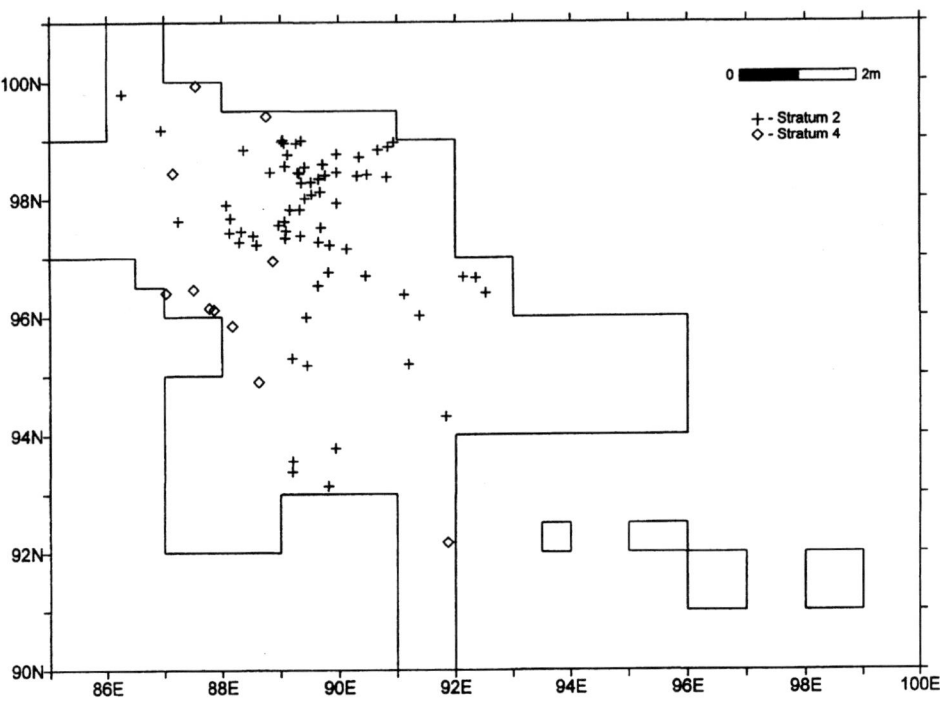

Figure 9-5. The distribution of all stone tools with Stratum 2 and Stratum 4 differentiated.

1990; Newman 1990; Newman and Julig 1989; Shafer and Holloway 1979). These analyses provide information concerning prehistoric diet and subsistence that is not always evident by conventional methods of analyses.

The successful identification of blood residues is dependent on the amount and condition of the antigen (immunoglobulin) retained on an artifact. However, these are extremely robust proteins that can survive harsh treatment outside the body, while still retaining their antigenicity and biological activity (Arquembourg 1975; Macey 1979; Sensabaugh et al. 1971; among others). This is important when dealing with archaeological materials where varying degrees of preservation occur.

The validity of applying conventional forensic techniques to archaeological materials has been demonstrated by the analysis of lithics from the Cummins Site, Thunder Bay (Newman and Julig 1989); Hidden Cave, Nevada (Newman 1990); and other sites in North America.

Crossover electrophoresis (CIEP) is widely used in forensic laboratories to identify the source of bloodstains, body fluids, and tissues (Culliford 1964). The principle of this test is that all animals produce antibodies (immunoglobulins) that recognize and bind with foreign proteins (antigens) as part of the body's defense system. The ability of these proteins to precipitate antigens from solution is one of their best-known properties, and it is this ability that is tested in CIEP. The test is sensitive (can detect 10^{-8} g of protein), is reasonably rapid, and lends itself to the processing of multiple samples (Culliford 1964). The procedure is discussed fully in Newman and Julig 1989.

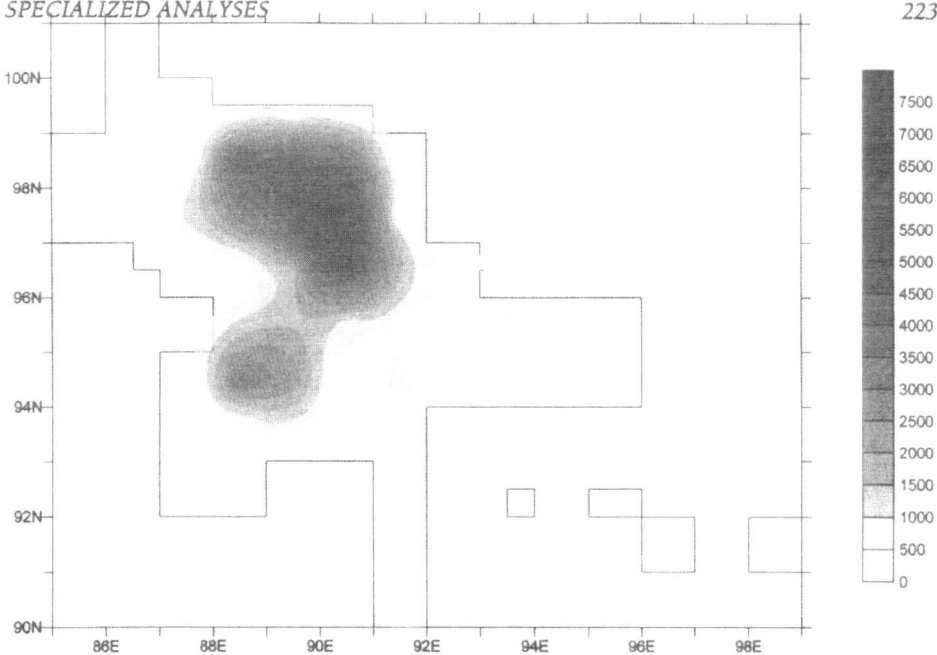

Figure 9-6. Shaded relief contour plot of the distribution of shell in Stratum 2.

Seven chipped stone artifacts from *Aetokremnos* were submitted for blood residue analysis. These were as follows: FN 984, thumbnail scraper; FN 1101, backed piece; FN 1025, side scraper; FN 1025, thumbnail scraper; FN 708, retouched piece; FN 782A, retouched piece; and FN 984, side scraper. All of these artifacts were from Stratum 2.

In this test, a 5% ammonia solution is used as extractant. This solution has been found to be the most effective in forensic cases where bloodstains are old or severely denatured (Dorrill and Whitehead 1979; Kind and Cleevely 1969).

The artifact is placed in a small plastic weigh boat, and 0.5 cc of the five percent ammonia solution is applied directly with a syringe and needle. Initial disaggregation of the residue is carried out by placing the weigh boat and contents in an ultrasonic bath for two to three minutes. Extraction is continued by placing the weigh boat and its contents on a rotating mixer for 30 minutes. The resulting ammoniacal solution is removed with a pipette and stored in a plastic vial prior to testing.

The animal antisera used in this analysis are, except where noted, prepared specifically for forensic medicine. These antisera are solid-phase absorbed to eliminate species cross-reactivity. However, the inevitable result of evolution is that all mammalian species have some serum protein antigenic determinants in common (Lowenstein 1986). Closely related species will cross-react strongly with antiserum made against one of them, while distant relatives will react weakly.

Three additional antisera—elephant, trout, and bison—were raised at the Department of Biological Sciences, University of Calgary (Ceri and Newman, principal investigators). The trout antiserum will give positive results to most members of the Salmonidae family, while the elephant and bison are species specific. Anti–pygmy hippopotamus serum was obtained from Jerold Lowenstein, University of California, San Francisco.

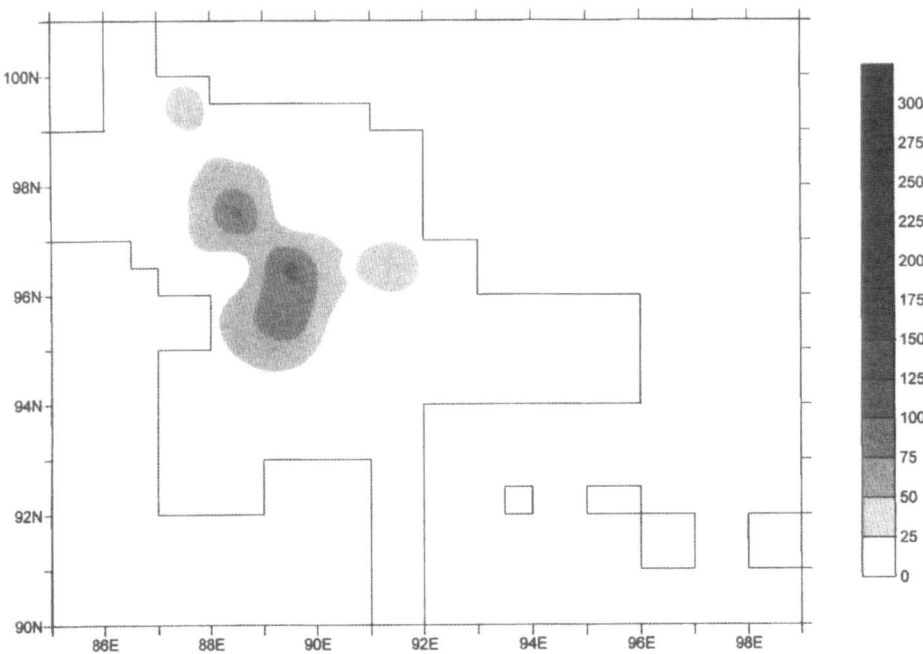

Figure 9-7. Shaded relief contour plot of the distribution of bird bones in Stratum 2.

All extracts are first tested against preimmune serum (i.e., serum from a nonimmunized animal). A positive result against this serum could arise from nonspecific protein interaction not based on the immunological specificity of the antibody. All extracts gave negative results. Analysis was continued by testing all extracts against the following antisera: antichicken/antideer, antimouse, antiguinea pig, antihuman, antibison, antielephant, antitrout, antipygmy hippopotamus.

One artifact—FN 984, a thumbnail scraper—tested positive to antihuman serum. This serum reacts only with humans and apes. The most likely explanation for positive tests for human blood results from accidental cuts during tool manufacture or resharpening. It also is possible that perspiration or other traces of recent handling may be responsible. However, as these artifacts have been handled extensively, more positive results would have been expected if this were the cause of the reaction.

None of the other artifacts elicited positive results to the antisera used.

THE PUMICE FROM *AETOKREMNOS* (*Vincenzo Francaviglia*)

There are two pieces of waterworn pumice from the *Aetokremnos* excavations. Stratum 2 (upper) produced FN 426 (N98E89, Feature 4), which measures 57 × 43 × 41.5 mm. Stratum 2 yielded SFN 66 (N97E89, Locus 2/7, SE quad), which measures 30 × 28 × 14.5 mm. Both pieces are probably naturally in the archaeological deposits and have not been modified by man. They are the earliest pumices to be found on an archaeological site

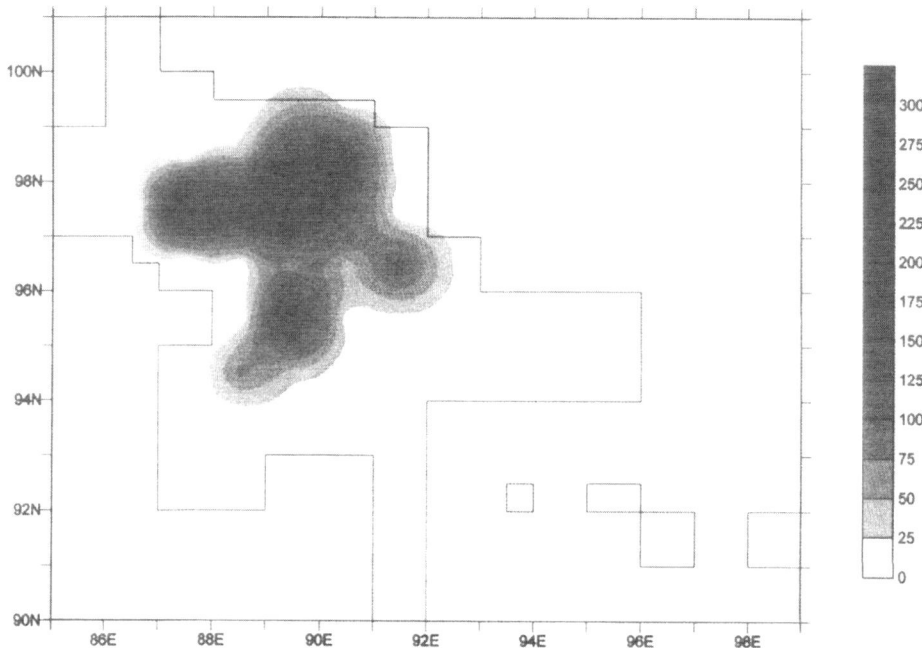

Figure 9-8. Shaded relief contour plot of the distribution of bird bones in Stratum 4. The same contour intervals were used in this figure as in Fig. 9-7.

on Cyprus.[3] They have been studied with the hope that their provenance and age could be determined.

At first glance, the two pieces appear different. The first (FN 466) is brownish, with evident plagioclase phenocrysts. The second (SFN 66) is whitish, with a less evident amount of phenocrysts.

The process of provenance identification of an unknown material involves a comparison of some of its features with those of some well-known materials. With this principle in mind, we have compared the two pumices in question with pumices originating from several Greek and Italian volcanoes. First of all, we deliberately ruled out as possible sources those volcanoes whose known eruptions are too recent as compared with the *Aetokremnos* archaeological material. Therefore, we ruled out the pumices from the Late Minoan Santorini eruption, the so-called Bo (Günther and Pichler 1973), dating to the seventeenth century B.C. (Hammer and Clausen 1990), and the pumices from Lipari Monte Pelato (Pichler 1980), dating to the eighth century A.D.

We have, however, taken into account the pyroclastics from three older Santorini eruptions: the Middle Pumice II or Bm II (Francaviglia and Di Sabatino 1990) or Ignimbrites

[3]Pumice has been found on other Cypriot archaeological sites on the island, but they date to much later periods (e.g., Elliott 1983:128, 1990:137; Francaviglia 1990:128). Previous suggestions for the use of the pumice from archaeological sites on Cyprus include polishing metal objects, cleaning cooking vessels, as a toilet aid (as also used today), or simply as an item of curiosity because of its lightness (D. Reese 1995).

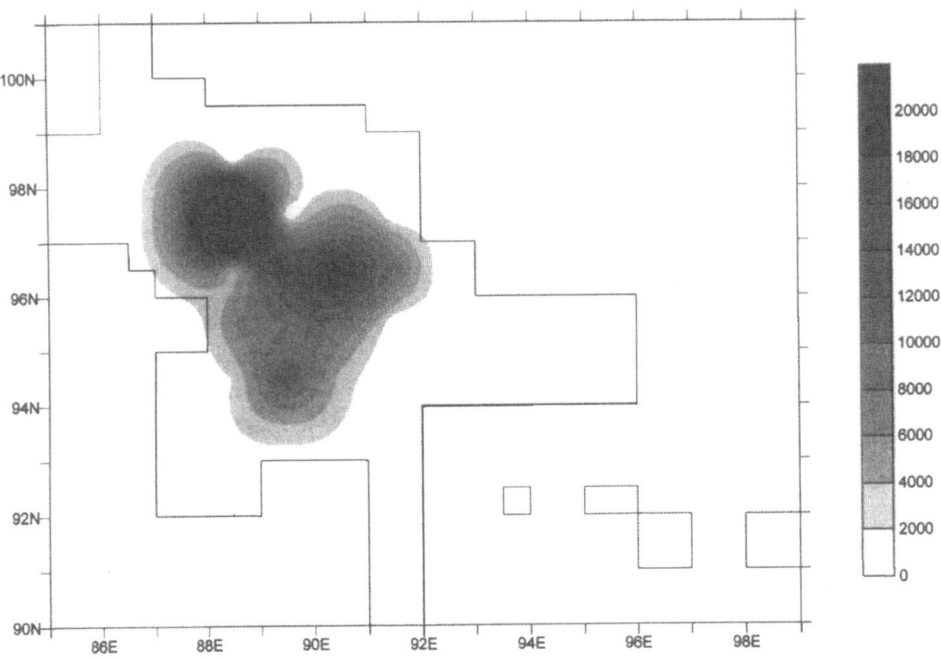

Figure 9-9. Shaded relief contour plot of the distribution of *Phanourios* bones in Stratum 4.

(Pichler and Friedrich 1976), the Middle Pumice I (Bm I), and the Bu1 (Günther and Pichler 1973). The age of these pyroclastics being, respectively, 18,500 B.P., 37,000 B.P., and more than 100,000 B.P. (Pichler and Friedrich 1976).

Pyroclastics of unknown age from Yali and Nisyros have also been taken into consideration. Finally, some sea-borne pumices, of unknown origin and age, which one can find everywhere along east Mediterranean beaches, have also been considered for comparison (Francaviglia 1990).

In order to determine their chemical composition, the two *Aetokremnos* pumices were compared with other Mediterranean pyroclastics by X-ray fluorescence (XRF) for 29 elements using the well-known method of Leoni and Saitta (1976). The loss of ignition (LOI) has been dosed by thermogravimetrical way. This analysis demonstrated that FN 426 and SFN 66 are two different things. From the petrological point of view, the first is a dacite and the other a rhydodacite.

The chemical data obtained through XRF were processed graphically and statistically, using ordinary binary plots and discriminant analysis (one of the so-called multivariate methods, Davis 1973). Though binary plots and discriminant analysis may appear to be two different approaches, they are substantially similar. A binary plot is a bidimensional representation of two quantities; a discriminating plot is a particular oriented projection of an *n*-dimension space onto a bidimensional space. As far as the discriminant analysis is concerned (Figs. 9-10–9-11), we have taken into account the major and minor elements (Na, Mg, Al, Si, K, Ca, Ti, Mn and Fe) on one side and some trace elements (Nb, Zr, Y, Sr, Rb, Ba, Ce, Nd, La) on the other.

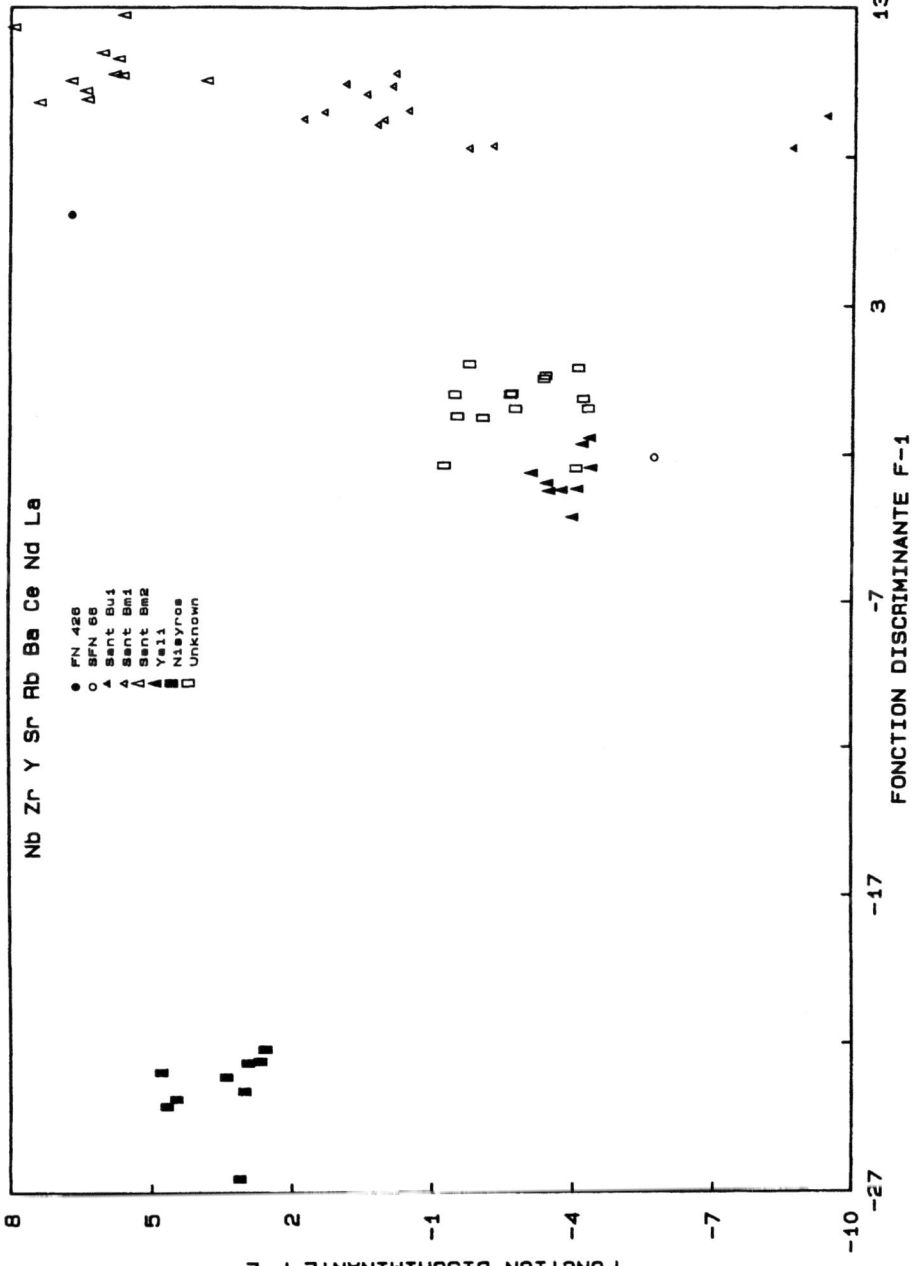

Figure 9-10. Discriminant function analysis for *Aetokremnos* and other pumices, using trace element abundances.

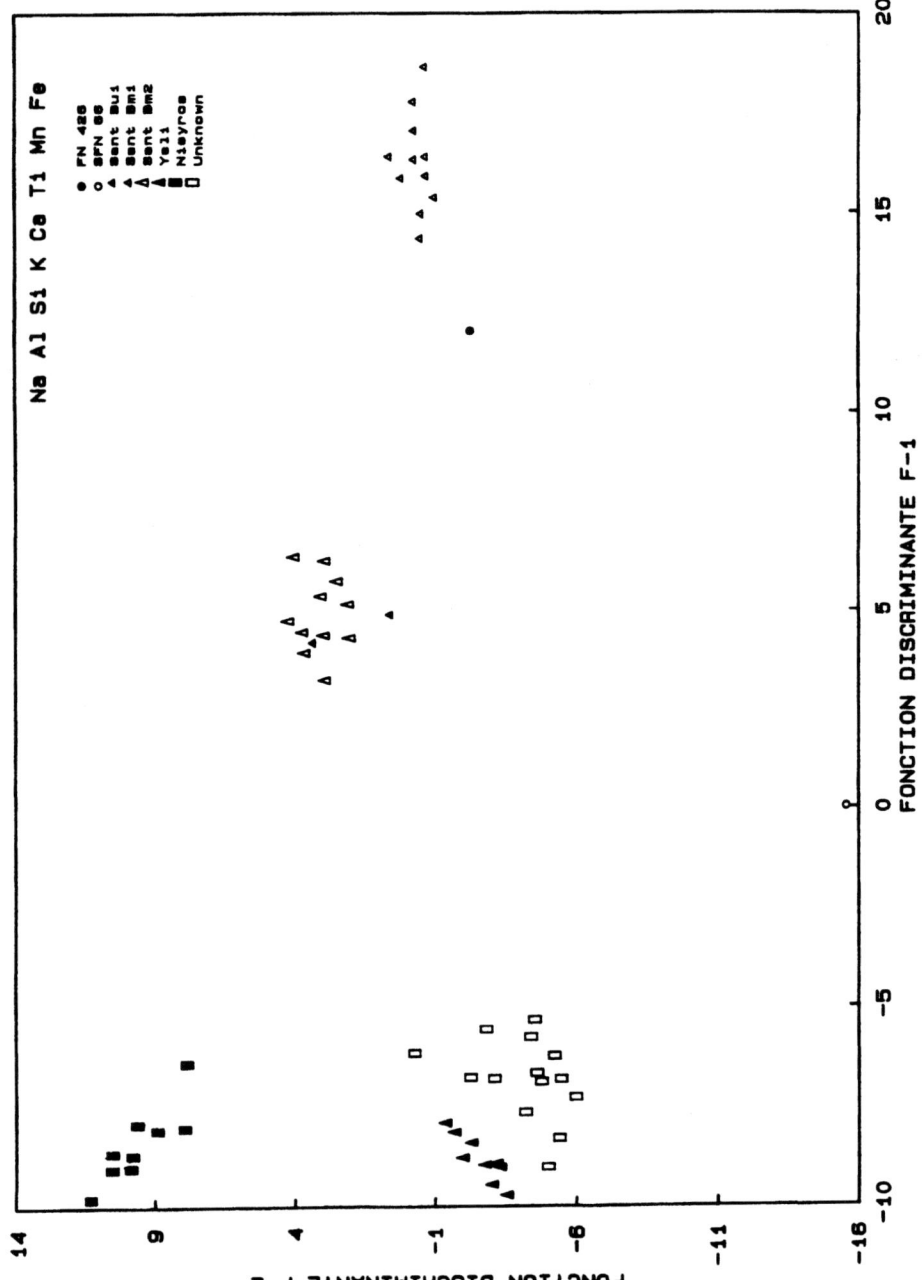

Figure 9-11. Discriminant function analysis for *Aetokremnos* and other pumices, major and minor elements.

The trace elements binary plots show that the *Aetokremnos* FN 426 pumice sample is akin to the Santorinian Middle Pumices II (Bm II) eruption, the pyroclastics of the Middle Pumices I (Bm I) being slightly different. The SFN 66 sample shows similarity with some unknown east Mediterranean sea-borne pumices.

The discriminant analysis leads us to the same conclusions. In the case of discriminant analysis using trace element abundances, by progressively increasing their number from 5 to 9, the position of FN 426 is always closer to the Bm II cluster than to that of Bm I (Fig. 9-10, the case for 9 trace elements).

In the case of discriminant analysis using major and minor elements, by progressively increasing their number from 5 to 8, some ambiguity remains; in other words, if we consider 5, 6, and 7 elements, there is no doubt that the FN 426 pumice belongs to the Middle Pumices II (Bm II) Santorini eruption (18,500 B.P.). But, by increasing up to 8 the number of elements computed, some ambiguity with the older Santorinian Middle Pumices I (Bm I) arises.

Whatever plot we use, the position of the SFN 66 sample is undefined. Sometimes it may be related to the unknown east Mediterranean sea-borne pumices, as in the case for discriminant analysis using trace elements (See Fig. 9-10); sometimes it appears totally isolated, as in the case for discriminant analysis using major and minor elements (Fig. 9-11).

PHYTOLITHS

In an attempt to characterize the local vegetation at *Aetokremnos* during its occupation, phytolith extraction was performed by David Rhode (Desert Research Institute) on two sediment samples from Strata 2 and 4. This was part of a larger pilot study investigating the utility of phytolith analyses for paleoenvironmental and archaeological reconstructions in Cyprus. Unfortunately, no phytoliths were identified in the extracted residue from the sediments at *Aetokremnos*. It is likely that this finding reflects actual absence of phytoliths in the *Aetokremnos* sediments, rather than laboratory technique, because samples from another early Cypriot site (Kholetria *Ortos*) were processed by Rhode during the same run, and these contained abundant phytolith preservation. The reasons for the lack of phytoliths at *Aetokremnos* remain unknown. Although these efforts were disappointing, phytolith analysis is likely to be useful in reconstructing vegetation formations and plant use by prehistoric Cypriots elsewhere on the island, and we hope to see its increased application.

FLOTATION AND POLLEN

Although numerous flotation samples were taken, results proved disappointing. Julie Hansen (Boston University) examined seven samples and found virtually no preserved remains. She was able only to identify very minute amounts of *Pinus* sp., *Genista*-type remains, and indeterminate conifer. Likewise, pollen samples, examined by Peter Wigand (Desert Research Institute) also had limited potential. Although his research identified the presence of some pollen, it was limited, and we decided to direct our limited resources toward the analysis of other materials, the results of which are presented throughout this volume.

INVESTIGATION OF THE *PHANOURIOS* BONES FOR EVIDENCE OF CULTURAL MODIFICATION (*Sandra Olsen*)[+]

During the excavations of 1990, over 16,000 bone fragments were examined for possible evidence of butchery and taphonomic processes. The purposes of this research were to delineate the impact that humans might have had on the faunal assemblage at *Aetokremnos* and to contribute to the understanding of the site formation processes.

Material from four areas of the site was investigated. This sample included 3,214 bone fragments from FN 359 (Stratum 4/2), 6,645 from FN 367 (Stratum 4B), 3,191 from FN 451 (Stratum 4B), and 3,551 from FN 490 (Stratum 4B), for a total of 16,601 bone fragments. The sample was selected from large mammal material that was not encrusted in matrix or soaked in acid by the excavators when removing the matrix. No other criteria were used in the choice of elements examined. Material that had been cleaned with acid was eliminated from the study because this process often etches the bone surface and erodes cultural and natural surface modifications. All of the material that was identifiable was from *Phanourios*, but it is possible that some of the more fragmentary bone was derived from pygmy elephants.

The methods that were employed began with examination of the bone surfaces with the eye and a 10× hand lens. Bone fragments bearing surficial modifications were then cleaned and inspected with a 40 power microscope. Cleaning consisted of lightly brushing the mark with alcohol, applied with a very soft camel hair brush. Silicone rubber molds were taken of the few striations that were ambiguous in nature. Epoxy casts were then made from the molds for examination in a scanning electron microscope.

The mammal assemblage is generally well preserved. Apart from the fact that some of the material, particularly that from the front of the shelter, has been loosely consolidated in a breccia, the *Phanourios* material has survived in fairly good condition.

The most destructive taphonomic process appears to be sedimentary abrasion, which has lightly scratched some of the bone (Fig. 9-12). In addition, some of the bone shows obvious rounding of broken edges and overall polishing (Fig. 9-13). The combination of abrasion, rounding, and polishing suggests either heavy pedoturbation, such as trampling by large mammals or humans (Andrews and Cook 1985; Olsen and Shipman 1988), or, less likely, short distance transport by fluvial action (Behrensmeyer 1988, 1990).[5] Surface scratches associated with sedimentary abrasion, like those shown in Figure 9-12, can normally be distinguished from humanly inflicted cutmarks by several criteria, especially the location and orientation of the marks, the morphology and depth of the marks, and their association with polish (Olsen and Shipman 1988: 549–552). As in actualistic experiments involving trampling, the *Phanourios* bones from *Aetokremnos* showed high frequencies of criss-crossing shallow marks, sweeping over the bone surfaces. These marks lacked any of the parallel longitudinal microstriations commonly witnessed in deep V-shaped grooves,

---

[+]This contribution was received after the other chapters in this volume had been prepared. The issue of cutmarks is an important one, and Olsen's contribution is included in its entirety here, although we clearly disagree with her interpretation. Although we acknowledge the lack of clear cutmarks, we deal with this in great detail in Chapter 12. The following extensive series of footnotes (fns. 5–15) has been appended as counterpoints to some of Olsen's conclusions.

[5]Mandel's contribution (Chap. 3) clearly discounts excessive pedoturbation. Furthermore, he shows that there has been only minimal, and very localized, fluvial action that could have moved the bones.

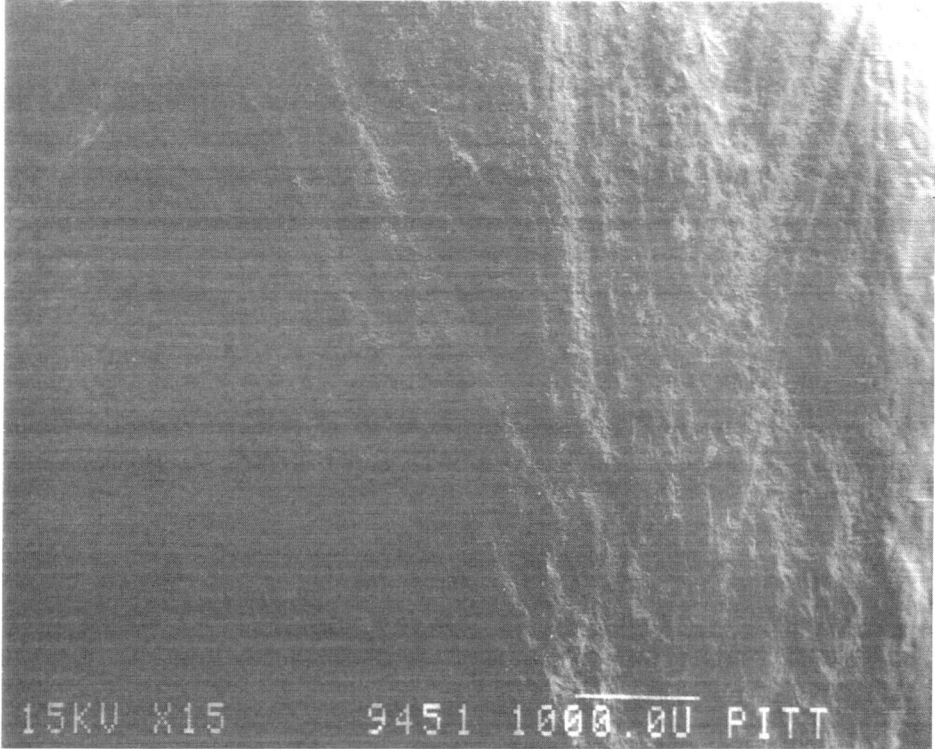

Figure 9-12. Sedimentary abrasion on the surface of a *Phanourios* bone from *Aetokremnos*.

which are characteristic of true cutmarks made with chipped stone tools. The striae were also not restricted to locations on bones where cutmarks often occur, that is in epicondylar regions or other surfaces where muscles, tendons, or ligaments are firmly attached, but instead they were widespread and showed no clear orientation or indication of patterning throughout the assemblage.

In the sample examined here, no spiral fractures or obvious fresh bone fractures were observed. Indications of postdepositional fractures, in which the collagen had been largely desiccated and denatured prior to breakage, were common. These were manifested in depressed fractures and longitudinal and transverse (as opposed to spiral) breaks. Thin bones, like ribs, often exhibited pitting and nibbling along their delicate margins, which appear to have been caused by small sharp pieces of stone, such as roof spalls, having been pressed into their surfaces. These markings did not look like carnivore gnawing or dynamically inflicted hammerstone impact scars.

The excavations did not reveal articulated limb bones or vertebral columns or even crania and mandibles. In fact, the elements appear to have been badly jumbled into disarray. There are at least three possible explanations for this fact. The first is that the hippopotami and elephants died one by one of natural causes in the rockshelter, and their remains were trampled by others who occupied the cave subsequently. This explanation would account for the mixing and disarticulating of the material, the postdepositional

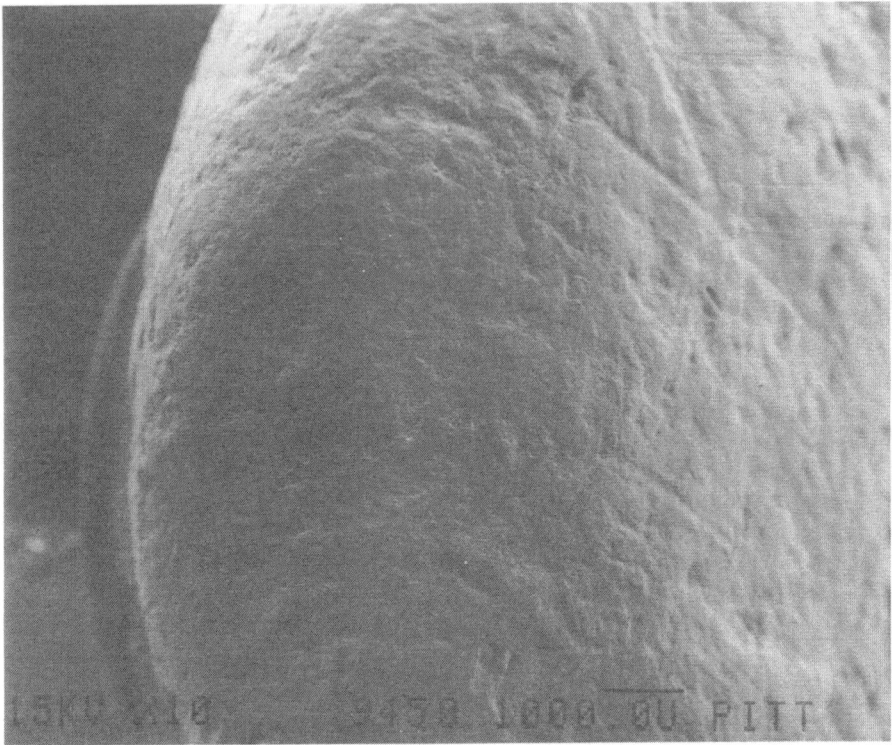

Figure 9-13. Broken end of a *Phanourios* pubis, showing rounding and multiple striations from sedimentary abrasion.

breakage, and the sedimentary abrasion (Olsen and Shipman 1988). Some articulation should be expected, however, unless trampling was fairly intense. A second hypothesis is that the hippopotamus and elephant bones were deposited through hydraulic transport or some other means, and that the rockshelter formed later in time, exposing the paleontological assemblage.

In either of these cases, human occupation would have taken place later and would have been only coincidentally located in the same place as the paleontological deposits. During use by the humans, further disarticulation, mixing, and sedimentary abrasion would have been likely, especially if any digging took place. The process of making hearths or lowering the shelter's floor to create more vertical space for upright humans could have contributed to the disturbance of the paleontological deposits. This activity would also explain the presence of *Phanourios* bones on the talus slope.

The third explanation is that human hunters killed and thoroughly butchered the hippopotami, ate the meat, and discarded the bones in the rockshelter. Such activity could account for the disarticulation of the hippopotami—if extensive butchery did take place—but fails to explain the complete absence of cutmarks on the bones examined or any evidence of marrow extraction (such as spiral fractures and hammerstone impact scars).

It must be said that in the 16,601 bone fragments from *Aetokremnos* I examined, no reliable evidence for butchery was observed. This lack of evidence has serious implications regarding the interpretation of the site formation processes and the relationship between the humanly produced artifacts, hearths, and other cultural traces and the deposits of hippopotamus and elephant remains.

In mass kill sites, because of the abundance of animals killed at one time, butchery tends to be relatively superficial compared with what takes place with single kills, so that cutmarks are usually low in frequency, and skeletons are often left partially articulated (Olsen 1989). In temperate regions, the extent of carcass utilization is highly variable because meat will spoil much more quickly in the summer than in the winter, limiting available processing time when the temperatures are high, the number of animals killed is high, and the number of people conducting the butchery is low.

At the Upper Paleolithic site of Solutré, France (Olsen 1989), which is interpreted as a palimpsest of multiple kills, butchery was slight. Cutmarks appeared on only 0.34% of the bones examined, but the marks were in typical locations indicating primarily skinning, disarticulation of the joints, and meat removal. With such a low percentage of cutmarks, it is not surprising that whole articulated limbs and vertebral columns were relatively common. Also, articulated crania and mandibles were frequently found, despite heavy sediment loading and movement due to solifluction. In comparison, at *Aetokremnos* there is extensive disassociation of elements from single individuals, yet no evidence of butchery. At Solutré, it is presumed, the animals were only lightly butchered, because a small hunting band would find it difficult to butcher and eat or preserve all of the meat before it spoiled in the summer heat. There, cutmarks were rare but still present, and articulated body segments were found. If *Aetokremnos* represents a mass kill event, and humans were processing the meat on site, then the butchery might have been only at the most superficial level.

This kind of light butchery would leave behind many articulated body segments, and at least a small percentage of bones would still show cutmarks. Then, the question arises as to how the body segments became disarticulated postdepositionally. Trampling and other activities by humans could explain some of this, but postdepositional breakage seems excessive if the bones were relatively fresh when humans trod on them. Experiments conducted to study the effects of human trampling on bones of ungulates in a variety of soil conditions failed to produce much breakage (Olsen and Shipman 1988).[6]

I am in strong disagreement with Simmons's (1991a:862) opinion that the thick skin and large fat deposits would have made it unlikely that cutmarks would be found on *Phanourios* bones.[7] Regardless of how thick the skin of an animal is or how much fat overlies the muscle, anatomy of any mammalian quadruped is organized around the same basic framework. The muscles attach either directly or via tendons to the bones and span

---

[6]We have explained the breakage and disarticulation of the *Phanourios* remains without recourse to excessive trampling scenarios. "Light" butchery would not necessarily have resulted in articulated body segments, depending on secondary uses of the bone (see Chaps. 12 and 13).

[7]In the cited preliminary report I did indicate that "butchering an animal as thick skinned and with as much fat as a pygmy hippopotamus would not necessarily have resulted in cut marks. This is particularly true if the butchering was not being done efficiently" (Simmons 1991a:862). I stand by these comments (see Chap. 12). However, not being a hunter or having experience in butchering, in this volume I have omitted reference to the "fat" aspect of butchering and cutmarks.

joints. In order to segment a large animal either to cook it or to eat it, cuts are usually made at the joints. To filet a muscle mass, it must be cut off the bone at its points of origin and insertion (i.e., where it is firmly attached directly or via a tendon to the bone surface). Either of these processes can leave cutmarks on the bones. Skin and fat only come into play in the initial stages of butchering and have no effect on disarticulating or fileting cutmarks, regardless of the species involved. Thick skin is often more difficult to remove from areas like the skull and feet than thin skin, which can be easily pulled off, so butchering an animal with thick skin might actually increase the number of skinning marks found on the bone in some places.

More relevant than the thickness of the skin or the quantity of body fat to the production of cutmarks with stone tools are the thicknesses of the periosteum and hyaline cartilage on the bones themselves. These tissues can protect the bone from cutmarks during processing with stone tools. Cutmarks are uncommon on the articular surfaces of large mammals because the hyaline cartilage is thick and resistant. Most cutmarks, therefore, occur around the joint, in the epicondylar region where ligaments, muscles, and tendons are cut. Cutmarks have been found with regularity on prehistoric horse (Olsen 1989), pig, and cow bones (Olsen 1994) butchered with stone tools, however, so there is no reason to expect that *Phanourios* would be dramatically different.

Although it is true that cutmarks usually occur on fewer than 15% of all of the faunal material from an archaeological site and can be very rare, some cutmarks should still be present in a collection of 16,600 well-preserved bones. Butchery can be light, in which case, cutmarks are scarce and the carcass is left mostly articulated. On the other hand, at times, butchery is quite intense. Fileting, by which the meat is cut off the bone with or without disarticulating the joints, often leaves high frequencies of cutmarks along the shafts of the bones (Olsen 1987). If the butchering involves disarticulated joints, with the exception of the shoulder, the butchering tools are likely to come into contact with bones.

While dismembering a carcass, the ligaments, muscles, and tendons are cut with the sharp edge of a stone tool. Some have argued that a knowledgeable butcher does not need to leave cutmarks on the bone because he or she "knows" the anatomy. This argument ignores the fact that the underlying bone acts much like a cutting board. The soft tissue is cut more easily if it is pressed against the surface of the bone by the stone flake or knife. That is why most people place meat on a cutting board rather than swinging at it while it's suspended in midair. Although using the bone for support does not always mean that the stone tool's edge will leave visible marks on the bone, it is difficult to avoid such marring every time. Nor is there any strong motivation on the part of the butcher to take extreme precautions against inflicting cutmarks on the bones, although excessive contact will eventually dull the stone implement.[8]

Finally, the stone tools from *Aetokremnos* are generally quite small blades and thumbnail scrapers. If the blades were hafted into slotted wooden handles, then they would be useful butchering tools; however, large bifaces would be more effective in removing the thick skin of a hippopotamus. The small scrapers seem to be better suited to processing mollusks than to butchering a hippopotamus.[9]

---

[8]See the discussion in Chapter 12, especially comments from research conducted by G. Haynes and G. Frison.
[9]I completely disagree with this statement, as discussed in Chapter 12.

Figure 9-14. Cow and pig bones from experimental campfire. Cleaned bones were placed in a pit and covered with 10–15 cm of soil. A wood fire was built on top of the soil and kept burning or six hours. Bones turned brown to black and cracked open from the heat, despite the absence of contact with any direct flame.

In recent years, doubt has been cast on the correlation between burnt bone and any cultural implications (Bennett 1999; Bennett and Klippel 1995). At *Aetokremnos*, there is an abundance of bones that appear to be burnt. With the quantity of ash in the site and the presence of hearths, this is not surprising. Experiments conducted by this author burying clean cow and pig bones in silt below an open campfire demonstrate that the bone need not be lying in direct contact with the fire to be cracked, split, and blackened by the heat (Fig. 9-14). Therefore, a paleontological deposit of *Phanourios* bones that was lying just under the surface or even as much as 10–15 cm below the surface of a hearth could be affected by a subsequent fire. The results obtained from my short actualistic study of burning have been duplicated in a more thorough experiment (Bennett and Klippel 1995).[10]

The nature of the burnt bone from *Aetokremnos* was unusual in a few specimens in which the interior of the bone appeared to be more seriously affected than the exterior (Fig. 9-15). In these cases, the fine trabeculae of the cancellous (or "spongy") bone were charred, while the external cortical surface showed little or no alteration. The finding of bone burnt internally fits with the hypothesis that the bones were already cracked open and free of insulating meat or marrow before the fire was built, as would be the case if the *Phanourios* remains were deposited long before the human utilization of the cave. Blackened bones occur

---

[10]See discussion of burning in Chapter 12, especially relating to the research of Stiner *et al.* (1995). I have not seen the Bennett and Klippel (1995) source, as this was a paper presented at a meeting.

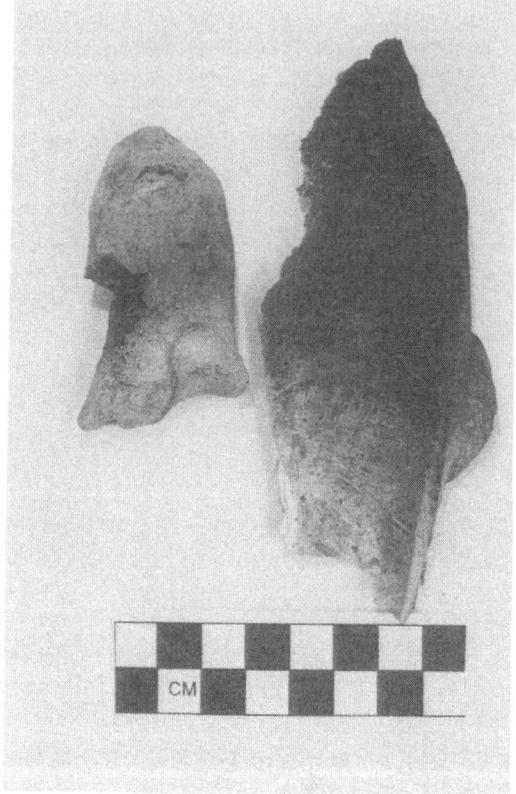

Figure 9-15. Comparison of unusual burning patterns in which the internal cancellous tissue is burnt without the exterior cortical bone browning. A *Phanourios* ulna from *Aetokremnos* (left) and a cow femur (right) from the modern experiment are shown

in other parts of the rockshelter a short distance from the main hearth and are more difficult to explain, but they may simply reflect periodic removal of accumulated ash and debris from hearths to other parts of the shelter.[11]

The findings of this study were that moderate sedimentary abrasion, rounding, polish, and postdepositional breakage suggest that a taphonomic process like trampling had occurred on some of the faunal material. No definitive humanly inflicted cutmarks or indications of marrow extraction, such as spiral fractures or impact scars, were observed. Burning was relatively common in bones, but this may have taken place long after the *Phanourios* bones were deposited because of their close proximity to the heat of later fires.

The interpretation that is most favored by this researcher, based on the faunal evidence, the lithic assemblage, the stratigraphy and distribution of artifacts, and the taphonomy of the site favors hypothesis 1 or 2. In other words, the hippopotamus and elephant bones accumulated naturally in the bottom stratum of the site, as has happened at nu-

---

[11]There is no direct relationship of burned bone to the hearths. We have provided discussion on the burning of the *Phanourios* remains in Chapter 12.

merous localities around the coast of Cyprus (Boekschoten and Sondaar 1972) and represent a paleontological deposit. The specific means by which this natural accumulation occurred have not been determined. In Cyprus, paleontological accumulations of hippopotami and elephants typically occur in two settings: rockshelters or caves and stream deposits. This species of hippopotamus has been interpreted as being primarily terrestrial because their remains have not been found in association with lake deposits (Boekschoten and Sondaar 1972). The bones were disarticulated, broken, abraded, and polished by some form of pedoturbation, like trampling by other hippopotami, or by whatever natural agent that transported them into the cave.[12] In other circumstances, carnivores would be suspected, but Cyprus had a deficiency of predators, and there is no evidence of carnivore gnawing on the bones.

According to this interpretation of the evidence, after some interval of time, humans entered the rockshelter and used it for preparing mollusks and large birds for consumption. Some of the paleontological deposits were dug out and pushed down the talus slope to lower the floor of the rockshelter. The ceiling of the shelter was quite low, and a hearth would quickly fill such a small area with heat and smoke, so enlarging the cave by the one method possible seems logical. A depression was made for hearths, and the birds and mollusks were processed, perhaps on a seasonal basis, repeatedly. The small rockshelter may therefore represent a short-term food processing site that may have been used on many occasions. From time to time, the hearth was cleaned out, distributing burnt *Phanourios* bones and ash around the floor and out on the talus slope.[13] This scenario may not be completely accurate, but it is not negated by the evidence and seems more plausible to me than the hypothesis that the hippopotami and elephants were killed by humans; butchered with diminutive stone tools to the point of completely disarticulating them without leaving a single cutmark, impact scar, or spiral fracture, and burning the bones in the unusual manner displayed at *Aetokremnos*.[14]

The dense quantity of *Phanourios* bones, the rarity of stone tools in the lower portion of the stratigraphic record, and the opposite trend in the upper levels support my reconstruction. Bird bones and mollusks are most concentrated in the upper levels, with the stone tools. During the excavations, it was clear that roots or burrowing invertebrates had made long vertical shafts that penetrated from the upper levels to the lower ones.[15] These agents, in addition to intrusion by human activities, could account for the few pieces of stone that do occur at the lower levels.

---

[12]As pointed out in Chapter 12, little systematically collected data are available for most of the paleontological sites known in Cyprus. Certainly in the case of *Aetokremnos*, we have ruled out natural agencies as an origin source.
[13]We have thoroughly discussed this possibility in Chapters 12 and 13 and have concluded that the data do not support such an interpretation.
[14]We obviously clearly disagree with this conclusion.
[15]As Mandel (Chap. 3) has convincingly demonstrated, there has been only minimal root or insect disturbance to the deposits at *Aetokremnos*.

Chapter *10*

Additional Archaeological Investigations on the Akrotiri Peninsula

ALAN H. SIMMONS, MICHAEL NEELY, AND DAVID S. REESE

PREVIOUS ARCHAEOLOGICAL INVESTIGATIONS ON THE AKROTIRI PENINSULA (*Alan H. Simmons*)

Prior to our investigations, archaeological study of the Akrotiri Peninsula had been limited (see Heywood 1982), with the notable exception of the survey conducted by Brian Pile that located *Aetokremnos*. Fortunately, RAF-Akrotiri has an active and professional amateur society, the Western Sovereign Bases Archaeological Society, and they are involved in a variety of archaeological investigations, as well as conservation matters. Most of their studies, however, concentrate on the remains of classic antiquity, the most notable of which are those from Curium, immediately west of the peninsula.

Before Pile's survey, some previous archaeological survey had been undertaken. The principal study was that of A. Megaw and Colonel J. Last, who was the military advisor within the Western Sovereign Base Area (WSBA). They conducted a survey in 1954; unfortunately, I was unable to locate a copy of this report. F. Haggerty (1991), one of the active amateur archaeologists on the base during our investigations, has summarized this survey.

Megaw and Last listed 18 sites but gave only limited information on the nature of these. Their survey was conducted prior to the airfield's being built, and, according to Haggerty, should have included most of the larger (i.e., visible) sites. These sites included a variety of "settlements," "tombs," "ruins," and "watch towers"; some of these were formally named, while others were not. Notably, their survey did not locate, nor in all likelihood did they look for, prehistoric occurrences.

As a result of the Megaw and Last survey, legislation known as the Antiquities Ordinance of 1975 was enacted. The ordinance divided the major sites located during the survey into three "lists." The first is "The Republic" (i.e., Republic of Cyprus), which included the stadium, Sanctuary of Apollo, and other lands at Kourion owned by the Republic, as well as the cemetery of Ayio *Ermoyenis*. The second list is "The Crown" (i.e., British), and included portions of Curium owned by the Crown, Kato *Katalymata*, and Pano *Katalymata*. The third list is "Private," and includes portion of Kourion on private land and the church and monastery of St. Nicholas ("Monastery of the Cats").

The Antiquities Ordinance regulated archaeological activity on RAF-Akrotiri, and Haggerty (1991:52) noted that due to the ordinance, there has been no active archaeology on the base other than observation and nondisturbance survey. Most clearly visible sites appear to date to the Roman period from between the first and fourth centuries A.D. The original inspection report of 1954 claimed that the Akrotiri Peninsula had been densely populated from the Hellenistic period to the end of the seventh century.

Haggerty (1991:52) goes on to state that other sites also had been discovered and reported to the Cypriot authorities, and that "one notable report was by Flt Lt Brian Pile of 34 Squadron. In 1981, he wrote a report on the evidence of early man and the locations of fossils sites on the base. One of the sites-'Site E' . . . was the location of fossil bones of pigmy [sic] hippopotami and pigmy [sic] elephant. This site has revolutionized the history of early man in Cyprus."

Haggerty's summary represents a relatively accurate statement on the nature of archaeological investigations on RAF-Akrotiri up to the *Aetokremnos* project. Although Haggerty refers to Pile's locating "fossil sites" (i.e., plural), we have found no record of other paleontological occurrences located on the Akrotiri Peninsula, by Pile or anyone else. This is confirmed by an examination of Held's recent work, which summarizes both paleontological and early prehistoric sites on Cyprus; none of the former are noted for the Akrotiri Peninsula (1992:36–37).

Pile's (1981) survey was remarkable for its thoroughness and emphasis on small, nonstructural sites, especially considering that it was conducted by an amateur. His report was more of a listing of recorded sites than an integrated summary of the results of his survey. He recorded 31 sites and 4 "areas," for a presumed total of 35 "sites." Of these, only 12 (34%) contained ceramics. Held's thorough evaluation of the Akrotiri Peninsula (1992:112–126) provided additional information on these, including proper site names. Although not all sites were visited during the *Aetokremnos* Project, a number were. Our impression of these is that they fit well within the rubric of rather nondescript "artifact scatters," with limited potential for in situ deposits.

In labeling sites, Pile used a somewhat confusing methodology—some were designated numerically, while others were designated alphabetically (thus "Site E"). To add to the confusion, some sites apparently were subdivided (e.g., "Site 16, Area A," etc.). Oddly enough, I could find no site form for *Aetokremnos*, although this clearly was a locality to which Pile paid a considerable amount of attention.

Pile collected several artifacts, particularly chipped stone, from most of these sites. He labeled many of the sites as "Chalcolithic" on his site map; the majority are located on the southeastern portion of the peninsula, near the cliffs. I analyzed the chipped stone among these artifacts, presently curated at the Kourion Museum in Episkopi village, using the methodology employed at *Aetokremnos*. Overall, they are rather nondescript. It consisted of 550 artifacts, broken down as follows: 19 cores, 47 primary flakes, 92 secondary flakes, 137 tertiary flakes, 4 bladelets, 6 secondary blades, 15 tertiary blades, 18 microflakes, 155 pieces of debris, and 38 tools. Of the 320 debitage blanks, only 25 (7%) are blades or bladelets. Virtually no diagnostic tools were noted; the lack of the "thumbnail" scrapers so apparent at *Aetokremnos* is striking. Such artifacts did occur, however, at some of Pile's sites that we subsequently tested.

THE AKROTIRI PENINSULA SURVEY, 1991 (*Alan H. Simmons*)

In addition to the excavations at *Aetokremnos* and the testing of three possibly related surface sites (see later), we conducted a limited survey during three weeks in July of 1991 (Simmons 1992d). The primary purpose of the survey was to supplement already known information and to determine if other prehistoric sites related to the Akrotiri Phase could be located. We also were interested in the occurrence of paleontological sites that might contain *Phanourios* remains, because the presence of these could affect the interpretation of *Aetokremnos*. As noted earlier, such paleontological sites are well known throughout Cyprus, but none have been recorded on the Akrotiri Peninsula or nearby. We wished to systematically examine small portions of the Peninsula where it was geomorphologically plausible that other ancient sites might be located. In particular, we focused on cliff edges similar to those where *Aetokremnos* is situated.

Based on our excavations at *Aetokremnos*, it appeared likely that any related sites would not contain architecture and would be of low archaeological visibility, probably consisting of scattered pieces of flint artifacts and possibly bone and shell. Accordingly, it was necessary to conduct the survey with these limitations in mind.

The survey was conducted by a crew of two to three individuals. It was pedestrian, with individuals walking transects at regular intervals. The spacing depended on the roughness of the terrain. For example, in precipitous areas along cliff faces, spacing was limited, while on wider open areas, spacing could be farther apart. Most of the survey was conducted in a systematic fashion, but in some cases, examination was more in the nature of a reconnaissance rather than a true survey. No collections were made.

The survey examined seven separate transects, covering a total of roughly 1.23 sq k, or 122.7 ha (Table 10-1). Of the seven areas, one was immediately adjacent to *Aetokremnos* and covered the dangerously eroding cliffs and cliff-top around that site; one was located around the cliffs and cliff-tops on the southwestern end of the Peninsula, near the Princess Mary Hospital at Cape Zevgari; another was around the cliffs and cliff-tops on the eastern end of the Peninsula at Cape Gata; one was immediately inland from the southeastern end

Table 10-1. Location and Size of Surveyed Transects

Transect	Location	Approximate area surveyed (ha)
I	*Aetokremnos* cliffs	14.25
II	North base periphery	49.10
III	Cape Zevgari	19.00
IV	Inland from east coast	27.17
V	Southeast Peninsula	7.17
VI	Cape Gata	0.60
VII	Southwest edge of Akrotiri Salt Lake	5.45
TOTAL AREA SURVEYED		122.74

of the Peninsula; another was slightly inland from the eastern coast; the sixth was along the northern periphery of RAF-Akrotiri; and the last was a reconnaissance of the southwestern end of the Akrotiri Salt Lake.

Much of the area surveyed has been impacted by continuous modern occupation of the base area; few pristine regions survive. In some portions of the survey zone, however, vegetation was heavy and visibility was accordingly limited.

Despite careful examination, no new sites were located. Only a few isolated flint artifacts were noted, and those could have come from several periods. They included a microlithic core and a few nondescript pieces of debitage, primarily flakes. Roman pottery, however, was ubiquitous.

One of the survey's goals was to verify the location of sites recorded by Pile. With the exception of one, all of the sites that he found that were situated in our survey transects were, in fact, relocated. This attests to the thoroughness of Pile's original survey. Most of these sites do not appear to have much in the way of intact deposits, although as the excavations at *Aetokremnos* have demonstrated, this can be misleading.

The site that could not be relocated was Pile's Site 5. According to the description and photograph, this is near a meteorological station and not too distant from both Site 2 (which was test excavated—see later) and *Aetokremnos*. Although some of the local archaeologists insist they had recently visited Site 5, it is my belief that this actually was Site 2. Site 5 has apparently been completely collected, or, more likely, completely eroded into invisibility.

Much of RAF-Akrotiri has been disturbed by modern activities. Despite this, there are numerous in-situ archaeological resources still intact on the base's and the WSBA's boundaries. The small area surveyed by the present study did not locate any new sites. This does not mean that they do not exist on the base, however, and if resources ever are available, we would recommend a basewide systematic survey and testing program designed to record archaeological sites from all periods. The Roman period is known to be especially rich, but earlier periods also are represented, if by more ephemeral remains, as *Aetokremnos* has amply demonstrated.

The fact that no new archaeological or paleontological sites were recorded is significant. This "negative evidence" suggests that *Aetokremnos* was not merely one of several paleontological sites that was later occupied by humans, as has been suggested by some critics of the site's association of cultural and faunal materials. There is no evidence to indicate the presence of other fossil beds on the Peninsula. Both our survey and previous, albeit less systematic, investigations confirm this.

Thus *Aetokremnos*, and possibly some of the small surface sites within a few kilometers of it, appear to represent the only manifestations of the Akrotiri Phase on the Peninsula. That no other archaeological sites were located dating to the Akrotiri Phase indicates that this occupation may have been ephemeral, although this is not necessarily the case. Low-visibility lithic sites are subject to a variety of postdepositional processes that could obscure them for modern discovery. In addition, we have to consider that related sites might be either under water or have eroded from the cliff areas into the sea. In any event, though, it would appear that those responsible for the Akrotiri Phase were not in the habit of leaving residues that would result in a substantial archaeological signature. This makes a solid definition of the phase all the more intriguing, if difficult.

TESTING OPERATIONS AT THREE SMALL SITES
(Alan H. Simmons, Michael Neeley, and David Reese)

Introductory Comments

Although the primary focus of investigations in this study was *Aetokremnos,* we test excavated three other sites in order to obtain potentially comparable data (Fig. 10-1). These sites, tested during the 1990 season, had all been previously recorded by Pile. Several of the sites he had recorded were visited during the excavations at *Aetokremnos.* We decided to conduct test excavations at three that appeared most likely to contain in situ cultural deposits.

Our investigations at these three sites were all quite limited, consisting of both surface collection and exploratory excavation units. Buried deposits were virtually nonexistent or, when they occurred, were not very deep. Furthermore, all of the sites have been disturbed by modern activities, and all indicate multiple occupations, apparent by the number of ceramics and other more recent materials. In our analysis of the chipped stone, we employed the same methodology used at *Aetokremnos* to ensure comparability. Other artifacts were analyzed in less detail. Names for the sites follow Pile's original designations. In addition, we provide the site's proper names, following Held's (1992:112–126) summary.

Site 2: Akrotiri *Vounarouthkia ton Lamnion 2*

Description. Site 2 is located on a small sand dune approximately 100 m north of the cliff edge from *Aetokremnos.* The area around the dune is relatively flat, though there is a slight slope south toward the cliff. The dune, less than 1 m in height and capped by a

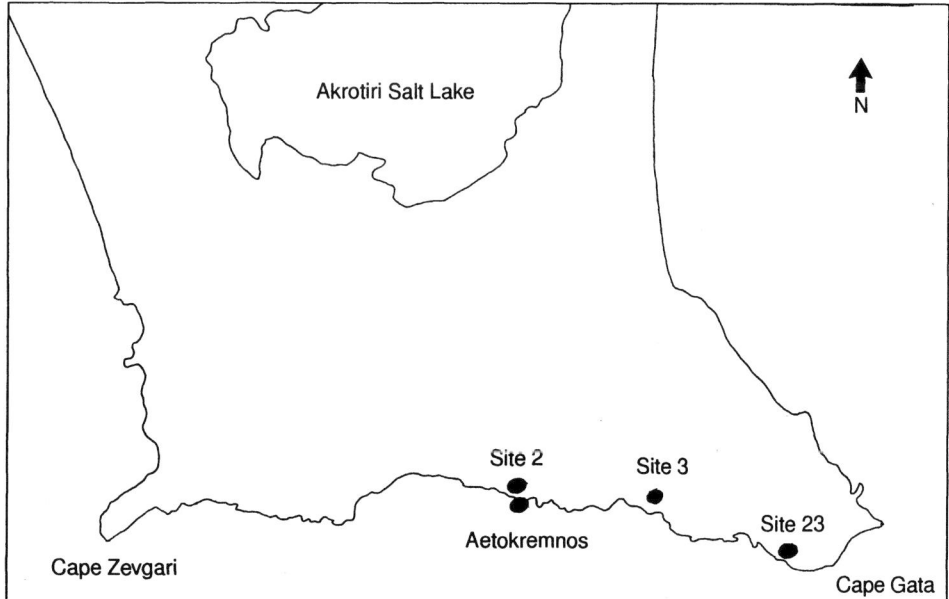

Figure 10-1. Location map of the three tested sites.

moderately dense growth of sagelike vegetation, covers an area approximately 10 × 120 m, though the artifact scatter is double this size, and is less than 1 m in height. Given this low height and the relatively flat surrounding area, the effects of water action on the transport of cultural materials is believed to be minimal. The decrease in artifact density about 10 m from the dune is evidence that supports this observation. At this distance, shell and chipped stone become scarce, which differs from the immediate dune area. Ceramics, however, which are ubiquitous along the cliffs, continue in low densities.

Methodology. In order to cover the entire dune and surrounding areas, a series of 5-x-5-m squares were laid out across the site. This configuration resulted in a site area, as defined by the grid system, of 20 m on all sides (400 m² total). Each of the 5-x-5-m grids was completely collected. The results of the surface collection indicated that the greatest density of material lay on the edges of the sand dune, particularly in areas with little to no ground cover. Farther from the dune, the density of materials decreased, except for ceramics, the density of which remained fairly constant. The classes of artifacts from the surface collection include chipped stone, ceramics, shell, igneous rock, glass, iron, and copper/bronze. The varied nature of these classes suggests several different occupational phases for the dune area.

A single 1-x-2-m unit was excavated on the south side of the dune. This unit was situated in an area that contained high densities of surface chipped stone and shell. It extended into the vegetated portion of the dune where lithic material is visible on the surface. Thus the excavation covered an area of the site with both high- and low-density surface materials.

Stratigraphy. The majority of artifacts at Site 2 come from its surface. There is, however, some buried deposition. The excavation indicated that there were two distinct strata within the dune. The first, Level 1, was a gray-brown organic stratum covering the northern portion of the unit. This area contained few surface artifacts and was covered by vegetation. Included in this sediment, which was filled with plant roots and (wild) onions, were high densities of shell and chipped stone, with lower densities of ceramics. Also found in the organic sediment were glass, igneous rock, and a silver coin with an Arabic inscription. This upper stratum obviously represents a mixture of temporal periods, possibly spanning prehistoric (chipped stone) to medieval (coin and ceramics) times. The heavy root activity has destroyed any discrete depositional levels within this organic topsoil and made the differentiation of horizons impossible.

The second stratum (Levels 2 and 3) is a light brown sand that is more consolidated than the overlying organic layer. This stratum is visible on the surface in the southern portion of the unit (the organic level either never formed here or was stripped away by natural processes) and is beneath the organic sediments in the north. It is notable that the density of cultural material, consisting of a low amount of chipped stone, shell, and ceramics confined to the upper portion of this stratum, decreases sharply in this level. Much of this material has probably worked its way down into this stratum from above and does not represent a distinct cultural horizon. Due to the declining frequency of cultural material, this excavation unit was reduced to 1 × 1 m (focusing on the northern half) and continued downward. The artifact density dwindled until sterile sediments were reached, about 35–40 cm below the surface.

Marine Shells. The 1980 surface collection by Pile and our 1990 surface collection and test excavations produced 5,438 marine shell fragments that come from at least 2,492 individuals. Unlike *Aetokremnos* and the other two sites tested, at Site 2 *Patella* (1,216 individuals) is found in almost equal numbers as *Monodonta* (1,260 individuals). There are actually more *Patella* (3,043) fragments than *Monodonta* fragments (2,378), but fewer actual individual shells. Of the total number of fragments, only 60 are found burnt. This is only 26 individual shells (13 *Monodonta*, 13 *Patella*) or 1.0%.

Together *Monodonta* and *Patella* account for 99.4% of the shell collection. There are 16 other shells and one crab present. All are probably food debris except for 1 waterworn *Cerithium*, 1 slightly worn *Murex*, and 1 *Mitra*, which was collected dead on the beach.

Chipped Stone. During the survey that recorded the site, Pile collected several chipped stone artifacts (Table 10-2). These are largely nondiagnostic artifacts, consisting primarily of debris (43%). Notable, however, is the presence of a thumbnail scraper, similar to the types that are so characteristic of *Aetokremnos*.

Table 10-2. Chipped Stone Assemblage from Site 2

Type	Pile sample n	Testing sample Surface	1	2	3	n	%	N
Tools								
TNS-V1		2				2		2
TNS-S/E	1							1
TNS		4	2			6		6
perforator	1							1
ret. bl.	1			1		1		2
ret. fl.		4				4		4
Subtotal	3					13	4.0	16
Debitage								
cor. fl.		2				2		2
sec. fl.	4	10	1			11		15
ter. fl.	11	10	6			16		27
sec. bl.	1							1
ter. bl.	1		1	1		2		3
bladelets		1	1			2		2
Subtotal	17					33	10.1	50
Other Waste								
debris	28	55	69	2		126	38.5	154
microflakes	10	45	72	9	1	127	38.8	137
cores	1	1				1	0.3	2
Akrotiri cores	6	22	5			27	8.3	33
Subtotal	45					281		326
Total	65					327	100.0	392

Note: "%" refers only to artifacts systematically collected during testing operations. Key: TNS=thumbnail scrapers, V1=variant 1, S/E= side/end, ret.=retouched, bl.=blade, fl.=flake, cor.=cortical, sec.=secondary, ter.=tertiary.

Systematic testing resulted in the recovery of over 300 chipped stone artifacts (Table 10-2). Among the 13 tools were another 6 thumbnail scrapers (Fig. 10-2). Because these have not been previously reported from other Cypriot sites and are so diagnostic of *Aetokremnos*, the temptation to suggest an affinity is strong. These scrapers, however, are not as well manufactured, on technological grounds, as are the *Aetokremnos* pieces. Their retouch is generally abrupt or steep, and not invasive, which is a predominant pattern at *Aetokremnos*. The edges of the Site 2 scrapers also are battered, possibly reflecting use. At *Aetokremnos*, on the other hand, the edges are generally fresh. Thus, there are distinct similarities with the *Aetokremnos* thumbnail scrapers, but these are primarily on general typological grounds.

Perhaps the most unique artifacts type from Site 2 is not the thumbnail scrapers, significant as they may be, but the presence of a peculiar artifact we have termed *exhausted*

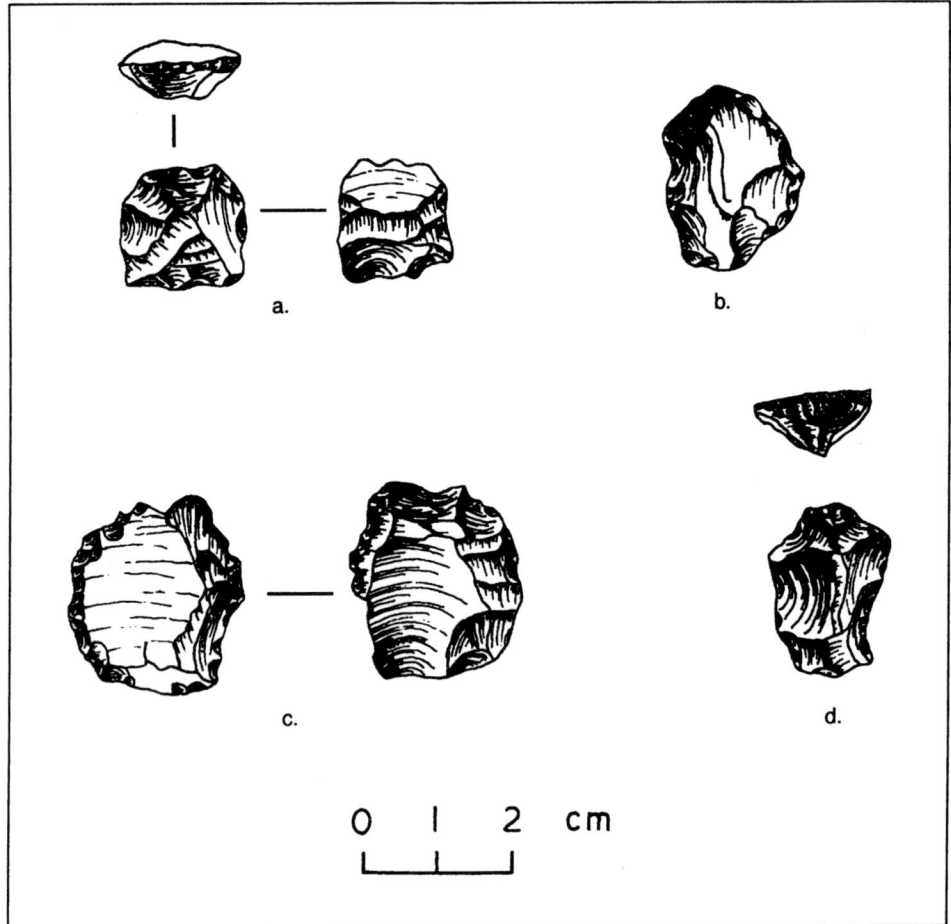

Figure 10-2. Site 2 thumbnail scrapers. (a) thumbnail scraper, side/end, variant 1; (b) thumbnail scraper, side/end; (c) thumbnail scraper, side/end, variant 1; (d) thumbnail scraper, end.

Akrotiri cores (Fig. 10-3). These are not similar to exhausted cores from *Aetokremnos*. There, small cores are distinct bladelet forms. At Site 2, however, these artifacts are uniformly small and globular or spheroidal; they almost resemble "marbles." Table 10-3 provides summary statistics on these artifacts. Most were manufactured on white cherts or quartzite. These artifacts also are abundant, forming over 8% of the total assemblage from Site 2.

The function of these unusual artifacts is unclear. We have classified them as cores, and they may simply represent parent materials that were very efficiently reduced. On the

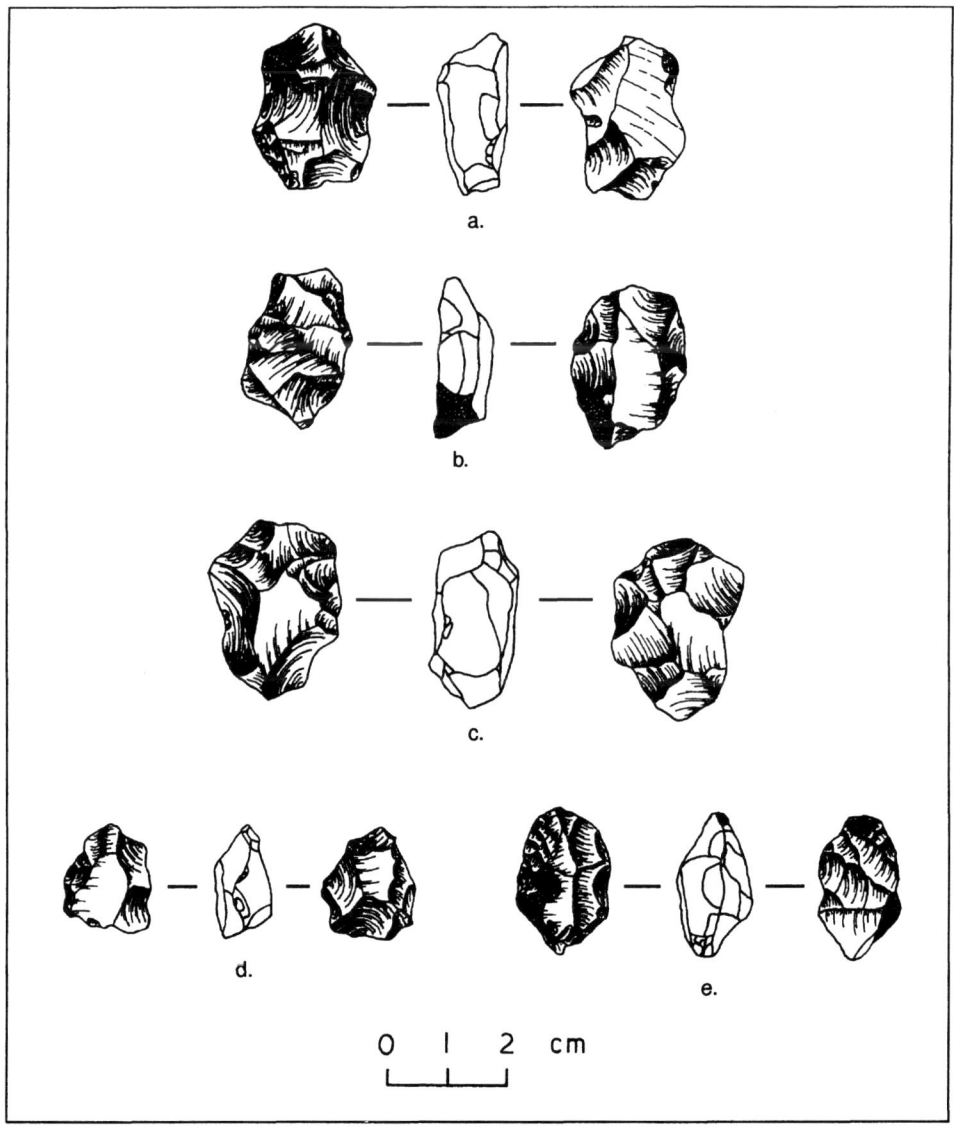

Figure 10-3. Site 2 cores. a–e: *Akrotiri cores.*

Table 10-3. Summary Statistics for Akrotiri Cores from Site 2

	Length	Width	Thickness
Average	22.5	17.5	11.0
Standard Deviation	4.4	2.9	2.0

other hand, it seems that a considerable effort was expended on their manufacture, and their abundance suggests that they might have been desired end products, used as some sort of tool. One impressionistic interpretation is that they could represent "ammunition" for slings. Some of these cores also could have been further "reduced" to thumbnail scrapers, although most of those artifacts are not on cores, but rather on flakes, albeit thick ones.

The remainder of the assemblage is rather nondescript, but the materials certainly fall within the typological and technological range represented by *Aetokremnos*. Many of the artifacts were manufactured on quartzite. Microflakes are quite common, and much of the debris is quite small. Final tool production and/or resharpening was a probable activity at the site.

Other Artifacts. A variety of other artifacts were recovered from Site 2. Foremost among these are ceramics. The majority of the ceramics, not surprisingly, are Roman. These are all highly rolled, abraded, and quite small. A tabulation of these was not made for Site 2. Several pieces of igneous, apparently not naturally available in the region, also were recovered, all from the surface. These included 10 fragments, 1 egg-shaped piece, 1 ovoid form, and 1 spheroid form. None of these exhibit clear human modification. Other miscellaneous artifacts include 2 coins (1 with the previously mentioned Arabic inscription and the other indecipherable), 1 copper or bronze pin, and 8 fragments of colored (opaque, brown, green, aqua) glass.

Chronology. Three radiocarbon determinations were obtained from Site 2, all on shell. These are "modern" (UCL-314), 750 ± 100 B.P. (UCL-306), and 750 ± 300 (UCL-313). The average is 750 ± 95 B.P. at one standard deviation (cal A.D. 1219–1304, average 1282). This clearly does not date a prehistoric occupation. The determinations could be accurate, reflecting an occupation in the A.D. 1200s, or, more likely, these determinations could be considered unreliable, coming from contaminated samples, and being dated with what some might consider an experimental method (i.e., "first-order" determinations—see Chap. 8).

Summary. Based on this small sounding of Site 2, several conclusions may be drawn. First, the site *may* be associated with the occupation of *Aetokremnos*, based on typological comparisons alone. The presence of thumbnail scrapers suggests an affinity to *Aetokremnos*, more so than any other tested site. Its location directly above the *Aetokremnos* rockshelter is further, if tenuous, evidence of a possible linkage. If the two sites are associated, it may well be that Site 2 represents either a temporary camp site or other specific activity locality. However, the assemblage is too nondescript to suggest any functional interpretation. The large number of spheroidal exhausted cores is intriguing and may suggest a very specialized activity. It is, however, one that we cannot determine.

Second, the depth of the cultural deposits are shallow, mainly confined to the surface sediments capping the dune, at < 20 cm. It is unlikely that any artifacts will be found below 50 cm, even at the center of the dune. Third, the presence of a variety of incongruous artifact classes on the surface and in the organic topsoil suggests that a certain amount of surface deflation had occurred in the past, as well as some subsurface mixing of material via root activity. The deflated surfaces appear to be located in the vicinity of the dune but not in the topsoil. The vegetated topsoil, while containing few surface artifacts, is laden with root activity, suggesting a less than ideal context for finding stratified deposits. Finally, given the effects of these natural processes, the likelihood of finding discrete subsurface deposits that correspond to the relatively discrete occupations of the site is very poor. Certainly the presence of ceramics and an Islamic coin indicates mixed deposits. Given the ubiquity of ceramics over the entire Akrotiri Peninsula, it is easy to explain their incorporation into what might have been an early prehistoric context. However, it is clear that postoccupational modifications to Site 2, primarily natural, but also some possibly associated with modern activity on the airbase, have left it with little integrity. Further excavation of this site is likely to provide little understanding of the occupational episodes of the dune outside of increasing the classes and frequency of artifacts.

Site 3: Akrotiri *Limassol Lighthouse*

Description. Site 3 is located on a sand dune near the lighthouse near the eastern cape of the Peninsula. The surface scatter begins north of the dirt track, though nothing is visible in the road section, and continues north up the dune about 20–25m and along the road roughly 35m. The site consists of three main areas: (1) a flat, sparsely vegetated area at the base of the dune, (2) the sparsely vegetated southern slope of the dune, and (3) the densely vegetated top of the dune. At first glance, it appeared that much of the surface material was eroding out of the dune and coming to rest down the slope. The areas of the greatest artifact density were on the slope and the base of the dune rather than at the top. This surface material, including the seemingly ubiquitous ceramics, also contains localized densities of shell and chipped stone.

Methodology. The surface collection consisted of a series of 5-x-5-m squares covering most but not all of the site. Those areas nearest the road cut were left uncollected, as were portions of the upper dune. In addition, two isolated units further east were collected to gain some understanding of the extent of the site. Nineteen 5-x-5-m units were collected for a total area of 475 m². The areas along the base of the dune were most productive, while those on the top of the dune were the least. The density of material was also lower in the western 10 m than in the other areas, which suggests that the main portion of the site is in the eastern grids.

Within each of the three main areas, a single excavation unit was placed: a 2-x-2-m unit at the base of the dune, a 1-x-5-m unit on the slope, and a 1-x-1-m unit on the top. In this way, the range of variation of artifact density (low to high) and vegetation cover (low to high) was sampled to determine the potential for stratified deposits and the effects of slope wash.

Stratigraphy. The 2-x-2-m square was situated in an area containing a high density of surface material. It was thought that this might be an accurate indication of subsurface deposits. However, on excavating, almost all of the cultural material came from the upper

7–10 cm, suggesting a deflated surface because more than one temporal phase appears to be represented. With increasing depth, the material became more scarce until sterile sediments were reached at about 40 cm below the ground surface. In this area, there were no stratified deposits, and the likelihood of material having been deflated or washed down is very high.

The area of the dune slope was sampled by a 1-x-5-m trench running north into the dune. This long unit was subdivided into a 1-x-3-m section in the lower south and a 1-x-2-m unit in the upper north end. The 1-x-3-m portion of this trench was not very rich in material, consisting of chipped stone and shell found mostly on or near the surface. Again, the possibility of the material being deflated or derived from the upper dune is quite high. This portion of the trench is similar in many respects to the 2-x-2-m unit near the road.

In the 1-x-2-m portion of the trench, there is a noticeable difference, especially near the top of the dune. There is a topsoil layer, nearly 20 cm thick, covering the north end of the unit, which overlies a distinct cultural layer. Within this cultural layer are large quantities of shell, moderate amounts of chipped stone and ceramics, and bits of carbon. We realize that these carbon specimens could be derived from other areas, given the active nature of sand dunes. However, at the base of this cultural layer is a gray lens that differs from the very homogeneous brown sand found throughout the entire site. It is believed that this lens corresponds to an occupational phase of the site and is not derived or disturbed. Below the lens and cultural level, the density of material decreases significantly until sterile sediments are once again reached. The cultural deposits in the northern end of this trench appear to be sealed (the topsoil) with a minimal amount of disturbance (e.g., deflation, water tolling) and are the best evidence in the dunes for subsurface deposits.

The final area of the site tested was the top of the dune. A 1-x-1-m square was excavated due north of the 1-x-5-m unit to see if the cultural deposits identified there continued into the dune. Below the topsoil level, a layer of shell, chipped stone, and ceramics was uncovered. It was believed that this represented the shell layer found in the 1-x-5-m trench because of the density of material. However, this layer appeared to be too high stratigraphically to be part of the same deposit. As excavation continued downward, a very thick (about 30 cm) sterile level was encountered. At the bottom of this level, several bits of carbon were recovered, along with increasing amounts of shell, chipped stone, and ceramics. It is this cultural level that appears to be a continuation of the level found in the trench. Also, as in the case of the trench, a gray lens was encountered along the bottom of the artifactual level. Below this point, the density fell until sterile sediments were reached. Based on this sounding, there is strong evidence supporting a stratified, buried deposit in the dune.

Marine Shells. The 1980 surface collection by Pile and our 1990 surface collection and test excavations produced 10,151 marine shell fragments, coming from at least 8,895 individuals. Like Akrotiri *Aetokremnos* (96.2% *Monodonta*, 3% *Patella*) and Site 23 (93% *Monodonta*, 6% *Patella*), the vast majority of shells here are *Monodonta* (92%, 8,203 individuals) and *Patella* (7.5%, 669 individuals). Unlike *Aetokremnos*, however, the *Monodonta* at Site 3 are not heavily smashed, and no shells are found burnt.

Together *Monodonta* and *Patella* account for 99.7% of the shell collection. There are 19 other shells and 4 crabs. All are probably food debris, except for 1 *Conus*, 1 *Euthria*, and the *Glycymeris* and *Donax*.

Chipped Stone. Pile's collection for Site 3 was relatively large and contained some diagnostic elements (Table 10-4). In particular, 2 thumbnail scrapers were recovered, as were 2 of the tiny exhausted cores so common at Site 2. Our systematic collection substantially augmented this sample. As with the other sites, most material came from, or near, the site's surface.

A total of 5 thumbnail scrapers were retrieved (Fig. 10-4:a,b,d). Other tools included 2 burins (Fig. 10-4:c,e), 2 microlithic tools (a trapezoid and a retouched bladelet), and 1 "tang" (Fig. 10-4:f). Finally, a total of 10 exhausted cores were represented in the assemblage (Fig. 10-5:a,b,d); several other cores also were recovered, including a bladelet core

Table 10-4. Chipped Stone Assemblage from Site 3*

Type	Pile sample n	Testing sample Surface	1	2	3	4	5	n	%	N
Tools										
TNS-V1										
TNS-S/E	2									2
TNS		3						3		3
S/E scraper		1						1		1
Side scraper		2						2		2
Burin			1					1		1
Burin/ret. fl.		1						1		1
Uniface			1					1		1
Tang		1						1		1
Trapezoid		1						1		1
Ret. bladelet		1						1		1
Truncation	1									1
Ret. bl.	2	1				1		2		4
Ret. fl.		3	1	1				5		5
Subtotal	5							19	7.1	24
Debitage										
sec. fl.	2	9	5	2				16		18
ter. fl.	12	19	5			1		25		37
cor. bl.	1									1
sec. bl.		1						1		1
bladelets		5	2					7		7
Subtotal	15							49	18.4	64
Other waste										
Debris	24	35	25	2	1	4		67	24.7	91
Microflakes	25	53	16	6	5	9	1	120	11.9	145
Cores/frags	6	4						4	1.5	10
Akrotiri cores	2	8						8	3.0	10
Burin spall		1						1	0.4	1
Subtotal	58							200		258
TOTAL	78							268	100.0	346

*Note and Key is the same as in Table 10-2.

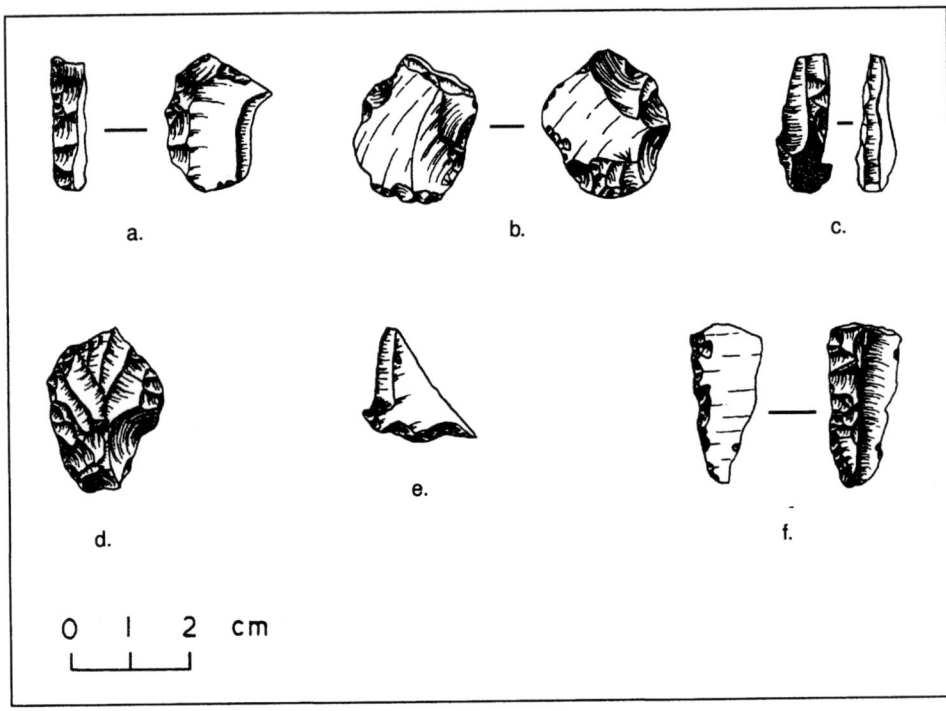

Figure 10-4. Site 3 tools. (a) thumbnail scraper, side; (b) thumbnail scraper, end; (c) single-blow straight burin; (d) thumbnail scraper, side/end; (e) single-blow straight burin on retouched flake; (f) "tang."

fragment (Fig. 10-5:c). Two important comments may be made about the composition of the assemblage from Site 3. First, it is very similar typologically and technologically to Site 2, and the comments made for that locality also pertain here. Second, the tools suggest an affinity to *Aetokremnos*. Once again, it is tempting to suggest an affinity amongst all three sites, but this can only be based on typological grounds. Although we are hesitant to force-fully make such comparisons, the fact remains that Sites 2 and 3 are the closest cultural manifestations to *Aetokremnos* yet recorded in Cyprus. Given their proximity, it is not un-reasonable to assume that the surface sites might represent either habitations camps or spe-ciality satellites associated with *Aetokremnos*. In any case, both sites, although technologically and typologically similar to *Aetokremnos*, combine the added element of the tiny spheroidal cores, which are not present at the latter site.

Other Artifacts.   Other artifacts recovered from Site 3 include 439 sherds; these are rolled, abraded, and quite small, but they are not as fragmentary as the ceramics from Site 2. Most (433, 98%) are Roman; 2 Chalcolithic and 4 unidentifiable sherds also were recov-ered. Igneous materials are not common at Site 3. The two pieces recovered are a fragment and an ovoid-shaped piece. None exhibit any clear human modification. Other materials recovered include a clear glass fragment, a small iron fragment, and a piece of metal shot; as with Site 2, 2 coins, 1 with an Arabic inscription, also were retrieved.

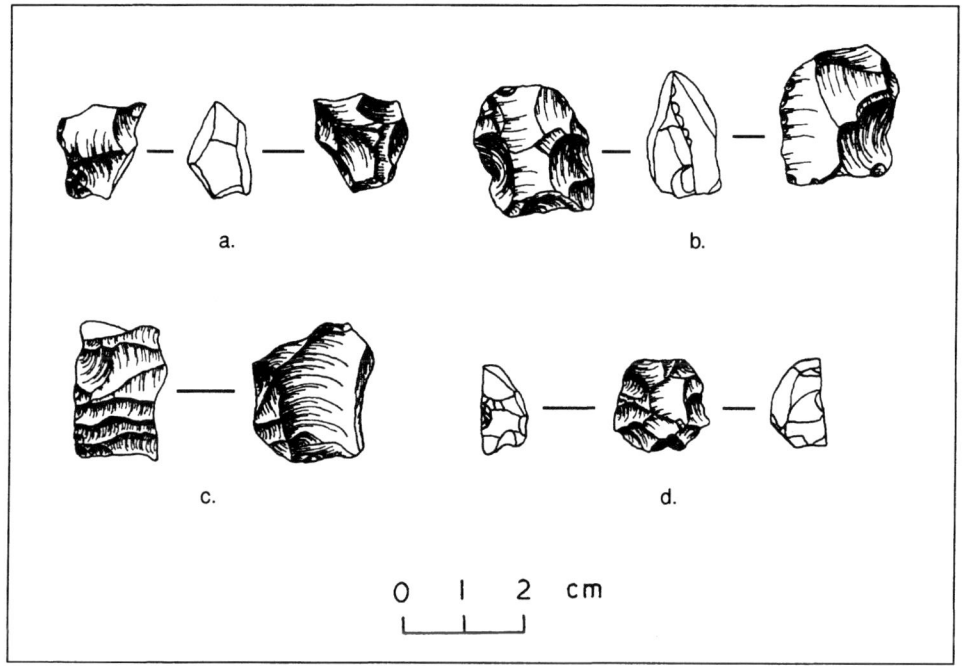

Figure 10-5. Site 3 cores. (a)–(b), (d) "Akrotiri" cores; (c) bladelet core.

Chronology. Five radiocarbon determinations were obtained from Site 3. These dates are (1) modern (shell, UCL-308 and shell, UCL-309); (2) 200 ± 250 B.P. (shell, UCL-312); (3) 250 ± 80 B.P. (charcoal, Beta-45243); and (4) 370 ± 90 (charcoal, Beta-45243). The latter date has several calibrated intercepts. These occur at B.P. 462, 341, and 339, with calibrated ranges of B.P. 509–303 for the earlier intercept and of B.P. 425-0 for the latter intercept. The intercept for this date when all intercepts are averaged is 256 ± 73 B.P. at one standard deviation or a calibrated range of about A.D. 1525–1945 with an average of A.D. 1655. All determinations suggests an essentially modern occupation. Although the shell determinations may be considered a less reliable marker, the two charcoal dates are striking in both their recentness and their overlap. These would appear to date a late occupation of the site. However, that occupation is totally at odds with the chipped stone composition of the site. Thus if one relies on typological comparisons for relative dating, Site 3 may, in fact, represent two discrete occupations. As with the other two tested sites, the chronology of Site 2 is ambiguous, a frustrating problem when dealing with such sites, which also have equivocal context and are heavily disturbed and largely surface manifestations.

Summary. The results of the test excavations at Site 3 indicate the presence of buried deposits in relatively undisturbed conditions in the dune area only. The lower slope and road area consist of shallow deposits and dense surface material, suggesting a deflated land surface in these areas. The notion that the surface material will provide a reliable indication of where to excavate is not valid for this site. We had hoped that the abundance of carbon from the deeper portions of the site would date the occupation(s), although the determinations obtained all suggest a recent use. That these determinations correspond to the temporal periods represented by the various artifact types is unlikely, given the nature of the chipped stone artifacts. They may, however, give some indication as to the extent of disturbance (naturally or culturally) occurring within the dune.

Site 23: Akrotiri *Vounarouthkia ton Lamnion* East

Description.   Site 23 is located on a fossilized sand dune, which has an active dune capping the peak. The site is situated approximately 1 km east of *Aetokremnos* along the south coast of the peninsula. The vegetation, consisting of sagelike scrub, covers parts of the active dune, while the remainder of the site area is barren. Site definition is based primarily on the presence and density of sherds over the site, though it had been previously collected by Pile. The sherd scatter continues downslope to the road, a distance of approximately 40 m south. The sherds continue west and southwest. A small drainage channel cuts the surface west of the site. Beyond this channel, the sherd scatter ceases. Approximately 10 m to the north is a barbed wire fence, and the ceramics continue in low densities up to this barrier. About 5 m from the east edge of the site, a large drainage cuts the land surface. Artifacts do not continue out to this drainage, but a few scattered items are found at its bottom. The location of the site on a small dune makes it probable that some of the artifacts in its vicinity, but not collected as part of the site itself, may have washed down from the dune's top. This probability suggests some destruction of the sand dune due to natural agents.

Methodology.   For the purposes of collecting the surface, a series of 5-x-5-m squares were laid out over the dune and nearby slopes. This resulted in a total of 16 5-x-5-m units comprising an area of 400 m² (20 x 20 m). The actual site demarcation is difficult to discern as there is a light sherd scatter over much of the area. For practical reasons, the areas of the dune and slope were defined as the "site." Because the site had been collected previously, the density of surface material was very low, consisting almost entirely of ceramics. Only a few isolated pieces of shell and chipped stone were collected, along with a sample of igneous cobbles that litter the entire surface. The vegetation covering part of the hill did not affect the visibility of surface finds.

Stratigraphy.   Test excavations consisted of two 2-x-2-m squares. Area 1 was placed on the south slope of the dune, while Area 2 was situated in the central portion of the top of the dune. Neither area yielded any indication of its subsurface possibilities in the surface collection, so the placement of these units was purely judgmental.

The upper portions of Area 1 yielded no cultural material and were filled with organics and wild onions. Stratigraphically, the sediments here are very homogeneous, a dark brown color with evidence of calcretions throughout. Due to the paucity of cultural material, two small soundings (1 x 1 m and 50 x 50 cm) were placed in the southeast and southwest corners, respectively. Although the consistency and compact nature of the sediments remained homogenous throughout these soundings, the density of cultural material increased with the recovery of shell (*Monodonta*) and chipped stone (though densities were still very low). These materials were not concentrated in any horizontal level but were present at various depths throughout the soundings, suggesting some natural displacement up and down or very ephemeral episodes separated by considerable depositional spans. The former seems more likely. Each sounding extended over 50 cm below the present surface. Of particular interest in the 1-x-1-m sounding was a large igneous cobble (> 20 cm) near the bottom, which may have been a lightly used quern. It is associated with two other large stones, though of very different material, in the southwest corner of the 1-x-1-m unit. This stone continues into the section, so it was not collected, and its actual size is unknown. The presence of this sort of stone in the lower, and nearly sterile, sediments of the unit is intriguing because there is only a scattering of chipped stone and shell in the preceding 40 cm, and no material is associated with or below it. Before this stone is to be considered "cultural," the possibility of natural abrasion via water and wind has to be refuted. It is noted that large quantities of worn, igneous rock (pebbles) cover the present land surface of this site and may be of a dubious nature culturally.

The excavations in Area 2, at the top of the dune, were in a more densely vegetated area. The sediments were very soft on the surface in the active portion of the dune. In these sediments, a few potsherds were found. Except for these few items, which probably have been trampled or displaced naturally, the upper portion of the unit is sterile. Below the active dune level, the sediments become streaked with carbonates and are much more consolidated. Because the artifacts consisted of a few sherds in the top 20 cm of the unit, two soundings (1 × 1 m and 50 × 50 cm) were excavated in the southeast and southwest corners, respectively. Each sounding continued downward an additional 35–40 cm, yielding a single piece of chipped stone in each. The strata in these soundings are the same as the upper level, very homogeneous. It is somewhat surprising to find isolated chipped stone artifacts 45–60 cm below the surface associated with nothing at all. If these are worked into the sediments, then the dune consolidation must be a relatively recent phenomena. It is possible that these artifacts correspond to an occupation that was very ephemeral or one that was missed in the placement of the soundings. The potential for stratified deposits at this site is not very good.

Marine Shell and Fauna.   The 1990 test excavations recovered 266 shell fragments from 100 individuals: 93 *Monodonta turbinata/M. articulata* individuals (topshell, 251 fragments, 93%), 6 *Patella* caerulea/*P. lusitanica* individuals (limpet, 14 fragments, 6%) and 1 *Cerithium vulgatum*. Unlike *Aetokremnos,* none of these shells have been burnt.

A single bone fragment was recovered during the excavations. This is an ovicaprid-sized rib, and has clearly been butchered with a metal implement.

Chipped Stone.   Pile apparently did not collect any artifacts from Site 23, according to all of the documentation we could find. One box of artifacts, however, was labeled "Site 23b." On Pile's map, this site was located some 70 m south of Site 23, on the side of the cliffs overlooking the sea. This collection, which was not diagnostic, included 2 tools—1 a possible "point" (see later) and 1 a backed blade—1 secondary blade, 1 tertiary blade, 4 tertiary flakes, 1 secondary flake, and 1 piece of debris. Pile apparently also collected a few other tools from Site 23 (Swiny 1988:10), but we could not relocate these.

Our test operations recovered only a small chipped stone assemblage, consisting of 31 artifacts (Table 10-5). A high proportion of tools is represented (nearly 20%), but, unlike Sites 2 and 3, none are diagnostic. The same can be said for the waste materials. Of note,

Table 10-5. Chipped Stone Assemblage from Site 23, Including Re-Analyzed Artifacts Collected by Pile and Labeled as "Site 23b"*

Type	Sample pile Site 23b n	Testing sample Surface	Subsurface	n	%	N
Tools						
Possible point	1					1
Backed blade	1					1
Ret. tip		1		1		1
Truncation on bl.		1		1		1
Ret. fl.		3		3		3
Notch		1		1		1
Subtotal	2	6		6	(19.4)	8
Debitage						
cor. fl.			1	1		1
sec. fl.	1		1	1		2
ter. fl.	4	1	4	5		9
sec. bl.	1		1	1		2
ter. bl.	1		5	5		6
Bladelets			1	1		1
Subtotal	7			14	45.2	21
Other waste						
Debris	1	3	6	9	29.0	10
Microflakes			1	1	3.2	1
Cores/frags			1	1	3.2	1
Subtotal	1			11		12
TOTAL	10			31	100.0	41

*Note and Key is the same as in Table 10-2.

however, are four artifacts previously described by Swiny in the vicinity of Site 23 (these apparently are from the Pile collection). One was termed a *double end scraper*. On reexamination by the author, and using the typology established here, this artifact is classified as a large secondary flake with some battering. Of more interest is a large pointed blade (Fig. 10-6:a). Swiny believed this was similar to Pre-Pottery Neolithic forms from the Levantine mainland (Swiny 1988:5, Fig. 4.1:11); indeed, in overall morphology, the artifact resembles a Byblos point. But it is crudely fashioned, and its typological classification as a projectile point is problematic. Also of interest is a backed and tanged blade (Swiny 1988:5, Fig. 4.2:11). The "tang" on this artifact is somewhat problematic, resembling more a notch (Fig. 10-6:b). Finally, a "retouched flake scraper" (Swiny 1988:5, Fig. 4.4:11) bears resemblance to a thumbnail scraper, but this artifact could not be relocated.

Other Artifacts. Ceramics are common at Site 23, as they are at Sites 2 and 3. A total of 310 were collected; these are highly abraded and small. The majority (292, 94%) are

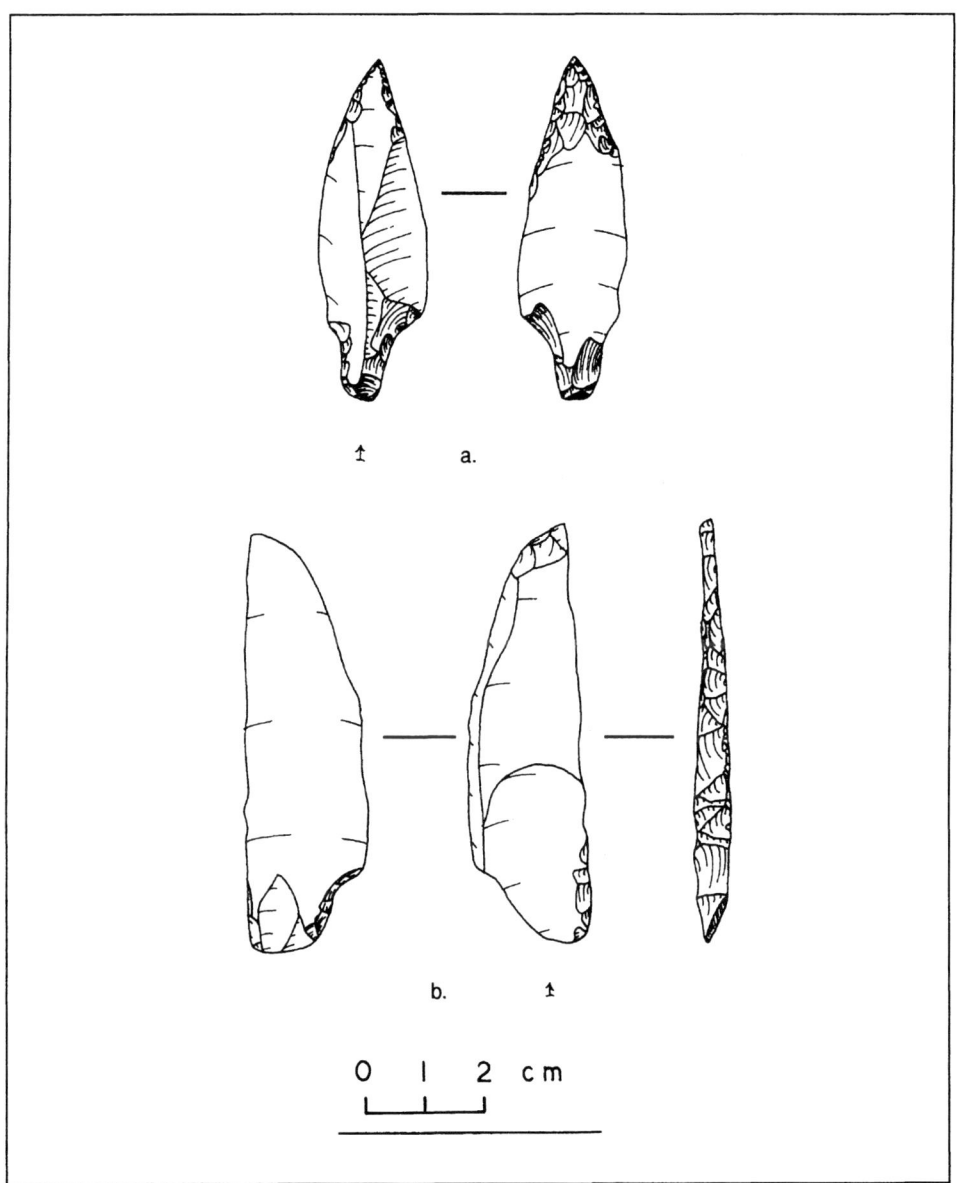

Figure 10-6. Site 23 artifacts. (a) "point"; (b) backed blade.

Roman; 2 Chalcolithic and 16 unidentifiable sherds also were collected. Igneous objects also are common, but the majority are fragments or unmodified pebbles. Those collected include 17 pebbles, 1 elongated pebble, 1 battered pebble, 1 egg-shaped pebble, and 18 fragments. Three possible handstones, with quite problematic working surfaces, also were recovered.

Chronology.   The chronology of Site 23 is intriguing. Two radiocarbon determinations were obtained, both on shell: 8350 ± 250 B.P. (UCL-307) and 9780 ± 80 B.P. (Beta-34370). Using the correction factor for the Reservoir Effect of 334 years proposed for the *Aetokremnos* radiocarbon shell determinations (Chap. 8), these determinations become 8684 ± 250 B.P. and 10,114 ± 80 B.P. At a two-sigma range, these determinations *nearly* overlap, but they are still separated by some 800 years. If both shell samples are ^{13}C corrected, however, they do overlap, and the average is 9647 ± 76 B.P. (cal B.C. 9027–8678, average 8678 at one standard deviation, and ca. B.C. 10,999–10,484, average 10,999 at two standard deviations).

The Site 23 radiocarbon determinations pose some interesting scenarios. Conservatively, one could maintain, as with the other tested sites, that the radiocarbon determinations on shell are all unreliable. Or, playing devil's advocate, one could assume that the Site 23 determinations are correct. If this is so, they either represent two early occupations, or, if averaged, represent an occupation that apparently is still be too young to relate to *Aetokremnos*, where it will be recalled that the weighted average of all subsurface radiocarbon determinations is 10,465 B.P. or 10,900 B.P. for shell alone (Chap. 8). However, when calibrated, the average is 8678 B.C. at one standard deviation, and 10,999 B.C. at two standard deviations. The calibrated average of the *Aetokremnos* determinations is cal B.C. 9703, thus the Site 23 determinations are roughly within the range of *Aetokremnos*. It is ironic that Site 3 has a closer typological affinity to *Aetokremnos*, but it is not supported chronologically by a single radiocarbon determination. Site 23, on the other hand, has a closer chronological affiliation, but it is not supported on typological grounds.

Summary.   To recapitulate, Site 23 contains a very low density of artifactual material. Most of it seems to be concentrated on the surface, suggesting a deflated site. It is interesting that ceramics, which are the predominant surface artifact, are found near the surface in only one excavation unit, suggesting that the deflation of the site may be a recent phenomena as none of this material has been worked into the compact, subsurface sediments (unlike the few lithic artifacts). The near absence of artifacts on the top of the hill suggest an occupation farther down the hill or the movement of material. Given out current information, Site 23 is not a good candidate for containing stratified deposits. The majority of the material comes from the surface, with very little subsurface material evident. Perhaps the only questionable aspect of this interpretation is the possible quern in Area 1. If this is a cultural artifact, it may indicate subsurface deposits at a depth not yet reached, which, in turn, suggests a more substantial site than that presented above, assuming grinding implements are not very portable artifacts. Also, this would say something about the rate of deposition and soil formation within the dune. If the "quern" is noncultural then further work is likely to be fruitless.

A Comparative Study of the Aetokremnos *Chipped Stone*

INTRODUCTION

After exhaustively examining available literature, we have concluded that the chipped stone assemblage from *Aetokremnos* thus far has no parallels on Cyprus. What remains to be demonstrated is documenting the distinct nature of the *Aetokremnos* assemblage. In this chapter, we provide several comparisons with other chipped stone materials from Cyprus and the Levant.

Our claim that the chipped stone from *Aetokremnos* has no counterparts in Cyprus requires verification, not an easy task because so few thorough studies have been conducted on this artifact class in Cyprus. The most obvious comparisons would be with materials from Aceramic Neolithic sites, but the chipped stone data generally are poorly published. When one looks farther afield than Cyprus, there are several similarities of the *Aetokremnos* chipped stone to other roughly contemporary assemblages. Due to differences among various researchers in analytic treatment, however, all our comparisons must be based on general categories rather than detailed comparison. Thus we concentrate on generalized comparisons, using both available published data and more specific comparisons from samples of a few Cypriot assemblages that were examined during the course of this study. This discussion will show just how unique the *Aetokremnos* materials are from other known assemblages.

We first consider materials from the Kyrenia region, where claims for a pre-Neolithic, even Paleolithic, occupation have been made. We then compare the *Aetokremnos* materials with those from the nearby tested sites. Following that is a comparison with *Aetokremnos*'s closest chronological period, the Aceramic Neolithic. Finally, we examine, in broader perspective, the *Aetokremnos* chipped stone in relation to some Epipaleolithic and Neolithic mainland assemblages, primarily from the Levant. Our intention here is to show how distinct the *Aetokremnos* materials are in relation to other documented sites on the island. This documentation, coupled with the chronological data presented in Chapter 8, serves to demonstrate why we have proposed a new phase designation for Cyprus based on the excavation of only one site.

KYRENIA

Given the attention they have received in the literature as an example of a possible pre-Neolithic occupation, it is useful to consider in some detail chipped stone from sites near Kyrenia, in northern Cyprus. The materials reported by Stockton (1968) often are cited as very early remains from Cyprus (see Chap. 1). Although most researchers have dismissed this claim as unreliable, a reanalysis of this material has not been undertaken until now. I had the opportunity to examine this material, albeit quickly, while in Nicosia. The collection is curated in the Cyprus Survey storeroom of the Cyprus Museum.

It is important to realize that the Kyrenia materials are not from one specific locality. Rather, they appear to have been collected from a variety of areas within the Kyrenia district. Stockton (1968:16) noted that most of the finds were from east of Kyrenia, near Khrysokava, in an area between two quarries. He also indicated that similar materials were located just west of Kyrenia in an area more disturbed by quarrying (presumably modern) activities. An additional 30 artifacts were located near the entrance to the Catholic Church (Kyrenia C). Finally, he noted that a few pieces were found at a helicopter pad at Tjiklos in the Kyrenia range and in plowed fields near Bellapais on the slopes of the Kyrenia range. Additional information is not provided, but it is clear that a considerable geographic span is involved. For example, in one of the boxes containing a few artifacts (1 core fragment, 2 flakes, and 1 noncultural item), the following handwritten note was present: "These peices [sic] were found at the [indecipherable] 6 1/2 mile beach east of Kyrenia [indecipherable] indicating a 14 mile strip of inhabited area during paleolithic times."

Stockton does not provide a detailed typology, but indicated that "just over a hundred implements [formal retouched tools?] were identified. Only a sampling of the tools and waste flakes were retained for study and museum purposes" (Stockton 1968:17). It was this sample, apparently, that is curated in the Cyprus Survey storeroom, and that I was able to reexamine. It consisted of 299 artifacts and 24 pieces I considered noncultural. Before addressing my study of this material, however, it is informative to reconstruct Stockton's typology, especially because he makes reference to "thumbnail scrapers" (Stockton 1968:17). (Table 11-1 summarizes his analysis.)

Several of these artifacts are illustrated in Stockton (1968). Unfortunately, I was unable to match many of the illustrations with his typology, and during my reanalysis, using the typology established for the *Aetokremnos* materials, quite a different result emerged. I was only able to identify confidently 2 tools, 1 small retouched flake, of near microlithic proportions, and 1 retouched blade, which contained only marginal retouch. It may be, however, that the tools identified by Stockton simply were not in the Cyprus Museum collection.

Although Stockton (1968) illustrated 21 artifacts, only 5 in the Cyprus Museum sample could be tied to his plates. Four of these were labeled and thus could confidently be tied to the illustrations. Unfortunately, none of the microliths and scrapers illustrated could be relocated. Because only a small portion of the illustrated artifacts could be relocated, it may well be that a separate box of "illustrated artifacts" contains the missing items, and that this

Table 11-1. Typology of Kyrenia Materials

Type	Number and comments
Scrapers	
Steep scrapers	23, including reused cores, 2 pointed scrapers, and a microlithic core scraper
Side scrapers	16, a "poor and motley group"
Round scrapers	9, including a "few" small enough to be considered "thumbnail"
Concave scrapers	11
Nosed scrapers	5
End scraper	1
Knives	
Long, pointed triangular sectioned flakes	6
Backed flake tools	
Small triangular sectioned flakes, semicircular in shape	10
Miscellaneous	
Bifacial chopper	1
Awl	1
Small geometrics	
Triangular	1
Rectangular	1
Cores	
Irregular	12
Flakes	Number unspecified, all with prominent bulbs of percussion; no blades observed

*From Stockton (1968:17)

box could not be found. Even with those pieces relocated, however, my typology does not always match Stockton's classification. The reanalysis is summarized in the following.

I reclassified the artifact Stockton typed as a "backed flake tool" (Stockton 1968: Plate VI, lower right) as a flake. I agreed with his classification of a "core" (Plate VII, top center) and typed this as a unidirectional flake core. The "backed flake tool" (Plate VI, right, second from top) was reclassified as noncultural (there was some question if this was in fact the piece illustrated, but I believe it is; the scale is "exploded" in Stockton's plate). Another "backed flake tool" (Plate VI, right, third from top) was reclassified as a flake; while yet another (Plate VI, bottom center) was reclassified as a retouched piece.

Table 11-2 presents the results of the reanalysis. The materials were in various boxes, but these were either missing locational labels or were unclear on provenience. Although the collection came from several localities, for the purposes of this analysis, these materials were lumped into two categories: Kyrenia and Kyrenia C. Kyrenia C was the only clearly marked specific locality, and undoubtedly it referred to the materials collected near the

Table 11-2. Typology Based on Reanalysis of Kyrenia Sites Collected by Stockton

Type	Kyrenia					Kyrenia C				
	C	B	N	%	R%	C	B	N	%	R%
Tools										
Retouched flake	1									
Retouched blade	1		2	0.7	1.7					
Debitage										
Primary flakes	1	2	3							
Secondary flakes	10	8	18			4		4		
Tertiary flakes	30	24	54			1	4	5		
Subtotal	41	32	75	27.8	62.5	5	4	9	31.0	37.5
Blades										
Secondary blades	3		3							
Tertiary blades	2		2							
Subtotal	5		5	1.9	4.2					
Microflakes			4	1.5	3.3			15	51.7	62.5
Debris			150	55.5	—			5	17.2	—
Cores										
Globular			4							
Exhausted			9							
Subdiscoidal			3							
Unidirectional			2							
Subtotal			16	12.6	28.8					
TOTAL			270	100.0	100.0			29	99.9	100.0

Note: R% excludes debris; C=complete, B=broken.

Catholic Church. Note that Stockton (1968:16) indicated the presence of 30 "small un-bleached flakes" from Kyrenia C; the reanalysis was based on the 27 artifacts in the box labeled "Kyrenia C."

The overall assemblage is not very convincing; in fact, I believe several items are non-cultural. Considering that many pieces were found in or near quarry locales strengthens an argument for a nonprehistoric origin. Despite this, however, some of the pieces appear to have been intentionally worked. The material is by and large coarse flint. Much of it is heavily rolled, indicating movement and a lack of in situ context. Much of the material is Lefkara in appearance, but also is quite vesicular. The "artifacts" are overall rather chunky and most were manufactured on undesirable raw materials. Technologically, none of the pieces are as well manufactured as are those from *Aetokremnos*—they have a much more "expedient" appearance.

Even though sample sizes are small, it is useful to consider some specific attributes of the Kyrenia materials in relation to *Aetokremnos*. Basic metrics were obtained on the com-

Table 11-3. Debitage Comparisons Between *Aetokremnos* and Kyrenia Materials

(A) Metrics (mm)	Length	SD	N	Width	SD	N	Thickness	SD	N
Aetokremnos									
Blades	44.2	14.6	26	16.2	3.6	73	4.4	2.3	76
Flakes	28.9	13.2	138	23.2	8.7	188	5.7	3.4	253
Cores	45.1	16.2	19	35.1	14.9	19	18.1	9.4	19
Kyrenia									
Blades	50.0	18.3	5	23.1	7.3	5	8.9	2.5	5
Flakes	33.0	11.4	38	26.6	7.9	38	9.7	3.8	38
Cores	54.8	16.2	8	41.5	11.0	8	35.6	9.9	8

(B) Platform Types	*Aetokremnos* % (N=247)	Kyrenia % (N=38)
Single	45.7	63.2
Dihedral	5.3	10.5
Punctiform	13.0	0.0
Multiple	0.4	2.6
Cortical	0.4	0.0
Crushed	21.9	13.2
Unidentifiable	13.4	10.5
TOTALS	100.1	100.0

plete debitage and a sample of the cores, summarized in Table 11-3(A). A comparison of those with the *Aetokremnos* metrics indicated no similarity whatsoever; the Kyrenia materials were larger in all dimensions. Additionally, a visual examination of a sample of the materials assessed their degree of patination. Of the 299 artifacts examined, only 48 (16.1%) were considered patinated, despite Stockton's belief that a majority were. I believe that he interpreted the natural color and texture of the raw material as patination. For comparative purposes, only 9.8% of the *Aetokremnos* material were patinated. Finally, platform types between the two assemblages (Table 11-3B) were quite dissimilar as well.

In summary, there are virtually no technological nor typological affinities between the Kyrenia assemblage and that of *Aetokremnos*. Much of the Kyrenia collection consists of pieces that one could reasonably argue as being of noncultural origin. Despite this, however, several have all the appearances of intentional workmanship, although it is quite crude. This undoubtedly is one reason that Stockton considered these materials as pre-Neolithic. Given limited contextual information, however, I believe that one cannot consider these pieces as indicative of any cultural period. They are, in my opinion, quite possibly remnants of modern "dhoukani," or threshing, flakes (cf. Pearlman 1984).

TESTED SITES

In this section, we make some comparisons of chipped stone from the three tested sites with the assemblage from *Aetokremnos*. Although a directly comparable analytical procedure was used, this comparison is hampered by small sample sizes, especially at Site 23. A further potential biasing factor is that some similarities may be more apparent than real simply *because* an identical analytical method was used. That is, the tested sites may appear more similar to *Aetokremnos* than some of the other sites addressed in this chapter simply due to the similarities in analysis. With these caveats in mind, we can turn to the comparisons.

In overall assemblage composition, there are few similarities between *Aetokremnos* and the tested sites (Table 11-4). *Aetokremnos* most closely resembles the assemblage from Site 23 in proportions of different classes of chipped stone materials, except for the virtual absence of microflakes at the latter site. The assemblage from Site 23, however, is only 41 artifacts, so correlations may be spurious. Sites 2 and 3 resemble one another rather well in overall composition, and *Aetokremnos* is strikingly different from both of these sites. In particular, there is a high proportion of tools at *Aetokremnos*, suggesting a specialized function. The relatively high number of cores and microflakes at Sites 2 and 3 suggest that a full range of chipped stone reduction occurred there. In addition, the presence of the small "Akrotiri cores" at Sites 2 and 3 is striking; while *Aetokremnos* has some exhausted cores, these bear only a superficial resemblance to the tiny cores from the other sites. All reduction stages are represented at *Aetokremnos*, but the numbers indicate that this was not a primary activity, especially when compared with Sites 2 and 3. Overall, at Sites 2 and 3, the composition of the chipped stone suggests more varied activities, perhaps reflecting some sort of base camp function.

In examining the debitage in more detail, additional distinctions stand out (Table 11-5). Site 23 should again be viewed suspiciously because of the small sample size, but it is clear that *Aetokremnos* is quite different from Sites 2 and 3. At *Aetokremnos*, blades are a significant component of the assemblage; likewise, blades are common at Site 23, while they are rarer at Sites 2 and 3 (Table 11-5A). Site 3 and *Aetokremnos*, however, both share relatively high proportions of bladelets, reflecting some emphasis on microlithic production. An examination of metric data on flakes from all three tested sites and *Aetokremnos* shows that *Aetokremnos* once again stands out (Table 11-5B), primarily because of the overall larger size of flakes from *Aetokremnos*. Once again, however, Site 23 shows the closest similarity to *Aetokremnos* in this attribute. Finally, ratios of flakes to blades/bladelets at the four sites are provided in Table 11-5C. Again, this simple comparison demonstrates that blade production at *Aetokremnos* was more common than at the other sites.

An examination of tool composition also is instructive (Table 11-6), although sample sizes are small at the tested sites. Perhaps the strongest linkage between *Aetokremnos* and

Table 11-4. Comparison of Tested Akrotiri Peninsula Sites with *Aetokremnos*

Class	Site 2		Site 3		Site 23		*Aetokremnos*	
	N	%	N	%	N	%	N	%
Tools	16	4.1	24	7.0	7	17.5	128	12.8
Debitage*	50	12.8	64	18.7	21	52.5	376	37.7
Cores	35	8.9	20	5.8	1	2.5	20	2.0
Debris	154	39.3	90	26.2	10	25.0	296	29.7
Microflakes	137	35.0	145	42.3	1	2.5	178	17.8
TOTAL	392	100.1	343	100.0	40	100.0	998	100.0

*Debitage includes only blades, flakes, and bladelets.

Table 11-5. Debitage Comparisons Between *Aetokremnos* and Tested Sites

(A) Debitage Composition	Site 2 N	%	Site 3 N	%	Site 23 N	%	*Aetokremnos* N	%
Flakes	44	88.0	55	85.9	12	57.1	256	68.1
Blades	4	8.0	2	3.1	8	38.1	78	20.7
Bladelets	2	4.0	7	10.9	1	4.8	42	11.1
(B) Metrics (mm)	N	Average/SD	N	Average/SD	N	Average/SD	N	Average/SD
Length	21	18.3/4.2	19	19.0/3.6	3	26.9/8.6	138	28.9/13.2
Width	24	16.9/3.2	34	18.9/7.8	6	23.6/4.5	188	23.2/8.7
Thickness	29	4.7/2.4	41	5.9/2.2	7	6.0/3.7	253	5.7/13.4
(C) Flake/Blade Ratios	7.3:1		6.1:1		1.3:1		2.1:1	

the tested sites is the presence of thumbnail scrapers; these have not been identified elsewhere in Cyprus. These implements, while absent at Site 23, occur in some abundance at Sites 2 and 3. Proportionally, thumbnail scrapers are the most common tool at all three sites. Coupled with other scraper forms, they clearly indicate a scraper focus at all sites.

Other tools provide less information. The tool assemblage from *Aetokremnos* is more varied than that at the other sites, but this simply may be a reflection of the higher number of implements at the former. Beyond retouched pieces, burins are the second most common tool at *Aetokremnos,* while they are poorly represented at the tested sites. Retouched blades and flakes are common at all sites, but this is to be expected. The so-called point at Site 23 has no parallels with any of the other sites under discussion here, or, for that matter, with any other sites in Cyprus.

There is a curious contradiction between tools and overall assemblage composition at these sites. One might interpret the figures in Tables 11-4 and 11-6 as indicating that the overall assemblage composition suggests a more specialized function for *Aetokremnos,* while the tools suggest more variety. That is, if Sites 2 and 3 represent limited base camps of some sort, where a variety of functions were conducted, one might reasonably expect to find a variety of tool classes represented. This is the case at Site 3; tool variety at Sites 2 and 23 is more restricted. The widest variety, however, occurs at *Aetokremnos.* Once again, variety simply may be a reflection of the larger sample size at *Aetokremnos.* It also could indicate that at *Aetokremnos,* which we argue is a specialized site, intensity of activity required a range of tools, with an emphasis on scrapers. The data on these sites are equivocal.

A final, and critical, question to ask of the tested sites is, Are they culturally related to *Aetokremnos*? Based on the detailed analyses of the chipped stone materials, we cannot satisfactorily answer this question. All sites share some similarities, but there are substantial differences between the assemblages, in typology, technology, and proportional occurrences of major classes. Whether these distinctions are minor enough to separate the sites culturally is debatable. Certainly, functional differences could account for many of the differences. We also cannot ignore the possibility that the tested sites represent chronologically mixed assemblages. It will be recalled that all tested sites contain ceramics, and some of these date to later (e.g., Roman) periods, clearly indicating mixture. The tested sites have proven

Table 11-6. Tool Typology for Tested Akrotiri Peninsula Sites and *Aetokremnos*

Types	Site 2		Site 3		Site 23		Aetokremnos	
	N	%	N	%	N	%	N	%
Thumbnail scrapers	9	56.2	5	20.8			36	28.1
End scrapers							3	2.3
Side scrapers			2	8.3			7	5.5
Side/end scrapers			1	4.2			4	3.1
Other scrapers							2	1.6
Burins			2	8.3			20	15.6
Truncations			1	4.2	1	14.3	3	2.3
Notches					1	14.3	3	2.3
Unifaces			1	4.2			2	1.6
Tangs			1	4.2				
Backed pieces							2	1.6
Points					1	14.3		
Perforators	1	6.3						
Retouched blades	2	12.5	2	8.3	1	14.3	16	12.5
Retouched flakes	4	25.0	7	29.2	3	42.8	22	17.2
Microliths			2	8.3			6	4.7
Others							2	1.6
TOTAL	16	100.0	24	100.0	7	100.0	128	100.0

difficult to date absolutely. Two radiocarbon determinations from Site 23 suggest a chronological affinity with *Aetokremnos,* but the other determinations from the tested sites do not. Thus, in many ways, Site 23 suggests the closest affinity with *Aetokremnos,* although proper interpretation is hampered by a small sample size. On the other hand, the strongest linkage with *Aetokremnos* is the presence of the distinctive thumbnail scrapers, which occur at Sites 2 and 3 but are absent from Site 23.

Based on all of these data, my conclusion is that the tested sites may be members of the Akrotiri Phase, but that they also are multicomponent, and with repeated re-use, resulting in a palimpsest of assemblages. This condition has made separation of individual components nearly impossible. If the tested sites are related to the Akrotiri Phase, they may reflect limited base camps rather than specialized sites. The assemblage mixing, however, may have distorted functional isolation beyond recognition. Resolution of this issue would require an extensive excavation program at other similar sites on the Akrotiri Peninsula.

CYPRIOT ACERAMIC NEOLITHIC SITES

We could perhaps expect to find the closest chipped stone similarities to *Aetokremnos* in the Cypriot Aceramic Neolithic. Close examination of published material, however, suggests that artifacts from *Aetokremnos* share very little with this period. In this section, we first summarize general characteristics of the chipped stone from Aceramic Neolithic sites and *Aetokremnos*. We do not, however, examine every Aceramic Neolithic site discussed in Chapter 1; in most cases, chipped stone from these sites is not well documented. Instead, we focus only on the major sites of Khirokitia *Vounoi* and Kalavassos *Tenta*. Following this generalized discussion, we then provide more specific comparisons with two Aceramic Neolithic sites where the chipped stone has been relatively well documented—*Cape Andreas Kastros* and Kholetria *Ortos*. At the latter site, an analytical approach was used that is nearly identical to that employed at *Aetokremnos*.

Typically, chipped stone from the Aceramic Neolithic is referred to as a blade industry, but few quantitative data are available to document this as certain. Although the Aceramic Neolithic in Cyprus has been characterized as a blade technology, it is clear from published data that flakes also were a major component. This pattern is similar to that at *Aetokremnos* as well. Limited aspects of technology and typology at Aceramic sites have been discussed by Cauvin (1984), Coqueugniot (1984), and Stekelis (1953) for Khirokitia; by Hordynsky and Todd (1987) and Hordynsky and Kingsnorth (1979) for *Tenta;* Guilaine *et al.* (1995) for *Shillourokambos;* and by Fox (1988) for *Ortos* (surface only). Other excavated or tested sites (see Chap. 1) have even more limited reports.

In general, one has the impression that Aceramic Neolithic materials, even blades, tend to be "clunky" and large, with limited technological sophistication. This impression, however, may be more of a research bias than a reflection of reality. Information from other cultural periods, such as the Chalcolithic, also has been scant, although recent efforts (e.g., Betts 1979, 1985, 1987; D'Annibale 1992, 1993, 1994) are beginning to rectify this deficiency. Studies such as these, and recent examinations of Aceramic Neolithic materials, suggest that there was more technological sophistication in Cypriot chipped stone than previously believed.

Information on Aceramic Neolithic tools also is limited. Unlike the mainland, where projectile points are a typical diagnostic of the Aceramic Neolithic, points are virtually absent in the Cypriot Neolithic (e.g., Cauvin 1984:85).[1] Other tools include a wide variety of types common to Near Eastern (and other) Neolithic sites. These include burins, scrapers, retouched pieces, rare perforators, "tanged" pieces, and denticulates, just to name principal classes (Cauvin 1984; Cooper 1997:71–73; Fox 1988; Guilaine *et al.* 1995; LeBrun 1981; Simmons 1994a; Stekelis 1953).

Certainly the best known Aceramic Neolithic site in Cyprus is Khirokitia. Although it has been under investigation for over 50 years, information on its chipped stone assemblages is limited. The most recent studies at the site have concentrated on areas other than chipped stone, thus some of the best information available remains Stekelis's (1953) discussion, published as an appendix in the original site report. Only slightly over 1,200 artifacts were discussed; that such a small sample is reported from such a large site clearly indicates that systematic collection of chipped stone was not a priority.

Stekelis concluded that the Khirokitia assemblage was essentially a simple one, composed of broad blades and flakes. Blades are abundant and tend to be large. Although they do not outnumber flakes, they are well manufactured and their "straightness and regularity are in striking contrast to he irregularity of the flakes. The blades have small unfaceted striking platforms" (Stekelis 1953:409). Many of the blades were retouched into tools. Cores are not abundant and are primarily "rough," often with only one striking platform. Although most of the raw material was brown or grey cherts, a few implements of obsidian, an imported material, were recovered.

Tools (*n*=291) included abundant side and end scrapers (*n*=24) and retouched pieces (*n*=119). Burins also apparently occurred, primarily as simple single-blow forms. I say

---

[1]Although "proper" points have recently been reported from *Shillourokambos* (Guilaine, personal communication 1998).

"apparently" because Stekelis makes no reference to these, although in a companion appendix, Waecheter (1953) noted their presence. Possibly the "gravers" noted by Stekelis are what Waecheter is referring to. The illustrations (Stekelis 1953, Plate CXLIX:15,16) seem to confirm this. Sickle blades also are common, many with irregular and deep denticulations and sheen. Interestingly, Stekelis noted the presence of four "arrow-heads." These are rounded, small implements with limited retouch. Those specimens illustrated (Stekelis 1953:414, Fig. 110:1,2, and 3) appear questionable as projectile points. Two of the three illustrated resemble perforators instead of projectiles.

Scrapers included several varieties manufactured on both blades and flakes. Curiously, perhaps ironically, Stekelis referred to one scraper as a "pigmy end-scraper with bulbar face retouch" (Stekelis 1953:412). This artifact is illustrated (Stekelis 1953:412, Fig. 110:4) and resembles more accurately a lightly retouched truncation. It bears no resemblance to the thumbnail scrapers found at *Aetokremnos*. No other thumbnail forms are noted or illustrated.

The most characteristic features of the Khirokitia assemblage, according to Stekelis, are large tanged "points" (or blades) and flakes, ranging in length from 70 to 177 mm. The "tang is produced by secondary flaking from the bulbar face on one or both edges. The rest of the flake was generally left untouched" (Stekelis 1953:412–413).

Stekelis concludes that the Khirokitia materials probably

> derive indirectly from the evolved Upper Paleolithic or Mesolithic source in the Near East. The Palaeolithic techniques continued to persist until a more recent date. It is noteworthy that the tanged blades of Khirokitia have typological parallels in the Lyngby culture of northern Europe. On the other hand, no comparative material has been found in the Mesolithic or Chalcolithic cultures of Syria, Palestine, or elsewhere in the Near East to provide cultural relationship between them and the industry at Khirokitia.

> The origin of the Khirokitia industry is for the moment obscure, and only further excavation can throw light on the roots of this very important flake industry. (Stekelis 1953:412–413)

It is clear from these statements that Stekelis found few similarities between the Khirokitia and presumably ancestral Levantine assemblages. Instead, broader parallels with Europe are implied, which in the context of contemporary archaeological thought offer few satisfactory origin explanations.

In the same volume, Waechter (1953) made a comparison between the Khirokitia and Erimi *Pamboula* (a Chalcolithic site whose chipped stone was studied earlier by Seton-Williams [1936]) materials, noting a considerable difference between the assemblages. A slight digression is warranted here, since at *Pamboula* some of the most characteristic implements are round or discoidal scrapers (Seton-Williams 1936:51; Waechter 1953:415). These frequently are well manufactured with clear and distinct retouch and are typed as both "round scrapers" and "thumb scrapers," described as follows:

> Round Scrapers . . . are quite as numerous as end scrapers and exhibit the finest flaking of the industry. In type they are rather large, 4–5 cms. in diameter, and resemble the late Neolithic type in Europe. . . . In some the striking platform has been removed and the flaking carried right round and also over the upper face. Others are only worked upon three sides, while in none does the retouch occur upon the bulbar face. . . . Thumb Scrapers . . . are few; they are of buff chert, about 1 1/2 x 2 cms. long and roughly circular in shape. They are steeply worked on two sides, but have no other noticeable characteristic." (Seton-Williams 1936:51)

The "thumb scrapers" are not illustrated, but the description does not match the *Aetokremnos* thumbnail scrapers except in size. In particular, few of the *Aetokremnos* specimens are "worked on two sides." Upon examination of the single illustrated "round scraper" (Seton-Williams 1936, Plate XXVII:6), it is clear that these also are not at all similar to those recovered from *Aetokremnos*. None of the *Aetokremnos* scrapers are retouched around the entire perimeter of the artifact, or even on "three sides," as described for *Pamboula*.

Along the same lines, at another Chalcolithic site, Kalavassos *Pamboules* in the Vasilikos Valley, chipped stone tools were characterized by a high number of scrapers of varying types (Hordynsky and Ritt 1978). These types included round and oval forms; at least two illustrated specimens resemble the *Aetokremnos* thumbnail forms (Hordynsky and Ritt 1978:191, Figs. 17:2 and 17:3), although the retouch does not appear as invasive.

More recent excavations at Khirokitia have only dealt with the chipped stone in cursory fashion. Coqueugniot (1984) was concerned primarily with wear patterns, while Cauvin (1984) discussed similarities, or more accurately, dissimilarities to the Levant. In short, although a huge chipped stone assemblage is known to exist from Khirokitia, very little of it has been published. Despite this, however, it seems clear that there are virtually no parallels with the assemblage from *Aetokremnos*.

Turning to the other major excavated Aceramic Neolithic site, Kalavassos *Tenta*, there is even less information. Although not yet reported in full, the initial approach taken to the large *Tenta* assemblage was promising. Hordynsky and Kingsnorth (1979) discussed a strategy largely based on Collins's (1975) "product groups" of chipped stone reduction. They noted that their study of the chipped stone from sites in the Vasilikos Valley (including, but not restricted to, *Tenta*) was intended to complement project goals of clarifying chronological, ecological, and technological developments. In particular, they sought to identify "sources of raw materials, the reconstruction of lithic reduction sequences . . . and the study of activity and discard patterns" (Hordynsky and Kingsnorth 1979:287). Their initial application of this approach to the excavated *Tenta* materials (in contrast to surface materials, see later) showed that raw material was plentiful in both the Vasilikos River bed and in fields several km upstream from *Tenta*. The most abundant raw material at the site is a coarse gray chert with a source of at least 5 km distance. Obsidian occurred, but it was rare. They also concluded that tools at *Tenta* were single components chosen for specific tasks. Hordynsky and Kingsnorth (1979:290) further noted the higher ratio of blades and coarse cherts at *Tenta* compared with nearby Chalcolithic sites; however, there is greater tool standardization amongst the latter.

In a later report, Hordynsky and Todd (1987) provided some information on the large assemblage, but it is based on surface materials only. They reported that 24,536 lithics were collected from the site's surface. This number is certainly more in line with what one would expect from a major habitation site, unlike the numbers reported from Khirokitia. At Khirokitia, though, there is a much larger sample of chipped stone than has thus far been published (LeBrun, personal communication 1990).

Most of the raw material from this surface collection at *Tenta* is Lefkara chert; which seems consistent with the excavated materials. Only two fragments of obsidian are reported from the surface. Hordynsky and Todd (1987:17) believed that the most likely source for the majority of materials is the nearby Vasilikos River bed. The initial typology they devised consisted of 6,217 of the reported 24,536 artifacts; they gave no information on the composition of the remainder, although a safe assumption might be that they were of generalized waste, shatter, or "debris" (as used in this volume). Although the information from *Tenta* is extremely limited, it would appear that few similarities exist between it and *Aetokremnos.*

More detailed comparisons can be made between *Aetokremnos* and two other Aceramic Neolithic sites, about which detailed published information on the chipped stone is available. At *Cape Andreas Kastros* (LeBrun 1981), basic categories of chipped stone can be compared with *Aetokremnos* with only minor modification. With materials from *Ortos* (Cooper 1997:61–96; Simmons 1994a) direct comparisons can be made with *Aetokremnos* because virtually the same classification systems were used at both sites. In addition, Fox's (1988) original description of *Ortos* had a good discussion on the chipped stone, albeit based only on surface materials.

Before examining the precise data, a few words on some subjective observations are useful. I had the opportunity to briefly examine some of the *Cape Andreas Kastros* materials in the Cyprus Museum in Nicosia. After looking at some of the material from Khirokitia (from Dikaios's excavations) at the Museum, my impression is that the chipped stone from *Cape Andreas Kastros* is considerably different from both *Aetokremnos* and Khirokitia. There were none of the large blades (at least in the Museum's collection) so characteristic of Khirokitia. They were, however, abundant cores, and much of the debitage resembles that from *Aetokremnos* in overall forms. By this, I mean that the debitage tends to be smaller than that from Khirokitia and consists of both flakes and blades. Technologically, the *Cape Andreas Kastros* assemblage is relatively simple and not as well developed as at *Aetokremnos.* It suggests a more expedient technology. It must be realized, however, that these are simply generalized impressions, based on a cursory examination of the materials.

A major research objective of the *Ortos* Project, as it was at *Aetokremnos,* was the systematic analysis of the chipped stone. At *Ortos,* both the typology and technology were more sophisticated than had been previously reported from Cyprus. This leads one to the inevitable conclusion that perhaps chipped stone technology was not as crude during the Aceramic Neolithic in Cyprus as some have implied. Rather, the deficiency may have been in the lack of detailed analyses. In spite of this possibility, however, there is no denying the fact that compared with the mainland Aceramic Neolithic, Cyprus does not exhibit the same degree of technological sophistication.

Table 11-7. Comparison of Major Chipped Stone Classes from *Aetokremnos*, *Ortos*, and *Cape Andreas Kastros*

Class	Aetokremnos		Ortos		Cape Andreas Kastros	
	N	%	*N*	%	*N*	%
Tools	128	24.4	1,250	4.1	829	8.7
Flakes	256	48.9	23,467	77.8	8,074	84.4
Blades	78	14.8	2,997	9.9	274	2.9
Bladelets	42	8.0	689	2.3	63	0.7
Cores	20	3.8	1,756	5.8	322	3.4
TOTAL	524	99.9	30,159	99.9	9,562	100.1

Note: Excludes debris, microflakes, and other classes where comparative data are not available; *Ortos* data from Cooper (1997:67, Table 5.1); *Cape Andreas Kastros* data compiled from LeBrun (1981:32).

What is important for the present discussion, however, is how these Neolithic materials compare to *Aetokremnos*. Tables 11-7 to 11-11 present information on various aspects of these assemblages. These tables reflect minor changes made to the original reports for consistency.

Table 11-7 shows some major distinctions between *Aetokremnos* and the Aceramic Neolithic sites. *Aetokremnos* clearly stands out from *Ortos* and *Cape Andreas Kastros* in its high proportion of tools. Furthermore, *Aetokremnos* has a relatively high proportion of blades and bladelets when compared with the other two sites, where flakes are a much more abundant form of debitage, suggesting an orientation toward more of a blade technology at *Aetokremnos*. It is only with cores that the proportions from all three sites are roughly similar.

Table 11-8 clearly demonstrates the emphasis on blades at *Aetokremnos* by showing the ratio of flakes to blades (and bladelets) at the sites. Data from Khirokitia also are included here for illustrative purposes, but they are undoubtedly skewed. At *Aetokremnos*, the ratio is roughly two to one, whereas it is much higher at the Aceramic Neolithic sites. At *Cape Andreas Kastros*, in particular, the ratio of flakes to blades is very high. Although blade production was more common at *Aetokremnos*, it is interesting that only 28.9% of the tools were manufactured on blade blanks. At *Ortos*, this figure is 49.6% (1993–94 sample only; Simmons 1994a:5), despite the fact that flakes constitute 76.7% of the debitage there (same sample). One reason for this difference appears to be the high percentage of thumbnail scrapers as tools at *Aetokremnos;* these were almost exclusively manufactured on flake blanks.

An examination of metrics on blades and flakes reveals some distinctions between assemblages (Table 11-9). This information was not available for *Cape Andreas Kastros*, but a sample of 50 blades from Khirokitia was measured, while 50 blades and 50 flakes from *Ortos* were measured. I obtained the Khirokitia data courtesy of the Cyprus Museum, while the *Ortos* data are taken from unpublished materials that I am presently analyzing.

At both Khirokitia and *Ortos*, blades are large in all dimensions. The figure for Khirokitia may be skewed by original selection for large blades, but it is clear that at both Neolithic sites, blade production was oriented toward large blanks. The blades from *Aetokremnos* are significantly smaller. With flakes, however, this distinction is much less pronounced. Overall, the flakes from *Aetokremnos* still are smaller than those from *Ortos*, but the differences are not as pronounced as with blades. Although the length is nearly the same from both sites, the Neolithic flakes tend to be wider and thicker.

We can also examine variability within major debitage classes between *Ortos* and *Aetokremnos* (Table 11-10). For comparative purposes, data from a sample of Khirokitia

Table 11-8. Ratios of Flakes to Blades and Bladelets, *Aetokremnos* and Neolithic Sites

Aetokremnos	2.1:1
Ortos	6.4:1
Cape Andreas Kastros	24.0:1
Khirokitia	6.3:1

Note: *Ortos:* Compiled from Cooper (1997:67, Table 5.1); *Cape Andreas Kastros:* LeBrun (1981:32, Table 6); and Khirokitia: Stekelis (1953:413).

**Table 11-9. Metric Comparisons of Flakes and Blades from *Aetokremnos*
with Samples from *Ortos* and Khirokitia (blades only)**

Site	Length			Width			Thickness		
	Avg.	SD	*N*	Avg.	SD	*N*	Avg.	SD	*N*
Aetokremnos									
Blades	44.2	14.6	26	16.2	3.6	73	4.4	2.3	76
Flakes	28.9	13.2	138	23.2	8.7	188	5.7	3.4	253
Ortos									
Blades	54.6	15.5	50	22.3	6.8	50	9.5	5.1	50
Flakes	29.5	15.9	50	28.8	11.9	50	7.0	3.7	50
Khirokitia									
Blades	83.1	16.3	50	25.3	5.6	50	8.0	2.7	50

**Table 11-10. Comparison of Debitage Types between *Aetokremnos*,
Ortos, and Khirokitia Samples**

	Aetokremnos		*Ortos**		Khirokitia	
	N	%	*N*	%	*N*	%
Flakes						
Primary	13	3.3	860	3.2	3	0.5
Secondary	79	19.8	4,816	17.7	53	8.1
Tertiary	164	41.2	17,791	65.3	182	27.7
Blades						
Primary	0	0	107	0.4	3	0.5
Secondary	13	3.3	1,039	3.8	116	17.6
Tertiary	65	16.3	1,851	6.8	286	43.4
Bladelets	42	10.6	689	2.5	8	1.2
Core trimming	6	1.5	35	0.1	5	0.8
Burin spalls	16	4.0	44	0.2	2	0.3
TOTAL	398	100.0	27,232	100.0	658	100.1

* Ortos data from Cooper 1997:67, Table 5.1.

chipped stone, examined at the Cyprus Museum, are included here. It should, however, be clear that this is a quite biased sample, judging from the high percentage of blades (61.5%). The data from *Ortos*, however, are directly comparable with those from *Aetokremnos*. At the former site, 74.2% of the flakes and blades are tertiary forms, while at *Aetokremnos* this figure is considerably less, 57.5%. At Khirokitia, the figure is 71.1%. Although these data are undoubtedly skewed, they do closely match the figures from *Ortos*. These data could suggest that a more consistent amount of total reduction occurred at *Aetokremnos* as compared with *Ortos* (and Khirokitia), where the evidence indicates that

Table 11-11. Comparison of Major Tools Classes from *Ortos*,
Cape Andreas Kastros, and *Aetokremnos*

Class	Cape Andreas Kastros		Ortos		Aetokremnos	
	N	%	N	%	N	%
End scrapers	68	8.1	35	2.8	3	2.3
Side scrapers	7	0.8	34	2.7	7	5.5
Thumbnail scrapers			5	0.4	36	28.1
Other scrapers			19	1.5	6	4.7
Sickles	216	25.8	208	16.7		
Burins	10	1.2	33	2.6	20	15.6
Backed pieces	89	10.6	36	2.9	2	1.6
Truncations	7	0.8	148	11.8	3	2.3
Tangs			24	1.9		
Perforators	43	5.1	6	0.4		
Pics/axes	10	1.2	2	0.2	1	0.8
Notches	20	2.4	85	6.8	3	2.3
Denticulates	91	10.9	25	2.0		
Retouched blades	83	9.9	125	10.0	16	12.5
Retouched flakes	189	22.5	179	14.3	22	17.2
Microliths			14	1.1	6	4.7
Others	6	0.7	272	21.8	3	2.3
TOTAL	839	100.0	1,250	99.9	128	99.9

Note: Figures from *Ortos* excludes tool fragments; *Ortos* data compiled from Cooper (1997:71–73, Table 5.4); *Cape Andreas Kastros* data compiled from LeBrun (1981:33).

decortification activities, as represented by primary (and to a lessor degree, secondary) elements, took place elsewhere.

This argument, however, is somewhat weakened by the considerable number of cores at *Ortos*. The proportion of bladelets also is much higher at *Aetokremnos*, as noted earlier. Finally, burin spalls are relatively abundant at *Aetokremnos;* this abundance might be anticipated, considering that burins are quite common at the site. Although not included in Table 11-10, the percentage of microflakes at *Aetokremnos* and *Ortos* also is interesting. This figure is 17.4% (N=178) at the former and 12.8% (N=8,327) at the latter, possibly indicating a greater emphasis on either or both final tool manufacture and resharpening activities at *Aetokremnos*. All of these figures, of course, must be viewed cautiously because, despite similar data recovery and analysis methods, the sample sizes varies considerably between assemblages (N=1,021 at *Aetokremnos* and N=64,867 at *Ortos*).

Finally, one can examine the composition of major tool classes between the sites (Table 11-11). All sites contain a wide variety of tool types, but once again, some major differences are readily apparent. First of all, the preponderance of scrapers at *Aetokremnos* stands out, with over 40% of all tools falling into that category. Within this class, the principal type of scraper at *Aetokremnos* is the thumbnail scraper, which apparently does not occur at *Cape Andreas Kastros.* It is interesting to note the limited presence of these small scrapers at *Ortos*, where a typology similar to that used at *Aetokremnos* was employed. These are not identical to the *Aetokremnos* scrapers, but they are similar, leading one to suspect that differences in analytical typologies may account for at least part of the distinctions. Although this may well be the case, it does not explain the preponderance of thumbnail scrapers at *Aetokremnos*. Indeed, although we may say that thumbnail scrapers do occur in Aceramic Neolithic assemblages (at least at *Ortos*), they were only a very small component of them.

There are two other glaring distinctions between the sites. The first is the lack of sickles at *Aetokremnos*, a class that forms a significant percentage of tools at the other sites. This discrepancy would in all likelihood be related to the agricultural orientation of the two Neolithic sites. The second is the high proportion of burins at *Aetokremnos*. Although these tools do occur at the Neolithic sites, they are not common.

Finally, there is a relatively high number of microlithic tools at *Aetokremnos*. Again, however, this may reflect an analytic bias. Note that microliths occur at *Ortos*, although in low proportions. Other tool classes seem not to indicate any particular patterns, although the relatively high number of perforators at *Cape Andreas Kastros* is interesting.

OTHER CYPRIOT MATERIALS

As reported in Chapter 10, several of the sites recorded by Pile on the Akrotiri Peninsula may be early ones. Unfortunately, there is little in the way of systematic comparisons that can be done with these small assemblages, particularly because we do not know if the collections are representative. The presence of thumbnail scrapers, however, at a few of these sites suggests possible affinities with *Aetokremnos*. If this is the case, it should come as no surprise, given their proximity to *Aetokremnos*. Such a connection must, unfortunately, remain a matter of conjecture.

Some chipped stone reportedly was present at the *Akanthou* fossil site found by Sondaar and Spaan in the northern part of Cyprus, near an Aceramic Neolithic site. Unfortunately, no detail is available on this (Reese, personal communication 1992).

Over the past several years, other presumably Aceramic Neolithic sites have been recorded, primarily by amateurs, in southern Cyprus. I had the opportunity to examine some of these, and visit one, near Pissouri. None of these collections (curated at the Kourion Museum) resemble the *Aetokremnos* materials, and the Pissouri site is a very dispersed scatter of chipped stone containing blades but lacking any other diagnostic elements. These collections could be either Aceramic Neolithic materials or could relate to later periods, representing specialized functions where ceramics were not used.

Finally, it is not terribly useful to make any comparisons to later cultural periods. Although the above discussion has not been exhaustive, it is clear from a review of the literature that chipped stone studies from post-Aceramic Neolithic occurrences have been even rarer than those from that period. Studies from Ceramic Neolithic sites have not concerned themselves in any great detail with chipped stone, even when detailed publications exists (e.g., Sotira:Dikaios 1961). Likewise, little detailed information has been published from Chalcolithic sites.

SUMMARY OF COMPARISONS WITH CYPRIOT NEOLITHIC MATERIALS

Several conclusions can be made regarding the *Aetokremnos* chipped stone assemblage when compared with other Cypriot materials:

1. The Kyrenia assemblages do not resemble *Aetokremnos* in the least. A careful examination of these materials suggests that many are not cultural, and that the remainder could date from virtually any cultural period. There is no evidence whatsoever that these are "Paleolithic." Convincing claims for pre-Neolithic materials on Cyprus must have sites in context, datable materials, systematic collections, and careful analysis. Kyrenia has none of these.

2. Assemblages from *Aetokremnos*'s nearest chronological neighbor, the Aceramic Neolithic, show few similarities, either typologically or technologically. Overall, *Aetokremnos* materials are smaller and more bladelike than those from Neolithic sites. Tools at *Aetokremnos* occur in distinctly different proportions than they do from the Neolithic sites, even when the same analytical procedure was used (as at *Ortos*).

3. One must be aware of potential reasons for these distinctions. First of all, the lack of published information on chipped stone from the Aceramic Neolithic sites presents an analytic problem. With the exceptions of *Cape Andreas Kastros* and *Ortos*, we have very little systematic information on complete assemblage composition. Second, with the exception of *Ortos*, different analytic methods may mask similarities. For example, the presence of thumbnail scrapers has been documented at *Ortos*, where a typology nearly identical with that used at *Aetokremnos* was employed. Third, one would not reasonably expect Neolithic village sites to have the same (or even similar) chipped stone compositions, either in tool classes or in overall configuration, as does a specialized site such as *Aetokremnos*.

4. There are some more convincing similarities reported between *Aetokremnos* and the three tested sites on the Akrotiri Peninsula, where identical analytical methods were used. Even here, however, *Aetokremnos* stands out in a number of ways. These sites may represent other components of the Akrotiri Phase, but they also have no *Phanourios* remains and are badly disturbed, thus presenting equivocal data.

5. While published data are rare, those existing show virtually no similarities between *Aetokremnos* and materials from other cultural periods, such as the Chalcolithic. Although "thumbnail scrapers" have been claimed from Chalcolithic *Pamboula*, for example, they do not resemble the types found at *Aetokremnos* or at *Ortos*, for that matter.

6. There may be more similarities of other Cypriot chipped stone materials with those of *Aetokremnos*, but we will not know this until the systematic treatment of such artifacts becomes a priority. The picture is, however, slowly changing with increased, albeit still preliminary, emphasis on chipped stone assemblages in studies presently underway, such as the Lemba Archaeological Project (Betts 1979, 1985, 1987; McCartney personal communication 1994), the Canadian Palaipaphos Project (D'Annibale 1992, 1993, 1994), the Malloura Survey (Kardulias 1993; Kardulias and Yerkes 1993), and the *Ortos* Project (Cooper 1997:61–96; Simmons 1994a,b,c). Additionally, innovative studies, such as McCartney's (1993) study of dhoukani and prehistoric chipped stone, are a welcome trend.

7. It is reasonable to conclude that the chipped stone from *Aetokremnos* is quite distinct from anything else reported on Cyprus, both in terms of typology and technology. It also weakens the argument that the materials from *Aetokremnos* were either washed in from sites above the rockshelters (which we have demonstrated is not stratigraphically possible in any case), or that they belong to a later cultural period (which the radiocarbon determinations have convincingly dispelled).

A COMPARISON WITH LEVANTINE MATERIALS (Alan H. Simmons and Martin Rose)

While the assemblage from *Aetokremnos* appears unique to Cyprus, it shares general similarities with several mainland Near Eastern materials. These similarities are perhaps to be expected if the occupants of *Aetokremnos* derived from a generalized Late Epipaleolithic or Early Neolithic population. It would be a fruitless task to try to specifically tie the *Aetokremnos* materials to any particular Near Eastern "culture." One could consult published reports, looking for similarities, and indeed one would probably come to the conclusion that *Aetokremnos* really does not stand out. If the site were on the mainland, it could fit comfortably within numerous identified chipped stone industries known throughout the region from about 12000 to 8000 B.C. What *Aetokremnos* lacks, however, are diagnostic artifacts, the time-honored *fossile directors* that so frequently are used to characterize specific (and presumed) cultural entities.

The most diagnostic elements from *Aetokremnos* are the thumbnail scrapers. These appear to be characteristic of the Akrotiri Phase and have not been identified at other Cypriot sites (beyond limited numbers at *Ortos* and the tested Akrotiri Peninsula sites, Chap. 10). On the mainland, however, thumbnail scrapers are not a rarity. Certainly, one can find general parallels with *Aetokremnos* at many sites throughout the Near East. The following is only a small sample: Thumbnail scrapers (even if not classified as such) similar to those from *Aetokremnos* have been illustrated in Anatolia: e.g., Upper Paleolithic Karain B and Oküzin:Albrecht 1988a:34, Figure 8:13–16; Albrecht 1988b:216, Figure 4:2, 219, Figure 7:23, 26, 28, and 220, Figure 8:9; Epipaleolithic AgaÇlg:Gatsov and Özdogan 1994:115, Figure 4:2, 3, 4, 117:4; PPNB Hayaz:Roodenberg 1989:96, Figure 3.29,30; Early Neolithic Hallen Cemi:Rosenberg 1994:232, Figure 6:9,10; the Levant: e.g., PPNB Divshon:Servello 1976:365, Figure 12-6a; Harifian Abu Salem:Scott 1977:298, Figure 11-8a,b,e; Natufian Saaide:Schroeder 1991:64, Figure 6.12; Epipaleolithic Khallat 'Anaza:Betts 1991:226, Figure 7:13; and the interior Near East: e.g., Neolithic Jarmo:Hole 1983: 275–276, Figure 118:15,17 and Figure 119:18; Epipaleolithic M'lefaat:Dittemore 1983: 689, Figure 242:2, 12.

One can continue the search for similarities far beyond the Near East. Thumbnail scrapers nearly identical to those found at *Aetokremnos* have been reported from sites as far away as Tasmania: e.g., Bone and Nunamira Caves: Cosgrove *et al.* 1990:70, Fig. 6). Such comparisons are clearly of limited utility. The point of this extended discussion is simply to note that thumbnail scrapers by themselves, while apparently diagnostic within Cyprus to the Akrotiri Phase, are not unique nor rare—they commonly occur in a widely ranging chronological and geographic span.

What we have attempted here is a generalized comparison for exploratory purposes. It is not intended as a comprehensive treatment, but rather an exercise in demonstrating just how different the *Aetokremnos* materials appear from other roughly contemporary assemblages. For the purposes of this analysis, we have tabulated basic assemblage characteristics from a series of Levantine sites that span the chronological range of *Aetokremnos*'s occupation. Selection of these sites was somewhat arbitrary, since a huge database exists from the Levant. We selected sites that had chipped stone classifications roughly comparable with those used at *Aetokremnos*. Data assembled from published reports are summarized in Table 11-12.

Table 11-12. Data Sources Used for Comparisons

All Harifian Sites	Henry 1989: Appendix C, Table C-1, pp. 269–271
All Natufian Sites	Henry 1989: Appendix C, Table C-2, pp. 269–271
Neolithic Villages	
'Ain Ghazal 1988	Rollefson *et al.* 1991: Table 1, p. 98 and Table 4, p. 100
'Ain Ghazal 1984	Rollefson and Simmons 1986: Table 1 (in situ materials only), p. 154 and Table 4, p. 156
Wadi Shu'eib	Simmons *et al.* 1989: Table 1, p. 32, Table 3, p. 32, and unpublished data in Simmons's possession; Cooper 1997: Table 4.2, p. 51 and Table 4.3, p. 52
Netiv Hagdud	Bar-Yosef *et al.*, 1991: Tables 1 and 2, p. 413
Cape Andreas	LeBrun 1981: Table 6, p. 32 and Table 8, p. 33
Kholetria *Ortos*	Simmons 1994a: Table 1, p. 4 and Table 2, p. 6; Simmons 1994c: Table 1, p. 40 and Table 2, p. 41; Simmons and Corona 1993: Table 1, p. 3 and Table 2, p. 5
Small Neolithic Sites	
Divshon	Servello 1976: Table 12.1, p. 345 and Table 12.4, p. 356; Simmons 1980: Table 13, p. 133
Nitzana, Nahal Boqer, and Atadim	Simmons 1980: Table 13, p. 133
Mushabi VIH, VIG, and VIK	Mintz and Ben-Ami 1977: p. 222, Table 59, p. 228–229, Table 60, and p. 234, Table 61

For the Late Epipaleolithic (Natufian and Harifian) sites, we use information for major tool classes only, with several classes lumped together for consistency (classified here as "other tools"). For Neolithic sites, we use data for both complete assemblages and for major tool classes. For comparative purposes, we also have included information from Cypriot Neolithic sites. Note that the sample sizes from all of these assemblages varies considerably, with *Aetokremnos* being on the smaller end. This is a potential biasing factor.

One of the original intentions of the exploratory statistical analysis was to examine the covariance between different Aceramic Neolithic sites with respect to either major tools or complete assemblages. Contrasts between Neolithic villages and limited activity sites could also be undertaken. Still other comparisons were made between Late Epipaleolithic sites with respect to major tool classes. We thought that if significant correlations existed, it might be possible to partition the sites into different groupings. Before undertaking a correlation analysis, however, pairwise visual comparisons between sites were made with simple scatterplots.

The scatterplots were very revealing in that they illustrated the futility that would have been involved in proceeding with correlation-based analyses. Because of the variable data recovery strategies used over time at the different sites, many of the samples were not directly comparable. Some of the differences can be relegated to the use of different sized screens, while others are based on limited sample sizes, in terms of the amount of the site actually excavated: The smaller the sampling fraction, the higher the probability that two similar sites could actually be characterized quite differently. Even one village site ('Ain Ghazal), excavated in different seasons using identical data recovery strategies, was not the same, probably due to spatial variability. Still other pairwise relationships appeared to be heavily influenced by non-normal distributions and the presence of outliers.

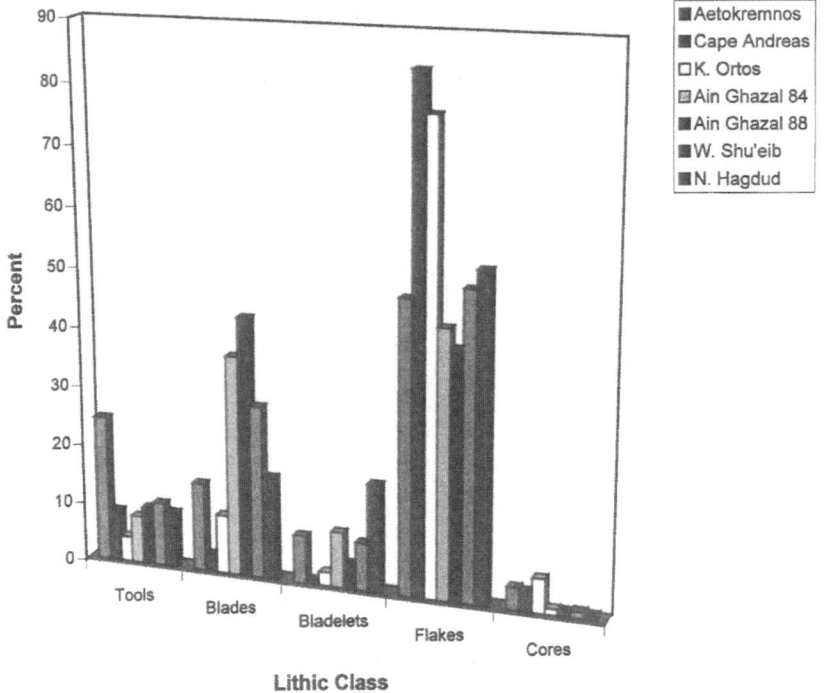

Figure 11-1. Comparisons of chipped stone from *Aetokremnos* to Neolithic village sites.

The most profitable comparisons simply graph both overall assemblage composition (e.g., tools, core, blades, flakes) and major tool classes (e.g., burins, microliths, notches, denticulates, scrapers, and others). This operation enables a quick visual assessment of assemblage variability within and between sites from different chronological periods and, for the Neolithic sites, different functions (i.e., village vs. limited activity). The overall configurations of various assemblages compared to *Aetokremnos* are illustrated in Figure 11-1 (village sites) and Figure 11-2 (nonvillage sites).

Compared with villages, *Aetokremnos* stands out most clearly as having a very high proportion of tools, not surprising at a specialized activity site. Another major distinction is the relatively low percentage of blades at *Aetokremnos* when compared with the mainland villages (but note the even lower percentage at *Cape Andreas Kastros* and Kholetria *Ortos*).

A less-clear picture emerges when examining *Aetokremnos* in relation to smaller, nonvillage sites, which is perhaps a more apt comparison (Fig. 11-2; no information available for bladelets). Once again, the relatively low percentage of blades is apparent at *Aetokremnos*. Tools, however, are more common at these smaller, limited activity sites than they are in villages. What is striking about these figures, however, is not so much how *Aetokremnos* differs, but rather how much variability there is between the sites. For example, in examining these data alone, one could surmise that Mushabi VI H is perhaps the most distinct of all assemblages. This conclusion simply points out the potential dangers of making too much of such broadscale comparisons.

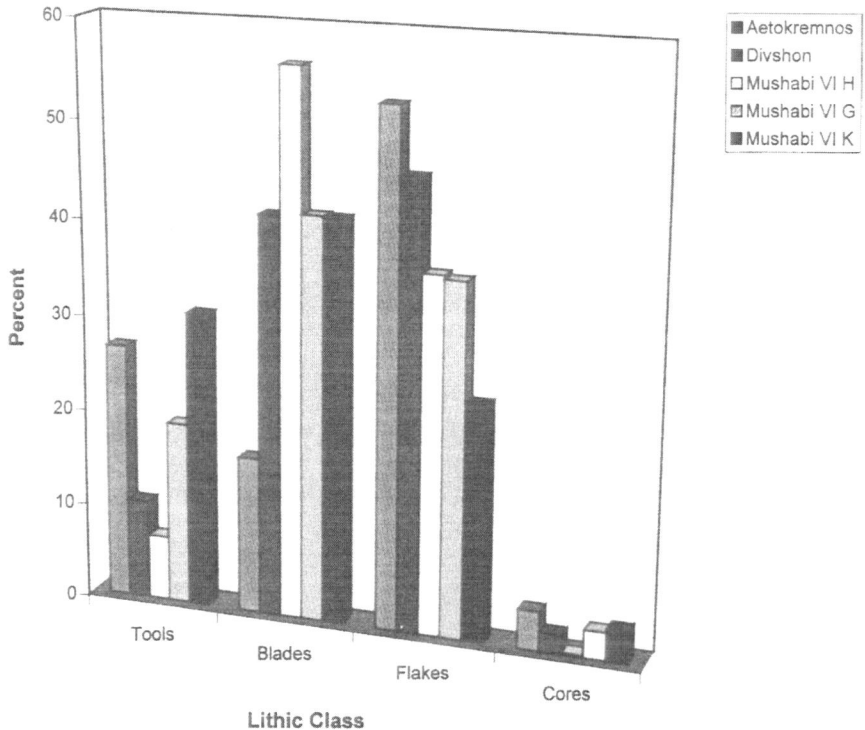

Figure 11-2. Comparisons of chipped stone from *Aetokremnos* to nonvillage sites.

In looking at tool compositions from Neolithic villages, Neolithic nonvillage special-ized-activity sites, and Epipaleolithic sites (Figs. 11-3–11-5), we used the lowest common denominator available for comparisons. Thus principal tool classes examined include mi-croliths, burins, scrapers, notches/denticulates, and "Others." *Aetokremnos* stands out in its high percentage of scrapers. This figure is higher than at any of the comparative sites. To a lessor degree, but still quite apparent, burins also are more common at *Aetokremnos* than at Epipaleolithic sites (Fig. 11-5), although they are quite abundant at most Neolithic sites, except the Cypriot ones (Figs. 11-3 and 11-4). The category "Others," which lumps all other tool classes, is highest at Neolithic villages, be they mainland or Cypriot, and at Ne-olithic specialized sites. Not surprisingly, microliths are abundant at Harifian and Natufian sites and less common at the others, including *Aetokremnos*. Some Mushabian Neolithic sites, however, have roughly comparable percentages of microliths in relation to *Aetokrem-nos*. When examining the tool compositions from Epipaleolithic sites, what is most appar-ent about this figure is the high degree of variability present. Microliths, of course, constitute a major tool class, but considerable variation also is apparent. Unlike *Aetokrem-nos*, where burins are very significant, they are overall a much more poorly represented class here. Likewise, scrapers, while quite common, come nowhere near the proportions here that they do at *Aetokremnos*. Only at sites G20 and K3 are there some similarities.

The comparisons made in this section have largely been done for heuristic purposes. A mass and somewhat confusing database was used, thus our conclusions can only be

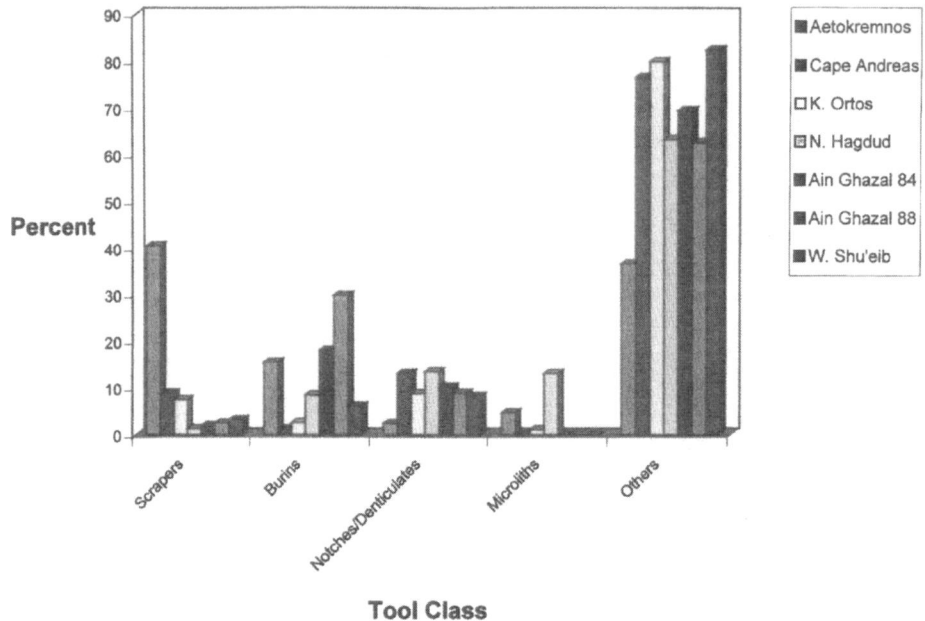

Figure 11-3. Tool composition between *Aetokremnos* and Neolithic villages.

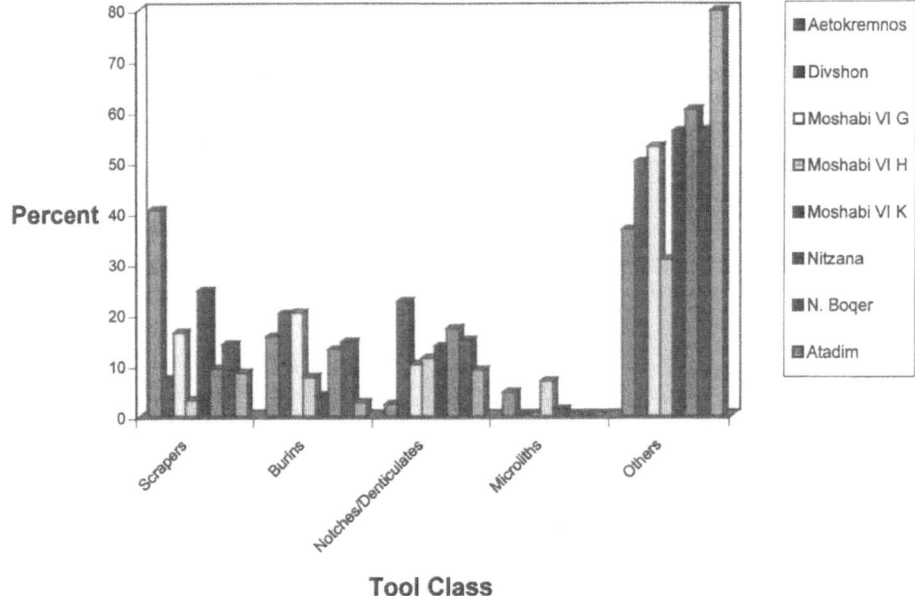

Figure 11-4. Tool composition between *Aetokremnos* and Neolithic specialized-activity sites.

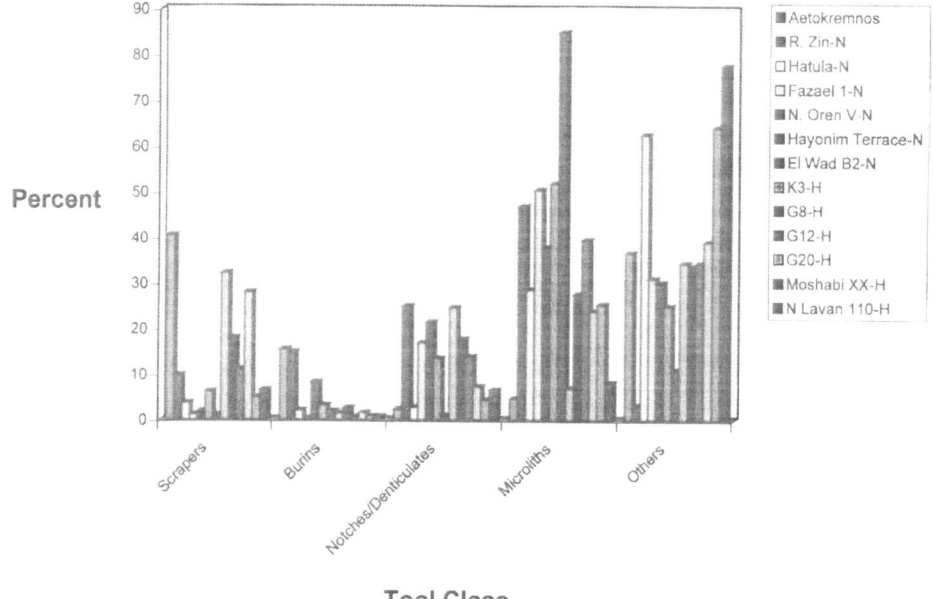

Figure 11-5. Tool composition between *Aetokremnos* and Epipaleolithic sites. H = Harifian and N = Natufian.

generalized. In terms of overall assemblage composition and specific tool classes, *Aetokremnos* exhibits no ready similarities to any of the mainland sites. Based on the data examined, we cannot say that the assemblage from *Aetokremnos* resembles more closely Neolithic, Harifian, or Natufian materials. Although there are some similarities, it would be a stretch to make too much of these.

CONCLUSION

In conclusion, then, no analogues in the chipped stone for *Aetokremnos* are apparent from either other Cypriot sites or from mainland sites that range in time from Late Epipaleolithic through Aceramic Neolithic. What does this mean? It would be a mistake to make too much out of generalized comparisons that are based only on artifacts. After all, *should* there be many similarities? In *Aetokremnos,* we are looking at a small and specialized assemblage used in the processing of a faunal suite with no mainland analogues. We feel that the data strongly support the specialized nature of the *Aetokremnos* assemblage. Taken as an isolated entity, one could drop these materials into one of the mainland cultural periods, and it would not stand out dramatically in terms of overall typology or technology. It would, however, present some major differences in its proportions of various elements. Most striking among these is the high percentage of scrapers, especially of the thumbnail type, and the high percentage of burins, suggesting to us that the major distinctions at *Aetokremnos* in comparison with other sites relate to functional variability.

Chapter *12*

Bitter Hippos of Cyprus?

Heaven knows how true all this was: but it was true for them. And the bibliography of Cyprus is so extensive and detailed that the truth must somewhere be on record. . . . Oddly enough, too, their stories provided true sometimes when they sounded utterly improbable; Andreas, for example, in describing ancient Cyprus to me produced a home-made imitation of a hippopotamus walking around and browsing in my courtyard which was worthy of Chaplin. It was nearly a year before I caught up with the report of the dwarf hippopotamus which had been unearthed on the Kyrenia range: a prehistoric relic. It was only justice, I suppose, that I myself should be disbelieved by them. (Durrell 1986 [originally 1957], *Bitter Lemons of Cyprus,* pp. 94–95)

INTRODUCTION

The preceding chapters have presented the primary data for Akrotiri *Aetokremnos.* What remains to be done in the final two chapters is to address several issues these data have posed. As Lawrence Durrell implied in his classic novel on Cyprus, sometimes the truth is stranger than fiction. With *Aetokremnos,* perhaps the most significant question to ask is, Have we created a myth (cf. Bunimovitz and Barkai 1996) by suggesting the association of extinct animals with early humans, or is there compelling and defensible archaeological data to support this claim beyond the proverbial reasonable doubt? We believe that the latter scenario is true.

The intent of this chapter is to justify our rationales for claiming the direct association of cultural materials with the faunal remains at *Aetokremnos.* We discuss in detail specific arguments made against the association of the *Phanourios* remains and cultural materials at *Aetokremnos* and provide counterarguments that support the association.

In any comparative treatment such as this chapter attempts, there is a huge literature available from both archaeological and natural history sources relating to taphonomy. In particular, the seminal works of Binford (1978, 1981, 1987), Brain (1981), and Haynes (1991), to name but a few key authors, have questioned many of the assumptions archaeologists make in looking at presumed archaeofaunas. Other authors have examined taphonomic issues from a broader perspective, with Bunn's (1991) and Lyman's (1994) works being some of the most comprehensive. Many current studies, often based on ethnographic and actualistic data, as well as archaeological information, have made great strides in identifying and controlling for noncultural processes in order to sort them from cultural ones, or, as Behrensmeyer (1993:3432) put it, "removing the taphonomic overprint." We hope to provide a convincing argument for *Aetokremnos*'s significance, one that will cause even the most ardent distractors to muster their own arguments as to why the site is *not* what it appears.

THE ASSOCIATION OF FAUNAL AND CULTURAL MATERIALS AT *AETOKREMNOS*

Perhaps the most critical question in assessing the significance of *Aetokremnos* is to ask the simple question well posed by Shipman, "What are all these bones *doing* here?" (Shipman 1979:42). By answering this, can the association of cultural materials with the remains of extinct endemic fauna at *Aetokremnos* be verified? The problem of recognizing humans as bone-accumulating agents is, of course, critical and involves analytically sorting out cultural bone from natural bone. The former includes bone deposited as a result of human activity, and the latter includes bone accumulated and deposited as the result of natural processes (Lyman 1994:216).

Here we summarize the data used as an argument for supporting the association of bone and cultural materials at *Aetokremnos*. In particular, we examine the following interrelated issues: *Phanourios* taphonomy as it relates to natural versus cultural deposition, stratigraphy and erosion, chronology, burning, and cutmarks. Lyman (1994:216–219) summarized various criteria used to recognize cultural bone. The final part of this section will assess how well *Aetokremnos* meets these criteria.

Phanourios Taphonomy and Deposition

In Chapter 1, we presented an argument made by Catherine Perlès for the in situ deposition and cultural association of the *Phanourios* remains at *Aetokremnos*. She made a succinct and compelling argument for the intact nature of the site and the association of the bones with cultural materials. Here we elaborate on this issue.

We know that there are numerous paleontological sites containing pygmy hippopotami and dwarf elephants throughout Cyprus and other Mediterranean islands. If these could be directly compared with *Aetokremnos*, one could determine how similar or dissimilar the sites are in the abundance of bones, articulation, MNI, age/sex distribution, preservation, and stratigraphy. Unfortunately, none of these have been systematically investigated, and it is only recently that attempts have been made to synthesize available information (e.g., Held 1992; Reese 1995). Most published reports are quite dated and relate to issues of paleontological concern rather than archaeological configuration. Many studies of paleontological sites have been concerned with obtaining diagnostic elements rather than on systematic excavation of complete deposits. What clearly is needed is taphonomic research along the innovative lines of Bonfiglio (1995) in Sicily.

A thorough review of the literature suggests that *Aetokremnos* is thus far unique. None of the paleontological sites have the combination of sheer abundance of bones and individual animals, stratified deposits, burning, exceptional preservation, nor, certainly, the presence of artifacts. Rather, one has the impression of, usually, small amounts of highly fossilized bone and lack of stratigraphy. The rich site of Akanthou *Arkhangelos Mikhail* (Tatlisu) in the northern part of Cyprus offers promise in addressing these issues, but has primarily concentrated on recovering material washed out of primary context (Bromage 1992; Reese 1995:86–131). Little detail is yet published on this site, however, and the unfortunate political circumstances of modern Cyprus have hindered proper investigation and dissemination of information. In any event, however, sites such as Akanthou appear to be the exception rather than the rule.

At issue for *Aetokremnos* is whether or not the primary deposit of *Phanourios* remains (Stratum 4) could be the result of a natural (noncultural) accumulation in a rockshelter that was later occupied by humans (Stratum 2). To properly address this, we need to understand the formation processes of natural sites that contain *Phanourios*. Unfortunately, such data are not present, but there are some general taphonomic "rules" relating to the accumulation of bones that are relevant to *Aetokremnos*.

Lyman, citing Badgley (1986a,b) and Behrensmeyer (1983), stated that there are two types of bone accumulating processes: active and passive. It is worth quoting him in full here:

> *Active accumulation* processes are those which, via transport or movement of skeletal parts (whether or not as complete carcasses/skeletons) significant distances from the location of animal death, result in relatively dense concentrations of bones and teeth in a spatially limited area. Such processes are labeled "spatially focused processes" by Behrensmeyer (1983:94). Active accumulation involves forces and energy external to the animal(s) whose bones are accumulated. *Passive accumulation* processes are those which do not involve transport of skeletal parts significant distances from the location of animal death; such process are not spatially focused, and have been considered to represent normal attritional mortality and deposition of animal remains close to the place of death (Behrensmeyer 1983). Passive accumulation involves forces and energy internal to the animal(s)-its behavior-whose bones are accumulated. (Lyman 1994: 162–163)

It is important to determine whether the *Phanourios* remains at *Aetokremnos* are the result of passive or active accumulation processes. Although neither process definitively argues for cultural versus noncultural accumulation, it is still useful to consider this distinction. An active accumulation might suggest a cultural origin, particularly if geological actions can be ruled out as a transport mechanism. A passive accumulation, on the other hand, could suggest an natural deposition, although a kill site certainly also can be a passive accumulation (Lyman 1994:163).

There is no doubt that there are a large number of individuals represented at *Aetokremnos*, and there certainly are well-known examples of large numbers of individuals that have been accumulated by passive processes. The LaBrea tar pits are perhaps the most famous multitaxon examples, while single-taxon assemblages include the abundantly documented African elephant die sites. The frequency of bones in such scenarios tends to be high (Lyman 1994:191–192).

Passive mass accumulations of bones have three distinguishing attributes: First, there must be some factor resulting in animals being attracted to a particular locale year after year; second, the probability that at least some of these animals will die in that attractive locale must be greater than in other areas; and, third, the animals must effectively accumulate themselves. This means that there is no accumulation agent that is external to the accumulated bones, but instead the process of accumulation involves the behaviors of the animals themselves (Lyman 1994:192).

In contrast to passive accumulation, active mass accumulations are created by bone-accumulating agents and processes that are external to the accumulated bones. Such processes can have several sources, including geological and human processes (Lyman 1994:193–216). We believe that the evidence from *Aetokremnos* strongly points to an active, human-induced accumulation process.

The considerable literature on modern elephant die sites is a possible analogy for *Aetokremnos*. Realizing the hazards of both ethnographic and naturalistic analogies, careful comparison can nonetheless be useful. It is, however, necessary to separate myth from truth, as there is a long history of exaggeration in African lore. In a classic work on the formation of bones that laid the foundation for modern taphonomic studies, Weigelt (1989:15, originally 1927) noted that

> the fact that we come across dead animals relatively seldom has given rise to many tales, especially in the case of elephants, whose valuable tusks cause people to devise preposterous schemes to search for their "dying grounds" or "graveyards." In fact, many early accounts note the lack of elephant carcasses. For example, the elephant hunter Sanderson, despite wandering throughout British India for several decades, came across elephants that had died a natural death only twice. In spite of this, however, rumors of rich elephant "graveyards" fooled more than one colonial expedition. (Weigelt 1989:15)

Certainly, the most detailed and well-conceived study of modern elephant die sites and their relevance to archaeology is by Haynes (1991). In particular, his actualistic studies of mass death and mass kill sites (Haynes 1991:111–191) make compelling reading. Although his actualistic data for kill sites were of mass kills for modern culling purposes, the resultant meat still was butchered and processed (Haynes 1991:177), thus many of Haynes's observations offer insight into the formation of *Aetokremnos*.

Before the reader becomes convinced that Haynes is a vocal advocate for archaeological kill sites, he has, in fact, questioned many claimed archaeological and faunal (elephant) associations, providing convincing evidence that shows how natural die sites may mimic presumed cultural associations. He stressed the need for critical assessment of patterning in both the modern and fossil record and noted that "the evidence for human hunting and processing of probosideans is that it appears to be far less substantial than has been claimed. The sites and assemblages of interest have inspired unreconciled and contradictory interpretations, because the excavation techniques and the types of data sought in each case were widely variable, resulting in much variation in the supportability of interpretive statements" (Haynes 1991:205).

In comparing kill (cultural) and die-off (natural) sites of modern elephants, Haynes (1991:190–191) made the following observations:

- Kill sites contain densely clustered bones with much higher concentrations of elements than do die-off sites. However, the die-off sites tend to contain either vertically dispersed or stratified clusters.
- Kill sites contain a nonselective sample of entire herd groups. They also contained skeletons of one or more very small calves and often several fetuses. Adults males occur in low proportions at kill sites, but they also are rare in die-off sites.

- Kill site skeletons contained few articulated units.
- Bone representation at kill and die-off sites is similar.
- Kill sites are not located near permanent water sources, while die-off sites are situated in stream channel depressions or spring-fed ponds.

How do these observations compare to *Aetokremnos*? The site shares many similarities to Haynes's kill sites. At *Aetokremnos* the following was observed:

- Virtually none of the bone is articulated (but see discussion later).
- A nonselective sample of a *Phanourios* herd (probably) is represented, including adolescent and fetus remains. Of over 500 MNI, 85 are under one year of age.
- The bone at *Aetokremnos* is abundant and densely clustered. Although it also is stratified, it is not vertically dispersed; rather, it is largely confined to the shelter's interior.
- The site is not located near permanent (drinkable) water.

We do not yet have sex information on the *Aetokremnos Phanourios* remains, although given the large number of MNI, it is likely that adult males are represented. Furthermore, at *Aetokremnos* virtually every skeletal element is represented. Haynes does not provide much specific information here, but it must be realized that in his African example, elephants at the mass kill sites were systematically butchered, which could have resulted in the absence of certain body elements. Additionally, there are numerous carnivorous scavengers in Africa that can disrupt the integrity of in situ remains.

Given these observations, the *Phanourios* remains from *Aetokremnos* resemble a kill site using Haynes's criteria. There also is at least one other important aspect that supports a cultural accumulation rather than a natural one to consider. This was an observation made by the project geomorphologist Rolfe Mandel during excavation. The bedrock floor of *Aetokremnos* had virtually no sediment on it. Rather, bone accumulations were in direct contact with the floor. It is unlikely that groups of *Phanourios* would have entered a shelter as "clean" as this. In fact, aeolian activity, as well as gradual disintegration of the roof, are both very active depositional agents, and the absence of such deposition on the floor below the bone remains practically guarantees that the floor was prepared to some degree.

All of these observations support the nonnatural deposition of *Phanourios* remains at *Aetokremnos*. It would be a rare depositional history indeed that could account for the accumulation of over 500 hippos in a shelter as small as *Aetokremnos*.

Stratigraphy

Related to the associational argument just presented, it could further be argued that the association of *Phanourios* and artifacts is more apparent than real, the result of people digging into Stratum 4 and disturbing a naturally deposited bed of *Phanourios*. Our justification as to why this is not the case has largely been presented in the preceding section and by Mandel (Chap. 3) in great detail; here we summarize stratigraphic issues.

There are two clear strata at *Aetokremnos*: Stratum 2 and Stratum 4. Few would question that the former is cultural, while the anthropogenic nature of the latter, consisting of the bone bed, is at issue. In many portions of the site, particularly those disturbed by erosion and rooffall, a mixed stratum (2/4) occurs, but in much of the shelter, Stratum 2 is clearly separated from Stratum 4 by the sterile Stratum 3. There is virtually no evidence that activities taking place in Stratum 2 caused any major disturbance to the underlying bone bed. The rationale for this conclusion may be summarized as follows.

First, beyond a few spatially isolated instances, there is no evidence that the materials from either Stratum 2 or 4 are the result of external depositional processes. For example, there is no way that the materials in either stratum could have been washed in. This is graphically illustrated by the presence of well-defined ash stains that make up hearths in Stratum 2. Instead, both strata are in situ depositions. Second, Stratum 4A is clearly the result of intense thermal alternation. Yet, there is no one to one spatial correlation between hearths in Stratum 2 and Stratum 4A, thus one cannot make the argument that the later is simply a result of heat penetrating from Stratum 2 hearths. Finally, the boundaries between the stratigraphic units, including Strata 2 and 4, are very distinct and abrupt, which indicate that there has been minimal mixing. Thus the chipped stone artifacts, which are typologically and technologically identical in both Strata 2 and 4, are indicative of separate occupations by the people with the same assemblage. The time between these occupations, however, was very short (see later).

One also cannot overlook the fact that features occur not only in Stratum 2, but also in Stratum 4. The areas of burnt bone that make up these lower features cannot be reasonably attributed to natural causes, nor can they be explained as a result of intrusive activity from Stratum 2. Certainly, the most parsimonious conclusion is that they are the result of human activity occurring at the time that Stratum 4 was deposited.

Thus the stratigraphic data alone indicate that Strata 2 and 4 are distinct entities. If there were no *Phanourios* in Stratum 2, or no artifacts in Stratum 4, then one could perhaps reasonably argue that these two stratigraphic units have no relationship whatsoever, but this is not the case, as has been demonstrated throughout this volume. Although the two units may be separable in time, the artifactual materials from both indicate the same cultural group bears responsibility for their formation. Furthermore, there is only a very limited amount of time separating both units.

Absolute Chronology

Related to the stratigraphic argument of near contemporaneity is the absolute chronology of *Aetokremnos*. We are fortunate in having a large series of radiocarbon determinations that form a consistent and close clustering. This is important because since Strata 2 and 4 are stratigraphically distinct in situ developments, a logical conclusion might be that they are separated by a considerable amount of time, which is not the case. The radiocarbon determinations on *Phanourios* bone are consistent with those on other, clearly cultural materials, such as charcoal and shell. Even acknowledging that there are difficulties in dating both bone and marine shell, the concordance between all of the *Aetokremnos* determinations is remarkable. If one argues that there is no relationship between the strata, the contemporary radiocarbon determinations on *Phanourios* bone and cultural materials demand explanation. If one concedes that Stratum 2 is cultural, one must also assume then that the first inhabitants of Cyprus coincidentally deposited their site upon one of the last remaining herds of *Phanourios*, as represented by Stratum 4. Such a coincidence seems unlikely. The absolute chronology cannot be ignored.

The absolute dates indicate that the chronological separation between Stratum 2 and Stratum 4 is of such a short duration that it cannot be measured in radiocarbon years. The entire occupational span at *Aetokremnos* could be a short as a few hundred years, if that. It stretches even the most imaginative scenario to envision that humans and *Phanourios* co-existed without knowledge of one another.

Burning

Over 29% of the bones from *Aetokremnos* are burned, which represents a large proportion, higher than seen in many indisputable cultural faunal assemblages. If the faunal assemblage is not the result of cultural deposition, it is necessary explain how so much of the bone could have been burned. We also must examine what is meant by "burning." While the temptation is great to associate burning with cooking, this is far too simplistic, as Lyman (1994:384) noted. Not all cooking necessarily results in burnt bone, and there are other ways by which bone can be burned.

It also is important to realize how archaeologists define *burned* bone. Lyman (1994:397) and others have cautioned against using color alone to determine burning. Lyman (1994:385) also noted, citing research by Shipman *et al.* (1984:314), that color may be a poor indicator of the *precise* temperature to which a bone was heated. Even noting these precautions, there is little question that the *Aetokremnos* bone is burned. There is no chemical indication in the surrounding matrix that could have discolored the bone, and the degree of burning is substantial and quite variable. It ranges from charred ends to completely burned pieces to the fragmentary "crinkly" bone of Stratum 4A, which suggest intense heat. Although there is no question that the bone from *Aetokremnos* is burned, at issue is how did it get that way?

A useful distinction here is made by Brain's (1981:54) experimental research, in which he concluded that there are two distinct stages of burning. As collagen is carbonized, the bone becomes black, or "carbonized." As heating continues, oxidization occurs, and the bone becomes white or "calcined" (Lyman 1994:385). Other researchers have proposed more burning categories, such as Johnson (1989:441), who distinguished four stages: unburned, scorched or superficial, charred or blackened, and calcined. Stiner *et al.* (1995:228–229) used six color levels for burning, from minimal (values 1–3) to more advanced partial and complete calcination (values 4–6).

The *Aetokremnos* bone was classified as burned on visual examination, and no distinctions between degrees of burning or burning stages were made. Based on our observations, however, the majority of burned bone would be characterized as carbonized, although calcined bone also occurs. Much of the burned bone also is burned into the interior, not just on its surface. This is important because "burning damage on bone normally extends deep into the cortex, and distinguishes burning damage from common types of superficial mineral staining" (Stiner *et al.* 1995:226). A few pieces of bone from *Aetokremnos* were a pale green color. There is no evidence to indicate that this color was the result of chemical changes; rather, we believe that they were very intensely burned. David (1990:68, 71) indicated that highly heated, calcined bones can be bluish-green (as well as gray, white, or blue) in color. Finally, the large amount of "crinkly" black bone that occurred in Stratum 4A appears to be somewhere in between the carbonized and calcined distinctions.

Certainly, there are instances where bone can be burned naturally, without human intervention. Lyman (1994:388) noted that bone can be burned naturally in three scenarios: proximity to anthropogenic fires, brush fires, or in situ burning of organic matrix.

At *Aetokremnos,* the latter two scenarios are unlikely. Terrestrial brush fires conceivably could trap animals in restrictive localities, such as the *Aetokremnos* shelter, burning them to death and charring their remains. There is, however, absolutely no supporting evidence for this scenario. Much of the intense burning is spatially restricted, not all of the bones are burned, there are different degrees of burning, and there is no geological or geomorphic evidence for a brush fire. Likewise, it is unlikely that the bone was resting in any natural organic matrix that burned. Again, there is no evidence for this. Vegetation is, and probably was, relatively sparse throughout the Akrotiri Peninsula.

Another possible natural cause of burning could be termed *catastrophic.* One visitor to the site, facetiously it is hoped, suggested that perhaps the *Phanourios* remains were burned by catastrophic lightning strikes. Again, there is no evidence for this, and it would have had to have been an apocalyptical storm indeed to have charred portions of the remains of over 500 hippos!

Burning due to proximity to anthropogenic fires must be taken more seriously. Some critics of *Aetokremnos,* when faced with the abundance of burnt bone, have suggested that this could be due to postdepositional factors. Essentially, the argument is that there are two discrete strata at the site: Strata 2 and 4. Stratum 2 is clearly cultural, while Stratum 4 consists primarily of *Phanourios,* and any associations between bones and artifacts are fortuitous, the result of mixing. In a previous section, "Stratigraphy," we have indicated why this scenario is unlikely.

For the time being, however, let us assume that this interpretation is accurate. The argument continues that the burning is the result of the bones' proximity to anthropogenic fires, in this case, hearths. For this to be correct, one would have to assume that hearths in Stratum 2 were so hot that they burned underlaying *Phanourios* remains. We argue against this on three counts.

First, if this scenario were correct, burned bone would only, or primarily, occur *under* Stratum 2 hearths, which is not the case. Burned bone is distributed throughout the deposits not only under hearths. Highly concentrated areas of burned bone (e.g., Feature 3) show no correlation with overlaying hearths. Furthermore, much of the *Phanourios* in Stratum 2 (46.3%) also is burned. In Stratum 4, the percentage burned is lower, at 31.9%, but it will be recalled that not all of the bone from this stratum has been examined, and it is likely that the figure will increase. The point is that if one argues the bone is burned because it is underneath hearths, then it cannot also be argued that the burning of Stratum 2 bone is due to the same process. A stratigraphic argument could be made that the Stratum 2 bone was burned while it was in Stratum 4 and then displaced into Stratum 2 by ancient pit excavation. This, however, is not a very parsimonious argument and would not likely account for the high percentage of burned bone in Stratum 2.

A second argument against the proximity scenario is purely stratigraphic. If the burned bone were the result of intense heat generated by overlaying hearths, then one would expect that the intervening Stratum 3 would exhibit signs of burning as well. It does not.

A third argument relates to the intensity of burning. Although we did not conduct any experimental studies, it is unlikely that hearths in Stratum 2 could have generated enough heat to cause the degree of burning observed on the bone. Lyman (1994:388–389) summarized an experiment examining the effects of different kinds of fires on bone. In this study, David (1990) compared proportions of burning on bones subjected to a brush fire, 25 minutes in a hearth and 6 hours in a hearth. He demonstrated that carbonization occurred on 98.9% of the bones exposed to the brush fire and 75.5% of the bones in a hearth for 25 minutes. Calcination occurred only in the hearths, at a rate of 24.5% in the 25 minute fire and 95.0% in the 6-hour exposure. Given these figures, it is unlikely that bone *beneath* hearths, with only indirect exposure to heat, would be severely burned. That over 30% of the Stratum 4 bone is burned simply cannot be realistically accounted for by indirect exposure to heat.

Further evidence against the bone being burned by overlaying hearths was provided by Stiner *et al.* (1995). In experimental hearths, using Mediterranean hardwoods, they buried fresh goat bones at depth up to 15 cm beneath the fire bed; they also exposed bone to the direct fires for a comparative base. They were cautious in interpreting their results, noting that "bones buried in sediments prior to when a fire is lit can be burned by that fire, implying that bone deposition and bone burning potentially represent unrelated events during the formation of archaeological sites" (Stiner *et al.* 1995:234). When examining their actual test results, however, they pointed out that "although bones were buried as deep as 15 cm below the coal bed, *only those specimens in the first 5 cm were affected much by heat from the fire.* Moreover, these shallowly buried bones were burned only to the point of carbonization" (Stiner *et al.* 1995:230, italic added for emphasis). They further observe that "we were unable to induce calcination on bones buried by any amount of soil, despite the fact that our control fires were comparatively hot (minimally 900°C)" (Stiner *et al.* 1995:231).

It will be recalled that at *Aetokremnos,* Stratum 4 often exceeds 50 cm in thickness, and that buried *Phanourios* occurs throughout the stratum, not only on the top of it. Furthermore, Stratum 2 frequently is separated from Stratum 4 by several cm of Stratum 3. In any event, the separation between the bottom of fire hearths in Stratum 2 and *Phanourios* in Stratum 4 almost always exceeds 15 cm, and yet much of this bone is burned. It is therefore exceedingly unlikely that the burning is the result of overlaying hearths.

Another observation made by Stiner *et al.* (1995:229–230) that is pertinent to *Aetokremnos* related to bone fragmentation as a function of burning intensity. It will be recalled that Stratum 4A is largely composed of highly fragmented burned bone with a granular appearance. We attribute this to intense burning, but it is also important to realize that burned bone is more likely to crumble than is fresh bone. Stiner *et al.*'s experimental studies included human trampling of bones buried beneath a cooled fire bed. They showed that the burned bones, particularly calcined ones, were extensively fragmented by trampling.

At *Aetokremnos,* it is possible that much of the fragmented Stratum 4A bone became so due to later human trampling in Stratum 2. This conclusion, however, does not rule out human involvement in the formation of Stratum 4, as argued throughout this chapter; rather, it merely notes that a stratigraphically later occupation (i.e., Stratum 2) could have caused the fragmentation. It will be recalled that occupation of the two strata was not separated by a considerable time span.

Finally, the accidental burning scenario does not take into account that 3 of the 11 features occur in Stratum 4, and thus they are horizontally as well as vertically associated with burned *Phanourios.* These include Feature 3, the huge and extremely burned bone feature. This feature is so horizontally extensive that it is difficult to argue that it is the result of an overlaying fire.

An alternative to the stratigraphic natural burning argument is that the *Phanourios* remains were intentionally burned, perhaps for fuel, by much later human occupants of the shelter. Although this argument is not so easily discarded, it does not fit the available evidence. Furthermore, it is unlikely that near fossilized, "paleontological" bone would have been used for fuel. Fresh, "green" bone, containing organic elements such as grease, burns much more easily. Thus, if the Stratum 2 occupants of the site were using bones from a paleontological site for fuel, not too much time could have passed between the deposition of the bone and the cultural event. It is unlikely that burning of bone deposited several thousand years earlier would have been very efficient. It also would have required a fuel source to initiate the burning. The fuel issue, however, is intriguing and will be addressed in Chap. 13.

To satisfactorily address the possibility that the burned bone was from a paleontological context, it is necessary to test the proposition that the bone was burned when dry. Lyman (1994:387–388), once again summarizing experimental data, provided supporting data for just the opposite conclusion, that is, that the *Aetokremnos* bone was burned fresh or "green." He noted that Buikstra and Swegle (1989) attempted to determine the condition of bones at the time of burning. Three conditions are identified: fleshed, green (or defleshed shortly before burning), and dry. Their data indicated that dry bone has insufficient organic substance to become uniformly carbonized; only green bone is uniformly smoked or blackened. Furthermore, green bone that has been calcined is white, blue, or gray, while dry calcined bone is light brown or tan. None of the *Aetokremnos* bones exhibit these latter hues. Thus it appears unlikely that the bone from *Aetokremnos* was burned when it was dry, as it would be if Stratum 4 were a paleontological deposit.

Finally, we should consider cooking methods as a way of burning bone. "Whether or not a bone is burned during cooking depends of course on how meat is cooked, and whether, say, bone in meat broiled over a fire will be burned depends on whether the bone is exposed to the heat" (Lyman 1994:216). If consumption was the only activity at *Aetokremnos*, it appears unusual that so much *Phanourios* is burned, no matter what methods of cooking were used. For example, if complete or near complete animals were roasted, we might not expect to find a high degree of burning. As has been pointed out by Gifford-Gonzalez (1989:193), different types of cooking might just char exposed articular surfaces of a bone, as soft tissues protect the rest of the bone from burning. Conversely, when entire bones are burned, as with some of the *Aetokremnos* materials, the flesh has probably already been removed. To burn as much bone as exists at *Aetokremnos* solely by cooking seems unlikely, even if tastes ran to well-done hippo steaks.

In conclusion, the huge amount of *Phanourios* and other bone that is burned cannot satisfactorily be explained by natural causes. Coupled with the other arguments advanced in this chapter, the most parsimonious explanation is that it is the result of cultural activity. The range of thermal alternation at *Aetokremnos* is interesting, as it indicates possible functional differences in the use of *Phanourios* (and other fauna), which is addressed more fully in Chapter 13.

Cutmarks

In a faunal assemblage of over 500 hippopotami, one might expect to find evidence of butchery marks if humans were consuming these animals, as proposed here. Such marks appear to be absent on the *Aetokremnos* fauna. Olsen (see Chap. 9), an expert on butchery marks on archaeofaunas, examined several thousand *Phanourios* bones and was not able to identify any clearly butchered bone to her satisfaction. Although the entire assemblage was not examined, if such marks occurred, it seems that they would have been apparent on this sample. Given the huge size of the assemblage, it was reasonable to expect some evidence of cutmarks, but this simply appears to be absent. Thus the apparent contradictory evidence of a huge faunal assemblage with no cutmarks requires careful examination.

First, a definition of butchering is required. Although many authors have described it in different ways, we use Lyman's definition of *butchering* as "the human reduction and modification of an animal carcass into consumable parts" (Lyman 1987:252). Having an acceptable definition of butchering, one must then ask "does all butchering leave cutmarks?"

There is an enormous, and contradictory, literature on the issue of butchery involving cutmarks and other bone modifications in archaeological fauna. Lyman (1994:294–353) provided a thorough summary, and Morlan (1984) discussed rigid criteria for recognizing artificial bone modifications. Although much research has focused on cutmarks, there are, of course, other examples of human modification to bone that have received considerable discussion, including the issue of spiral fractures and other forms of bone breakage, for example. The *Aetokremnos* assemblage, however, was not examined for these modifications. One reason for this is that in spite of excellent preservation, rooffall had crushed many of the bones, thus making an examination of breakage patterns and fractures difficult.

Thus attention here focuses only on cutmarks. After even a brief review of the literature, it rapidly became apparent that one can muster a number of pro or con arguments that explain either the lack or presence of cutmarks. Indeed, after examining much of this literature, I sometimes feel that we are fortunate *not* to have cutmarks, as there is heated debate on whether or not modifications that some archaeologists have identified as cut marks are, in fact, cultural rather than natural. It is clear that there are many instances in which butchery marks may be absent, and that one must be cautious in making any generalizations.

Much of the literature dealing with this issue is concentrated on detecting cutmarks, often with the use of scanning electron microscopes (SEM); on determining whether or not observable marks on bone are the result of human activity or natural agents; or on documenting the way such marks (both human or natural) are produced. More rarely have authors thoroughly discussed the *lack* of cutmarks on presumed archaeofaunas. Because we have no clear cutmarks at *Aetokremnos* (assuming the sample examined by Olsen is representative), however, it is precisely this issue with which we must deal.

An important point must be made here. Although critics may question the apparent absence of cutmarks at *Aetokremnos*, such marks often are relatively rare, even in many well-documented butchery assemblages, because soft tissues frequently shield bone from being marked (Shipman and Rose 1983:86). Indeed, one might consider cutmarks on bone the signature of unskilled and inefficient butchers.

Unfortunately, there are few examples of archaeological instances of hippopotamus butchering in the literature, and virtually none of pygmy hippopotamus. The exception to this is an intriguing article on the extinct Madagascar pygmy hippopotamus (MacPhee and Burney 1991, see later). Of the studies that do exist, many relate to Lower Paleolithic examples of full-sized hippopotami (e.g., Bunn 1982; Hill 1983; Issac 1977, 1978), although there certainly are instances of more recent archaeological associations of hippopotami with cultural materials, including examples from the Levant (Horwitz and Tchernov 1990) and even Cyprus (e.g., Reese 1985). Most of these, however, do not deal explicitly with cutmarks. Hill's (1983) study did examine this issue, but was based on a single bone of extinct *Hippopotamus gorgops* from Olduvai Gorge, where he makes a convincing argument for human modification.

After an exhaustive review, the only observation of cutmarks on an extinct pygmy hippopotamus I could find comes from Madagascar. Here, MacPhee and Burney (1991) reported on four dwarfed hippopotamus (probably *Hippopotamus lemerlei*) bones originally collected by Grandidier (1905). They make a convincing argument that these bones were cut while green with metal implements. The cuts are clustered in the midshaft, usually in the form of a partial or complete ring of incisions. They are long, straight, and planar (MacPhee and Burney 1991:700–701). The authors conducted an experimental study to test the hypothesis that the bone was cut when green rather than dry (or old). They produced cuts with a metal hatchet on a fresh cow femur that mimicked marks found on the hippopotamus. Furthermore, hacking at newly excavated hippopotamus long bones with a bush axe resulted in rapid splintering, but not in the long, straight, planar cuts seen in the Grandidier specimens. Thus MacPhee and Burney conclude that the latter were cut while green with metal implements, noting that it is improbable that stone tools could have produced the types of marks observed on the Grandidier samples (1991:701). Thus there are few parallels to the *Aetokremnos* materials with regard to specific butchering practices. (Other implications of the Madagascaran data will be examined in the next chapter.)

Lacking clear-cut archaeological data, we must turn to ethnographic examples and experimental studies, in which it becomes apparent that cutmarks are not at all a necessary criterion for defining butchery. As with our discussion on natural die sites, elephants once again offer perhaps the closest analogies. Crader (1983:135) has pointed out that the paucity or lack of cutmarks is simply not a very reliable guide for understanding the degree of butchering of many carcasses. There are several variables that can account for this. As but one example, because conarticulated elephant elements can be separated without the need for wedging them apart or cutting into periosteal bone on limb shafts, epiphyses, or articular surfaces, cutmarks should not even be expected (Haynes 1987).

Haynes noted further that:

> one reason mammoth bones may not be cutmarked is that they are not assembled or connected at the joints the same way as bison or deer bones. They are much more easily taken apart without the need for cutting deeply into bone surface. Also, the cartilage is so thick on epiphyses that even deep nicks or cuts do not remain after the soft tissue has decayed. In experimental studies in Africa during culling operations, I have butchered 40 elephants and watched another 600 being butchered by *steel knives* in the field. None of these carcasses had cutmarked bones. (Haynes 1988:148, italic added for emphasis)

Frison provided additional evidence from modern elephant butchery experiments. He noted that "once the thick joint capsule is cut through, which was done with the same quartzite reduction flake used in cutting the hide and stripping the meat, the joint literally fall apart. This can be done leaving no cut marks on the bone" (Frison 1989:778).

It is significant that in many modern examples of elephant butchering using steel tools, cutmarks still may be absent. If steel tools often do not produced cutmarks, how likely is it that stone ones will? During the intense African herd culling that Haynes summarized, experienced culling crews did not, deliberately or accidentally, cut bones. Other, less experienced butchery crews, however, did leave bones deeply chopped and cutmarked

(Haynes 1991:185). Even in his own experiments, disarticulating femora and humeri did not produce cutmarks, despite the fact that

> I did cut against epiphyses at times to force the knife edge through connective tissue. Articular cartilage is thick on elephant limbs, and when it had decayed on the elements that I disarticulated, even knife marks that had appeared to be deep were no longer preserved. The cortical bone surface itself has never preserved cut marks. I have also examined hundred of ribs, vertebrae, and innominates at cull sites where experienced crews butchered carcasses, and none were cut-marked. (Haynes 1991:186)

The examples cited above all involve elephants. Unfortunately, there are fewer explicit accounts of modern hippopotamus butchery, at least from ethnoarchaeological perspectives. Part of the reason for this may be due to the fact that have not been culled as extensively as have elephants. Crader (1983) provided one of the rare examples in her interesting examination of single carcass bone scatters of elephants and hippopotami in the Nabwalya region of Zambia. Of the four hippopotamus sites she examined, only one was a possible butchery site. She believes the latter reflected a rapid butchery event. Crader identified three classes of butchery marks: cutmarks, chop marks, and shear faces, all of which were produced by metal implements. None of the hippopotamus bones at the one butchery site had cutmarks, although chop marks and shear faces were present on some bone. Crader attributed this to hasty butchering (Crader 1983:134–135).

Thus far, attention has focused on the process of butchering and cutmarks. A related issue involves cooking processes. *Cooking* includes the preparation of food for eating by boiling, roasting, baking, etc. (cf. Marshall 1989:17). Clearly, how an animal is cooked can relate to how it is butchered. If, for example, *Phanourios* were roasted whole at *Aetokremnos*, there may have been little need for butchering so invasive as to scar the bone, since the meat could have been pulled apart at articular joints with minimal cutting of tissue.

In summary, the lack of clear butchery marks on the *Aetokremnos* fauna is not of grave concern. This is a fact of the data with which we must deal. A review of the ethnographic and experimental literature indicates that the presence of such marks is highly variable and is largely dependent on the methods used in butchery as well as the skill of the butcherers. There are many scenarios that can explain the absence of butchery marks at *Aetokremnos:*

- There was sufficient meat obtained at one time, relative to human group requirements, so that the animals were not fully processed. This is particularly true if the butchering was not being done efficiently, a possible condition if *Phanourios* were locally abundant and, being unaccustomed to any predators, were "easy" kills.
- An animal such as a *Phanourios* had abundant meat, and efficient butchering that might result in cutmarks was unnecessary.
- The techniques used in butchering and cooking did not require cutmarks.
- The preservation of the bones is too poor to show cutmarks.
- The tools used for butchering were not of the type that typically would result in cutmarks, which is the next issue to examine.

Artifact Assemblage

An issue related to cutmarks involves the *Aetokremnos* chipped stone assemblage. Essentially, the argument is that an assemblage dominated by small thumbnail scrapers is an unlikely one for use in a hippopotamus butchering/processing site. These tools are simply too small and the chopping or hacking implements one might expect with such a function are absent.

In the preceding section, we have demonstrated that the lack of cutmarks is not a convincing argument against the cultural nature of *Aetokremnos*. Can an argument now be made that the implements from the site could have functioned as efficient *Phanourios* processing tools? We believe that the answer to this is yes. Of course, it will be recalled that the majority of chipped stone occurs in Stratum 2, not Stratum 4, which contains most of the *Phanourios* remains. We have already shown, however (in Chap. 6), that the assemblage from Stratum 2 is not different from Stratum 4; thus, we feel confident in asserting that the site's assemblage was used for similar functions throughout its occupation. Another important observation to keep in mind is that raw material availability may, to some extent, have dictated the overall small size of chipped stone implements at *Aetokremnos*.

The problem of equating chipped stone function with typology is, of course, something that has occupied considerable attention in the archaeological literature. There is little consensus in determining which type of implements could have performed certain tasks. Specialized studies, such as blood or other residues on chipped stone, also have not always proven convincing (e.g., Eisele *et al.* 1995; Fiedel 1996).

One compelling argument that the *Aetokremnos* assemblage could easily have functioned as *Phanourios* processing implements comes from an important work by Frison (1989), in which he demonstrated the facility of butchering modern African elephants with the simplest of chipped stone implements. He also noted that perishable components of butchery might not be preserved in the archaeological record (Frison 1989:768). Although much of his experimental work was directed toward demonstrating the efficiency of Clovis points and atlatl and dart weaponry (Frison 1989:768–777), the section of most interest here related to butchery of deceased animals. The main effort in elephant butchering is cutting the hide. In his experiment, the tools that Frison used in butchering experiments were large biface reduction flakes, which performed their tasks adequately, although not as efficiently as a metal knife. These chipped stone tools also had to be resharpened frequently. Once the necessary cuts were made in the hide, its removal was relatively easy and required little resharpening of tools (Frison 1989:777–779; Frison and Todd 1986:128–134). Frison's observation is important with regard to *Aetokremnos*, as the site contains an abundance of microflakes, which could represent resharpening activities and thus initial hide processing as well as subsequent removal.

In another experimental study, Frison again demonstrated that "butchering in known communal procurement sites was accomplished with the simplest of both tool assemblages and processes of carcass handling" (Frison 1979:260). He pointed out that the greatest differences in tool use in butchering is often determined by the size of the animal. In this study, he butchered a bison calf (about 350 lb, which may be roughly comparable to *Phanourios*) in a short period of time with light tools. Larger animals, such as an adult bison, were more difficult to handle, although it was still possible to butcher these with simple cutting tools. This task, however, was facilitated by the addition of simple chopping and breaking tools (Frison 1979:260). As with the African experiment, Frison noted that in processing, a sharp tool is initially desirable for cutting open the hide, but once this is done, a duller implement can be used in subsequent skinning (Frison 1979:261).

The implements used by Frison in the African experiment (1989) were "large biface reduction flakes." Their dimensions were not provided. In the bison experiment, Frison used two chipped stone implements. One was a "skinning knife" 15.1 cm long, while the other was a unmodified flake. No measurements were given for the second artifact, although from the illustration, it appears to be 6–7 cm long (Frison 1979:263–263, Fig. 5). At *Aetokremnos*, we lack direct analogues for such implements (with the exception of the unmodified flake), and overall the assemblage is small in size. It is not, however, so small as to preclude efficient butchery.

There is ample archaeological evidence of the use of small, unspecialized tools associated with presumed kill or butchery sites. It is particularly well documented in North American Paleo-Indian sites (e.g., Frison 1991, especially pp. 289–325). For example, at the Horner site in Wyoming, Frison (1987) noted that the tool assemblage is comprised largely of flakes, many of which are relatively small. At this site, Todd *et al.* (1987:49) noted the relatively short average length (<40 mm) of a sample of tools and debitage. For comparison, at *Aetokremnos* the mean length of blades is 44.2 mm, 28.9 for flakes, and 24.9 for thumbnail scrapers. An interesting parallel to *Aetokremnos* at the Horner Site is the presence of very small end scrapers, some of which resemble thumbnail forms. Many of those illustrated are under 30 mm in length, and the smallest is roughly 15 mm (Frison 1987:245–249, Fig. 7.11).

Other examples of the use of small implements in presumed butchering activities are provided by Guthrie (1990:281), who noted that in Alaska, bison dating to circa 11,000 B.P. is found in association with microblades often less than 2 cm long. He suggested that these could have been composite tools used in cutting. Guthrie (1990:283) noted that further evidence of the use of such small tools comes from Siberia, where composite projectile points of reindeer antler and microblades were found in bison scapula (Abramova 1982), and from northern Germany (Bosinski 1981). Such microblades, as well as small bifacial points and small burins, are characteristic of assemblages in extreme north North America and Siberia at the end of the Pleistocene.

We must, however, be cautious about assigning too much importance to the use of extremely small (microlithic) tools, presumably hafted. Frison (1979:262, 1991: 314–315) noted that hafted tools were not always efficient, as the "blood and guts" involved in butchering can effect the binding and damage a tool. He believed that "it is much easier and efficient to use a simple non-hafted tool that is short-lived but quite functional" (Frison 1979:262).

A study of Mousterian assemblages from Italy (Kuhn 1991, 1993; Stiner and Kuhn 1992:322–328) also is relevant here. Kuhn demonstrated that at sites with prolonged occupations in which entire carcasses were introduced into caves, the chipped stone assemblages tended to be associated with less-intensive tool reduction and greater reliance on immediately available raw materials. One observation potentially pertinent to *Aetokremnos* was as follows:

> More stable residential patterns would entail less reliance on transported toolkits, reducing the need to repeatedly renew a limited toolkit and making it less beneficial to produce the largest possible tool blanks. . . . [I]t might well have been possible to stockpile scarce pebble raw materials at residential locations and to employ numerically more productive platform core reduction techniques to make smaller blanks destined for light use and little transport. . . . [T]he processing of animal carcasses might also have created a special demand for unretouched or lightly resharpened edges. (Kuhn 1993:29)

At *Aetokremnos,* we have evidence for a roughly similar sort of technological strategy. Although there is evidence for resharpening, many of the artifacts are small and would appear to fit within the type of scenario described by Kuhn. Furthermore, good raw material may have been at a premium on the Akrotiri Peninsula.

In examining *Aetokremnos,* we also must consider that possibility that the assemblage is not representative, consisting primarily of discards, as Held (1989a:9) has observed. Although this is possible, given that the entire site was excavated, we have as representative an assemblage as exists.

Another observation is that the assemblage from *Aetokremnos* undoubtedly was not used exclusively in the processing of *Phanourios.* There are other fauna elements present that the assemblage also would have to accommodate. For example, the large number of burins, and possibly burin spalls, may reflect a usage related to marine shell processing, as these implements could have effectively pried open the shell lips. The majority of these implements occur in Stratum 2, which contains the majority of shell as well.

A final point to recognize is that the chipped stone assemblage from *Aetokremnos* is unique to Cyprus. Thus far, nothing like it has been documented, so one cannot make the argument that the tools and other chipped stone artifacts that occur with *Phanourios* are simply fortuitous, representing intrusive items from a later occupation. The implication here would be that this later occupation was from a period already documented on the island, which is clearly not the case, particularly in light of the radiocarbon dates. Even if this scenario were correct, the "later occupation" would still be something that has not previously been observed on Cyprus. That such a coincidence would occur is highly unlikely.

The point of this discussion is that there are ample examples of the use of small, unsophisticated chipped stone implements that apparently functioned quite well as butchery tools. The assemblage from *Aetokremnos* easily fits within a multifunctional use pattern in which butchering was a major activity. Certainly, the preponderance of scrapers at the site suggests intense skinning and hide-scraping activities. Although it is naive to suggest that archaeologists' typologies connote direct function, certain correlations do seem clear. As Frison and Bradley (1980:128) have noted, "End scrapers are still probably the best stone tools for scraping hides." The combination of thumbnail scrapers, other scrapers, and sharp flakes and blades at *Aetokremnos* would have made up an efficient *Phanourios* processing kit. They also could have served similar functions with the other mammalian fauna, such as elephants and birds. Other implements, such as burins and perhaps the few microliths, could have functioned in the processing of smaller fauna, such as marine shells.

Frison's (1979:262) obvious, but perhaps often overlooked, observation that butchering covers a wide range of tool use is relevant here. As he noted, "The possibilities for butchering a bison are many; the emphasis on tool types are, likewise, many. It is possible to use a simple flaked tool and butcher an entire bison. In fact, once a person butchers one in this manner it is tempting to adopt this as a method which some groups apparently did" (Frison 1979:261).

Finally, one also must remember that there are other artifacts present at *Aetokremnos* beyond chipped stone. The very undiagnostic igneous pebbles could have been used for a variety of functions related to pounding or breaking bone. There also are numerous ornaments present that clearly have nothing to do with food processing. We can only explain their presence as perhaps broken necklaces worn by the occupants of the site as they went about their business of processing *Phanourios.*

CONCLUSION

When one examines all of the disparate data sources from *Aetokremnos*, there appears little doubt of the direct relationship between humans and *Phanourios*. Taken individually, there might be some question, but collectively all of the data point to the same inevitable conclusion. What is somewhat ironic at *Aetokremnos* is that if the site were located on the mainland, fell within an established cultural historical framework, and contained, say, sheep instead of pygmy hippopotami, few would even give second thought to the direct relationship. It is, of course, incumbent on us to justify our claims for the association of humans and *Phanourios*. Some critics have claimed that the relationship is circumstantial. Of course it is, as are most archaeological interpretations. One must make reasoned arguments based on a careful consideration of the hard data. That is the nature of archaeological inquiry. Given the constellation of evidence, however, to claim that there is no relationship between people and *Phanourios* requires as much justification as the converse.

Our justification for the direct relationship between people and an extinct Pleistocene species is summarized below. Lyman (1994:216–219) cited the following commonly used criteria to distinguish cultural and natural bone: burning or charring; bone comminution; mineralization, weathering, and staining; butchering and technology marks; ethnological analogy; skeletal completeness; and context and associations. How well does *Aetokremnos* meet these criteria?

There is little question that much of the bone from *Aetokremnos* is burned. Burning is not restricted solely to *Phanourios*, but includes all species represented. The degree and intensity of burning, as well as stratigraphic associations, rules out accidental, postdepositional causes.

Comminution, or small fragmentation, of bone, can result by boiling it to extract grease (Lyman 1994:217). This does not necessarily require that the bone fragments be burned. At *Aetokremnos*, much of the bone is both comminuted and burned. A condition that is not direct evidence for grease extraction, but strongly suggestive of cultural intervention. Furthermore, the fragmentation of some of the bone (e.g., Stratum 4A) could have been at least partially caused by trampling, as noted earlier (Stiner *et al.* 1995:229–230).

The degree of weathering, mineralization, or staining of bones can vary between naturally and culturally deposited bone. Lyman (1994:217) noted that cultural bone should be more heavily weathered than natural bone. At *Aetokremnos*, there is little variation in the degree of weathering on the bone, with the exception of the heavily mineralized specimens that occur on the surface. This weathering pattern includes not only *Phanourios*, but all of the bone, and suggests a consistent mode of deposition.

Clear cutmarks or other modifications to bone obviously are an indication of a human agency, either for butchering or the production of bone tools or ornaments. At *Aetokremnos*, such marks are absent, and only one *Phanourios* bone was modified. Lyman (1994:218) noted, however, that not all culturally deposited faunal remains will possess these traits.

Ethnographic analogy is useful in interpreting archaeofaunas, but has at least two problems. First, ethnozoological data may be ambiguous, and, second, cultures evolve and change, so what people were consuming when ethnographic data were compiled may not be what the ancestors of those people consumed (Lyman 1994:218). We have relied heavily on ethnographic and wildlife data, not so much for whether or not people consume hippopotami (they clearly do), but rather to indicate the range of variation in deposition and butchering processes.

The completeness of skeletal elements represented at a site may give a clue to human involvement. There is, however, a considerable behavioral range involved in the ways that people process and consume animals; they do not always accumulate and deposit only portions of carcasses, for example (Lyman 1994:218). At *Aetokremnos*, complete, or nearly complete, *Phanourios* skeletal elements are present. Although one could argue that this indicates a natural deposition, one could just as well argue that it reflects processing and consumption patterns.

Finally, context and associations are critical is assessing the relationship of human and animal remains. Lyman's comments on this are worth repeating in detail here:

> Variously burned, comminuted, mineralized, and butchered bone is readily believed to have been modified and deposited by cultural processes when such bones are associated with undisputed evidence of hominids, such as artifacts. . . . The combined attributes of burning, fragmentation, similar mineralization or staining across multiple specimens, butchery marks, and association with artifacts, all point to the same accumulation agent. As more of these attributes fail to be present, the inferences that the remains represent culturally accumulated bone progressively weakens. (Lyman 1994:218–219)

In light of these observations, the evidence overwhelmingly points to a cultural origin for the *Aetokremnos* fauna, including not only the pygmy hippopotamus but also the dwarf elephant, birds, and other faunal materials.

In addition, we also offer the following arguments as to why the *Phanourios* accumulation at *Aetokremnos* is *not* natural:

- There is no geological evidence for a sinkhole.
- There is no geomorphic evidence for sources of *Phanourios* from outside of shelters (e.g., water movement, erosion).
- The precipitous location of *Aetokremnos* argues against the natural accumulation of *Phanourios* in the shelter, even for such a "mountain"-adapted species.
- If *Aetokremnos* were a natural mass die site, one would expect to find aged/sick individuals. This is not the case; 27% of the *Phanourios* individuals analyzed are under one year old.
- The lack of vertical spreading of the *Phanourios* remains argues against a mass die site.
- There are no features on the cliffs or plateau above *Aetokremnos* to account for a repeated natural jump site.
- The shelter probably never was large enough to offer abundant protection from the elements. There is nothing about the location of *Aetokremnos* to make it particularly attractive to *Phanourios* as a place to accumulate.
- Why would only *Aetokremnos* be occupied by *Phanourios* when other shelters were nearby?
- None of the faunal remains are articulated. There is no evidence in Cyprus for scavengers or predators prior to the arrival of man. Lacking these, as well as geological evidence for disturbance, one must account for the disarticulation in some other (i.e., cultural) manner.

- If the *Phanourios* fell off the cliffs over time, resulting in an accretional deposit at *Aetokremnos*, why are they concentrated only in the shelter and not elsewhere in the site's area? Furthermore, how could they have fallen off the cliffs to a resting location *inside* the shelter?
- If the *Phanourios* did fall off the cliffs, why is there no lateral spread of their remains along the cliff, both above and below the site?

In conclusion, we feel that the evidence overwhelmingly supports the direct association of *Phanourios* with cultural activities at *Aetokremnos*. This is demonstrated by:

- Dense accumulation of over 500 individuals with the small confines of a rockshelter.
- Near total disarticulation of all faunal remains.
- Burning of about 30% of the *Phanourios* remains.
- The high amount of phosphorous in Stratum 4 (and Stratum 2); it is unlikely that a natural deposit of bone would be so high in phosphorous.
- "Clean" floor of shelter—no accumulation of sediments between floor and *Phanourios* suggests a prepared floor.
- Virtual contemporaneity of Stratum 2 and Stratum 4, based on abundant radiocarbon determinations.
- Presence of artifacts directly associated with *Phanourios.*
- Presence of an assemblage never before described in Cyprus
- Presence of cultural features.
- The stratigraphic integrity of Strata 2 and 4 argues against mixing.
- Presence of other associated fauna, including an inverse stratigraphic relationship in number of birds to *Phanourios.*

Although a few of these observations alone might be problematic, the constellation of evidence provides overwhelming evidence for a direct association between humans and *Phanourios* beyond reasonable doubt. Occam's Razor dictates this as the most parsimonious explanation. Given this association, it is no small wonder that the endemic fauna of Cyprus might have become bitter indeed on their first, and apparently brief, exposure to humans.

Chapter *13*

The Function of Akrotiri
Aetokremnos *and Its Place in*
Colonization and Extinction Events

Ku ala tomu, u tunamanine
(Look at the hippo, he is dead)
—Lozi-western Zambia-myth, Prins 1980:126

INTRODUCTION

In the preceding chapter, we argued for the association of humans and fauna at *Aetokremnos*. In this final chapter, we discuss the site's probable function and examine broader issues, including the possible origins of the "Akrotiri Phase" and the implications of *Aetokremnos* for extinction and colonization studies. In order to provide a proper context, we first discuss behavioral inferences for *Phanourios* and how they relate to the site.

BEHAVIORAL ASPECTS OF *PHANOURIOS*

There are few pygmy hippopotami existing today. These bear little resemblance to the extinct forms, of which *Phanourios* was one, making it difficult to reconstruct behavioral patterns. This is unfortunate because studies of animal behavior can contribute significantly to our understanding of how humans manipulated and exploited them. In this section, we summarize what little is known of the habits of extinct pygmy hippopotami. We also discuss modern forms as possible analogues for some basic behavioral characteristics of extinct pygmy hippopotami. We do this with some trepidation, realizing the dangers of loosely formed analogies. Some insight, however, might be gained into the *Aetokremnos* hippopotami by examining certain behavioral proclivities of modern forms.

Before doing so, we may ask, Is there any behavioral information available for *Phanourios* or any of the other dwarfed extinct forms of hippopotami? Unfortunately, most available data refer only to physical characteristics, and only very limited generalizations exist regarding behavior.

The specialized foot and leg bones of *Phanourios* indicate that it was well adapted to mountainous terrain. It was, in fact, better adapted to walking than swimming. Having no natural predator, these animals did not have to be fast runners, and their short legs gave them better stability in the rugged environment characteristic of many of the Mediterranean islands (Boekshoten and Sondaar 1972:335–336; Sondaar 1986:53–54). Sondaar (1986:54) also suggested that their short legs allowed the Mediterranean dwarf ruminants (including *Phanourios*) to carry extra seasonal weight. Although we know very little of the diet of these animals, Boekshoten and Sondaar (1972:335–336) believed that *Phanourios* may have had different requirements from the grasses of other hippopotami, subsisting instead on weeds and leaves from small shrubs. They make this observation based on *Phanourios* dentition and concluded that "the odontology and the morphology of *Phanourios* suggests a mode of living like a leaf-eating pig" (Boekshoten and Sondaar 1972:336).

Thus it appears that *Phanourios* may have been more terrestrially adapted than modern common hippopotami. As such, it probably was not directly tied to permanent sources of water, paralleling the modern pygmy hippopotamus. Its diet, however, may have differed from both (i.e., common and pygmy) modern forms.

One critical behavioral element that is lacking for *Phanourios* is information on group composition. This is important as it has implications for hunting strategies. It also is one of the most distinct behavioral differences between modern forms of hippopotami: The common hippopotamus (*Hippopotamus amphibius*) is a herd animal, while the pygmy hippopotamus (*Choerposis liberiensis* [Morton]) is a solitary animal. Is any herd information available for extinct forms of pygmy hippopotami? Many of the paleontological sites in Cyprus contain the remains of numerous individuals (although not approaching the proportion seen at *Aetokremnos*), but the context of these is questionable and may represent accretional accumulations rather than individual "herds."

Some recent hints at extinct pygmy hippopotamus behavior have emerged from intriguing research being undertaken in Madagascar. Here, at the "Hippo Site," excavation of a 2-sq-m area produced partial skeletons of at least eight individuals. These included five adults and three immatures. Additional individuals also are present in unexcavated portions of the site. The remains from the excavated area were partially articulated, and the investigators believe that a herd of hippopotami became trapped in the cave and died together. There was, incidentally, no evidence of human involvement in the death of these animals (Burney *et al.* 1997). The implications of the Madagascar material are significant. They suggest that at least on that island, pygmy hippopotami existed in small herds, unlike their modern counterparts.

For additional information on behavioral characteristics, we must turn to the modern hippopotamus. It is, of course, dangerous to reconstruct behavior of an extinct species on the basis of living related forms, thus what follows must be considered as being very generalized. There is, of course, a huge amount of information that exists on modern hippopotami in the natural history and African ecology literature (see Dorst and Dandelot 1970:171–173; Estes 1991:222–226; Frädrich 1967; Frädrich and Lang 1972; Verheyen 1954; and Walker 1975 for thorough summaries). Here we only present some basic information that might shed at least some insight into the behavioral proclivities of *Phanourios*. Our task is rendered more difficult by the fact that there are two extant species of hippopotamus, the common hippopotamus and the pygmy hippopotamus, and, unfortunately, they share few behavioral characteristics. Thus, while the temptation is to compare *Phanourios* to the modern pygmy hippopotamus, this cannot be done directly. *Phanourios* has characteristics distinct from either form of modern hippopotamus (particularly in locomotion), and although it shares some similarities with the modern pygmy hippopotamus, it actually is more closely related to the large animal, at least skeletally (Boekschoten and Sondaar 1972:326–331; Reese 1975a; Sondaar 1986:53).

Relatively little is known of the modern pygmy hippopotamus. It is important to note that *Choeropsis* is not a proper dwarfed species, and despite its common name, it is not simply a proportional dwarf of the common hippopotamus; indeed, it belongs to a different genus (Reese 1975:65). There are notable structural differences in the shape of the head, dentition, and feet (Walker 1975:1370). Much of the following is taken from three works describing *Choeropsis* (Dorst and Dandelot 1970:172–173, Frädrich and Lang 1972, and Walker 1975:1367–1368, 1370), realizing that so little is known of these animals that different authors often provide different information.

Given the controversial nature of *Aetokremnos*, it is perhaps ironic that the very existence of modern pygmy hippopotami was initially questioned. It is worth a small diversion to briefly examine the history of their documentation to the western world. The first scientific description of the pygmy hippopotamus appeared in 1841, although it took fifty years to resolve its status. The vice-president of the Philadelphia Academy of Natural Sciences, Dr. Samuel Morton, had heard from a traveler of a little hippopotamus from the inland rivers of Liberia. It was said that this animal was hunted for its meat, and the traveler had not only seen it, but also tasted it. Dr. Morton, however, was rather skeptical about the story, but in 1843, his friend Dr. Goheen sent him a set of mammals' skulls from Monrovia, which included two skulls similar to a hippopotamus, but much smaller. He described them in 1849, naming the species *Hippopotamus liberiensis*, but his colleague Joseph Leidy soon demonstrated that it was so different in size and teeth characteristics from the ordinary hippopotamus that is deserved to be a new genus, *Choeropsis*. Despite these two skulls, however, most scientists still denied its existence (Heuvelmans 1995:23–24, originally 1955).

Initially the pygmy hippopotamus was believed to be just an extremely small species of the common hippopotamus. Professor Sir Richard Owen, a distinguished British paleontologist and fervent disciple of Georges Cuvier, the French zoologist often credited with establishing the science of paleontology, did not believe in the existence of a separate genus for this animal. Owen was "a man who could deny evidence when it was before his eyes, and, unfortunately, like Cuvier's, his word was taken as gospel" (Heuvelmans 1995:24). Despite this dogmatic view, however, evidence, often in the form of living specimens, gradually accumulated that the Liberian pygmy hippopotamus was, indeed, distinct from the common hippopotamus.

Around 1870, a young pygmy hippopotamus, which weighed barely 15 kg, was sent to the Dublin Zoo, where it lived for several weeks. In 1879 and 1886, the Swiss zoologist Johann Büttikofer made observations on live pygmy hippopotami in Liberia and returned to Europe with several skulls and skeletons "in a rather poor state" (Heuvelmans 1995:24). In 1912, the German explorer Hans Schomburgk was able to capture five live specimens for the animal trader Carl Hagenbeck in Stellingen (Frädrich and Lang 1972). The feat was not achieved easily. At first, local Liberians refused to help Schomburgk, thinking he was mad to want to capture such a monster, which they described as a *nigbve,* thought to be a very fierce black pig with teeth sharp enough to cut a person in two. Some people apparently felt that this creature might have been the pygmy hippopotamus, except that it was known that the *nigbve* was a forest dweller and, by definition, hippopotami were aquatic, and even by this time, the existence of pygmy hippopotami had not been firmly established (Heuvelmans 1995:47–48). Ultimately, however, Schomburgk was able to persuade the locals to help and

> after months of searching, he came upon the creature 10m away in the forest. It was a shiny black and did look like a big pig, but it was obviously related to a hippopotamus. Unfortunately, Schomburgk—who was the first white man to see a pygmy hippopotamus in its natural surroundings—had no means ready to catch it and had scruples about shooting an animal which was thought to be extinct and was certainly very rare. . . . Back in Monrovia no one believed his story: the *nigbve* was a mere superstition, or at best a legend based on a long- extinct animal . . . he had to return to Hamburg empty-handed. But now he knew he was not hunting a myth, and by Christmas 1912 he was in Liberia again. This time he was luckier. On 28 February 1913, having made sure that the species was much less rare than he had thought, he shot the first specimen. The next day he managed to capture one alive and found that . . . it was actually much easier to tame than an ordinary hippopotamus. . . . Five months later Hans Schomburgk confounded the sceptics [sic] by bringing back five live pygmy hippopotami. . . . [He] thus proved that at least one native legend was well-founded. (Heuvelmans 1995:48–50, 429)

So, at the beginning of the twentieth century, there were at least a score of skeletal samples plus some captive live specimens. Despite this, several naturalists still thought *Choeropsis* was more or less mythical, some alleging it was just a young hippopotamus or an individual freak. One natural history museum even classified a badly mounted specimen with the fossils, thus denying its current existence (Heuvelmans 1995:24).

Since that time, however, the scientific community has accepted the existence of these enigmatic creatures. Much of what we know of the pygmy hippopotamus has been made from observations in zoos. They are presently rare, even in their home range in West Africa, where they are still hunted for their meat (Frädrich and Lang 1972:110). They are classified as "rare" by the International Union for the Conservation of Nature and Natural Resources (Delany and Happold 1979:386).

The pygmy hippopotamus is a hippolike creature, but, as noted earlier, not at all a mere reduction of the common hippopotamus. It is more piglike, about the size of a wild boar. It body is massive, but lightly built; it is almost torpedo shaped. The legs are short and sturdy, and its head is comparatively smaller and rounder than that of the common hippopotamus. Its height at the shoulder varies from 50 to 100 cm; its length is between 150–175 cm, and its tail length is about 16 cm. Weight ranges from approximately 180–270 kg. At birth, they weigh 3 to 4.5 kg (Walker 1975:1368, 1370). The body is naked, with hair only at the ears, on the upper lips, and on the tassel. They can feed under water as well as on land, and their diet consists of aquatic plants, leaves of bushes, algae, shoots, fallen fruits, and short grass. The gestation period is 190–210 days, and they have a life span of 17 to 40 years. Unlike the common hippopotamus, the pygmy hippopotamus is not gregarious. They never live in herds, but singly or in pairs, although Frädrich and

Lang (1972:116) noted that they can occur in "small families." Another major dissimilarity from the common hippopotamus is that *Choeropsis* is not aquatic; rather they generally live in streams, dense wet forests, and swamps (Walker 1975:1367, 1370). They do, however, usually stay near water (Estes 1991:223). They are nocturnal, as is the common hippopotamus. At night, they wander along fixed paths through the undergrowth that with time comes to resemble tunnels. They are good swimmers, but are far less aquatic than their huge relative (Dorst and Dandelot 1970:172–173; Frädrich and Lang 1972:110).

The pygmy hippopotamus is difficult to observe in the wild, as are many animals living in forests. Some researchers have noted that if pursued, they take refuge in dense thickets, but more recent information is contradictory. For example, two collectors who in the 1960s managed to capture several pygmy hippopotami indicated just the opposite—when the pygmies encountered people, they fled immediately into the nearest river or swamp (Frädrich and Lang 1972:114). Virtually nothing is known of aggressive behavior in the pygmy hippopotamus, although it is assumed to be similar to that of the common hippopotamus (see later) (Leuthold 1977:128). Walker (1975:1370) noted that they are not unduly vicious, but that they can be dangerous if disturbed.

Pygmy hippopotami do very well in captivity (Frädrich and Lang 1972:115). Whether or not this is the case in the wild is unknown, but the common hippopotamus, when protected in reserves, can become so numerous that they cause severe environmental deterioration and habitat change (Delany and Happold 1979:46). The damage they cause includes reduction of grass cover, erosion of soil, and increase in the number and density of scrubby bushes that previously were prevented from spreading by grass fire (Delany and Happold 1979:129–130; Owen-Smith 1988:233–234).

The pygmy hippopotamus becomes quite tame in captivity (Frädrich and Lang 1972:116), as the explorer Schomburgk noted on their discovery (Heuvelmans 1995:50). There is no suggestion that they were or could be domesticated, but their "shy" and tame nature may have archaeological implications in terms of hunting strategies.

In contrast to the pygmy hippopotamus, the common hippopotamus has quite different behavioral patterns. They are, of course, much larger, and can weight up to 3,200 kg. The common hippopotamus is an aquatic animal, unlike *Choeropsis*, and is an excellent swimmer and diver. They spend practically the entire day sleeping and resting in or near water. They also are equally at home in fresh or salt water (Walker 1975:1367–1369). Like the pygmy hippopotamus, they are nocturnal, but they also are quite gregarious and territorial. Even in times of temporary food shortages, they do not migrate (Frädrich and Lang 1972:117). They live in herds of 5–15, sometimes up to 30, which during certain seasons may join together in even larger herds. Females form "schools" with their young (Dorst and Dandelot 1970:171; Leuthold 1977:209–210; Walther 1984:4). Some researchers, however, have observed groups with several adult males as well (Olivier and Laurie 1974). Of interest is that these groups tend to remain fairly constant over periods of a month or two. During times of stress, however, such as when rivers dry up, animals may be forced together in aggregations of up to 150 individuals (Owen-Smith 1988:104).

It is difficult to obtain accurate data reflecting age and sex structure of hippopotamus herds, although some information is available as the result of culling activities. In a sample of 585 hippopotami of both sexes shot in the Luangwa River in Zambia, 78% were over age 10 (i.e., adult), while of 225 culled in the Kruger Park in South Africa, 68% were adult. These figures may be somewhat skewed, as young individuals are difficult to shoot and retrieve from the water, so an overestimation of adults may be the result (Owen-Smith 1988:203).

Common hippopotami are bulk and roughage eaters, or grazers, and need to drink fairly regularly (Leuthold 1977:22). They are an aquatic animal, although they are not what Frädrich and Lang (1972:117) referred to as "a high performance swimmer but rather, as H. Hediger put it, a 'fresh water' buoy." These animals prefer water that is only about $1^{1}/_{2}$ m deep and areas with little or no current. At night, they will leave the water and come to land to feed. They will travel up to 7 km from their river or lake homes for this activity (Delany and Happold 1979:124). During feeding, they often travel solitarily or in very small groups of females with one or more young (Owen-Smith 1988:104). Like the smaller versions, they create well-worn trails and defecation/marking sites, which attest to the frequent use of the same paths to move to and from nocturnal feeding areas, implying considerable regularity in these movements (Hediger 1951; Verheyen 1954).

Due to their large size, hippopotami have few predators. Although they can be aggressive, much of their defensive behavior is more in the form of threats rather than actual aggression, and they apparently have not developed a ritualized fighting technique (Leuthold 1977:128–129). Threatening behavior includes wide-open mouths (which also can simply be yawning). During this particular threat posture, the hippopotamus is said to belch malodorous intestinal gas in the direction of its opponent (Walther 1984:208); oral tradition from Madagascar also notes the destructive power of "awesome flatulence" from possibly extant pygmy hippopotami (Burney and Ramilisonina 1998:961). Hippopotami also do fight, however, and can cause great damage to one another or other animals (Frädrich and Lang 1972:119; Leuthold 1977:128–129). They also are known to attack humans with little or no provocation, although they usually do so when escape routes are blocked (Frädrich and Lang 1972:127).

Although hippopotami appear to breed at all times of the year, many give birth during the wet season months. For example, in the Kruger Park in South Africa, 70% of births occur during October–March, with a peak in January–February. In Uganda, the peaks are in October and April, during the early rains (Owen-Smith 1988:118).

Population density among hippopotami varies considerably. Densities of 18 animals per sq km have been recorded along the shorelines of Lakes Edward and George in Uganda and Zaire, but local concentrations reached effective densities of up to 31 per sq km. Under these high densities, grassland degradation occurred. Along an 88-km section of the Nile River above Murchison Falls in Uganda, density averaged 19 per sq km, with peaks of 26. Along the Semliki River in Zaire, the hippopotamus density was over 10 per sq km, and along the Luangwa River floodplain in Zambia, effective density was about 8 per sq km. Along various rivers in the Kruger Park, densities averaged 1.1 per sq km. (Owen-Smith 1988:223, citing several primary sources). Studies suggest that the potential rate of population increase in hippopotamus exceeds 10% per year (Owen-Smith 1988:214). Note that these figures are for the common hippopotamus, which is aquatic. The figures are tied to water sources, and the effective ecological densities are generally calculated assuming that the grazing range extends 3.2 km from the river or lake margin (Owen-Smith 1988:223). Similar figures for the more terrestrial pygmy hippopotamus are more difficult to obtain.

A final aspect to consider with modern hippopotami is use by humans. This, of course, is not difficult to demonstrate; the ethnographic literature contains many examples of human use of the hippopotamus. The primary use is in the form of food, but hippopotami also have served as status or tribute items. For example, the ceremonial allocation of parts of royal game animals, including hippopotami, to specific office holders as a form of tribute has been documented (Prins 1980:93, 272). In addition, the use of hippopotamus parts, particularly ivory, is well documented, even in the archaeological record. Horwitz and Tchernov (1990), for example, demonstrated such a usage in the Levant since at least the Chalcolithic period. Insoll (1995) documented a similar usage of hippopotamus ivory in trade in medieval Mali.

Use of hippopotamus as food, however, is perhaps more common. They have been hunted for the abundance of their meat and fat (90 kg/average per animal). The flesh is highly prized by many, and the hide is said to make excellent soup. Their teeth also are composed of superior ivory (Walker 1975:1369). It is curious, though, that some groups, at least, apparently do not like the taste of hippopotamus. The Bisa of the Nabwalya region of Zambia claim that they do not hunt hippopotamus, nor do they eat their meat. There is a stigma attached to eating hippopotamus meat, and they claim that it has a terrible odor. They will, however, kill animals that are found raiding their gardens. When confronted with butchery marks on a recently killed hippopotamus, however, an informant admitted that some Bisa did eat hippopotamus meat, but "not his family" (Crader 1983:110–112, 130).

There is apparently little economic value to pygmy hippopotami. Their flesh, however, is prized and is said to taste like that of the wild pig (Walker 1975:1370).

Techniques for butchering and cooking hippopotamus also are quite varied. Crader (1983:130–132) noted the rather sloppy and furtive butchering of hippopotami in Zambia, while Frädrich and Lang (1972:129) cited instances of controlled cropping on a near commercial level, where hippopotamus meat is sold on the market. They suggested the possibility of hippopotamus farms from which regular meat supplies could be obtained, raising hippopotami like pigs, so that they could be bred, raised, and butchered on demand. The hippopotamus, they say, is well suited for this purpose, requiring no special food and needing little space—they can be kept together with many others in a relatively small enclosure. Frädrich and Lang also provide at least one example of cooking techniques, quoting R. Sachs, an assistant to Bernhard Grzimek, the compiler of the massive *Animal Life Encyclopedia*, "Large chunks of hippo meat, which perishes easily in the African climate, are placed on a wire grill over a simple fire and covered. The heat and the smoke preserve the meat and at the same time cover it with a crust that keeps flies from the meat. Meat which has been treated in this manner keeps for several days and is sold on the market as fresh meat" (Frädrich and Lang 1972:129).

Although modern analogues cannot be directly applied to *Phanourios*, a reasonable assumption can be made that some behavioral characteristics also are applicable to the extinct forms. It is clear that both species of modern hippopotami, although possessing considerably different behavioral patterns, share characteristics that make them amenable to human predation. This is particularly true in relation to their relatively restricted territories, the marking of large and obvious trails, and in their predictable behavioral proclivities. Furthermore, the ethnographic literature is full of references to the consumption of hippopotamus. Certainly, there is no reason to suspect that *Phanourios* would not have made for nutritious meals, perhaps even more so than modern hippopotami, if in many ways it resembled a large pig, as Boekshoten and Sondaar (1972:336) believed. They would be especially valued in an island setting like Cyprus, where other protein sources were limited.

SITE FUNCTIONAL INTERPRETATIONS

If one assumes that the association of fauna with cultural materials at *Aetokremnos* is valid, as we believe we have demonstrated, what can we determine regarding the site's function? Does any of the behavioral information discussed earlier, as well as the artifact assemblage and features, provide enough data to generate a functional model?

It seems clear that the primary focus of *Aetokremnos* involved the use of *Phanourios* and other faunal materials. The data, however, do not point toward *Aetokremnos* functioning as a kill site. We believe that the animals were killed elsewhere and brought to the shelter for processing. Given their relatively small size, and the completeness of skeletal elements recovered at the site, we furthermore believe that entire *Phanourios* carcasses were transported to the site. As noted in Chapter 7, there is no evidence of a "Schlepp Effect." Although transporting a several-hundred pound animal may seem like a substantial task, there is ample ethnographic documentation for the movement of large animals or substantial portions thereof. Although there does appear to be a threshold of transportability based on the size of an animal, Crader (1983:138–139) noted that the Bisa of Zambia will carry hippopotamus bones, while this is not the case with elephants. Certainly, the evidence from *Aetokremnos* indicates that moving entire *Phanourios* carcasses was not a major difficulty. The question one must ask, however, is why go through this trouble, instead of simply dismembering preferred portions?

We believe that the answer to this question is that the occupants of *Aetokremnos* used virtually every part of the animal, not only for consumption, but also as secondary products. The early human occupants of Cyprus found themselves in a land with relatively few resources. Although *Phanourios* may have been plentiful, other resources were more scarce, thus an efficient exploitation strategy would have involved using the entire carcass. Lyman (1994:295) tabulated the many carcass parts that are exploitable by humans, as well as various activities directed toward extracting consumable parts. We have summarized these in Table 13-1. This example makes clear that humans can be very efficient in their total utilization of prey animals, and we suggest that this was the case with *Phanourios*.

Even the heads of *Phanourios* contained potentially consumable materials. Stiner (1991:471–474, 1993:152–158) and Stiner and Kuhn (1992:328–330) have graphically and convincingly demonstrated that head parts of ungulates in Middle Paleolithic contexts were important dietary components. They believed that when food energy sources were periodically or seasonally scarce, the high fat content of soft tissues in the head of prey animals could have been important resources. Significantly, much of this content persists even in animals that are malnourished, as *Phanourios* may have been (see later). Stiner and Kuhn

---

Table 13-1. Exploitable Carcass Resources and Selected Carcass Processing Activities for Extracting Them

A. Exploitable resources: hide, hair, sinew, bone, horn/antler, marrow, grease, blood, teeth, viscera, fat/blubber, meat, juice, brains, hooves

B. Processing activities: evisceration, disarticulation/dismemberment, bone extraction, marrow extraction, bone grease extraction, periosteum removal, skinning/hide removal, defleshing/filleting/meat extraction, brain extraction, blood extraction, bone juice production, sinew or tendon removal

Source: Modified from Lyman 1987, 1994:295.

(1992:328) noted that the "fat/protein ratio in head tissues, particularly the brain, is both high and stable throughout the year, because the fat-rich myelin sheaths enclosing the cranial nerves cannot be metabolized under conditions of food stress." Another source of protein also could have been the marrow found in long bones, which, along with cranial elements, are amply represented at *Aetokremnos*.

In addition to providing food resources, the brains could have been useful in hide processing, as is amply documented in the ethnographic literature. Reed (1972) certainly has demonstrated the complexity that may be involved in hide working, and there is no reason to believe that the occupants of *Aetokremnos* would not have used *Phanourios* hides as items of clothing, especially in an environment with few resources (it will be recalled that the few pig and possible deer phalanges recovered from the site have been interpreted as remnants of clothing; certainly the abundant amounts of *Phanourios* phalanges could have served a similar function).

We propose that the occupants of *Aetokremnos* used virtually every part of the *Phanourios* that they hunted. Note, however, that there is not a one-to-one correspondence between efficient *use* and efficient butchery. One could argue that efficient butchery might have resulted in penetrating the carcasses deep enough to leave cutmarks, which are not present at *Aetokremnos*. This reasoning is fallacious, however. Indeed, efficient butchers often do not leave cutmarks. Furthermore, if *Phanourios* were locally abundant, obtaining every usable piece of meat, which may have required thorough butchering and possibly resultant cutmarks, may not have been necessary. Finally, butchering efficiency may have been linked with the manner in which the animals were cooked; if they were roasted whole, butchery could have been minimal (see Chap. 12).

Even so, why was the bone apparently cached at the site instead of being discarded after consumption? This issue has been a vexing one for us. Given the location of *Aetokremnos*, would it not have been an easy task to simply discard the bone, throwing it out of the shelter into the sea? Instead, we have a shelter filled with bones. How can this be explained?

We believe that the bone was intentionally cached for subsequent use after consumption. In particular, *Phanourios* bone would have made an adequate source of fuel, particularly if fresh. Indeed, there are historic accounts of paleontological sites being mined for fossilized bone that was then commercially processed as fuel (Leighton 1989:191). For example, Hugh Falconer noted that in Sicily "in 1829 there was a great demand for bones for manufacture of lamp-black for sugar-refining . . . within the first six months 400 quiutals [40,000 kg] were procured from San Ciro. The great majority belong to two species of *Hippopotamus*" (Murchison 1868:544).

Although we do not suggest exploitation on this scale, it is possible that *Phanourios* bones were used as fuel, both for warmth and, ironically, for the cooking of freshly killed *Phanourios*. Although fossilized bone can be burned (as in the modern Sicilian example), fresh bone certainly would have been a more efficient fuel (see discussion in Chap. 12).

One also could argue that bone was cached for future use as a trade item, either locally or more regionally, such as on the mainland. This scenario is unlikely because realistically the only trade value of *Phanourios* bone might have been ivory. Even if the bone was valuable as fuel, there is absolutely no evidence to support its being traded. If *Phanourios* were traded, one might reasonably expect to find evidence for this in the form of *Phanourios* bones at mainland sites, and this has never been reported. It appears likely that *Phanourios* was cached for future use *at the site*.

Evidence for caching at *Aetokremnos* comes from several of the features where bone was intensely burned. Although some may have been burned to dispose of food waste, it is equally plausible that bone actually was also the *source* of fuel. Such a scenario is particularly plausible in an environmental context in which wood for fuel may have been scarce, as it may have been on the Akrotiri Peninsula. Unfortunately, paleoenvironmental data indicating vegetation density are lacking, but it is unlikely that the peninsula ever was exceptionally rich in wood sources.

In summary, *Phanourios* provided attractive "packages" that contained a variety of economic prizes. Fig. 13-1 outlines a model for the possible "life cycle" of butchered *Phanourios*.

In assessing the function of *Aetokremnos*, we also cannot forget that there are other resources represented at the site, particularly, marine shell, several species of bird, and small numbers of dwarfed elephant. The abundance of the first two resources in the upper strata may reflect a gradual diminution of the availability of *Phanourios*. The importance of marine shell as a dietary component should not be overlooked. At *Aetokremnos*, marine resources clearly were important, although usage was certainly restricted to shell: It will be recalled that only one fish bone was recovered!

This increasing scarcity of resources contributed to the abandonment of *Aetokremnos*, and, perhaps ultimately, of the Akrotiri Peninsula and Cyprus itself. Coupled with this resource scarcity, however, another variable in the abandonment of the site may simply be that the shelter was disintegrating, as Mandel (Chap. 3) has noted. It will be recalled that rooffall was abundant in the cultural deposits, and the site simply may have become too dangerous to continue to use. Another point to consider relates to hunting. If *Aetokremnos* was not a kill site, but rather an area of intensive *Phanourios* (and other animal) processing, how were the animals killed? We have very little evidence of the answer to this question. Indeed, it will be fruitless to enter into the hunting/scavenging debate that has consumed so much attention in recent years. Suffice it to say, however, that by approximately 10,000 years ago, humans were well-skilled hunters. This skill does not preclude scavenging the odd deceased pygmy hippopotamus, but the shear abundance of these animals at *Aetokremnos* suggests a more systematic hunting scenario.

Although we have painfully little evidence regarding specific hunting procedures, perhaps some of the limited behavioral information on modern hippopotami can provide clues, albeit in a speculative manner. A critical issue is whether *Phanourios* was a herd animal. Clearly, human hunting strategies will vary according to whether or not prey animals occur singly or in groups. Although modern pygmy hippopotami are solidary, the evidence, scant as it may be, suggests that *Phanourios* may have been more gregarious. We come to this conclusion from three lines of evidence: First, when *Phanourios* are encountered at paleontological sites, there tends to be several individuals represented, although not as many as at *Aetokremnos*. This statement, of course, must be made with great caution, because detailed information on these paleontological sites is rare. Furthermore, most of these sites are derived and may represent accretional rather than contemporaneous events. Nonetheless, this evidence suggests that these animals may have been group oriented rather than solitary. Even if many of the paleontological sites are accretional events, the probability of several individuals being deposited in the same locality seems unlikely if they were solitary creatures. Clearly, what is required here is more systematic investigation of paleontological sites.

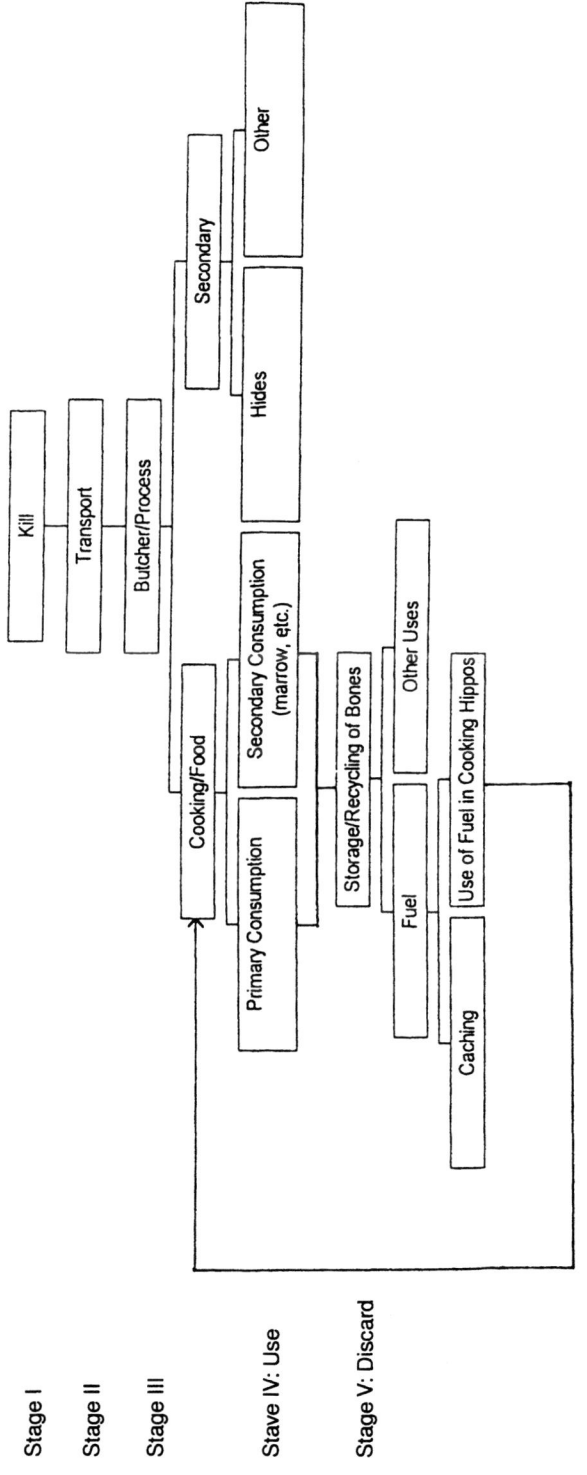

Stage I

Stage II

Stage III

Stave IV: Use

Stage V: Discard

Figure 13-1. Model for the "life cycle" of butchered *Phanourios*.

The second line of reasoning suggesting group rather than solitary behavior is simply the huge number of individuals represented at *Aetokremnos*. Although it is not impossible that solitary animals could have been hunted and eventually would have accounted for this number over time, a more likely explanation is that they were killed in groups. *Aetokremnos* is a small site. If individual animals were hunted by a presumably small group of people, it might have taken quite some time for the accumulation of *Phanourios* present at *Aetokremnos* to have occurred. This is not an impossibility, as the site may have been occupied for up to a few hundred years; however, one also has to weigh the economic options available to the occupants of the Akrotiri Peninsula. Although it was not necessarily an impoverished environment, its resources probably were relatively restricted. Would the cost-benefit ratio have been worthwhile if the primary prey resource were a solitary animal, given the apparent lack of domestic resources and paucity of other abundant wild plants or animals? Clearly, this type of argument can rapidly turn tautological, but it does tend to support group rather than solitary behavior.

Finally, the exciting new evidence coming out of Madagascar (see earlier) supports the notion that the extinct pygmy hippopotamus was a herd rather than a solidary animal, at least on that island. Of course, in Madagascar, an entirely different species of pygmy hippopotamus is present, and one must be cautious in making comparisons. However, the evidence is intriguing.

Herd behavior also may have occurred if environmental conditions had deteriorated to the degree that resources were becoming scarce. Again, specific paleoenvironmental data are lacking, but consensus opinion favors some degree of deterioration at the end of the Pleistocene. The suggestion that herd behavior may have been adaptive is supported by modern African evidence, where it has been demonstrated that hippopotami can form into herds of up to 150 individuals during time of environmental stress (Owen-Smith 1988:104). If indeed *Phanourios* were forced into herd behavior, this behavior also could have had an increasingly deleterious effect on an already fragile environment. When modern hippopotami are protected and increase in population, they can cause severe environmental damage (Delany and Happold 1979:46).

If, for the sake of argument, *Phanourios* were a herd animal, do we have any clue as to how they were hunted? Again, nothing direct is available. Based on the behavioral patterns of both modern common and pygmy hippopotami, however, it certainly would have been easy to determine where these animals congregated. Their behavior is quite predictable, and they leave abundant traces in preferred localities in the form of trails, which become quite distinct, and droppings. Hippopotami are notorious in their defecation habits, often marking territory quite dramatically. Such predictable habits certainly would not have been lost to the occupants of *Aetokremnos* and could have facilitated hunting.

Another question to ask is, What were the preferred habitats of *Phanourios?* Again, the differences between modern common and pygmy hippopotami are striking, with the former being much more aquatic than the latter. The location of paleontological sites throughout Cyprus does not show a preference for aquatic habitats—indeed, many of the sites occur in mountainous areas, and the foot bones of *Phanourios* indicate an adaptation to hilly areas (Boeschoten and Sondaar 1972). Thus the Akrotiri Peninsula at first glance might seem an unlikely ideal habitat for *Phanourios:* It is relatively flat, except for the cliff areas on its southern extension. And yet this is precisely where *Aetokremnos* is located. Although we do not believe that the animals were killed at the site, it is unlikely that they were transported a great distance. Thus it is apparent that the Akrotiri Peninsula supported a rather substantial *Phanourios* population.

Although these animals may not have been overly aquatic, the Akrotiri Salt Lake would have represented a favorable habitat. Water still was necessary for their survival. Alternatively, the Kouris River, a few km to the north, which until quite recently was perennial, also could have served as a habitat (Swiny 1982:2). It will be recalled that modern hippopotami are at home in both fresh and salt water bodies. If *Phanourios* congregated around the salt lake, we can infer that they would have ventured several km from this "base" for food, as do modern hippopotami, both common and pygmy. *Aetokremnos* is only slightly over 3 km from the lake, and if the leafy resources apparently preferred by *Phanourios* were available within the vicinity of the site, its location is ideal, as both a feeding and hunting area.

The location of *Aetokremnos* cannot be evaluated on the basis of *Phanourios* alone. The Akrotiri cliffs may have been attractive to the many birds present at *Aetokremnos*, although the majority of species represented appear to be more marsh-loving forms. As such, the Salt Lake would also have been a preferred bird habitat. One must ask that if the Akrotiri Salt Lake were a preferred habitat for both *Phanourios* and birds, why is the site located some 3 km to the south, along the cliffs? The answer may lie in the obvious importance of marine shell resources to the inhabitants of *Aetokremnos*, especially during its late stage of occupation. Marine shell would have been plentiful along the rocky coast and potentially expanded shoreline (cf. Gomez and Pease 1992) of the southern portion of the Akrotiri Peninsula. Finally, the location of the site within a rockshelter may have provided protection from the elements and bounded space for the storage of materials, such as *Phanourios* bone, for future usage (see earlier). Thus the site's location may have actually optimized proximity to a variety of resources. We have not attempted a site catchment analysis (cf. Vita-Finzi and Higgs 1970), but Figure 13-2 illustrates a tentative model of the potential scenario we have sketched.

The admittedly speculative nature of this discussion does little to directly address the question posed a few pages ago: How were *Phanourios* hunted? We simply do not know. Lacking projectiles, it is unlikely that they were speared or "shot." Although we cannot prove it, *Phanourios* may have been quite easy to dispatch. They had no predators on the island until the arrival of the ultimate predator: humans. As such, they would likely have been quite "naive" animals, expressing little fear of humans. They may have been easy to approach and simply clubbed to death. Of course, this is entirely conjectural; we have no way to prove it. Equally speculative is the possibility that they could have been run off the Akrotiri Cliffs to their death. Although the image of a "hippo jump" may seem comical, there certainly are archaeological precedents for animals either being driven over steep edges or into box canyons and then dispatched. Of course, if a run over the cliffs did occur, many of the animals probably would have fallen into the sea, no doubt facilitated by their rotund morphologies. If this happened, the occupants of *Aetokremnos* would have been forced to "fish" them out of the sea and transport them to the site. If Gomez and Pease's (1992) reconstruction is correct, however, there would have been a wider coastal beach at the time of occupation. In any event, the idea of a "hippo jump" is an admittedly imaginative scenario, but it also is a possible one.

A final consideration regarding to the function of *Aetokremnos* relates to season of occupation. Was it a permanent, year-round occupation, or was it occupied seasonally? Again,

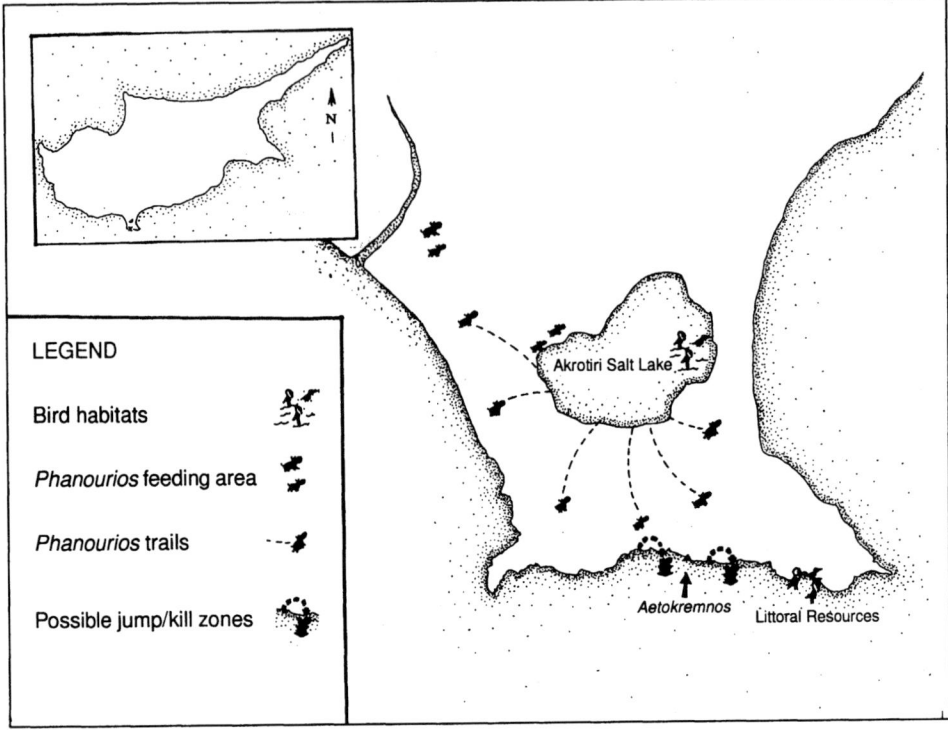

Figure 13-2. Model of *Aetokremnos* exploitation pattern.

this is a difficult question to answer, but there are clues from the faunal remains and modern analogues.

Unfortunately, little is known of seasonality in modern pygmy hippopotamus, so our comparisons must come from the larger forms, and much of this information is contradictory. Common hippopotami are not overly seasonal, but herd compositions do change in response to environmental conditions. Like other ungulates, changes in the distribution and abundance of food and water supplies largely determines the nature and extent of the home ranges and population movements (Leuthod 1977:227). Modern common hippopotami are always near water. They congregate at rivers during the dry season and at early rains, and remain there throughout the rainy season. They will follow the rising flood waters that gradually cover the floodplains during the rainy season, and they will move out to floodplains at the end of the rains and the beginning of the dry season (Delany and Happold 1979:202, 205). Estes (1991:223) noted that crowding around water is greatest during the dry season, and that hippopotami will disperse more widely during the rainy season. Conversely, other researchers have indicated that during dry seasons, hippopotami may travel up to 10 km from water sources (Owen-Smith 1988:62). Clearly, local conditions are an important variable here.

In relation to *Aetokremnos*, one could argue that its distance from the Akrotiri Salt Lake suggests a dry season (summer) occupation, on the assumption that *Phanourios* would have traveled farther from water during times of resource scarcity. Alternatively, the end of the dry season (fall to early winter) and into the rainy season could also have seen *Phanourios* venturing farther away from the lake, if modern analogies have any bearing. Of course, this further assumes that the Salt Lake was a preferred *Phanourios* habitat, which remains a tenuous assumption. In other words, the modern data really are quite contradictory and could be used either way.

Hippopotami also tend to follow the typical early dry season mating-wet season calving pattern typical of smaller ungulates (Owen-Smith 1988:184). They may have been more susceptible to predation during this period. The presence of several *Phanourios* individuals under one year of age at *Aetokremnos* suggests that the site could have been occupied at least during the rainy (i.e., winter) season.

Specialized studies of certain elements of the *Aetokremnos Phanourios* remains, particularly the dentition, also might contribute to seasonality information. We have not yet, however, been able to conduct these.

Seasonal implications also come from the avifauna from *Aetokremnos* (see Mourer-Chauviré, Chap. 7). *A. anser* and *A. fabalis,* which were not definitively identified at the site, are both migratory species. *Anser* probably would only have been present during its breeding season during the spring and summer, while *fabalis* likely wintered on the island. There is an abundance of bustard at the site, and these probably were present on Cyprus all year. Based on the avifauna, Mourer-Chauviré concluded that the site was occupied throughout the year.

Little seasonal information is available from the large marine shell assemblage from *Aetokremnos*. Over 99% of the species recovered have rocky shore/littoral habitats (see Reese, Chap. 7), but the types of analyses that might indicate seasonality have not yet been done.

Finally, the artifact assemblage does little to elucidate any seasonal patterns. Durand's study (Chap. 9) suggests possible summer/winter usages of the shelter. There is some patterning of lithics at *Aetokremnos,* and a concentration of these artifacts toward the back of the shelter (as seen in Stratum 2) may indicate a winter usage; the back would have offered more protection from the elements. Conversely, the concentration of lithics toward the front and west, as seen in Stratum 4, could suggest a summer, or at least fair-weather, usage. These conclusions are consistent with the distribution of subsistence remains as well, although the relatively low number of *Phanourios* in Stratum 2 offers little in interpretative value. Both shell and avifauna tend to concentrate toward the back of the shelter, a pattern consistent with the artifacts. If these patterns have any meaning, they might suggest that *Phanourios* was primarily hunted during the summer (Stratum 4), while a more diverse economic base consisting of birds and shells, but still some *Phanourios*, indicates a winter usage during Stratum 2.

Viewing this disparate database, we cannot reach a clear conclusion on the seasonality of *Aetokremnos*. The artifacts provide very tentative suggestions of a chronological distinction in seasonal use (e.g., Stratum 4, summer; Stratum 2, winter). The faunal remains suggest that the site could have been occupied throughout the year. There may have been an emphasis toward dry season occupation, based on the assumption that *Phanourios* would have traveled farther afield in search of resources. Conversely, the dry season may in fact have involved the formation, and congregation, of *Phanourios* herds *near* water sources. If this water source was the Akrotiri Salt Lake or the Kouris River, then a wet season occupation may be suggested for *Aetokremnos*. In other words, we simply cannot time make a definitive statement about the seasonality of occupation at *Aetokremnos*.

There is one more functional possibility that we must consider, albeit briefly. Some scholars have suggested, not entirely facetiously, that the vast amount of *Phanourios* remains may indicate some sort of ceremonial function for *Aetokremnos*. Certainly, there is some evidence for ceremonialism during this time period on the mainland, and cultic activity is well known from later periods of Cypriot prehistory. Although the concept of an ancient pygmy hippopotamus worship cult may have some inherent satisfaction, there is absolutely no supporting data for this interpretation at *Aetokremnos*. Some have felt that the number of beads might indicate this sort of activity, but we have no evidence linking the use of beads to, on, or with *Phanourios*! Nothing in the configuration of the site, the artifacts, or the faunal remains indicates any sort of cultic orientation.

In summary, *Aetokremnos* was not a kill site. Rather, it was the locus of intense *Phanourios* processing that involved not only butchering for consumption but also additional processing, possibly for "secondary resources." Once this activity was accomplished, the bone may have been cached, to be used as fuel for additional cooking and other activities at a later time. The abundance of *Phanourios* suggests a very specialized hunting focus toward these animals. Abundance alone is not necessarily an indicator of specialization; it "is at least as likely to reflect the response of a generalist forager to a situation or locality in which few prey species are available" (Stiner 1992:447). Although Stiner's observations are significant, they may not be relevant in the case of *Aetokremnos*, a site located on an island with few prey choices. Specialization does, indeed, appear to be a supportable conclusion in this case.

Other resources, however, also were consumed at *Aetokremnos*, including a substantial amount of birds and marine shell, as well as smaller amounts of other resources. Their remains are most abundant in Stratum 2, and this abundance reflects a more variable diet latter in the site's occupation. Seasonality of occupation cannot be determined, but the site could have been occupied throughout the year. *Aetokremnos* undoubtedly was part of a larger settlement system. Unfortunately, the archaeological reflection of this system is one of extremely low visibility. Sites such as those dune occurrences tested on the Akrotiri Peninsula may represent other components of this system. *Aetokremnos*, however, was optimally situated so as to take advantage of a range of resources, including those available from the rocky coast and shore (shell and other marine resources) and terrestrial forms, such as *Phanourios*. In addition, the cliffs surrounding the site could have been a favored habitat for the abundant bird species represented. The site may have served as a central-processing and storage base, but there is little evidence to indicate that it was any sort of permanent habitation.

Ultimately, however, resource depletion may have caused abandonment of both the site and the island. As Sondaar (1987:160) has noted, dwarfed endemic fauna could have been quickly reduced in number by human predation. The impact of human activity would have been particularly acute because many of these animals have low reproduction rates. On generally impoverished islands, once such a resource was no longer abundant, human populations may have had to leave the island. This, indeed, may be what occurred at *Aetokremnos*.

ORIGINS AND COLONIZATION

A question that has not yet been addressed is, "Where did those responsible for *Aetokremnos* come from"? Unfortunately, this is a difficult issue to satisfactorily resolve. Indeed, from our perspective, we are more interested in knowing what these people did once they arrived in Cyprus, rather than their origin. Nonetheless, one must ask, why Cyprus? There is a very large and interesting literature on initial human colonizations of islands that is far beyond the scope of this work. Pertinent issues have been addressed in Chapter 1, but some review is useful here. It will be recalled that Cherry (1990:192–203, 1992:32–33) provided excellent summaries and discussion of this issue as it relates to the Mediterranean, while Keegan and Diamond (1987) had a more global examination of why and how humans ultimately colonize islands.

An important point must be made here: Many researchers have hinted, if not explicitly stated, that the Mediterranean islands were too impoverished to have supported hunter/gatherer populations beyond perhaps a few short "visits" (e.g., Cherry 1981:58–59; Evans 1977:14). Rather, some scholars assumed that most of the islands were not permanently occupied until the Neolithic or later. Certainly, there is scant archaeological evidence to suggest the contrary. Lewthwaite (1989) dealt with this in some detail, proposing that the western Mediterranean islands were more conducive to foraging populations, who were "pre-adapted" to subsequent Neolithic economies. Although he presented a compelling argument, the data from *Aetokremnos* require modification of his model in that these data indicate a consistent pre- (or Early) Neolithic occupation of an eastern Mediterranean island. Finally, we also note as an aside, the argument against hunter/gatherer occupation of apparently "marginal" islands loses some of its strength when one considers the quite permanent occupations by hunter/gatherers of far more marginal environments, such as Australia or the North American Great Basin. The variability and complexity of prehistoric hunter/gatherer adaptations is well attested to in current literature (e.g., Bailey 1983; Bettinger 1991; Kelly 1983, 1995; Peterkin *et al.* 1993; Price and Brown 1985; Winterhalder and Smith 1981).

In any case, the initial human occupation of Cyprus was undoubtedly an early example of sea-faring abilities. But, as noted in Chapter 1, it certainly was not *the* oldest, either in the Mediterranean or elsewhere. Even if Cyprus presented a difficult "target," the inescapable fact is that is was occupied by mainlanders sometime in the tenth millennium B.C. (calibrated). But, is there any way to determine where these people came from?

There are two primary lines of evidence to help address this: typological/technological and chronological. Chronological comparisons can likewise prove elusive, yet they can provide perhaps a stronger regional comparative base. What do the artifacts and the chronology of *Aetokremnos* tell us of their origin?

As shown in Chapter 11, the lithic assemblage from *Aetokremnos*, while unique to Cyprus, could easily fit within a multitude of Late Pleistocene/Early Holocene mainland cultures. The distinctive thumbnail scrapers that characterize *Aetokremnos* occur, albeit in lower proportions, in many Anatolian and Levantine assemblages of roughly comparable dates. The remainder of the assemblage does not radically differ from mainland groups, both in typology and technology. At *Aetokremnos*, however, two distinct elements seen in the mainland are missing: an emphasis on microlithic tools, as seen, for example, with

Natufian groups, and an absence of projectile points, as seen, for example, with Early Neolithic groups. There really is no satisfactory explanation for this absence, except that the assemblage from *Aetokremnos* represents a very specialized adaptation to the conditions posed by Cyprus, and that this assemblage was specifically geared toward the efficient exploitation of a relatively restricted fauna. Of course, one could argue that projectile points would have made an ideal *Phanourios* hunting implement. We cannot disagree beyond noting the apparent widespread contradiction that throughout the Near East (and elsewhere), projectile points only become very common during the Neolithic, *after* hunting presumably declined in the face of farming and animal husbandry.

An origin from somewhere other than the Levant or Anatolia is unlikely, given the geography of Cyprus. We tend to favor a Levantine origin, a rather tenuous conclusion, based in part on the fact that *Aetokremnos* is located in southern Cyprus, and that the Akrotiri Peninsula may have been a suitable "target" for Levantine mariners. If an Anatolian source were likely, one might reasonable expect to have found a site like *Aetokremnos* in northern, not southern, Cyprus. As there are no other clear examples of sites dating to the Akrotiri Phase, it is unlikely to assume an Anatolian origin that left no traces until *Aetokremnos* was produced in the south. This reasoning, of course, can be faulted because few systematic archaeological surveys, as characterize modern research endeavors, have been conducted in the north since the Turkish invasion of 1973.

A Levantine origin also is supported, albeit indirectly, by subsequent Neolithic populations. Although the origins of Cypriot Neolithic groups are not definitively known (see Chap. 1), many researchers favor the Levant (LeBrun 1989; Rollefson 1989). This issue is a difficult one because the Cypriot Neolithic is so distinct from its mainland counterparts. This distinction has prompted Ronen (1995), in an intriguing but difficult to verify model, to propose that the Aceramic Neolithic peoples of Cyprus, who he terms *Asprots,* were a very conservative lot indeed—fundamentalists who chose insularity as a means of maintaining cultural isolation and fending off outside influences.

In any case, supporting data for a Levantine origin also are found in the presence of fallow deer at Cypriot Neolithic sites. There are similar to the Mesopotamian fallow deer from Syria/Lebanon (Davis 1984:152) rather than Anatolian forms.

Another facet of "negative" evidence favoring a Levantine origin is simply that our knowledge of Late Epipaleolithic/Early Neolithic cultures along the southern Anatolian coastline is limited. Recent research, however, at sites such as Karain (Albrecht 1988a,b) and Öküzini (Albrecht *et al.* 1992; Otte *et al.* 1995) in southwest Anatolia, is beginning to shed more light on the Early Holocene of this region. Research elsewhere in Anatolia also is shedding new light on Early Neolithic adaptations, including the possibility that pigs were one of the first domesticates, at least at Hallan Çemi Tepesi in eastern Anatolia (Rosenberg *et al.* 1995). In the Levant, however, a considerable amount of information already exists for cultures contemporary with *Aetokremnos.*

For these reasons, we lean toward a Levantine origin. If such a genesis is proposed, can we determine what specific cultural affinity it was? Again, the artifact assemblage is of little use because the materials from *Aetokremnos* can fit easily within a wide range of Natufian or Pre-Pottery Neolithic A, or even Kebaran, assemblages. We do know, however, that during the Pre-Pottery Neolithic in the Levant, a substantial coastal adaptation is represented, at least during the latter Pre-Pottery Neolithic B period (cf. Galili *et al.* 1993). This adaptation suggests a familiarity with the sea.

Turning to the chronological issue, *Aetokremnos* is well dated to at least the early ninth to late tenth millennium B.C., calibrated (see Chap. 8). This fits perfectly within a Late Natufian or early Pre-Pottery Neolithic scenario, with an edge toward the latter (Byrd 1994; Kuijt and Bar-Yosef 1994).

Another admittedly tenuous observation that indirectly supports a Neolithic affinity is that at *Aetokremnos,* a few pig bones were recovered. We have interpreted these as perhaps reflecting cloaks or some other form of clothing, rather than as an economic resource. The small sample precludes determining if these phalanges were from domesticated animals, but their presence, used as clothing, may suggest a domestic "secondary product" use. There is no evidence that pigs were domesticated during the Natufian, thus supporting the Neolithic affinity.

All this indicates that the people responsible for *Aetokremnos* were very early Neolithic farmers or very late Natufian hunter/gatherers. This may suggest a reason for their "flight" to Cyprus (whether from the Levant or Anatolia), although it is admittedly speculative.

The Late Natufian and Pre-Pottery Neolithic Periods were times of economic turmoil. The inception of the irreversible "Neolithic Revolution" was at the doorstep, and peoples were faced with dramatic economic decisions. Virtually the entire history of humans up to this point had been based on hunting and gathering. Abandoning this proven economic strategy was no easy decision. The reasons for the adoption of economies based on the domestication of plants and animals have filled many volumes and are beyond the scope of this work. Many researchers, however, believe that people were ultimately forced into domestic economies because of population increase or other variables that may have been related to climatic changes that occurred during the Early Holocene. Whatever the causes, however, hunting remained an important activity throughout the Neolithic, and, indeed, many small specialized Pre-Pottery Neolithic sites devoted to hunting are well documented (e.g., Betts 1991; Simmons 1980). Thus hunting was not a "lost art"; rather, it appears that it remained an important economic supplement. Certainly, in Cyprus during the Pre-Pottery Neolithic, hunting was very significant, with consensus opinion supporting the importation of mainland deer to the island (e.g., Davis 1984:152, 1989:206, 1994:305).

We propose that those responsible for *Aetokremnos* were a conservative group of early Levantine Neolithic peoples; earlier in fact that the subsequent Neolithic Asprots suggested by Ronen (see earlier). Perhaps they did not want to become part of the wider "Neolithic economy" that forced many people to congregate in sedentary villages and focus much of their energy on farming and herding. In the face of increasing pressure from these sedentary groups, many more mobile peoples may have been pushed to marginal zones, where they could continue the lifestyle that they were used to, which consisted of hunting and gathering. Indeed, gathering may have assumed less importance due to the paucity of floral resources in these zones. Thus hunting may have become even more important. We know from extensive survey and excavation in the southern, more arid portions of the Levant that substantial Late Epipaleolithic and Early Neolithic groups occupied much of this region (e.g., Bar-Yosef and Phillips 1977; Betts 1991; Goring-Morris 1987, 1991; Scott 1977; Simmons 1980).

Thus it may be that a few perhaps more adventurous groups of these people, favoring the traditional lifestyle over the new domestic economies, and not wanting to compete with people already occupying some of the available, if marginal lands, opted to set out to sea. Their destination was the Akrotiri Peninsula. There they found an unspoiled habitat occupied by relict herds of pygmy hippopotami and other Pleistocene endemics, which, although they may have been in decline due to deteriorating climatic conditions, provided these hunters with an ample, if short-lived economic opportunity. We have termed this occupation the *Akrotiri Phase.*

If this is an accurate scenario, is there any way to reconstruct how many people were involved? Unfortunately, prehistoric population estimates are difficult even with good data. On the basis of only one certain site (i.e., *Aetokremnos*) belonging to the Akrotiri Phase, we are reluctant to provide any estimates. Abundant ethnographic data indicate that hunter/ gatherer band size often falls between 25–50 people, and it certainly seems reasonable to assume this as a minimum number for the Akrotiri Phase. In all likelihood, far more individuals were involved. Again, ethnographic analogies suggest that a minimum of 500 people are necessary for a sustainable population (but see Kelly 1995:209–213). If this were the case for the Akrotiri Phase, it is unlikely that they were all concentrated on the Akrotiri Peninsula. Until more research can document additional sites, we simply cannot address this issue further.

Another question to ask is, What happened to these people? Again, conclusions are equally tenuous and speculative. It is here that distinctions between "colonization" and "utilization" made by scholars such as Cherry (1990:197–199) are important variables. Cherry believes that the earliest "occupation" of an island is different from the earliest "utilization." An occupation, or colonization episode, involves the point when the island becomes a group's major source of subsistence throughout the year, while utilization involves short-term or seasonal visits to procure resources or perhaps even accidental, unsuccessful attempts at colonization.

Where does *Aetokremnos* fit within this scenario? Even examining the radiocarbon dates liberally, one cannot make an argument that the site was occupied for more than about 1,500 years. In fact, we believe it was far briefer occupation. There is absolutely no evidence that the occupants of *Aetokremnos* remained on the island after the site's abandonment, possibly as founders of the aceramic Khirokitia Culture. We make no claim for this. Although new sites may be discovered providing such a linkage (such as *Shillourokambos* [Guilaine, *et al.* 1955]), there currently is no chronological evidence supporting a direct ancestral relationship between the Akrotiri Phase and the Khirokitia Culture.

Was *Aetokremnos* then reflective of mere "utilization" of Cyprus? It may be a semantic argument, but the evidence suggests that the Akrotiri Phase does not represent an actual colonization episode. Certainly, it was "occupied," probably for several hundred years. It would appear, however, that this occupation was largely restricted to the coastal areas, as are, in fact, most large Aceramic Neolithic sites. We do not believe that those responsible for *Aetokremnos* were seasonal visitors to the island, however. The difficulty of the voyage precludes a consistent return to the island on an annual, or even less-frequent, basis. Although the site itself may have been seasonal, we suspect that people of the Akrotiri Phase occupied other sites, possibly ones such as those tested on the Akrotiri Peninsula, at other times of the year. *Aetokremnos*, however, appears to have been the center of attention, at least as can be determined by extant archaeological evidence.

The most parsimonious explanation may be that once the primary resource, *Phanourios*, was no longer available, or became scarcer, the site, and probably the island, were abandoned. Although it is difficult to make such sweeping generalizations on the basis of a single site, there is supporting evidence in the stratigraphy at *Aetokremnos*. It will be recalled that other species, notably birds, became much more common in the upper strata of the site, while *Phanourios* declined dramatically. If one rules out stratigraphic mixing of deposits, this may imply an economic shift to a broader base as the primary resource became less plentiful, in no small part due to human predation. Ultimately, a point was reached at which it was no longer economically viable to continue occupation. Coupled with this was the physical deterioration of the shelter as well, undoubtedly another component contributing to its abandonment.

One can only presume that the occupants of *Aetokremnos* either returned to their original homeland or set out elsewhere. If indeed they returned to their homelands, certainly they took with them memories of Cyprus. Although there presently is no way to archaeological verify this, this "residual memory" may have been passed down for several generations. With knowledge of the existence of an unoccupied island, perhaps those responsible for the founding of the Khirokitia Culture were in some elusive manner related to the original occupants of the island. Consideration of why Cyprus was subsequently occupied, and probably colonized, by later Neolithic peoples is, however, beyond the scope of this discussion. We note, though, that occupation of the supposed marginal Mediterranean islands by Late Neolithic mainland groups because of ecological stress (cf. Cherry 1981; Evans 1977) requires modification in light of data from *Aetokremnos*. If the scenario proposed here is correct, the stress (perhaps social as well as environmental) may have had a much earlier origin.

EXTINCTION

Modern humans have caused enough extinctions that we should have had ample opportunity to study the process...Ultimately a species goes extinct when its last individual dies, but this is the relatively trivial endpoint of a much more complicated and interesting chain of events. Whenever the death rate exceeds the birth rate, extinction is inevitable. . . . (Brown 1995:159)

Introduction

The issue of whether or not humans were the primary causal agents of the extinction of several species on a global basis at the end of the Pleistocene is one of the most controversial topics in modern archaeology. The argument essentially boils down, in simplest form, to two models: humans were responsible for these extinctions, or the extinctions were brought about by other factors, primarily climatic change. Those who blame humans usually attribute extinction to direct predation in the form of hunting (the so-called "overkill" or "blitzkrieg" model of Paul Martin) or to indirect causes, such as resource competition, often brought about by imported domestic animals. Proponents of the climatic model usually invoke the demonstrable climatic changes at the end of the Pleistocene and beginning of the Holocene to explain the extinction episodes. There is an enormous literature by proponents and antagonists on this issue, and we certainly can not examine this extremely complex topic here. Many relevant citations have already been provided in Chapter 1.

We should note the distinction between *extinction* (global loss of a species) and *extirpation* (loss of a species from an island or region, with one or more populations surviving elsewhere) (Steadman 1995b:1123). For purposes of this discussion, we prefer the term *extinction.* Certainly, *Phanourios*, a species unique to Cyprus, did go extinct. One might argue that other species of pygmy hippopotami apparently survived until later, as in Madagascar, for example (where they may *still* exist [Burney and Ramilisounina 1998]), and this could suggest extirpation instead, but we consider this a semantic argument in the context of this study.

So, does *Aetokremnos* have a role to play in this debate? The time frame certainly is perfect, falling precisely within the chronological framework proposed by advocates of the overkill model. The presence of Pleistocene pygmy hippopotami and elephants with Holocene cultural remains at *Aetokremnos* is clear, and it is one of the best-documented cases of such an association yet documented in the archaeological record. Clearly, the role of humans in the extinction of these species must be reevaluated. Prior to the documentation of *Aetokremnos*, it was assumed that these island-adapted endemics had gone extinct long before humans entered the scene.

Island Extinctions and Humans

Island faunas are ideal candidates for extinction at the hand of humans. Indeed, it is ironic that, in many cases, isolated islands, despite having extinction-prone biogeorgraphies, often were the last places to be so affected (Burney 1993b:535–536,539). Because of the lack of carnivores, genetically fixed behavior patterns for flight and attack often are lost in island herbivores. Once these reactions are lost, the individual animal cannot regain them. In the absence of predators, high reproduction rates are useless and also will be lost. A new predator [such as humans] with normal behavioral patterns and reproduction rates will therefore reproduce quickly on islands and soon exterminate the slowly reproducing, unwary species (Schüle 1993:406; 1989, 1992).

Schüle (1993) believed that when humans arrived on some Mediterranean islands, their hunger put an end to the pygmy elephants, hippopotami, and cervids living there. The menu was augmented by the more or less flightless giant swans on Malta, Sardinia, and Sicily, and all kinds of giant tortoise and giant rodents on most islands. When the "big animals" were gone, there was not much left to live off. Before the introduction of domesticates, hunters had little chances of survival once the endemic fauna was depleted (Schüle 1993:406). If an essential resource was overexploited, colonizers had to adapt to the new conditions or else disappear (Schüle 1993:401).

Schüle (1993:408) acknowledges, however, that this scenario is only supported on Cyprus (by *Aetokremnos*) and Sardinia. His contention that *Homo erectus* was responsible for the extinctions of endemics on Corso-Sardinia, however, cannot be supported archaeologically (see Cherry 1992). Nonetheless, he posited an intriguing model for extinction.

Where does *Aetokremnos* fit within this type of scenario? In placing *Aetokremnos* within the larger global extinction process, it is important to remember that the site is located on an island. There are certainly examples of humans causing the extinction of a wide variety of animal species both in modern times and in the archaeological record. This process is most graphically illustrated in island contexts, where it has been time and time again demonstrated that human predators were an efficient extinction machine, as Schüle had proposed. There is a large and well-documented literature demonstrating human-induced extinctions within the constraints of island biogeographies, particularly within historic contexts. Indeed, Martin (1984) considered Holocene island extinctions as part of the "blitzkrieg" model proposed for continents (cf. Moismann and Martin 1975). Examples of such "quick" (i.e., 1,000 years or less, cf. Stuart 1991:460) island extinctions are numerous (e.g., see individual contributors in Martin and Klein 1984).

Although historic cases clearly demonstrate that humans were capable of causing devastating extinctions of island faunas, can these serve as models for earlier extinctions, either continental or island? That is, many of the relatively recent island extinction episodes were caused by humans arriving on islands who practiced economies based on domestication, supplemented by hunting. Thus, these peoples were presumably able to maintain much higher populations than they could by hunting and gathering alone (Stuart 1991:458–459). They may be, therefore, an inappropriate model for pre-Neolithic examples.

Not all island extinctions, however, were so rapid. Of interest here is the demonstrated coexistence of humans and island endemics during the Holocene. There are several Mediterranean examples in which humans ultimately caused extinctions, but only after several hundreds, or even thousands, of years of coexistence. Clearly in these cases, rapid extinction was not a variable, and Diamond's (1989b:169) suggestion of a "sitzkrieg," or slow attrition, model may be appropriate.

Examples of relatively long-term coexistence in the Mediterranean often cited include Mallorca and *Myotragus*, an extinct antelope-like ruminant (Burleigh and Clutton-Brock 1980; Waldren 1982, 1991, 1994). Although many of the archaeological details of relevant sites are not well documented, and in some cases the direct association of humans with *Myotragus* is less than compelling, it seems clear that humans were ultimately involved in the eradication of these animals (see Cherry 1991:184–189). There is little evidence indicating that the initial settlers of the island were anything earlier than Neolithic farmers.

One implication of such a coexistence is the operation of some type of "game-farming" strategy, ultimately resulting in extinction. Schüle notes that

> not even farmers could be expected to eat their goats or sheep when unsuspecting suppers walked everywhere. Like the Dodo, giant tortoises and so many other island vertebrates, *Myotragus* was harvested rather than hunted by the newcomers—it could not possibly have survived a second generation of human settlers. There is no undisputed proof that man hunted them, but in view of the time-span concerned in the extinction of these fearless animals, archaeological evidence can hardly be expected. The fossil evidence lies in negative rather than in positive proof: the edible fauna disappeared. (Schüle 1993:406)

Schüle (1993:406–407), however, did question the scenario of a long relationship between people and *Myotragus* on Mallorca, believing that the arguments were not convincing. Many other researchers are less sanguine, comfortable with a long-term coexistence between *Myotragus* and humans (cf. Cherry 1991:184–189; Waldren 1994). They believe that there is adequate archaeological support of such a scenario. They further feel that extinction ultimately was a result of human activity, whether it was from overhunting, unsuccessful competition with goats for similar niches, or from extermination by diseases brought to the island by domestic livestock (Cherry 1990:189; Clutton-Brock 1984).

Other examples come from Sardinia and Corsica, where the exemplary research of Vigne (e.g., Vigne 1983; 1987a,b; 1988; 1989; 1990; 1992; Vigne and Alcover 1985) serves as a model for careful zooarchaeological interpretation. In Corsica, hunting pressures apparently led to rapid extinction of *Megaceros* deer and probably *Cynotherium*, a canid. Several species, however, such as *Prolagus* (a harelike animal), *Episoriculus*, and two rodents, succeeded in resisting hunting and competition with humans during eight millennia. They coexisted with the complete modern fauna until after the sixth century, finally becoming extinct after being unable to resist the combined effects of predation by humans and by the new animal immigrants (such as dogs, foxes, and weasels); competition with invaders; and vegetation changes due to pastoralism and agriculture. Their extinctions probably did not result from a single factor because all the primary causes existed as early as the Neolithic. Rather, it was the combined effects that ultimately proved their demise (Blondell and Vigne 1993:144).

In Sardinia, the data are more controversial. Much depends on interpretation of Corbeddu Cave and claimed association of *Prolagus* and *Megaceros* with Epipaleolithic cultural remains. Claims also have been made for human-induced extinction of Lower/Middle Pleistocene fauna at approximately 200,000–300,000 years ago (Martini 1992; Sondaar 1986, 1987), presumably by *Homo erectus*. Cherry (1992) has convincingly questioned many of the claims for such extremely ancient human occupations and for the association of humans with much of the extinct Sardinian fauna.

Sicily is not considered here, as it in a sense is a "false-island," having been joined to the mainland for much of the Pleistocene (Cherry 1990:189). Sicily does have a lineage of pygmy elephants and hippopotami, dwarf deer, and two species of giant dormouse, as well as a long human occupation, which stretches back to the Acheulean (Cherry 1990:190). There is, however, virtually no evidence for direct human predation of dwarfed forms. At sites such as Uzzo Cave, where human hunting appears well documented, there are no Pleistocene endemics in the faunal assemblage (Tagliacozzo 1993).

Even if some of the early claims for humans and extinctions cannot be archaeologically verified, Sondaar (1987:160) made the interesting observation that for sustained occupation on a island with few resources, a prey animal should be one with a rapid reproduction rate. Such may have been the case in Sardinia with *Prolagus*. Given the demonstrable procreation habits of ochotonids, such creatures may have been able to sustain a high population in spite of human predation. Conversely, animals with low-reproduction rates, such as *Phanourios*, would have been much more susceptible to extinction.

Some the best direct archaeological evidence for island extinction comes from New Zealand. Here, over 300 sites contain the remains of butchered moas (Anderson, 1984, 1989, 1991, 1995; Caughley 1988; Cumberland 1962; Lockerbie 1959; McCulloch and Trotter 1975; Trotter and McCulloch 1984). This abundance has allowed for the development of eloquent models of extinction that are supported by actual archaeological data.

Anderson (1989, 1991, 1995) had perhaps provided the most thoughtful investigation of this, examining both the radiocarbon chronology and the quantification of overexploitation of moa populations. By modeling moa and human population sizes and culling and consumption levels, he concluded that substantially more moas must have been killed than is apparent in the archaeological evidence to satisfy the requirement of an overkill "blitzkrieg" explanation. Rather, he favors extinction as a "series of local events in which over-hunting in one valley was succeeded by over-hunting in another" (Anderson 1989:143).

There are some implications of Anderson's research for *Aetokremnos* that disallow for any direct comparisons. First, his estimates of moa populations ran into the "tens and some hundreds of thousands" (Anderson 1989:145). Second, he considered a "high" moa MNI as 2.2/sq m; using even smaller figures of 0.1 MNI and 0.2 MNI in his calculations, he estimated the total size of the moa catch at between 108,000–336,000 individuals (Anderson

1989:147). At *Aetokremnos,* the approximate MNI/sq m is much higher, at 12.6 (based on a total MNI of 505 and an area of about 40 sq m). These figures are important because it unlikely that there were anywhere near even 100,000 *Phanourios* on the Akrotiri Peninsula. Finally, Anderson (1989:147) estimated a minimum human population of at least 1,000. This again is a much higher figure than probable for the Akrotiri Peninsula (see later). Anderson's research is instructive because "in short, what seems plausible in what is acknowledged as one of the most convincing cases of overkill is still not yet demonstrable in terms of tangible evidence" (Anderson 1989:149).

In summary, it is clear that islands are susceptible to human-induced extinction episodes. This is particularly well documented in cases of recent extinctions, although even in these, directly supporting archaeological data are rare. One cannot, of course, automatically assume human predation as being the primary extinction stimulus, even on islands. This must be demonstrated, and other variables certainly must be important. In spite of this, however, *Aetokremnos* has demonstrated the *antiquity* of island extinctions.

Extinctions of Other Dwarfed Mammals

Beyond Keith's (1925,1931) fanciful, and wholly unsupported, images of Neanderthals in Malta slaughtering pygmy hippopotami and other endemics, is there any direct evidence for human predation, and subsequent extinction of, *dwarfed* island mammals? The answer is that there are indeed very few. In fact, as Diamond (1984:851–852) noted several years ago, there are only four examples of undoubted human "waves" directly implicated in island extinctions: Hawaii, New Zealand, Chatham Island, and Madagascar. Of these, only Madagascar overwhelmingly drew its victims from megafauna, including dwarfed forms.

In Madagascar, pygmy hippopotami and other endemics apparently coexisted with humans for up to a 1,000 years before the former became extinct (Dewar 1984; MacPhee and Burney 1991; but see Burney and Ramilisonina 1998). Despite this, however, direct archaeological evidence for the association of humans with pygmy hippopotami is lacking. Archaeological sites contain few subfossils (Dewar 1984:580), and the best evidence for association comes from only *seven* apparently butchered hippopotamus bones from very insecure contexts (MacPhee and Burney 1991).

In the Mediterranean, there is little evidence of human association with the dwarfed Pleistocene endemics so well known on many of the islands, including either examples of presumed "quick" extinctions or longer term coexistences. The possible coexistence of humans and dwarfed elephants on the island of Tilos remain unverified. The dwarfed antelope of Mallorca remains the most convincing evidence of human association with an extinct dwarfed island endemic, outside of *Aetokremnos.* Indeed, the association of humans with other, nondwarfed endemics is questionable in all but a few instances, such as Corsica, where rodents, shrew, and pika ultimately became extinct as a result of human activity (Vigne 1987a). The evidence from Sardinia is intriguing, if controversial. For Crete, Lax and Strasser (1992) provided a reasonable theoretical model of extinction being the indirect results of human activities, such as land clearance and the introduction of domesticated animals. They concede, however, that there is little direct evidence to support a temporal association between humans and these animals (Lax and Strasser 1992:209; Strasser and Lax 1993).

Elsewhere in the Near East, there also is little evidence for an association of humans with dwarfed mammals. A possible exception is a painting from an Egyptian tomb that *may* represent a dwarfed elephant (Rosen 1994). If this is accurate, it could suggest that these forms were present until only a few thousand years ago. It is, however, a quite tenuous argument.

In North America, despite some claims to the contrary (e.g., Berger 1980; Orr 1968), the well-documented dwarfed elephants of the Channel Islands (Madden 1977; Wenner and Johnson 1980) do not appear to ever have been hunted by humans (e.g., Wendorf 1982). In a sense, this is curious, given the island's short distance from the mainland. This, of course, presupposes a chronological synchronicity of humans and the dwarfed forms, which has not been convincingly demonstrated.

Finally, some very tantalizing evidence has emerged from an unlikely source. Dwarfed elephants have recently been reported from Wrangle Island in the Siberian Arctic. The intriguing thing about these is their apparent persistence until roughly 3,700 years ago (Lister 1993; Long *et al.* 1994; Vartanyan *et al.* 1993). Vartanyan *et al.* indicated there was no evidence that the Wrangle mammoths were hunted by humans and preferred an ultimate extinction caused by climatic and vegetational changes. One could argue, however, that they indeed were able to persist so long precisely because they were under no predation pressure from humans. Continued research on Wrangle Island will no doubt contribute to the discussion of extinction and Holocene longevity.

A SPECULATIVE MODEL FOR *PHANOURIOS* EXTINCTION ON THE AKROTIRI PENINSULA

Given this discussion, could the occupants of *Aetokremnos* have caused the extinction of *Phanourios?* We believe the answer to this question is yes. The following is intended only as a speculative exercise. It makes no attempt to emulate the elegant nutritional models exemplified by the work of researchers such as Speth (1983) or Jochim (1976), for example.

As a starting point, we can attempt to reconstruct the density of *Phanourios* on the Akrotiri Peninsula. Several assumptions are important here: First, we assume that the Peninsula itself represented a relatively isolated habitat for these animals. Second, we assume that the Salt Lake was present. Third, we assume that densities for modern hippopotami are rough analogous to those of *Phanourios*. The density of modern common hippopotami ranges considerably—from about 1.1 to 31 individuals per sq km. These are themselves estimates, as there is relatively little such information available for modern hippopotami—probably due, in part, to the difficulty of getting accurate counts for semi-aquatic animals (cf. Leuthod 1977:209–210). Virtually no density information is available for modern pygmy hippopotami.

One important aspect of this model is that it assumes meat was a primary dietary source, given the relative lack of wild plant resources on Cyprus. Although this assumption goes against the commonly held view of the importance of plants versus animals in hunter/gatherer diets, as originally articulated in the classic work by Lee and DeVore (1968), there certainly are abundant examples in the ethnographic literature of situations in which meat formed a major dietary component. Various Eskimo groups (cf. Draper 1977) are perhaps the most extreme examples, but the North American protohistoric bison hunters are another (e.g., Speth 1983).

Certainly, the importance of fat to prehistoric diets cannot be overestimated; fats not only tend to be high in protein but are also high-energy sources (Jochim 1981:81–83; Speth

1983:148–159). Thus if *Phanourios* contained an abundant amount of fat, It may have been valued as an attractive high-energy/protein package. We cannot, of course, reconstruct the fat content of *Phanourios,* and it is well known that wild game animals have less total fat than domesticated ones (e.g., just over 4 grams fat per 100 grams of wild meat, as compared with 29 grams of fat per 100 grams of domestic meat) (Eaton *et al.* 1988a:80). If we can use a rough analogy to *Phanourios,* wild boars contain 16.8 grams of protein and 8.3 grams of fat per 100 gram portions (Eaton *et al.* 1988a:108). Thus *Phanourios* could have been an excellent source of these important nutrients, even though its fat context (despite the image of "fat" hippopotami) probably was less than that of domesticated animals.

Based on these assumptions, the following scenario can be presented: The Akrotiri Peninsula is roughly 9 by 12 km (108 sq km). It will be recalled that the southern portion of the Akrotiri Peninsula may have actually been an island in the past. If it was, the area on which *Aetokremnos* is located would obviously have been even smaller that 108 sq km. If, however, it was an island, the separation between it and the "mainland" (i.e., the northern portion of the present-day Akrotiri Peninsula) would have been minimal. Thus we will use the geographic boundaries of the Peninsula as it presently exists for this exercise.

Using modern estimates (1.1 to 31), *Phanourios* density on the Akrotiri Peninsula could have ranged from 118.8 to 3,348. For convenience, we will use a relatively high average density of 25/sq km on the assumption that these animals had no predators. Using this figure gives a density of 2,700 animals. Given an optimistic growth rate of 10% (cf. Owen-Smith 1988:214), 270, animals could be added to this figure annually. Of course, one also must subtract for mortality. Hippopotami, however, have relatively long life spans, so we might assume a relatively low mortality rate.

A complicating variable here is the minimum population size required for long-term survival. Many researchers have addressed this issue, although there is little consensus on a acceptable figure. Often cited is that at least 500 randomly mating individuals are required for survival. Recent research, however, suggests that a species must number 10,000 or more to maintain its evolutionary viability (Culotta 1995). This clearly has implications for Cyprus and the Akrotiri Peninsula. If the 500 figure is reliable, *Phanourios* could have survived on the Peninsula, assuming a population of 2,700. If, however, the 10,000-individual figure is more correct, extinction may have occurred without interference by humans. What is obviously required are better estimates of the total population of *Phanourios* on the entire island; at this point, such data are not available. These are issues beyond the scope of the present work, and the following is provided as only one explanatory scenario based on admittedly scant data.

If a population of approximately 2,700 pygmy hippopotami roamed the Akrotiri Peninsula, human predation would have had to exceed the 10% growth rate to induce extinction. Such predation would require killing over 270 animals on an annual basis. It will be recalled that over 500 individuals are represented at *Aetokremnos.* Thus the question becomes, How many people were on the Akrotiri Peninsula and for how long? Would there have been enough people to consume nearly 270 animals on an annual basis, even given the paucity of other resources?

Further calculations are necessary to address these questions. It would be useful to know how much usable meat could be obtained per carcass. Although there are many ways by which to calculate this, Frison's (1979:262) experimental butchering of a roughly 455-kg adult bison yielded about 182 kg of fresh meat, or roughly 40% of total body weight. Assuming an average adult weight of about 200 kg for *Phanourios,* 40% would yield nearly

80 kg of meat per adult animal. If 270 kills/year or more were necessary to induce extinction, this would yield 21,600 kg of meat per annum.

It is difficult to estimate per person consumption of meat for any time span, but to paraphrase an old adage, "Man cannot live by meat alone." For argument's sake, we use figures provided by an intriguing, if perhaps unconventional, source, *The Paleolithic Prescription* (Eaton *et al.* 1988a) and related works (Eaton and Konner 1985; Eaton *et al.* 1988b). Although many calculations of nutritional intake assume a diet of 2,000 calories/day, Eaton *et al.* (1988a:79–80) preferred 3,000 calories, due to the presumably increased activity levels of prehistoric preagricultural peoples. They further make the assumption of a 35% meat and 65% vegetal diet, then concluded that about 2,250 g (2.25 kg) of food had to be consumed every day. They noted, however, that these percentages could be reversed (i.e., 65% meat, 35% plants) with no significant change in the energy intake because there is a close caloric similarity between game meat (as opposed to domestic meat) and plant foods.

For argument's sake, let us assume then that 60% of the Akrotiri diet consisted of *Phanourios*. This gives an allowance for other animals making up the other 5% of the total 65% meat consumption, as well as 35% for possible plant resources. Using Eaton *et al.*'s (1988a) figures of 3,000 calories and 2,250 grams of daily consumption, approximately 1,350 grams, or 1.35 kg (i.e., 60%) would be from *Phanourios*, translating to 9.45 kg per person, per week, or an annual average consumption of 491 kg. The estimated meat yield of 21,600 would thus support 44 people.

So, what are the implications of these very speculative figures? Were there over 40 people living on the Akrotiri Peninsula during the Akrotiri Phase? This seems a very reasonable assumption, even given the virtual absence of recognizable sites dating to this period (beyond *Aetokremnos*). Although calculating population densities of hunter/gatherer groups is fraught with difficulties (e.g., Bettinger 1991:157–160; Kelly 1995:205–259; Smith 1981), many researchers are comfortable with an estimated average density of 25–50 people per "band." Thus these figures seem very reasonable. The often cited "maximal band" figure of 500 individuals, however, has, according to Kelly (1995:258), little empirical or theoretical evidence to support it. Thus for the Akrotiri Peninsula, we may postulate "bands" of up to 50 people, but a "sustaining" maximal band of 500 is unnecessary.

If there is any meaning to these figures, they suggest that even if only one band of people occupied the Akrotiri Peninsula, they could easily have decimated the population of *Phanourios* in a short time. But what happens if *Phanourios* were already on the verge of extinction, this being the "natural" result of their own vegetational destruction, coupled with climatic deterioration at the end of the Pleistocene? If we used the low-density figures presented earlier, an even more dramatic scenario emerges. For example, assuming a density of 2 animals/sq km provides a population of only 216 animals on the Peninsula. Using the same calculations made earlier, a 10% hunting rate would require the demise of 21 animals annually, with a meat yield of 1,680 kg (80kg/animal × 21 individuals). This yield could support a population of only 3.4 humans! Because it is unlikely that less than a minimum band of, say, 20 people would have occupied the Peninsula, a far higher than 10% hunting rate would have had to have been achieved; even a 50% rate would only have supported only about 18 people. In this scenario, extinction could be a rapid event indeed.

As this is a purely illustrative example, what happens if we modify some of these numbers? Table 13-2 presents a few different scenarios, using both the 40% meat-to-weight ra-

Table 13-2. Speculative Scenarios for *Phanourios* Hunting Rates and Supportable Human Populations on the Akrotiri Peninsula

Phanourios density	40% usable meat rate=80 kg/animal	Number of humans supportable	50% usable meat rate=100 kg/animal	Number of humans supportable
High				
25/km2; 10% hunt rate=270	21,600 kg		27,000 kg	
60% diet		44.0		55.0
30% diet		88.0		110.0
Medium				
15/km2; 10% hunt rate=162	12,960 kg		16,200 kg	
60% diet		26.4		33.0
30% diet		52.8		66.0
Low				
2/km2; 10% hunt rate=21	1,680 kg		2,100 kg	
60% diet		3.4		4.3
30% diet		6.8		8.6

Note: Animal hunt rates are based on 10% of total possible density; assumes *Phanourios* consumption of 9.45 kg/wk, 491/year (at 60%); or 4.7 kg/wk, 245.5/year (at 30%) (see p. 329–331 for explanation).

tio suggested by Frison and the larger 50% ratio suggested by Jochim (1976:133) for red deer. If the concept of people consuming nearly 10 kg of *Phanourios* weekly seems overwhelming, these additional scenarios assume a lower percentage of *Phanourios* in the diet, including only a 30% *Phanourios* rate, more in line with Eaton *et al.'s* (1988a:79–80) suggestion of a 65% plant-35% animal ratio for many prehistoric hunter/gatherer groups. Although the figures change substantially depending on the scenario, the end result really does not. Even when using these more modest figures for *Phanourios* hunting and human population levels, it seems clear that local populations of pygmy hippopotamus could have been decimated relatively rapidly.

A scenario such as that presented earlier must be evaluated against a backdrop of the environmental change associated with the end of the Pleistocene and beginning of the Holocene. Although not large in comparison with modern hippopotami, *Phanourios* was one of the largest animals inhabiting Cyprus. Certainly, research suggests that large body size is a characteristic associated with high rates of extinction during episodes of environmental change. Large size has at least two correlates increasing susceptibility to extinction: First, large size severely constrains population density and hence total population size. As a result, any environmental change that further reduces populations increases the probability of extinction. Second, large organisms have life history traits that make them susceptible to environmental change (Brown 1995:162). Thus with the presumed environmental changes during the transition to the Holocene, *Phanourios* could have been poised on the brink of extinction.

Phanourios was clearly the preferred resource at *Aetokremnos,* and even a "healthy" population could have rapidly succumbed to small groups of hunters. There is little archaeological evidence to suggest an intense human occupation of the Peninsula (or indeed Cyprus) at the time. Coupled with deteriorating climatic conditions, however, humans may have rapidly accelerated an inevitable extinction, being the "straw to break the hippo's back" if these animals were already under stress. Indeed, the Akrotiri Peninsula may have served as a refugia for remnant *Phanourios* populations. To document this, however, other paleontological sites containing *Phanourios* would have to be radiometrically dated. Thus humans still are the principal variable. If they had not occupied the Akrotiri Peninsula, even if only for a short period of time, *Phanourios* still may have been present when permanent occupation of Cyprus occurred during the Aceramic Neolithic.

CONCLUSIONS

Where does *Aetokremnos* fit within Diamond's (1989a:39–41) "Evil Quartet" of recent extinction mechanisms: overkill, habitat destruction and fragmentation, impact of introduced species, and chains of extinction? It appears, based on the present evidence, that only the overkill mechanism was very significant in the case of Cyprus. Habitat destruction may already have begun due to the destructive habits of both *Phanourios* and *Elephas*, which could have been accelerated by deteriorating climatic conditions. Habitat destruction by humans, however, is especially severe only with the introduction of agriculture, and there is no evidence that the occupants of the site practiced this economic strategy. Introduction of agriculture did not occur until the Cypriot Neolithic. Likewise, there is little to suggest that the occupants of *Aetokremnos* introduced any new species that could have competed with *Phanourios*. They *may* have had pigs and possibly deer, based on the few bones of these species recovered from the site, but we believe that these were probably introduced into the site as remnants of clothing rather than living animals. Finally, the chains of extinction noted by Diamond may be inapplicable to Cyprus, as there were few indigenous species living on the island. Perhaps the extinction of *Phanourios* accelerated the population increase in birds, which primarily occurs in abundance late in the stratigraphic record at *Aetokremnos*, but this relationship seems tenuous.

Another variable that Diamond does not consider in his "Evil Quartet," since he is dealing with recent extinctions, is, of course, climate change (which he deals with elsewhere: e.g., Diamond 1984:834–838, 1989b:171–174). Climate undoubtedly was also an extinction mechanism in the case of *Aetokremnos*. We do not, however, consider it primary, as there is presently no evidence to indicate climatic changes at approximately 12,000–10,000 B.P. that were any more severe than previous fluctuations. As noted previously, however, the state of paleoenvironmental research in Cyprus requires far more research before precise patterns can be observed, and their roles in extinctions can be assessed. Along these lines, the exemplary interdisciplinary and paleoenvironmental research currently being conducted (e.g., Burney 1993a; Patterson *et al.* 1995) in Madagascar should serve as models for the way in which this complex problem should be approached.

It is evident that extinction, even on islands, is not a clear-cut process. Burney's (1993b) so-called "recipe for disaster" involves at least four variables, which complement those posed by Diamond (earlier). They are climate change, human predation, changes in fire regime and vegetation structure, and the arrival of exotic species. Other authors have elaborated on variants of these variables in quite some detail (e.g., Burney *et al.* 1988; Diamond 1984, 1989b:169–170; Sondaar 1987, to name but a few). At *Aetokremnos*, however, human predation appears to have been the overriding factor. Thus we still must come to the conclusion that humans were the significant factor in the extinction of *Phanourios*.

Certainly, the extinction of these animals involved a complex interaction of both human and natural variables, including the human impact on the supporting environment and direct predation. It seems clear, however, that when undisturbed by humans, the natural processes of dispersal, colonization, and evolution may result in a very low rate of extinction, at least on tropical islands (Steadman 1995b:1129). Equally clear is that "how long it takes for a species to be obliterated by people depends on a multitude of local factors" (Steadman 1995a:46). We believe that at *Aetokremnos*, these "local factors" favored a rapid extinction event.

Excavation of one site, even one as rich as *Aetokremnos*, will not support (or refute) a model of Pleistocene overkill, but it will certainly add to the limited database. *Aetokremnos* ironically presents something of a contradiction to Martin's (1984; Moismann and Martin 1975) classic "blitzkrieg" model. Martin proposed that extinction occurred so rapidly that it would be unlikely to find sites containing the remains of the extinct animals. It was the paucity of butchered skeletons that prompted the "blitzkrieg" model (cf. Diamond 1984:855). Diamond (1984:855) further noted that there are examples of human-linked extinction that left few skeletons (as proposed by Martin), but there also are cases of hunting that left abundant skeletons, while not causing extinction. *Aetokremnos*, with its abundance of bone, certainly falls in the latter category. This is, however, perhaps a moot point as *Aetokremnos* is not unique here. In New Zealand, at least, relatively rapid extinction of moas is reflected by archaeological sites containing large numbers of skeletons (Anderson 1984, 1989).

It may be that pygmy hippopotami were already on the verge of extinction in Cyprus, and that human presence accelerated this. The introduction of competing animal species by people may also have been a variable. In any event, it is likely that the hippopotami, unused to any predators, would have been a naive fauna, easy prey to human hunters. A concept of island biogeography that is particularly relevant here involves niche shifts. Colonizing animals (in this case, humans) are faced with a new array of resources and can cause abrupt changes in the distribution of endemic flora and fauna (Diamond 1970; Diamond and Marshall 1977). The most rapid of these "are immediate behavioral responses by an individual colonizing animal confronted with new food resources harvestable by a foraging technique already practiced by the animal" (Keegan and Diamond 1987:75). In the *Aetokremnos* scenario, human hunters, presumably with an established "foraging" (or hunting in this case) technique, could have caused a near catastrophic decimation of the pygmy hippopotamus population. The evidence at *Aetokremnos* certainly points to an abundant hippopotamus "harvest" over a relatively short period of time.

In summary, there is virtually no evidence similar to that of *Aetokremnos*. Many claims may have been made for the association of humans and Pleistocene island endemics, but these are not well supported by actual archaeological data. In many cases, the arguments for coexistence are implied by analogy, relying on roughly synchronous chronologies. What *Aetokremnos* provides is an actual archaeological site that contains both early human artifacts and extinct endemics, making it unique in the extinction argument, at least as it relates to an island and an Early Holocene site. Thus the significance of *Aetokremnos* is not in demonstrating an extinction episode, but rather in demonstrating its *antiquity* and its causation by a people who were preagricultural.

FINAL REMARKS

This book has tried to be both a comprehensive site report and a broader interpretative document. By trying to be all things, we are certain to have omitted discussion on some aspects of *Aetokremnos* that other scholars might have considered critical. For this, I must accept responsibility. I believe, however, that we have accomplished a formidable task in this work. I also hope that the absolute necessity of interdisciplinary research has been well demonstrated here. Even if the downside of such an approach is that it often takes longer to complete a project, because one must rely on numerous researchers who all have other commitments, the final results are, we hope, worth the wait.

Certainly, one of the problems in having a considerable time lag between excavation and publication of the final report (in this case, over five years) is the very real possibility of having one's conclusion being second-guessed or, worse yet, usurped by other researchers. There is no one to blame for such a predicament other than ourselves, however. Given the controversial nature of the site, it should come as no surprise that other investigators, using data presented in preliminary reports, have come to their own conclusions about *Aetokremnos*. Sometimes these conclusions have been at odds with ours but overall these have been reasoned and in line with available data.

Aetokremnos has not escaped the critical eye of John Cherry, who is perhaps the leading proponent of using caution and well-structured archaeological methodology to verify claims of antiquity throughout the Mediterranean Islands. His insightful articles (particularly Cherry 1990 and 1992) have cast more than reasonable doubt on many claims of great antiquity on the islands. In assessing *Aetokremnos*, he reached many of the conclusions that we did. However, we disagree with one of his assessments. In addressing evidence for Mediterranean Island "pre-Neolithic" human occupation, he states that such phenomena are characterized by

> (1) heavy reliance on endemic, Pleistocene mammalian fauna which, not being adapted to the pressures of predation, may have been "naive," easily taken, and therefore readily driven to extinction by overkill; and (2) a very rudimentary and impoverished material culture, which bears little resemblance either to contemporary assemblages on adjacent mainland areas or to those of succeeding Neolithic cultures. (Cherry 1992:34)

We have no qualm with the first statement, and indeed believe that *Aetokremnos* provides compelling evidence for precisely such an extinction event. With the second statement, however, we do disagree. The assemblage from *Aetokremnos* is not "rudimentary and impoverished." Indeed, in many ways, it is more sophisticated than succeeding Aceramic Neolithic assemblages in Cyprus, and, as argued in Chapter 11, it would fit comfortably within mainland late Epipaleolithic or early Aceramic Neolithic groups, although it lacks the characteristic projectile points of the latter.

In any event, we are fully in agreement with Cherry's warning on terminology. What are early assemblages such as that from *Aetokremnos* to be called? Although *pre-Neolithic* is perhaps the most neutral, it also is quite vague. Cherry (1992:34) was absolutely correct in stating that *Paleolithic* is not an appropriate term, as it has connotations of considerable antiquity and possibly pre-*Homo sapiens* hominids. We prefer neutral terms, and until more data are available, regionally defined characterizations, such as the *Akrotiri Phase,* are perhaps the most realistic solution. What is important is that groups such as those responsible for *Aetokremnos* belonged to a Late Pleistocene/Early Holocene world that was undergoing rapid and dramatic changes. The site of *Aetokremnos* represents the material manifestation of one of the more unique adaptive responses to this world.

What then is the ultimate disposition of Akrotiri *Aetokremnos?* Why is it so controversial? In the final perspective, *Aetokremnos* is perhaps most significant not because it represents the earliest site in Cyprus, or even because it provides compelling evidence that humans were at least partially to blame for the extinction of endemics. Flannery (1973:308) long ago pointed out the futility of searching for the "oldest" of anything, and human-induced extinctions are well documented, at least in on islands and in historic times. Rather, *Aetokremnos* is a methodological case study showing how difficult it is to thoroughly document the complex interplay between humans and animals. In spite of these caveats, however, we believe that *Aetokremnos,* to date, *is* the earliest site in Cyprus, and that people indeed *were* responsible for pushing an extinction event. We know that people began having irreversible ecological impacts during the Neolithic (cf. Köhler-Rollefson and Rollefson 1990; Simmons *et al.* 1988); we now know that even nonagriculturalists, at least in the constricted confines of an island ecosystem, could have caused equally devastating environmental consequences.

Many researchers have noted that in proving a claim of antiquity that is contrary to consensus opinion, certain criteria must be met that are beyond what is required under "normal" archaeological circumstances (e.g., Cherry 1981,1990:201–203, 1992:36; Cordell 1984:122; Dincauze 1984; Grayson 1984; Haynes 1969; Mead and Melzer 1984; Meltzer 1986; Meltzer and Mead 1983, 1985). These "*must* include sound stratigraphy coupled with a series of chronometric determinations of artifacts indisputably of human manufacture in direct association—i.e., *artifacts, stratigraphy* and *dates*" (Cherry 1992:36). Akrotiri *Aetokremnos* exceeds all of these criteria beyond any reasonable doubt.

In an excellent discussion on how claims for antiquity can become assumed models without undergoing critical scrutiny, Cherry (1992) pointed out several fallacies and problems that could be resolved by the application of rigorous scientific archaeological methodology. Unfortunately, claims for controversial sites, whether they be for great antiquity or something else, often have "a tendency to dissolve into stalemate over the nature and use of evidence" (Cherry 1992:28). By the application of precise and multidisciplinary data recovery, we hope we have avoided this problem with *Aetokremnos.*

Perhaps an even deeper issue related to various paradigmatic approaches, depending on schooling, theoretical perspective, or even nationality. To claim the contrary is naive, as pointed out for the circum-Mediterranean region by Clark (1991). This issue has been directly addressed for *Aetokremnos* (Simmons 1991b), where it was suggested that at least some of the initial skepticism for the site was tied to a lack of knowledge regarding the nature of hunter/gatherer sites lacking architecture. Certainly, there is a wide range of interpretative variability within the discipline of archaeology. In an area such as the Mediterranean, where anthropological archaeology has often been superseded by nonanthropological approaches, the end result can be a paradigm clash between differing perspectives on the nature and assessment of archaeological data. *Aetokremnos* certainly has been a victim of this cross-disciplinary polemic. Saying this does not denigrate any of these approaches, but rather acknowledges that strict adherence to any one can lead to theoretical and interpretive intolerance and blindness.

Perhaps Akrotiri *Aetokremnos,* in the final analysis, has helped to bridge this disciplinary chasm. In the end result, it is not important if we have convinced every researcher that *Aetokremnos* is an archaeological site; that it is the oldest, well-established such site in Cyprus; and, indeed, on any of the Mediterranean Islands; or that people were responsible for the extinction of a unique endemic species. The evidence presented in the previous chapters will either do this or not. We hope, however, that we have caused a serious rethinking of the nature of archaeological evidence, showing that it is variable and need not be bound by any particular school of thought, as long as it can be defended with rigorous adherence to scientific methodology. If we have accomplished this, we are content that we have made a major contribution to rewriting the unique history of humans and their interactions with islands.

References

Abramova, Z. (1982). Zur jagd im jungpalaolithikum: nach beispielen des jungpalaolithischen fundplatzes Koko-ervo I in Sibiren. *Archäologisches Korrespondenblatt* 12: 1–9.

Acra, M. , Martini, F. , Pitzalis, G. , Tuveri, C. , and Ulzega, A. (1982a). Il Paleolitica dell'Anglona (Sardegna Settentrionale). Richerche 1979–1980. *Quadrani* 12: 58.

Acra, M. , Martini, F. , Pitzalis, G. , Tuveri, C. , and Ulzega, A. (1982b). Il depositio Quaternario con industria del Paleolitico Inferiore di sa Padrosa-Pantallinu (Sassari). *Rivisita di Scienze Preistoriche* 37: 31–53.

Adovasio, J. , Fry, G. , Gunn, J. , and Maslowski, R. (1975). Prehistoric and Historic Settlement Patterns in Western Cyprus (with a Discussion of Cypriot Neolithic Stone Tool Technology). *World Archaeology* 6: 339–364.

Adovasio, J. , Fry, G. , Gunn, J. , and Maslowski, R. (1978). Prehistoric and Historic Settlement Patterns in Western Cyprus: An Overview. *Reports of the Department of Antiquities, Cyprus 1978*: 39–57.

Albrecht, G. (1988a). An Upper Paleolithic Sequence from Antalya in Southern Turkey: Results of the 1985 Cave Excavations at Karain B. *La Mutation—L'Homme de Neandertal* 8: 23–35.

Albrecht, G. (1988b). Preliminary Results of the Excavation in the Karain B Cave near Antalya/Turkey: The Upper Paleolithic Assemblages and the Upper Pleistocene Climatic Development. *Paleorient* 14: 211–222.

Albrecht, G. , Albrecht, H. , Burger, D. , Moser, J. , Rähle, W. , Schoch, W. , Storch, J. , Verpmann, H. , and Urban, H. (1992). Late Pleistocene and Early Holocene Finds from Öküzini: A Contribution to the Settlement History of the Bay of Antalya, Turkey. *Paléorient* 18/2: 123–141.

Alcover, J. (1991). Island Colonization in the Western Mediterranean: The Balearic Islands. In *2nd Deya Conference of Prehistory: Archaeological Techniques, Technology and Theory*, Vol. 2, edited by W. Waldren, J. Ensenyat, and R.-C. Kennards, pp. 251–266. British Archaeological Reports, International Series 574, Oxford.

Alcover, J. , Florit, F. , Mourer-Chauviré, C. , and Weesie, P. (1992). The Avifauna of the Isolated Mediterranean Islands During the Middle and Late Pleistocene. *Natural History Museum of Los Angeles County, Science Series* 36: 273–283.

Altevogt, R. , Grzimek, B. , and Thenius, E. (1972). Die russeltiere. In *Grzimeks Tierleben: Enzyklopadie des Tierreiches*, vol. 12, Saugetiere 3, edited by B. Grzimek, pp. 479–514. Kindler Verlag, Zurich.

Andel, T. van. (1987). The Adjacent Sea. In *Fascicle 2: Landscape and People of the Franchthi Region*, edited by T. van Andel and S. Sutton, pp. 31–54. Indiana University Press, Bloomington.

Andel, T. van. (1989). Late Quaternary Sea-Level Changes and Archaeology. *Antiquity* 63: 733–745.

Andel, T. van. (1990). Addendum to 'Late Quaternary Sea-Level Changes and Archaeology. *Antiquity* 64: 151–152.

Andel, T. van and Lianos, N. (1983). Prehistoric and Historic Shorelines of the Southern Argolid Peninsula: A Sub-bottom Profiler Study. *International Journal Nautical Archaeology Underwater Exploration* 12: 303–324.

Andel, T. van and Shackleton, J. (1982). Late Paleolithic and Neolithic Coastlines of Greece and the Aegean. *Journal of Field Archaeology* 9: 445–454.

Andel T. van, and Sutton, S. (Eds.). (1987). *Fascicle 2: Landscape and People of the Franchthi Region*. Indiana University Press, Bloomington.

Anderson, A. (1984). The Extinction of Moa in Southern New Zealand. In *Pleistocene Extinctions: A Prehistoric Revolution*, edited by P. Martin and R. Klein, pp. 728–740. University of Arizona Press, Tucson.

Anderson, A. (1989). Mechanics of Overkill in the Extinction of New Zealand Moas. *Journal of Archaeological Science* 16: 137–151.

Anderson, A. (1991). *Prodigious Birds: Moas and Moa Hunting in Prehistoric New Zealand*. Cambridge University Press, Cambridge.

Anderson, A. (1995). Current Approaches in East Polynesian Colonisation Research. *The Journal of the Polynesian Society* 104: 110–132.

Andrews, P. and Cook, J. (1985). Natural Modifications to Bones in a Temperate Setting. *Man* 20: 675–691.

Anonymous. (1910). *Annals of the Cyprus Natural History Society* II.

Arquembourg, P. (1975). *Immunoelectrohporesis. Theory, Methods, Identification, Techniques*. S. Karger, Basel-Munich.

Åström, P. (1957). The Middle Cypriote Bronze Age. *Swedish Cyprus Expedition* (Vol. IV/IB). Ohlsson, Lund.

Åström, P. (1972). Summary and Historical Conclusion. In *Swedish Cyprus Expedition* (Vol. IV/ID), pp. 763–781. Berlingska Boktryckeriet, Lund.

Audley-Charles, M. and Hooijer, D. (1973). Relation of Pleistocene Migrations of Pygmy Stegodonts to Island Arc Tectonics in Eastern Indonesia. *Nature* 241: 197–198.

Axelrod, D. (1967). *Quaternary Extinctions of Large Mammals*, University of California Publications in Geological Sciences, Vol. 74. University of California Press, Berkeley and Los Angeles.

Azzaroli, A. (1980). About Pygmy Mammoths of the Northern Channel Islands and Other Island Faunas. *Quaternary Research* 16: 423–425.

Azzaroli, A. (1981). Cainozoid Mammals and the Biogeography of the Island of Sardinia, Western Mediterranean. *Palaeogeography, Palaeoclimatology, Palaeoecology* 36: 107–111.

Azzaroli, A. and Guazzone, G. (1979). Terrestrial Mammals and Land Connections in the Mediterranean Before and During the Messinian. *Palaeogeorgaphy, Palaeoclimatology, Palaeoecology* 29: 155–167.

Baales, M. (1992). Accumulations of Bones of Lagopus in Late Pleistocene Sediments: Are They Caused by Man or Animals? *Cranium* 9/1: 17–22.

Bacher, A. (1967). Vergleichend morphologische untersuchungen an einzelknochen des postkranialen skeletts in mitteleuropa verkommender schwane und ganse. Ph.D. dissertation, Universität München, München.

Bachmayer, F. and Symeonidis, N. (1974). Eigenartige abspaltungen von strobzahnen der zwergelefanten aus der hohle "Charkadio" auf der insel Tilos (artefakte?). *Annales Geologiques des Pays Helleniques* 26: 320–323.

Bachmayer, F. , Symeonidis, N. , Seemann, R. , and Zapfe, H. (1976). Die ausgrabungen in der zwergelefanten-höhle Charkadio auf der insel Tilos in den jahren 1974 und 1975. *Annalen des Naturhistorischen Hofmeseums, Wien* 80: 113–144.

Badgley, C. (1986a). Counting Individuals in Mammalian Fossil Assemblages from Fluvial Environments. *Palaios* 1: 328–338.

Badgley, C. (1986b). Hunter-Gatherer Behavior in Prehistory: Problems and Perspectives. In *Hunter-Gatherer Economy in Prehistory*, edited by G. Bailey, pp. 1–6. Cambridge University Press, Cambridge.

Bailey, G. (1983). *Hunter-Gatherer Economy in Prehistory: A European Perspective*. Cambridge University Press, Cambridge.

Bailon, S. (1991). *Amphibiens et reptiles du Pliocène et du Quaternaire d'Espagne et de France: mise en place et évolution des faunes*. Thèse (non publiee), Universite Paris, Paris.

Baird, D. (1992, April 18). Aspects of Continuity from the PPNB to the Early Late Neolithic—The Evidence from Wadi Jilat and Azraq. Paper presented at the Late Pre-Pottery Neolithic to Early Neolithic Recent Research in Jordan Workshop, Yarmouk University, Irbid, Jordan.

Bannerman, D. and Bannerman, W. (1958). *The Birds of Cyprus*. Oliver and Boyd, London.

Bar-Yosef, D. (1994). The Marine Shells. In *Le Site de Hatoula en Judée Occidentale, Israël*, edited by M. Lechervallier and A. Rosen, pp. 233–238. Mémoires et Travaux de Centre de Recherche Français de Jérusalem 8, Paris.

Bar-Yosef, O. and Phillips, J. (Eds.). (1977). *Prehistoric Investigations in Gebel Maghara, Northern Sinai*. QEDEM 7, Monographs of the Institute of Archaeology, Hebrew University. Ahva Co-op Press, Jerusalem.

Bar-Yosef, O. , Gopher, A. , Tchernov, E. , and Kislev, M. (1991). Netiv Hagdud: An Early Neolithic Village Site in the Jordan Valley. *Journal of Field Archaeology* 18: 405–424.

Bard, E. , Hamelin, B. , Fairbanks, R. , and Zindler, A. (1990). Calibration of the 14C Timescale over the Past 30,000 Years Using Mass Spectrometric U-Th Ages from Barbados Corals. *Nature* 345: 405–410.

Barfield, L. (1991). Hot Stones: Hot Food or Hot Baths? In *Burnt Mounds and Hot Stone Technology*, edited by M. Hodder and L. Barfield, pp. 59–68. Sandwell, England.

Barfield, L. and Hodder, M. (1991). Burnt Mounds or Saunas, and the Prehistory of Bathing. *Antiquity* 61: 370–379.

Barnosky, A. (1989). The Late Pleistocene Event as a Paradigm for Widespread Mammal Extinction. In *Mass Extinctions: Processes and Evidence*, edited by S. Donovan, pp. 235–254. Columbia University Press, New York.

Bate, D. (1903a). Preliminary Note on the Discovery of a Pigmy Elephant in the Pleistocene of Cyprus. *Proceedings of the Royal Society of London* 71: 498–500.

Bate, D. (1903b). The Mammals of Cyprus. *Proceedings of the Zoological Society of London* 1903(2): 341–348.

Bate, D. (1903c). On an Extinct Species of Genet (*Genetta plesictoides*, Sp. N.) from the Pleistocene of Cyprus. *Proceedings of the Zoological Society* 2: 121–124.

Bate, D. (1903d). On the Occurrence of Acomys in Cyprus. *The Annals and Magazine of Natural History* II: 565–567.

Bate, D. (1903, December). *III. Zoological Society of London. The Geological Magazine* X: 332 (abstract).

Bate, D. (1904a). Further Note on the Remains of *Elephas cypriotes*, from a Cave-Deposit in Cyprus. *Philosophical Transactions of the Royal Society* 197: 347–360.

Bate, D. (1904b). On the Ossiferous Cave-Deposits of Cyprus. *Geological Magazine* (Decade 5) 1: 324–325.

Bate, D. (1904c). Further Note on the Remains of *Elephas cypriotes, Bate,* from a Cave-Deposit in Cyprus. *Proceedings of the Royal Society* 74: 120–122.

Bate, D. (1904d). Further Note on the Remains of *Elephas cypriotes, Bate,* from a Cave-Deposit in Cyprus. *The Geological Magazine* (Decade 5) 1: 325–326.

Bate, D. (1906). The Pygmy Hippopotamus of Cyprus. *Geological Magazine* (Decade 5) 3: 241–245.

Bate, D. (1916). On a Small Collection of Vertebrate Remains from the Har Dalam Cavern, Malta; With Note on a New Species of the Genus *Cygnus. Proceedings of the Zoological Society of London:* 421–430.

Bate, D. (1937). Palaeontology: The Fossil Fauna of the Wady-el-Mughara Caves. In *The Stone Age of Mount Carmel*, I, edited by D. A. E. Garrod and D. M. A. Bate, pp. 137–233. Clarendon Press, Oxford.

Baudou, E. (1982). Fouilles d'Ayia Irini, District de Larnaca. In V. Karageorghis, *"Chronique des Fouilles et Découvertes Archèologiques à Chypre in 1981." Bulletin de Correspondance Hellénique* 106: 713.

Baudou, E. (1983). Fouilles d'Ayia Irini, District de Larnaca. In V. Karageorghis, *"Chronique des Fouilles et Découvertes Archèologiques à Chypre in 1982." Bulletin de Correspondance Hellénique* 107: 918.

Baudou, E. and Englemark, R. (1983). The Tremithos Valley Project: A Preliminary Report for 1981–82. *Report of the Department of Antiquities, Cyprus 1983:* 1–8.

Baudou, E. , Engelmark, R. , Niklasson, K. , and Wennberg, B. (1985). The Tremithos Valley Project. In *Acts of the Second International Congress of Cypriot Studies* (Nicosia, April 1982), edited by T. Papadopoulos and S. Hadjistyllis, pp. 369–371. Society of Cypriot Studies, Nicosia.

Beck, H. (1937). Report on Four Beads from Layer B of the Mughared el-Wad. In *The Stone Age of Mount Carmel*, vol. I., D. A. E. Garrod and D. M. A. Bate, p. 125. Clarendon Press, Oxford.

Behrensmeyer, A. (1983). Patterns of Natural Bone Distribution on Recent Land Surfaces: Implications for Archaeological Site Formation. In *Animals and Archaeology: I. Hunters and Their Prey*, edited by J. Clutton-Brock and C. Grigson, pp. 93–106. British Archaeological Reports, International Series 163, Oxford.

Behrensmeyer, A. (1988). Vertebrate Preservation in Fluvial Channels. *Palaeogeography, Palaeoclimatology, Palaeoecology* 63: 183–199.

Behrensmeyer, A. (1990). Transport-Hydrodynamics: Bones. In *Paleobiology: A Synthesis*, edited by D. Briggs and P. Crowther, pp. 232–235. Blackwell Scientific Publications, Oxford.

Behrensmeyer, A. (1993). Discussion: Noncultural Processes. In *From Bones to Behavior*, edited by J. Hudson. pp. 342–348. Southern Illinois University, Center for Archaeological Investigations, Occasional Paper 21, Carbondale, Illinois.

Bennett, J. (1999). Thermal Alteration of Buried Bone. *Journal of Archaeological Science* 26:1–8.

Bennett, J. and Klippel, W. (1995). Thermal Alteration of Subsurface Faunal Remains. *Society for American Archaeology, Abstracts of the 60th Annual Meeting:* 36.

Berger, R. (1980). Early Man on Santa Rosa Island. In *The California Islands: Proceedings of a Multidisciplinary Symposium*, edited by D. Power, pp. 73–78. Santa Barbara Museum of Natural History, Santa Barbara.

Beta Analytic. (1991). Report of Radiocarbon Dating Analyses for *Aetokremnos* AMS Samples (Reports on file). Quaternary Research Center, Desert Research Institute, Reno, Nevada.

Bettinger, R. (1991). *Hunter-Gatherers: Archaeological and Evolutionary Theory.* Plenum Press, New York.

Betts, A. (1979). The Chipped Stone from Lemba *Lakkous* and Kissonerga *Mylouthkia* (1976–77). *Report of the Department of Antiquities of Cyprus, 1979:* 100–111.

Betts, A. (1985). The Chipped Stone. In *Lemba Archaeological Project: 1. Excavations at Lemba Lakkous, 1976–1983,* edited by E. Peltenburg, pp. 94–95, 196–197, 276–278. Studies in Mediterranean Archaeology 70:1. Paul Åströms Förlag, Göteborg.

Betts, A. (1987). The Chipped Stone. In E. Peltenburg *et al.*, Excavations at Kissonegra Mosphilia 1986 (pp. 5–10). *Report of the Department of Antiquities, Cyprus 1987:* 1–18.

Betts, A. (1991). The Late Epipaleolithic in the Black Desert, Eastern Jordan. In *The Natufian Culture in the Levant,* edited by O. Bar-Yosef and F. Valla, pp. 217–234. International Monographs in Prehistory, Archaeological Series 1, Ann Arbor, Michigan.

Binford, L. (1978). *Nunamiut Ethnoarchaeology.* Academic Press, New York.

Binford, L. (1981). *Bones: Ancient Men and Modern Myths.* Academic Press, New York.

Binford, L. (1984). *Faunal Remains from Klasies River Mouth.* Academic Press, New York.

Binford, L. (1987). Were There Elephant Hunters at Torralba? In *The Evolution of Human Hunting,* edited by M. Nitecki and D. Nitecki, pp. 47–105. Plenum Press, New York.

Bintliff, J. (1977). *Natural Environment and Human Settlement in Prehistoric Greece* (Vols. 1 and 2). British Archaeological Reports, Supplement Series 28, Oxford.

Bjerrum, L. and Jorstad, F. (1968). Stability of Rock Slopes in Norway. *Norwegian Geotechnical Institute Publication 79:* 1–11.

Blondel, J. and Vigne, J. (1993). Space, Time, and Man as Determinants of Diversity of Birds and Mammals in the Mediterranean Region. In *Species Diversity in Ecological Communities,* edited by R. Ricklefs and D. Schluter, pp. 135–146. University of Chicago Press, Chicago.

Blueweiss, L. , Fox, H. , Kudzama, V. , Nakashima, D. , Peters, R. , and Sams, S. (1978). Relationships Between Body Size and Some Life History Parameters. *Oecologia* (Berlin) 37: 257–272.

Blumler, M. (1993). Successional Pattern and Landscape Sensitivity in the Mediterranean and the Near East. In *Landscape Sensitivity,* edited by D. Thomas and R. Allisons, pp. 287–305. Wiley, New York.

Boccaletti, M. and Manetti, P. (1978). The Tyrrhenian Sea and Adjoining Regions. In *The Ocean Basins and Martins 4B,* edited by A. Nairn, W. Kanes, and F. Stehli, pp. 149–199. Plenum Press, New York.

Bocheński, Z. (1989). Ptaki-aves. *Folia Quaternaria:* 59–60, 89–108.

Boekschoten, G. and Sondaar, P. (1966). The Pleistocene of the Katharo Basin (Crete) and Its *Hippopotamus. Bijdragen tot de Diekunde* 36: 17–44.

Boekschoten, G. and Sondaar, P. (1972). On the Fossil Mammals of Cyprus. *Proceedings of the Koninklijke Nederlanse Adademie van Wetenschappen* (Series B) 75: 306–338.

Boessneck, J. and von den Driesch, A. (1978). Preliminary Analysis of the Animal Bones from Tell Hesbân. *Andrews University Seminary Studies* 16/1: 259–287.

Boessneck, J. and von den Driesch, A. (1987). Analyse der vogel-, reptilien-, amphibien-und fischknochen. In *Die Ergenbisse der Ausgrabungen 1975–1978, Band II: Naturwissenschaftliche Untersuchungen,* edited by M. Korfmann, pp. 43–52. Von Zabern, Mainz.

Bonfiglio, L. (1995). Taphonomy and Depositional Setting of Pleistocene Mammal-Bearing Deposits from Acquedolci (Northeastern Sicily). In *First European Palaeontological Congress: Geobios—Mémoire Spécial No. 18,* edited by M. Gayet and B. Courtinat, pp. 57–68. Édition de l'Université Claude-Bernard, Lyon.

Bonifay, E. (1983). Circonscription de la Corse. In *Informations Archeologiques. Gallia Prehistoire* 26: 511–524.

Bonnichsen, R. and Sorg, M. (Eds.). (1989). *Bone Modification.* Peopling of the Americas Publications, Center for the Study of the First Americans, Institute for Quaternary Studies, University of Maine, Orono, Maine.

Bons, J. , Cheylan, M. , and Guillaume, C. (1984). Les reptiles méditerranéens. *Bulletin de la Societe Herpetolofie de France* 29: 7–17.

Bordaz, J. (1970). *Tools of the Old and New Stone Age.* Natural History Press, Garden City, New Jersey.

Bordes, F. (1961). *Typologie du Paleolithique Ancien et Moyen.* Publication de l'Institut de Prehistoire de l'Universite de Bordeaux, l'Universite de Bordeaux, Bordeaux.

Bosinski, G. (1981). *Gönnersdoft: eiszeitjager am mittelrhein.* Landesmuseum Koblenz, Rheinlandpfalz.

Bottema, S. (1966). Palynological Investigation of a Settlement near Kalopsidha (Cyprus). In P. Åström, *Excavations at Kalopsidha and Ayios Iakovos in Cyprus,* pp. 133–134. Studies in Mediterranean Archaeology 2, Göteborg.

Bottema, S. (1976). Note on Pollen. In P. Åström, D. Baley, and V. Karageorghis, *Hala Sultan Tekké 1*. Studies in Mediterranean Archaeology 45: 1.

Boulenger, G. (1888). Second List of Reptiles and Batrachians from Cyprus. *The Annals and Magazine of Natural History* 6, XII (ser. 2): 505–506.

Braidwood, R. (1983). Jarmo Chronology. In *Prehistoric Archaeology Along the Zagros Flanks*, edited by L. Braidwood, R. Braidwood, B. Howe, C. Reed, and P. Watson, pp. 537–540. The University of Chicago Oriental Institute, Chicago.

Brain, C. (1981). *The Hunters or the Hunted?* University of Chicago Press, Chicago.

Bremner, M. and Mulvaney, C. (1982). Salicylic Acid Thisolfate Modification of Kjeldahl Method to Include Nitrate and Nitrite. In *Methods of Soil Analysis* (Pt. 2), edited by A. Page, R. Miller, and D. Keeney (Eds.), p. 621. American Society of Agronomy, Madison, Wisconsin.

Brézillon, M. (1971). *La denomination des objects de pierre taillee* (2nd ed.), IVᵉ supplement a "Gallia-Prehistoire." Centre National de la Recherche Scientifique, Paris.

Brice, W. (Ed.). (1978). *The Environmental History of the Near and Middle East Since the Last Ice Age*. Academic Press, New York and London.

Briuer, F. (1976). New Clues to Stone Tool Function: Plant and Animal Residues. *American Antiquity* 41: 478–484.

Broderick, M. (1979), Ascending Paper Chromatographic Technique in Archaeology. In *Lithic Use-Wear Analysis*, edited by B. Hayden, pp. 375–383. Academic Press, New York.

Bromage, T. (1992). Northern Cyprus Pleistocene Research Expedition (NORCYPRE): Statement of Purpose and Intent (unpublished manuscript). Department of Anthropology, Hunter College, New York.

Bromage, T. , Dreghorn, W. , and Erojoment, H. (1988). Renewed Research on Northern Cyprus Pleistocene Deposits. In *International Conference, Early Man in Island Environments, Oliena (Sardegna), Abstracts*, edited by M. Sanges, pp. 85–86. Stampa Industria Grafica Stampacolor, Sassari, Sardinia.

Broodbank, C. and Strasser, T. (1991). Migrant Farmers and the Neolithic Colonization of Crete. *Antiquity* 65: 233–245.

Brown, J. (1995). *Macroecology*. University of Chicago Press, Chicago and London.

Buchholz, H. (1969). Naissance d'une civilisation. *Archeologie Vivante* II/3: 19–28.

Buchholz, H. and Karageorghis, V. (1973). *Prehistoric Greece and Cyprus: An Archaeological Handbook*. Phaidon Publishers, New York.

Buikstra, J. and Swegle, M. (1989). Bone Modification Due to Burning: Experimental Evidence. In *Bone Modifications*, edited by R. Bonnichen and M. Sorg, pp. 247–258. Center for the Study of the First Americans, University of Maine, Orono, Maine.

Buitenhuis, H. (1988). Archaeozoölogisch onderzoek langs de Midden Eufraat. Ph.D. dissertation. Rijksuniversiteit Groningen, Groningen.

Bunimovitz, S. and Barkai, R. (1996). Ancient Bones and Modern Myths: Ninth Millennium B.C. Hippopotamus Hunters at Akrotiri *Aetokremnos*, Cyprus? *Journal of Mediterranean Archaeology* 9: 85–96.

Bunn, H. (1982). *Meat-eating and Human Evolution: Studies on the Diet and Subsistence Patterns of Plio-Pleistocene Hominids in East Africa*. Unpublished Ph.D. dissertation, University of California, Berkeley.

Bunn, H. (1991). A Taphonomic Perspective on the Archaeology of Human Origins. *Journal of Anthropological Archaeology*: 433–467.

Burleigh, R. and Clutton-Brock, J. (1980). The Survival of *Myotragus balearicus* (Bate, 1909) into the Neolithic on Mallorca. *Journal of Archaeological Science* 7: 385–388.

Burney, D. (1993a). Late Holocene Environmental Changes in Arid Southwestern Madagascar. *Quaternary Research* 40: 98–106.

Burney, D. (1993b). Recent Animal Extinctions: Recipes for Disaster. *American Scientist* 81: 530–541.

Burney, D. and Ramilisonina (1998). Research Report. The *Kilopilopitsofy, Kidoky,* and *Bokyboky:* Accounts of Strange Animals from Belo-sur-mer, Madagascar, and the Megafaunal "Extinction Window." *American Anthropologist* 100:957–966.

Burney, D. , MacPhee, R. , Rafamantanantsoa, J. , Rakotondrazafy, T. , and Kling, G. (1988). The Roles of Natural Factors and Human Activities in the Environmental Changes and Faunal Extinctions of Late Holocene Madagascar. In *International Conference, Early Man in Island Environments, Oliena (Sardegna), Abstracts*, edited by M. Sanges, pp. 127–128. Stampa Industria Grafica Stampacolor, Sassari, Sardinia.

Burney, D. , James, H. , Grady, F. , Rafamantanantsoa, J. , Ramilisonina, Wright, H. , and Cowart, J. (1997). Environmental Change, Extinction, and Human Activity: Evidence from Caves in NW Madagascar. *Journal of Biogeography* 24: 755–767.

Byrd, B. (1994). Late Quaternary Hunter-Gatherer Complexes in the Levant Between 20,000 and 10,000 B.P. In *Late Quaternary Chronology and Paleoclimates of the Eastern Mediterranean*, edited by O. Bar-Yosef and R. Kra, pp. 205–226. Radiocarbon and American School of Prehistoric Research, Tucson, Arizona, and Cambridge, Massachusetts.

Cadastral Survey of Cyprus. (1988). 1:50,000 scale map, Series K717, Sheet 23, Edition 4-GSGS. Limassol.

Caloi, L. and Palombo, M. (1983). Osservazioni sugli Ippopotami Nani delle Isole del Mediterraneo. *Geologico Romana* 22: 45–83.

Caloi, L. , Kotsakis, T. , and Palombo, M. (1986). La fauna a vertebrati terrestri del Pleistocene delle isole del Mediterraneo. *Geologica Romana* 25: 235–256.

Camps, G. (1988). *Préhistoire d'une île: les origines de la Corse*. Editions Errance, Paris.

Carrington, R. (1962). *Elephants*. Penguin Books, Harmondsworth, Middlesex, U.K.

Carson, M. and Kirkby, J. (1972). *Hill Slope Form and Process*. Cambridge University Press, Cambridge.

Carter, P. (1989). Fauna from the 1976 Season. Part II.B In *American Expedition to Idalion, Cyprus 1973–1980*, edited by L. Stager and A. Walker, pp. 244–251. Oriental Institute, Chicago.

Case, T. and Cody, M. (1987). Theories of Island Biogeography. *American Scientist* 75: 402–441.

Cassels, R. (1984). Faunal Extinction and Prehistoric Man in New Zealand. In *Quaternary Extinctions: A Prehistoric Revolution*, edited by P. Martin and R. Klein, pp. 741–767. University of Arizona Press, Tucson.

Cataliotti-Valdina, J. (1994). La malacofaune marine de Cap Andreas-Kastros. In *Fouilles Récentes à Khirokitia (Chypre), 1988–1991*, edited by A. LeBrun, pp. 361–392. Éditions Recherches sur les Civilisations, ADPF, Paris.

Catling, H. (1966). Cyprus in the Neolithic and Chalcolithic Periods. In *The Cambridge Ancient History*, pp. 1–21. Cambridge: University Press, Cambridge.

Caughley, G. (1988). The Colonisation of New Zealand by Polynesians. *Journal of the Royal Society of New Zealand* 18: 245–270.

Cauvin, M. (1984). L'outillage lithique de Khirokitia (Chypre) et le Levant, In *Fouilles Recentes A Khirokitia (Chypre), 1977–1981*, edited by A. LeBrun, pp. 85–87. Editions Recherche Sur Les Civilisations, Memoire 41, Paris.

Chapman, R. (1977). Analysis of the Lithic Assemblages. In *Settlement and Subsistence Along the Lower Chaco River: The CGP Survey*, edited by C. Reher, pp. 371–452. University of New Mexico Press, Albuquerque.

Chauvin, P. (1975). La genette (*Genetta genetta* L.) sa morphologie-son comportement et sa protection: quelques aspects en milieu vendéen. Thèse. Ecole Nationale Vétérinaire D'Alfort, Alfort.

Cherry, J. (1979). Four Problems in Cycladic Prehistory. In *Papers in Cycladic Prehistory*, edited by J. Davis and J. Cherry, pp. 22–47. University of California, Los Angeles.

Cherry, J. (1981). Pattern and Process in the Earliest Colonisation of the Mediterranean Islands. *Proceedings of the Prehistoric Society* 47: 41–68.

Cherry, J. (1984). The Initial Colonisation of the West Mediterranean Islands in the Light of Island Biology and Paleogeorgraphy. In *The Deya Conference of Prehistory: Early Settlement in the Western Mediterranean Islands and Their Peripheral Areas*, edited by W. Waldren, R. Chapman, J. Lewthwaite, and R. Kennard, pp. 7–27. British Archaeological Reports, 229L, Oxford.

Cherry, J. (1985). Islands Out of the Stream: Isolation and Interaction in Early East Mediterranean Insular Prehistory. In *Prehistoric Production and Exchange in the Aegean and East Mediterranean*, edited by B. Knapp and T. Stech, pp. 12–29. Institute of Archaeology, Monograph 25, University of California, Los Angeles.

Cherry, J. (1987). Island Origins: The Early Prehistoric Cyclades. In *Origins: The Roots of European Civilisation*, edited by B. Cunliffe, pp. 16–29. BBC Books, London.

Cherry, J. (1990). The First Colonization of the Mediterranean Islands: A Review of Recent Research. *Journal of Mediterranean Archaeology* 3: 145–221.

Cherry, J. (1992). Paleolithic Sardinians? Some Questions of Evidence and Method. In *Sardinia in the Mediterranean: A Footprint in the Sea*, edited by R. H. Tykot and T. K. Andrews, pp. 29–39. Sheffield Academic Press, Oxford.

Cherry, J. (Ed.). (1995). Colonization of Islands. *World Archaeology* 26, entire issue.

Christodoulou, D. (1959). *The Evolution of the Rural Land Use Pattern in Cyprus*. Geographical Publications Limited, Bude, England.

Clark, G. (1987). From the Mousterian to the Metal Ages: Long-Term Change in the Human Diet of Cantabrian Spain. In *The Pleistocene Old World: Regional Perspectives*, edited by O. Soffer, pp. 293–316. Plenum Press, New York.

Clark, G. (Ed.). (1991). *Perspectives on the Past*. University of Pennsylvania Press, Philadelphia.

Clark, R. (1973). Report on a Collection of Reptiles from Cyprus. *British Journal of Herpetology* 5/1: 357–360.

Clot, A. and Mourer-Chauviré, C. (1986). Inventaire systématique des oiseaux quaternaires des Pyrénées françaises. *Munibe* 38: 171–184.

Clutton-Brock, J. (1981). *Domesticated Animals from Early Times*. Heinemann, London.

Clutton-Brock, J. (1984). Preliminary Report on the Animal Remains from Ferrandell-Oleza, with Comments on the Extinction of *Myotragus balearicus* and on the Introduction of Domestic Livestock to Mallorca. In *The Deya Conference of Prehistory: Early Settlement in the Western Mediterranean Islands and the Peripheral Areas*, edited by W. Waldren, R. Chapman, J. Lewthwaite, and R.-C. Kennard, pp. 99–118. British Archaeological Reports, International Series No. 229, Oxford.

Clutton-Brock, J. (1988). *The British Museum Book of Cats, Ancient and Modern*. British Museum Publications, London.

Clutton-Brock, J. and Burleigh, R. (1983). Some Archaeological Applications of the Dating of Animal Bone by Radiocarbon with Particular Reference to Post-Pleistocene Extinctions. In *PACT 8: 14C and Archaeology* (Vol. 2). Council of Europe, Parliamentary Assembly, Strasbourg.

Cluzan, S. (1984). L'outillage et les petits objets en pierre. In *Fouilles récentes à Khirokitia (Chypre), 1977–1981*, edited by A. LeBrun, pp. 111–124. Editions Recherches sur les Civilisations, ADPF, Memoire no. 41, Paris.

Cobham, C. (1908). *Excerpta Cypria, Materials for a History of Cyprus*. Cambridge University Press (Reprinted, 1969 by Kraus Reprint Co., New York).

Cobham, C. (Trans.). (1909). *Travels in the Island of Cyprus by Giovanni Mariti*. Cambridge University Press, London. (Originally published in 1896)

Cohen, M. (1975). Archaeological Evidence of Population Pressure in Pre-Agricultural Societies. *American Antiquity* 40: 471–475.

Cohen, M. (1977). *The Food Crisis in Prehistory*. Yale University Press, New Haven.

Coleman, J. , Barlow, J. , Mogelonsky, M. , and Schaar, K. (1996). *Alambra. A Middle Bronze Age Settlement in Cyprus. Archaeological Investigations by Cornell University, 1974–1985*. Studies in Mediterranean Archaeology 118. Paul Åströms Förlag, Jonserd.

Colledge, S. (1980). Plant Species from Kissonerga-Mylouthkia, Feature 16.3, Appendix 1. In E. Peltenburg, *Lemba Archaeological Project, Cyprus, 1978: Preliminary Report. Levant* 12: 18–20.

Colledge, S. (1981). Kissonerga-Mylouthkia 1979: Paleobotancial Report. In E. Peltenburg, *Lemba Archaeological Project, Cyprus, 1979: Preliminary Report. Levant* 13: 47.

Colledge, S. (1982) Lemba-Kakkous 1980-Flora, Appendix 3. In E. Peltenburg, *Lemba Archaeological Project, Cyprus, 1980: Preliminary Report. Levant* 14: 53.

Collins, M. (1975). Lithic Technology as a Means of Processual Inference. In *Lithic Technology: Making and Using Stone Tools*, edited by E. Swanson, pp. 15–34. University of Chicago Press, Chicago.

Constantinou, G. (1982). Geological Features and Ancient Exploitation of the Cupriferous Sulphide Orebodies of Cyprus. In *Early Metallurgy in Cyprus, 4000–500 B.C.*, edited by J. Muhly, R. Maddin, and V. Karageorghis, pp. 13–24. Pierides Foundation, Larnaca.

Contenson, H. de. (1971). Tell Ramad, a Village Site of Syria of the 7th and 6th Millennia B.C. *Archaeology* 24: 278–283.

Cooper, J. (1997). Unwrapping the Neolithic Package: Wadi Shu'eib and Kholetria *Ortos* in Perspective. M.A. thesis, Department of Anthropology, University of Nevada at Las Vegas, Las Vegas, Nevada.

Coqueugniot, E. (1984). Premiers elements concernant l'utilisation des outils en silex de Khirokitia (Chypre). Campagne de 1981. In *Fouilles Recentes A Khirokitia (Chypre), 1977–1981*, edited by A. LeBrun, pp. 89–93. Editions Recherche Sur Les Civilisations, Memoire 41, Paris.

Cordell, L. (1984). *Prehistory of the Southwest*. Academic Press, Orlando, Florida.

Cosgrove, R. , Allen, J. , and Marshall, B. (1990). Paleo-Ecology and Pleistocene Human Occupation in South Central Tasmania. *Antiquity* 64: 59–78.

Cox, C. , Healey, I. , and Moore, P. (1973). *Biogeography: An Ccological and Evolutionary Approach*. Blackwell Scientific Publications, Oxford.

Crabtree, D. (1972). An Introduction to Flintworking. *Occasional Papers of the Idaho State University Museum* 28, entire volume.

Crabtree, P. and Campana, D. (1990a). A Note on the First Season of Excavation at the Late Natufian Site of Salibiya I, Jordan Valley. *Paléorient* 16/1: 111–114.

Crabtree, P. and Campana, D. (1990b). The Late Natufian Site of Salibiya I in the Jordan Valley: Preliminary Investigations. *AnthroQuest* 42: 20–22.

Crader, D. (1983). Recent Single-Carcass Bone Scatters and the Problem of "Butchery" Sites in the Archaeological Record. In *Animals and Archaeology: 1. Hunters and Their Prey,* edited by J. Clutton-Brock and C. Grigson, pp. 107–141. British Archaeological Reports, International Series No. 163, Oxford.

Cramp, S. (Ed.). (1985). *The Birds of the Western Palearctic:* IV. Oxford University Press, Oxford.

Cramp, S. and Simmons, K. (Eds.). (1977). *The Birds of the Western Palearctic:* I. Oxford University Press, Oxford.

Cramp, S. and Simmons, K. (1979). *The Birds of the Western Palearctic:* II. Oxford University Press, Oxford.

Croft, P. (1979). Preliminary Comments on the Faunal Remains from Lemba Project Sites. Appendix 1 in E. J. Peltenburg, Lemba Archaeological Project, Cyprus, 1976–77: Preliminary Report. *Levant* II: 37–40.

Croft, P. (1982). Faunal Remains from Tenta and Ayious. In I. Todd Vasilikos Valley Project; Fourth Preliminary Report, 1979–80, pp. 60–63. *Journal of Field Archaeology* 9: 35–77.

Croft, P. (1989a). A Reconsideration of Fauna from the 1972 Season: Part II.C. In *American Expedition to Idalion, Cyprus 1973–1980,* edited by L. E. Stager and A. M. Walker, pp. 259–270. Oriental Institute, Chicago.

Croft, P. (1989b). The Osteology of Neolithic and Chalcolithic Cyprus. Ph.D. dissertation, University of Cambridge, Cambridge.

Croft, P. (1990). Appendix VIII: Faunal Remains from Palaepaphos-*Teratsoudhia.* In *Tombs at Palaepaphos,* edited by V. Karageorghis, pp. 154–155. A. G. Leventis Foundation, Nicosia.

Croft, P. (1991). Man and Beast in Chalcolithic Cyprus. *Bulletin of the American Schools of Oriental Research* 282/283: 63–79.

Croft, P. (1995). Faunal Remains from Kholetria *Ortos* (Unpublished manuscript on file). Department of Anthropology, the University of Nevada, Las Vegas.

Culliford, B. (1964). Precipitin Reactions in Forensic Problems. *Nature* 201: 1092–1094.

Culotta, E. (1995). Minimum Population Grows Larger. *Science* 270: 31–32.

Cumberland, K. (1962). Moas and Men: New Zealand about A.D. 1250. *The Geographical Review* 52: 151–173.

Cutler, D. (1982). Charcoal and Silica. In *Vrysi: A Subterranean Settlement in Cyprus,* edited by E. Peltenburg, pp. 433–434. Aris and Phillips Ltd., Warminster.

D'Annibale, C. (1992). Lithic Analysis. In D. Rupp, Clarke, J. , D'Annibale, C. , and Stewart, S. , *Canadian Palaipaphos Survey Project: 1991 Field Season* (pp. 300–312). *Report of the Department of Antiquities, Cyprus:* 285–317.

D'Annibale, C. (1993). Lithic Analysis. In D. Rupp, Clarke, J. , D'Annibale, C. , Croft, P. , and King, R. , *The Western Cyprus Project: 1992 Field Season* (pp. 399–404). *Report of the Department of Antiquities, Cyprus 1993:* 381–412.

D'Annibale, C. (1994). Chipped Stone Assemblage. In D. Rupp, Clarke, J. , D'Annibale, C., Critchley, J. , and Croft, P. , *Preliminary Report of the 1993 Field Season of the Western Cyprus Project at Prastio-Agios Savvas Tis Karonis Monastery A' (Paphos District, Cyprus)* (p. 323). *Report of the Department of Antiquities, Cyprus 1994:* 315–328.

David, B. (1990). How Was This Bone Burnt? In *Problem Solving in Taphonomy,* edited by S. Solomon, I. Davidson, and D. Watson, pp. 65–79. University of Queensland Anthropology Museum, St. Lucia.

Davis, J. (1973). *Statistics and Data Analysis in Geology.* John Wiley & Sons, New York.

Davis, S. (1984). Khirokitia and Its Mammal Remains: A Neolithic Noah's Ark. In *Fouilles Récentes à Khirokitia (Chypre), 1977–1981,* edited by A. LeBrun, pp. 147–162. Éditions Recherche sur les Civilisations, ADPF, Paris.

Davis, S. (1985, 3 January). Tiny Elephants and Giant Mice. *New Scientist* 105/1437: 25–27.

Davis, S. (1987a) La faune. In A. Le Brun, S. Cluzan, S. Davis, J. Hansen, and J. Renault-Miskovsky, Le Néolithique Préceramique de Chypre. *L'Anthropologie* 91/1: 305–309.

Davis, S. (1987b). *The Archaeology of Animals.* Yale University Press, New Haven.

Davis, S. (1989). Some More Animal Remains from the Aceramic Neolithic of Cyprus. In *Fouilles Récentes à Khirokitia (Chypre) 1983–1986,* edited by A. LeBrun, p. 221. Éditions Recherche sur les Civilisations, Memoire No. 81, Paris.

Davis, S. (1994). Even More Bones from Khirokitia: The 1988–1991 Excavations. In *Fouilles Récentes à Khirokitia (Chypre) 1988–1991,* edited by A. LeBrun, pp. 305–333. Éditions Recherche sur les Civilisations, Paris.

Delany, M. and Happold, D. (1979). *Ecology of African Mammals.* Longman, New York and London.

Demetropoulos, A. (1984). Marine Molluscs, Land Snails, Etc. In *Fouilles Récentes à Khirokitia (Chypre), 1977–1981,* edited by A. LeBrun, pp. 169–182. Editions Recherches sur les Civilisations, ADPF, Paris.

Desse, J. (1984). L'ichthyofaune du site Neolithique de Khirokitia (Chypre). In *Fouilles Récentes à Khirokitia (Chypre), 1977–1981*, edited by A. LeBrun, pp. 167–168. Éditions Recherches sur les Civilisations, ADPF, Paris.

Desse, J. and Desse-Berset, N. (1989). Les poissons de Khirokitia (campagnes 1983, 1984, et 1986). In *Fouilles Récentes à Khirokitia (Chypre), 1983–1986*, edited by A. LeBrun, pp. 223–233. Éditions Recherches sur les Civilisations, ADPF, Paris.

Desse, J. and Desse-Berset, N. (1994). Stratégies de pêche au 8ᵉ millénaire: les poissons de Cap Andres-Kastros. In *Fouilles Récentes à Khirokitia (Chypre), 1988–1991*, edited by A. LeBrun, pp. 335–360. Éditions Recherche sur les Civilisations, ADPF, Paris.

Desse, J. , Desse-Berset, N. , and Rocheteau, M. (1987). *Contribution à l'ostéométrie du Mulet Liza (Liza) ramada Risso, 1826 (=Mugil capito Cuvier, 1829)*. APDCA, Juan-les-Pins, France.

Dewar, R. (1984). Extinctions in Madagascar. In *Quaternary Extinctions*, edited by P. Martin and R. Klein, pp. 574–593. University of Arizona Press, Tucson.

Diamond, J. (1970). Ecological Consequences of Island Colonization by Southwest Pacific Birds: I. Types of Niche Shifts. *Proceedings of the National Academy of Sciences, U.S.A.* 67: 529–536.

Diamond, J. (1984). Historic Extinctions: A Rosetta Stone for Understanding Prehistoric Extinctions. In *Quaternary Extinctions*, edited by P. Martin and R. Klein, pp. 824–862. University of Arizona Press, Tucson.

Diamond, J. (1989a). Overview of Recent Extinctions. In *Conservation for the Twenty-First Century*, edited by D. Western and M. Pearl, pp. 37–41. Oxford University Press, New York and Oxford.

Diamond, J. (1989b). Quaternary Megafaunal Extinctions: Variations on a Theme by Paganini. *Journal of Archaeological Science* 16: 167–175.

Diamond, J. and Marshall, A. (1977). Niche Shifts in New Hebridean Birds. *Emu* 77: 61–72.

Dikaios, P. (1936). The Excavations at Erimi, 1933–1935, Final Report. *Report of the Department of Antiquities, Cyprus* 1936: 1–81.

Dikaios, P. (1953). *Khirokitia*. Oxford University Press, London.

Dikaios, P. (1961). *Sotira*. The University Museum, Philadelphia.

Dikaios, P. (1962). The Stone Age. *The Swedish Cyprus Expedition IV/1A*. Hakan Ohlssons Boktryckeri, Lund.

Dikaios, P. (1969). *Enkomi Excavations 1948–1958:* I. Verlag Philipp von Zabern, Mainz am Rhein.

Dincauze, D. (1984). An Archaeo-Logical Evaluation of the Case for Pre-Clovis Occupations. In *Advances in World Archaeology* (Vol. III), edited by F. Wendorf and A. Close, pp. 275–323. Academic Press, Orlando, Florida.

Dittemore, M. (1983). The Soundings at M'lefaat. In *Prehistoric Archaeology Along the Zagros Flanks*, L. Braidwood, R. Braidwood, B. Howe, C. Reed, and P. Watson, pp. 671–692. The University of Chicago Oriental Institute Publications, Volume 105, Chicago.

Donahue, J. and Adovasio, J. (1990). Evolution of Sandstone Rockshelters in Eastern North America: A Geoarchaeological perspective. In *Archaeological Geology of North America*, edited by N. Laska and J. Donahue, pp. 231–251. The Geological Society of American, Boulder, Colorado.

Donovan, S. (Ed.). (1989). *Mass Extinctions: Processes and Evidence*. Columbia University Press, New York.

Dorrill, M. and Whitehead, P. (1979). The Species Identification of Very Old Human Bloodstains. *Forensic Science International* 13: 111–116.

Dorst, J. and Dandelot, P. (1970). *A Field Guide to the Larger Mammals of Africa*. Collins, London.

Downs, E. (1985). An Approach to Detecting and Identifying Blood Residues on Archaeological Stone Artifacts: A Feasibility Study. (Manuscript on file). Center for Materials Research in Archaeology and Ethnology, Massachusetts Institute of Technology, Cambridge.

Doyel, D. and Debowski, S. (Eds.). (1980). *Prehistory in Dead Valley, East-Central Arizona: The TG&E Springerville Report*. Arizona State Museum Archaeological Series 144. University of Arizona, Tucson.

Draper, H. (1977). The Aboriginal Eskimo Diet in Modern Perspective. *American Anthropologist* 79: 309–316.

Dreghorn, W. (1981). Recent Uplift in North Cyprus. *Geologie en Mijnbouw* 60: 281–284.

Durrell, L. (1986). *Bitter Lemons of Cyprus*. Faber and Faber Ltd., London. (Originally published in 1957)

Eaton, S. and Konner, M. (1985). Paleolithic Nutrition: A Consideration of Its Nature and Current Implications. *New England Journal of Medicine* 312: 283–289.

Eaton, S. , Shostak, M. , and Konner, M. (1988a). *The Paleolithic Prescription*. Harper and Row, New York.

Eaton, S. , Konner, M. , and Shostak, M. (1988b). Stone Agers in the Fast Lane: Chronic Degenerative Diseases in Evolutionary Perspective. *American Journal of Medicine* 84: 739–749.

Eisele, J. , Fowler, D. , Haynes, G. , and Lewis, R. (1995). Survival and Detection of Blood Residues on Stone Tools. *Antiquity* 69: 36–46.

Ekman, J. (1977). Animal Bones from a Late Bronze Age Settlement at Hala Sultan Tekke, Cyprus. *Hala Sultan Tekke* 3, edited by P. Åströms, pp. 166–178. Studies in Mediterranean Archaeology 45:3 (pp. 166–178). Paul Åströms Förlag, Göteborg.

Elliott, C. (1983). Appendix IX: Stone Objects from Palaepaphos-Skales. In V. Karageorghis, *Palaepaphos-Skales, an Iron Age Cemetery in Cyprus* (Alt-Paphos 3), pp. 426–432. Universitätsverlag Konstanz GmbH, Konstanz.

Elliott, C. (1985a). General assessment of the ground stone industry. In *Lemba Archaeological Project* (Vol. 1) edited by E. Peltenburg, pp. 271–275. Studies in Mediterranean Archaeology, 70. Paul Åströms Förlag, Göteburg.

Elliott, C. (1985b). The Ground Stone Industry. In *Lemba Archaeological Project* (Vol. 1), edited by E. Peltenburg, pp. 70–93, 161–194. *Studies in Mediterranean Archaeology* 70, Paul Åströms Förlag, Göteborg.

Elliott, C. (1990). Appendix V: The Ground Stone Industry. In *Tombs at Palaepaphos*, V. Karageorghis, pp. 129–143. A. G. Leventis Foundation, Nicosia.

Elliott, G. and Dutton, R. (1962). *Know Your Rocks: An Introduction to Geology in Cyprus*. Zavallis Press, Nicosia.

Ericson, P. (1987). Interpretations of Archaeological Bird Remains: A Taphonomic Approach. *Journal of Archaeological Science* 14: 65–75.

Estes, R. (1991). *The Behavior Guide to African Mammals*. University of California Press, Berkeley.

Evans, J. (1973). Islands as Laboratories of Culture Change. In *The Explanation of Culture Change: Models in Prehistory*, edited by C. Renfrew, pp. 517–520. University of Pittsburg Press, Pittsburgh.

Evans, J. (1977). Island Archaeology in the Mediterranean: Problems and Opportunities. *World Archaeology* 9: 12–26.

Ewald, P. (1984). Contribution a l'histoire naturelle de l'île de Chypre; les reptiles. *Biocosme Mesogeen* 1/3: 71–92.

Farrand, W. (1985). Rockshelter and Cave Sediments. In *Archaeological Sediments in Context*, edited by J. Stein and W. Farrand, pp. 21–39. Center for the Study of Early Man, Institute for Quaternary Studies, University of Maine, Orono, Maine.

Facchini, F. and Giusberti, G. (1988). Sur la presence de l'homme dans l'île de Crete au cours du Wurm Moyen. In *International Conference, Early Man in Island Environments, Oliena (Sardegna), Abstracts*, edited by M. Sanges, p. 147. Stampa Industria Grafica Stampacolor, Sassari, Sardinia.

Faure, M. , Guerin, C. , and Sondaar, P. (1983). *Hippopotamus Minutus Cuvier*, mise au point. In *Actes du Symposium Paleontologique Georges Cuvier, Montbeliard*, edited by E. Buffetaut, J. Mazin, and E. Salmon, pp. 157–183. Montbeliard, France.

Fick, O. (1974). *Vergleichend morphologische untersuchungenan einzelknochen eurpaischer Taubenarten*. Ph.D. dissertation, Universität Munchen, Munchen.

Fiedel, S. (1996). Blood from Stones? Some Methodological and Interpretive Problems in Blood Residue Analysis. *Journal of Archaeological Science* 26: 139–147.

Flannery, K. (1973). The Origins of Agriculture. *Annual Review of Anthropology* 2: 271–310.

Flemming, N. (1972). Relative Chronology of Submerged Pleistocene Marine Erosion Features in the Western Mediterranean. *Journal of Geology* 80: 633–662.

Flemming, N. (1978). Holocene Eustatic Changes and Coastal Tectonics in the Northeast Mediterranean: Implications for Models of Crustal Consumption. *Philosophical Transactions of the Royal Society, London* 289A: 36–458.

Flemming, N. and Webb, C. (1986). Tectonic and Eustatic Coastal Changes during the Last 10,000 Years Derived from Archaeological Data. *Zeit. fur Geomorph., Suppl.* 62: 1–29.

Flemming, N. , Raban, A. , and Geotschel, C. (1978). Tectonic and Eustatic Changes on the Mediterranean Coast of Israel in the Last 9,000 Years. *Progr. Underwater Sci.* 3: 33–93.

Flint, P. and Stewart, P. (1983). *The Birds of Cyprus: An Annotated Check-List*. (B.O.U. Check-list No. 6.) British Ornithologists' Union, London.

Flint, R. (1974). Pleistocene Epoch. In *Encyclopedia Britannica*, (Vol. 14), pp. 14, 558–569. Chicago, Illinois.

Florit, X. , Mourer-Chauviré, C. , and Alcover, J. (1989). Els ocells pleistocenics d'es Pouas, Eivissa. Nota preliminar. *Bulleti de la Instició catalana d'Història natural* 56 (Sec. Geol.): 35–46.

Forsyth Major, C. (1902). On the Pygmy Hippopotamus from the Pleistocene of Cyprus. *Proceedings of the Zoological Society of London* II/I: 238–239; II/II: 107–112.

Fox, W. (1987). The Neolithic Occupation of Western Cyprus. In *Western Cyprus: Connections*, edited by D. Rupp, pp. 19–44. *Studies in Mediterranean Archaeology* 77, Paul Åströms Förlag, Göteborg.

Fox, W. (1988). Kholetria *Ortos:* A Khirokitia Culture Settlement in the Paphos District. *Report of the Departments of Antiquity, Cyprus, 1988:* 29–42.

Frädrich, H. (1967). Das verhalten der schweine (Suidae, Tayassuidae) und flusspferd (Hippopotamidae). *Handbook of Zoology* 8: 10, 1–44.

Frädrich, H. (1968). Das flusspferd. In *Grzimeks Tierleben: Enzyklopadie des tierreiches,* vol. 13, Saugetiere 4, edited by B. Grzimek , pp. 120–141. Kindler Verlag, Zurich.

Frädrich, H. and Lang, E. (1972). Hippopotamuses. In *Grzimek's Animal Life Encyclopedia,* vol. 13, Mammals IV, edited by B. Grzimek , p. 129. Van Nostrand Reinhold Company, New York.

Francaviglia, V. (1990). Sea-Borne Pumice Deposits of Archaeological Interest on Aegean and Eastern Mediterranean Beaches. In *Thera and the Aegean World III* 3 *(Chronology),* edited by D. Hardy, with C. Renfrew, pp. 127–134. The Thera Foundation, London.

Francaviglia, V. and Di Sabatino, B. (1990). Statistical Study on Santorini Pumice-Falls. In *Thera and the Aegean World III 3 (Chronology),* edited by D. Hardy, with C. Renfrew, pp. 29–52. The Thera Foundation, London.

Fredericksen, C. (1988). Gas Chromatography and Prehistoric Tool Use Residues. *Archaeology in New Zealand* 31: 28–34.

Frison, G. (1979). Observations on the Use of Stone Tools: Dulling of Working Edges of Some Chipped Stone Tools in Bison Butchery. In *Lithic Use-Wear Analysis,* edited by B. Hayden, pp. 259–268. Academic Press, New York.

Frison, G. (1987). The Tool Assemblage, Unfinished Biface, and Stone Flaking Material Sources for the Horner Site. In *The Horner Site: The Type Site of the Cody Cultural Complex,* edited by G. Frison and L. Todd, pp. 233–278. Academic Press, Orlando, Florida.

Frison, G. (1989). Experimental Use of Clovis Weaponry and Tools on African Elephants. *American Antiquity* 54: 766–784.

Frison, G. (1991). *Prehistoric Hunters of the High Plains* (2nd ed.). Academic Press, San Diego.

Frison, G. and Bradley, B. (1980). *Folsom Tools and Technology at the Hanson Site, Wyoming.* University of New Mexico Press, Albuquerque.

Frison, G. and Todd, L. (1986). *The Colby Mammoth Site: Taphonomy and Archaeology of a Clovis Kill in Northern Wyoming.* University of New Mexico Press, Albuquerque.

Galili, E. , Weinstein-Evron, M. , Hershkovitz, I. , Gopher, A. , Kislev, M. , Lernau, O. , Kolska-Horwitz, L. , and Lernau, H. (1993). Atlit-Yam: A Prehistoric Site on the Sea Floor Off the Israeli Coast. *Journal of Field Archaeology* 20: 133–157.

Garcia, L. (1972). *The Balearic Islands.* Thames and Hudson, London.

Garrod, D. (1937). Description and Archaeology: Part I. In *The Stone Age of Mount Carmel* I, edited by D. Garrod and D. Bate, pp. 3–124. Clarendon Press, Oxford.

Gass, J. (1968). Is the Troodos Massif of Cyprus a Fragment of Mesozoic Ocean Floor? *Nature* 220: 39–42.

Gatsov, I. and Özdogan, M. (1994). Some Epi-Paleolithic Sites from NW Turkey. *Anatolica* 20: 98–120.

Gebel, H. and Kozlowski, S. (1994). *Neolithic Chipped Stone Industries of the Fertile Crescent,* Studies in Early Near Eastern Production, Subsistence, and Environment 1. Ex oriente, Berlin.

Georgiades, C. (1989). *Nature of Cyprus: Environment-Flora-Fauna.* Ch. Georgindes, Nicosia.

Geyh, M. (1980). Holocene Sea-Level History: Case Study of the Statistical Evaluation of ^{14}C Dates. *Radiocarbon* 22: 695–704.

Gifford, J. (1978). Paleogeography of Archaeological Sites of the Larnaca Lowlands, Southeastern Cyprus. Unpublished Ph.D. dissertation, University of Minnesota, Duluth.

Gifford-Gonzalez, D. (1989). Ethnographic Analogues for Interpreting Modified Bones: Some Cases from East Africa. In *Bone Modification,* edited by R. Bonnichsen and M. Sorg, pp. 179–246). Center for the Study of the First Americans, University of Maine, Orono, Maine.

Gjerstad, E. (1926). The Stone Age in Cyprus. *Antiquaries Journal* 6: 54–58.

Gjerstad, E. (1934). Petra tou Limniti. In *The Swedish Cyprus Expedition* (Vol. I), pp. 1–12. The Swedish Cyprus Expedition, Stockholm.

Gjerstad, E. , Lindros, J. , Sjoqvist, E. , and Westhom, A. (1934). *The Swedish Cyprus Expedition: Finds and Results of the Excavations in Cyprus 1927–1931* (Vols. 1 and 2). The Swedish Cyprus Expedition, Stockholm.

Glover, E. , Glover, I. , and Vita-Finzi, C. (1990). First-Order ^{14}C Dating of Marine Molluscs in Archaeology. *Antiquity* 64: 562–567.

Gomez, B. and Pease, P. (1992). Early Holocene Cypriot Coastal Palaeogeography. *Report of the Department of Antiquities, Cyprus 1992:* 1–8.

Goring-Morris, A. (1987). *At the Edge: Terminal Pleistocene Hunter-Gatherers in the Negev and Sinai.* British Archaeological Reports, International Series 361, Oxford.

Goring-Morris, A. (1991). The Harifian of the Southern Levant. In *The Natufian Culture in the Levant*, edited by O. Bar-Yosef and F. Valla, pp. 173–216. International Monographs in Prehistory, Archaeological Series 1, Ann Arbor, Michigan.

Grandidier, G. (1905). Recherches sur les lémuriens disparus et en particuliers sur ceux qui vivaient á Madagascar. *Nouvelles Archives de la Muséum de l'Histoirie Naturelle, 4è sér* 8: 1–140.

Grayson, D. (1984). Archaeological Associations with Extinct Pleistocene Mammals in North America. *Journal of Archaeological Science* 11: 213–221.

Grayson, D. (1989). The Chronology of North American Late Pleistocene Extinctions. *Journal of Archeological Science* 16: 153–165.

Grayson, D. (1991). Late Pleistocene Mammalian Extinctions in North America: Taxonomy, Chronology, and Explanations. *Journal of World Prehistory* 5: 193–231.

Guilaine, J. , Coularou, J. , Briois, F. , Carrère, I. , and Philibert, S. (1993). Fouille Néolithique. *Bulletin de Correspondance Hellénique* 117: 716–717.

Guilaine, J. , Briois, F. , Coularou, J. , and Carrère, I. (1995). L'etablissement Neolithique de *Shillourokambos* (Parekklisha, Chypre). Premiers résultats. *Report of the Department of Antiquities, Cyprus 1995:* 11–32.

Gunnis, R. (1936). *Historic Cyprus: A Guide to Its Towns and Villages, Monasteries and Castles.* Methuen, London and K. Rustem & Brothers, Nicosia.

Günther, D. and Pichler, H. (1973). Die obere und untere bimsstein-folge auf Santorin. *Neues Jahrbuch für Geologie und Paläontologie* 7: 394–415.

Guthrie, R. (1984). Mosaics, Allelochemics and Nutrients: An Ecological Theory of Late Pleistocene Megafaunal Extinctions. In *Quaternary Extinctions*, edited by P. Martin and R. Klein, pp. 259–298. University of Arizona Press, Tucson.

Guthrie, R. (1990). *Frozen Fauna of the Mammoth Steppe: The Story of Blue Babe.* University of Chicago Press, Chicago and London.

Hadjistavrinou, Y. and Constantinou, C. (1977). Hydrogeology of the Akrotiri Peninsula. In *Bulletin No. 7 of the Geological Survey Department*, pp. 45–74. Ministry of Agriculture and Natural Resources, Nicosia.

Hadjisterkotis, E. and Reese, D. (1994). Palaeontological and Archaeological Evidence for Turtles on Cyprus, with New Information on Living Tortoises. *British Herpetological Society Bulletin* 49: 16–18.

Haggerty, F. (1991, December). The Archaeological Sites of Akrotiri. *RAF Akrotiri-Flamingo:* 52.

Halstead, P. (1987). Man and Other Animals in Later Greek Prehistory. *The Annual of the British School of Archaeology at Athens* 82: 71–83.

Halstead, P. (1992). Dimini and the "DMP": Faunal Remains and Animal Exploitation in Late Neolithic Thessaly. *The Annual of the British School of Archaeology at Athens* 87: 29–59.

Halstead, P. and Jones, G. (1987). Appendix I: Bioarchaeological Remains from Kalythies Cave, Rhodes. In A. Sampson, *I Neolithiki periodhos Dhodhekanisa* (pp. 135–150). Dhimosievmata tou Arkheolovikou, Ministry of Culture, Athens.

Hammer, C. and Clausen, H. (1990). The Precision of Ice-Core Dating. In *Thera and the Aegean World III* 3 *(Chronology)*, edited by D. Hardy, with C. Renfrew, pp. 174–178. The Thera Foundation, London.

Hansen, J. (1987). Les restes vegeteaux. In A. LeBrun, S. Cluzan, S. Davis, J. Hansen, and J. Renault-Miskovsky, "Le Neolithique Preceramique de Chypre." *L'Anthropologie* 91: 309–312.

Hansen, J. (1989). Khirokitia Plant Remains: Preliminary Report (1980–1981, 1983). In *Fouilles Recentes a Khirokitia (Chypre), 1983–1986*, edited by A. LeBrun, pp. 235–250. Editions Recherche sur les Civilisations, ADPF, Paris.

Hansen, J. (1991). Paleoethnobotany in Cyprus: Recent Developments. In *New Light on Early Farming: Recent Developments in Paleoethnobotany*, edited by J. Renfrew, pp. 225–236. Edinburgh University Press, Edinburgh.

Haynes, C. (1969). The Earliest Americans. *Science* 166: 709–715.

Haynes, G. (1987). Elephant-Butchering at Modern Mass-Kill Sites in Africa. *Current Research in the Pleistocene* 4: 75–77.

Haynes, G. (1988). Spiral Fractures, Cutmarks, and Other Myths About Early Bone Assemblages. In *Early Human Occupation in Far Western North America: The Clovis-Archaic Interface* (Anthropological Papers Number 21), edited by J. Willig, C. Aikens, and J. Fagan, pp. 145–151. Nevada State Museum, Carson City.

Haynes, G. (1991). *Mammoths, Mastodonts, and Elephants: Biology, Behavior, and the Fossil Record.* Cambridge University Press, Cambridge.

Hediger, H. (1951). *Observations sur la psychologie animale dan les Parcs Nationaux du Congo Belge.* Inst. Parcs. Nat. Congo, Bruxelles.

Held, S. (1982). The Earliest Prehistory of Cyprus. In *An Archaeological Guide to the Ancient Kourion Area and the Akrotiri Peninsula,* edited by H. Swiny, pp. 6–11. Department of Antiquities, Cyprus, Nicosia.

Held, S. (1983). Contributions to the Early Prehistoric Archaeology of Cyprus: Vol. 1. Environmental and Chronological Background Studies. Unpublished manuscript, Library of the Cyprus American Archaeological Research Institute, Nicosia.

Held, S. (1989a). Colonization Cycles on Cyprus: 1. The Biogeographic and Paleontological Foundations of Early Prehistoric Settlement. *Report of the Department of Antiquities, Cyprus, 1989:* 7–28.

Held, S. (1989b). Early Prehistoric Island Archaeology in Cyprus: Configurations of Formative Culture Growth from the Pleistocene/Holocene Boundary to the Mid-3rd Millennium B.C. Unpublished Ph.D. dissertation, Institute of Archaeology, University College, University of London, London.

Held, S. (1990). Back to What Future? New Directions for Cypriot Early Prehistoric Research in the 1990s. *Report of the Department of Antiquities, Cyprus, 1990:* 1–43.

Held, S. (1992). *Pleistocene Fauna and Holocene Humans: A Gazetteer of Paleontological and Early Archaeological Sites on Cyprus.* Studies in Mediterranean Archaeology 95. Paul Åströms Förlag, Jonsered, Sweden.

Helmer, D. (1981). Appendix IV: Les rongeurs du Cap Andreas-Kastros. In *Un site neolithiques preceramique en Chypre: Cap Andreas Kastros,* edited by A. LeBrun, pp. 91–92. Editions Recherches sur les Grands Civilisations, ADPF, Paris.

Henry, D. (1989). *From Foraging to Agriculture: The Levant at the End of the Ice Age.* University of Pennsylvania Press, Philadelphia.

Herscher, E. (1995). Archaeology in Cyprus. *American Journal of Archaeology* 99: 257–294.

Hesse, B. , Ogilvy, A. , and Wapnish, P. (1975). The Fauna of Phlamoudhi-Melissa: An Interim Report. *Report of the Department of Antiquities, Cyprus, 1975:* 5–29.

Hesse, B. , Ogilvy, A. , and Wapnish, P. (1983). Appendix I: Report on the Fauna from Phlamoudhi Vounari. In *Phlamoudhi Vounari: A Sanctuary Site in Cyprus.* Studies in Mediterranean Archaeology 65, pp. 116–118. Paul Åströms Förlag, Göteborg.

Heuvelmans, B. (1995). *On the Track of Unknown Animals* (3rd rev. ed.). Kegan Paul International, London and New York. (Originally published in 1955 as *Sur la Piste des Bêtes Ignorées*)

Heywood, H. (1982). The Archaeological Remains of the Akrotiri Peninsula. In *Ancient Kourion Area,* edited by H. Swiny, pp. 162–175. Zavallis Press, Nicosia.

Heywood, H. , Swiny, S. , Whittingham, D. , and Croft, P. (1981). Erimi Revisited. *Report of the Department of Antiquities, Cyprus, 1981:* 24–42.

Hill, A. (1983). Hippopotamus Butchery by *Homo erectus* at Olduvai. *Journal of Archaeological Science* 10: 135–137.

Hinz, G. (1979). *Neue tierknochenfunde aus der Magula Pevkakia in Thessalien. I. Die Nichtwiederkauer.* Unpublished Ph.D. dissertation, Universität München, München.

Hofmeijer, G. and Sondaar, P. (1992). Pleistocene Humans in the Island Environment of Sardinia. In *Sardinia in the Mediterranean: A Footprint in the Sea.* Monographs in Mediterranean Archaeology 3, edited by R. Tykot and T. Andrews, pp. 49–55. Sheffield Academic Press, Sheffield.

Hofmeijer, G. , Sondaar, P. , Alderliesten, C. , Van der Borg, K. , and De Jong, A. (1987). Indications of Pleistocene Man on Sardinia. *Nuclear Instruments and Methods in Physics Research* B, 29: 166–168.

Hofmeijer, G. , Alderliesten, C. , Van Der Borg, K. , Houston, C. , De Jong, A. , Martini, F. , Sanges, M. , and Sondaar, P. (1989). Dating of the Upper Pleistocene Lithic Industry of Sardinia. *Radiocarbon* 31: 986–991.

Hole, F. (1983). The Jarmo Chipped Stone. In *Prehistoric Archaeology Along the Zagros Flanks* (Vol. 105), edited by L. Braidwood, R. Braidwood, B. Howe, C. Reed, and P. Watson, pp. 233–284. The University of Chicago Oriental Institute Publications, Chicago.

Honea, K. (1975). Prehistoric Remains on the Island of Kythnos. *American Journal of Archaeology* 79: 277–279.

Hordynsky, L. and Kingsnorth, A. (1979). Lithic Reduction Sequences in the Vasilikos Valley: Methods and Preliminary Results. *Journal of Field Archaeology* 6: 265–300.

Hordynsky, L. and Ritt, M. (1978). The Chipped-Stone Industry of Kalavasos-Pamboules. In Ian Todd and Project Staff Members, Vasilikos Valley Project: Second Preliminary Report, 1977 (pp. 190–191). *Journal of Field Archaeology* 5: 161–195.

Hordynsky, L. and Todd, I. (1987). The Surface Survey of the Site. In *Vasilikos Valley Project: 6. Excavations at Kalavasos Tenta* (Vol. 1), edited by I. Todd, pp. 17–20. Studies in Mediterranean Archaeology 71:6, Paul Åströms Förlag, Göteborg.

Horwitz, L. and Tchernov, E. (1990). Cultural and Environmental Implications of Hippopotamus Bone Remains in Archaeological Context in the Levant. *Bulletin of the American School of Oriental Research* 280: 67–76.

Houtekamer, J. and Sondaar, P. (1979). Osteology of the Fore Limb of the Pleistocene Dwarf Hippopotamus from Cyprus, with Special Reference to Phylogeny and Function. *Koninklijke Nederlandse Akademie van/Wetenschappen* (Series B) 82: 411–448.

Hsü, K. (1977). Tectonic Evolution of the Mediterranean Basins. In *The Oceanic Basins and Margins: Vol. 4A. The Eastern Mediterranean*, edited by A. Nairn, W. Kanes, and F. Stehli, pp. 29–75. Plenum Press, New York.

Hüe, F. and Ethecopar, R. (1970). *Les oiseaux du Proche et du Moyen-Orient.* Editions N. Boubée & Cie, Paris.

Hyland, D. , Tersak, J. , Adovasio, J. , and Siegel, M. (1990). Identification of the Species of Origin of Residual Blood on Lithic Material. *American Antiquity* 55: 104–112.

Insoll, T. (1995). A Cache of Hippopotamus Ivory at Gao, Mali, and a Hypothesis of Its Use. *Antiquity* 69: 327–336.

Issac, G. (1977). *Olorgesailie: Archaeological Studies of a Middle Pleistocene Lake Basin in Kenya.* University of Chicago Press, Chicago.

Issac, G. (1978). The Food-Sharing Behavior of Protohuman Hominids. *Scientific American* 238: 90–108.

Jánossy, D. (1977). Subfossil Bird Remains from the Kermanshah Valley Sites. In *The Animal Remains from Four Sites in the Kermanshah Valley, Iran: Asiab, Sarab, Dehsavar and Siahbid* (pp. 119–132). British Archaeological Reports, Supplement Series 34, Oxford.

Jarman, M. , Bailey, G. , and Jarman, H. (1982). *Early European Agriculture: Its Foundation and Development.* Cambridge University Press, Cambridge.

Jochim, M. (1976). *Hunter-Gatherer Subsistence and Settlement: A Predictive Model.* Academic Press, New York.

Jochim, M. (1981). *Strategies for Survival.* Academic Press, New York.

Johnson, D. (1980). Problems in the Land Vertebrate Zoogeography of Certain Islands and the Swimming Powers of Elephants. *Journal of Biogeography* 7: 383–398.

Johnson, D. (1983). The California Continental Borderland: Landbridges, Watergaps, and Biotic Dispersals. In *Quaternary Coastlines and Marine Archaeology: Towards the Prehistory of Land Bridges and Continental Shelves*, edited by P. Masters and N. Flemming, pp. 481–527. Academic Press, New York.

Johnson, E. (1989). Human-Modified Bones from Early Southern Plains Sites. In *Bone Modification*, edited by R. Bonnichsen and M. Sorg, pp. 431–471. Center for the Study of the First Americans, University of Maine, Orono, Maine.

Johnstone, P. (1980). *The Sea-Craft of Prehistory.* Routledge and Kegan Paul, London.

Joleaud, L. (1920). Contribution a l'etude des hippopotames fossiles. *Bulletin de la Societe Geologique de France* serie 4, 20: 13–26.

Jones, D. , Merton, C. , Poore, M. , and Harris, D. (1958). *Report on Pasture Research Survey and Development in Cyprus.* Government of Cyprus, Nicosia.

Jonsson, L. (1983). Appendix III: Animal and Human Bones from the Bronze Age Settlement at Hala Sultan Tekke. In *Hala Sultan Tekke* 8, edited by P. Åströms. Studies in Mediterranean Archaeology 45, pp. 222–246. Paul Åströms Förlag, Göteborg.

Karageorghis, V. (1982). *Cyprus from the Stone Age to the Romans.* Thames and Hudson, London.

Kardulias, P. (1993). Identifying Early Human Occupation on Cyprus: The Lithic Evidence. *American Journal of Archaeology* 97: 311.

Kardulias, P. and Yerkes, R. (1993). Identifying Early Human Occupation of Cyprus (Abstract). *American Journal of Archaeology* 97: 311.

Kardulias, P. , Toumazou, M. , and Yerkes, R. (1992). Excavation and Survey in the Malloura Valley, Central Cyprus: The 1991 Season. *Old World Archaeology Newsletter* 15: 18–23.

Keckler, D. (1994). *SURFER for Windows: User's Guide.* Golden Software, Inc., Golden, Colorado.

Keegan, W. and Diamond, J. (1987). Colonization of Islands by Humans: A Biogeographical Perspective. In *Advances in Archaeological Method and Theory* (Vol. 10), edited by M. Schiffer, pp. 49–92. Academic Press, New York.

Keith, A. (1925, February 28). When Malta Was Part of the Eur-African Land-Bridge: A Prehistoric Big-Game Drive. *London Illustrated News*: 349–351.

Keith, A. (1931). *The Antiquity of Man.* J. B. Lippincott, Philadelphia.

Kelly, R. (1983). Hunter-Gatherer Mobility Strategies. *Journal of Anthropological Research* 3: 277–306.

Kelly, R. (1995). *The Foraging Spectrum: Diversity in Hunter-Gatherer Lifeways.* Smithsonian Institution Press, Washington, D.C. and London.

Kersten, A. (1991). Birds from the Palaeolithic Rock Shelter of Ksar 'Akil, Lebanon. *Paléorient* 17/2: 99–111.

Kilmer, V. and Alexander, L. (1949). Methods of Making Mechanical Analyses of Soil. *Soil Science* 68: 15–24.

Kind, S. and Cleevely, R. (1969). The Use of Ammoniacal Bloodstain Extracts in ABO Groupings. *Journal of Forensic Sciences* 15: 131–134.

King, J. (1953). Appendix III: Mammal Bones from Khirokitia and Erimi. In *Khirokitia,* pp. 431–437. Oxford University Press, London.

King, R. (1987). Western Cyprus: The Paleoenvironment. In *Western Cyprus: Connections.* Studies in Mediterranean Archaeology, Vol. 77, edited by D. Rupp, pp. 7–17. Paul Åströms Förlag, Göteborg.

Kirch, P. (Ed.). (1988). *Island Societies: Archaeological Approaches to Evolution and Transformation.* Cambridge University Press, Cambridge.

Kirkbride, D. (1966). Five Seasons at the Pre-Pottery Neolithic Village of Beidha in Jordan. *Palestine Exploration Quarterly* 88: 8–72.

Klein, R. (1994). The Tor Hamar Fauna. In *Prehistoric Cultural Ecology and Evolution: Insights from Southern Jordan,* edited by D. Henry, pp. 405–416. Plenum Press, New York.

Knapp, A. , Held, S. , and Manning, S. (1994). The Prehistory of Cyprus: Problems and Prospects. *Journal of World Prehistory* 377: 377–453.

Köhler-Rollefson, I. (1989). Resolving the Revolution: Late Neolithic Refinements of Economic Strategies in the Eastern Levant. *Archaeozoologia* III/1–2: 201–208.

Köhler-Rollefson, I. , Gillespie, W. , and Metzger, M. (1988). The Fauna from Neolithic 'Ain Ghazal. In *The Prehistory of Jordan: The State of Research in 1986,* edited by A. N. Garrard and H. G. Gebel, pp. 423–430. British Archaeological Reports, International Series 396(1), Oxford.

Köhler-Rollefson, I. and Rollefson, G. O. (1990). The Impact of Neolithic Subsistence Strategies on the Environment: The Case of 'Ain Ghazal, Jordan. In *Man's Role in the Shaping of the Eastern Mediterranean Landscape,* edited by S. Bottema, G. Entjes-Nieborg, and W. van Zeist, pp. 3–14. A. A. Balkema, Rotterdam.

Kopper, J. (1984). Canet Cave, Esporles, Mallorca. In *The Deya Conference of Prehistory: Early Settlement in the Western Mediterranean Islands and the Peripheral Areas,* edited by W. Waldren, R. Chapman, J. Lewthwaite, and R.-C. Kennards, pp. 61–69. British Archaeological Reports, International Series 229, Oxford.

Koucky, F. and Bullard, R. (1974). The Geology of Idalion. In *American Expedition to Idalion, Cyprus, First Preliminary Report: Seasons 1971 and 1972,* edited by E. Stager, A. Walker, and G. Wright, pp. 11–25. American Schools of Oriental Research, Cambridge, Massachusetts.

Kowalski, K. and Rzebik-Kowalska, B. (1991). *Mammals of Algeria.* Institute of Systematics and Evolution of Animals, Polish Academy of Sciences, Wroclaw.

Kraft, J. , Aschenbrenner, S. , and Rapp, G. (1977). Paleogeographic Reconstructions of Coastal Aegean Archaeological Sites. *Science* 195: 41–47.

Krinsley, D. and Doorkamp, J. (1973). *Atlas of Quartz Sand Surface Textures.* Cambridge University Press, Cambridge.

Kuhn, A. (1993). Mousterian Technology as Adaptive Response: A Case Study. In *Hunting and Animal Exploitation in the Later Palaeolithic and Mesolithic of Eurasia,* edited by G. Peterkin, H. Bricker, and P. Mellars, pp. 25–31. Archaeological Papers of the American Anthropological Association, Washington, D.C.

Kuhn, S. (1991). "Unpacking" Reduction: Lithic Raw Material Economy in the Mousterian of West-Central Italy. *Journal of Anthropological Archaeology* 10: 76–106.

Kuijt, I. and Bar-Yosef, O. (1994). Radiocarbon Chronology for the Levantine Neolithic: Observations and Data. In *Late Quaternary Chronology and Paleoclimates of the Eastern Mediterranean,* edited by O. Bar-Yosef and R. Kra, pp. 227–245. Radiocarbon and American School of Prehistoric Research, Tucson, Arizona, and Cambridge, Massachusetts.

Kurten, B. (1968). *Pleistocene Mammals of Europe.* Weidenfield and Nicholson, London.

Kurten, B. (1972). *The Age of Mammals.* Columbia University Press, New York.

Kuss, S. (1973). Die Pleistozanen saugetierfaunen der ostmediterranean inseln. Inr alter und ihre herkunft. *Ber. Naturf. Ges., Freiburg i. Br.* 63: 49–71.

Kyllo, M. (1982). The Botanical Remains. In *Vrysi: A Subterranean Settlement in Cyprus,* edited by E. Peltenburg, pp. 415–436. Aris and Phillips Ltd., Warminster.

Lanfranchi, F. (1967). La grotte sepulcrale de Curacchiaghiu (Levie, Corse). *Bulletin Societe Prehistoire Francaise,* 64: 587–612.

Lanfranchi, F. (1974). Le Neolithique Ancien Mediterraneen, facies Curacchiaghiu, a levie. *Cahiers Corsica* 43: 39–48.

Lanfranchi, F. and Weiss, M. (1973). *La civilisation des Corses: les origines.* Cyrnos et Mediterranee Ed., Ajaccio.

Lanfranchi, F. and Weiss, M. (1977). *Araguina-Sennola, dix annees de fouilles prehistoriques a Bonifacio.* Archeologie Corsa 2.

Lang, E. (1968). Das zwergflusspferd. In *Grzimeks Tierleben: Enzyklopadie des Tierreiches,* vol. 13: Saugetiere 4, edited by B. Grzimek, pp. 118–120. Kindler Verlag, Zurich.

Lang, S. (1992). *An Investigation of Image-Processing Techniques at Pincevent Habitation No. 1, A Late Magdalenian Site in Northern France.* Arizona State University Anthropological Research Paper No. 43. Arizona State University, Tempe.

Larje, R. (1992). The Bones from the Bronze Age Fortress at Nitovikla, Cyprus. In *Nitovikla Reconsidered* (Memoir 8). Medelhavsmuseet, Stockholm.

Larson Jr. , P. (1978). Ornamental beads from the Late Natufian of Southern Israel. *Journal of Field Archaeology* 5: 120–121.

Laville, H. , Rigaud, J. , and Sackett, J. (1980). *Rockshelters of the Perigord.* Academic Press, New York.

Lax, E. and Strasser, T. (1992). Early Holocene Extinctions on Crete: The Search for the Cause. *Journal of Mediterranean Archaeology* 5: 203–224.

LeBrun, A. (1971). *Cape Andreas Kastros* (Rapport preliminaire). *Report of the Department of Antiquities, Cyprus, 1971:* 1–23.

LeBrun, A. (1974). *Cap Andréas Kastros* (Rapport preliminaire 1970–72). *Report of the Department of Antiquities, Cyprus, 1974:* 1–23.

LeBrun, A. (1981). L'industrie lithique. In *Un Site Neolithique Preceramique en Chypre: Cap Andreas Kastros,* edited by A. LeBrun, pp. 31–41. Recherche Sur les Grandes Civilisations, Éditions ADPF, Paris.

LeBrun, A. (Ed.). (1984). *Fouilles recentes à Khirokitia (Chypre), 1977–1981.* Editions Recherche sur les Civilisations, ADPF, Paris.

LeBrun, A. (Ed.). (1989). *Fouilles recentes à Khirokitia (Chypre), 1983–1986.* Editions Recherche sur les Civilisations, ADPF, Paris.

LeBrun, A. (1993) Recherches sur le Néolithique Précéramique de Chypre. In *Kinyras—L'Archéogie Française à Chypre,* edited by M. Yon, pp. 55–80. Travaux de la Maison de L'Orient, Lyon.

LeBrun, A. (Ed.). (1994) *Fouilles récentes à Khirokitia (Chypre), 1988–1991.* Éditions Recherche sur les Civilisations, ADPF, Paris.

LeBrun, A. , Cluzan, S. , Davis, S. , Hansen, J. , and Renault-Miskovsky, J. (1987). Le Néolithique Précéramique de Chypre. *L'Anthropologie* 91: 283–316.

Lee, R. and DeVore, I. (1968). *Man the Hunter.* Aldine Press, Chicago.

LeGarff, B. (1991). *Les amphibiens et les reptiles dans leur milieu.* Bordas Ed, Paris.

Legge, A. (1982a) Ayios Epikitos: The Recent Farming Economy. In *Vrysi, A Subterranean Settlement in Cyprus,* edited by E. Peltenburg, pp. 14–20. Aris & Phillips Ltd., Warminster.

Legge, A. (1982b). The Vertebrate Fauna. In *Vrysi, A Subterranean Settlement in Cyprus,* edited by E. Peltenburg, pp. 76–88. Aris & Phillips Ltd., Warminster.

Lehavy, Y. (1974). Excavations at Neolithic Dhali-Agridhi. In *American Expedition to Idalion, Cyprus—First Preliminary Report: Seasons of 1971 and 1972,* edited by L. E. Stoger, A. Walker, and G. E. Wright, pp. 95–102. Bulletin of the American Schools of Oriental Research Supplement 18. Cambridge, Massachusetts.

Lehavy, Y. (1989). Dhali-Agridhi: The Neolithic by the River. In *American Expedition to Idalion, Cyprus 1973–1980,* edited by L. E. Stager and A. Walker, pp. 203–243. American Schools of Oriental Research, Cambridge, Massachusetts.

Lehmann, E. von and Nobis, G. (1979). Subfossile mauswiesel, *Mustela nivalis* Linne, 1766 aus Enkomia-Alasia auf Zypern. *Bonner Zoologische Beiträge* 30/1–2: 32–38.

Leighton, R. (1989). Antiquarianism and Prehistory in Western Mediterranean Islands. *Antiquaries Journal* 69: 183–204.

Leoni, L. and Saitta, M. (1976). X-Ray Fluorescence Analysis of 29 Trace Elements in Rock and Mineral Standards. *Rendiconti Società Italiana di Mineralogie e Petrologia* 32/2: 497–510.

Leuthold, W. (1977). *African Ungulates: A Comparative Review of Their Ethnology and Behavioral Ecology.* Springer-Verlag, Berlin, Heidelberg, New York.

Lewthwaite, J. (1989). Isolating the Residuals: The Mesolithic Basis of Man-Animal Relationships on the Mediterranean Islands. In *The Mesolithic in Europe,* edited by C. Bonsall, pp. 541–555. John Donalds Publishers Ltd., Edinburgh.

Lister, A. (1993). Mammoths in Miniature. *Nature* 326: 288–289.

Livingston, S. (1989). The Taphonomic Interpretation of Avian Skeletal Part Frequencies. *Journal of Archaeological Science* 16: 537–547.

Lockerbie, L. (1959). From Moa-Hunter to Classic Maori in Southern New Zealand. In *Anthropology in the South Seas,* edited by J. Freeman and W. Geddes, pp. 75–110. New Plymouth, Avery.

Long, A. and Rippeteau, B. (1974). Testing Contemporaneity and Averaging Radiocarbon Dates. *American Antiquity* 39: 205–215.

Long, A. , Sher, A. , and Vartanyan, S. (1994). Holocene Mammoth Dates. *Nature* 369: 364.

Lort, J. (1977). Geophysics of the Mediterranean Sea Basins. In *The Oceanic Basins and Margins: Vol. 4A. The Eastern Mediterranean,* edited by A. Nairm, W. Kanes, and F. Stehili, pp. 151–213. Plenum Press, New York.

Lowenstein, J. (1986). Evolutionary Applications of Radioimmunoassay. *American Biotechnology Laboratory* 4: 12–15.

Lyman, R. (1987). Archaeofaunas and Butchery Studies: A Taphonomic Perspective. In *Advances in Archaeological Method and Theory* (Vol, 10), edited by M. Schiffer, pp. 249–337. Academic Press, San Diego.

Lyman, R. (1994). *Vertebrate Taphonomy* (Cambridge Manuals in Archaeology). Cambridge University Press, Cambridge.

MacArthur, R. and Wilson, E. (1967). *The Theory of Island Biogeography.* Princeton University Press, Princeton.

Macey, H. (1979). The Identification of Human Blood in a 166-Year-Old Stain. *Canadian Journal of Forensic Sciences* 12: 191–193.

MacPhee, R. and Burney, D. (1991). Dating of Modified Femora of Extinct Dwarf *Hippopotamus* from Southern Madagascar: Implications for Constraining Human Colonization and Vertebrate Extinction Events. *Journal of Archaeological Science* 18: 695–706.

Madden, C. (1977). Elephants of the Santa Rosa Channel Islands. Southern California Geological Society of America.

Maglio, V. (1975). Pleistocene Faunal Evolution in Africa and Eurasia. In *After the Australopithecines,* edited by K. Butzer and G. Isaac, pp. 419–476. The Hague: Mouton.

Mandel, R. and Simmons, A. (1997). Geoarchaeology of the Akrotiri *Aetokremnos* Rockshelter, Southern Cyprus. *Geoarchaeology* 12: 567–605.

Manning, S. (1991). Approximate Calendar Date for the First Human Settlement of Cyprus? *Antiquity* 65: 870–878.

Marks, A. (1976). Glossary. In *Prehistory and Paleoenvironments in the Central Negev, Israel: Vol. 1. The Avdat/Aqev Area, Part 1,* edited by A. Marks, pp. 371–383. Southern Methodist University Press, Dallas.

Marks, A. and Simmons, A. (1977). The Negev Kebaran of the Har Harif. In *Prehistory and Paleoenvironments of the Central Negev, Israel* (Vol. 2), edited by A. Marks, pp. 233–269. Southern Methodist University Press, Dallas.

Marshall, L. (1989). Bone Modification and "The Laws of Burial." In *Bone Modification,* edited by R. Bonnichsen and M. Sorg, pp. 7–24. Center for the Study of the First Americans, University of Maine, Orono.

Martin, P. (1984). Prehistoric Overkill: The Global Model. In *Quaternary Extinctions: A Prehistoric Revolution,* edited by P. Martin and R. Klein, pp. 354–403. University of Arizona Press, Tucson.

Martin, P. and Klein, R. (Eds.). (1984). *Quaternary Extinctions: A Prehistoric Revolution.* University of Arizona Press, Tucson.

Martin, P. and Wright, H. (Eds.). (1967). *Pleistocene Extinctions: The Search for a Cause.* Yale University Press, New Haven.

Martini, F. (1992). Early Human Settlement in Sardinia: The Palaeolithic Industries. In *Sardinia in the Mediterranean: A Footprint in the Sea,* edited by R. Tykot and T. Andrews, pp. 40–48. Sheffield Academic Press, Sheffield.

Martini, F. and Pitzalis, G. (1980). Il Paleolitico Inferiore in Sardegna. *Att. 23 Riunione Sci. Ist. Ital. Preist. Protost. Firenze:* 249–255.

Martini, F. and Pitzalis, G. (1981). Il Paleolitico in Sardegna. In *Ichnusa: La Sardegna dalle Origini all' Età Classica,* edited by E. Atzeni, F. Barreca, M. Ferrarese Ceruti, E. Contu, G. Lilliu, F. LoSchiavo, F. Nicosia and E. Schnedier, pp. 603–604. Scheiwiller, Milan.

Martini, F. and Pitzalis, G. (1982). Il Paleolitico Inferiore in Sardegna. In *Atti del XXIII Riunione Scientifica 'Il Paleolitico Inferiore in Italia, Firenze, 7–9 Maggio 1980,* pp. 249–255. Istituto Italiano di Preistoria e Protostoria, Firenze.

McCartney, C. (1993). An Attribute Analysis of Cypriot *Dhoukani* "Teeth": Implications for the Study of Cypriot Chipped Stone Assemblages. *Report of the Department of Antiquities, Cyprus 1993:* 349–364.

McCulloch, B. and Trotter, M. (1975). The First Twenty Years: Radiocarbon Dates for South Island Moa-Hunter Sites, 1955–74. *New Zealand Archaeological Association Newsletter* 18: 2–17.

Mead, J. and Meltzer, D. (1984). North American Late Quaternary Extinctions and the Radiocarbon Record. In *Quaternary Extinctions: A Prehistoric Revolution*, edited by P. Martin and R. Klein, pp. 440–450. University of Arizona Press, Tucson.

Mead, J. and Meltzer, D. (Eds.). (1985). *Environments and Extinctions: Man in Late Glacial North America.* Center for the Study of Early Man, University of Maine, Orono.

Meadow, R. (1983). Appendix G: The Vertebrate Faunal Remains from Hasanlu Period X at Hajji Firuz. In *Hajji Firuz Tepe, Iran: The Neolithic Settlement*, pp. 369–422. The University Museum, Philadelphia.

Megaw, A. and Last, J. (1954). Field Survey of Akrotiri—Inspection Report (ms. on file). RAF-Akrotiri, Cyprus.

Meiggs, R. (1982). *Trees and Timber in the Ancient Mediterranean World.* Clarendon Press, Oxford.

Meikle, R. (1977). *Flora of Cyprus: Vol. 1.* The Bentham-Moxon Trust, Royal Botanic Gardens, Kew.

Meikle, R. (1985). *Flora of Cyprus: Vol. 2.* The Bentham-Moxon Trust, Royal Botanic Garden, Kew.

Meltzer, D. (1986). Pleistocene Overkill and the Associational Critique. *Journal of Archaeological Science* 13: 51–60.

Meltzer, D. and Mead, J. (1983). The Timing of Late Pleistocene Mammalian Extinctions in North America. *Quaternary Research* 19: 130–135.

Meltzer, D. and Mead, J. (1985). Dating Late Pleistocene Extinctions: Theoretical Issues, Analytical Bias, and Substantive Results. In *Environments and Extinctions: Man in Late Glacial North America*, edited by J. Mead and D. Meltzer, pp. 145–173. Center for the Study of Early Man, University of Maine, Orono.

Miller, N. (1984). Some Plant Remains from Khirokitia. In *Fouilles Recentes a Khirokitia (Chypre), 1977–1981*, edited by A. LeBrun, pp. 183–188. Editions Recherche sur les Civilisations, ADPF, Paris.

Millman, J. and Emery, K. (1968). Sea-Levels During the Past 35,000 Years. *Science* 162: 1121–1123.

Mintz, E. and Ben-Ami, D. (1977). Neolithic Occurrences. In *Prehistoric Investigations in Gebel Maghara, Northern Sinai*, edited by O. Bar-Yosef and J. Phillips, pp. 219–244. QEDEM 7, Monographs of the Institute of Archaeology, Hebrew University. Ahva Co-op Press, Jerusalem.

Mitchell, P. (1903). Note on the Cypriote Spiny Mouse. *Proceedings of the Zoological Society of London* II: 260–261.

Morel, S. (1960). The Geology and Mineral Resources of the Apsiou-Akrotiriarea. In *The Geology and Mineral Resources of the Agros-Akrotiri Area.* Geological Survey Department, Cyprus. Government Printing Office, Nicosia.

Morlan, R. (1984). Toward the Definition of Criteria for the Recognition of Artificial Bone Alternations. *Quaternary Research* 22: 160–171.

Morrison, I. (1982). Aspects of the Geomorphology of Lemba, Mosphilia, and Mylouthkia. *Levant* 14: 54–57.

Morrison, I. and Watkins, T. (1974). Kataliondas-*Kourvellos*: A Survey of an Aceramic Neolithic Site and Its Environs in Cyprus. *Palestine Exploration Quarterly* 106: 67–75.

Mosimann, J. and Martin, P. (1975). Simulating Overkill by Paleoindians. *American Scientist* 63: 304–313.

Mourer-Chauviré, C. (1975a). Le oiseaux du Pléistocène moyen et supérieur de France. Lyon: *Documents des Laboratoires de Géologie de la Faculté des Sciences de Lyon* 64: 2 fascs.

Mourer-Chauviré, C. (1975b). Les oiseaux (*Aves*) du gisement pléistocène moyen des abîmes de la Ffage à Noailles (Corrèze). *Nouvelles Archives du Muséum d'Histoire naturelle de Lyon* 13: 89–112.

Mourer-Chauviré, C. (1981). Les oiseaux de la grotte de Kitsos (Attique Grèce). In N. Lambert, *La grotte préhistorique de Kitsos (Attique)* Vol. II, pp. 595–606. Editions ADPF, Paris et Ecole Française Athenes.

Mourer-Chauviré, C. (1983). Les oiseaux dans les habitats préhistoriques; gibier des hommes ou proies des racaces? In *Animals and Archaeology 2 Shell Middens, Fishes and Birds*, edited by C. Grigson and J. Clutton-Brock, pp. 111–124. British Archaeological Reports, International Series 183, Oxford.

Murchison, C. (Ed.). (1868). *Palaeontological Memoirs and Notes of the Late Hugh Falconer, A.M., M.D.: Vol. II. Mastodon, Elephant, Rhinoceros, Ossiferous Caves, Primeval Man and His Contemporaries.* R. Hardwicke, London.

Neeley, M. and Clark, G. (1993). The Human Food Niche in the Levant over the Past 150,000 Years. In *Hunting and Animal Exploitation in the Later Paleolithic and Mesolithic of Eurasia*, edited by G. Peterkin, H. Bricker, and P. Mellars, pp. 221–240. Archaeological Papers of the American Anthropological Association No. 4, Washington, D.C.

Neev, D. , Bakler, N. , and Emery, K. (1987). *Mediterranean Coasts of Israel and Sinai.* Taylor and Francis, New York.

Neeve, D. , Bakler, N. , and Emery, K. (1987). *Mediterranean Coasts of Israel and Sinai.* Taylor and Francis, New York.

Neophytou, P. (Ed.). (1976). *Fifth Bird Report 1974.* The Cyprus Ornithological Society, Nicosia.

Nesse, W. (1991). *Introduction to Optical Mineralogy.* Oxford University Press, Oxford.

Newman, M. (1990). The Hidden Evidence from Hidden Cave, Nevada. Ph.D. dissertation, University of Toronto, Toronto.

Newman, M. and Julig, P. (1989). The Identification of Protein Residues on Lithic Artifacts from a Stratified Boreal Forest Site. *Canadian Journal of Archaeology* 13: 119–132.

Nicholson, S. (1978). Climatic Variations in the Sahel and Other African Regions During the Past Five Centuries. *Journal of Arid Environments* 1: 3–24.

Nicholson, S. and Flohn, H. (1980). African Environmental and Climatic Changes and the General Atmospheric Circulation in Late Pleistocene and Holocene. *Climatic Change* 2: 313–348.

Nitecki, M. (Ed.). (1984). *Extinctions.* University of Chicago Press, Chicago and London.

Nobis, G. (1985). Appendix IX: Tierreste aus dem präphönizischen Kition. In *Excavations at Kition V/II*, pp. 416–433. Department of Antiquities, Nicosia.

Nobis, G. and von Lehmann, E. (1979). Ein geweihstück vom rothirsch, *Cervus elaphus* Linne, 1758, aus Kition, Zypern. *Säugetierkundliche Mitteilungen* 27/2: 158–160.

Northcote, E. (1988). An Extinct "Swan-Goose" from the Pleistocene of Malta. *Palaeontology* 31/3: 725–740.

Oberhummer, E. (1903). *Die Insel Cypern, eine landeskunde auf historischer grundlage.* Theodor Ackermann, Munich.

Olivier, R. and Laurie, W. (1974). Habitat Utilization by Hippopotamus in the Mara River. *East African Wildlife Journal* 12: 249–271.

Olsen, S. (1987). Magdalenian Reindeer Exploitation at the Grotte des Eyzies, Southwest France. *Archaeozoologia* 1: 171–182.

Olsen, S. (1989). Solutré: A Theoretical Approach to the Reconstruction of Upper Paleolithic Hunting Strategies. *Journal of Human Evolution* 18: 295–327.

Olsen, S. (1994). Exploitation of Mammals at the Early Bronze Age Site of West Row Fen (Midenhall 165), Suffolk, England. *Annals of the Carnegie Museum* 63: 115–153.

Olsen, S. and Shipman, P. (1988). Surface Modification on Bone: Trampling versus Butchery. *Journal of Archaeological Science* 15: 535–553.

Orr, P. (1968). *Prehistory of Santa Rosa Island, California.* Santa Barbara Museum of Natural History, Santa Barbara.

Otte, M. , Yalcinkaya, I. , Leotard, J. , Kartal, M. , Bar-Yosef, O. , Kozlowski, J. , López, I. , and Marshack, A. (1995). The Epi-Palaeolithic of Öküzini Cave (SW Anatolia) and Its Mobiliary Art. *Antiquity* 69: 931–944.

Owen-Smith, R. (1987). Pleistocene Extinctions: The Pivotal Role of Megaherbivores. *Paleobiology* 13: 351–362.

Owen-Smith, R. (1988). *Megaherbivores: The Influence of Very Large Body Size on Ecology.* Cambridge University Press, Cambridge.

Patterson, B. , Goodman, S. , and Sedlock, J. (Eds.). (1995). *Environmental Change in Madagascar.* The Field Museum, Chicago.

Patton, M. (1996). *Islands in Time: Island Sociogeography and Mediterranean Prehistory.* Routledge, London and New York.

Pearlman, D. (1984). *Threshing Sledges in the East Mediterranean: Ethnoarchaeology with Chert Knappers and Dhoukanes in Cyprus.* Unpublished M.A. thesis, Center for Ancient Studies, University of Minnesota, Minneapolis.

Peltenburg, E. (1978). The Sotira Culture: Regional Diversity and Cultural Unity in Late Neolithic Cyprus. *Levant* 10: 55–74.

Peltenburg, E. (1979a). The Prehistory of West Cyprus: Ktima Lowlands Investigations 1976–1978. *Report of the Department of Antiquities, Cyprus, 1979*: 69–99.

Peltenburg, E. (1979b). Troulli Reconsidered. In *Studies Presented in Memory of Porphyrios Dikaios*, edited by V. Karageorghis, pp. 21–45. Lions Club, Nicosia.

Peltenburg, E. (1982a). Early Copperwork in Cyprus and the Exploitation of Picrolite: Evidence from the Lemba Archaeological Project. In *Early Metallurgy in Cyprus, 4000–500 BC.*, edited by J. D. Muhly, R. Maddin, and V. Karageorghis, pp. 41–62. Pierides Foundation, Larnaca.

Peltenburg, E. (1982b). *Vrysi: A Subterranean Settlement in Cyprus.* Aris & Phillips Ltd., Warminster.

Peltenburg, E. (1991). Local Exchange in Prehistoric Cyprus: An Initial Assessment of Picrolite. *Bulletin of the American Schools of Oriental Research* 282/283: 107–126.

Perkins, D. and Daly, P. (1968). A Hunters' Village in Neolithic Turkey. *Scientific American* 219: 97–106.

Perlès, C. (1979). Des navigateurs Méditerranéens il y a 10,000 ans. *La Recherche* 10: 82–83.

Perlès, C. (1988). *Akrotiri, Site E* (Unpublished report on file). Quaternary Sciences Center, Desert Research Institute, Reno, Nevada.

Peterkin, G. , Bricker, H. , and Mellars, P. (Eds.). (1993). *Hunting and Animal Exploitation in the Later Palaeolithic and Mesolithic of Eurasia.* Archaeological Papers of the American Anthropological Association, No. 4. American Anthropological Association, Washington, D.C.

Pianese, S. (1968). Rassegna storica delle ricerche sul Paleolitico in Sicilia. *Quaternaria* 10: 213–250.

Pichler, H. (1980). The Island of Lipari: In The Aeolian Islands—An Active Volcanic Arc in the Mediterranean Sea. *Rendiconti Società Italiana di Mineralogie e Petrologia* 36/1: 415–440.

Pichler, H. and Friedrich, W. (1976). Radiocarbon Dates of Santorini Volcanics. *Nature* 262: 373–374.

Pichon, J. (1984a). *L'avifaune natoufienne du Levant. Systématique, paléoécologie, palethnographie.* Université Pierre et Marie Curie, Paris.

Pichon, J. (1984b). Les oiseaux du site de Khirokitia (Chypre). In *Fouilles récentes à Khirokitia (Chypre), 1977–1981,* edited by A. LeBrun, pp. 163–165. Editions Recherches sur les Civilisations, ADPF, Paris.

Pichon, J. (1987). L'avifaune de Mallaha. In *La Faune du Gisement Natoufien de Mallaha (Eynan) Israël,* edited by J. Bouchard, pp. 115–150. Mémoires et Travaux du Centre de Recherche Français de Jérusalem 4. Association Paléorient, Paris.

Pile, B. (1981). *Akrotiri Peninsula Sites: Record Data* (Unpublished report on file). RAF Akrotiri, Cyprus.

Piper, C. (1942). *Soil and Plant Analysis.* Hassell Press, Adelaide, Australia.

Polach, H. (1971). Radiocarbon Dating of Bone Organic and Inorganic Matter. *Proceedings of the Radiocarbon Users Conference, 1971,* pp. 180–211. Wellington, New Zealand.

Polach, H. and Golson, J. (1966). *Collection of Specimens for Radiocarbon Dating and Interpretation of Results.* Australian Institute of Aboriginal Studies, Canberra.

Poole, A. and Robertson, A. (1991). Quaternary Uplift and Sea Level Change at an Active Plate Boundary. *Journal of the Geological Society of London* 148: 909–921.

Poole, A. , Shimmield, G. , and Robertson, A. (1990). Late Quaternary Uplift of the Troodos Ophiolite, Cyprus: Uranium-Series Dating of Pleistocene Coral. *Geology* 18: 894–897.

Price, T. and Brown, J. (1985). *Prehistoric Hunter-Gatherers: The Emergence of Cultural Complexity.* Academic Press, New York.

Prins, G. (1980). *The Hidden Hippopotamus.* Cambridge University Press, Cambridge.

Redding, R. (1988). A General Explanation of Subsistence Change: From Hunting and Gathering to Food Production. *Journal of Anthropological Archaeology* 7: 56–97.

Reed, R. (1972). *Ancient Skins, Parchments, and Leathers.* Seminar Press, London and New York.

Reese, D. (1975a). Dwarfed Hippos: Past and Present. *Earth Science* 28: 63–69.

Reese, D. (1975b). Men, Saints, or Dragons? *Expedition* 17: 26–30.

Reese, D. (1977). Additional Comments on the Pleistocene Fauna of Cyprus (Manuscript on file). Cyprus American Archaeological Research Institute, Nicosia.

Reese, D. (1978). Molluscs from Archaeological Sites in Cyprus: "Kastros" Cape St. Andreas, Cyprus and Other pre-Bronze Age Mediterranean Sites. *Fisheries Bulletin* 5: 3–112.

Reese, D. (1982). Marine and Fresh-Water Molluscs from the Epipaleolithic Site of Hayonim Terrace, Western Galilee, Northern Israel, and Other East Mediterranean Sites. *Paléorient* 8: 83–90.

Reese, D. (1985). Appendix 8: Hippopotamus and Elephant Teeth from Kition. In *Excavations at Kition V* (Part 2). Department of Antiquities, Nicosia.

Reese, D. (1988). The Early Holocene Fauna of Cyprus: Dwarfed Hippopotami and Elephants from Akrotiri *Aetokremnos.* In *International Conference, Early Man in Island Environments, Oliena (Sardegna), Abstracts,* edited by M. Sanges, p. 81. Industria Grafica Stampacolor, Sassari.

Reese, D. (1989a). Appendix D: The Natufian Shells from Beidha. In *The Natufian Encampment at Beidha: Late Pleistocene Adaptation in the Southern Levant,* pp. 102–104. Jutland Archaeological Society Publications XXIII:1, Moesgard, Århus (Denmark).

Reese, D. (1989b). Tracking the Extinct Pygmy Hippopotamus of Cyprus. *Field Museum of Natural History Bulletin* 60: 22–29.

Reese, D. (1990). Review of *Marine Molluscan Remains from Franchthi Cave, with a Report on the Oxygen Isotope Analysis of Marine Molluscs from Franchthi Cave* by J. C. Shackleton, M. R. Deith, and N. J. Shackleton. *American Journal of Archaeology* 94: 682–683.

Reese, D. (1991). Marine Shells in the Levant: Upper Paleolithic, Epipaleolithic, and Neolithic. In *The Natufian Culture in the Levant,* edited by O. Bar-Yosef and F. Valla, pp. 613–628. International Monographs in Prehistory, Ann Arbor.

Reese, D. (1992a). The Earliest Worked Bone on Cyprus. *Report of the Department of Antiquities, Cyprus, 1992:* 13–16.

Reese, D. (1992b, July). Tale of the Pygmy Hippo. *Cyprus View* 6: 50–53.

Reese, D. (1993). Marine Shells. In *The Land of the Paphian Aphrodite: 2. The Canadian Palaipaphos Survey Project. Artifact and Ecofaunal Studies,* edited by L. Sørensen and D. Rupp, pp. 207–209. Studies in Mediterranean Archaeology 104, Paul Åströms Förlag, Göteborg.

Reese, D. (1995). *The Pleistocene Vertebrate Sites and Fauna of Cyprus.* Geological Survey Department, Ministry of Agriculture, Natural Resources and Environment, Nicosia.

Reese, D. (1996). Cypriot Hippo Hunters No Myth. *Journal of Mediterranean Archaeology* 9: 107–112.

Regteren Altena, C. van. (1962). Molluscs and Echinoderms from Palaeolithic Deposits in the Rock Shelter of Ksar'Akil, Lebanon. *Zoologische Medelingen* XXXVIII/5: 87–99.

Renault-Mikovsky, J. (1985). Palynologie: evolution de la vegetation et du climat au Chalcolithique dans le sud-ouest de L'Ile de Chypre. In *Lemba Archaeological Project 1: Excavations at Lemba Lakkous 1976–1983,* edited by E. Peltenberg, pp. 306–311. Studies in Mediterranean Archaeology 70, Paul Åstrom Förlag, Göteborg.

Renault-Mikovsky, J. (1989). Étude paléobotanique, paléoclimatique et palethnographique du site Néolithique de Khirokitia dans le sud-ouest de L'Ile de Chypre. In *Fouilles Néolithique à Khirokitia (Chypre) 1983–1986,* edited by A. LeBrun, pp. 251–263. Editions Recherches sur les Civilisation, ADPF, Paris.

Reyment, R. (1983). Palaeontological Aspects of Island Biogeography: Colonization and Evolution of Mammals on Mediterranean Islands. *OIKOS* 41: 299–306.

Ringrose, T. (1993). Bone Counts and Statistics: A Critique. *Journal of Archaeological Science* 20: 121–157.

Robertson, A. (1977). Tertiary Uplift of the Troodos Massif, Cyprus. *Geological Society of America Bulletin* 88: 1763–1772.

Rollefson, G. (1984). 'Ain Ghazal: An Early Neolithic Community in Highland Jordan. *Bulletin of the American Schools of Oriental Research* 255: 3–14.

Rollefson, G. (1985). The 1983 Season at the Early Neolithic Site of 'Ain Ghazal. *National Geographic Research* Winter, 1985: 44–62.

Rollefson, G. (1989). The Late Aceramic Neolithic of the Levant: A Synthesis. *Paleorient* 15: 490–495.

Rollefson, G. and Simmons, A. (1985). The Early Neolithic Village of 'Ain Ghazal, Jordan: Preliminary Report on the 1983 Season. *Bulletin of the American Schools of Oriental Research Supplement* 23: 35–52.

Rollefson, G. and Simmons, A. (1986). The Neolithic Village of 'Ain Ghazal, Jordan: Preliminary Report on the 1984 Season. *Bulletin of the American Schools of Oriental Research Supplement* 24: 145–164.

Rollefson, G. and Simmons, A. (1988). The Neolithic Settlement at 'Ain Ghazal. In *The Prehistory of Jordan: The State of Research in 1986,* edited by A. Garrard and H. Gebel, pp. 393–421. British Archaeological Reports, International Series 396, Oxford.

Rollefson, G. , Kafafi, Z. , and Simmons, A. (1991). The Neolithic Village of Ain Ghazal, Jordan: Preliminary Report of the 1988 Season. *Bulletin of the American Schools of Oriental Research Supplement* 27: 95–116.

Ronen, A. (1991). Letter to S. Swiny, Director, Cyprus American Archaeological Research Institute, Nicosia. University of Haifa, Haifa, Israel.

Ronen, A. (1995). Core, Periphery, and Ideology in Aceramic Cyprus. *Quartar* 45–46: 178–206.

Roodenberg, J. (1989). Hayaz Höyük and the Final PPNB in the Taurus Foothills. *Paleorient* 15: 91–101.

Rosen, B. (1994). Mammoths in Ancient Egypt? *Nature* 369: 364.

Rosenberg, M. (1994). A Preliminary Description of Lithic Industry from Hallan Çemi. In *Neolithic Chipped Stone Industries of the Fertile Crescent,* edited by H. Gebel and S. Kozlowski, pp. 223–238. ex oriente, Berlin.

Rosenberg, M. , Nesbitt, R. , Redding, R. , and Strasser, T. (1995). Hallan Çemi Tepesi: Some Preliminary Observations Concerning Early Neolithic Subsistence Behaviors in Eastern Anatolia. *Anatolica* 21: 1–12.

Runnels, C. (1995). Review of Aegean Prehistory IV: The Stone Age of Greece from the Palaeolithic to the Advent of the Neolithic. *American Journal of Archaeology* 99: 699–728.

Rupp, D. (1981). Canadian Palaipaphos Survey Project: Preliminary Report of the 1979 Season. *Report of the Department of Antiquities, Cyprus:* 251–268.

Rupp, D. (1987a). Introduction. In *Western Cyprus: Connections*, edited by D. Rupp, pp. 1–5. Studies in Mediterranean Archaeology 77. Paul Åströms Förlag, Göteborg.

Rupp, D. (Ed.). (1987b). *Western Cyprus: Connections.* Studies in Mediterranean Archaeology 77. Paul Åströms Forlag, Göteborg.

Rupp, D. , Sørensen, L. , King, R. , and Fox, W. (1984). Canadian Palaipaphos (Cyprus) Survey Project: Second Preliminary Report, 1980–1982. *Journal of Field Archaeology* 11: 133–154.

Rupp, D. , Sørensen, L. , Lund, J. , King, R. , Fox, W. , Gregory, P. , and Stewart, S. (1987). Canadian Palaipaphos (Cyprus) Survey Project: Third Preliminary Report, 1983–1985. *Acta Archaeologica* 57: 27–45.

Sanchiz, F. (1984). Algunas batracofaunas pleistocénicas de islas del Mediterraneo oriental. *Actas II Reunion Ibero-americana sobre conservacion y zoologia du vertebrados*, pp. 59–69. Caceres.

Schätti, B. (1985). Eine neu zornnatter aus Zypern, *Coluber cypriensis* n. sp. (Reptilia, Serpentes, Colubridae). *Revue suisse de zoologie* 92/2: 471–477.

Schroder, H. (1991). Natufian in the Central Béqaa, Lebanon. In *The Natufian Culture in the Levant*, edited by O. Bar-Yosef and F. Valla, pp. 43–80. International Monographs in Prehistory, Ann Arbor, Michigan.

Schüle, W. (1989). Simulation of Population Dynamics as a Means of Paleoanthropological Research. In *Microcomputers in Paleontology*, edited by D. Burton and D. Harper, pp. 82–115. Contributions to Palaeontology, Museum of the University of Oslo, Oslo.

Schüle, W. (1992). Vegetation, Megaherbivores, Man and Climate in the Quaternary, and the Genesis of Closed Rain-Forests. In *Tropical Forests in Transition: Ecology of Natural and Anthropogenic Disturbance Processes*, edited by J. Goldammer, pp. 45–76. Birkhäser, Basel.

Schüle, W. (1993). Mammals, Vegetation and the Initial Human Settlement of the Mediterranean Islands: A Palaeoecological Approach. *Journal of Biogeography* 20: 399–412.

Schutt, J. and Vierra, B. (1980). Lithic Analysis and Methodology. In *Human Adaptations in a Marginal Environment: The UII Mitigation Project*, edited by J. Moore and J. Winter, pp. 45–65. University of New Mexico, Office of Contract Archaeology, Albuquerque.

Schwartz, J. (1973a). Palaeo-Zoology at Idalion. *American Journal of Archaeology* 77/2: 226–227.

Schwartz, J. (1973b). The Palaeozoology of Cyprus: A Preliminary Report on Some Recently Analyzed Sites. *World Archaeology* 5: 215–220.

Schwartz, J. (1974a). Faunal List from Dhali-Agridhi. In *American Expedition to Idalion, Cyprus—First Preliminary Report: Seasons of 1971 and 1972*, edited by L. Stager, A. Walker, and G. Wright, pp. 103–118. Bulletin of the American Schools of Oriental Research, Supplement 18.

Schwartz, J. (1974b). The Paleo-Osteology of Cyprus. In *American Expedition to Idalion, Cyprus—First Preliminary Report: Seasons of 1971 and 1972*, edited by L. E. Stager, A. Walker, and G. Wright, pp. 119–121. Bulletin of the American Schools of Oriental Research, Supplement 18. Cambridge, Massachusetts.

Scott, T. (1977). The Harifian of the Central Negev. In *Prehistory and Paleoenvironments of the Central Negev, Israel* (Vol. II), edited by A. Marks, pp. 271–322. Southern Methodist University Press, Dallas.

Sensabaugh, G. , Wilson, A. , and Kirk, P. (1971). Protein Stability in Preserved Biological Remains: Parts 1 and 2. *International Journal of Biochemistry* 2: 545–568.

Servello, A. (1976). Nahal Divshon: A Pre-Pottery Neolithic B Hunting Camp. In *Prehistory and Paleoenvironments in the Central Negev, Israel* (Vol. I), edited by A. Marks, pp. 349–370. Southern Methodist University Press, Dallas.

Seton-Williams, V. (1936). The Implements of Flint and Chert. In *The Excavations at Erimi 1933–1935*, edited by P. Dikaios, p. 53. *Report of the Department of Antiquities, Cyprus, 1936, Part I.*

Shackleton, J. (1985). Macro- and Micro-Level Approaches to the Reconstruction of Palaeoshorelines. In *Palaeoenvironmental Investigation: Research Design, Methods, and Data Analysis*, edited by N. Fieller, D. Gilbertson, and N. Ralph, pp. 221–228. British Archaeological Reports, 58, Oxford. Symposia of the Association for Environmental Archaeology, No. 5A.

Shackleton, J. , van Andel, T. , and Runnels, C. (1984). Coastal Paleogeography of the Central and Western Mediterranean During the Last 125,000 Years and Its Archaeological Implications. *Journal of Field Archaeology* 11: 307–314.

Shackleton, J. , Deith, M. , and Shackleton, N. (1988). *Marine Molluscan Remains from Franchthi Cave, with a Report on the Oxygen Isotope Analysis of Marine Molluscs from Franchthi Cave.* Franchthi vol. 4. Indiana University Press, Bloomington.

Shackleton, N. (1968). Knossos Marine Mollusca (Neolithic). *Annual of the British School of Archaeology in Athens* 63: 264–266.

Shackleton, N. (1969). Preliminary Observations on the Marine Shells. In *Hesperia* 38: 379–380.

Shafer, H. and Holloway, R. (1979). Organic Residue Analysis in Determining Stone Tool Function. In *Lithic Use-Wear Analysis*, edited by B. Hayden, pp. 385–399. Academic Press, New York.

Shea, J. (1989). A Use-Wear Study of a Sample of Chipped Stone Artifacts from Akrotiri *Aetokremnos*. Letter report on file, Department of Anthropology, University of Nevada, Las Vegas.

Shipman, P. (1979). What Are All These Bones Doing Here? Confessions of a Taphonomist. *Harvard Magazine*, Nov.–Dec.: 42–46.

Shipman, P. and Rose, J. (1983). Early Hominid Hunting, Butchering, and Carcass-Processing Behaviors: Approaches to the Fossil Record. *Journal of Anthropological Archaeology* 2: 57–98.

Shipman, P., Foster, G., and Schoeninger, M. (1984). Burnt Bones and Teeth: An Experimental Study of Color, Morphology, Crystal Structure and Shrinkage. *Journal of Archaeological Science* 11: 307–325.

Silence, T. (1996). Study of Sedimentation Processes Within the Akrotiri *Aetokremnos* Rockshelter, Cyprus (Report on file). Department of Anthropology, University of Nevada, Las Vegas.

Simmons, A. (1980). Early Neolithic Settlement and Economic Behavior in the Western Negev Desert of the Southern Levant. Unpublished Ph.D. dissertation, Southern Methodist University, Dallas.

Simmons, A. (1981). The "Other" Archaeology of Northwestern New Mexico—Perspectives on the Aceramic Occupation of the San Juan Basin. *Contract Abstracts and CRM Archaeology* 2: 12–20.

Simmons, A. (1982). Lithic Analysis. In *Prehistoric Adaptive Strategies in the Chaco Canyon Region, Northwestern New Mexico* (3 vols.), A. Simmons (assembler), pp. 187–251. Navajo Nation Papers in Anthropology, No. 9. Window Rock, Arizona.

Simmons, A. (1988a). Extinct Pygmy Hippopotamus and Early Man in Cyprus. *Nature* 333: 554–557.

Simmons, A. (1988b). Fouilles d'Akrotiri *Aetokremnos*. In V. Karageorghis (Ed.), Chronique des fouilles et Decouvertes Archeologiques a Chypre en 1987. *Bulletin de Correspondance Hellenique* 112: 817–820.

Simmons, A. (1989a). Preliminary Report on the 1988 Test Excavations at Akrotiri *Aetokremnos*. *Report of the Department of Antiquities, Cyprus*: 1–5.

Simmons, A. (1989b). Fouilles d'Akrotiri *Aetokremnos*. *Bulletin de Correspondance Hellenique* 113: 815–817.

Simmons, A. (1989c). Excavations at Akrotiri *Aetokremnos*. In *Annual Report of the Department of Antiquities for the Year 1988*, edited by V. Karageorghis, pp. 41–42. Department of Antiquities, Nicosia.

Simmons, A. (1991a). Humans, Island Colonization, and Pleistocene Extinctions in the Mediterranean: The View from Akrotiri *Aetokremnos*, Cyprus. *Antiquity* 65: 857–869.

Simmons, A. (1991b). One Flew Over the Hippo's Nest: Extinct Pleistocene Fauna, Early Man, and Conservative Archaeology in Cyprus. In *Perspectives on the Past*, edited by G. Clark, pp. 282–304. University of Pennsylvania Press, Philadelphia.

Simmons, A. (1991c). Preliminary Report on the Interdisciplinary Excavations of Akrotiri *Aetokremnos* (Site E): 1987, 1988, 1990. *Report of the Department of Antiquities, Cyprus*: 7–14.

Simmons, A. (1992a). Akrotiri *Aetokremnos* and Early Cypriot Prehistory. In *Acta Cypria. Acts of an International Congress on Cypriote Archaeology*, edited by P. Åström, pp. 348–355. Paul Åströms Förlag, Jonsered.

Simmons, A. (1992b). Global Cultural Resource Archaeology in the Early 21st Century. In *Quandaries and Quests: Visions of Archaeology's Future*, edited by L. Wandsnider, pp. 79–97. Center for Archaeological Investigations, Southern Illinois University, Occasional Paper No. 20. Carbondale, Illinois.

Simmons, A. (1992c). Les plus anciens habitants de Chypre chassaient-ils l'hippopotame? *La Recherche* 248: 1318–1320.

Simmons, A. (1992d). Preliminary Report of the Akrotiri Peninsula Survey, 1991. *Report of the Department of Antiquities, Cyprus, 1992*: 9–11.

Simmons, A. (1993). Early Cypriots and Extinct Pygmy Hippopotami. *National Geographic Research and Exploration* 9: 123–125.

Simmons, A. (1994a). Early Neolithic Settlement in Western Cyprus: Preliminary Report on the 1992–1993 Test Excavations at Kholetria *Ortos*. *Bulletin of the American Schools of Oriental Research* 295: 1–14.

Simmons, A. (1994b). The 1994 Kholetria *Ortos* Excavations. *Biblical Archaeologist* 57: 244.

Simmons, A. (1994c). Preliminary Report on the 1993 Test Excavations at Kholetria *Ortos*, Paphos District. *Report of the Department of Antiquities, Cyprus 1994*: 39–44.

Simmons, A. (1996). Whose Myth? Archaeological Data, Interpretations, and Implications for the Human Association with Extinct Pleistocene Fauna at Akrotiri *Aetokremnos. Journal of Mediterranean Archaeology* 9: 97–105.

Simmons, A (1998a). Exposed Fragments, Buried Hippos Assessing Surface Archaeology. In *Surface Archaeology,* edited by A. Sullivan, pp. 159–167. University of New Mexico Press, Albuquerque.

Simmons, A. (1998b). Test Excavations at Two Aceramic Neolithic Sites in the Uplands of Western Cyprus. *Report of the Department of Antiquities, Cyprus, 1998:* 1–16.

Simmons, A. and Corona, R. (1993). Test Excavations at Kholetria *Ortos,* a Neolithic Settlement Near Paphos. *Report of the Department of Antiquities, Cyprus 1993:* 1–10.

Simmons, A. and Reese, D. (1993). Hippo Hunters of Akrotiri. *Archaeology* 46: 38–43.

Simmons, A. and Wigand, P. (1994). Assessing the Radiocarbon Determinations from Akrotiri *Aetokremnos,* Cyprus. In *Late Quaternary Chronology and Paleoclimates of the Eastern Mediterranean,* edited by O. Bar-Yosef and R. Kra, pp. 247–254. Radiocarbon and American School of Prehistoric Research, Tucson, Arizona, and Cambridge, Massachusetts.

Simmons, A. , Reese, D. , and Held, S. (1988). Extinct Pygmy Hippopotamus, Early Man, and the Initial Human Occupation of Cyprus. In *International Conference, Early Man in Island Environments, Oliena (Sardegna), Abstracts,* edited by M. Sanges p. 81. Industria Grafica Stampacolor, Sassari.

Simmons, A. , Rollefson, G. , Kafafi, Z. , and Moyer, K. (1989). Test Excavations at Wadi Shu'eib, a Major Neolithic Settlement in Central Jordan. *Annual of the Department of Antiquities of Jordan* 33: 27–42.

Simmons, A. , Rollefson, G. , Köhler-Rollefson, I. , Mandel, R. , and Kafafi, Z. (1988). 'Ain Ghazal: A Major Neolithic Settlement in Central Jordan. *Science* 240: 35–39.

Simpson, G. (1940). Mammals and Land Bridges. *Journal of the Washington Academy of Science* 30: 137–163.

Simpson, G. (1965). *The Geography of Evolution.* Chilton Books, New York.

Smith, E. (1981). The Application of Optimal Foraging Theory to the Analysis of Hunter-Gatherer Group Size. In *Hunter-Gather Foraging Strategies: Ethnographic and Archeological Analyses,* edited by B. Winterhalder and E. Smith, pp. 36–65. University of Chicago Press, Chicago.

Soil Survey Staff. (1982). *Procedures for Collecting Soil Samples and Methods of Analysis for Soil Survey,* Soil Survey Investigations Report No. 1. USDA-SCS, U.S. Government Printing Office, Washington D.C.

Solecki, R. (1977). Predatory Bird Rituals at Zawi Chemi Shanidar. *Sumer* 33/1: 42–47.

Sondaar, P. (1977). Insularity and Its Effect on Mammal Evolution. In *Major Patterns in Vertebrate Evolution,* edited by M. Hecht, P. Goody, and B. Hecht, pp. 671–707. Plenum Press, New York.

Sondaar, P. (1986). The Island Sweepstakes. *Natural History* 95: 50–57.

Sondaar, P. (1987). Pleistocene Man and Extinctions of Islands Endemics. *Memoire Societe Geologique de France,* N.S. 150: 159–165.

Sondaar, P. , Hofmeijer, G. , and Sanges, M. (1989). The Dramatic End of the Sardinian Paleolithic Island Economy. In *People and Culture in Change,* edited by I. Hershkovitz, pp. 517–521. British Archaeological Reports, International Series No. 508(i), Part i, Oxford.

Sondaar, P. , Sanges, M. , Kotsakis, T. , Esu, D. , and deBoer, P. (1984). First Report on a Paleolithic Culture in Sardinia. In *The Daya Conference of Prehistory: Early Settlement in the Western Mediterranean Islands and Their Peripheral Areas,* edited by W. Waldren, R. Chapman, J. Lewthwaite, and R. Kennard, pp. 29–47. British Archaeological Reports, International Series, No. 229, Oxford..

Sondaar, P. , Sanges, M. , Kotsakis, T. , and deBoer, P. (1986). The Pleistocene Deer Hunter of Sardinia. *Geobios* 19: 17–25.

Sondaar, P. , Martini, F. , Ulzega, A. , and Hofmeijer, G. (1991). L'homme Pléistocène en Sardaigne. *L'Anthropologie* 95: 181–200.

Sørensen, L. and Rupp, D. (Eds.). (1993). *The Land of the Paphian Aphrodite: Vol. 2. The Canadian Palaipaphos Survey Project—Artifact and Ecological Studies.* Studies in Mediterranean Archaeology 104:2. Paul Åstroms Förlag, Göteborg.

Speth, J. (1983). *Bison Kills and Bone Counts: Decision Making by Ancient Hunters.* University of Chicago Press, Chicago.

Spoor, C. and Sondaar, P. (1986). Human Fossils from the Endemic Island Fauna of Sardinia. *Journal of Human Evolution* 15: 399–408.

Spoor, C. and Sondaar, P. (1987). The First Palaeolithic Human Fossils from Sardinia. *Bones: Treasuries of Human Experience in Time and Space* 1: 69–71.

Stafford, T. , Brendel, K. , and Duhamel, R. (1988). Radiocarbon, ^{13}C and ^{15}N Analysis of Fossil Bone: Removal of Humates and XAD-2 Resin. *Geochimica et Cosmochimica Acta* 52: 2257–2267.

Stahl, U. (1989). Tierknochenfunde vom Hassek Höyük (Sudostanatolien). Ph.D. dissertation, Ludwig-Maximilians-Universität, München.

Stanley, S. (1987). *Extinctions*. Scientific American Library, New York.

Stanley, D. (1977). Post-Miocene Depositional Patterns and Structural Displacement in the Mediterranean. In *The Oceanic Basins and Margins: Vol. 4A. The Eastern Mediterranean*, edited by A. Nairn, W. Kanes, and F. Stehili, pp. 77–150. Plenum Press, New York.

Stanley-Price, N. (1976). Some Observations on the Marine Molluscs at Khirokitia. *Report of the Department of Antiquities Cyprus, 1976:* 1–10.

Stanley-Price, N. (1977a). Colonisation and Continuity in the Early Prehistory of Cyprus. *World Archaeology* 9: 27–41.

Stanley-Price, N. (1977b). Khirokitia and the Initial Settlement of Cyprus. *Levant* 9: 66–69.

Stanley-Price, N. (1979a). *Early Prehistoric Settlement in Cyprus: A Review and Gazetteer of Sites, c. 6500–3000 B.C.* British Archaeological Reports. International Series No. 65, Oxford.

Stanley-Price, N. (1979b). On Terminology and Models in Cypriote Prehistory. In *Studies Presented in Memory of Porphyrios Dikaios*, edited by V. Karageorghis, pp. 1–11. Lions Club, Nicosia.

Stanley-Price, N. and Christou, D. (1973). Excavations at Khirokitia, 1972. *Report of the Department of Antiquities Cyprus, 1976:* 1–33.

Stead, I. (1967). A La Tène Burial at Welwyn Garden City. *Archaeologia* CI: 1–62.

Steadman, D. (1989). Extinction of Birds in Eastern Polynesia: A Review of the Record and Comparisons with Other Pacific Island Groups. *Journal of Archaeological Science* 16: 177–205.

Steadman, D. (1995a). Extinction of Birds on Tropical Pacific Islands. In *Late Quaternary Environments and Deep History: A Tribute to Paul S. Martin*, pp. 33–49. The Mammoth Site of Hot Springs Dakota, Hot Springs, South Dakota.

Steadman, D. (1995b). Prehistoric Extinctions of Pacific Island Birds: Biodiversity Meets Zooarchaeology. *Science* 267: 1123–1131.

Stekelis, M. (1953). The Flint Implements. In *Khirokitia*, pp. 409–413. Oxford University Press, London.

Stewart, R. (1974). Paleobotanic Investigation, 1972 Season. In *American Expedition to Idalion, Cyprus, First Preliminary Report: Seasons 1971 and 1972*, edited by L. E. Stager, A. Walker, and G. Wright, pp. 123–129. Bulletin of the American Schools of Oriental Research, Supplement 18. Cambridge, Massachusetts.

Stewart, S. (1987). A Model for Prehistoric Chert Acquisition in the Paphos District, Cyprus. In *Western Cyprus: Connections*, edited by D. Rupp, pp. 43–51. Studies in Mediterranean Archaeology 77. Paul Åströms Förlag, Göteborg.

Stiner, M. (1991). Food Procurement and Transport by Human and Non-Human Predators. *Journal of Archaeological Science* 18: 455–482.

Stiner, M. (1992). Overlapping Species "Choice" by Italian Upper Pleistocene Predators. *Current Anthropology* 33: 433–451.

Stiner, M. (1993). The Place of Hominids Among Predators: Interspecific Comparisons of Food Procurement and Transport. In *From Bones to Behavior*, edited by J. Hudson, pp. 38–61. Center for Archaeological Investigations, Southern Illinois University at Carbondale, Carbondale.

Stiner, M. and Kuhn, S. (1992). Subsistence, Technology and Adaptive Variation in the Middle Paleolithic. *American Anthropologist* 94: 306–339.

Stiner, M. , Kuhn, S. , Weiner, S. , and Bar-Yosef, O. (1995). Differential Burning, Recrystallization, and Fragmentation of Archaeological Bone. *Journal of Archaeological Science* 22: 223–237.

Stockton, E. (1968). Pre-Neolithic Remains at Kyrenia, Cyprus. *Report of the Department of Antiquities, Cyprus:* 16–19.

Strasser, T. and Lax, E. (1993). Holocene Faunal Extinctions on Crete. *American Journal of Archaeology* 97: 343.

Stuart, A. (1991). Mammalian Extinctions in the Late Pleistocene of Northern Eurasia and North America. *Biological Review* 66: 453–562.

Stuiver, M. and Becker, B. (1993). High-Precision Calibration of the Radiocarbon Time-Scale A.D. 1950–6000 B.C. *Radiocarbon* 35: 35–65.

Stuiver, M. and Braziunas, T. (1993). Modeling Atmospheric 14C Influences and 14C Ages of Marine Samples Back to 10,000 B.C. *Radiocarbon* 35: 137–189.

Stuiver, M. and Polach, H. (1977). Discussion, Reporting of ^{14}C Data. *Radiocarbon* 19: 355–363.

Stuiver, M. , Pearson, G. , and Braziunas, T. (1986). Radiocarbon Age Calibration of Marine Samples Back to 9000 Cal Yr B.P. *Radiocarbon* 28(2B): 980–1021.

Stuiver, M. , Braziunas, T. , Becker, B. , and Kromer, B. (1991). Climatic, Solar, Oceanic and Geomagnetic Influences on Late-Glacial and Holocene Atmospheric $^{14}C/^{12}C$ Change. *Quaternary Research* 35: 1–24.

Stylianou, A. and Stylianou, J. (1980). *The History of the Cartography of Cyprus.* Zavallis Press, Nicosia.

Swiny, H. (Ed.). (1982). *Ancient Kourion Area.* Zavallis Press, Nicosia.

Swiny, S. (1982). The Environment. In *Ancient Kourion Area,* edited by H. Swiny, pp. 1–5. Zavallis Press, Nicosia.

Swiny, S. (1986). *The Kent State University Expedition to Episkopi Phaneromeni* (Part 2). Mediterranean Archaeology 74:2. Paul Åströms Förlag, Nicosia.

Swiny, S. (1988). The Pleistocene Fauna of Cyprus and Recent Discoveries on the Akrotiri Peninsula. *Report of the Department of Antiquities, Cyprus 1988*: 1–14.

Swiny, S. (1989). Prehistoric Cyprus: A Current Perspective. *Biblical Archaeologist* 52: 178–189.

Swiny, S. (1995). Giants, Dwarfs, Saints or Humans, Who First Reached Cyprus? In *Visitors, Immigrants, and Invaders in Cyprus,* edited by P. Wallace, pp. 1–19. Institute of Cypriot Studies, University at Albany, SUNY, Albany.

Symeonides, N. (1972). Die entdeckung von zwergelefanten in der Höhle charkadio auf der Insel Tilos. *Annales Geologiques des Pays Helleniques* 24: 445–461.

Symeonides, N. (1988). Nanoi elephantes stin niso Tilo (Dodekanisa). *Anthropologika Analekta* 49: 77–83.

Symeonides, N. , Bachmayer, F. , and Zapfe, H. (1973). Grabungen in der zwergelefanten-Höhle charkadio auf der Insel Tilos. *Annalen des Naturhistorischen Hofmuseums, Wien* 77: 133–39.

Szyndlar, Z. (1984). Fossil Snakes from Poland. *Acta zoologica Cracoviensis* 28/1: 1–156.

Tagliacozzo, A. (1993). *Archeozoologia della Grotta dell'Uzzo, Sicilia* (Supplemento al Bulletinno di Paletnologia Italiana, Vol. 84, Nuova Serie II). Istituto Poligrafico E Zecca Dello Stato, Rome.

Talbot, G. (1983). Appendix K: Beads and Pendants from the Tell and Tombs. In K. M. Kenyon and T. A. Holland, *Excavations at Jericho:* V. British School of Archaeology in Jerusalem, pp. 788–801. Oxford University Press, Oxford.

Tamers, M. (1991). Letter Report to A. Simmons, Desert Research Institute, Reno, Nevada. Beta Analytic, Miami.

Tchernov, E. (1980). *The Pleistocene Birds of 'Ubeidiya, Jordan Valley.* The Israel Academy of Sciences and Humanities, Jerusalem.

Tchernov, E. (1993). Exploitation of Birds During the Natufian and Early Neolithic of the Southern Levant. *Archaeofauna* 2: 121–143.

Terrell, J. (1976). Island Biogeography and Man in Melanesia. *Archaeology and Physical Anthropology in Oceania* 11: 1–17.

Terrell, J. (1977). Geographic Systems and Human Diversity in the North Solomons. *World Archaeology* 9: 62–81.

Teschner, H. , Wiedl, H. , and Bohme, W. (1992). Wiederentdeckung der ringelnatter (*Natrix natrix* ssp.?) auf Zypern—vorlaufiger Bericht. *Herpetofauna* 14/80: 6–10.

Theodorou, G. (1990). The Dwarf Elephants of Tilos. *The Athenian,* May: 17–19.

Thurston, H. 1971. *The Travellers' Guide to Cyprus.* Jonathan Cape, London.

Tixier, J. (1963). *Typologie de l'Epipaleolithique du Maghreb.* Memoires du Centre de Recherches Anthropologiques, Prehistoriques et Ethnographiques. Arts et Metier Graphiques, Paris.

Todd, I. (1977). Vasilikos Valley Project: First Preliminary Report, 1976. *Report of the Department of Antiquities Cyprus, 1977:* 5–32.

Todd, I. (1978). Vasilikos Valley Project: Second Preliminary Report, 1977. *Journal of Field Archaeology* 5: 161–195.

Todd, I. (1979). Vasilikos Valley Project, 1977–1978: An Interim Report. *Report of the Department of Antiquities Cyprus, 1979:* 13–68.

Todd, I. (1982). Vasilikos Valley Project: Fourth Preliminary Report, 1979–1980. *Journal of Field Archaeology* 9: 35–79.

Todd, I. (Ed.). (1987a). *Vasilikos Valley Project 6: Excavations at Kalavasos Tenta: Vol. 1.* Studies in Mediterranean Archaeology, Vol. 71:6. Paul Åströms Förlag, Göteborg.

Todd, I. (1987b). Chronology, Foreign Relations, and Comparisons. In *Vasilikos Valley Project 6: Excavations at Kalavasos Tenta: Vol. 1,* edited by I. Todd. Studies in Mediterranean Archaeology, Vol. 71: 6. Paul Åströms Förlag, Göteborg.

Todd, I. (1987c). Appendix I: Summary Listing of Excavated Aceramic Neolithic Sites in Cyprus. In *Vasilikos Valley Project 6: Excavations at Kalavasos Tenta: Vol. 1,* edited by I. Todd, pp. 186–188. Studies in Mediterranean Archaeology, Vol. 71:6. Paul Åströms Förlag, Göteborg.

Todd, L. , Witter, R. , Frison, G. (1987). Excavation and Documentation of the Princeton and Smithsonian Horner Site Assemblages. In *The Horner Site: The Type Site of the Cody Cultural Complex*, edited by G. Frison and L. Todd, pp. 39–91. Academic Press, Orlando, Florida.

Trotter, M. and McCulloch, B. (1984). Moas, Men, and Middens. In *Quaternary Extinctions: A Prehistoric Revolution*, edited by P. Martin and R. Klein, p. 727. University of Arizona Press, Tucson.

Tucker, M. (1989). *Techniques in Sedimentology*. Blackwell Scientific Publications, Boston.

Tufte, E. (1983). *The Visual Display of Quantitative Information*. Graphics Press, Cheshire, Connecticut.

Tukey, J. (1977). *Exploratory Data Analysis*. Addison-Wesley, Reading, Massachusetts.

Tusa, S. (1985). The Beginning of Farming Communities in Sicily: The Evidence of Uzzo Cave. In *Papers in Italian Archaeology IV: Part ii. Prehistory*, edited by C. Malone and S. Stoddart, pp. 61–82. British Archaeological Reports. International Series No. 244, Oxford.

Uerpmann, H. (1987). *The Ancient Distribution of Ungulate Mammals in the Middle East*. Beihefte zum Tübinger Atlas des Vorderen Orients. Reihe A (Naturwissenschaften), Nr. 27. Dr. Ludwig Reichert Verlag, Wiesbaden.

Vartanyan, S. , Garutt, V. , and Sher, A. (1993). Holocene Dwarf Mammoths from Wrangel Island in the Siberian Arctic. *Nature* 362: 337–340.

Vaufrey, R. (1929). Les éléphants nains des îles Méditerranéennes et la question des isthmes Pléistocénes. *Archives de l'Institut de Paléontologie Humaine, Mémoire:* 6. Masson et C^{le}, Editeurs, Paris.

Vaughan, P. (1985). The Burin-Blow Technique: Creator or Eliminator? *Journal of Field Archaeology* 12: 488–496.

Verheyen, R. (1954). *Monographie éthologique de l'hippopotame (Hippopotamus amphibius L.)*. Inst. Parcs Nationaux Congo, Bruxelles.

Vigne, J. (1983). Les mammifères terrestres non-volants du post-Glaciaire de Corse et leurs rapports avec L'homme: étude paléo-ethno-zoologique fondée sur les ossements. Thèse 3e Cycle, P. et M. Curie Universitie, Paris.

Vigne, J. (1987a). L'extinction Holocène du fonds de peuplement mammalien indigène des îles de Mediterranée occidentale. *Mémoires de la Société Géologique de France* N.S. 150: 167–177.

Vigne, J. (1987b). L'origine du peuplement mammalien de Corse: quelques réflexions biogéographiques. *Bulletin de la Société Zoologique de France* 111(3–4): 165–178.

Vigne, J. (1988). *Les mammifères post-Glaciaires de Corse—étude archéozoologiue*. XXVIe Supplément à Gallia Préhistoire. Éditions du Centre National de la Recherche Scientifique, Paris.

Vigne, J. (1989). Le peuplement Paléolithique des îles: le débat s'ouvre en Sardaigne. *Les Nouvelles de L'Archélogie* 35: 39–42.

Vigne, J. (1990). Biogeographical History of the Mammals on Corsica (and Sardinia) Since the Final Pleistocene. In *International Symposium on Biogeographical Aspects of Insularity*, pp. 369–392. Atti Dei Convegni Lincei 85. Accademia Nazionale dei Licei, Rome.

Vigne, J. (1992). Zooarchaeology and the Biogeographical History of the Mammals of Corsica and Sardinia Since the Last Ice Age. *Mammal Review* 22: 87–96.

Vigne, J. and Alcover, J. (1985). Incidence des relations historiques entre l'homme et l'animal dans la composition actuelle du peuplement amphibien, retilien et mammalien des îles de Méditerranée occidentale, pp. 79–91. *110e Congrès National des Sociétés Savanates*, Montpellier. *Sciences, Fasc. 11.*

Vilette, P. (1983). Avifaunes du Pléistocène final et de l'Holocène dans le sud de la France et en Catalogne. *Atacina* 11, entire issue. Carassone.

Vita-Finzi, C. (1969). *The Mediterranean Valleys. Geological Changes in Historical Times*. Cambridge University Press, Cambridge.

Vita-Finzi, C. (1973). Paleolithic Finds from Cyprus? *Proceedings of the Prehistoric Society* 39: 453–454.

Vita-Finzi, C. and Higgs, E. (1970). Prehistoric Economy in the Mount Carmel Area of Palestine: Site Catchment Analysis. *Proceedings of the Prehistoric Society* 36: 1–37.

Vogel, J. (1984). Letter Report to S. Swiny, Director, Cyprus American Archaeological Research Institute, Nicosia, Cyprus. National Physical Research Laboratory, Pretoria.

Vogel, J. and Visser, E. (1981). Pretoria Radiocarbon Dates II. *Radiocarbon* 23: 43–80.

Volf, J. (1959). La réproduction des genettes au Zoo de Prague. *Mammalia* 23: 168–171.

Voous, K. (1960). *Atlas of European Birds*. Nelson, London.

Waechter, J. (1953). Appendix 1a: A Comparison Between the Flint Implements of Khirokitia and Erimi. In P. Dikaios, *Khirokitia*, pp. 414–415. Oxford University Press, London.

Waines, G. and Stanley-Price, N. (1977). Plant Remains from Khirokitia in Cyprus. *Paleorient* 5: 281–284.

Waldren, W. (1982). *Balearic Prehistoric Ecology and Culture*. British Archaeological Reports. International Series No. 149, Oxford.

Waldren, W. (1991). Age Determination, Chronology and Radiocarbon Recalibration in the Balearic Islands. In *2nd Deya Conference of Prehistory: Archaeological Techniques, Technology and Theory* (Vol 2.), edited by W. Waldren, J. Ensenyat and R.-C. Kennards, pp. 45–78. British Archaeological Reports. International Series No. 574, Oxford.

Waldren, W. (1994). *Survival and Extinction: Myotragus Balearicus, an Endemic Pleistocene Antelope from the Island of Mallorca*. Donald Baden-Powell Quaternary Research Center, Pitt Rivers Museum, University of Oxford, Oxford, and Deìa Archaeological Museum and Research Centre, Deìa, Mallorca, Baleares, Spain.

Waldren, W. and R.-C. Kennard (Eds.). (1987). *Bell Beakers of the Western Mediterranean: Definition, Interpretation, Theory and New Site Data*. British Archaeological Reports, International Series 331, Oxford.

Waldren, W. , Chapman, R. , Lewthwaite, J. , and Kennards, R. (Eds.). (1984). *The Deya Conference of Prehistory: Early Settlement in the Western Mediterranean Islands and the Peripheral Areas*. British Archaeological Reports, International Series No. 229, Oxford.

Waldren, W. , Ensenyat, J. , and Kennards, R. (Eds.). (1991). *2nd Deya Conference of Prehistory: Archaeological Techniques, Technology and Theory* (2 vols). British Archaeological Reports, International Series No. 573–574, Oxford.

Walker, E. (1975). *Mammals of the World* (3rd ed., vol. II). The Johns Hopkins University Press, Baltimore and London.

Walther, F. (1984). *Communication and Expression in Hoofed Mammals*. Indiana University Press, Bloomington.

Ward, A. (Ed.). (1978). *Limited Activity and Occupation Sites*. Center for Anthropological Studies, Contribution to Anthropological Studies 1, Albuquerque.

Ward, G. and Wilson, S. (1978). Procedures for Comparing and Combining Radiocarbon Age Determinations: A Critique. *Archaeometry* 20:19–1.

Watkins, T. (1973). Some Problems of the Neolithic and Chalcolithic Period in Cyprus. *Report of the Department of Antiquities, Cyprus, 1973:* 34–61.

Watkins, T. (1979). Kataliondas-*Kourvellos*: The Analysis of the Surface Collected Data. In *Studies Presented in Memory of Porphyrios Dikaios*, edited by V. Karageorghis, pp. 12–20. Lions Club, Nicosia.

Watkins, T. (1981a). The Economic Status of the Aceramic Neolithic Culture of Cyprus. *Journal of Mediterranean Anthropology and Archaeology* 1: 139–149.

Watkins, T. (1981b). The Chalcolithic Period in Cyprus: The Background to Current Research. In *Chalcolithic Cyprus and Western Asia*, edited by J. Reade, pp. 9–20. British Museum, London.

Watson, J. , Stanley-Price, N. , and Arnold, E. (1977). Vertebrate Fauna from the 1972 Sounding at Khirokitia. *Report of the Department of Antiquities, Cyprus, 1977:* 232–260.

Weesie, P. (1982). A Pleistocene Endemic Island Form Within the Genus *Athene*. *Athene cretensis* n.sp. (Aves. Strigiformes) from Crete. *Proceedings of the Koninklijke Nederlandse Akademie van Wetenschappen* B, 85/3: 323–336.

Weesie, P. (1988). The Quaternary Avifauna of Crete, Greece. *Palaeovertebrata* 18/1: 1–94.

Weigelt, J. (1989) (trans. by J. Schaefer). *Recent Vertebrate Carcasses and Their Paleobiological Implications*. University of Chicago Press, Chicago and London. (Originally published in 1927)

Wendorf, M. (1982). The Fire Areas of Santa Rosa Island: An Interpretation. *North American Archaeologist* 3: 173–180.

Wenner, A. and Johnson, D. (1980). Land Vertebrates on the California Channel Islands. In *The California Islands: Proceedings of a Multidisciplinary Symposium*, edited by D. Power, pp. 497–530. Santa Barbara Museum of Natural History, Santa Barbara.

Werner, F. (1936). Reptiles from Mount Troodos, Cyprus. *Proceedings of the Zoological Society of London* 2: 655–658.

Westbrook, S. (1979). Ethnographic Study in Kalavasos Village, 1978. In *Vasilikos Valley Project, 1977–1978: An Interim Report*, edited by I. Todd, pp. 39–43. *Report of the Department of Antiquities*.

Wettstein, O. von. (1953). Herpetologia aegaea. *Sitzungsberichten der Österreichischen Akademie der Wissenschaften Mathematisch-Naturwissenschaftliche Klasse* 162: Bd 9 & 10.

Wheeler, M. (1983). Appendix J: Greenstone Amulets. In *Excavations at Jericho:* V., edited by K. M. Kenyon and T. A. Holland, pp. 781–787. Oxford University Press, Oxford.

Whitehead, P. , Bauchot, M. , Hureau, J. , Nielsen, J. , and Tortonese, E. (1986). *Fishes of the Northeastern Atlantic and the Mediterranean III*. Unesco, Paris.

Wiedl, H. and Eugster, U. (1991). *Exhibition of Amphibians and Reptiles of Cyprus*. Herpetological Society of Cyprus, Paphos.

Wilkins, G. (1953). Appendix IV: Shells from Khirokitia and Erimi. In *Khirokitia*, edited by P. Dikaios, pp. 438–440. Oxford University Press, London.

Williamson, M. (1981). *Island Populations*. Oxford University Press, Oxford.

Winterhalder, B. and Smith, E. (Eds.). (1981). *Hunter-Gatherer Foraging Strategies: Ethnographic and Archeological Analyses*. University of Chicago Press, Chicago.

Xenophontos, C. (1982). Steatite Versus Picrolite. In E. J. Peltenburg, Early Copper-work in Cyprus and the Exploitation of Picrolite: Evidence from the Lemba Archaeological Project. In J. D. Muhly, R. Maddin, and V. Karageorghis, eds. , *Early Metallurgy in Cyprus, 4000–500 B.C.* (p. 59). Pierides Foundation, Larnaca.

Zeist, W. van. (1981). Plant Remains from Cape Andreas-Kastros (Cyprus). In *Un Site Néolithique Précéramique en Chypre: Cap Andréas-Kastros,* edited by A. LeBrun, pp. 95–99. Paris Editions ADPF, Paris.

Zeuner, F. and Ellis, A. (1961). Appendix 3: Animal Bones. In *Sotira*, edited by P. Dikaios, pp. 235–236. The University Museum, Philadelphia.

Zohary, M. (1973). *Geobotanical Foundations of the Middle East*. Gustav Fischer, Stuttgart.

Index

INTERDISCIPLINARY CONTRIBUTIONS TO ARCHAEOLOGY
Chronological Listing of Volumes

CHESAPEAKE PREHISTORY
Old Traditions, New Directions
Richard J Dent, Jr.

PREHISTORIC CULTURAL ECOLOGY AND EVOLUTION
Insights from Southern Jordan.
Donald O. Henry

STONE TOOLS
Theoretical Insights into Human Prehistory
Edited by George H. Odell

THE ARCHAEOLOGY OF WEALTH
Consumer Behavior in English America
James G. Gibb

STATISTICS FOR ARCHAEOLOGISTS
A Commonsense Approach
Robert D. Drennan

DARWINIAN ARCHAEOLOGIES
Edited by Herbert Donald Graham Maschner

CASE STUDIES IN ENVIRONMENTAL ARCHAEOLOGY
Edited by Elizabeth J. Reitz, Lee A. Newsom, and Sylvia J. Scudder

HUMANS AT THE END OF THE ICE AGE
The Archaeology of the Pleistocene–Holocene Transition
Edited by Lawrence Guy Straus, Berit Valentin Eriksen, Jon M. Erlandson, and David R. Yesner

VILLAGERS OF THE MAROS
A Portrait of an Early Bronze Age Society
John M. O'Shea

HUNTERS BETWEEN EAST AND WEST
The Paleolithic of Moravia
Jiři Svoboda, Vojen Ložek, and Emanuel Vlček

MISSISSIPPIAN POLITICAL ECONOMY
Jon Muller

PROJECTILE TECHNOLOGY
Edited by Heidi Knecht

A HUNTER–GATHERER LANDSCAPE
Southwest Germany in the Late Paleolithic and Mesolithic
Michael A. Jochim

FAUNAL EXTINCTION IN AN ISLAND SOCIETY
Pygmy Hippopotamus Hunters of Cyprus
Alan H. Simmons and Associates